The Machinery of Government

T0355192

The Machinery of Government

Public Administration and the Liberal State

JOSEPH HEATH

OXFORD
UNIVERSITY PRESS

OXFORD
UNIVERSITY PRESS

Oxford University Press is a department of the University of Oxford. It furthers
the University's objective of excellence in research, scholarship, and education
by publishing worldwide. Oxford is a registered trade mark of Oxford University
Press in the UK and certain other countries.

Published in the United States of America by Oxford University Press
198 Madison Avenue, New York, NY 10016, United States of America.

© Oxford University Press 2020

First issued as an Oxford University Press paperback, 2022

Library of Congress Cataloging-in-Publication Data
Names: Heath, Joseph, 1967– author.
Title: The machinery of government : public administration and the liberal state /
Joseph Heath.
Description: New York, New York, United States of America : Oxford University Press, 2020. |
Includes bibliographical references and index.
Identifiers: LCCN 2019055825 (print) | LCCN 2019055826 (ebook) | ISBN 9780197509616 (hbk) |
ISBN 9780197628324 (pbk) | ISBN 9780197509630 (epub) | ISBN 9780197509623 (updf) |
ISBN 9780197509647 (online)
Subjects: LCSH: Public administration—Decision making. | Civil service ethics. | Public interest.
Classification: LCC JF1525.D4 H44 2020 (print) | LCC JF1525.D4 (ebook) |
DDC 352.3/301—dc23
LC record available at https://lccn.loc.gov/2019055825
LC ebook record available at https://lccn.loc.gov/2019055826

Contents

Preface

It is possible to go a long way in political philosophy without actually knowing very much about how the state works. To take just one example, the first time that I was contacted by a former Clerk of the Privy Council, I had to look up the job title to see what the position was. I remember the occasion quite well, because I had recently been hired at the Université de Montréal. The previous year, I had published a popular book, *The Efficient Society*, offering some philosophical arguments in defense of the welfare state in Canada. My ability to communicate with a broader public in both official languages quickly put me on the radar in Ottawa. And so, somewhat to my surprise, I found myself getting called by federal civil servants, asking me to share with them my thoughts on a range of different topics.

The most daunting invitation that I received during this period was from Jocelyne Bourgon, the aforementioned former Clerk of the Privy Council. She was at the time the head of an agency called the Canadian Centre for Management Development, whose mission was essentially to provide management training within the federal civil service. One of the events that she organized was a monthly dinner for the federal deputy ministers, to which a guest speaker was always invited to animate the discussion. She wanted to know whether I would like to come and discuss my book.

At this point, I should pause to explain some of these job titles. In Canada, a Deputy Minister (DM) is the highest-ranked civil servant within a particular department (equivalent to a Permanent Secretary in the United Kingdom). The Prime Minister, by contrast, does not have a department, but rather presides over the Privy Council Office. The Clerk of the Privy Council is the highest-ranked civil servant within the Privy Council Office, and so is essentially the Deputy Minister to the Prime Minister. The Clerk is also the official head of the public service, and is therefore the highest-ranked unelected official within the executive branch (save for the Queen and her Representative, the Governor-General).

Anyone who followed this should be able to see just how terrifying Bourgon's invitation was. It's one thing to write a book defending the welfare state, it's quite another to sit down for dinner with the people who actually *run* the welfare state. Figuring out what to say to them that would not be considered either impractical or banal was enough to induce a minor crisis of self-confidence.

I had plenty of time to ponder these questions. Since Ottawa is not far from Montreal, the easiest way to get to the dinner was to drive. And so, for two hours in the car, I wracked my brain trying to think up something to say to these people that would be less than completely useless. The mere fact that I had no idea who any of them were, or what their jobs entailed, was inauspicious. Philosophy trains you to think about the state in terms of very abstract normative principles. It most emphatically does not teach you to think in terms of policy, much less in operational terms.

In the end, the conversation did not go at all the way I had envisioned. One of the claims I had made in *The Efficient Society* was that efficiency was the most important "value" underlying the welfare state (a claim that I will revisit and defend, in greater detail, in chapter 4 of the present work). I was, in fact, cutting corners there, just a bit, for the sake of the popular audience, by using the vague term "value" to describe any sort of normative standard. Over the course of dinner, I happened to say, as an aside, something along the lines of "strictly speaking, efficiency is a principle, not a value." One of the DMs immediately picked up on this and asked, "What do you mean, a principle and not a value?" I went on to give a somewhat potted explanation of the distinction between the right and the good, which then turned into a discussion of John Rawls.

I could see that not all the DMs were interested in this conversation, but that quickly changed once I began to explain the importance of the distinction in terms of the liberal commitment to "neutrality." The conversation was taking place just a few years after Will Kymlicka had published his book *Multicultural Citizenship*, a work that had a significant impact in Canada, and so I illustrated the idea of neutrality by showing how it guided multiculturalism policy, and the expectation that immigrants will integrate into the institutions of Canadian society without necessarily assimilating into the culture or religion of the majority.[1] I went on to explain how the same sort of constraint generalized across every domain of state activity.

I could see that at this point I had everyone's attention, and we spent the rest of the evening discussing the concept of liberal neutrality. I found myself explaining things that in the academic world were considered rather obvious, but that clearly had not worked their way into the vocabulary of state officials. As things were wrapping up, one of the DMs thanked me quite earnestly for the conversation. "This idea of neutrality is something that I think we all understand, as part of how we go about our work, but we didn't have the words to explain what we were doing."

On the long drive home, I had ample time to reflect upon the experience. As I suspected, the things that I had planned to say were not that useful or interesting to the DMs. It turned out, however, that I did have something to offer, though it was not what I thought it would be. The biggest surprise was that the conversation had been a lot more "philosophical" than I expected, in the sense that it had focused almost entirely on abstract normative concepts. I had been trying to think of more practical, less abstract things to say, whereas the DMs actually wanted to talk about big ideas. The difference was that they were more interested in the vocabulary I was using than in the specific arguments I had developed. My "value added" as a philosopher, it turned out, stemmed from the centuries-long tradition of reflection and debate about political power that has equipped us with the vocabulary and the conceptual apparatus required to express certain aspects of our institutional practices.

As a former student of Charles Taylor and Jürgen Habermas, I was certainly familiar with the idea that the central role of philosophy is the expressive one, of making explicit what is otherwise only implicit in our practices. Until that point though, I had not realized how important this methodological precept could be. Helping other people to express their understandings of the world is, of course, less exciting than handing down normative principles from on high, or acting as a legislator in the kingdom of ends. It does, however, stand a better chance of being useful. In a social context in which professional philosophers have been almost completely sidelined in all public discussions of both politics and morality, this is not a small virtue.

This experience helps to explain the somewhat unusual method that I employ in this book. The work began as a set of reflections on "the ethics of public administration," understood broadly as a question about the norms that should govern the exercise of administrative power by members of the state bureaucracy. My approach, however, is reconstructive. I am not interested in telling civil servants how to do their jobs, or how to behave more "ethically" as they go about them. Apart from the fact that they know a lot more about how to do their jobs than I ever will, they also have an extremely rich professional work culture, which includes a strict list of "dos and don'ts."

There is, however, an enormous gap between the sophistication of this professional culture and the quality of the attempts that have been made to codify or articulate the "values" that are implicit in it—starting with the fact that civil servants love to talk about "values," even when what they mean is actually something more like "principles"! Part of this owes to a lack of sophistication in dealing with abstract normative concepts. Part of it stems from the political context in which they are writing, in particular, the need to appear suitably deferential to politicians, which has the unfortunate effect of preventing any acknowledgment, much less frank discussion, of the enormous power that is wielded by unelected officials.

I did not get going on the project, however, until many years later, after having moved (back) to the University of Toronto. There I became involved in discussions to create a public policy program. The founding director of the new School of Public Policy and Governance, Mark Stabile, invited me to teach a course on ethics for the public policy students. At the time, I had for several years been teaching business ethics in the philosophy department, and my views on that topic were reasonably well-developed. There is a group of business ethics theorists who attempt to generalize beyond the corporation, to think more abstractly about the ethics of "bureaucratic organizations" (a category that would obviously include the state). So I agreed to teach the public policy course, based on the assumption that some of what I knew about business ethics would be relevant to thinking about the moral obligations of state employees.

I quickly discovered how mistaken I was—the business ethics literature turned out to be of practically no use. The next big surprise occurred when I went to the library to check out the background literature, only to discover that, sitting next to the hundreds and hundreds of books on business ethics, were fewer than a dozen books dealing with the ethics of public administration. Almost all were very "hands-on" treatments by practitioners in the field. Moral questions arising from the behavior of *elected officials* have been the subject of reasonably intense discussion, but the question of how state employees (i.e., the "permanent" civil service) should act remains a surprisingly neglected topic.

And yet, while few of the specific doctrines that I had developed in the field of business ethics carried over to public administration, those who are familiar with my work in the former area will recognize that the method employed here is the same. One of the major problems with traditional business ethics is that it treats morality as something entirely external to the practice of business. As a result, the pronouncements of ethicists tend to arrive like an alien imposition, which in turn gives businesspeople license to ignore them, on the grounds that the expectations are simply incompatible with the demands of running a successful business. My approach, therefore, has been to focus on the moral obligations that are already implicit in market relations, and that are advanced through commercial and competition law, as well as regulation.[2] Business ethics, on this view, involves articulating the "implicit morality of the market." To do this, however, it is necessary to have something of a "big picture" view of the role the market plays in society, in order to see how it came to be structured in the way that it is.

My approach to the ethics of public administration is roughly the same, in that it represents an attempt to articulate the "implicit morality of the state," based on the practices of those who make up the overwhelming majority of public officials (i.e., members of the executive branch) in a well-governed polity. Unfortunately, the only way to get clear on this is also to have a "big picture" view of the role of the state in society. As a result, a substantial portion of this book is not about public administration per se, but rather about the history of the liberal-democratic state, and how it came to assume the major functions that it currently discharges in our society. For those who feel that this is digressive, at this point all I can offer are my assurances that, in my own mind at least, it is not.

Trying to figure out how civil servants think about questions of professional morality, I should note, is considerably more difficult than it is with business-people. Successful businesspeople tend to be both gregarious and opinionated, which makes them eager to discuss how their world works. The civil service, however, selects for the exact opposite qualities. The traditional "Whitehall ethos" that governs the civil service in Westminster-style parliamentary dem-ocracies is one that prizes discretion, secrecy, and anonymity. There are, as we shall see, very good institutional reasons for this, but one of the untoward effects is that it makes it extremely difficult for outsiders to figure out how the civil ser-vice operates. These people are, if not positively secretive, then at least extremely discrete.

One of the great advantages of teaching in a school of public policy, I have discovered, is that these institutions tend to accumulate a fair number of retired and furloughed civil servants, who, after a certain amount of deprogramming, start to become more gregarious and opinionated. Thus I have benefited enor-mously from conversations and interactions with my colleagues at the University of Toronto School of Public Policy and Governance (now the Munk School of Global Affairs and Public Policy), most importantly Mel Cappe (another former Clerk of the Privy Council). (I should mention as well that the DM who picked up on my equivocation regarding principles and values was Alex Himelfarb, who went on to become the Clerk under Prime Minister Paul Martin. I had a number of rewarding intellectual exchanges with Alex, both while he occupied that posi-tion and afterward.)

Lest I be accused of fraternizing only with former Clerks, I should note that, as a Fellow of the Trudeau Foundation, I have also had the opportunity to interact with a number of the public servants who serve as mentors for graduate students funded by the foundation. There were too many interesting exchanges to recall in detail, but certain conversations with Susan Cartwright and Morris Rosenberg stand out as having been particularly illuminating.

Finally, I should mention another, somewhat unusual, source of insight. For several years, I participated as a lecturer in an exchange program for civil servants, organized between the Asian Institute at the University of Toronto and Sun Yat-sen University in Guangzhou, China. It was part of a month-long exec-utive training program, which brought to Canada approximately forty relatively senior managers from across all sectors of the Chinese state, together with some state-owned enterprises, to study our practices of public administration.

There was something extremely clarifying about having to explain how "our system" works to a relatively skeptical audience of managers, who knew a great deal about how the world works, but practically nothing about how Western sys-tems of government work. Their inclination was to treat all our talk about de-mocracy as roughly equivalent to Communist Party ideals—important for the self-image of the society but saying practically nothing about how real decisions get made. Seeing our system through their eyes—which parts they found exciting, which parts they found unbelievable, which parts they found culturally most foreign—was enormously illuminating.

I have also benefited over the years from countless interactions with my public policy students. Most of this book has been used, at one time or another, as accompanying material for my public policy course, and so I have benefited from the comments, corrections, observations, and criticisms of literally hundreds of students. I would like to extend my deepest appreciation to them all. I would also like to thank Mark Stabile, Carolyn Tuohy, Michael Baker, and Peter Loewen, for their unflagging support for including this perspective in the curriculum.

As for specific individuals, I have benefited greatly from comments, conversations, and professional courtesies extended by Abraham Singer, Wayne Norman, Bernardo Zacka, Joel Anderson, Sareh Pouryousefi, Daniel Weinstock, Andrew Potter, James Radner, Rutger Claassen, Ian Clark, Xavier Landes, Vida Panitch, Jack Knight, Hamish Russell, and Audrey Macklin. My colleague David Dyzenhaus has also been an invaluable resource on administrative law. I would also like to thank Hamish Russell for research assistance. Material from this book has been presented at Carlton University, the Princeton University Center for Human Values, University of Copenhagen, SUNY Buffalo, the University of Maryland, as well as the conference for *Nomos LX*. Chapter 4 represents a revised version of material that was published as "Three Normative Models of the Welfare State" (*Public Reason* 3 [2011]: 13–43).

Finally, a note on the title of the book. The phrase "machinery of government" was coined by John Stuart Mill, who used it to refer to the ordinary operations of state bureaucracy.[3] Since that time, however, it has acquired a specialized meaning within the civil service in several countries. Canada, for instance, has an administrative unit known as the Machinery of Government Secretariat, whose job is to provide advice on any proposed reorganization of personnel or responsibilities between ministries. I've always found it amusing to think that there are people walking around with this phrase on their business cards. Nevertheless, the sense in which I am using the phrase is not the technical one, but rather the ordinary English-language sense originally used by Mill.

The Machinery of Government

1

Taking Public Administration Seriously

Thomas Hobbes famously described the state as an artificial creation, like a person writ large: "by Art is created that great Leviathan called a Common-wealth, or State (in latine Civitas), which is but an Artificiall Man."[1] The sovereign, he claimed, was equivalent to the soul, which gave "life and motion to the whole body." When properly ordered, "every joynt and member is moved to perform his duty" through a system of reward and punishment. He compared this system to the nerves and sinews that control the extremities in the human body. There is nothing mysterious about these motions, he claimed, "for what is the Heart, but a Spring; and the Nerves, but so many Strings; and the Joynts, but so many Wheeles, giving motion to the whole Body, such as was intended by the Artificer?"

This picture of the state as something artificial, rather than natural, marked a decisive break with the prior tradition of Western political philosophy. But this is not the only aspect of Hobbes's description that made a powerful impression. Although later thinkers were more comfortable assigning sovereignty to a dem-ocratically elected assembly than to a monarch, the image of the state as a mech-anism, or a machine, whose only objective should be to carry out the will of the sovereign, has been a lasting one. Indeed, as Western states became increasingly well-organized over time, and especially with the development of "rational" bu-reaucracy in the 19th century, the image of the state as a mechanism, and indi-vidual officials as cogs in a giant machine, became more widespread.

Yet despite the popularity of these images, political philosophers have always known that they represent at best an idealization, or, more likely, a distortion, of how the state really operates. A cog is able to transmit motion but has no motive force of its own. Yet a state bureaucracy is made up of people, who, no matter how well supervised and controlled, are nevertheless capable of recalcitrance, initia-tive, independence, and insubordination. With the rapid growth of the state in the 20th century, along with the changes in its role associated with the rise of the welfare state, the question of how much control elected assemblies actually exer-cise over the state bureaucracy became a topic of interest to academics. A sophis-ticated empirical literature has developed on this very subject.[2] Unfortunately, the question has been of surprisingly little interest to *normative* political theorists, who have had a great deal to say about democracy, sovereignty, and even judicial authority, but practically nothing to say about public administration. Yet a great

The Machinery of Government. Joseph Heath, Oxford University Press (2020). © Oxford University Press.
DOI: 10.1093/oso/9780197509616.001.0001

deal of public policy is made, not by elected officials, but by bureaucrats. This is a feature of our political systems that, at some level, everyone is aware of, and yet we have barely begun to reflect upon its normative significance.

1.1. Inside the machine

As a prelude to any philosophical reflection on the state, it makes sense to examine the "machinery of government" a bit more carefully, to see what sorts of things the cogs have been up to. What follows are three stories—by no means unusual or unrepresentative—that provide a sense of how state bureaucracy actually functions, and how complex policy questions are decided. We begin with the military, the branch of the executive that is, at least in theory, most committed to the principle of following orders.

1.1.1. The military

US Army General Creighton Abrams is remembered today primarily because of the battle tank—the M1 Abrams—that was named in his honor. Whatever the merits of this vehicle, his most important legacy has nothing to do with military hardware. It arises from a bureaucratic reorganization of the US Army that he oversaw—the so-called Total Force structure, adopted in 1973. Abrams's contribution occurred as part of a more general restructuring of the US military that was undertaken in reaction to the humiliation suffered in Vietnam. From an American perspective, the war in Vietnam had been a disaster in almost every way possible. The brunt of the suffering was, of course, felt by the people of Vietnam. But the war also created intense conflict within American society, much of it centered on the draft (i.e., conscription), which was extremely unpopular. Adding salt to the wound was the hostile reception that many American soldiers received upon returning from tours of duty. Soldiers in uniform routinely encountered hissing, verbal abuse, and confrontation in public places. For years, Pentagon staff had to walk through a gauntlet of protesters on the way to work, who were calling them "baby killers" and war criminals.[3] To say that morale was low would be a serious understatement.

The first and most obvious conclusion to be drawn from this was that conscription had been a terrible idea. Although Richard Nixon had promised to end the draft during the 1968 electoral campaign, once elected he oversaw a continuation of the practice. In 1973, however, when the bill that had authorized the draft expired, President Nixon allowed it to lapse. The administration officially committed itself to the principle of an all-volunteer force, based on widespread agreement that the draft had become a needlessly divisive issue in American society. Within the military, however, some went even further. The domestic acrimony and conflict that had developed, they believed, was not just a consequence of an unpopular draft. The deeper problem was that the civilian leadership had committed American forces to a war that did not enjoy general public support. Much of the lack of support owed to the fact that there had been no official congressional declaration of war, just a gradual escalation of forces by successive presidents, authorized by the vague wording of the 1964 Gulf of Tonkin resolution.

Abrams was among those who shared these convictions. He vowed that elected officials would never again be permitted to undertake a major military operation without first securing the broad support of the American people. The commitment to an all-volunteer force required a large-scale reorganization, and under the auspices of this initiative, Abrams concluded the so-called Golden Handshake agreement with the secretary of defense, James Schlesinger.[4] Abrams secured approval to increase the number of army divisions from thirteen to sixteen, in return for a commitment to achieve this using only existing human resources. Observers were initially puzzled by the agreement, since it seemed to be impossible based on the existing model. There simply were not enough active service members to staff that many positions. The way Abrams achieved it was by transferring most of the army's traditional support functions to reserve units. For instance, he made reservists responsible for all the core transportation functions, operating seaports, airports, and railways. Again, to some observers this seemed strange: "For the Army, Abrams's unilateral decision to commit the Army to fielding sixteen divisions without an increase in overall strength was stunning for the degree to which it [made] the active Army dependent upon the reserves."[5] Indeed, after the Total Force restructuring undertaken by Abrams was complete, "a reserve call-up would be needed on practically the first day of any crisis."[6]

Increasing the role of the reserves was, in fact, the primary objective of Abrams's initiative. By putting almost the entire transportation infrastructure in the hands of reservists, he made it impossible to deploy the army without calling up reserves. This, in turn, made it more difficult for civilian authorities to commit the United States to large-scale military action without first securing broad-based public support.[7] As one commentator described it:

> By making reliance on the reserves so profound that the Army could not function without them even in the early days of a major crisis, Abrams was also fundamentally limiting a president's flexibility in committing military forces. Even activating the reserves temporarily required a presidential proclamation, a politically charged move guaranteed to spark intense debate on Capitol Hill and in

governors' mansions across the country, where control of the National Guard resides short of a national emergency. Committing them to a theater of operations for longer than 180 days required the direct approval of Congress. Because of the nature of the reserve structure, National Guardsmen and Army and Air Force Reservists are also generally older than their active-duty counterparts, and mobilizing them meant abruptly depriving families across the country of husbands and fathers. It was exactly the type of polarizing debate and national hardship that Lyndon Johnson had hoped to avoid by not ordering a major mobilization of the reserves during Vietnam.[8]

As Schlesinger later observed, Abrams was strongly committed to the principle of civilian control of the armed forces. At the same time, he believed that Lyndon Johnson's refusal to call up the reserves had been one of the worst decisions made during the Vietnam conflict. So, while maintaining deference to civilian authority, Abrams's objective was, as Schlesinger put it, "to fix the incentives so that the civilians would act appropriately."[9] Others have described Abrams's force restructuring as creating an "extra-constitutional tripwire on the presidential use of military power."[10]

1.1.2. Transportation

In 1897, in an attempt to encourage the economic development of coal fields in southern British Columbia, the Government of Canada entered into an agreement with the Canadian Pacific Railroad (CPR) to secure construction of a railroad from Lethbridge, in southern Alberta, to Nelson, in British Columbia, passing through the Crow's Nest Pass. The government ceded 3.75 million acres of land to the railroad, and provided a large cash subsidy. In return, the railroad agreed to a bundle of rate-control measures, including a reduction and then a freeze on transportation rates for the shipping of grain grown on the prairies to all the major export ports. Fatefully, in what remained common practice in the 19th century, these rate reductions were all specified in (nominal) dollar terms. No one thought much of this, in part because of the expectation that rail rates would fall, but also because Canada was on the gold standard at the time, and so the possibility of significant price inflation was not considered.

And indeed, for the next fifty years, the "Crow Rate," as it was called, had much the desired effect, constraining monopolistic pricing practices without imposing significant hardship on the railroads. In the late 1940s, however, after wartime wage-and-price controls had been lifted, there was a sudden bout of price inflation, which, in turn, began to cause financial hardship for the CPR. By 1961, losses from hauling grain were estimated to be in the millions of dollars per year.

The response from the railroad was predictable. Unable to make money hauling grain, it essentially stopped all new investment in and maintenance of the grain-hauling infrastructure. The company refused to upgrade its old boxcars to the more efficient new hopper cars; but more significantly, it stopped all maintenance work on the intricate network of branch lines that connected the major trunks to the grain elevators (and small towns) spread across the prairies (a decision that inspired the classic Canadian farm anthem, "Goddamn the CPR").[11]

This put the Canadian government in a difficult position. The Crow Rate had been negotiated before the provinces of Alberta and Saskatchewan entered the confederation. Over time, the rate had come to be seen as one of the essential terms of that entry, giving it something akin to constitutional status in those provinces—at least as far as popular perception was concerned. Yet the arrangement it created was clearly unsustainable. Not only did it make grain transportation entirely uneconomical, but the price distortion had increasingly negative effects on the economies of the Western provinces. By massively subsidizing the export of grain, it discouraged both value-added food processing and livestock production in the West. It also limited diversification into new crops such as soy beans and canola, which were not eligible for the subsidy. Yet the government was just as locked into the agreement as the railroad. Any politician foolish enough to even suggest that the rate be reconsidered was immediately and decisively punished at the polls. Thus the Government of Canada began paying subsidies to the railroads and, over time, became more deeply involved in railroad operations, taking over the maintenance of numerous branch lines and purchasing thousands of hopper cars.

With the advent of double-digit inflation in the 1970s, it became clear to officials in the Departments of Transportation and of Finance that the arrangement could not continue. Yet the issue of abolishing the Crow Rate seemed like a political non-starter. Canada's first-past-the-post electoral system, not to mention the decentralized structure of the federation, gives concentrated regional interests enormous sway over federal government policy. In 1974, the minister responsible for the Canadian Wheat Board, Otto Lang, was persuaded to give a speech proposing the abolition of the Crow Rate (combined with one-time compensation to farmers).[12] He was thoroughly vilified for his efforts, and promptly deposed by his Saskatchewan constituents in the next election. When the Progressive Conservative Party of Canada was elected in 1979, Don Mazankowski of Alberta was appointed minister of transport, an arrangement that essentially made any movement on the issue impossible.

The snap election of 1980, which brought the Liberal Party of Canada headed by Pierre Trudeau back to power, created a unique opportunity. First, because of their overwhelming sweep of ridings in Quebec, the Liberals were able to form a majority government despite having lost every seat west of Winnipeg.

Thus there was literally no one in the government beholden to Western voters. (Trudeau resorted to appointing unelected senators to the cabinet to represent Western interests.) Second, Trudeau's primary focus was on constitutional issues, a preoccupation that made him broadly permissive with respect to other policy areas and ministries. Finally, Trudeau appointed Jean-Luc Pépin to the Transport Ministry, a Quebec MP whom he wanted to sideline because of their disagreements over constitutional questions. Pépin was an extremely capable minister, who was looking for a big policy issue with which to leave his mark. Officials in the Department of Transportation had already, over the course of the previous decade, been engaged in intensive negotiations with stakeholder groups in Western Canada, trying to build some agreement around changes in the Crow. They quickly moved to bring Pépin up to speed on the file and integrate him into the discussions.

Pépin proved adept, and quickly earned a reputation as an "honest broker" among interest groups on all sides of the issue. (As Arthur Kroeger, the deputy minister of transportation from 1980 to 1983, observed, "During this period Pépin displayed increasing mastery of transport issues; after six months as minister, he was beginning to find his feet. When we went to Cabinet committees together, I found him articulate and able to hold the attention of his colleagues when he spoke.")[13] The civil service also invested a tremendous amount of time and effort in mediating relations between representatives of Western farmers and members of the government. For instance, upon learning that the executive of the Western Agricultural Conference (WAC) was holding a meeting in Ottawa, transport officials arranged for a series of additional meetings with members of Cabinet and Prime Minister Trudeau. Kroeger recalls making careful preparations for the meeting with Trudeau:

> Having observed that some of the executive's meetings with ministers had strayed off to peripheral issues, I decided to draft a list of key questions that should be addressed during the meeting with the prime minister. I sent them to Janet Smith in the Privy Council Office, who incorporated them into the prime minister's briefing note. I then passed the same set of questions to the WAC executive, as a means of ensuring that both sides would use their limited time together to discuss the things that really mattered. When I subsequently told Pépin what I had done, he fully concurred.[14]

Unfortunately, the reform effort was dealt a serious setback in 1982–83, when farmers in Quebec decided to oppose changes to the Crow, on somewhat convoluted grounds. By the 1980s, Western farmers were paying less than 20 percent of the cost of transporting their grain to port. Increasing the price of transportation would have decreased the *local* price of grain, which would, in turn, have benefited Western livestock producers. Quebec farmers concluded that this would expose them to unwanted competition, and as a result, they began to oppose changing the Crow Rate. The Liberal government, being highly sensitive to opinion in Quebec, quickly folded, rejecting a draft bill that Pépin had presented. Kroeger describes the reaction in the department:

> For officials in the department, as much as for our minister, the Cabinet's refusal on producer payments came as a body blow. The qualities of objectivity and political neutrality that are mandatory for those who wish to serve as government officials should not be confused with an indifference to public policy outcomes. We were particularly dismayed because the fears felt by the farmers in Quebec, which had driven the Cabinet's decision, were clearly unfounded, as would be demonstrated in later years. So far as we were concerned, the Cabinet's decision was a clear case of politicians knowing the better and choosing the worst.[15]

Officials responded by modifying the bill, agreeing to pay the transitional subsidy directly to the railroads rather than to farmers, an arrangement that mollified Quebec interests by preserving the competitive disadvantage suffered by the Western livestock industry. This was a second-best policy, but it was widely understood to be the only politically feasible arrangement. In this form, the Western Grain Transportation Act was eventually passed, in November 1983, and with it the Crow Rate was abolished. (Since that time, soy beans have become the third-largest farm crop in Canada, in terms of cash receipts, and annual production in Manitoba and Saskatchewan has increased from zero to over 2.5 million tonnes in 2017.[16] That same year, canola displaced wheat as the most widely seeded crop in Canada.[17])

1.1.3. Regulation

One of the benchmarks of economic development is the extent to which states exercise regulatory authority and control over the sale of food and medicine within their territory. With respect to medicines in particular, all developed nations have a sophisticated review process, particularly for new drugs, which must undergo clinical trials and secure approval *prior* to sale. Many of these procedures were pioneered by the US Food and Drug Administration (FDA), which developed the model of the regulator possessed of gatekeeping authority, and also designed the system of procedures new drugs would have to undergo to obtain approval (such as the sequence of "phase I," "phase II," and "phase III" clinical trial protocols). Indeed, despite various attempts to weaken its authority over the past two decades, the FDA remains one of the most powerful regulatory agencies of its type, with both the highest level of in-house scientific expertise and the most demanding standards in the world.[18] This is sometimes thought to be paradoxical, or at least surprising. As Daniel Carpenter asks, "Why in the Unites States—the reputed 'weak state' of the Western world . . .—has the national government displayed the most far-reaching and stringent regulations on medicines? Why, for most of the twentieth century, has the FDA exercised a greater degree of formal power and informal discretion over drug development and marketing than have other national regulators?"[19]

The answer to this question is complex, but a central feature of it involves the power the FDA had to redefine and expand its mandate over the course of the 20th century. Food adulteration, for example, was a long-standing problem in early capitalism, and some of the earliest regulatory interventions were aimed at limiting it. The 1906 Food and Drugs Act extended this mandate to include drugs. The act, however, conferred very little authority, and the country saw a large-scale expansion of the "patent medicine" market. The number of different products being sold increased from hundreds in the 19th century to thousands in the early 20th. After several well-publicized episodes of poisoning, in particular, the deaths of 107 people in 1937 who had used a product called Dr. Massengill's Elixir Sulfanilamide, Congress was pressed to create an agency with gatekeeping authority, so that new drugs would require approval before being marketed. Thus the FDA was officially created in 1938, by the Federal Food, Drug and Cosmetic Act.

A key feature of the legislation is that it authorized the FDA to evaluate the safety of all prospective new drugs. What it did *not* do, however, was authorize the FDA to assess the efficacy, or therapeutic value, of proposed medicines. Naturally, the manufacturers of patent medications resisted such an extension of FDA power; but the prerogative of judging clinical efficacy was also jealously guarded by doctors, who did not like the idea of government officials telling them what medications they could and could not prescribe to patients. This was an unfortunate state of affairs, because the overwhelming majority of drugs being sold at the time, though not positively toxic, were nevertheless entirely useless. As Carpenter notes, "With the possible exception of aspirin (whose contents were usually published) and several analgesics, no widely sold patent medicine of the late nineteenth to early twentieth century was later shown to have clinical curative power for its consumers."[20]

This, combined with a simple professional aversion to hucksterism and the exploitation of consumers, no doubt led many FDA scientists to want to expand the agency's mandate. At the same time, the emergence and development of pharmacology as a scientific discipline—led in no small measure by FDA employees—resulted in a situation in which government scientists were often in a much better position to make judgments of clinical efficacy than doctors.

Doctors were notorious for falling prey to anecdotal evidence, and for offering "testimonials" for drugs that in fact had no therapeutic value. The only solution—as FDA officials could clearly see—was to introduce clinical trials using control groups, to separate out the effects of a treatment from the background tendency of patients to recover on their own.

Thus the FDA began, in the postwar era, to expand its mandate beyond merely keeping toxic substances off the market. As early as 1949, the head of the agency's New Drug Section, Erwin E. Nelson, began pressing to expand the FDA mandate to include efficacy as well as safety. One argument appealed to the FDA's authority over labeling: "While the fundamental concern of the new drug application is with the evidence for safety, the law also has a requirement to the effect that direction for use must be supplied. And these will have to do with both the safest and most efficacious way of using the drug."[21] The labeling rule thus offered a back door through which an assessment of efficacy could be introduced. The more powerful argument, however, which later came to predominate, was that the mandate to assess safety *presupposed* a determination of efficacy, because one could not assess safety without knowing the dose the individual would be taking.[22] The suggestion was that, if a drug lacked efficacy, then an individual might take an arbitrarily large dose, and that nothing could be judged "safe" in such quantities. Thus any assessment of safety required a precursor investigation to determine the clinically effective dose. Only once the effective dose size was determined could one go on to determine whether the drug was safe.

On the basis of this appeal to "the procedural inseparability of safety and efficacy," along with the fact that the agency was already mandating clinical trials to prove safety, the FDA was able to gradually expand its requirements and force manufacturers to provide proof of clinical efficacy. It achieved this through a series of modifications of the NDA (New Drug Application) form, which determined the requirements that needed to be met for drug approvals. It should be noted that the inseparability argument achieved greater force over time, particularly with the invention of early chemotherapy agents, which were of necessity toxic, since chemotherapy works by killing cells. Thus one could not say that they were "safe" in the abstract; their use could only be justified on the grounds that the clinical benefits outweighed their negative side effects. Here, it is less controversial to say that safety and efficacy are intertwined. Nevertheless, one could imagine a system in which the FDA merely oversaw a process through which toxicity would be assessed at various dose levels, publicized the results, and left the decision of whether the benefits outweighed the harms up to doctors and patients.

For this reason, the FDA continued to campaign, in various ways, for changes to the enabling statute that would officially authorize it to assess efficacy. It was able to achieve this in 1962, with the so-called Kefauver-Harris Amendments, which among other things, gave the agency the desired mandate to assess the efficacy of new drugs. Yet it is clear that the FDA would never have been able to achieve this legislative outcome—given the lobbying power of the American Medical Association (AMA), as well as of the nascent pharmaceutical industry— without the near miss that Americans experienced with the drug thalidomide. The manufacturer, William S. Merrell & Co., had submitted thalidomide for approval in the United States (under the generic name Kevadon) in 1961, but FDA scientist Frances Kelsey had rejected the initial application, demanding that more extensive clinical trials be performed. During the period of delay, evidence of serious side effects associated with the drug began to accumulate in Europe, particularly in Germany, where it was in widespread use. Women who had used it during the first trimester of pregnancy as an anti-nausea drug gave birth to babies with phocomelia, or serious birth defects in their extremities. Kelsey was quickly hailed as a national hero for having protected Americans from this scourge. She was profiled in virtually every major newspaper and magazine in the country, and became the subject of a famous photograph when she was awarded a Distinguished Civilian Medal of Honor by President John F. Kennedy.

The FDA worked to parlay this increased moral authority into an expansion of its statutory powers. Senator Estes Kefauver had previously tried to pass a set of amendments to the 1938 Food, Drug and Cosmetic Act, but his efforts had been blocked by lobbying from the AMA and the pharmaceutical industry. After Kelsey was summoned to testify to Congress, "presidents, senators and House members pushed one another aside to shower ever more praise and ever more discretion upon the officers of the Food and Drug Administration."[23] The amendments were passed, granting the FDA not only the authority to demand proof of efficacy, but also substantial discretion (or delegation of powers). In particular, legislators left a large number of key concepts undefined. As a result, "national politicians handed to the Administration the power of interpretation and concept definition, all but ensuring that the key developments in American pharmaceutical policy would come not from statute but from administration rule-making and regulatory practice."[24]

Critics have sometimes charged that these amendments were adopted in a hurried fashion, in the aftermath of a crisis. This is not the case. The statutory changes had in fact been drawn up years in advance, and the FDA had been actively (but unsuccessfully) lobbying Congress to enact them. As Kelsey later described it:

The Department's proposed legislation, which served as the basis for most of the provisions in the law as enacted which relate to drug testing, was very carefully drafted by experts and widely studied within the Executive Branch of the Government before it was sent to Congress by our Secretary. Similarly the proposed investigational drug regulations were carefully prepared on the basis of many years of experience with the new drug law before the thalidomide situation came to public attention.[25]

It is important to be clear about what Kelsey is saying here: the FDA basically wrote the law, and when the time was right—that is, when the averted thalidomide catastrophe gave it the public profile and moral authority it needed— strong-armed Congress into passing it. This episode illustrates a more general trend in the development of regulatory law in the United States. As Carpenter puts it, "The transformation of efficacy regulation demonstrates a growing pattern of the post–New Deal American state: federal rulemaking and statutes frequently encode administrative practices that were established years before."[26]

1.2. Beyond discretion

The stories of ending the draft in the United States, abolishing Canada's Crow Rate, and expanding the mandate of the US FDA took place in different jurisdictions, at different times, and involved different branches of the state. At first glance, they may appear to have little in common. And yet they do share something. They are all instances of democratic states making good decisions, but not making them in the way that conventional democratic theory says they should. According to the standard textbook story, a democratic society is "self-governing" in that the people, via their elected representatives, exercise sovereignty and decision-making authority. This means that major decisions about the use of state power are supposed to be made by the legislature, and by elected officials. According to this theory of the state, elected officials stand at the apex of power and have the responsibility to decide all questions of "policy." These decisions are then handed down to officials whose job is simply to implement the policies that have been adopted.[27]

It is, of course, generally understood that the "real world of democracy" is never quite so simple, and that these basic organizational principles are often violated in practice. This is often regarded as a defect, or an imperfection, in the organization of democratic states. Yet if one examines more closely the way that public policy is developed—in particular, if one speaks to public officials and civil servants—these "imperfections" seem to be much more the rule than the exception.[28] Furthermore, while a great deal has been written about how the judiciary serves as a countermajoritarian institution, curbing the occasional excesses of popular democracy, the civil service in many instances plays the same role. More striking, however, is simply the level of autonomy that the civil service enjoys in its day-to-day activities (which in turn lends a degree of consistency, stability, technical expertise, and long-term planning to state action that it might otherwise lack).

This autonomy takes several different forms. The first, illustrated by Abrams's reorganization of the US Army, is that public officials often have a great deal of *discretion* in how they carry out their orders. In the military, for instance, an enormous range of operational questions are decided by officers, not by the civilian leadership. Such questions as who will operate ports or run the meal services are of much too low a level of granularity to be dealt with by White House officials, much less Congress. But as Abrams showed, decisions made at this level can have enormous ramifications and, indeed, can dramatically restrict the range of options that are available at the top policy level. Furthermore, while the principle of civilian oversight remains inviolate, there has been a general push over the past few decades to increase the amount of discretion exercised by the military. The image of US President Johnson hunched over a map of Vietnam, literally choosing which targets to bomb, is one that made many people very uncomfortable, for multiple reasons. Increasingly, there is the sense that these sorts of operational decisions should be made by military professionals.

The second attribute of civil servants—illustrated by Kroeger's account of the attempts to retire the Crow Rate—is that they are able to play a "long game," which gives them significant *control over the policy process*. Unlike politicians, civil servants are often in a position to work on an issue for decades, and to wait until circumstances are propitious—and the government likely to be sympathetic—before moving on a particular proposal. The civil service is also in a position to cultivate long-term relationships with the major players in civil society, to fund research and analysis, to study and collaborate with officials in other jurisdictions, and to draw upon academic or technical expertise. Compared to politicians, they are often better organized, better informed, and less beholden to short-term political pressure. This is especially true in jurisdictions where there is a tradition of executive-branch political neutrality, which results in very little turnover of personnel with changes of government.

The third feature is the most diffuse and difficult to characterize. Carpenter, in his study of the FDA, tries to describe it with his twin notions of "reputation and power." The phenomenon he is after, which is well illustrated in the case of the FDA, is that government departments or agencies are able to become a locus of genuine political power, and perhaps even authority, in part through their success at solving problems. This power can, in turn, be used to bring pressure to bear on elected officials, through numerous channels.[29] If one looks at attitude surveys of the general public, one sees that it is common for Americans to express much higher levels of trust in various administrative agencies of the US federal government than in their elected officials (indeed, Congress as an institution usually has the lowest approval rating of all). This is in part due to peculiar design features of the US legislative system, but it also reflects a more general phenomenon. Unelected officials, such as the governor of the central bank, the chief medical officer, or the auditor-general, are often highly authoritative figures, not just because of their technical expertise, but because they are seen as discharging the central obligation of public officials—namely, to serve the public interest—more effectively than elected leaders. This gives them the ability to bring pressure to bear on elected officials and, more generally, to influence legislative outcomes.

There is, I should note, a long-standing discussion about the issue of discretion in public administration.[30] The phenomenon of administrative discretion is not new; it arose pretty much simultaneously with the development of administrative capacity in the modern state. In Britain, for instance, when legislators began to take an interest in regulating various social and economic questions in the early 19th century, they quickly discovered that standing in the halls of Westminster and saying "make it so!" did not, in general, result in it coming to be so. Whether the issue concerned building codes, railway safety standards, health and sanitation matters, provision of foodstuffs on transatlantic voyages, or encouraging counties to create local police forces, acts of Parliament were passed, and then subsequently ignored by everyone, whether it be individuals, local governments, or the nascent joint-stock enterprises. It became clear that if the state wanted to regulate such matters, it would need to do more than just pass laws; it would need to create the administrative capacity to ensure that the laws were actually put in effect.

Yet in trying to create effective administrative capacity, British legislators found themselves also endowing administrative officials with wide-ranging discretion. For instance, the responsibilities of the well-known 19th-century figure of the "factory inspector" entailed much more than what we would now consider to be an inspector's duties. The combination of changing technology and poor communications meant that inspectors in the 19th century had to be able to make a great number of decisions on the spot, without conferring with either Whitehall or Parliament. Thus British inspectors enjoyed quasi-judicial power, including the ability to create rules and regulations, and to mandate specific technologies and remedies.[31] (They also served as an important source of technical advice and information about best practices, in an era in which there was relatively little diffusion of knowledge among business owners.)

In many cases, discretionary powers such as those enjoyed by factory inspectors were written right in to legislation. For instance, the 1832 Act for the Prevention of Cholera delegated the power to make "rules and regulations" for the containment of the disease to the Privy Council office, on the grounds that "it may be impossible to establish such rules and regulations by the authority of parliament with sufficient promptitude to meet the exigency of any case as it may occur."[32] The 1844 Railroad Regulation Act left the formulation of several standards to the Board of Trade, specifying that "the Lords of the said Committee shall have a discretionary Power" in those domains. For instance, in setting standards for passenger cars, the statute stated that "the Carriages in which Passengers shall be conveyed by such Train shall be provided with Seats, and shall be protected from the Weather, in a Manner satisfactory to the Lords of the said Committee."[33] This is an early instance of a formulation that became typical over the course of the century.

When central banking arrangements were formalized in the early 20th century, a similar decision was made to insulate these institutions from direct political control. Thus the US Congress gave the Federal Reserve a very broad mandate. The members of its Board of Governors are appointed by the president and ratified by the Senate. Beyond that, they operate with almost as much independence from the government of the day as do Supreme Court justices, enjoying fourteen-year terms that cannot be revoked or cut short by elected officials. Similarly, the Governor of the Bank of Canada is appointed by the government for a seven-year term with no provision for removal from office. Canada's minister of finance has the power to issue written directives to the bank, which it must comply with, but this power has never been exercised. In keeping with constitutional tradition, central bank independence remains more of a convention in Canada than in the United States, and yet it is a convention that has evolved for a reason.

It is sometimes thought that banking is a merely technical matter, which is why it can be removed from the remit of democratic politics. The legislature, according to this view, sets the basic policy objective of the bank, leaving officials with only "technical discretion," concerning the choice of the appropriate means to realize these ends. And yet this is manifestly not the case. The current mandate of the US Federal Reserve is to "maintain long run growth of the monetary and credit aggregates commensurate with the economy's long run potential to increase production, so as to promote effectively the goals of maximum employment, stable prices, and moderate long-term interest rates." It is often referred to as a "dual mandate," since the objectives of maintaining "maximum employment" and "stable prices" (i.e., low inflation) often push in opposite directions, leaving to the Board of Governors, and the Reserve Board Chair, the very political task of deciding how these two objectives should be balanced. Similarly, the Bank of Canada has a complex mandate—namely, "to regulate credit and currency in the best interests of the economic life of the nation, to control and protect the external value of the national monetary unit and to mitigate by its influence fluctuations in the general level of production, trade, prices and employment, so far as may be possible within the scope of monetary action, and generally to promote the economic and financial welfare of Canada." The use of open-ended language, such as the injunction to promote "the best interests of the economic life of the nation," is clearly intended to grant much more than technical discretion to the bank.

The rationale for taking central banking out of the hands of politicians was relatively straightforward. Sound management of the national monetary system requires resisting several temptations to which politicians have been known to succumb, particularly once countries have gone off the gold standard and so have the ability to print money. The concern is that elected officials will favor "easy money" policies in order to relax fiscal constraints, and therefore will tend to adopt policies that are inflationary. Central bankers are often in a position of having to make extremely unpopular decisions, such as to maintain high interest rates to control inflation. As a result, it makes sense to want to insulate them, to some degree, from the populist backlash that usually develops during such periods. The amount of democratic control over this segment of the executive has therefore been adjusted, based largely on the perception that democratic majorities cannot be trusted to make decisions in this domain that are in their own long-run interest.[34]

Indeed, the demand to "keep politics out" of particular domains of public administration is surprisingly long-standing and, in many cases, a popular demand, despite the fact that it flies directly in the face of the principle of democratic legitimacy.[35] With the development of the welfare state in the 20th century, it became increasingly common for entire administrative agencies to be set up in an arms-length relationship to elected officials. For example, when the US Congress created the Consumer Product Safety Commission in 1981, it went to some lengths to ensure that the agency would function in a way that was free from political interference. This was reflected in the decision to create an independent agency rather than place it within the Department of Health, Education, and Welfare. The committee report defending the decision explained it in the following terms:

This decision reflects the committee's belief that an independent agency can better carry out the legislative and judicial functions contained in this bill with cold neutrality that the public has a right to expect of regulatory agencies formed for its protection. Independent status, and bipartisan commissioners with staggered and fixed terms, will tend to produce greater insulation from political and economic pressures than is possible . . . in a cabinet-level department. The Commission's decision under the legislation will necessarily involve a careful meld of safety and economic considerations. This delicate balance, the committee believes, should be struck in a setting as far removed as possible from partisan influence.[36]

This is just one example of a more general trend in US public admin-istration, which reached its apogee in the 1970s with the creation of the Environmental Protection Agency (EPA) and the Occupational Safety and Health Administration, both of which were established with very broad mandates. Given the way that American politics functions, protecting regulatory agencies from "capture" by regulated interests often means protecting them from *politicians*. Yet this obviously runs contrary to the desire to maintain democratic accountability. Thus an important body of critical literature emerged, during the 1970s, arguing, as one commentator put it, that "Congress had reached a point of abdicating its responsibilities to govern by creating one new bureaucracy after another while constraining them with little more than a directive to 'Go forth and do good.'"[37]

Another major trend in public-sector management during the 20th cen-tury, particularly during the 1960s and 1970s, was "corporatization," whereby segments of the state bureaucracy were hived off and placed in semi-autonomous corporations—state-owned enterprises (SOEs), or "crown corporations" in Westminster parlance—with independent boards of directors appointed by the government. The British General Post Office (or the Royal Mail), for instance, was a government department throughout most of the 19th and 20th centuries (often with a minister, who sat in Cabinet). In 1969 its assets were transferred to an independent statutory corporation, which has operated at arms-length from the government ever since. Similarly, many Western states in the postwar period came to own airlines, railroads, shipping lines, coal mines, electrical generation facilities, telegraph services, and oil companies, many of which were subject to direct political administration (e.g., at the cabinet level). To pick a particularly notorious example, most Western states owned a national airline (e.g., British Overseas Airway Corporation, which became British Airways; Trans-Canada Airlines, which became Air Canada, etc.). Administration of these airways, in-cluding major decisions about routes, fares, maintenance facilities, and purchase of new aircraft, was undertaken at the cabinet level, by elected officials. During the 1970s, however, there was a concerted push to remove these types of admin-istrative decisions from political control. The standard remedy was corporat-ization, which involved the partitioning of assets and liabilities between the SOE and line departments, creation of a board of directors to mediate relations be-tween elected officials and managers, self-financing of capital investment by the SOE, increased focus on economic efficiency (i.e., break-even or profitability) as a managerial objective, and finally, the use of contracting to implement the "so-cial responsibility" mandate of the SOE.[38]

Needless to say, these reforms dramatically increased managerial autonomy in the public sector. It should be noted, as well, that these trends in public man-agement had all been put in place long before the rise of the reform movement known as "new public management" (NPM; or, later, in the United States, "reinventing government"), which pushed the hiving-off process even further, resulting in the creation of agencies with various degrees of autonomy from the original line departments. It would be something of an understatement to describe the reforms as having increased the amount of discretion exercised by public officials. In many cases, it directly granted them the ability to take initiatives or to set policy in particular domains. For instance, under the old system, in which the activities of SOEs were integrated into one or more government departments, there was no separation between the budget of the "firm" and that of the department in which it was embedded (with the implication that operating losses were simply absorbed by departmental budgets). "Capital investment by state enterprises was, alongside road building, current expenditure on police and so on, part of public expenditure programmes, whilst their operating surpluses were, along with taxes, social security payments and so on, part of government income."[39] It follows from the structure of these arrangements that their budgets were, in the end, subject to parliamentary approval. The removal of budgets from the line departments therefore meant that projects could be undertaken, in principle, without the consent of elected officials.

Those familiar with this history will know that these initiatives were undertaken, not by self-aggrandizing bureaucrats trying to maximize budgets, but as a broad-based response to the range of new responsibilities taken on by the state as part of a good-faith effort to serve the public interest more effectively. Furthermore, they were undertaken with the full knowledge and consent of elected officials. Even the NPM reforms, which were largely motivated by the desire to *curb* bureaucratic entrenchment and budget maximization, wound up dramatically increasing the autonomy of civil servants. Indeed, there was something rather paradoxical in UK Prime Minister Margaret Thatcher's desire to crack down on what she saw as an unresponsive and splenetic civil service, while at the same time promoting greater "risk-taking" and "innovation" among public-sector managers.[40] Since it is impossible to identify successful innovations or good risks in advance, the only way to achieve these objectives is to increase managerial discretion (and to develop increased tolerance for failure).

As a consequence of these various trends, an enormous gap has opened up between the way democratic states are supposed to function—or at least the way their operations are represented in normative political theory—and the way they actually do operate. This brings to mind Michel Foucault's claim that "despite the differences in epochs and objectives the representation of power has remained under the spell of monarchy. In political thought and analysis we still have not cut off the head of the king."[41] There is a persistent tendency to imagine the state as a single vertically integrated hierarchy, in which all major decisions are taken at the apex of power. This in turn leads to an overwhelming emphasis on legislatures as the primary locus of public decision-making.[42] Yet if one looks at institutions like the military, which are supposed to be a best-case scenario for a hierarchical model of administration, one can see that the "org chart" provides a very misleading picture of how power is actually exercised. The same is true of the police (where sociological studies established, long ago, that the culture of street-level policing involves a commitment to various policy objectives that are not, strictly speaking, part of their mandate, such as the preoccupation with the preservation of "social order").[43] It is striking that in both cases, these arrangements are not obviously dysfunctional. Indeed, elected officials are flawed in many ways, and it is not difficult to think of good policy reasons for wanting certain questions to be decided at lower levels of state administration.

Unfortunately, the "democratic self-governance" picture remains the dominant normative model of the modern liberal-democratic state. As a result, much of the actual policymaking process within the state occurs in a "wink-wink nudge-nudge" fashion, where everyone understands the implicit structure of decision-making, but nothing is ever made explicit, because that would run contrary to the dominant *normative* understanding of how democratic states are supposed to function. My own view, which I intend to defend over the course of this book, is that the relative autonomy of public administration is not an embarrassment to democratic principles, only to certain misinterpretations that have become widespread. My hope is that showing how existing arrangements can be normatively justifiable will make it possible to articulate, or to make explicit, the actual processes through which decision-making occurs. This should, in turn, permit more critical self-reflection upon these arrangements than has previously been possible.

1.3. Administrative power

Many of the examples of administrative action that have been presented here are not easily classified as merely the exercise of discretion. High-level administrative discretion arises when legislation either grants it directly, or when it is written in such abstract language that further specification is needed for it to have practical effect. The latter is a pervasive feature of the American approach to regulation.[44] For instance, the US Pollution Prevention Act specifies that "Congress hereby declares it to be the national policy of the United States that pollution should be prevented or reduced at the source whenever feasible."[45] The statute is silent, not just on how the term "feasible" is to be interpreted, what it means to "prevent or reduce," but also on the meaning of the term "pollution." The result is a significant delegation of power to the EPA to define how these terms are to be interpreted and to promulgate specific regulations (an issue that came to the fore in 2009, when the EPA chose to classify carbon dioxide as a pollutant to allow President Barack Obama to take action aimed at mitigating climate change without congressional approval). This kind of administrative unilateralism is clearly a feature, not a bug, of these statutes. As John Rohr has observed, "To a considerable extent, this administrative independence is the product of legislative intent. Congress was surely aware of the consequences that would inevitably result from the decision to sprinkle statutes creating administrative agencies with such discretion-conferring words as adequate, advisable, appropriate, beneficial, competent, detrimental, expedient, equitable, fit, practicable, proper, reasonable, reputable, safe, sufficient, wholesome, and their opposites."[46]

On the other hand, when the FDA created the system of phased clinical trials, or when the Canadian public service laid the groundwork for the abolition of the Crow Rate, it was not just filling in the blanks of existing legislation or providing a precisification of vague terms. These public officials were doing much more than exercising discretion; they were taking the initiative, developing a set of practices or policy positions that would become the subject of subsequent legislative ratification. This is also a pervasive feature of contemporary public administration—"legislative proposals often originate through administrative initiative," as Terry Cooper has observed.[47] To capture this broader set of administrative activities, I will follow Jürgen Habermas in speaking of the exercise of "administrative power," a construct that can be taken to include discretion and policy development, as well as influence on the political process.[48] The question then becomes how the exercise of such power could be legitimate, as opposed to merely a form of domination, or a usurpation of legislative authority?

What is needed, in order to answer this question, is essentially a "philosophy of the executive." This phrase evokes the classic liberal division of powers of the state into three branches: the legislative, the judicial, and the executive. According to the ideal-typical formulation, the task of the legislature is to promulgate general rules; the role of the judiciary is to interpret and apply them; and the job of the executive is to enforce them. If one adopts the Weberian view of the state as the institution that exercises a monopoly over the legitimate use of force in a territory, then the actual use of force is strictly the prerogative of the executive—the other two branches merely specify the conditions that make one or another exercise of it legitimate. Thus under conditions of a liberal division of powers, the coercive power of the state is in all cases wielded by the executive. It is not just that the police, the prison system, and the military all belong to the executive branch; it is that almost all state employees are members of the executive branch.

Given that the state is constituted largely by the executive, it is surprising how undertheorized this branch of government is. Indeed, between the publication of Hegel's *Philosophy of Right* in 1821 and Pierre Rosanvallon's *Democratic*

Legitimacy in 2010, one struggles to find any extended treatment of the subject by a major political philosopher.[49] The legislature attracts the lion's share of attention, based on the perception that it is "the place where decisions are made." Whatever energy is left over seems to get directed to the courts. For example, from reading the literature on crime and punishment, one can learn a great deal about how judges think, and practically nothing about how prison wardens think, even though the latter are extremely powerful and important figures in the criminal justice system. Much of this neglect is based on the simple perception that the executive is theoretically uninteresting, because of its subordinate role vis-à-vis the other two branches. It is also based on the view that the executive is *merely* in the business of exercising power, but that the conditions of legitimacy for the exercise of this power are determined entirely by the other two branches. According to this view, the executive is not a *source* of legitimacy or political authority, it merely inherits these normative statuses from the other branches, which in turn implies that normative theorists should only be interested in the latter. I intend to challenge this view, in part by showing how the executive serves as an independent source of political authority.

Before I pursue this line of thinking further, however, it is necessary to clarify some institutional details. The ideal-typical picture of the three branches of the state that one finds in classical liberal theory is institutionalized in ways that sometimes obscure the underlying principles. English-language debate over the status of the executive is clearly impaired by the fact that the Anglosphere is divided by two quite different systems—namely, the Westminster (parliamentary) and the American (presidential) systems. Although they differ on many points, both systems remain British in origin, and as a result, the branch of government officially known as "the executive" is a descendant of the royal power, which is to say, the power of the monarch; whereas "the legislature" is a descendant of Parliament. This results in a number of peculiarities in the way that power is divided up between them—most obviously, in the fact that the executive exercises a number of prerogatives (such as the conduct of foreign affairs) that are essentially outside statutory control.[50] This is a consequence of the fact that the British Parliament never succeeded in wresting all power away from the monarch. (And in the United States, it is a consequence of the fact that the Constitution adopted in 1787 roughly entrenched the division of powers that existed at the time in Britain. Thus the contemporary division of powers between the president and the House of Representatives in the United States essentially reproduces the division that existed in the late 18th century between the British king and Parliament. The British system, by contrast, underwent considerable evolution over the course of the 19th century.)

The most significant source of confusion, however, is the fact that, under both systems, the highest members of the executive are democratically elected.

Consider first the Westminster system (variants of which are used throughout the world, most prominently in the United Kingdom, Canada, New Zealand, and many Caribbean nations, along with modified versions in Australia, South Africa, India, and Pakistan). Under the original arrangement, the official head of state remains the monarch (or the monarch's representative), and all legislation must receive royal approval in order to become law. The "Government" is headed by the Cabinet (composed largely of ministers, each responsible for a different department), which technically serves the Crown and is the de facto head of the executive branch. Members of Cabinet are *by convention* members of Parliament, although they need not be. Apart from the fact that members of the upper house (lords in the United Kingdom, senators in Canada and Australia) often serve in the Cabinet, it is not unheard of for private individuals to be appointed directly to Cabinet—although it is also conventional that once appointed they will seek election to the House of Commons at the earliest opportunity or, failing that, be appointed to the upper chamber. The general point is that the upper tier of the executive branch—the prime minister, ministers, and other members of the Cabinet—are normally elected officials.

Because of this structure, it is quite easy to assume that the legitimacy of the executive branch is inherited from that of the legislature. And yet the phenomenon that I am interested in is not the Cabinet, but rather the role that the civil service plays. Immediately below the minister is the class of officials often known as the permanent civil service—on the grounds that civil servants are expected to retain their positions through changes of government. Thus every minister in the United Kingdom is assisted by a "permanent secretary" (or a "departmental secretary" in Australia, "chief executive" in New Zealand, or "deputy minister" in Canada—from here on, I will refer to all as simply "deputy ministers" or DMs). DMs are appointed by the prime minister, but astonishingly, all departmental personnel decisions made at the sub-DM level are made by the DM, and are technically outside the control of the minister. (In this respect, a Cabinet minister has far less power over his or her department than the CEO of a private corporation has over the organization.) The permanent civil service, with its own internal and autonomous system of hiring, appointment, and promotion, constitutes the core of the executive branch, and its powers pose the greatest challenge to our conception of how democratic states are supposed to function. As George Wallas observed as far back as 1908: "The real 'Second Chamber,' the real 'constitutional check' in England, is provided, not by the House of Lords or the Monarchy, but by the existence of a permanent Civil Service, appointed on a system independent of opinion or desires of any politician, and holding office during good behavior."[51] In contemporary discussions, it has become conventional to distinguish the "political executive" (ministers and political staff) from this "civil" or "public service."[52]

The system in the United States is quite different, starting with the fact that the head of the executive branch, the president, is elected separately from members of Congress. More consequential, in some ways, is that the system of cabinet government used throughout the Commonwealth, with its characteristic structure of ministers and departments, is a 19th-century innovation, and thus evolved after the bifurcation of the American and British systems. As a result, the American system resembles a democratized version of the constitutional monarchy of 18th-century Britain, in which the president directly appoints the members of a cabinet, who operate with near-total independence from the legislature. There is no permanent civil service in the upper echelons—that is, again, a 19th-century British innovation—instead there is a system of political appointments (what is often referred to, less charitably, as a "spoils" system[53]). An incoming president normally makes over 4,000 appointments directly, at least 1,000 of which require Senate approval.[54] These appointments have knock-on effects down the hierarchy, which play out over time, making it difficult to assess the overall effects of a presidential transition. Common estimates put the total number of personnel who change at around 50,000.

As a result, even though the organization chart of the US government suggests a greater separation of the executive branch from the legislative branch, in practice, the institution of the permanent civil service at a senior level in parliamentary systems gives unelected officials much greater power and autonomy than in the US. Nevertheless, there are some distinctive features of the US system that increase the autonomy of the executive branch. First of all, the United States has been at the forefront of the movement to create agencies that function with considerable autonomy from the departments represented in the cabinet (and thus from White House control). Although the leaders of these agencies are politically appointed, it is unclear in many cases how much control they actually exercise. Second, when elected officials other than the president want to know what is going on in various branches of government, they are often reduced to calling officials in for questioning before congressional committees (where they may or may not get straightforward answers). They are also forced to rely much more heavily on legislation to control the executive, precisely because the system lacks the kind of authority structure that one finds between ministers and their departments in the Westminster system. Finally, the increased "gridlocking" of Congress with respect to the passage of much ordinary legislation, along with the evolution of a de facto supermajoritarian constraint in the Senate has led to a steady expansion of executive power.

Thus the question of administrative power largely corresponds to the question of executive power, in both Commonwealth countries and in the United States, although in neither case is the equation straightforward. The significant institutional differences between the two systems make it difficult to develop a "philosophy of the executive" that generalizes across the two. In the discussion that follows, I will therefore focus primarily on the Westminster structure, making reference to the American structure only on certain topics. There are several reasons for this. First, there is the simple fact that as a Canadian, I am more familiar with the Westminster system. Second, and more controversially, is the fact that the Westminster system is the most widely copied in the world. Third, and most controversially, it is because I consider the parliamentary arrangement to be normatively superior to the presidential one, in no small measure because of the higher quality of public administration facilitated by the institution of the permanent civil service. Since my goal is to focus on best practices in public administration, the American system is of less interest because of the overall poor quality of public administration in that country. (As Steven Teles has argued, the US government is best described as a "kludgeocracy," which for any given policy question has an astonishing ability to generate "the most gerry-rigged, opaque and complicated response" possible.[55])

It is noteworthy, in this context, that while the United States has sometimes sought to promote democracy abroad, it generally does not encourage other countries to adopt the specific structure of its political system. For instance, following the 2003 invasion of Iraq, the new governance structure imposed on the country by the United States was essentially parliamentary (with a cabinet government composed of ministers who are all members of the Council of Representatives, which is the main elected body). This suggests that the attitude of most American officials to their own system of government is one of resignation, rather than of enthusiasm or endorsement.

The most well-known problem in American public administration stems from the appointment of politically well-connected incompetents to positions of administrative authority. Yet the negative effects of the spoils system are felt not just at the top, but all the way down the organizational hierarchy. One of the significant features of the US system is that in many domains of the public service there are very poor prospects for internal promotion, precisely because the most senior positions are monopolized by individuals who come from outside, through patronage appointments. As a result, it is much more difficult to recruit talented and ambitious young people to the civil service, because there is no career path from entry-level positions to senior management.[56]

Thus there is a great deal to be said for the institution of a permanent civil service that enjoys substantial independence from the government of the day. Even though the Westminster system is sometimes said to suffer from an incomplete separation of powers, because of the dual role of cabinet ministers, it in many respects exhibits a more complete separation, because of the convention of civil service neutrality. And since I consider this to be the more desirable arrangement, I will focus on the normative challenge that it poses to our conventional understanding of how democratic states are supposed to function.

The institution of the permanent civil service clearly involves a quid pro quo—politicians get the benefit of stable, competent, and knowledgeable administrators, but this is inevitably accompanied by a reduction in their own power (or at least their *marge de maneouvre*). There is a tendency in the literature to treat this as an essentially "realist" concern, a necessary evil. To the extent that the benefits are acknowledged, it is often somewhat begrudgingly. I take a more positive stance. The presence of permanent officials in senior administrative roles, I argue, corrects some of the major deficiencies of democratic governance, and makes an important contribution to the success and stability of liberal democratic states. In particular, it serves as a major bulwark against the inconstancy that is one of the major weaknesses of populist democracy. Far from serving as a source of legal uncertainty, administrative discretion instead increases the stability and predictability of the state and enhances its capacity for long-term commitment.

In some domains, I should note, the advantages of appointment over election are practically taken for granted. One need only consider, for instance, the pathologies generated by the election of district attorneys (i.e., crown prosecutors) and local judges in United States. Candidates' desire to be seen as "tough on crime," and the competitive dynamic that informs these elections, is seen as a major factor contributing to what some observers have described as "the collapse of American criminal justice."[57] There is, in any case, no appetite anywhere in the world to reproduce this system, even though it is, strictly speaking, more democratic. Similarly, it is difficult to imagine a scenario in which capitalism could have survived without the steadying influence of central banks, in particular, central banks with the autonomy to defy public opinion when necessary. The idea that the overriding priority of the state during an economic crisis should be to maintain the solvency of banks is always going to be a difficult sell with the general public. Thus we settle for an arrangement under which central bankers are significantly insulated—not exempted, but insulated—from public control.

In other policy domains, the advantages of permanent officials are perhaps less obvious, but they are nevertheless significant. It is sometimes said that professional administration contributes "rationality" to state activity. This description is obviously quite vague, intended to capture a number of different effects. It usually means some combination of the following, which might be described as the major contributions of the executive branch:

1. *Keeping the show on the road.* This self-deprecating expression, commonly used in the UK civil service (i.e., "How are things in your department?" "Oh you know, we're keeping the show on the road"), actually captures an

important aspect of the activities of the executive. There are often significant periods of time in democratic societies in which there is no government, or where the one that exists is dysfunctional. (In Belgium, for instance, it often takes months, and on one occasion more than a year, for the various parties elected to the Chamber of Representatives to negotiate a coalition that is able to form a government.) Obviously, the business of government cannot come to a halt during these periods. It is not just that programs need to be administered, but that planning and policy development must continue, foreign affairs must be conducted, and so on.

2. *Doing long-term planning.* It is a common criticism of democratic politicians that they have a very short planning horizon, because of the relatively short electoral cycle in most jurisdictions. This leads many observers to assume that government policy will also be short-sighted—in particular, that there will be an irresistible temptation to put off paying for projects, and thus ever-increasing deficits. And yet the actual performance of democratic states in this regard is far more mixed than such an analysis leads one to expect.[58] Much of this is a consequence of the civil service, which evinces a standing concern for the *sustainability* of government operations. Indeed, the executive branch is perhaps the most powerful source of fiscal discipline on the state.

3. *Maintaining consistency over time.* Depending upon the political system, governments can alternate quite rapidly, and even with fixed election dates, the complexion of the government can change dramatically. Politicians as well may have a tendency to "oversteer" in their decision-making, deciding one thing, then quickly retreating in the face of public backlash. The state can easily find itself lurching back and forth (e.g., initiating projects, then canceling them), often at great cost in both time and resources. To the extent that it is possible, the civil service can act as a moderating force (simply by virtue of there being a class of permanent officials able to make up their mind with respect to a particular policy, and pursue it despite changes in government or the political climate). While politicians often complain about the sluggishness of the civil service, or the difficulty of getting their policies implemented, one can see how this same tendency could be a virtue in an unstable political climate.

4. *Using better information.* Commentators on the legislature and the judiciary often note that the effectiveness of both branches of government is diminished by their very limited capacity to collect and process information. The implicit comparison is to the executive branch, which is teeming with analysts who can be assigned to research any issue. It is also important to keep in mind that the chief statistical agencies (such as Statistics Canada, CBS in the Netherlands; the National Institute of Statistics and Economic

Studies, or INSEE, in France; and Destatis in Germany) are part of the executive, and so the civil service largely takes the initiative in collecting the data that can, in turn, be used as the basis for advocating and assessing particular policies. The executive also administers the national census and the tax system, and imposes an identification system (with varying degrees of intrusiveness) on the population.

5. *Conducting evidence-based policy analysis.* Politicians are highly responsive to what is written in the press, to the pressure of current events (e.g., "sympathetic victims" in case of healthcare resource allocation, or highly mobilized constituencies), and increasingly, to what appears in social media. This leaves them prey to many cognitive biases, as well as to the everyday perils of anecdotal evidence. The civil service, by contrast, has increasingly cultivated a commitment to using empirical evidence to evaluate the effectiveness of policies (up to and including the use of randomized control trials to assess outcomes). Widespread use of cost-benefit analysis has also contributed to the practice of making explicit all the factors that speak in favor of and against any policy, which in turn makes the quality of the underlying evidence more amenable to assessment.

6. *Focusing on the general interest.* Again, because it is not beholden to any particular constituency, the higher civil service often finds itself acting as the "lawyer for society" in discussions with politicians. Theorists who focus exclusively on the democratic side of governance often assume that highly organized interest groups will be able to extract significant rents, when the costs are born by diffuse, poorly organized groups.[59] This is particularly true if the rent-seeking group is geographically concentrated (e.g., corn farmers, coal miners, etc.), because they will be able to "capture" local politicians (in electoral systems with geographically based ridings). To the extent that this tendency is checked—and the dystopia imagined by public choice theory not realized—it is often thanks to the civil service, which is free to take a broader view of the matter.

7. *Resisting democratic pandering.* There are of course many instances of straightforward demagogues winning popular elections. Even in more mature or affluent democracies, there is a constant temptation among politicians to pander to some of the public's more ignoble sentiments. Hatred of immigrants and foreigners, for instance, can easily be inflamed. Taxation is also an area in which rich veins of public resentment lie waiting to be tapped. The civil service, again, is in a position to act as a moderating influence in these domains. Indeed, in some areas, such as taxation policy, it has been argued that more arms-length agencies should be created—on the model of central banking—to determine policy.[60]

8. *Maintaining constitutionality.* The role of the courts in being able to veto unconstitutional legislation is well-known (and has been growing in many jurisdictions, with the increasing popularity of written constitutions that include an enumerated list of justiciable rights). And yet the courts are a blunt mechanism for controlling unconstitutional legislation, in part because they provide only "after the fact" correction, rely on challenges arising from civil society, and are only able to strike down legislation, not rewrite it. By contrast, civil servants (in particular, staff of the Department of Justice or its equivalent) are intimately involved in the drafting of legislation, and are constantly raising the question of constitutionality (or as we say in Canada, "Charter-proofness"[61]). The courts function much more like a fail-safe mechanism, rather than being the primary bulwark against unconstitutional behavior by the state.

If one were a consequentialist in political philosophy, it would not be difficult to justify the power and influence that administrative officials wield—one could simply point to these beneficial effects. Most political philosophers, however, adopt a more principled approach to normative theory, believing that institutional arrangements such as democratic elections or judicial oversight based on constitutional norms have more than just instrumental value. Administrative power, from this perspective, might have beneficial consequences, yet still be illegitimate. Of course, some conservative theorists have been deeply troubled by what they describe as "the rise of the administrative state."[62] Although they claim to have a principled basis for this opposition, it is surely not a coincidence that they are also opposed to its effects.[63] Among theorists who are not opposed to its effects—that is, those who are broadly supportive of socialized medicine, environmental regulation, consumer protection, etc.—the tendency has been simply to pass over it all in silence. And yet the growth of administrative power poses an obvious challenge to all our received normative accounts of political authority, regardless of whether we are broadly supportive or critical of its effects.

The first step to fruitful philosophical engagement with this question lies in an acknowledgment that, no matter how determined one is to reject consequentialist modes of normative reasoning, principles of political philosophy are nevertheless not deduced from pure reason, they remain idealizing reconstructions of existing practices. Liberal theories of justice are of interest to us in no small measure because of the success of liberal societies, not just at creating wealth, but also at respecting individual freedoms and promoting a wide range of different forms of human flourishing. If it turns out that a great deal of this success is due to the unheralded efforts of career officials—in other words, if administrative power is a central feature of our most successful practices—then it behooves us to find some place for their contributions in our *normative* accounts of the state.

1.4. The permanent civil service

The same independence from the public that allows the civil service to take a more impartial view of the public interest can also become a serious problem. Indeed, merely enumerating the virtues of the permanent civil service runs the risk of encouraging the "good king" fallacy (i.e., that monarchy is the best system of government, as long as the king is good). Official corruption, for instance, when it becomes systemic, can be an extraordinarily serious, damaging, and intractable social problem and, indeed, is generally regarded as a chief factor in keeping many countries in a state of relative underdevelopment.[64] Similarly, many nations are unable to achieve effective control of their militaries, and almost every nation has some degree of difficulty controlling its police forces.

Elected officials have also been known to complain about insubordination or general noncompliance, even in mature democracies. And yet these problems do not pose that much of a *theoretical* challenge. Straightforward insubordination contradicts the principle of parliamentary supremacy, should not be tolerated—and, under only slightly idealized conditions, should not occur. The more theoretically challenging forms of administrative power are the ones that cannot, and should not, be eliminated, even under idealized conditions. Consider, for instance, the more subtle, and arguably more pervasive issue, which arises in mature democracies, sometimes referred to as the "Sir Humphrey" problem. The name is taken from the British comedy series, *Yes, Minister*, which became extraordinarily influential in government and in public perceptions of the civil service. The series followed the relations between a minister, the Right Honorable Jim Hacker, and his permanent secretary (i.e., DM), Sir Humphrey Appleby. The central comedic premise is that, although the minister is formally in charge, Sir Humphrey is in fact making all the decisions. The reasons for this are predictable:

> First of all, Hacker was new to government and Sir Humphrey was a veteran civil servant. Sir Humphrey knew his way around government. Secondly, Hacker did not really know anything about his department, whereas Sir Humphrey knew a great deal, and even when he did not know something about the department he controlled the flow of information to the minister. Thirdly, Sir Humphrey, not the minister, controlled the future career paths of the public servants working in the department. So everyone on staff had a direct interest in pleasing the permanent secretary rather than the minister. Fourthly, Sir Humphrey was very close to the cabinet secretary, the prime minister's top civil servant, so he had his own channel to the prime minister and most days it functioned better than Hacker's. And finally, of course, Sir Humphrey took a first at Cambridge, whereas poor Hacker finished with a third from the London School of Economics.[65]

One of most hackneyed jokes within the civil service is that *Yes, Minister* was not a comedy, but rather a documentary. The reason this joke has been told so many times is that it contains more than a small grain of truth. One of the by-products of having a "sterling" civil service is that it often attracts a more capable class of individual than the legislature does. By way of illustration—and without the intention of picking on anyone in particular—consider the state of affairs, at the time of writing, in the Ministry of Health and Long-Term Care in the Canadian province of Ontario. There have been, I should note, extraordinary mismatches between ministers and their staff during the time that I have lived in Ontario, such as when a high-school dropout was appointed minister of education, or the owner of a small-town car dealership appointed minister of transportation.[66] In contrast, at the time of writing both the minister of health, Dr. Eric Hoskins, and his deputy minister, Dr. Robert Bell, are well educated and accomplished individuals. If one compares their background experiences, however, one can see some important differences. Hoskins, after graduating from medical school at McMaster, and later earning a Doctor of Philosophy at Oxford in public health and epidemiology, moved to the Sudan, where he immersed himself in development work, and eventually became co-founder of an NGO (War Child Canada) that focused on international relief efforts. He was elected to the provincial legislature in 2009 and appointed to cabinet in 2010, where he held two other ministries before becoming minister of health in 2014. Bell, the DM, is nearly a decade older than Hoskins, with a medical degree from McGill, and subsequent specialization as an orthopedic oncologist. After more than two decades of clinical practice, he went on to become chief operating officer at Princess Margaret Hospital and chair of both Cancer Care Ontario's Clinical Council and the Cancer Quality Council of Ontario (both powerful government agencies in the province). He subsequently served for nine years as president and chief executive officer of University Health Network, Canada's largest research hospital.

There are subtle differences between these two CVs (the status differential between a general physician with a degree from McMaster and an orthopedic surgeon with a degree from McGill is comparable to the difference between a third from the London School of Economics and a first from Cambridge). The really significant difference, however, comes down to work experience. Hoskins, the minister, never really practiced medicine in Ontario. Bell, in addition to having worked within the system for decades, also ran two of the most important hospitals, and was intimately involved in high-level administrative work, including at two of the major funding agencies. Indeed, the fact that the public service is in a position to recruit such an accomplished individual is an extraordinarily positive thing. (In moving to the DM position, Bell took a salary cut of almost 50 percent.[67] This is in addition to the millions of dollars he was already foregoing just by working in the public sector—either as a hospital CEO or a DM.)

And yet there is an obvious trade-off, in terms of democratic control. To the extent that one succeeds in attracting capable people to the public service, a natural consequence will be an increase in the power of unelected officials. As a result, if one were to ask who was really running the healthcare system in Ontario, the answer would clearly be Bell. In fact, Hoskins was widely perceived as a "weak minister," who focused more on personal projects, while Bell was managing the large-scale initiatives for cost-control and reorganization of the healthcare system.[68]

I have presented this example in some detail because it illustrates several points. The first thing to observe is that the asymmetry between this particular minister and DM was not especially extreme, yet it still had significant effects. One of the important qualities of electoral democracy is that, ideally, it brings people from all walks of life to government. In practice, the outcomes fall short of the ideal, but it remains the case that an enormous range of people with different backgrounds and life experiences wind up becoming cabinet ministers. This is a positive feature of the system, which I doubt many would be interested in changing. And yet the state is a very large, very complex bureaucratic organization. Dealing with complex bureaucratic organizations requires a highly specific skill set, which most people do not possess. The civil service, however, promotes people for possession of precisely this ability. The higher civil service is therefore populated, not just by capable individuals, but by people who are expert at getting things done in a bureaucracy (i.e., at running meetings, making personnel decisions, reading and extracting key information from reports, etc.) As a result, there will always be an asymmetry between elected officials and the permanent civil service. This is the Sir Humphery problem. One can see it just as clearly in Kroeger's remark that after six months in the position, Minister Pépin (himself a former university professor, and therefore no stranger to bureaucracy) "was beginning to find his feet." Despite Kroeger's evident regard and even affection for Pépin, it is difficult not to detect a trace of condescension in his observation that, when Pépin spoke at Cabinet, "I found him articulate and able to hold the attention of his colleagues."

I dwell on these issues in part to make it clear that I am not dismissing or minimizing the very real concern about bureaucratic domination that informs a great deal of commentary on the powers of the executive branch.[69] At the same time, it is important to recognize that administrative power is not just an unfortunate inevitability, or a lamentable by-product of the complexity of modern nation-states. It is difficult to imagine wanting to solve the Sir Humphrey problem by degrading the quality of the public service. Autonomous public administration makes a crucial contribution to the success of liberal-democratic societies, and in many ways makes democratic governance possible, by serving as a counterweight and corrective to many of the more dysfunctional tendencies of popular sovereignty. Thus it is important to offer a normative reconstruction of the liberal-democratic state that sticks closer to existing practices. This includes not just acknowledging the positive contributions the executive branch makes, but also offering an affirmative justification for those arrangements. This is important for various reasons, not the least of which is that without such an analysis, it is impossible to distinguish good exercises of administrative power from bad ones.

Luckily, it is not so difficult to find an account that offers precisely the desired normative reconstruction, at least in outline. If one considers Montesquieu's original presentation of his division of powers doctrine, one can find an ideal template for thinking about the relations between the executive branch and the other two branches of the state. In Montesquieu's view, there is no perfect arrangement that can guarantee that the state will be committed to defending individual liberty (or to promoting the public interest more generally). The legislature, even when democratically elected, is capable of acting tyrannically, as are the courts, and as is the executive. A division of powers between these three branches is thus recommended, for two reasons. First, it means that in order for the state to use its powers of coercion, all three branches must be, in a sense, "on the same page"—the legislature must pass the law, the courts must interpret and apply it, and the administration must enforce it. More importantly, however, Montesquieu thought that there should be ongoing tension, even a degree of antagonism, among the three branches, so that each could serve as a check on the others. A free society will be one in which this productive tension is maintained without any one branch ever managing to subordinate the others.

On this model, in the same way that the executive serves as a corrective to certain pathologies of the legislature (e.g., the excesses of popular sovereignty), the legislature also provides a corrective to characteristic pathologies of the executive (e.g., the problem of bureaucratic rigidity and entrenchment). The latter point is widely recognized in the civil service. As Kroeger put it, "Being a senior official does not tempt one to think that government by technocrats would be a great idea. On the contrary, the experience tends to reinforce one's democratic instincts."[70] The division of powers, in this respect, represents an attempt to secure the benefits of technocratic rule, while avoiding some of the major liabilities. As far back as 1861, Sir Charles Wood observed of the British system:

> The permanent public servants . . . are the advisers of, and to a certain extent, a check upon, the new political chiefs who come in without experience; while, on the other hand, the tendency of all permanent officers is to get into a certain routine, and a change of the heads, from time to time, checked by the permanence of those who are always in office, tends very much to produce an improved system of administration of any department.[71]

One can see even in private-sector management that the tendency of large firms to become out of touch with consumers over time is a very serious problem.

The problem is even more severe in the case of state bureaucracies, which are entirely immune to the forces of creative destruction in the marketplace that impose outside limits on the disconnect that can develop between firms and their customers. Democratic elections, and with them a replacement of the top personnel within departments (not just new ministers, but a shuffling or replacement of DMs), serve the purpose of limiting bureaucratic entrenchment and ossification. Democracy is the public-sector analog of creative destruction.

Apart from mitigating the problem of bureaucratic entrenchment, democracy also serves to limit pathological features of the state bureaucracy that may arise at all levels. I have, at numerous points in this discussion, emphasized the benefits that flow from having segments of the executive insulated from public opinion and control. Yet this insulation can just as easily become a problem, in that it gives state officials the power to ignore both legitimate and illegitimate demands from the public. Furthermore, because of the state's coercive power and monopolistic position, individuals often have no choice but to deal with public officials, which can in turn increase the degree of nonresponsiveness. (The clients of a private business are, by and large, assets to the organization, and are treated accordingly. The structure of government budgeting is such that the "clients" of the state—be they school children, hospital patients, unemployed workers, social-work cases, or pensioners—are, by and large, liabilities to the organization. Thus the inevitable bias of state bureaucracies is to treat them accordingly.) One of the most important roles that elected officials play involves so-called constituency work, which essentially amounts to troubleshooting problems in the state bureaucracy on behalf of citizens.[72] Crucially, elected officials can serve as a counterweight to the problem of bureaucratic rigidity or unresponsiveness. They function as "free agents," who can generate action at any level of the bureaucracy and also demand flexibility, or exemptions, in particular cases. Citizens who are caught in Kafkaesque situations are often able to get movement by contacting their elected officials.

Thus the best way to characterize a liberal-democratic state is not to imagine it as one in which the people or their representatives get together and democratically decide all major questions of public policy, which state officials then go off and implement. Nor is it plausible to characterize the state, as Habermas does (under the influence of Niklas Luhmann), as an autonomous, self-steered subsystem, which can only be pinned down and controlled at the periphery by democratic publics.[73] It is, instead, best to think of the state—at least, a successful, well-administered, and reasonably responsive liberal state—as the product of an ongoing internal tension between an essentially technocratic executive branch, an elected legislature that is highly responsive to public opinion, and a judiciary endowed with important supervisory functions. The key point is that each brings its own considerations and concerns to the table, and policy is ultimately determined through the interaction that results. What is often mistakenly described as "democratic self-governance" is in fact just the principle of "legislative supremacy" (or "parliamentary supremacy"), which states that in the event of intractable conflict between the three branches, it is ultimately the legislature that gets to decide.[74] But from the fact that, in principle, any question can be decided by the legislature, it does not follow that, in practice, every question is, or ought to be, decided by the legislature.[75] As John Stuart Mill observed long ago, "There is a radical distinction between controlling the business of government and actually doing it."[76]

1.5. Political neutrality

The institution of the permanent civil service, I have suggested, generates significant benefits for the quality of public policy, delivery of public services, and ultimately, promotion of social welfare. It is also, one might add, an arrangement that seems objectively rather improbable. Clearly, the more natural impulse of politicians is to bring in partisans, or individuals of demonstrated loyalty, to fill major staff positions. Of course, back in the 18th century, when public offices were bought and sold, politicians had no choice but to accept the existence of permanent officials—evicting someone from office would have been akin to depriving him of his property. In the modern world, however, what makes permanence possible is the institution of *civil service neutrality*. I describe this as an "institution" because, while there are a few explicit rules and regulations that public servants must follow, the bulk of the commitment to neutrality takes the form of an unwritten code of conduct, a component of the system of *professional ethics* that governs administrative behavior. And while this conduct has not been officially codified, it is of sufficient importance to the practice of Westminster-style government that many commentators have taken to describing it as a "constitutional convention."[77]

At the most superficial level, the commitment to neutrality just means that civil servants should not support particular political parties or engage in partisan political activity. This cuts in two directions: civil servants should not engage in partisan opposition to the government of the day or in partisan activities in support of the ruling party. Thus the issue is not just one of not demonstrating disloyalty to the minister, but also of avoiding excessive loyalty.[78] (In Canada, the prohibition of political party membership for civil servants has been, predictably, challenged in the courts, as a violation of the rights of expression and association of civil servants. These challenges have been defeated, but have resulted in some stipulations, for example, the explicit prohibition on engaging in partisan activity extends only to work hours. The more extensive prohibition, however, persists within the unwritten ethos of the civil service. A civil servant who engaged in significant partisan activity in her spare time would find it a significant obstacle to promotion—and for good reason. An incoming minister is asked to vest an enormous amount of trust in permanent officials, given how easily a departmental scandal can destroy a politician's career. How could any politician reasonably be expected to trust a senior official who, in his or her spare time, has actively and publicly supported the opposition? As a result, ambitious civil servants almost uniformly adopt a veneer of political inscrutability.[79])

At a deeper level, the ethic of neutrality requires much more than just prescinding from partisan political activity. Adrian Ellis, who has written one of the few modern articles on the topic, defines *political neutrality*, in its most minimal form, as "the capacity to serve differing administrations with equal effectiveness."[80] The term "capacity" is a bit weak. The more usual expectation is that the civil service will exhibit loyalty to the government of the day, and be vigorous in advancing its agenda (thus exhibiting "the capacity to serve the incumbent administration with maximum efficiency"). Max Weber articulated this idea even more forcefully, describing it in what we would now call agency-theoretic terms: "The honour of the civil servant is vested in his ability to execute conscientiously the order of the superior authority, exactly as if the order agreed with his own convictions."[81]

Of course, anyone who has ever worked in an organizational hierarchy has no doubt dreamed of having subordinates possessed of a sense of "honor" that impelled them to act as Weber describes. In reality, this type of selfless devotion is likely to be an unobtainable ideal. Similarly, Ellis notes that his own account of neutrality rules out an "independently pursued bureaucratic agenda,"[82] which, again, posits a level of self-effacement on the part of civil servants that is very seldom realized. Thus many theorists have instead chosen to describe civil service neutrality as something more like an arrangement, or a set of conventions, between politicians and permanent officials, that includes an element of quid pro quo. Donald Savoie, for instance, describes it as an implicit agreement, which he refers to as "the traditional bargain." This arrangement "calls on public servants to provide the government of the day non-partisanship, loyalty, impartiality, discretion and professionalism, in return for anonymity and security of tenure."[83]

On Savoie's view, the institution of neutrality is closely tied to the doctrine of ministerial accountability. The latter is simply the convention that cabinet ministers are held accountable, to the public and in Parliament, for everything that happens in their department, regardless of whether they knew about it or could have done anything to prevent it. It is sometimes misrepresented as the convention that ministers will resign whenever anything goes wrong in their departments. Resignation is actually less important than the fact that they are the ones who have to stand up in Parliament to face a barrage of criticism, as well as answer questions while they seek to defend the government. The key feature of this convention is that they are expected specifically to refrain from "naming and blaming" officials, even if they know who made the mistake.[84] This is, in fact, a highly functional arrangement for the bureaucracy as a whole. One of the classic problems of bureaucratic organization is that bad news generally does not travel up the organizational hierarchy, simply because officials want to avoid being punished for accidents or ineptitude. The problem is endemic in authoritarian regimes, and it often dramatically exacerbates political problems. The first SARS epidemic in China and the Chernobyl nuclear disaster in the former Soviet Union, for example, were both made much worse by the difficulty political leaders and senior public officials had obtaining accurate information, or even any information at all, about what was going on. One way of getting people to tell the truth is to promise that they will not be punished for doing so. This is what underlies the commitment to "anonymity" that Savoie mentions. It is not just that the civil servants seek to keep their contributions anonymous, it is that they are guaranteed (public) anonymity, as well as freedom from summary dismissal, in the event that they make mistakes. The minister takes responsibility.[85]

One can see here the structure of the quid pro quo that informs the relationship. The minister's position is, in effect, "If I'm going to protect you, then you must serve me loyally." The commitment to discretion, and even secrecy, on the part of civil servants, follows from this commitment to avoid doing or saying anything that could embarrass the minister. The arrangement is mutually advantageous for the parties, and beneficial for the nation as a whole, to the extent that it allows for a greater degree of experience and sophistication to develop among those in senior administrative positions. It should also be noted that in certain cases, when highly partisan elected officials have failed to uphold their end of the bargain by dismissing officials and bringing in loyalists to achieve what they hope will be greater responsiveness to political direction, the consequences have generally been a reduction in their capacity to achieve the government's objectives. Although political appointees are more likely to share a personal commitment to the government's agenda, their lack of expertise, institutional memory, knowledge of procedures, and poor stakeholder networks, have generally made them less effective at getting that agenda implemented.[86]

The "traditional bargain" has, however, become frayed in other ways over the past few decades. Indeed, the lack of trust in the civil service on the part of elected officials is reflected in the fact that political staff have become a feature of every minister's office. In Canada, each minister now has both a DM and a "chief of staff," the latter being a partisan political appointment (called "exempt staff," i.e., they are paid for out of the public treasury but are exempt from all the normal rules governing the civil service). Most ministers now have between twenty and thirty political staff members in their offices (although, for various reasons, these

individuals tend to be young and inexperienced, which is why they are often referred to, derisively, as "the kids in short pants"). Several factors have contributed
to this shift, including the growth of public-sector unionization, the effects of
new public management reforms, and the rise of partisan or quasi-partisan think
tanks able to take on policy-development roles.

It should be noted that the higher civil service has made some effort to discourage the suggestion that there was ever a "bargain" with elected officials, on
the self-effacing grounds that the executive has no authority to make demands,
and thus no ability to bargain.[87] At the same time, it is difficult to find anyone
who is prepared to defend a model of unconditional deference to ministerial
whim. Unfortunately, various attempts to articulate a set of civil service "values,"
or to clarify what normative commitments do not violate neutrality, have been
unsophisticated at best. Thus there is, at the moment, a strong tradition of political neutrality within the civil service; at the same time, there is a sense that there
remains a range of issues on which it is legitimate for the civil service to "have a
view." Kroeger summed up the prevailing attitude quite well when he said that
"objectivity and political neutrality . . . should not be confused with an indifference to public policy outcomes." In particular, there is within the civil service
widespread endorsement of a self-standing notion of "good public policy," which
is independent of the specific preferences of the government of the day. Similarly
(and in part since DMs in the United Kingdom and Canada have been made
financial "accounting officers" for their departments, reporting directly to a parliamentary committee), the civil service has in recent years become emboldened
on the subject of the fiscal sustainability of government programs. So while the
civil service is obliged to remain neutral on certain questions, it is decidedly *not*
neutral on others, such as finances. But because there is no satisfactory articulation of the basis for distinguishing such cases, much less a politico-theoretic
justification for it, it tends to be propagated as merely an implicit understanding,
or a set of institutional practices that lack explicit justification.

My central ambition is to clarify this issue—to specify the objectives that the
civil service may pursue without usurping powers that are legitimately reserved
for the legislative branch, and without violating the terms of the traditional bargain that underlies the convention of civil service neutrality. Of course, when
a theorist like Ellis says that there should be no "independently pursued bureaucratic agenda," people generally nod their heads in agreement, because no
one likes the sound of "bureaucratic agenda." But this is not how state officials
describe their objectives. What they take themselves to be motivated by is an
independent conception of the public interest, along with the aforementioned
commitment to good public policy. The suggestion that state officials should
have no conception of, or commitment to, the public interest, or "good policy,"
is considerably more dubious. Indeed, if we had to rely entirely upon elected

officials to take the initiative to get things done, and to define the public interest, the quality of the public sector would deteriorate in myriad ways.

Consider just one example. Officials at Health Canada have worked assiduously over the past decade to raise public awareness of the health hazards posed by indoor radon gas, the second most common cause of lung cancer in the country (after smoking). Radon is a colorless, odorless, but unfortunately radioactive gas, which enters buildings through basements. In modern, high-efficiency "sealed-envelope" dwellings, it tends to become trapped and can reach dangerous levels. Unfortunately, persuading people to take radon gas seriously, much less pay money to have their homes tested for it, is extremely difficult.[88] It is also not an issue in which politicians take much interest, simply because the public has no interest. There are, as they say, no votes to be had in dealing with it. To make matters worse, an effective policy response to the hazard must be orchestrated at all three levels of jurisdiction (federal, provincial, and municipal), because of the need to adjust building codes and inspection practices. To the extent that Canada has a national strategy for protecting its citizens from indoor radon gas, it can fairly be described as a consequence of the initiative and persistence of officials at Health Canada. One might choose to call this an "independently pursued bureaucratic agenda," but it would be important then to acknowledge that this sort of independence makes an important contribution to the health and well-being of the public.

At the same time, it should be recognized that Health Canada's work on radon gas levels is not entirely apolitical. If one looks at the recommendations coming out of the program, one sees that many of them involve adding additional complexity to building codes and workplace safety regulations, imposing new inspection requirements, using taxpayer funds to subsidize home inspections, and creating new requirements for commercial property owners and landlords. This expansion of the regulatory state was actively opposed by the Conservative party, which formed the federal government in Canada from 2006 to 2015—the period during which the National Radon Program was adopted and implemented. So while the minister of health would no doubt have been aware of the program's existence, and would probably even have been briefed on it, its basic objectives could hardly be regarded as an expression of the political ideology or will of the government. Most likely, the program was advanced because neither the topic nor the budget ever rose to a level at which it acquired political significance.

And yet if one were to interpret the concept of civil service neutrality strictly, one might be inclined to think that Health Canada bureaucrats should not be out trying to cultivate public awareness of the dangers of radon gas, much less pressing for regulatory changes through complex negotiations with municipal and provincial levels of government; they should instead be sitting on their hands, waiting for instructions from the minister. This is, thankfully, not how things work. Increasingly, the civil service works out on its own what a good policy would be in a particular domain, drawing on a combination of in-house expertise and consultation, as well as policy experts in universities, think tanks, and civil society organizations. Often, the details of "good policy" are known years in advance of its actual implementation. Politicians then act as brokers between this policy community and the general public. It often happens that, for one reason or another, good policy is resisted, which may limit what is politically possible. Politicians will then engage in negotiation, trying to reach agreement on a policy that is as close to good policy as possible, making the compromises required by various interest groups and the public more generally.

This is not a bad arrangement, and one certainly would not want a system in which experts were able to directly impose their preferred policies, without any need to negotiate with the perspectives and interests of the public. In other words, there is a lot to be said for the system as it has evolved. The problem is that our existing theories of democracy are completely inadequate to address this reality. According to the received view, politicians are supposed to be channeling the "general will," transforming it into policy ideas, legislating, and then calling on the civil service to implement the rules. This is probably a fair characterization of how the system works for a handful of signature policy initiatives, which politicians actively campaign on and which are often adopted for strategic or ideological reasons. But when it comes to day-to-day policy changes, the overwhelming majority of initiatives run in the opposite direction, from the executive branch to the legislature. As a result, there is a pervasive sense of bad faith among civil servants, based on the feeling that they are, in their everyday affairs, usurping political authority or doing something that they should not be doing. It is instructive, for example, to compare the various reports and inquiries conducted within the civil service on the subject of civil service values to the reflections of retired civil servants. The former are invariably written with a strong awareness of how they will be received by the government of the day and, as a result, tend to dramatically underplay the level of autonomy and influence that the civil service enjoys. Memoirs written by retired civil servants, by contrast, come across as much more honest accounts. Consider, for example, the way that Brian Cubbon, a retired UK civil servant, describes the type of policy direction provided by ministers:

> In polite company, we wrap up our role by using the dignified phrase "policy advice" to describe the contribution of officials, constantly emphasizing that policy is for ministers to decide. Policy-making is not a satisfactory term for describing the daily role of ministers. I suspect that it was invented by civil servants to flatter ministers into thinking that ministers' contributions are

more coherent and rational than they really can be. Ministers think in terms of ideas and prejudices and headlines, rather than policies.[89]

This statement may be somewhat uncouth, but if we take it as an accurate reflection of a situation that often arises in democratic states, then it follows that unelected officials wield substantial power. Indeed, in Cubbon's view, even describing civil servants as *servants* is misleading, as it "clouds the essential coarseness of acts of government. I prefer to describe the business I was in as the exercise of power within a democratic system."[90] The question then becomes how civil servants should be guided in their reasoning when thinking about how they exercise the power of the state.

The answer to this question, I will argue, follows from certain fundamental principles of political philosophy. Modern democracies are not regimes of unrestricted popular sovereignty. They are usually described as liberal-democratic states, a reflection of the fact that the power of the "democratic" part is tempered by a set of constraints that reflect the "liberal" part. It follows from this that the civil service is justified in maintaining adherence to the basic normative principles that define a liberal political order. This is consistent with the institution of civil service neutrality, because these bedrock liberal principles are outside the scope of legitimate political contestation. So while the civil service must be deferential to the legislature, it is also justified in maintaining independent adherence to basic liberal principles and to advancing policies that flow from those principles. These two imperatives may conflict, and when they do, the civil service may be justified in "pushing back" against the legislature, or elected officials more generally.

Something like this view has been defended by John Rohr, in a series of classic contributions to the literature on the ethics of public administration. In his view, the "constitution," along with a more general set of "constitutional" values, provides a set of principles that can guide the practice of public administration.[91] This way of articulating the idea has its strengths and weaknesses. On the one hand, by tying things directly to the constitution, he alleviates some of the discomfort associated with the suggestion that the executive should be anything less than entirely subordinate to the legislature. After all, nearly everyone agrees that civil servants, if asked to do something unconstitutional, should resist those orders. On the other hand, by focusing so narrowly on the constitution, Rohr risks implying that the civil service is beholden to two masters, not just to the legislature but to the judiciary as well. Furthermore, because he is writing in an American context, he focuses exclusively on the written constitution, and on Supreme Court jurisprudence. My own view is that, while the constitution represents a good point of departure for understanding more general liberal principles, it does not constitute the entirety of them, and certainly not if one focuses only on the written portion.

Thus my approach in what follows is to begin by articulating a very general theoretical characterization of liberalism, along with the core principles of a liberal theory of justice. From there, I will proceed reconstructively, trying to show that the prevailing conception of "best practice" within the civil service can be understood as reflecting a commitment to such principles. This may seem to be merely a methodological point, but it has political significance as well. I am not going to elaborate an abstract philosophical theory, then suggest that civil servants should act like Plato's philosopher king and rule in accordance with that theory. On the contrary, my task is the maieutic one, of making explicit what is presently only implicit.[92] I will propose an articulation and justification of the norms that *already* guide the practice of public administration in liberal-democratic states. There is no need to bring normative principles to bear upon the civil service from the outside, since the practice of public administration is already saturated with, and deeply structured by, a set of essentially normative ideas about the appropriate role of public officials. My goal is merely to articulate these implicit understandings at a higher level of abstraction, to connect them to broader principles that have been developed in modern political philosophy, and to defend them against certain objections and misunderstandings. This is intended to facilitate a more reflexive practice, but also to provide the expressive resources necessary for critical reflection on, and if necessary, reform of these practices.

I say this in part to pre-empt the objection to the argument that follows that I assign far too much power to the executive branch, and that I am promoting a form of unaccountable, technocratic rule. I would like to be clear that I do not recommend expanding executive power. I am for the most part just offering a justification of the status quo in successful welfare states, in recognition of the fact that the executive already wields enormous power in typical liberal democracies, and that this is a large part of the success of these societies. Furthermore, it is important to my project that the normative commitments I articulate are compatible with the institution of civil service neutrality, correctly understood. After all, no matter how highly placed they are, it remains the case that civil servants serve at the pleasure of elected officials. Not only can individuals be replaced, but career civil servants as a whole can be displaced by partisans and political staff. So if the autonomy of the civil service becomes too great, to the point where it generates obstructionism or the development of an entrenched mandarin class, the likely consequence would be diminished willingness on the part of politicians to accept the traditional bargain, based on the perception that the civil service no longer respects neutrality. The further consequence would be erosion of the quality of public administration, to the extent that the breakdown

in the traditional bargain would result in the substitution of young, inexperienced political staff or patronage appointments for experienced, trained officials.

Because of this, I do not think that the vision of a civil service "run amok" is
so much a threat to democracy as it is a threat to the quality of public services,
because of the backlash that it would generate from elected officials. The ideal arrangement, in my view, is one in which an experienced cadre of public officials,
enjoying the substantial security of tenure, advances an independent conception
of the public interest, but in a way that avoids taking positions on issues that are
the legitimate objects of political contestation and disagreement, and is thus appropriately deferential to the will of elected officials. My ambition in what follows
is to show that there is nothing internally contradictory or threatening to democratic self-government in this ideal.

1.6. Liberalism or democracy?

It may be helpful to contrast the view that I have sketched out with the only sustained modern attempt to grapple with the normative status of administrative
power, which is that developed by Pierre Rosanvallon, in a four-volume series
on the subject of democracy (*Counter-Democracy, Democratic Legitimacy, The
Society of Equals*, and *Good Government*).[93] My own view maintains at least a residual attachment to the principle of division of powers, and to the idea that there
may be a tension between the liberal and the democratic components of liberal
democracy. The democratic principle is institutionalized first and foremost in
the legislature, whereas both the judiciary and the executive (i.e., the permanent
civil service) maintain adherence to liberal principles, which means that they
adhere to a conception of justice that is relatively independent of public opinion,
to the point of sometimes serving as a countermajoritarian check on elected
officials. Rosanvallon, by contrast, has a much broader conception of democracy, which he considers to be only partially institutionalized by the legislature,
and therefore needs to be supplemented by a wide range of other institutional
arrangements, including the power of the executive. Thus he endorses a system
of executive supremacy, but argues that this arrangement, far from being anti-
democratic or countermajoritarian, is actually the most effective way of realizing
democratic principles.[94]

Rosanvallon's basic normative vision of the state is Rousseauian—he believes
that government should advance the general will. The general will in turn corresponds to what "the people" desire, which suggests that the underlying principle
of democratic decision-making is actually one of *unanimity*.[95] This is, of course,
impractical, and so existing democracies have chosen to settle for the practice of
majority rule in determining both the appointment of the government and the

enactment of legislation. Because of this, Rosanvallon regards the legislature as having a very partial, and in some respects defective, claim to democratic legitimacy. "Majority rule was introduced into democratic constitutions almost surreptitiously, as a sort of practical necessity, which in the beginning was never fully theorized. It took hold despite the fact that the concept of the majority had no philosophical foundation or authentic constitutional status."[96] As a result, to be described as "democratic," a society must include a large number of other institutional arrangements, which either correct the defects of majority rule or make their own independent contribution to the realization of the general will.

Rosanvallon's conception of "counterdemocracy," for instance, points to the role that various civil society groups, including the media, protestors, NGOs, and unions, can play in blocking or impeding legislation, and argues that this is part of the democratic system, because of the way that it stops numerical majorities from riding roughshod over the will of significant minorities. This countervailing power brings the democratic system as a whole closer to the ideal of unanimity. His analysis of the other branches of the state—the judiciary and the executive—follows the same basic logic. In the case of the executive, he claims that it promotes the realization of the general will primarily through its commitment to *impartiality*. A central feature, but also in certain respects a central defect, of the legislature is that it is dominated by political actors who exhibit high levels of partisanship. This quality of the legislature, which Rosanvallon describes as "its reflexive obedience to sectarian impulses," is one that is both disliked and mistrusted by the public. Indeed, Rosanvallon at one point quotes with approval Charles de Gaulle's description of parliament as "a delegation of special interests."[97] The legislature is, in many respects, the opposite of an impartial or disinterested institution. For Rosanvallon (as for de Gaulle), "the natural function of the executive, by contrast, on account of its unified structure, is to represent the general will and unity of the country."[98] He describes the authority that the executive derives from this as grounded in the "legitimacy of impartiality."[99]

Apart from its disinterestedness and nonpartisan nature, Rosanvallon also values the executive for its capacity to express the unity that he associates with the general will. The legislature, by contrast, tends merely to reproduce internally the divisions that exist within society. This problem is exacerbated in countries that have adopted proportional representation electoral systems, which usually block the formation of even majority governments. When such nations are divided, and yet some decision must be taken, the legislature often lacks the resources or the procedures necessary to take decisive action. For this and other reasons, the executive benefits also from the "legitimacy of efficacy," because of its ability to act decisively and to achieve results.[100]

Rosanvallon's vision is of an executive that functions as an important *component* of the broader constellation of institutional arrangements that together make up a democratic political system. There is, of course, an obvious difficulty with this idea. If the legislature exhibits internal division and partiality, it is largely because it is accountable to the public. The conception of the general will that the legislature works with can only stray so far from what the public actually wants. The executive, by contrast, has the autonomy to formulate its own conception of the general will, independent of the sometimes intemperate desires of the public. Unfortunately, it risks becoming completely untethered from anything that the public cares about or desires. Similarly, though the executive differs from the legislature in not being beholden to any particular group, the problem is that it may not be beholden to anyone at all. What is to stop its members from simply substituting their own interests for those of the public, or more insidiously, coming to identify their own parochial concerns with the general will?

Rosanvallon's response to this question, unfortunately, undermines the boldness and originality of his initial project. He claims that to overcome these difficulties, it is essential that the head of the executive branch be *popularly elected*. As a result, he regards presidentialism—along essentially Gaullist lines—as the uniquely favored arrangement of democratic institutions. And so despite all the talk about democracy being instantiated in a distributed fashion across a wide range of different institutions, each contributing a different element to the legitimacy of the whole, democratic election winds up being the gold standard of legitimacy, not just for the legislature but for the executive as well.[101]

This is a peculiar position for several reasons. First, the president of the republic, just like members of the legislature, is elected by majority rule, which as we have seen, Rosanvallon regards as an extremely flawed decision procedure.[102] Thus it is not clear how assigning control of the executive to an elected president accomplishes anything that could not be achieved by assigning control to the legislature (or to the head of the ruling party or coalition in the legislature). By contrast, the creation of two leadership positions—typically, the president and the prime minister—each with a claim to democratic legitimacy, without any principled procedure for resolving disputes that may arise, generates the potential for gridlock. This can produce either political paralysis, such as we have seen in the United States, or political instability, such as we have seen throughout Latin America. As Juan Linz has observed, in an influential critique of presidentialism, the lack of a clear decision procedure, or principle of precedence, in cases of conflict between the legislature and the executive is what generates the temptation for the armed forces to intervene, in order to act as a "mediating power."[103] Thus there is a clear connection between presidentialism and the susceptibility of political systems to military coups.

Rosanvallon's preferred solution to this problem is to strengthen the hand of the president (again, in the style of the French Fifth Republic) so that true gridlock with the legislature is not possible. (The American system has been drifting in a similar direction, which accounts for the ongoing hand-wringing about the "imperial presidency."[104]) Thus Rosanvallon endorses the principle of "executive supremacy." This in turn gives rise to a concern over "Caesarism," since the easiest way to achieve unity, and to overcome the internal divisions within society, is simply to have one person control the state. This shift in power to the executive generates a serious threat to the rule of law. Because the executive is not able to legislate, it typically rules by decree (e.g., "executive order" in the United States).[105] Indeed, this has become the standard template for "illiberal democracies" throughout the world, in which a popularly elected president subordinates the legislature and judiciary, then proceeds to rule as a dictator. (The flaws of parliamentary systems seem rather pedestrian in comparison. The greatest threat posed by the executive in a parliamentary system is not that it will seize the reins of power and subordinate the other two branches of the state, but merely that it will become an entrenched technocratic elite with an unhealthy fondness for the status quo.)

One might put forward various theories about how Rosanvallon winds up endorsing such a deeply unattractive position, but an obvious candidate would be that it follows from his initial impulse to bring the executive under the umbrella of democratically legitimate institutions, which then sets up the inevitable conflict with the legislature. Some have argued, to my mind persuasively, that the best way to avoid such a conflict—which, it should be noted, the executive usually wins—is to deprive the executive of democratic legitimacy entirely, by not allowing any of its members to be elected.[106] This, in turn, imposes a clearer division of authority on the branches of the state, forcing permanent officials to focus on their specific contribution, which is the problem-solving capacity that Rosanvallon aptly describes as subtending the "legitimacy of efficacy."

It is the latter arrangement that I intend to analyze here. Since my focus in this work is on parliamentary systems, some of the discussion that follows is simply orthogonal to Rosanvallon's (whose normative framework essentially requires presidentialism). More generally, however, my intention is to consider the executive as a sui generis source of political authority, the normative basis of which is best expressed in the language of liberalism, and of a commitment to liberal principles of justice, not to democracy. In this respect, my view represents "the road not taken," and is the obvious alternative to Rosanvallon's most basic approach to the question.

1.7. Conclusion

The best way to mitigate the risks inherent in the growth of administrative power is to develop a set of principles and rules aimed at guiding and constraining its exercise. This is precisely what has happened, congruent with the rise of the administrative state. These rules take two forms: administrative law and professional ethics. The former has as its core the set of ordinary laws, passed by the legislature, whose objective is to govern how the executive interprets and implements *other* laws. In addition to this, there is a body of case law, which has developed over time as the judiciary has considered challenges to the executive's interpretation of the law and use of its power. Together these make up the field of administrative law. The second major body of rules takes the form of a system of professional ethics, which is reproduced informally through the institutional culture of the civil service (and forms part of the "public-sector ethos"). It is, in many ways, just as constraining as administrative law, and yet it has received significantly less attention. In part, this is because it is not explicitly articulated, but is merely implicit in the practices of the various branches of the civil service. It is also because the enforcement mechanisms are informal, and so it can be difficult for an outsider even to recognize breaches of the norms. And finally, there is the fact that the commitment to a rather stylized conception of how democracy is supposed to function leads many theorists to want to downplay or deny the importance of purely self-imposed moral constraints in limiting the exercise of arbitrary power by the executive. Thus my goal is to articulate a set of normative ideals able to guide a professional ethic of public administration, which I take to be more-or-less implicit in existing best practices, but which seldom rises to the level of explicit articulation.

More generally, my goal is to answer the question, how it is possible for experts to develop a self-standing conception of what "good policy" looks like, without relying upon guidance from politicians? The tempting answer is to say that they have a purely technical perspective, and so they can work it out without making any value judgments. This is clearly not true, as we have seen. Even with central banking, perhaps one of the most technical fields of public administration, there are normative questions that must be answered. The better answer, I will argue, is that there are certain normative principles that, within a liberal polity, fall outside the scope of reasonable disagreement. These are the principles of efficiency, equality, and liberty, which form the normative core of modern liberal theories of justice. Although there is considerable disagreement over the correct conception of these principles, there is widespread agreement on the basic concepts. When formulated in an appropriately minimal fashion, they can provide the foundation for a self-standing conception of the public interest.

2

A General Framework for the Ethics of Public Administration

Compared to the field of business ethics, the field of "public administration ethics," or "ethics for civil servants," is relatively underdeveloped. Although there have been some noteworthy contributions, there are no distinguishable schools of thought, nor is there much sustained engagement between thinkers with different points of view.[1] There is some literature on "public integrity"; however, the discussion tends to focus disproportionately on the behavior of politicians and elected officials, at the expense of any concern over the behavior of civil servants.[2] Some attempts have been made to develop a general framework for the "ethics of management" or the "ethics of bureaucratic organizations" that would encompass both the private and public sectors, yet these tend to founder when confronted with the extreme heterogeneity that one finds within the public sector, in terms of its many different branches, the tasks they must discharge, and the complex relations they stand in toward both citizens and elected officials.[3] The state is not best described as an organization, but rather an "organization of organizations."[4] Some departments, agencies, or state-owned enterprises (SOEs) are almost fully autonomous from the government of the day; others are very closely tied to the enactment of policy. Some are engaged in the production of goods and services, others only regulate, and still others are engaged primarily in income transfers or in administering insurance systems. Some have thousands of employees, some almost none. Some deal directly with the public, others do not. Some have a service orientation toward their "clients," and others have a relationship that is essentially adversarial.[5] Thus is it difficult to generalize about the obligations that civil servants have, not just from jurisdiction to jurisdiction, but even from one branch to another in the same jurisdiction. The resulting intractability is reflected in many of the codes of ethics that have been developed for civil servants, which often wind up being a laundry list of dozens of "values," with no particular guidance about how they are to be implemented, much less reconciled in cases of conflict.[6]

And yet it is not difficult to see that the basic question of which principles or values should guide the deliberations of civil servants as they go about their duties, and how they should conceive of their obligations toward elected officials, state institutions, and the public more generally, is of the utmost

The Machinery of Government. Joseph Heath, Oxford University Press (2020). © Oxford University Press.
DOI: 10.1093/oso/9780197509616.001.0001

significance. Indeed, considering that almost all state employees work for the executive branch, it is extraordinary how much attention has been lavished on the legislature and the judiciary, to the exclusion of the executive.[7] There are three levels at which the ethics of civil servants matter. First, because a great deal of compliance with the law is morally motivated, ethical conduct on the part of state employees tends to be prophylactic against various forms of corruption, ranging from petty bribery at one extreme to military coups at the other. (In this context, it is worth keeping in mind that the "men with guns" on the state payroll are, almost without exception, members of the executive branch.) Public-sector ethics in this sense tends to be a preoccupation in underdeveloped and developing countries, particularly where systemic corruption is a major problem. The second major issue is executive discretion. The problem is not just that laws are often written in very general language. All the way down the organizational hierarchy civil servants have enormous latitude when determining how they carry out their responsibilities, and thus they require some set of principles that can guide their decision-making and conduct within these interstices or, in some cases, lacunae, of the law. Finally, there is the fact that civil servants, particularly in the upper echelons, or within powerful agencies, have the capacity to exercise significant influence over the legislative process. In liberal democracies, most serious or complex policy initiatives originate within the civil service.[8] Furthermore, the civil service is often deeply engaged with the interest groups and political constituencies that have a stake in these initiatives. This issue is particularly important in Westminster-style systems, in which the tradition of civil service neutrality creates a permanent class of officials with considerable expertise; whereas the structure of parliamentary elections generates significant turnover among elected officials, resulting in sometimes serious information asymmetries between members of the executive and their supposed political masters. Thus the civil service is often the source of highly effective policy entrepreneurship.[9] At the same time, misuse of this power gives the executive the capacity to undermine accountability to the public, and in the extreme, to subvert democracy.

Seen from this perspective, public administration ethics does not deal with small or inconsequential questions of personal morality, but rather with major issues concerning the disposition of state power. John Rohr articulated the stakes quite well when he observed that "the bureaucrat's position is sharply distinguished from that of the elected official, even though . . . he or she shares governing power with the elected official. The combination of these two ingredients—governing power and independence from the electorate—presents a significant problem for a democratic society. It is a problem that cannot be answered without a serious look at the ethical norms bureaucrats bring to their governing role."[10] In the discussion that follows, I shall defend my own framework for organizing the various strategies that have been proposed to address this problem.

Abstractly, there is little disagreement that the civil servant should be committed to serving "the public interest," or "the general good." Things get difficult when it comes to the institutional specification of this ideal, both how it gets defined and who has the authority to define it. Typically, civil servants have available three distinct poles of allegiance. The first is to elected officials, the second is to the public directly, and the third is to some independently determined interests of the state. Under happy circumstances, the three will be aligned: politicians will be tolerably responsive to the wishes of the public, while the public will prefer outcomes that can reasonably be construed as serving the general good, and professional norms will therefore recommend allegiance to all three. Difficult circumstances arise when the three become misaligned, so that the civil servant is forced to choose one over another, perhaps even over the other two. It is when confronting these "hard cases" that questions about the fundamental obligations of the civil servant arise.

2.1. Preliminary clarification

I would like to begin with a clarification that may seem rather abstruse, but is actually quite important for understanding some of the constraints that structure the argument that follows. My intention is to discuss the *professional* morality of civil servants, which is to say, the moral obligations that arise specifically from their institutional role. In philosophical terms, this qualification is typically expressed by saying that the inquiry is into the moral obligations of the civil servant *qua* civil servant (as opposed to qua individual, or qua member of society). Crucial here is the thought that the institutionally defined role of the civil servant imposes not just legal obligations on the individual occupant of that role, but moral obligations as well. Furthermore, these moral obligations are sometimes distinctive to the role; they are not obligations that fall on members of the public generally, or even on the occupants of other professional roles. I would therefore like to distinguish the demands of professional morality (that the individual is subject to qua civil servant) from those of everyday morality (that the individual is subject to qua member of society).

This way of looking at things is somewhat at variance with a common-sense view, which regards the "moral problems" that civil servants typically encounter as involving a conflict between, on the one hand, some set of institutional demands (e.g., an order from a superior to destroy a document), and on the other hand, some private moral conviction (e.g., the belief that the public has a "right to know" the contents of that document) arising from everyday morality. Faced with such a conflict, the dominant impulse—at least among those who are out-side observers of the conflict—is to recommend that the individual "do the right thing," which is to say, act in accordance with the private moral conviction. Yet this response, far from constituting a solution to the problem, is in my view actu-ally a reductio of the conceptual framework that generates it. If the answer to the question, "When should I do what I'm told?" is simply, "When what you're told to do is right," and if the answer to the question, "When shouldn't I do what I'm told?" is "When what you're told to do is wrong," then whatever view generates these answers is simply failing to take institutional roles seriously. Most obvi-ously, if people actually acted this way, then organizational hierarchy would be impossible. (If people obey orders only when they happen to agree with the or-ders, then there is no point giving orders.) Thus the view is anti-authoritarian in the strict sense of the term.[11] There may be something to be said for anti-authoritarianism as a personal philosophy, but it stands to reason that anti-authoritarianism cannot be a governing philosophy *for employees of the state*.[12]

The major problem with the anti-authoritarian stance is that it fails to ac-knowledge the division of moral labor that exists within our institutions. Instead of making everyone responsible for every bad thing that can happen (which often results in nobody doing anything), we generally find it advantageous to parcel out tasks, so that *some* people are assigned special responsibility for *some* of the bad things that can happen (which more often results in somebody doing something, even if it is not the ideal intervention). The tough problems that arise all involve this institutional differentiation of role. And yet the conventional un-derstanding of moral problems clearly fails to articulate the institutional aspect, because it treats institutions as a source of demands that are entirely external to morality, and so locates morality only in the private convictions of the indi-vidual (qua individual). It never really grapples with the hard problem, which is to understand the *moral* obligations individuals are subject to as occupants of institutional roles.

The idea that an institutional role can generate sui generis moral obligations should not be entirely foreign. It is widely understood, for instance, that a doctor has special obligations to her patients (e.g., confidentiality), which she is sub-ject to qua doctor, that a lawyer has special obligations toward his clients (e.g., advocacy), which he is subject to qua lawyer, and so on. The contrast between professional morality and everyday morality in this case is obvious, because the role obligation requires overt partiality to the interests of those with whom the professional has a specified relationship, a form of partiality that is not only un-licensed by everyday morality but may even come into conflict with it. (We typ-ically articulate this partiality by saying that there is a "fiduciary relationship" between the doctor and the patient, or the lawyer and the client, which entails a "duty of loyalty" to the latter's interests.) This makes it fairly easy to distinguish the professional moral obligations from the everyday (though it should be noted that, to the extent that professional education is in part a socialization process through which individuals come to internalize these norms of conduct, the distinction may not be introspectively available to practitioners).

The situation is somewhat confusing in the case of the civil servant, however, because this sort of explicit partiality is largely absent from the civil servant's role. Because the state is taken to serve "the public interest," and the basic thrust of everyday morality is to promote "the general good," the institutional demands placed upon the civil servant, as an employee of the state, are often quite similar to the demands of everyday morality—they both seem to involve doing what's best for "society." Indeed, where the professional obligations show up most clearly are the cases in which the civil servant is called upon to *resist* the partial moral obligations that arise from everyday morality, and, instead, to respect impartiality. For example, many of the difficult cases encountered by civil servants involve circumstances in which the strict application of a rule will disadvantage some morally sympathetic individual.[13] The potential for this conflict to arise is sometimes not given adequate consideration, because of the strong tendency to think of everyday morality as being always impartial (concerned with maximizing aggregate social welfare, or following a set of universalizable maxims, etc.). This makes it easy to conflate the role morality of the civil servant with the rules of everyday morality, and therefore to imagine that an injunction to "do the right thing"—according to the conventional or everyday understanding of what "the right thing" consists of—constitutes useful advice in resolving questions of professional conduct.

My own view is that the role morality of the civil servant can conflict with everyday morality, even when both are aimed at the general good, impartially construed. This is because the role morality arises in part from a division of moral labor within our institutions. One feature of this division of labor is that it is not left up to each individual to decide where the general good lies; instead, procedures have been put in place for making that determination. These procedures generate duties, even in cases where the individual believes that the procedures have, in this particular instance, failed to track the good. (And to repeat: unless these procedures carry *some* weight with the individual—i.e., unless she feels some moral obligation to respect their determinations—then there is very little point in having them.)[14]

Few people doubt that role morality can generate a variety of prima facie conflicts with everyday morality. There is a very rich debate, for example, on the question of whether and when lawyers are allowed to lie (and if they are, how that could be so).[15] The dominant impulse has been to try to show that the conflict is only prima facie, but that upon closer examination the obligations can be shown to be compatible. This typically takes the form of a rather casuistic justification (e.g., showing that the action is essential to the role, and that the role is required by some abstract moral consideration that outweighs or trumps everyday moral obligation).[16] Personally, I have doubts about these arguments, but that is not important for our purposes. It is sufficient to observe that philosophical arguments of this kind, by virtue of their esoteric quality and indirect structure, are typically not available to the *occupants* of the various professional roles. As a result, when these individuals are called upon to respect their professional obligations, *from their perspective*, it will sometimes involve violating rules of everyday morality. In the case of civil servants this can take myriad forms, but a typical example would be the obligation to strictly impose administrative rules, even when ordinary compassion pushes in the direction of bending or violating those rules.

This has a number of important implications, but the one that I would like to draw attention to here is that it makes the standard philosophical theories developed in the field of "normative ethics"—Kantianism, utilitarianism, and virtue theory—of very limited use in thinking about professional morality. This is because these theories were all developed in an attempt to provide a rational reconstruction of everyday morality (focusing primarily on our basic norms prohibiting harm, dishonesty, and indifference to suffering). Because professional morality can conflict with everyday morality, practitioners are unlikely to regard a particular question as settled just because some course of action would conventionally be regarded as unethical. (For example, the *mere* fact that a particular press release is likely to mislead the public does not mean that one may not be obliged to issue it. Or the *mere* fact that certain individuals are in desperate need does not mean that one can enroll them in a program for which they fail to meet the eligibility requirements.[17]) Now, to the extent that normative-ethical theories are just systematizations of everyday morality, they are not likely to be regarded as any more decisive by practitioners. To provide useful clarification, what philosophers need to offer is a rational reconstruction *of professional morality*. I will try to provide this in what follows.

2.2. Three models of accountability

As mentioned above, many of the ethics exercises undertaken in the civil service wind up producing a laundry list—which is to say, an unsystematic collection—of abstract values. It is therefore a common strategy in the theoretical literature, among those who adopt a "bottom up" approach, to start with these values and then try to impose some type of systematic order on them. One influential approach involves grouping these values in accordance with the branch of government from which they originate, or with whose operation they seem most strongly associated.[18] Thus it is common to distinguish juridical values (e.g., rights, liberty, equality) from political values (e.g., responsiveness, represent-ativeness, accountability) and from "bureaucratic" or "administrative" values (e.g., efficiency, economy, effectiveness).[19] Unfortunately, this taxonomic ap-proach tends to create more problems than it solves. By associating certain values with other branches of government, it treats them as exogenous to the practice of public administration, which suggests that they should function more as ex-ternal constraints than as internal features of the "ethic" of the executive branch. Furthermore, by associating "bureaucratic" values like efficiency so strongly with the executive branch, it raises perplexing questions about the legitimacy of those values. Particularly when a conflict arises between democratic and bureau-cratic values, it becomes difficult to see where the executive gets the authority to impose "its" values, or even what could justify a balancing of the two.[20] This, of course, can only be answered by addressing more basic questions of political philosophy. It therefore speaks in favor of a more "top-down" approach, starting with certain first principles, such as the fundamental structures of liberal democ-racy, then deriving from them guidance for the practice of public administration.

This is the approach adopted by John Rohr and Terry Cooper and, in a partic-ularly explicit form, in the work of Dennis Thompson. Again, starting from the idea that civil servants are committed to promoting the "public interest," the fun-damental question becomes how this commitment is institutionalized. I take it as relatively uncontroversial that at a sufficiently high level of abstraction, one can say that both the state and everyday morality are committed to promoting the "general good." There are, of course, many differences, one of the most impor-tant being that the state actually institutionalizes procedures for specifying what constitutes the general good and for determining where it lies. The state may also decide to pursue some less idealized objectives, in recognition of the weakness, indeterminacy, or contentiousness of these procedures. So while civil servants may inherit an obligation to promote the general good, it is almost never up to them to decide what it is or where it lies. This is what underlies the classic dis-tinction between "policy" and "administration"—the implication being that civil servants should be in the business of administering, or implementing, policy, but not in the business of setting it. This distinction gets at something impor-tant, but as we have seen, it tends to understate the amount of discretion civil servants enjoy when it comes to deciding how they will discharge their respon-sibilities.[21] There are many circumstances in which civil servants are clearly engaged in policy setting, not just implementation. Indeed, John Huber and Charles Shipan suggest that statutes are better understood, not as policies, but rather as "blueprints for policymaking."[22] And as Michael Lipsky argued in his classic study *Street-Level Bureaucracy*, even civil servants working at the lowest level of the organizational hierarchy—those involved in direct interactions with the public—are constantly making policy decisions. Furthermore, "when taken together the individual decisions of these workers become, or add up to, agency policy. Whether government policy is to deliver 'goods'—such as welfare or public housing—or to confer status—such as 'criminal' or 'mentally ill'—the discretionary actions of public employees are the benefits and sanctions of government programs or determine access to government rights and benefits."[23] This is why public administration is almost always subject to overarching systems of *accountability*, designed to ensure that there is an appropriate alignment of objectives between civil servants and those who are more formally charged with determining where the general good lies.

Accountability in government, however, is no simple affair. Indeed, over the past half-century there has been significant dissatisfaction in many democratic countries with the inherited system of accountability, which has in turn motivated several attempts to develop different patterns of organization. As a result, it is common in the literature on public administration to describe different "models" of accountability. Thompson, for instance, in an important contribution on the subject, distinguishes three distinct models of administrative accountability, which he calls the hierarchical, the participatory, and the professional.[24] In the familiar hierarchical model, accountability flows up the chain of command, and ultimately ends with the elected official who presides over a particular branch of government. In parliamentary systems, the hierarchical model corresponds to the well-known doctrine of "ministerial accountability." The participatory model—or as I prefer to call it, the "popular" model—reverses the lines of accountability, and tries to make the civil service directly accountable to the public, without the mediation of elected officials. And finally, the professional model requires that civil servants be held accountable to an independent set of professional norms, which express, in some form, "the universal interest of the state."[25] (In a Westminster context, this view is the one that takes seriously the fact that civil servants owe allegiance to "the Crown," not to Parliament.) Again, the term that Thompson uses is potentially confusing, since all three models are ways of understanding the "professional" morality of civil servants. To introduce a terminological distinction, I will refer to this last model as the "vocational" model (which captures the idea that public servants are committed to a "higher good," though, in this case, a secular one).

To visualize the difference between these models, one need only imagine an individual situated somewhere in the middle of an organizational hierarchy, wondering where his allegiances lie. The suggestion is that these loyalties can either flow "up" the organizational hierarchy toward the minister, "down" the hierarchy toward the public, or "across" to a group of peers who maintain the set of professional norms (see Figure 2.1).

These models also provide a useful template for thinking about professional ethics, since any argument that shows why explicit accountability should flow in

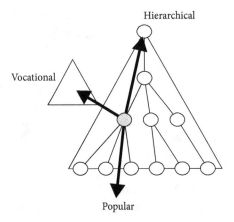

Figure 2.1 Three different models of accountability: hierarchical, popular, and vocational.

one way or another would appear to work equally well as an argument for why moral responsibility should do the same.[26] I will evaluate each of the models in turn. The hierarchical model, I suggest, is the least attractive in theory, but it remains influential as the official ideology of the civil service. The popular model is the most attractive in theory, but the least important in practice. Much of the literature, however, regards these two options as exhaustive. What I will attempt to show is that the vocational model, despite being the most often overlooked, is in fact the most defensible, and is best able to capture and articulate what is correct about the other two. The major impediment to its more widespread acceptance is that it does not tie the obligations of the civil servant directly to an explicitly democratic source of legitimacy. The major burden of proof therefore lies in showing that this should not undermine its normative authority.

2.3. The hierarchical model

The hierarchical model is without doubt the most straightforward way of thinking about the obligations of the civil servant. According to this view, where the "public interest" lies is determined through the democratic process. Parties and politicians compete for votes; those who attract the most votes are entitled to form the government. Having formed the government, they appoint leaders to each branch of the civil service—ministers, in the parliamentary tradition. The civil servant serves the public by serving the minister, or by serving those who exercise authority delegated by the minister. Thus allegiance and loyalty flow up the chain of command. Furthermore, there is no independent conception of the "general good" or the "public interest"; these are fully exhausted by the minister's specification. The civil servant may have *private* views on the matter, but the professional ethic of the civil servant has no notion of it other than the minister's. So loyalty to elected officials is not only an institutional expectation, it is the *moral obligation* of the civil servant.[27] This is the model at the heart of the doctrine of ministerial accountability, which forms the core of the so-called Whitehall ethos in the civil service of parliamentary systems.[28]

This way of thinking about professional obligation is obviously a natural fit with a Weberian model of bureaucracy (where the job of civil servants is to deliberate about "means," but not to set "ends"), as well as the classic distinction between "policy" and "administration" (in which civil servants are tasked with implementing policy, but not setting it). On the latter view, expressed canonically by Woodrow Wilson, public administration involves a neutral set of technical skills that can be applied to any goal.[29] This is, of course, a 19th-century argument, which is not entirely accidental, since many regard the basic view as hopelessly outdated. During the 1940s, in particular, influential critiques by Carl Friedrich and Paul Appleby were taken to have demonstrated the impossibility of drawing any clear distinction between policy and administration.[30] The view has, however, received some recent affirmations, such as the Armstrong Memorandum, circulated to an insubordinate civil service in the United Kingdom in 1985:

> Civil servants are servants of the Crown. For all practical purposes the Crown in this context means and is represented by the Government of the day. There are special cases in which certain functions are conferred by law upon particular members or groups of members of the public service; but in general the executive powers of the Crown are exercised by and on the advice of Her Majesty's Ministers, who are in turn answerable to Parliament. The Civil Service as such has no constitutional personality or responsibility separate from the duly constituted Government of the day. It is there to provide the Government of the day with advice on the formulation of the policies of the Government, to assist in carrying out the decisions of the Government, and to manage and deliver the services for which the Government is responsible.

For those who are unused to reading such documents, this may sound like a series of platitudinous claims. Upon closer examination, one can see that the memorandum is very strongly worded. (It was issued under the Thatcher Government, in response to several episodes in which civil servants acted in ways that exhibited disloyalty to their ministers—including a "whistleblowing" episode in the UK Ministry of Defence that resulted in government prosecution of the civil servant who had spoken out.) The claim that the civil service "has no constitutional personality or responsibility separate from the duly constituted Government of the day," for example, is quite striking (and not obviously true).[31]

Unfortunately, the hierarchical model receives very little serious consideration among academics, and even less among students, because it is so easy to dismiss by "playing the Nazi card" (also known as the *reductio ad nazium*).[32] People have great difficulty seeing how there could be any *moral* obligation to follow orders. On the contrary, "just following orders" is more often regarded as an excuse for immorality.[33] After all, weren't the German concentration camp guards "just following orders" when playing their part in the plan to exterminate European Jewry? Wasn't this how Adolf Eichmann defended his role in implementing the final solution? And didn't the Milgram experiments show that people are far too easily influenced by authority, and need to learn to exercise independent moral judgment?

This argument is not so much wrong as it is jejune. From the fact that some individuals have on some occasions been given orders that are outrageous and unconscionable (paradigmatically, an order to kill an innocent), it moves immediately to the conclusion that whenever anyone receives an order, she should evaluate it from the standpoint of her own moral code, and obey only if the action is considered permissible. This conclusion fails to take hierarchy seriously; it is simply a statement of the anti-authoritarian position (which, I have argued, is a reductio of the conceptual framework that generates it). If part of the institutional division of labor in the state involves giving some people special responsibility for determining what "the right thing to do" is, it necessarily follows that other people are going to have to follow orders, without deciding themselves whether that action is, in fact, the right thing to do. The alternative simply makes the division of labor impossible (and rules out, inter alia, representative democracy).

Yet anti-authoritarianism is so pervasive in our culture, and hierarchy is given so little serious consideration as a model of obligation, that many aspiring civil servants no doubt experience a rude shock on their first day at work. For not only is the civil service quite hierarchical, but its cultural ethos also involves much greater deference to authority than one finds in many other familiar social institutions, including many corporations. Many of its strongest traditions are essentially organized around the principle of loyalty to the minister of the day. For example, one of the reasons that "transparency" or "openness" in government is so difficult to achieve is that it runs headlong into one of the oldest and most prized virtues of the civil service, which is secrecy. Secrecy and discretion have historically been regarded as important moral obligations of the civil servant, because they are seen as a way of preserving both neutrality and loyalty of service to the minister.[34] So one can find civil servants engaged in elaborate precautions to avoid "access to information" requests, not because they reject the public's right to know, but because they regard it as the minister's prerogative to decide what the public should know. In other words, they do not conceive of their obligation as being to the public directly, but rather to the public indirectly, up the chain of command and through the minister.

The most interesting philosophical defense of hierarchy as a source of moral obligation in recent years has been Allan Buchanan's "agency-cost minimization" approach to the ethics of bureaucratic organizations.[35] A hierarchical organization can be modeled as a set of recursively embedded principal-agent relations. Principal-agent relations involve situations "in which one individual (the agent) acts on behalf of another (the principal) and is supposed to advance the principal's goals."[36] There is typically a degree of goal incongruity between principal and agent, resulting in the need to provide the agent with some incentive to advance the principal's goals rather than her own. These external "carrots and sticks" are typically supplemented by efforts to restructure aspects of the agent's internal motivation, either to reduce the level of goal incongruity between herself and the principal, or to provide some overriding source of motivation that will lead her to assign primacy to the principal's goals. This effort is almost never entirely successful (e.g., employees still waste time at work, exercise less care with their employer's property than their own, etc.), but whenever one does see an extremely effective organization, it is almost always because it has a successful formula for overcoming its internal agency problems.[37]

This conceptual framework is useful in that it suggests that the central issue in a hierarchical organization is not how to promote obedience to authority, but simply how to achieve a *delegation of tasks* without creating huge inefficiencies. The source of these inefficiencies lies in so-called agency costs, which come in two types: first, there is the direct cost of providing the carrots and sticks required to achieve incentive alignment (e.g., payment of supervisors, bonus pay schemes, etc.), and of cultivating the appropriate inner motivation (e.g., retreats, team-building exercises, etc.); second, there is the hidden cost of unresolved collective-action problems, or counterproductive behavior caused by a failure to achieve adequate incentive alignment. Buchanan observes that "to a large extent the most important and distinctive ethical principles that are applicable to bureaucratic organizations express *commitments* on the part of persons working in bureaucracies that function to *reduce the risks* that the behavior of bureaucrats, understood as agents, imposes upon the principals whose agents they are."[38] Thus he advances the somewhat functionalist-sounding view that these principles arise precisely because they reduce agency costs.[39] For example, he cites what he calls "the principle of stewardship," which serves "to impress upon the bureaucrat that the resources she controls are not her property but rather are owned by others for whom she serves as trustor or steward."[40] Similarly, if one were to look at the seven "Nolan principles" developed by the UK's Committee on Standards in Public Life, one can see that they all, in one way or another, have the effect of promoting more loyal agency.[41]

In an interesting twist, Buchanan goes on to observe that many organizations put in place control mechanisms aimed at reducing agency costs, which in turn may generate second-order agency problems when employees engage in counterproductive forms of behavior aimed at subverting these control mechanisms (e.g., destroying surveillance equipment, failing to maintain written records, etc.). Thus Buchanan argues that there arise norms aimed at minimizing these second-order agency costs. For example, he argues that the somewhat moralizing attitude adopted within effective bureaucracies toward perspicuous documentation of activities and decisions reflects an internalized norm that serves to protect the integrity of control mechanisms aimed at reducing first-order agency costs. Or, given the well-known tendency within bureaucracies to diminish the sense of personal responsibility among their members, Buchanan argues that there arises a second-order obligation to establish clear assignments of responsibility, in order to prevent the problem of "many hands" from emerging.[42]

Working through Buchanan's analysis, one quickly becomes aware of how thoroughly the ethos of bureaucratic organizations is permeated by norms and expectations that are essentially oriented toward the smooth operation of the hierarchy (which is to say, a reduction in agency costs and an avoidance of agency problems). Even if it is never given a principled articulation, the hierarchical model is "in the water"—implicit in the norms of the workplace. Furthermore, in states that suffer from various forms of systemic corruption, the central organizational challenge essentially is to achieve a set of effective agency relations, which is to say, a functional hierarchy. To take just one particularly dramatic example, the state of India has a very extensive primary school system, but has enormous difficulty getting its teachers to actually teach. On any given day, it is estimated that a quarter of all teachers do not show up for work, and even among those who do, only a fraction perform their classroom duties.[43] Here it is clear that the central challenge faced by the educational bureaucracy involves getting people to do what they are being told to do, or what they are being paid to do. The example also helps to show how many of the virtues associated with organizational hierarchy are simply taken for granted in many societies—in most developed countries, for instance, the idea that one might take a job as a public school teacher, and then simply not show up for work (perhaps paying off the school principal in order to avoid trouble) would simply never occur to most people.

Thus part of the reason the hierarchical model of accountability has difficulty being taken seriously in wealthy countries with low levels of corruption is that in those cultural contexts it is possible to take for granted that civil servants will not be particularly aggressive in taking advantage of agency relations, but will behave in appropriately deferential ways to their superiors. This is, of course, a bad reason for neglecting the model. There are, however, some good reasons for the disfavor it has increasingly been shown. Indeed, over the past few decades there has been a strong current of institutional and political opposition to the hierarchical model—not because of any principled objection to the idea of obedience to authority, but because there is a sense that it "no longer works" as a model of accountability. It is these influences that have resulted in the Armstrong memorandum sounding distinctively old-fashioned. There are four principal grounds for criticism.

2.3.1. Unrealistic

The fact that civil servants show *deference* to those above them in the chain of command does not mean that they meekly accept the policies that are handed down to them, or that they have any genuine commitment to advancing the goals of their political masters. There has always been considerable skepticism about the idea that "policy," in any meaningful sense of the term, is set by politicians, while civil servants limit themselves to "administration" or "implementation."[44] (Carol Lewis describes this dichotomy as having been relegated "to the realm of delusion."[45]) Thus Herman Finer's well-known assertion that "only the Minister has views and takes actions," understood descriptively, is simply false.[46] Understood normatively, the question is whether it is a reasonable aspiration, given the rather low probability that it could ever be satisfied.

Part of the difficulty stems from the unusual structure of the civil service as an organization, one in which the lower ranks of management typically have a near-total monopoly over information, and ministers are brought in from the outside, often having little or no experience of government, no idea how their own department works, no experience working in large organizations, and sometimes very little formal education. As Brian Cubbon described it, "Our system of government defies all management models. Where else would you have a board of directors consisting mainly of marketing men conducting all the key operations themselves, with the thinking at a much lower level in the organization?"[47]

Reflections of this sort have fueled a growing perception, in the postwar period, that the old ministerial accountability model was more appropriate to the late 19th century than it is to the contemporary world. (This perception was very much exacerbated by the *Yes, Minister* series, which played a not-insignificant role in the decline of faith in the traditional Whitehall model.) There was a time when ministers could develop a clear understanding of how any department of government functioned, and were even in a position to personally supervise all but the lowest-level employees. The growth of the state, in terms of both scale and complexity, has led to a steady increase in what Henry Parris refers to as "the fictitious element in the minister's responsibility for his department."[48] With the rise of the administrative state, ministers are not just failing to provide guidance for civil servants that is sufficiently concrete for them to be genuinely bound by these directives; in principle, they cannot provide such guidance, because they simply do not have enough information at their disposal to make expert decisions. Government departments exhibit an extreme form of what Oliver Williamson referred to as "information impactedness,"[49] and so cannot be managed in a top-down fashion. Indeed, there is a large empirical literature focused on the question of whether and to what degree politicians exercise meaningful control over the public-sector bureaucracy.[50] (This question, it should be noted, recurs all the way down the bureaucracy. Like ministers, senior-level civil servants often formulate policy objectives and goals at an extremely high level of abstraction, and thus serve as little more than sources of "ideas," which must be transformed into concrete policy at much lower levels of the bureaucracy.[51])

To give just one example, in the Canadian province of Ontario approximately 250,000 public-sector employees work in "health and social service institutions" (at the time of writing).[52] These institutions all have complex relations with the state, but almost all of them are under the budgetary control and nominal supervision of the Ministry of Health and Long-Term Care, which is subject to the authority of a single elected official—namely, the minister. The minister is, in turn, assisted by a number of very senior public servants: a deputy minister, an associate minister, two associate deputy ministers, and an assistant deputy minister, as well as a chief medical officer. These officials oversee a budget of approximately $51 billion in 2016 (which includes the single-payer insurance plan, which has a budget of around $17 billion). With an organization on that scale, it is difficult to imagine the role of the minister being adequately characterized as "giving orders" or "setting policy" that the rest of the organization merely implements. For instance, most hospitals in the province are independently managed nonprofit corporations, over which the government has practically no operational control (the state has only recently begun shifting away from global budgeting to more contractual and performance-based funding schemes). Short of closing them down entirely—which is virtually politically impossible—the minister has literally no control over how money is spent or decisions are made within these institutions. (This is quite normal in the public sector, as the extensive literature on the "soft budget constraint" has emphasized.[53]) Considering the vast organizational scale and complexity of the system, it would take an unusually capable or committed minister to be able to even *influence* policy in any meaningful way (as opposed to simply making changes in the "org chart," which is what politicians often wind up doing, in order to project, and perhaps to experience, a sense of efficacy).

Most politicians, it should be noted, are well aware of how little control they have. Consider the following reflections from Graham Steele, former minister of finance in the province of Nova Scotia:

> When your party is finally elected, and when you become a minister, you discover that the provincial government is a huge machine in motion and that almost everything is committed in advance—money, wages, programs, buildings, methods. There's not a lot of discretionary decision-making left ... The truth is that the provincial budget, in any given year, is virtually identical to the budget of the year before. My guess is that the budget is 98 percent the same from one year to the next. The only reason we might believe otherwise is that politics requires that differences be exaggerated. From one year to the next, no matter who is in government, and even if there is a change of government, the same civil servants do the same work the same way they did it the previous year.[54]

Steele presents this merely as a description of how things work, he does not offer any normative assessment. Similarly, it does not require a normative assessment to see that, to the extent that this "huge machine in motion" forms the context in which civil servants are currently working, it reveals quite clearly the limitations of the hierarchical model of accountability.

2.3.2. Increasing discretion

Not only are large segments of the civil service effectively exempt from direct ministerial authority, but many have been intentionally removed from its scope, often to counteract populist tendencies that are judged to be inimical to the formulation and implementation of good policy. The most important example of this, as we have seen, is central banking, where the governor of the central bank typically enjoys almost as much independence from democratic control as supreme court justices. Yet while central banking arrangements such as this are obvious, there are an enormous number of more subtle arrangements designed to provide an expert veto over the decisions of elected politicians. In Ontario, for example, there is (again, at the time of writing) a provincially appointed, quasi-judicial tribunal, the OMB (Ontario Municipal Board), with the power to hear appeals and to reject all planning and zoning decisions made at the municipal level. This is partly to provide regional integration, but also to check the strong tendency toward the "not in my backyard" attitude, or NIMBYism, that occurs in local politics. For example, municipal councilors may support a regional plan that calls for increased residential density, but then oppose all development projects in their own wards that would actually increase density (based on local mobilization against buildings that are deemed "too tall" for the neighborhood). These council decisions are then systematically overruled by the administrative tribunal, which, as a result, winds up making all the major local planning decisions in the province. Although politicians complain about this, it is not clear how many of them are genuinely opposed to the arrangement, because it allows them to pander to their constituents, while at the same time allowing their true preferences (for development and increased density) to prevail.

Furthermore, many of the major branches of the welfare state have an arms-length relationship to the government of the day, or the relevant ministry. In Canada, for instance, just as a provincial Ministry of Health has very little control over what goes on in hospitals, the Ministry of Education has practically no control over what happens in the universities, which are typically independently incorporated nonprofits. And so, despite the fact that the government exercises a near-monopoly in both sectors—there are, with a few minor exceptions, no privately funded hospitals or universities—administrators in these institutions are not actually a part of any "chain of command" that ends with a minister or other elected official. As a result, governments often have to regulate the operations of these organizations in the same way that they would with private corporations. Similarly, many SOEs are administered by appointed officials, but operate at arms-length from the government, and an independent board of directors makes all major decisions. In certain jurisdictions, there were experiments with cabinet-level control of SOEs, but these were largely rejected on grounds of inefficiency.[55] Beyond this, there has been a trend in law-making toward granting increased discretion to agencies, through so-called delegated or "secondary" legislation. In many cases, this takes the form of an explicit grant of discretion or rule-making authority.[56] This is often done for technical reasons, but it is also sometimes done to push controversial policy questions down to the executive level.[57] Sometimes, the use of very abstract language is the only way that those who are sponsoring the legislation can get a majority to agree to it. Sometimes, it is because legislators feel that they cannot get their own view to prevail at the legislative level, and so may have better luck achieving their goals through the bureaucracy (possibly through backdoor channels of influence). In other cases, it is because legislators do not want to be on the record supporting an unpopular policy or compromise, even though they actually do support it, and so they are more than happy to pass the job of imposing it along to civil servants (preserving for themselves a state of plausible deniability).[58]

2.3.3. Judicial review

Administrative decisions are subject to judicial review. Initially, the objective of judicial review was merely to ensure that administrative agencies were not exceeding their statutory authority, and to provide redress when they were. The model was one in which there was a clear set of rules, and the courts were charged with ensuring that administrators were applying them reasonably and impartially. With the growth of delegated legislation and administrative rule-making, however, courts found themselves dealing with litigants who were contesting, not the application of the rules to their specific case, but rather the rules themselves. This left the judiciary caught between two unpalatable options. One was to refrain from interfering, on the grounds that the power of courts extended no further than the written word of the statute; and so if the statute granted an administrative agency discretion, the court had no authority to supervise the details of how that discretion was used. The problem with this option is that it involved sometimes standing by idle in the face of patently unreasonable administrative actions, and in the extreme, what appeared to be violations of the rule of law (such as inconsistent, capricious, or discriminatory exercises of administrative authority). The other option, however, which seemed equally unpalatable, was to assess each contested rule and decision on its substantive merits. This, however, largely defeats the purpose of having specialized administrative agencies, which exist in many cases to bring together the expertise and information needed to make decisions in complex environments. To second-guess the decisions of these agencies, courts would essentially have to recapitulate the entire process of deliberation that led to the decision, something they generally lack the resources and capability to do. At very least, it would be a recipe for paralysis in state decision-making.

The compromise that emerged in most jurisdictions has involved the development of a body of law that imposes a set of *procedural constraints* on administrative agencies and decision-making. In particular, it imposes a complex set of requirements on rule-making exercises that involve a duty to consult, and in some cases take into consideration, the interests of all affected parties. One way of thinking about this is to say that, as legislatures have handed increased rule-making authority over to administrators, courts have, in turn, imposed upon administrators many of the deliberative burdens that have traditionally been associated with legislatures, such as duties of publicity, consultation, and accountability to the public (or to interest groups). Much of this emergent body of administrative law, however, governs all administrative action, not just cases of explicit delegation. As a result, it winds up also constraining the behavior of legislators, because they are unable to preempt or override the constraints on administration. Ministerial authority, for instance, is often limited by these required administrative procedures (and the civil servant, being the more conversant with them, may find herself in the position of saying to the minister, "We can't do that" or "We can't do it that way," in cases where a proposal violates them).

Thus an effective public administrator must be concerned, not just about the policy preferences of elected officials, but also about what the courts will accept—based not just on the established body of administrative law, but also on expectations about what will survive judicial review, including constitutional challenge. Indeed, one of the most important "guidance" documents published by the UK civil service is a pamphlet entitled *The Judge over Your Shoulder* (JOYS, for short).[59] It begins by listing no fewer than twenty distinct legal constraints that administrative decision-making is subject to (i.e., that could serve as a basis for legal challenge and review). The hierarchical model, at least in its straightforward variant, lacks the ability to articulate this new reality.

2.3.4. Weakness of democratic legitimacy

Finally, there is the fact that the connection between "the minister" and "the public interest" is much more attenuated in modern mass democracies. Part of this has to do with scale, and the fact that governments are elected only periodically, with political parties that aggregate the interests and positions of literally millions of individuals. There is also the fact that electoral competition has become increasingly strategic over time. The most obvious consequence of this has been increased partisanship. A more subtle effect has been that political parties seldom present themselves to the public with a comprehensive package of policy ideas. They instead tend to focus their energies on the personality of the leader, along with a small number of "wedge issues" they calculate will actually change voting decisions. And finally, there is the fact that many governments are elected by plurality, or through coalitions of parties that have each received a relatively small share of the popular vote. Thus there are many circumstances in which ministers have only a very weak claim to be "representative" of the interests of the people.

There is also the fact that in parliamentary systems, ministers have in certain symbolic ways stopped taking responsibility for what occurs in their departments. The practice of resigning whenever a serious scandal or breach of faith occurs on their watch is little more than a relic of the past.[60] Some ministers even adopt an adversarial stance toward their own officials, in order to mobilize voters and party contributions. The increased use of political staff in the minister's office also draws a distinction between those who owe loyalty to the minister and those who do not. All of this has the effect of alienating ministers from the civil service, by eroding the system of reciprocity that was at the heart of the traditional bargain.[61] These are all examples of how the partisan and strategic intensity of modern politics has led many elected officials to become increasingly withdrawn from the actual practice of governing. Yet power, like nature, abhors a vacuum, and to the extent that elected officials are no longer interested in running the state, someone else will usually step forward to do it for them.

2.4. The popular model

The suggestion that there has been a breakdown in the traditional relationship between ministers and civil servants is not confined to academic observers. Since the early 1980s, wave after wave of civil-service reform movements have been initiated, all loosely based on the suspicion that the traditional ministerial accountability model had become unrealistic and unworkable, given the realities—particularly the scale—of the modern welfare state.[62] As the civil service began to provide more services directly to the public (health, education, electricity and gas, transportation, pensions, etc.), it became increasingly strained to suggest that the lines of accountability in front-line service organizations should run up the organizational hierarchy, through the minister and parliament, and then back to the public through periodic elections. It seemed to many that the lines of accountability should be reversed, to run down instead of up. Why not have direct accountability to the public for the delivery of government services? This would appear to promote, at the very least, a government that was more responsive to the needs of its citizens. (This line of thinking received additional support from the "customer service revolution" that was taking place in private-sector management, which was also concerned with the tendency of large organizations to become unresponsive over time to the public that they served.[63])

Thompson refers to this as the "participatory" model of accountability, although I prefer the term "popular" to emphasize that it comes in both right-wing and left-wing versions. Both share a desire to reverse the direction of accountability in the civil service, so that it runs down to the public instead of up to elected officials. The left-wing version tries to do this by increasing citizen participation in executive decision-making, through exercises in direct and deliberative democracy. The right-wing version tries to do the same by focusing on economic incentives, giving the public the ability to "vote with their pocketbook," and tying the compensation of public-sector managers to their ability to satisfy consumer demand. In terms of Albert Hirschman's well-known distinction, left-wing reforms were focused on increasing citizens' "voice," whereas right-wing ones were more focused on creating opportunities for "exit." (Forming a parent's council at a local public school to advise on curriculum choices is an example of the former; introducing charter schools with competing curricula, and tying funding to the number of students enrolled, is an example of the latter.)

2.4.1. New Public Management

The most sustained attempt to implement the right-wing version of bu-reaucratic populism occurred under Prime Minister Thatcher in the United Kingdom, creating the template for a set of new public management (NPM) reforms that were subsequently imitated in many other parliamentary dem-ocracies. The most important element involved breaking up traditional departments and making parts of them independent agencies that would no longer be under direct ministerial control, but would instead engage in ex-plicit contracting with the government. The goal was to shift the public ser-vice away from a process-oriented model of administration to one that was more outcome-oriented. Under the slogan "let managers manage," the heads of these new agencies were to be given significantly more discretion and con-trol over most aspects of operations. In return, they were expected to engage in contracting over objectives, and to implement a set of performance measures that would allow for more precise evaluation of their activities. This was typi-cally accompanied by compensation arrangements tied to these performance measures. The changes in the "vertical" accountability relationship to ministers were generally supplemented with reforms aimed at increasing the responsive-ness of the bureaucracy to the public.[64] For example, instead of global budgets, public institutions would be shifted toward activity-based funding, meaning that they would be paid by the number of "clients" served—whether it be the number of students enrolled in a university, the number of surgical procedures performed in a hospital, or the number of driver's licenses renewed. This was expected to empower the public, by giving individual citizens a way of influen-cing the behavior of the state bureaucracy.

Had this initiative been more successful, we might now be thinking of some decentralized popular model as the most appropriate way of conceiving the moral obligations of civil servants. The general consensus, however, is that NPM did not succeed in changing the way that the civil service operates. In some cases, this was explicitly acknowledged—many of the independent agencies that had been created were folded back into the departments from which they had emerged. In other cases, it was merely de facto—civil servants simply worked around the new organizational structures, in order to preserve traditional lines of accountability.[65] In other cases, elected officials refused to let managers manage—or, they let them manage until a problem developed, at which point they reasserted control. Regardless of the particular scenario, it is now generally accepted that NPM reforms did very little to change traditional structures of ac-countability in the public sector.

There were four central weaknesses with the NPM model.

2.4.1.1 Information problems

Any discussion of NPM should be prefaced by the observation that a great many of the reform efforts were motivated by skepticism about the very idea that there is a "public-sector ethos," or the belief that morality plays a useful role in motivating civil servants. The traditional public-sector employment model is characterized by very dull pecuniary incentives combined with a professional ethic that is supposed to motivate high levels of dedication and work effort. What many critics of this model saw, instead, was simply a set of dull incentives generating a low level of work effort. Their response was to want to introduce a sharper set of incentives, keyed to the specific performances that the public would want to elicit from the bureaucracy.

Incentives, of course, are easy to create. The tricky part is to create the right incentives that will encourage the behavior that one wants to encourage and to discourage the behavior that one wants to discourage. To do this, one must have *information* about what the agent is doing. Unfortunately, with any complex task, the behavior one wants to encourage is seldom directly observable. There may, however, be other behaviors that are strongly correlated with it, which are much easier to observe. There is a temptation to take these other behaviors as proxies, and to develop a system of reward and punishment based on them. The problem with such an arrangement is that it encourages the agent to reallocate effort away from the task that one is trying to encourage, toward the behavior that one is using as a proxy for it. This erodes the underlying correlation, so that what started out as a reliable proxy becomes less so over time. Furthermore, the net effect of the system can be entirely perverse, if it results in less effort being expended upon the task that one is trying to encourage.

Consider the following concrete example. One typically wants a lawyer to be diligent and thorough. But to determine whether a lawyer has been diligent and thorough in preparing, say, a brief, one would essentially have to do the job all over again, to see if anything was missed. However, diligence and thoroughness are typically correlated with other qualities. For example, it often *takes longer* to do a thorough job. Thus law firms often reward associates for spending long hours at the office, under the assumption that in so doing they are rewarding especially diligent and thorough workers. In reality, associates may just be adjusting their work intensity, and spreading their tasks over a longer workday. This is a lose-lose outcome, for both employees of the firm and their clients.

The classic example of perverse incentives in the public sector arises when employees are given performance targets, or performance-based compensation, as a result of which they shift their attention away from more difficult cases toward easier ones, even if the former are the more important from an organizational standpoint. Immigration officials, for instance, given an incentive to increase the rate of deportations, may shift their attention away from individuals with criminal ties (who are often very difficult to find), toward individuals who have children, jobs, or close ties to the community (which makes them easy to locate). Or, factory inspectors given performance targets may shift their attention to small businesses, which are typically much less complicated to deal with, even though the activities of large firms have a far more significant impact on social welfare.[66] The result of these distortions may be a serious erosion of organizational effectiveness in the public sector, where the amount of work being done increases, but the achievement of actual policy objectives declines.

The theoretical literature on principal-agent theory articulates the basic problem succinctly: sharp incentives based on bad information are generally worse than dull incentives.[67] Although dull incentives may fail to motivate people to do the right thing, sharp incentives based on bad information will encourage them to do the wrong thing. This suggests that before implementing a performance pay scheme to "incentivize" employees, one must be extremely confident about one's information. It is difficult to see how there could be any basis for such confidence throughout most of the public sector, except when it comes to the management of the lowest-level service employees. As Friedrich observed, back in 1940, in the public service "responsible conduct of administrative functions is not so much enforced as it is elicited."[68]

Setting aside the obvious difficulties concerning the variety and complexity of government policy objectives, there was an even broader point that went largely unappreciated in the debates over NPM. Public management is difficult precisely because the public sector as a whole is a victim of adverse selection when it comes to the types of management problems it confronts. This is because the collective action problems the state is typically called upon to resolve are not a representative sample, or a randomly chosen subset, of the set of collective action problems individuals confront in their day-to-day lives. People have a wide range of institutional tools that they can use to resolve these problems—first and foremost, private contracting—which do not require explicit state intervention. Thus all the "easy" collective action problems tend to be solved privately, between individuals, through markets, within corporations, and even in communities through informal social control. One of the features that makes a problem "easy" is that free riding is readily observable, which in turn facilitates contractual solutions or tort remedies.

This means that the problems that the state is called upon to fix are typically the most intractable, because the costs and benefits are the hardest to identify, measure, and control. It is no wonder, then, that it is difficult to develop a set of performance measures to assess the civil service. If the outputs could be measured so easily, or if it were possible to draw up a complete contract, then there is probably no reason for the work to be done in the public sector! This was, in some ways, what was learned. One of the major institutional legacies of NPM was extensive contracting out and the development of purchaser/provider splits, which were often a salutary development. Yet as a model of public-sector *management*, NPM turned out to be hugely deficient. Not only did it fail to take the information problems any large-scale bureaucracy faces seriously, it failed almost completely to consider specific public-sector information challenges.

In response to this, the dominant impulse was to create a new layer of bureaucracy (known in Canada as "program evaluation"), whose primary function was to overcome the information asymmetry by collecting information about activities. Considerable effort was invested in creating this reporting system, despite the fact that there is essentially no evidence it is able to perform its assigned function. As Donald Savoie has argued, the fact that governments still rely upon downsizing to control spending is evidence that the accountability structure captures no relevant information about program effectiveness. If the central government were capable of discovering inefficiencies, then it would naturally tend to target cuts to those areas. Relying on across-the-board cuts means that whatever information there may be about inefficiencies in programs (e.g., overstaffing) is simply not transmitted up the hierarchy.[69]

2.4.1.2 Motivational crowding-out

The introduction of performance pay into the public service is perhaps the most enduring legacy of the NPM reforms. Underlying the commitment to performance pay is the idea that public servants should be materially rewarded for doing their jobs well. Yet it has struck many observers that this principle can easily be misconstrued as an invitation to corruption.[70] After all, the idea that performance should be linked to individual material reward implies that public servants, when making decisions, not only may, but *should* take their personal material advantage into consideration. From there, it is not such a leap to thinking that the government's pay offer is simply an expression of how much it values that individual's performance, and if some other party is willing to pay more, then it must value those services more highly, and so the greater good will be achieved by serving the latter. This suggests that the loyalty of the public servant should be available to the highest bidder. At very least, then, any government that makes the services of its officials available to the highest bidder would want to be extremely confident that it will always be the highest bidder. Unfortunately, there is no basis for such confidence—partly because of the logic of state action, where elected officials often wind up having to represent the interests of the more diffuse party in a conflict, while the more concentrated interest is able to form a lobby group. This is reflected in the fact that the "material incentives" offered under the NPM schemes are often quite small compared to the material rewards that may be available through various forms of official corruption.

Proponents of NPM typically overlooked this problem because of a widespread fallacy, the belief that as long as the material incentives are *aligned* with the existing "intrinsic" or moral incentives (i.e., they are both aimed at promoting the same forms of behavior), then the two will naturally complement one another, and thus enhance performance. This encouraged the view that one can take the existing level of performance as a baseline and simply enhance it by layering on additional material incentives. This analysis overlooked the phenomenon—now well-documented and repeatedly reproduced under experimental conditions—of "motivational crowding-out," whereby individuals who are given material incentives may *lose* whatever moral incentive they once had to perform a task.[71] In one experiment, for instance, students who were asked to perform a task "as a favor" for the professor worked quite hard, whereas those who were offered a cash payment worked less.[72] This occurs because the material incentive causes people to frame the interaction differently, which in turn brings out a different set of motives. Material incentives may crowd out moral ones because they may prompt the individual to shift from a "duty and obligation" framing to a "material advantage" framing of the interaction. As a result, they may lose whatever moral incentive they had, at the same time that they acquire the material one. So unless the material incentive is quite large, the net result may be a reduction in overall motivation, and hence and reduction in the quality or intensity of task performance. (This led Dan Ariely to observe that money "is often the most expensive way to motivate people. Social norms are not only cheaper, but often are more effective as well."[73])

2.4.1.3. Problem of capture

NPM drew upon many of the same rhetorical tropes as the customer-service revolution in business management. In general this is not a bad thing, since there can be little doubt that the absence of competition in the provision of government services makes it very difficult to motivate either front-line employees or managers to take customer service very seriously. The big difference between the state and the private sector, however, is that the state is not in a voluntary relationship with all of its "clients." In many cases, the state has an essentially adversarial attitude toward the people with whom the civil servant has day-to-day interactions. Consider, for example, a food inspector stationed at a meat-packing plant. He serves "the public," but he does not interact with the public at all in his official capacity. The people he interacts with are those he is charged with regulating, whose business and jobs he has the power to destroy by closing down the plant. The social structure of this and similar occupations creates an acute danger of "regulatory capture"—that is, the state employee will stop serving the public and become an advocate for the interests of the regulated industry. This is why the American Society for Public Administration code of ethics suggests that "to strengthen resistance to conflict of interest, public employees should avoid frequent social contact with persons who come under their regulation" and recommends periodic staff rotation to break up whatever social bonds or sympathies may have formed.[74]

Even more difficult are cases in which a particular department, agency, or bureau has both customer-service and regulatory responsibility. This is common, for instance, in the delivery of means-tested social services. Here the same employee is often responsible both for determining eligibility (a process that can be quite adversarial), and delivering the service once eligibility is established. Balancing the two requirements can be very difficult, and the usual nostrums that come from the business world (e.g., "the customer is always right") are of little use in guiding responsible decision-making. This is, of course, a management problem. What it suggests, however, is that designing an incentive scheme to reward the right forms of conduct is going to be extremely difficult. Consider, for example, the "special operating agency" Canada Passport (which is charged with processing passport applications). The public would naturally like to see quick turnaround times and quality customer service (which is, of course, one of the reasons the agency was created). At the same time, it would be imprudent to create a performance pay scheme that linked compensation to the number of applications processed, since part of the function of the bureau is to analyze applicants and *reject* those who are ineligible for a passport. Proper scrutiny is time-consuming. And one would not want the bureaucracy to be beholden to those who are most visibly being served (i.e., those who are standing in long lines at the passport office) to the detriment of the more diffuse group being served— those who benefit from having the state exercise care and attention in issuing passports. The latter group, however, will never be an organized interest. One of the major functions of electoral democracy is to create a group of representatives who will speak for these diffuse groups. But this means that the civil servant still has obligations that run up the organizational hierarchy, as well as some that run down to the public directly. Creating a system of incentives that can balance the two in a mechanical fashion, without creating an enormous amount of discretion, is difficult if not impossible.

2.4.1.4. Lack of political buy-in

Finally, for NPM to work it must be a two-way street. Managers must accept the responsibilities that come with increased autonomy, but ministers must also be willing to relinquish control over various segments of the bureaucracy. What many countries discovered, however, was that when scandals erupted in a particular area, ministers tended to get blamed, even when they had "let the managers manage," and were not directly involved in decision-making.[75] This may be due to the political culture being slow to adjust to the organizational changes that had occurred. Scandals tended to stick to the party in power, and to the minister responsible (or, in some cases, the minister formerly responsible). Thus ministers were often being presented with a demand in the form of "let managers manage, but if they screw up you get the blame." It is not difficult to understand, therefore, why many ministers continued to insist on asserting control, even over agencies that were nominally independent.[76] Over time, therefore, the slogan tended to become (as Savoie puts it), "Let the Manager Manage So Long as It Squares with RPPs, DPRs, MAF, OCG, PCO, TBS, OAG, OLA, IBP, PSC, ATIP, CIEC, OPSICC, DAGs, QFR and That It Does Not Create Problems for the Minister and Deputy Minister or Draw the Attention of the Prime Minister and His Advisers."[77] Furthermore, many performance pay systems have had the direction of accountability reversed, so that they now promote greater responsiveness to ministerial direction, by rewarding officials for achieving government objectives.[78]

It is also worth noting that a large segment of the public has very confused and contradictory views about compensation in the public sector. This produces, among other things, hostility to large pay packages for public employees, regardless of what people doing comparable jobs in the private sector may be earning. (This is what motivates salary disclosure acts in many jurisdictions, which require that all public-sector salaries above a certain threshold be made publicly available.) To the extent that performance-linked compensation sometimes generates very large bonus payments to individuals, it often becomes politically controversial. Furthermore, despite the fact that the demand for performance pay typically comes from conservative parties, there is an element on the populist right that is vociferously opposed to it (on the grounds the civil servants should simply do what they are told, without requiring special "incentives" for good performance).[79] Thus performance pay systems have a tendency to generate negative headlines for the party in power, no matter how long ago they were adopted. This can easily produce the impression that the NPM approach as a whole is a political liability.

2.4.2. Participatory government

The participatory version of the popular model was based on a healthy skepticism about the power of incentives (combined, in many cases, with a somewhat hypertrophied aversion to anything resembling a market pattern of organization). Many jurisdictions have therefore undertaken a variety of initiatives aimed at involving the public more directly in decision-making. There was, of course, the long-standing tradition of holding public hearings to solicit *input* from the public, particularly before a controversial decision had to be made. These meetings were early on expanded to include tools developed in the field of market research, such as public surveys and focus groups. Many deliberative initiatives, however, were designed to go beyond mere consultation to give the public some degree of control over decision-making. Traditional measures like citizen ballot initiatives were thus supplemented with negotiated rule-making exercises, citizen review boards, and citizen advisory committees, as well as citizen juries or panels.[80] (In the United Kingdom, the use of these tools increased most prominently in the mid-1990s, in part reflecting the declining faith in NPM initiatives.[81])

There is widespread acknowledgment that the increase in direct citizen participation can have salutary effects. First and foremost, it helps to provide policymakers with better information, so that the goods and services provided by the state more closely match the needs and desires of citizens. It can also prove quite valuable in persuading communities to accept the results of decision-making exercises (a phenomenon that has often been observed in the area of environmental protection, particularly with renewable-energy initiatives). In both respects, public participation serves to facilitate the provision of more responsive government. At the same time, it is very difficult to find many theorists who are willing to claim that this type of citizen participation allows the public to exercise effective *control* over state bureaucracies, or that participatory institutions are able to function as a governance mechanism. Even Thompson, who is quite sympathetic to these initiatives, admits that "the model bristles with problems."[82] These fall into five major categories:

2.4.2.1. Pathologies of direct democracy

For all the talk of "deliberation" and "deliberative democracy" associated with this tendency, it is important to remember that in almost all cases, deliberation by itself is not a decision procedure. Deliberation may help to educate citizens and improve the quality of preferences; however, it seldom succeeds in eliminating all disagreement. At some point, deliberation must stop and a vote must be taken. When this happens, all the well-known pathologies of aggregative democracy reassert themselves.[83] For example, there is a potential for cyclical majorities to form (when no option attracts a simple majority over others, and more than one option can win in pairwise comparison against all other options). This is exacerbated by the often ad hoc character of community or neighborhood decision-making, where there is no fixed quorum, and different people may show up on different occasions. This means that when a majority decides in favor of a particular option, it can be fairly easy to find and mobilize another majority that favors some other option. Thus the decision-making can be extremely unstable (reflected in the fact that "communities" often reverse themselves on decisions when given the opportunity to do so). More traditional democratic institutions have a variety of stopping rules and kluges designed to counteract these defects of majority decision-making. An open public forum typically lacks these resources, and therefore is very unlikely to produce a stable "general will."

2.4.2.2. Problem of capture (again)

The standard public-choice model of regulatory capture is based on the observation that concentrated interests tend to win out over diffuse interests in the quest for political favors, simply because they are subject to less serious collective action problems when mobilizing to advance their interests. Thus industry tends to win out over consumers when it comes to a particular regulation or rule change, because the potential benefit to each individual producer may be significant, whereas the loss to each individual consumer will be slight. Consumers are less likely to band together to defend their interests. (This is why industry spends so much more money on lobbying than consumers, even though both groups have roughly the same amount at stake. Industry is simply better organized.) As a result, there is a tendency within the political system as a whole to generate the exploitation of the unorganized by the organized.

One of the major functions of representative democratic institutions is to diminish the advantage going to the organized—to counteract the fact that the general public is at a structural disadvantage when it comes to defending its interests. If elected representatives are being cut out of the picture, then the participatory model is going to have to explain how groups that are diffuse and unorganized are supposed to assert themselves. Especially because participation in a deliberative forum is both costly and time-consuming, the deliberative model seems more likely to exacerbate the collective action problem faced by these large groups than to help resolve it. Unless it functions with hand-picked representatives (the way some citizen assemblies are), participatory forms of decision-making seem to suffer, at very least, from a squeaky wheel bias. Generally speaking, the individuals who show up to participate are those whose time has a very low opportunity cost (e.g., retirees), or else those with a significant economic stake in the decision (e.g., industry spokespeople). This has long been observed as a defect of public hearings, namely, that the public one would like to hear from is typically not the public that shows up.[84] Participatory exercises in which the public is involved in decision-making are typically even more time-consuming, and so the problems are likely to be greater. Thus there is a significant danger that the process will be controlled by those who have a concentrated economic interest in the outcome, and so "participatory democracy," in practice, will become a form of "corporatism," or interest group brokerage.[85]

2.4.2.3. Not a governance mechanism

There is also the fact that public participation seems to be incapable of serving as a genuine governance mechanism. It is one thing to call upon the public to provide *input*, quite another to expect that same public to exercise *control* over the behavior of public servants.[86] The problem is that effective governance is time-consuming and resource intensive, and so the public faces a serious collective action problem when it comes to exercising governance. Furthermore, if it is correct that the state is subject to an adverse selection problem with respect to the collective action problems it is called upon to resolve, this creates a problem not just for the NPM but for the participatory model as well. Government inherits all the most difficult collective action problems, where individuals and communities are unable to implement a solution using only private contracting and informal social control. But in these cases, the same collective action problem that makes individuals and communities unable to find a solution is likely to undermine their ability to exercise effective governance. Put the other way around, if the public were able to spontaneously organize to exercise effective control over the officials charged with resolving a particular collective action problem, then it probably would be able to resolve the collective action problem directly, without the need for state officials to get involved.

A second major problem shows up if one pays attention to the sort of information asymmetries that rendered the hierarchical model dubious. The central issue there, one may recall, is that ministers often had trouble effectively supervising their subordinates because of information impactedness. But to have any confidence in the participatory model, one must have some reason to think that the information asymmetries between civil servants and the public will be less serious than those between civil servants and the minister. And while one can imagine this to be true in certain very specific instances—pertaining to the quality of service delivery primarily—there are many, many more instances in which one can only think it false. Not only is the public less likely than the minister to be well-informed and more easily manipulated through selective information disclosure, but it also faces an enormous collective action problem when it comes to collecting and processing information. Again, because the public has interests that are extremely diffuse, very few individuals have any incentive to do the research and spend the time required to acquaint themselves with the file on any particular issue. The minister, by contrast, has a very powerful interest in keeping tabs on what is happening in her department. So, what are the chances that members of the public, who have no such interest, will be able to do a better job of it?

One can find both of these problems reflected in the fact that citizens express very little interest in various participatory exercises.[87] Not many people want to spend their evenings attending meetings. (Indeed, studies in several countries have shown that approximately 1 percent of the population regularly participates in deliberative political activities.[88]) Most people would much rather have some intelligent, civic-minded state official take care of problems that arise—which is, of course, precisely what the traditional system of representative democracy and ministerial accountability is designed to accomplish. Recognition of this fact has been one of the forces driving the movement toward "representative bureaucracy."[89] The thinking is that if the bureaucracy could be reconstituted in such a way that it more closely resembles the public, then its own internal deliberative processes might substitute for the more problematic ones involving the actual public. (Terry Cooper's conception of "responsible administration," which involves the public servant aiming to act as an idealized citizen, also seems to draw inspiration from this set of ideas.[90]) This is, of course, not an unreasonable ambition, but it constitutes a tacit acknowledgment of the limits of the participatory approach.

2.4.2.4. Laundering of elite preferences

Since the public is typically not well-informed on many policy questions, deliberative exercises normally include various forms of expert testimony. This creates an obvious opportunity to manipulate the process, especially since the procedures are invariably nonadversarial, and as a result, there is seldom much cross-examination or presentation of opposing testimony. Thus the participants may be quite vulnerable to suggestion, something that is reflected in the fact that reports and decisions issued by deliberative assemblies seldom contain many surprises, and often bear a suspicious resemblance to the central current of opinion among the bureaucrats who organized them. This gives rise to the worry that these exercises will be used only to give a cover of democratic legitimacy to what are, in effect, the preferences of the civil service.

Consider, for instance, the results of a citizen panel assembled by the City of Edmonton, in collaboration with researchers at the University of Alberta, as part of the Alberta's 2010–2011 budget process. The panel consisted of forty-nine randomly selected citizens, who met on Saturdays for a period of six weeks. They were given presentations by city officials, along with access to budget documents, growth projections, infrastructure plans, and so on. After intensive discussion and deliberation, the panel produced two "new directions" and four "recommendations" intended to guide the city's budgeting process. These were as follows:

- *Citizen Panel New Direction 1.* Citizens, City Council and Administration will need to adopt a change in thinking if we are to increase livability. A change in thinking should be achieved through both incentives and disincentives created by the public and private sectors.

- *Citizen Panel New Direction 2.* We need to act in ways that demonstrate and strengthen the interconnectedness of community life.
- *Recommendation 1.* Continue to increase the density of our city through long-term planning.
- *Recommendation 2.* Ensure that our transportation system emphasizes the convenience of users and the uniqueness of Edmonton's climate.
- *Recommendation 3.* Use environmental and economic sustainability as the basis for policy decisions aimed at livability.
- *Recommendation 4.* Use proactive and preventative methods to reduce crime and increase safety.[91]

One can see many of the weaknesses of deliberative exercises on display here. First, it is important to note how anodyne, bordering on vacuous, both the recommendations and the directions are. For instance, the document calls for a "change in thinking," without any specification of what that change is. This change is to be effected "through both incentives and disincentives created by the public and private sectors," a description that effectively excludes nothing. Because of this—what might charitably be described as the "open texture" of the language employed—it is difficult to see how these outputs could impose any meaningful constraint on the subsequent budgeting exercise. In particular, most of the points are conjunctive, in a way that would allow them to be enlisted in support of any policy or its opposite. Second, several points are clearly just echoing bureaucratic priorities and modes of expression. For instance, people randomly pulled off the street seldom express a strong concern for "the interconnectedness of community life." Thus there are strong grounds for suspicion that the panel was being used, in effect, to launder the opinions of the experts who briefed it and assisted in its deliberations. The asymmetries of power and information between civil servants and ordinary citizens are so great, it is difficult to see how a deliberative exercise such as this could significantly limit the power of the former.

2.4.2.5. Encouraging bureaucratic overreach

Closely related to the previous point is the concern that giving the state bureaucracy an opportunity to claim its own source of democratic legitimacy, independent of the legislature, is likely to encourage overreach, and in some cases, open defiance of elected officials.[92] There is already a general inclination among public servants to err on the side of overconfidence when comparing their own sense of where the "public interest" lies to that of politicians. One of the major factors that encourages greater modesty, or at least discourages civil servants from acting on their elevated self-perception, is that, though they may claim to know where the public interest lies, they are not actually authorized to speak on its behalf. To the extent that they have any claim to authority, they must rely upon superior knowledge, technical expertise, institutional memory, or instrumental efficacy. And yet politicians still hold the ultimate trump card, which is the fact that they were elected while civil servants were not. This does not stop the civil service from taking normative positions, but it does mean that on a certain range of partisan issues, there is an obvious obligation to defer to elected officials. However, exercises in participatory democracy have the potential to muddy the water on this point. Certain variants give civil servants an opportunity to rebut the politician's claim by saying, "We've held our own consultations with the public, and have been authorized to advance the following policies." The worst-case scenario, in many ways, would be if public participation generated a high level of democratic legitimacy for the bureaucracy, yet failed to achieve effective control over it, producing a civil service that is emboldened to advance its own agenda even against the explicit directives of elected officials.

2.4.3. Summary

All of this institutional detail should not be allowed to obscure the basic point. With the growing complexity of government and the declining trust in democratic institutions, there has been a natural tendency to turn away from hierarchical organizational forms and to imagine that a more responsible, more responsive civil service could be created by promoting an organizational culture in which public employees are held directly accountable to the public that they serve. Although the associated institutional reforms have no doubt led to a number of improvements in the operations of government (e.g., the flattening of organizational structures, increased public consultation, greater focus on quality service delivery, etc.), the attempt to change the structures of *accountability*, to make the civil service literally accountable or answerable to the public, has not been met with great success and, in some cases, has been an abject failure. The major problem is that "the public" is an extremely diffuse, often conflicted body, whose capacities for collective action are in many areas quite limited. It is precisely these difficulties that the traditional apparatus of representative democracy is intended to overcome. Attempts to bypass this, in order to create mechanisms through which the public can directly control elements of the public service (through either incentives or having a voice) have largely foundered, for precisely the reasons that one would expect. As a result, the reforms that were enacted tended to create an unsatisfactory situation, in which civil servants were partially accountable to the public, but remained partially accountable to elected officials. Because these two lines of accountability run in opposite directions, the net effect was often just to increase administrative discretion.

Because the popular model has been so difficult to institutionalize, a civil service *ethic* that encourages public-sector employees to think of their moral obligations in terms of service to "the public" seems likely to create a situation of enormous indeterminacy. One must put into place at least some procedures for determining what the public wants or needs; otherwise, this kind of an ethic winds up being all too similar to saying to the public servant, "Do what you think is right." Furthermore, because elected officials remain important players, with significant institutional authority, some account is required of how the will of the public is to be reconciled with that of its representatives, in cases of conflict. The popular model of accountability, at least in its existing incarnations, lacks the resources to explain how this integration is to be achieved.

2.5. The vocational model

This brings us to the third, somewhat neglected model of public-sector morality, the vocational model.[93] The vocational approach to the ethics of public administration looks to the example set by other classes of professionals, such as doctors and lawyers, in thinking about the constraints that the civil servants should be subject to. Generally speaking, the need for "professional" ethics arises when there is a class of workers engaged in tasks for which a division of labor is advantageous, but information asymmetries make it impossible (or exceedingly costly) for a principal to effectively supervise an agent or to assess the quality of her work. This makes complete contracting impossible, leaving the parties without a legal mechanism to resolve their agency problems. As a result, the task may not get delegated, or may not get performed at all. Faced with this potential inefficiency, the parties can both benefit from institutional arrangements that allow the agent to credibly commit to refraining from acting opportunistically, thereby creating trust between the parties. The various trappings of the official professions are all designed to create a legitimate basis for this trust, which in turn allows the parties to overcome the agency problem. These "trappings" may include a professional code of ethics, a set of licensing requirements, a complaints bureau, as well as a quasi-judicial body invested with the power to punish (typically through license revocation).[94] Central to all of this is a system of peer assessment. When a doctor is accused of malpractice, it is other doctors who are brought in to decide whether the complaint has merit. When a lawyer is accused of impropriety, it is other lawyers who consider the case for disbarment. This is precisely because of the information asymmetry. Patients usually cannot tell if a doctor has done a good job, only other doctors can, which is why the professional body has doctors who do the assessment.

One of the most characteristic features of professional groups is this horizontal structure of accountability, where the individual is called upon to justify her conduct, not to the principal, or to a superior, but rather to her peers. This is an obvious feature of the most highly structured professions, like law and medicine, but one can see it equally well in less formally structured professions, such as among university professors. One of the consequences of this arrangement is that a professional group must come up with its own, relatively autonomous conception of what counts as doing the job well and what counts as doing it poorly. Physician services, for instance, are organized around a clearly defined "standard of care," which is used to assess instances of alleged malpractice, but more importantly, guides many aspects of clinical decision-making and resource allocation. They do not determine this standard by interviewing patients or consulting hospital administrators (i.e., people above or below them in the organizational hierarchy). It is developed independently by physicians, based not just on their scientific knowledge but also on their assessment of the resource constraints that they are, on average, subject to. Of course, the goals of the patient figure prominently within this system of professional norms; the point is merely that the norms are not subordinate to or entirely instrumental to the realization of those goals. Thus patients have an important say in the treatment that is provided, but they do not get the last word.

In the case of civil servants, professional morality is also just as clearly organized around an *independent* conception of what it means to "do the job" well. One must, as Arthur Applbaum puts it, start with the question, "What values and purposes does the institution of the role of public servant aim to realize?"[95] The answer, generally speaking, will be that the civil servant's role is to serve the state, not just in any way but in such a way as to help the state achieve *its* purposes. These purposes, in turn, cannot be defined as simply "whatever the minister says" or "whatever the government of the day happens to want," because our system of government is not one of unlimited popular sovereignty. Thus, as Applbaum goes on to observe, answering the question about the role of the civil servant requires "at least a rough notion of legitimacy, justice, and goodness in government."[96] Furthermore, this notion must necessarily be *prior* to whatever specific political ideologies acquire influence through the democratic process, precisely because it is these background notions that will specify the particular role that democracy is to be assigned in the overall state structure (most importantly, it determines which decisions will be made democratically and which will not). So while the professional ethic of civil servants must accord an important place to the goals of elected officials, it is not entirely subordinate to those goals.

The obvious objection to this analysis is that modern liberal societies are characterized by pluralism with respect to fundamental values, and therefore the liberal state has no single "purpose" or, at least, none that can be specified uncontroversially.[97] The dominant response among proponents of the vocational model has not been to deny this, but rather to observe that a liberal state is nevertheless committed to certain principles, which are thin enough to be neutral with respect to the most contested values, yet thick enough to serve as the basis for a robust conception of civil service morality. Rohr refers to these as "regime values," and claims (in a US context) that they are articulated most clearly in the constitution. He therefore advocates a form of civil service morality organized around a commitment to the constitutional values of "equality," "freedom," and "property," further specified through careful attention to Supreme Court jurisprudence.

There are various problems with this formulation, but it is perhaps sufficient to observe that it does not generalize very well beyond the US context, particularly not to countries that have no written constitution or supreme court review of legislation. Thus the more common approach has been to identify a "political morality" for civil servants based simply on abstract liberal principles, as both Katherine Denhardt and, in a somewhat different way, Applbaum, have suggested.[98] What Applbaum is thinking of, for instance, when he talks about rough notions of "legitimacy, justice, and goodness in government" is something along the lines of John Rawls's theory of justice, which is intended to be neutral with respect to the various private moral views (or "comprehensive doctrines") held by citizens.[99] It is worth observing that Rawls's political philosophy derives a set of principles of justice to govern the "basic structure" of society—first and foremost, the state—without making any essential reference to democracy or to the output of democratic decision procedures. Thus it offers the type of self-standing account of what the state does and how it should be doing it that an independent professional conception of morality for the civil service would require, without the danger of collapse into either the hierarchical or the popular models.

The most glaring problem with Applbaum's approach is that it relies on an abstract philosophical theory of justice to specify the concept of "good government." Grounding a professional morality for civil servants in a controversial political philosophy is somewhat better than grounding it in the personal moral convictions of civil servants, but it is still subject to many of the same objections. A more reconstructive approach would focus instead on institutionalized practices, in an attempt to articulate the understandings that inform the existing professional morality in the civil service of liberal states. There are a variety of angles from which to approach this, but a particularly promising one involves an analysis of the reflections that have developed around the *legitimacy* of the liberal state, because this taps into broader public perceptions and expectations about the role of the state in society. In other words, the focus on legitimacy provides a different angle of approach for answering the questions of what the purposes of the state are, and what "goodness" in government consists in. One can then ask the more specific question about what role the executive plays in securing state legitimacy.

Recent philosophical literature on the state has been marked by an overwhelming emphasis on democracy, and democratic practices, as the source of legitimacy. This often translates, crudely, into an inability to conceive of ways that the exercise of state power could be legitimate other than through democratic election of the person exercising the power or the delegation of authority from a person so elected. From this perspective, the legitimacy of the executive branch depends entirely upon the legitimacy generated by the legislative through its periodic election.[100] This naturally lends support to the hierarchical model of accountability. This is, however, not the only way, or even the most plausible way, to think about legitimacy.[101] Indeed, it is widely held that the judiciary makes its own, distinctive contribution to the overall legitimacy of the state (one that is not reducible to the fact that judges are appointed by democratically elected politicians). It is, of course, possible to tell a more complex story, where the judiciary plays an essential role in creating the preconditions for democratic autonomy, and so again, its legitimacy derives from its contribution to the democratic legitimacy of the state.[102] A more defensible view would be that the judiciary generates its own form of legitimacy for the state, by ensuring that the rule of law is respected, that the treatment of citizens is fair and transparent, that individual rights are respected, and that the powers exercised by the legislature are appropriately circumscribed in accordance with constitutional norms.

My view is that the executive branch also makes its own distinctive contribution to the legitimacy of the state, which is not reducible to its role in facilitating democratic governance. As Ian Shapiro has argued, an important aspect of the legitimacy of any political order "depends on the problems it solves, and promises to solve, for people who are subject to it."[103] This is what Pierre Rosanvallon is describing when he refers to the "legitimacy of efficacy," which the state acquires through its capacity to solve pressing social problems.[104] The state is the central agent of *collective action* in the society, and citizens naturally look to it to solve a certain set of collective action problems, to provide solutions that are not only preconditional for the emergence of stable democratic institutions but also create the social conditions required for the development of nonstate solutions to many other problems. As the United States discovered in Iraq, for instance, democratic elections are of limited use in securing legitimacy for the state, if the state is simultaneously failing to discharge its more basic responsibilities, such as providing security or arranging for essential public services, such as electricity, to be provided without interruption.[105]

This aspect of legitimacy has been discussed rather extensively in the case of the European Union, which exercises regulatory powers that in many ways outstrip its democratic legitimacy.[106] Fritz Scharpf, for instance, has distinguished "input" from "output" legitimacy, where the former is established through procedures that give citizens input, or a "voice" in the political process, while the latter is established through the actual problems, confronted by citizens in their day-to-day lives, that the state is able to solve. In Scharpf's view, the central requirement of output legitimacy is "that government should be capable of achieving effective solutions to collective-action problems."[107] On this view, a government may be able to compensate for weakness on one side by strengthening the other—so a transnational body like the EU, with a relatively neglected and dysfunctional parliament, could (in principle) make up for the deficit on the "input" side with highly effective regulatory performances on the "output" side (e.g., by resolving collective action problems that the more democratically legitimate EU nation-states are unable to resolve).

From this concept of output legitimacy, one can develop the notion of the civil service having a "job to do," one that can be specified independently of the particular wishes of the government of the day. The central task lies in ensuring that the state discharge its basic obligations to its citizens. It has often been observed, for instance, that the approval ratings of various branches of the US federal government are almost inversely related to the level of democratic accountability of those agencies. Thus institutions like the Centers for Disease Control (CDC), the National Aeronautic and Space Administration (NASA), and the Food and Drug Administration (FDA), which enjoy substantial independence from congressional oversight, are among those that have the highest popular approval ratings.[108] Francis Fukuyama has suggested that "part of the reason they are admired is that they actually get things done," in large measure because they are not hobbled by the numerous veto points on decision-making that lead the American political system to generate such incoherent legislative outcomes.[109] Similarly, Bo Rothstein has argued that "electoral democracy is overrated when it comes to creating political legitimacy. Instead, political legitimacy is created, maintained, and destroyed not so much by the input side of the political system as by the output side."[110]

Generalizing, one can say that when the state takes over the task of providing education, or healthcare, or transportation service to the population, it also acquires an obligation to do so in a reliable, efficient manner, on terms that are fair to all citizens—regardless of the complexion of the particular political party that is in office.[111] This is, I would argue, the insight that was at the heart of NPM thinking, but that was misconceived in populist terms. The correct idea was the thought that state officials acquire direct obligations to the public—that is, obligations that are not mediated through representative democratic institutions. The mistake lay in thinking that the public's *conception* of these obligations should be determinative of their content or that the public somehow bore responsibility for ensuring that they were discharged. This is simply not institutionalizable. Doctors have obligations to their patients, but it is not up to the patients to decide what those obligations are, even though patients have *input* at various points in determining their care. Similarly, civil servants have obligations to the public, but it is not entirely up to the public to decide what these are, although the public will naturally have input into the proceedings.

If the central role of the state in modern societies is to solve the most intractable collective action problems—where individual contracting and informal community action fail—then there will also be substantive normative principles governing administrative action, which arise from the purposes that the state is committed to pursuing. When it comes to resolving collective action problems, the central principle (or, perhaps better yet, the guiding idea) is that of Pareto efficiency.[112] This is the rule that says that, if it is possible to make some people better off (by their own lights), without making anyone else worse off (again, by their own lights), then one should do so. Collective action problems are simply cases in which, owing to the structure of the interaction, individuals fail to bring about a Pareto efficient outcome through self-interested action. This gives each individual a reason to accept some form of constraint, on the grounds that when everyone does so, it results in an outcome that is better for each individual, including all those subject to the constraint.

Of course, using the word "efficiency" invites misunderstanding, since Pareto efficiency is easily confused with technical efficiency, which is a purely instrumental principle. This in turn evokes images of the old "policy/administration" distinction. Within that framework, it was uncontroversial to say that civil servants should be concerned about efficiency, but what was meant by this was just the economical implementation of policies handed down from on high. Pareto efficiency, however, is a normative principle that guides both policy choice and implementation. It commits one not only to a reduction of agency costs within the organization (as Allan Buchanan emphasized), and to the principle of subsidiarity when thinking about jurisdictional questions, but also to a broadly "public economic" understanding of the role of the state in society. After all, wanting to correct market failure is just another way of articulating the goal of solving collective action problems, and most of the major economic activities and regulatory interventions of the modern state represent attempts to correct market failure. Thus, under certain rather standard empirical conditions, one cannot be committed to the principle of efficiency without at the same time being an advocate of key welfare-state policies (such as environmental regulation, social insurance, mass transit, and so on).

It is important, therefore, when thinking about the contribution that the executive makes to the output legitimacy of the state, not to regard it as being indifferent on the question of which outputs the state should be producing. This is the central problem with Rothstein's influential work on the "quality of government." On the one hand, he sees quite clearly that "the main sources of political legitimacy are situated on the output side of the political system and have to do with the quality of government."[113] And yet he goes on to define the latter negatively, as merely "the absence of corruption, discrimination, and similar violations of the principle of impartiality."[114] There is an important insight here, which is that "citizens generally come into contact with the output side of the political system—with the administration—far more frequently and intensively than with its input side. Moreover, what happens to them on the output side is often crucial for their well-being."[115] This observation helps to explain the otherwise puzzling fact that many voters seem prepared to overlook antisocial and even criminal behavior in elected officials that they would never tolerate in, say, the principal of their child's school. Thus it matters a great deal that rule-of-law values (i.e., "impartiality" in Rothstein's sense)[116] be respected by the executive. At the same time, Rothstein himself acknowledges that people are concerned not just with the *way* outputs are provided but also *that* certain outputs be delivered. A state that decided it was no longer interested in providing security services would suffer an enormous deficit in output legitimacy, even if it withdrew from those activities in an orderly and scrupulously impartial manner. Thus we need a more complete normative model of the state, in order to specify the principles that should guide the exercise of administrative power.

The natural place to turn for this is to liberal political philosophy, although, as Rothstein notes with some disappointment, historically there has been practically no engagement between researchers interested in the quality of government institutions and philosophers doing work in normative political theory.[117] As a result, there is no "off-the-shelf" theory of political liberalism to which one can appeal to address the question of which normative principles should inform the practice of public administration. One cannot (pace Applbaum) simply plug in Rawls, or some other normative conception of justice, to do the job. Thus my approach, in the discussion that follows, is to engage reconstructively with the practices that have emerged over time within the public service, rearticulating them in the language of modern liberal theories of justice.

The ultimate goal is to vindicate an arrangement such as the one shown in Figure 2.2, which presents each of the three branches of government as making its own contribution to the overall legitimacy of the state, animated by its own central principles. The important point is that the executive branch is not just a neutral bystander or a servant of the legislature. The executive brings something distinctive to the table, in the same way that the judiciary does, which must be weighed against the contributions and demands made by the other branches. Good policy emerges out of the productive tension that arises between all three branches.

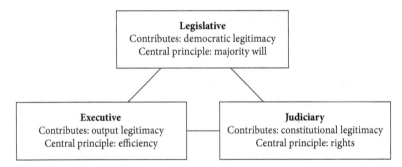

Figure 2.2 Three branches of the state.

Finally, although I have been emphasizing its distinctive features, it is important not to overstate the differences between the vocational model of accountability and the hierarchical and popular models. It is absolutely central to the professional self-understanding of civil servants that they regard themselves as working in the service of a *democratic* nation-state. Thus an enormous degree of deference to the minister, combined with a commitment to the ultimate supremacy of elected officials, is going to be built into the professional ethics of civil servants even on the vocational conception. (In the same way, many of the "agency cost minimization" norms that figured centrally in the hierarchical model will also figure prominently in any reconstruction of the vocational ethic of civil servants.) For example, the Tait Report on public-sector values in Canada lists "respect for the authority of elected office holders" next to "respect for the Constitution, the rule of law, and the institutions of Parliament and the courts" as the set of core "public-service values."[118] Thus "loyalty to the state" is not being proposed as an *alternative* to "loyalty to the minister" or "loyalty to the public." It is just that there must be, in the latter two cases, limits on the scope of these loyalties, and the most persuasive way of defining this is through an independent conception of what constitutes professional obligation, defined in terms of the basic organizational principles of the liberal state.

A model such as this raises a number of important concerns, and so despite my overall endorsement of the vocational model as an approach to thinking about the ethics of civil servants, it is worth noting some significant objections that have been raised:

2.5.1. Obstructionism

The most obvious problem with this model is that by essentially authorizing the executive to pursue an independent agenda based on its own conception of the state's role in society, state officials become less responsive to democratic control. The vocational model suggests that civil servants are entitled to "push back" against policies that they consider unjustifiable. At the same time, they are not entitled to become obstructionist, by thwarting the clearly expressed will of the people and their democratically elected representatives. As Cubbon puts it, the civil servant "must be neither a courtier nor an obstruction."[119] How is this balance to be struck?

In Canada, the traditional formula for thinking about this issue is summed up by the phrase—commonly used in the public service—"fearless advice and loyal implementation." The idea is that civil servants are entitled to verbally push back against a superior—including the minister—as hard as they like, up until the point at which a clear decision has been made.[120] Once a decision has been made, it then becomes their obligation to implement that decision, with the same degree of enthusiasm with which they may previously have opposed it. As Michael Quinlan (another retired British civil servant) put it: "One may think a particular policy concept to be a square circle, and indeed within the confidence of Whitehall one may argue fervently to that effect; but once the decision is taken, it is a matter not just of duty but of professional pride to help make the very best square circle that effort and imagination can contrive."[121]

Obviously, this formula relies upon the same policy/administration distinction that is generally thought to have been discredited so long ago. Institutionally, it does not really describe the way things work. It is, of course, important that the ethics of public service preclude the use of transparently obstructionist tactics, such as responding to a minister's orders by striking a committee to study the question, consigning it to bureaucratic limbo, and then hoping that the minister will fail to revisit the issue. Yet there is a great deal of space between this sort of bureaucratic obstruction and obediently following orders. For instance, Quinlan's phrase "once the decision is taken" does not have an entirely clear meaning, as decisions can always be revisited. DMs who find themselves in serious disagreement with their minister will seldom just give up on the issue, but will instead discuss it with the clerk of the Privy Council, who may then ask the prime minister to intervene and possibly overrule the minister (again, keeping in mind that most DMs have better lines of communication to the Prime Minister's Office than their ministers). The DM may also file a letter with the Treasury Board, which may in turn be shared with the auditor general (an independent parliamentary officer).[122] This creates a permanent record, making it clear that the minister was acting contrary to advice—a boon to the opposition, should things turn out poorly, and the right freedom-of-information requests are made. Given that most ministers would prefer to avoid all of these outcomes, they often find themselves engaged in something much more akin to "negotiation" with senior bureaucrats.

The perspective I have been developing here suggests that the right way to think about the obstructionism issue is not to frame it as a dilemma arising out of the personal interactions between civil servants and elected officials, but rather to conceive of it as a question about the appropriate relationship between the various branches of the state (along the lines suggested in Figure 2.2). In other words, it is not a question of "obedience or defiance" for the individual occupying a particular role, but rather how much the legislature should reasonably be expected to compromise with the executive in seeking to advance its agenda. This is, of course, an extremely difficult question, each time it arises. My only contribution here is to have suggested what I take to be a better way of *framing* the question than the one suggested by the traditional formula used in the civil service. Bureaucrats should not be obstructionist. But at the same time, the executive branch possesses a certain measure of political authority, grounded in its own sources of legitimacy. Thus the question of obstructionism is really a question about how power and authority should be balanced among the three branches of government.

2.5.2. The Problem of Pluralism

One characteristic of the vocational model that sets it apart from both the hierarchical and the popular is that it requires a theoretical specification of where the public interest lies. Both of the other two models allow one to evade the question by deferring to the "will of the people" to provide that specification. Thus the vocational model is subject to an obvious challenge arising from what Rawls referred to as "the fact of pluralism," namely, that there is in the population widespread yet reasonable disagreement about what constitutes "the good." The vocational model appears to take sides on a question that should be settled through the democratic process (and thus it could stand accused of "politicizing" the civil service).[123]

The central response to this has been to organize the vocational model around a set of principles that are widely thought to be *neutral* with respect to this pluralism. (This sort of liberal neutrality—neutrality with respect to rival conceptions of the good—is not to be confused with civil service neutrality—neutrality with respect to partisan political disagreement.) It is a defining feature of collective action problems, for instance, that individuals embroiled in them need not agree about very much to see that they are nevertheless engaged in a self-defeating pattern of interaction with respect to their own individual goals and projects. Thus a cooperative solution to the collective action problem—such as the Pareto principle recommends—can be judged superior from the standpoint of each individual, by his or her own lights. So while the Pareto principle may still be controversial, it must certainly be less controversial than the first-order value judgments that got the individuals into the collective action problem. (This is why, for example, one can support "economic growth," without necessarily supporting all the specific things that people are likely to do with an increase in their individual wealth.)

This, of course, is the standard liberal response when confronted with the fact of pluralism. And though I think it is essentially correct, it is important to recognize that these principles may still be politically (and philosophically) controversial. Merely declaring one's principles to be "neutral" does not magically dissolve all objections to them. This is most obvious in the case of equality, which is structurally similar to efficiency in not requiring any agreement over first-order value judgments, but is inevitably more controversial, because it attempts to resolve distributive conflict, which necessarily has a win-lose structure. There is, unfortunately, not all that much more that can be said here, other than the rather platitudinous injunction to refrain from dogmatism in thinking about these principles, and to be open to the possibility that they may require reformulation. Beyond that, it is perhaps worth observing that, in Western societies, basic liberal principles are a lot more controversial in theory than they are in practice. And finally, it is worth keeping in mind that purely democratic mechanisms for dealing with pluralism are not obviously any better, since they lack a normatively compelling aggregation mechanism.

2.5.3. Mandarin problem

Apart from the concern that the civil service will become obstructionist vis-à-vis the political program being pursued by the government of the day, there is also the concern that, if freed from the constraints of strict accountability to elected officials, it will become *an interest group*. This is a concern that is no doubt exacerbated by the growth of public-sector unionization in the past few decades. Although the public discussion tends to focus on economic aspects of unionization, the more serious issue, as far as professional ethics is concerned, is the workplace *culture* that unionization introduces, as well as the legal labor-relations paradigm, which tends to be strongly adversarial. There are enormous tensions between this culture (with its emphasis on wages and work hours, rules and regulations, seniority-based promotion, etc.) and the professional ethos that is appropriate to the role of the civil servant. (As Lorne Sossin has observed, judicial proceedings generated by labor-relations grievances are "not an ideal environment for the interpretation of the constitutional duties of civil servants."[124])

Most importantly, the adversarial culture is extremely hostile to anything that resembles discretion on the part of the employer, and therefore pushes in the direction of complete contracting—an ideal that is, as we have seen, both unobtainable and pernicious in the public sector.

One can see how an adversarial culture would arise in the private sector, where management is partial to a set of purely private interests that are frequently opposed to the interests of employees. Yet in the public sector, where management represents the public interest, a strongly adversarial orientation is likely to turn employees into just another rent-seeking group. This obviously has a deleterious impact on public-sector efficiency, making private-sector solutions more attractive by comparison. But more subtly, turning the civil service into an interest group in the eyes of the public makes it more difficult for the executive branch to do its part in securing the state's legitimacy, and therefore contributes to the long-term decline of confidence in government. This is further exacerbated by the involvement of public-sector unions in partisan politics, through funding political parties or paying for campaign advertising.

As far as the higher civil service is concerned, the greater danger is that of becoming overly disconnected or detached from the society that it ostensibly serves. This may lead to the style of "social engineering" or "high modernism" that generated many of the fiascos of mid-20th-century planning.[125] As Cooper puts it, "Administrative specialists can become narrow and isolated from the texture of the political community. They may be overly influenced by client groups and too firmly convinced of the 'one best way' of getting the job done. They may forget the importance of political support, not only in adopting policy but also in carrying it out. Legislative proposals, administrative rules and regulations, and agency implementation plans may need to be informed regularly by political realities."[126] For instance, there are several notorious cases of city planners acquiring enormous power—largely as a result of their technical expertise—then using it to implement disastrously ill-conceived "schemes of improvement."[127]

Politicians are, of course, often accused of suffering from the same detachment. And yet there is a crucial difference, in that politicians cannot escape the need to engage in "retail politics"—whether it be knocking on doors during an electoral campaign, giving speeches, holding townhalls, or dealing with constituency work—that brings them face-to-face with ordinary people. Civil servants, by contrast, are often insulated from any significant contact with members of the broader public. So even if they remain zealously committed to promoting the public interest, they may over time find themselves adopting an increasingly prescriptive conception of that interest, losing track of how the public itself understands its interests.[128]

2.6. Conclusion

The vocational model of public administration ethics is essentially a response to the fact that many civil servants are effectively unsupervisable—from either above or below—in the way that they carry out their responsibilities and in how they exercise their (sometimes enormous) power. This is not just a consequence of information impactedness, it also reflects the complex web of accountability relations that civil servants find themselves in. A DM in Canada is formally accountable not just to the minister, but also to the clerk of the Privy Council, the prime minister, as well as to certain parliamentary committees (as financial accountability officer) and, in some cases, parliamentary officers and government agencies. The DM also has obligations to employees in the department, to peers (i.e., fellow DMs), as well as to the public (e.g., service recipients). As Jacques Bourgault has observed, "a single action, in its various dimensions, can trigger a series of simultaneous accountability requirements to different parties with sometimes divergent points of view."[129] With this many "principals," it is impossible for DMs to think of themselves as "agents" in any meaningful sense of the term. (As the saying goes, a manager told to serve two masters has been freed from both and is answerable to neither.[130]) And yet, since such divided loyalties are inevitable in the public sector, it is important that civil servants have a strong, independent conception of where their professional obligations lie.

At the same time, it is important that civil servants not be conceived of as modern philosopher kings, acting on the basis of their own interpretation of abstract liberal principles (or worse, summoning their own *raisons d'état* to justify arbitrary power). Liberal principles are privileged in my account, not on philosophical grounds, but because they are actually institutionalized in the basic structure of the modern welfare state, as well as in the prevailing ethos of the executive branch. The need for philosophical reflection arises from the fact that these principles have not been adequately articulated. In other words, liberal principles are, to varying degrees, implicit in the structure of the modern welfare state, as well as the prevailing ethic of public administration. Yet because they are not fully explicit, they tend to be reproduced through continuation of practices and reproduction of institutional cultures, rather than through explicit teaching and deliberation. And when they are challenged, the various actors involved often lack the conceptual resources required to mount an explicit defense of these practices. This is the state of affairs that I hope to remedy in the discussion that follows.

I will develop the analysis by attempting to show how the modern welfare state is both an expression of, and arises as a consequence of a commitment to, modern liberalism. This is not an entirely uncontroversial claim, since there are many who think that key features of the modern state represent a deviation from liberal principles. Thus I begin, in chapter 3, with an attempt to bring some conceptual clarity to the question, by providing an historical account of how liberal principles emerged, what their distinctive characteristics are, and how they evolved over time. This analysis culminates in the characterization of modern liberalism as involving a commitment to the three basic principles of efficiency, equality, and liberty. In chapter 4, I go on to show how these three principles, but above all the commitment to efficiency, guided the expansion of the economic role of the state in the 20th century. The welfare state, on this view, arises as a consequence of a rather single-minded focus on improving social welfare by resolving collective action problems, while setting aside other conflicts. The overall goal of these two chapters is to show that "small-l liberalism," for an employee of the state, is like "water to the fishes." It serves as the taken-for-granted background, as well as providing the platitudinous conception of the public interest that informs the best practices of public administration.

Subsequent chapters then turn to the task of articulating the most important normative commitments that have arisen within the executive branch in the modern welfare state. My goal is to show how these can be interpreted as a consequence of these same, abstract liberal commitments to efficiency, equality, and liberty. I begin in chapter 5 with the administrative use of cost-benefit analysis, in order to show how it arises from the pursuit of efficiency, against a background commitment to equality and liberal neutrality. I begin with this because it represents the most clear-cut example of how the civil service is committed to the basic project of the welfare state. It therefore serves as the most important guide and constraint on the power that civil servants exercise over policy-making. In chapter 6, I discuss "rule of law" values, and argue that they constitute an interpretation of the idea of equal citizenship. Equality is a far more controversial principle than efficiency, as a result of which the commitment to political neutrality limits the extent to which the civil service can pursue any "thick" notion of equality. The idea of the rule of law, I will argue, incorporates the most substantial notion of equality compatible with non-partisanship. And finally, in chapter 7, I discuss the anti-paternalism constraint that tacitly structures a great deal of public decision-making. This anti-paternalism constraint, I will argue, is best understood as a consequence of the commitment to individual liberty that informs modern liberalism.

The discussion in chapters 3 and 4 is, admittedly, somewhat circuitous. The complexity of the modern welfare state makes it such that the civil service cannot avoid being guided by a relatively independent conception of the public interest. And yet this appears to be in tension with the most basic principle of democratic legitimacy, as well as the commitment to non-partisanship within the civil service. The idea that the civil service should have normative commitments, but no political commitments, seems inherently contradictory. The key to the solution,

I will argue, lies in the principle of liberal neutrality, which generates a set of more specific normative commitments that, while not always politically neutral, nevertheless have a strong claim to *priority* over the democratic principle. Unfortunately, the principle of liberal neutrality is often regarded as either an implausible or an inessential feature of that doctrine. What these criticisms often wind up showing, however, is not that liberal neutrality is problematic, but rather that it has become such a deep structural feature of the societies in which we live that many of its consequences have become taken for granted. In order to appreciate its significance, it is necessary to situate the principle historically, in order to see what a revolutionary change it represented with respect to the political systems that preceded it.

3

Liberalism

From Classical to Modern

If one were to take a typical Western country, such as Canada, and ask what political system the society is governed by, the standard answer would be that it is a
"liberal democracy." And if one were to ask the average citizen of such a country
what that means, many would be able to give a reasonably coherent account
of the "democracy" part, but would find it difficult to explain precisely what it
means for a state to be "liberal." This is in many ways a surprising failure, since
most liberal democracies have been liberal for a lot longer than they have been
democracies. Indeed, if one takes "democracy" to require something close to
universal adult suffrage, then the major liberal democracies only became fully
democratic—by extending the voting franchise to women—in the early to mid-
20th century. By contrast, many of the central features of the liberal political
order had been put in place at least a hundred years earlier.

On the other hand, if one were to turn to the academic literature to try to pin
down the meaning of the term "liberal," one would immediately be struck by the
bewildering array of views that get called liberal, and by the number of strikingly
different theoretical accounts of the normative core of these views. One would
no doubt come away with the impression that liberalism has something to do
with individual rights, or with constitutional limits on state power, but beyond
that it would be difficult to find any consensus. Indeed, if one were to ask what
John Locke, John Stuart Mill, and John Rawls have in common, such that they
all count as major figures in the tradition of liberal political thought, one would
be hard-pressed to find a core set of shared views that qualify them as liberals.
Furthermore, there has been a proliferation of "isms" within the broad scope of
liberal views (e.g., neoliberalism, classical liberalism, etc.), not to mention the
development of pejorative and polemical uses of the label, which has led some to
question whether the term still has any value.

This is an unfortunate state of affairs, particularly for our purposes, since,
as I will attempt to show, a proper understanding of what it means for a state
to be liberal is crucial for the exercise of public administration within such a
state. Indeed, one way of understanding the limitations of both the hierarchical
and the populist models of public-sector accountability is to see that they put
the onus entirely on democracy as the source of legitimacy for administrative

The Machinery of Government. Joseph Heath, Oxford University Press (2020). © Oxford University Press.
DOI: 10.1093/oso/9780197509616.001.0001

decision-making. Yet it is not the case, in liberal states, that the "people," much less their representatives in the legislature, get to do whatever they want. On the contrary, their decisions are subject to a number of what are sometimes called "countermajoritarian" constraints. The most well-known source of these is, of course, the judiciary, since it has been a major trend in democratic societies for courts to acquire the power to strike down legislation that they deem unconstitutional (with particular emphasis on potential violations of individual and minority rights). The traditional doctrine of the separation of powers also puts limits on the legislature, by reserving particular powers for the other branches of government—the prohibition on "bills of attainder" (legislation that directly imposes a punishment upon a group or individual) is one clear-cut example. Although it may seem a bit exotic, underlying the example is an extremely important principle, which is that the legislature does not have the power to *directly* exercise the state's powers of compulsion.

Yet as we have seen, it is not just the judiciary that enjoys a degree of independence from the legislature. The executive branch also enjoys substantial autonomy, which serves to check certain majoritarian tendencies. Administrative tribunals, for example, function very much like courts; they can in some cases overturn legislative decisions, and they have decision-making powers that the legislature does not. There are many other areas in which branches of the administration have been specifically isolated from political control (or, to use the slightly question-begging term, "political interference"). Thus if one were to ask how a civil servant should act, in some area in which there is clear administrative discretion, the answer cannot be "whatever the people want," or even "whatever the people's representatives want." That might be the correct answer if we lived in a system of unrestricted popular sovereignty (or a so-called illiberal democracy), but in liberal democracies things are not so simple. Any answer to the question must start, not with democracy, but rather with the background set of principles that inform the organization of the state, and that specify both the role and the constraints on democratic decision-making. The theory that attempts to articulate these principles, and guide their development, is what we refer to as "liberalism."

So despite the difficulty and confusion surrounding the term, a working understanding of liberalism is essential to the practice of public administration. My goal in this chapter is to bring some order to the chaos, in order to pick out what I consider to be the essential strand in the liberal political tradition. Rather than pursue this as a definitional exercise, I will provide a historical account of the development of what I take to be the key ideas in liberalism. The best way to understand the core of the doctrine is to see what liberalism arose as a reaction *against*—or, more specifically, which elements of the ancient and medieval political tradition European liberals were rejecting. The other major advantage of the historical perspective is that it allows us to see how the liberal idea evolved over time in response to changing social circumstances—first and foremost, in response to the Industrial Revolution and the rise of capitalism. I focus on two forms of liberalism: the "classical liberal" view, which is associated with the social contract doctrines of the Enlightenment, and the "modern liberal" view, which accompanied the rise of the welfare state in the 20th century. These two views are sufficiently different that many commentators have difficulty seeing what they have in common to both merit the term "liberal." Putting things into a historical perspective provides the basis for a more satisfactory response to this question.

3.1. Before liberalism

Max Weber's central methodological principle for understanding social institutions was to regard them as the product of a confluence of ideas and interests.[1] Ideas taken alone tend to be motivationally inert—they appeal to intellectuals, but not to a broad enough segment of the population to achieve widespread social change. Interests, by contrast, are motivationally powerful, yet cannot alone produce the *legitimacy* that is the hallmark of successful insti-tutionalization. A stable social order depends on some constellation of power and advantage, yet power is only effective when a critical mass of people—both those who wield it and those who are subject to it—believe that it is being rightly exercised.

  With this in mind, it is important to be wary of philosophical accounts of lib-eralism that treat it as purely an intellectual doctrine, and its emergence as the consequence of a conceptual revolution. Liberalism achieved preeminence in Europe during the 17th and 18th centuries, not as an abstract idea, but rather as a solution to a pressing social problem. The problem in question is sometimes described as that of religious intolerance, but this is not entirely accurate. By the 16th century, Christians had a long history of exhibiting intolerance toward in-ternal dissidents (the suppression of Lollardy, the burning of Jan Hus), in their dealings with Jews (numerous restrictions, expulsions, and pogroms), and in their treatment of Muslims (the Crusades, forcible conversion in Spain, the ex-pulsion of the Moriscos). As we shall see, there were actually powerful reasons, internal to the theology of the time, for this intolerance. None of these episodes led to a fundamental rethinking of the received ideas about the proper orga-nization of the state. Indeed, much of the repression was a *consequence* of the dominant way of thinking about the role of the state in society. The problem that drove the rise of liberalism was not religious intolerance, but religious *warfare*, and civil war in particular. What characterized earlier episodes of intolerance is that orthodoxy was able to prevail through force of arms. With the Protestant

Reformation of the 16th century, however, Christians found themselves, for the first time since the 11th century, with a schism that could not be resolved by force. The result was more than a hundred years of essentially nonstop warfare, both internal and external, affecting all the major regions of Western Europe.

There is considerable confusion on this score, because the Protestant Reformation is often cited as the source of a more "liberal" form of Christianity. Yet Protestantism *as such* did not give rise to liberalism, or inspire any fresh thinking on the question of tolerance.[2] There is some temptation to think that religious dissidents, such as Martin Luther or John Calvin, having experienced persecution at the hands of the church, would in turn have been less inclined to persecute those who disagreed with them. Yet this would be entirely mistaken. Protestants proved to be just as intolerant as Catholics, and equally zealous in pursuing and executing heretics. (Consider, for instance, the case of Michel Servet, a physician who wrote several tracts questioning the doctrine of the Holy Trinity. Forced to flee the Inquisition in France, he took refuge in Geneva in 1553, where, at Calvin's instigation, he was seized, tried, and burned at the stake.[3]) This is because Protestants shared with Catholics the same basic theory about the appropriate uses of coercion, and thus of state power. When they found sympathetic rulers (as Calvin did with the Council of Geneva), they behaved in much the same way that Catholics had.

To understand Christian attitudes toward the state, and the uses of state power, it is important to recognize that Christianity as such does not have a clear political philosophy. Jesus Christ's sole pronouncement on political questions— "render under Caesar what is Caesar's, render unto God what is God's"—is entirely quietist. Early Christians, including St. Paul, were basically satisfied with this approach, which preached passivity and withdrawal from the world, because they were expecting the "kingdom of Heaven" to appear on earth any day. The apostolic model, giving up all one's worldly possessions and abandoning one's family and friends to follow Christ, remained the dominant ideal. Yet as the centuries passed, and the influence of Christianity grew, this became both less plausible and less realistic. The conversion of the Roman Emperor Constantine in AD 313 posed the growing dilemma most sharply. Jesus's pronouncement gave advice to Christians on how to deal with a ruler, but it offered no advice to a Christian ruler on how to govern an empire. Christians had to look elsewhere to find guidance on how to organize their political affairs.

They looked, quite naturally, to existing Roman institutions and political ideas. Christians took over many of the institutional structures of Rome (indeed, one can still find within the Catholic Church institutional arrangements that trace their lineage, with unbroken continuity, directly back to the Roman empire). More importantly, they took over many of the ideas that had informed these institutions, ideas that were ultimately derived from classical Greek philosophy—Plato and Aristotle, along with their Roman interpreters. For if Christianity lacked a political philosophy, the Greeks had excelled in this area, producing a deep and comprehensive body of work, at whose center were Plato's *Republic* and *Laws* and Aristotle's *Ethics* and *Politics*. Furthermore, classical Greek political philosophy was an integral part of a broader cosmology that constituted the most sophisticated science of the time. In other words, Greek and Roman views on how human society should be governed fit within a broader view of the organization of nature and the universe. (It is not an accident that Plato's *Republic* contains substantial discussion of geometry, physics, and astronomy, or that Aristotle reached constantly for biological analogies.) Again, there was no correlate of this in Christian teachings. Thus Christians did much more than take over Greek political philosophy. They actually took over—in Christianized form—the entire philosophical cosmology of the Greeks, of which the political philosophy was but a part.

In this way, Christians inherited a worldview, which they modified to render compatible with monotheism and the idea of an intelligent creator, but which retained its essential features. This is what accounts for the remarkable stability and continuity—some might say, rigidity—of Christian thought throughout the first millennium and well into the second. Because it all fit together into a more-or-less cohesive whole, attempts to change just one part of it had the effect of creating enormous cognitive dissonance. This goes some distance toward explaining the stability of medieval political philosophy—or of the basic approach underlying that political philosophy—even in circumstances in which an impartial observer would judge it to have become highly dysfunctional. People simply could not imagine another way of thinking, because the revisions that would be required in their worldview by any change were too extensive.

As every student of philosophy knows, the central concept in the work of both Plato and Aristotle is that of "the good." When we encounter this term now, we are inclined to classify it as a moral concept. Yet for both Plato and Aristotle it was not only a moral idea; it was the animating principle of the *natural* order as well. There is a simple reason for this, which is that they did not see any distinction between the natural and the moral order. Of course, they recognized a distinction between the way that things are and the way that things should be. But in Aristotle's view, the only way to understand how things are is to understand them as striving for the way that they should be. The "good," in other words, provides the animating principle of all things. Physical motion, for instance, can be explained as a consequence of objects striving to achieve some end state. The flame rises because it seeks to be one with the heavens, the stone falls because it wants to be reunited with the earth. The end state that is sought can be described as what is "good" for the thing. This served as the basis for Aristotle's distinction between "natural" and "unnatural" motion. When the stone is thrown into the air, the motion is "unnatural," because it runs contrary to the stone's inner tendency. When it falls back to earth, the motion is "natural," because it conforms to and expresses the stone's true nature.

Rocks, of course, are very simple objects, and so the good that they seek exhibits little in the way of perfection. As one ascends the hierarchy of being, however, one encounters more complex forms, which have the capacity for higher degrees of perfection. There are plants, which have nutritive processes, and hence are alive; animals, which have desires as well, and so are capable of motion; and finally, humans, who possess not only the capabilities of the lower forms, but reason as well, which allows us to acquire knowledge, and thus to transcend the material realm. Thus the good *for us* takes the form of a set of explicitly articulated precepts—what we would describe as a "moral" ideal, or an explicitly articulated good. But it is not fundamentally different from the good that serves as the animating principle of all living things, and that directs the behavior of inanimate nature as well. Thus what we describe as moral action is simply the type of "natural" motion appropriate to humans.

Because of this way of thinking, when the Greeks turned their attention to political philosophy, and to the question of how human society should be organized, their point of departure was always to ask what "good" was served by political association. What was its telos? What do we strive to obtain through political association? The answer, not surprisingly, is that human society exists to promote the human good, if not individually, then corporately. For individuals who have the potential, society is to facilitate their attainment of the highest degree of individual perfection. For those who have a more debased nature, or an inferior soul, society is to compensate for their natural deficiencies, to rule them in a way that they are incapable of ruling themselves, so that at least their external behavior will be in conformity with what would be dictated by the good. This allows the political association as a whole to be good, even when not all of its individual members are.

Both Plato and Aristotle used the term "virtue" to describe the set of behavioral dispositions that were conducive to the attainment of the good. Thus an alternative way of describing the goal of political association is to say that it is aimed at the promotion of virtue. In the case of superior men, this meant providing the conditions under which virtue could develop and flourish. In the case of inferior men (and all women), it meant providing an exterior supplement to their own deficient self-governance. In other words, the role of the state was to provide an external framework of incentives—that is, of coercion—that would bring the conduct of the less innately virtuous in line with what virtue would dictate. Thus the core function of the *law*—to the extent that it reflects the organized coercive capacity of society—was to reward virtue and to punish vice.

In contemporary political philosophy this view is referred to as "perfectionism," in recognition of the fact that it begins with an ideal of human perfection, or a view of what people should be striving toward (in the current jargon, a "particular conception of the good"), then argues that political society should be organized around the promotion of that ideal. Several features of this view are worth drawing attention to. First of all, it is not a liberal view. Indeed, to put things this way is anachronistic, since liberalism arose as a reaction against perfectionism, and as a rejection of key features of that view. But it is worth being more specific about the particular features of perfectionism that lead us to classify it as illiberal. The first is that it posits one and the same ideal for both morality and politics. Indeed, the conception of the good that is taken to animate the political realm is fundamentally a moral one. As a result, written laws are regarded as just codified and enforced moral rules—and all moral obligations are, at least in principle, subject to state enforcement. Closely tied to this is the idea that there are no limits on the extent of state power. There is no recognition of what we now think of as a "private sphere," a realm of individual choice, outside the scope of coercive intervention by the state. Wherever there is immorality, there the state is seen as having a legitimate interest in intervening. If, for instance, the moral code is one that includes duties to self, then it seems entirely natural to the perfectionist that the state should have jurisdiction over various forms of private, self-regarding behavior.

Furthermore, there is no reason to think that there should be "freedom of speech," "freedom of association," or any other protected individual rights under a perfectionist view. The question is always whether the specific conduct promotes the good. If what a person is saying is good, or if the purpose for which people are assembling is good, then they can expect permission to proceed, and if not, not. Thus an institution such as censorship of publications, which is often now regarded as little more than a tool of tyrants, was actually part of a more general normative understanding of how political society should best be organized. Why should an individual be allowed to publish something that is antithetical to the good? Perfectionism simply lacked the conceptual resources to mount a convincing argument in defense of such a freedom. Since the whole purpose of political association, and the guiding idea of the law, was to promote the good, it just seemed obvious that the permissibility of publishing something should be determined by the substantive merits of the proposed publication, and that it was the duty of state officials to be as diligent as possible in assessing those merits.

One can also see, then, why perfectionism tended toward intolerance, at least with respect to dissenting ideas about the good. Humans are unique in that the good for us is explicitly articulated. This means, however, that one way of turning people away from the good is by confusing them, proposing "unnatural" courses of action, or seductive misinterpretations of the good. Since the objective of legal regulation is to promote a particular conception of the good, it stands to reason that the state should want to punish those who seek to promote deviant interpretations. Even just questioning the good, on this view, looks like a vice, one that should be punished along with every other form of vice. The fact that it is a crime of "thought" rather than of "action" is, at best, an irrelevant distinction (and, at worst, an exacerbating factor, because thought corrupts the individual's soul, while action affects only the body).

These are, in broad brush strokes, the set of ideas that constituted the "classical inheritance" of early Christian political thinking. In certain respects, the Christian appropriation of these ideas was straightforward; but in other regards, more complex. For instance, the monotheistic assumption of a divine intelligence and creator provided an attractive reinterpretation of Plato's rather unintuitive claim that abstract objects exist in a "realm of the Forms." These Platonic Forms became "ideas in the mind of God," which, through God's act of creation, became embodied in the world.[4] This not only provided a more plausible understanding of what the "Forms" might be, it provided the basis for a reconciliation between Plato's view of the forms as abstract objects and Aristotle's view of form as being embedded in all material objects. Under the Christian reinterpretation, this gave rise to the image of nature as a providential order, with everything both possessing and being animated by a divine purpose, forming an ascending hierarchy that culminates in God the creator.

There were, however, two points on which Christian thinking was significantly more pessimistic than that of the Greeks, which in turn lent added complexity to the appropriation of classical thought. Both are related to the "otherworldliness" of the Christian religion. In the first place, the doctrine of judgment and salvation *after death* meant that Christians situated the highest good outside the material realm, displacing it into the afterlife. Thus they were inclined to take a very dim view of how much could be accomplished, in the way of virtue, during this life. The legend of the fall, the doctrine of original sin, and the idea that divine "grace" is required for salvation, all tended to erode and undermine the Greek vision of the "great-souled" man, striding through the *agora*, exhibiting perfection and self-mastery. As a result, Christians put a great deal more emphasis on vice than they did on virtue—or on the related but slightly different notion of "sin."[5] Whereas moral thinking among the Greeks and Romans had often taken the form of compiling lists that focused on the virtues, then debating which ones were more or less important, Christians were more inclined to focus on sin, compiling typologies of sin (carnal versus spiritual; sins of thought, word and action; and, most famously, venial versus mortal sins).[6] Thus the Greek ethic of virtue became, in Christian hands, largely an ethic of vice (or sin). This carried with it a shift in political thinking and led to much greater focus on the punitive features of law and the need to protect against evil.

The second major difference in Christian thinking stemmed from the doctrine of divine judgment, which claimed that only God was able to bring about true justice. This, combined with a view of the world as being mired in sin, suggested that there was no chance of the highest good being achieved through the state. This raised very serious questions about what earthly political authority was *for*, or what it should be aiming toward. The most straightforward view was a theocratic one, which said that the earthly city should strive toward the good, to get as close as possible to realizing the divine purpose, even if that turns out to be not very close. On this view, there would be no distinction between political, moral, and religious authority—all would be part of a unified scheme to promote the good. The theocratic view, however, was not the one that early Christians settled on. Indeed, it acquired very little influence until the late Middle Ages (when doctrines like "the divine right of kings" were developed).[7] The dominant view throughout most of the Middle Ages was the Augustinian one, which found institutional embodiment in the so-called Gelasian arrangement, under which authority was divided between church and state (or pope and emperor), with neither being clearly in the ascendant. Again, the thinking underlying this arrangement reflected a greater measure of pessimism about the amount that the state could plausibly be thought to accomplish.

As a result of this conceptualization, most of the positive moral and political energies that had been directed toward the classical Greek polis were, in the Christian world, directed toward the church, not the state. This was a major factor in the move away from solitary hermeticism toward communal monasticism in early Christianity—an important trend at the time Augustine was writing. Since the state seemed irredeemably corrupt, the monastery emerged as the form of political association that could be organized around promotion of the highest good. (In this respect, the self-governing Greek city-state never disappeared, it just reinvented itself as a monastery.) The Aristotelian ideal of the virtuous individual—one who has achieved true happiness—provides the template for the Christian ideal of the saint. That true happiness can only be achieved after death and in the presence of God were simply amendments made to reconcile these older philosophical ideas with the Christian eschatology.

This may help to shed some light on why, throughout the Middle Ages, Christianity was, first and foremost, a monastic religion, with what Weber described as a strong "world-rejecting" character.[8] Given the fallen condition of humanity, one could only achieve virtue by distancing oneself from worldly concerns. Whereas Plato and Aristotle had identified a life of contemplation— again, removed from worldly concerns—as the primary candidate for the most virtuous life, Christians reinterpreted the practice of contemplation as that of *prayer*, and so identified the most virtuous life as one dedicated to prayer and worship, unencumbered by the distractions of family life. Thus the monasteries in Medieval Europe were not merely an accretion, a refuge for those suffering an excess of religiosity. They were the institutional embodiment of the highest aspirations of humanity. What eventually came to be thought of as "privileges" enjoyed by these monasteries—such as exemption from taxation—were not regarded that way until after they had come under attack during the Reformation. Prior to that, sustaining and supporting the monasteries was seen as one of the most important duties that the Christian state could perform.

Because of the complex division of labor that was established among the state, the church, and the various monastic orders, medieval Christian political thinking is also extremely complex. The obvious weakness of medieval political institutions is that, precisely because they were not theocratic, they had no principled way of resolving conflicts of authority between the pope and the "emperor" (in practice, the various kings and princes), or jurisdictional conflicts between the legal regime of the state and that of the church (and its "civil" and "canon" law). It is thus possible throughout the Middle Ages to find theories of state power that, to the modern ear, sound extremely secular. For example, certain theories of property were entirely conventionalist, making no appeal whatsoever to divine will or grant (the latter being the idea that, after the initial act of creation, God gave Adam possession of the earth).[9] Yet it is important to recognize that the basic framework of all these theories remains entirely perfectionist. The point of departure is always the good. It is just that when it comes to promoting this good, the church is given the predominant role, while the state usually remains a secondary actor.

There is some temptation to think that Western liberalism arose out of this "secular" strand of thinking, and thus to overestimate the continuity of the philosophical tradition in this regard.[10] Yet rather than the development of the secular strand, the late Middle Ages instead saw a sharp rise in theocratic thinking. Much of this owed to the rediscovery of Aristotle's *Ethics* and *Politics* in the 12th century. The manuscripts of these works had been available in the Arab and Islamic world throughout the Middle Ages, but not in Latin Christendom. Thus Christians had been much more influenced by Plato's sharply dualistic way of thinking. Islamic political philosophy, by contrast, was from the beginning highly theocratic—partly because the role of "prophet" and "king" had been unified in the person of the Prophet Mohammed, but also because of the vast influence of Aristotle. Thus there was an admirable simplicity in views such as those articulated in the early 10th century by Abu Nasr al-Farabi in his *Opinions of the Inhabitants of the Virtuous City*, where religious and political authority are completely undifferentiated, and all of society is organized into a single hierarchy, based on relative proximity to the divine.[11] Contact with these views led to an important shift in Christian thinking, which one can see clearly in the work of St. Thomas Aquinas. The result was that European kings became far more likely to see their authority as springing from the divine will, and to see themselves as directly charged with using the tools of the state to promote the highest good—construed now in religious terms.

These trends were, if anything, amplified by the Protestant Reformation. One of the central features of Luther's thinking was his intense hostility to monasticism.[12] Partly this was based on his perception that the institution had become wealthy and corrupt, but much of it was based on a fundamental disagreement about the nature of the good life. Luther was perhaps the most influential proponent of the transvaluation of values that Charles Taylor has referred to as "the affirmation of ordinary life."[13] The good life, according to this view, was one that was lived in a way that was fully engaged with the world, placing positive value on both work and family. From this perspective, the monastic life—secluded from the world, dedicated to contemplation and prayer—was both incomplete and potentially corrupting. This thinking was reflected in Luther's decision to help a group of nuns escape from a Cistercian monastery and, ultimately, to marry one of them. By denying that the highest good should be pursued only by religious specialists, but rather should be sought by all, Protestants wound up breaking down many of the barriers that had separated church and state, thereby encouraging a more theocratic understanding of political authority. Hence the insight at the heart of Voltaire's remark on Calvin and his followers, that "if they condemned celibacy in the priests, and let open the gates of the convents, it was only to turn all society into a convent."[14]

In certain respects, Protestants and Catholics were merely adopting two different visions of "the highest good" that one can find competing in Aristotle. In one passage of the *Nicomachean Ethics*, Aristotle claims that the best life is one that exhibits all of the virtues in combination. Later he describes the best life as dedicated to the exercise of the highest virtue—namely, contemplation.[15] One might be tempted to think of this as a rather esoteric and ultimately inconsequential inconsistency. But within a perfectionist political order, it had immediate and important consequences, because people thought the primary function of the legal order was to enforce the correct conception of the good. This was reflected most obviously in the commitment to the punishment of heresy. A long-standing Christian argument, dating back to Augustine, regarded heresy as a more serious crime than murder, because the latter only destroyed the body, while the former corrupted the soul and condemned its victims to eternal damnation.[16] Within this frame of thinking, the conclusion that heresy should be forcefully suppressed was practically inescapable. The suggestion that it should go unpunished would have been horrifying, much worse than the suggestion that murderers should be able to walk freely among us.[17] Indeed, one can find Aquinas repeating the "heresy is murder of the soul" argument, in almost

exactly the same terms, eight hundred years after Augustine. His only modification was to suggest that the heretic be given one or two opportunities to recant.[18]

As a consequence of this way of thinking, disagreement about religious
questions tended to erupt into violence, including organized state violence. It is
important to recognize, however, that this was not because of people's religious
views per se, but rather their political philosophy. There were, of course, powerful interests at work in these conflicts as well, but the prevailing political philosophy played a crucial role, because it provided an understanding of the proper
use of state power. One can see this constellation of forces at work in the way that
the status of monasteries became a flashpoint for conflict. Medieval Europe did
not just happen to have monasteries, these institutions were actively supported
by the state, based on a widely shared understanding about the nature of the
good life. Having rejected this conception, Protestants quite naturally felt entitled to use state power to dissolve the monasteries, and to seize their lands and
income. This conveniently aligned with the interests of certain parties (for Henry
VIII in England, Protestantism largely provided ideological cover for the seizure
of monastic lands).[19] Because of the *main morte* phenomenon—where land that
was left to the church remained there forever—monasteries had grown in size
and importance. In France, it is estimated that as much as 20 percent of the land
was owned by the Catholic Church at the time of the Reformation. This meant
that there was an enormous amount at stake in the debate over the disposition of
church lands.

The important thing to recognize is that the religious conflict provoked by
the Reformation was not driven solely by doctrinal debates. Because of the prevailing political philosophy, these deep disagreements about the nature of the
good life translated into state policies that had very serious economic and political consequences. The result was a series of extremely destructive conflicts.
The Thirty Years' War in the German states, for instance, which began with the
attempt of the Holy Roman Empire to impose religious uniformity throughout
its domain, resulted in an appalling loss of life. The combined toll of combat,
pestilence, and famine resulted in the death of approximately one-third of the
population, including more than half of the male population. Warfare erupted
in Switzerland and the low countries, as well as France (achieving particular
savagery in the St. Bartholomew's Day massacre). The civil war in England,
though materially less destructive, generated a series of succession crises that
destabilized the monarchy, and ultimately led to its replacement by a military
dictatorship.

What is particularly astonishing in retrospect is that these conflicts dragged
on for so long. The "wars of religion" in France, for instance, are conventionally divided into eight distinct wars, over a period of roughly three decades. The
persistence of these conflicts had much to do with the participants' inability to

see a way out except through victory of their own side. In part, this was because they subscribed to what John Stuart Mill would later describe as the logic of the persecutors ("we may persecute others because we are right, . . . they must not persecute us because they are wrong."[20]) Similarly, when pressed to find a solution to the problem of religious warfare, both sides were inclined to regard the solution as simple—everyone just needed to accept the authority of the one true church. More importantly, however, Europeans did not see how political order could be established without a definitive resolution of the question of who was right and who was wrong. The idea that one could have a stable polity without a thick religious consensus struck them as impossible. It did not help, of course, that the doctrine of religious toleration was itself declared a heresy, giving license to persecute its proponents. [21] Tolerance, in other words, was not tolerated. Not only did Christians consider themselves justified in persecuting their opponents, they could see no defensible alternative to doing so.

3.2. The rise of classical liberalism

If one were looking for an ideological factor to fault for the "wars of religion" in Europe, it would make more sense to blame the prevailing political philosophy than to focus on the religious issues. Religious disagreement was obviously an important element, and Protestantism was particularly unhelpful in its insistence that all Christians should read the Bible and draw their own conclusions about its meaning. Given the fragmentary, inconsistent and sometimes frankly contradictory nature of the Christian Bible, this proved to be little more than a recipe for generating schism.[22] At the same time, the perfectionist view of politics served as the "transmission belt" that took these doctrinal disagreements and transformed them into armed conflicts involving major states. This analysis is bolstered by the observation that the problem of religious warfare in Europe was resolved, not by an overcoming of religious disagreement, or by a decline in religiosity, but rather by a change in political philosophy. It was political liberalism, not ecumenism, much less atheism, that put an end to what was, at the time, the greatest curse afflicting European civilization.

It is also important to acknowledge that, at the outset, the rise of liberalism did not involve significant intellectual innovation. The major ideas had been in circulation for a long time. For instance, it has often been noted that one of the signature doctrines of liberal political philosophy, namely, social contract theory, had already been sketched out with exemplary clarity by Plato in the opening pages of the *Republic*.[23] There Glaucon suggests that justice involves a type of compromise. For each individual, the best outcome would be to commit injustice with impunity, while the worst outcome would be to suffer injustice and be incapable of revenge. Yet for one person to get the best outcome, someone else must get the worst one. If the harm suffered by the victim is greater than the benefit enjoyed by the perpetrator, then everyone has an incentive to accept an agreement under which everyone refrains from committing injustice, in return for the assurance that he will not have to suffer it. Thus justice can be seen as a type of compromise between individuals, where they agree to live together under rules that *all* can accept. As Plato's dialogue continues, however, this view is quickly rejected, not because there is any flaw in the underlying reasoning, but simply because it is second best. It fails to show why justice is *intrinsically* desirable, or that it is the highest good.

The significance of the wars of religion is not that they gave rise to an explosion of new thinking in political philosophy, but that they made people more receptive to the idea of settling for second best. This can be seen most clearly in the developing literature on tolerance—where the dilemma is posed in almost the exact same terms that led to its hasty dismissal in the *Republic*. The ideal arrangement is, of course, to live in a community in which everyone follows the teachings of the one true church, and where virtue is rewarded and vice is punished. The worst arrangement, by contrast, is to live in a community in which an ignorant majority seeks to impose its heretical views on believers, perverting and distorting the true word of Christ. The compromise is toleration: everyone agrees not to impose their views on others by force. From a doctrinal perspective, it is impossible to regard this as the best outcome. It is only when people come to see the close-knit community of believers, united by a shared pursuit of virtue, as *practically* unobtainable, that they begin to take proposals for accommodating religious pluralism seriously.[24]

Thus it is always possible to find intellectual antecedents of liberalism prior to the early modern era, just as one can find many formulations in medieval or early Renaissance works of political philosophy that sound liberal. The rise of liberalism was not due to the introduction of new ideas, but rather to the reconsideration of ideas that had long been in circulation. A great deal of the impetus for this reconsideration was the fatigue of war, which provided the "interest" considerations. This was, of course, accompanied by a reformulation of the ideas in more persuasive terms, as people began to take them seriously. One can see this clearly in the 16th and 17th centuries, already prefigured in Thomas Hobbes's *Leviathan*, where the idea of the social contract found its most influential modern articulation. Indeed, notwithstanding that Hobbes was a monarchist and an authoritarian, several of the most important ideas of the liberal tradition can be found in his work.

Hobbes's overriding objective, in his great book *Leviathan*, is to banish the specter of civil war. To accomplish this, it is necessary to overcome the fragmentation of political authority.[25] In Hobbes's view, this requires eliminating the major sources of political disagreement, because that is what generates the chaos and confusion. The first step in his strategy for doing so is to displace "the good" from the central role it had played in political philosophy. This necessarily requires a sharp break with the entire history of Western political philosophy emanating from ancient Greece. The major problem with what he calls the philosophy of "the schools"—by which he means scholasticism, the strand of Christian thinking strongly influenced by Aristotle, which was dominant at the time—is that it starts out on the wrong foot. It tries to build a political order based on a shared conception of the good, yet it lacks the intellectual resources to produce agreement about the nature of that good. Everything is basically downhill from there. What "the schoolmen" fail to recognize, Hobbes claims, is that there is no objective basis for "the good," at least, not as philosophers since Aristotle had conceived of it. Thus any attempt to base political authority on some shared conception of the good becomes a recipe for chaos.

Undermining the centrality of the "the good" in political philosophy is the purpose of the rather lengthy discourse on epistemology and philosophy of mind that occupies the opening chapters of the *Leviathan*. Hobbes's strategy is to show that even if there were such a thing as an objective good in nature, we could have no knowledge of it. The argument ends with his dramatic conclusion, that "whatsoever is the object of any man's appetite or desire, that is it which he for his part calleth 'good'; and the object of his hate and aversion, 'evil'; and of his contempt 'vile' and 'inconsiderable.' For these words of good, evil, and contemptible, are ever used with relation to the person that useth them, there being nothing simply and absolutely so; nor any common rule of good and evil, to be taken from the nature of the objects themselves."[26]

Contemporary readers sometimes fail to appreciate how dramatic a move this is. To start out a work of political philosophy by dismissing the concept of "the good" was to repudiate the entire classical and medieval tradition. One can, of course, find a similar move in Machiavelli's *The Prince*—a work that no doubt influenced Hobbes. The difference is that Machiavelli was merely offering advice to princes on how they should manage their affairs, one of his major pieces of advice being to ignore traditional moral constraints. Hobbes, by contrast, set out to do normative political philosophy in the traditional vein. He was attempting to reconstruct political morality, not dismiss it. He saw himself as offering a vindication of the idea of natural law, not a repudiation of it. The difference is merely that he wanted to do it without assigning any foundational role to the concept of the good (or evil).

Two key ideas drive Hobbes's construction, and when followed to their logical conclusion, they wind up producing many of the characteristic features of liberal political thinking. The first is the idea of the state as an *artificial* construct.[27] This is an explicit repudiation of the Aristotelian view, which regarded the state as something natural, or as the expression of human nature. Contact with hunter-gatherer societies in the Americas had familiarized Europeans with the idea that humans could get along without institutionalized political authority. And though Europeans invariably looked down on these groups as "savages," they also drew the correct inference that the social structures they were observing offered a glimpse of the prehistory of their own societies. In contrast to the Biblical narrative, according to which there had always been kings and cities, Europeans began to realize that their ancestors had also at one point lived as hunter-gatherers, without agriculture, metallurgy, or literacy, and without political authority. (Thus when Locke says, "In the beginning, all the World was America," he was articulating an important insight about social structure, the correctness of which we now take for granted.[28]) And so, in the same way that farming is not "the human condition," but rather an innovation that was introduced at a specific time and place, subjection to political authority is also not the human condition; it is an innovation that was introduced at a specific time and place. The question then becomes, Why did people accept it?

The second key idea concerns *how* the state might have arisen. Here, Hobbes makes the influential suggestion that the state arises when individuals agree to transfer to a person (the "sovereign") some of the powers that they enjoyed in the state of nature. The crucial constraint is that they are only willing to surrender these powers on the condition that everyone else does so as well—this is what can make it advantageous. Individuals alone would never benefit from surrendering any of their powers to someone else. Yet if everyone else is prepared to do the same, and if everyone's willingness is conditional on the willingness of everyone else to, then it can be advantageous to surrender a power. The loss that one suffers from no longer being able to exercise the power is made up for by the assurance that one will no longer have to suffer the negative consequences of others exercising it. In certain cases, the net effect of this will be positive, and so everyone will agree to grant the sovereign the entitlement to exercise some power on his or her behalf.

A good example of this is the power to break one's promises. Hobbes refers to powers exercised in the state of nature as "natural rights," and he regards people as having a natural right to do whatever they want. This includes the right to make promises and then break them. The possession of this right turns out to be disadvantageous, however, because knowing that no one can be compelled to keep his or her promises, no one will bother to make them, and so people will be deprived of the benefits that could come from any practice that involves contracts, such as long-distance trade. Thus, everyone has an interest in surrendering this right to the sovereign, giving the state the power to compel performance of agreements.

One can imagine property arising in a similar way. Hobbes asserts that in the state of nature, there will be no agriculture, or cultivation of the land, because "the fruit thereof is uncertain." If everyone has a natural right to take whatever they want, whenever they want, then people are unlikely to invest the time and energy required to clear land and plant seeds. "If one plant, sow, build, or possess a convenient seat, others may probably be expected to come prepared with forces united to dispossess and deprive him, not only of the fruit of his labor, but also of his life or liberty."[29] In the state of nature there will be very little theft, but only because no one will bother to create anything worth stealing. So again, individuals have an interest in surrendering to the sovereign their natural right to trespass and steal, giving the state the power to impose a system of property ownership.

This line of reasoning allows Hobbes to provide a new answer to an age-old question about political authority. It is natural to wonder why it is necessary for the state to use *force*, or why the law must be coercively imposed. The traditional answer was to say that if everyone were good, then there would be no need for coercion. Yet because some people are evil, they cannot be expected to do what is right on their own, and so they must be threatened and punished. From this perspective, there is an extremely close connection between the state's powers of coercion and the need to control evil—indeed, it is the existence of evil that ultimately justifies the power of the state. Hobbes, however, starts out by saying that evil is, more or less, in the eye of the beholder. The real problem is disagreement, or different people wanting incompatible things. For example, because of scarcity, when two people spot a good (say, a ripe apple hanging from the branch of an apple tree), they both immediately want it for themselves. Neither aspiration really merits the description "evil," although to the extent that either one frustrates the other's ambitions, that person is likely to describe the other as evil. Hobbes's great insight is that one can make the case for state regulation of such interactions—such as imposing a system of property that will determine whom the apple belongs to—without getting into the question of good and evil. Both parties have an interest, not only in there being a set of rules, but in having those rules coercively imposed.

In this way, Hobbes arrives at the rather unobvious conclusion that two people, despite being entirely pure of heart and motive, might nevertheless find it in their interest to submit themselves to the power of a third—to authorize that person to coerce them, because without the threat of coercion, the lack of trust between them would prevent them from engaging in mutually beneficial cooperation. And so, to the seemingly puzzling question, "Why would anyone ever agree to let someone else coerce him?" Hobbes provides a simple and straightforward answer: Because it's often in our interest to have others exercise coercive power over us.

In this way, Hobbes provides a justification for state power that avoids the troublesome language of good and evil. Yet in changing the argument for state power, he also changes, rather dramatically, the *practical forms* of state power that can be justified. Whereas the intellectual tradition that culminated in scholasticism is inclined to view legal compulsion as merely the enforcement of morality, Hobbes's view of law is necessarily going to be more constrained. To the extent that people disagree about moral questions, or about the nature of the good, they are unlikely to transfer the power to impose a single conception to the state. So, despite his ideological commitment to absolutism, Hobbes winds up laying out the basic architectonic for the idea of *limited government*, and of *constitutionalism* (ideas that found fuller expression in the work of Locke). The thought is that individuals start out with a set of "natural rights," some but not all of which they transfer to the sovereign, which then constitutes the power of the legal authority. The "social contract" is what specifies the rights that are surrendered and those that are not. This contract is then codified, taking the form of a *constitution*, the central function of which is to distinguish the domains of action in which the state may exercise legitimate power from those in which it may not. A central feature of such a constitution will be a *bill of rights*, which enumerates the domains in which individuals have not surrendered their natural rights, and thus, where the state may not legitimately regulate conduct. In domains that are not subject to constitutional protection, the state may make *laws* that constrain individual behavior.

This conception of limited government is undoubtedly the most powerful and influential idea in the liberal tradition. It is present in Hobbes's work *in nuce*— but only as elaborated by subsequent generations of explicitly liberal thinkers, and with the uptake it received in the American and French revolutions, did it become the basic template for the construction of a modern liberal state. Yet even in Hobbes's work one can see the force of the social contract idea, which pressed in the direction of limited government, beginning to be felt. Although Hobbes was an absolutist, the structure of his argument required that the sovereign exercise power only as an *agent* of the citizens, and so for any given power, it was necessary to tell some story about why people would have seen fit to surrender it. Generally speaking, Hobbes makes the case for this simply by appealing to the horrors of civil war and claiming that anything short of a total surrender of rights will lead inevitably to that outcome. In some cases, however, even that seemed dubious to him. An example would be the death penalty, which under social contract theory began to seem problematic in a way it never had before. The ancient Greeks found it perfectly self-evident that the state should have the power to kill its own citizens—so much so that they never even discussed the issue. (Plato's *Crito*, for instance, is focused on the question whether Socrates is obliged to submit to the death sentence that has been imposed upon him by the

Athenians, but the question of the legitimacy of the punishment never arises.) Medieval thinking worried about it occasionally, but only because of the prima facie tension between executions and the fifth commandment ("thou shalt not kill"). This is why canon law traditionally featured the absence of capital punishment. But no one ever doubted that the monarch or magistrate should be able to impose the death penalty; the question was just how this could be reconciled with Christian morality.

With Hobbes, the concern that it might be *illegitimate* for the state to kill its subjects arises for the first time. This is a thought that could only make sense if one endorses the idea of limited government, because it is only when one thinks that state power is somehow constrained—that there is a "line" the state must not cross—that one can begin to wonder whether a particular power falls on one or the other side of the line. If the state possesses only those powers that individuals would unanimously agree to surrender in a social contract, and their motive for entering into such a contract is their own advantage, then it is not entirely obvious that they would want to grant the sovereign the power to execute them. Hobbes does ultimately think that it would be in their interest—without the power to "overawe" his subjects, the commands of the sovereign will not be respected—but the point is that, for the first time, an *argument* needs to be provided to justify the use of state power that finds expression in the imposition of the death penalty. Furthermore, while Hobbes argues that transferring the power of life and death to the sovereign is rational *ex ante*, when the sovereign actually tries to use this power he cannot expect those he targets to comply willingly. As a subject, once the sentence of execution is passed, one cannot be obliged to go willingly to one's own death—because there is no longer any advantage to be had in respecting the terms of the social contract. Hobbes allows, therefore, that one is entitled to kick and scream as one is dragged to the gallows.[30] This is, as it were, a right that one can never be thought to have surrendered—or as we would now say, an "inalienable right."

The latter point may seem like little more than an amusing aside, but in fact the distance between this Hobbesian conception of inalienable rights and the Enlightenment conception—the one that can be found in the American Bill of Rights and the French Declaration of the Rights of Man and of the Citizen— is not that large. The important component missing in Hobbes's conception of rights is that he does not consider them to be *justiciable*. To the extent that they are individual rights, which one possesses in the state of nature, Hobbes thinks that getting other people to respect those rights is also something that is up to individuals, using whatever resources would be available to them in the state of nature. This is why one is able to kick and scream on the way to the gallows, but not to file an appeal with the courts. Because Hobbes thinks that all social cooperation is made possible by the sovereign, there is no way that one can appeal to other people to assist in securing one's rights *against* the sovereign.

Authority is completely undivided in Hobbes's scheme, and so there are only two forces, the will of the sovereign—which encompasses all possible modes of social cooperation—and the will of isolated individuals. Even if individuals retain certain natural rights after entering the civil condition, these rights are not worth much, because individuals must rely on their own force for the defense of these rights.

All this changes with the development of two very closely linked ideas: the *rule of law* and the *division of powers*. One of the central features of Hobbes's theory was that he subscribed to a "command" theory of law, according to which legal rules were essentially just an expression of the sovereign's will. There was, however, an older tradition, dating back to Aristotle at least, which tried to understand law on the model of social norms, as a set of standing rules governing the community, from which the sovereign could add or subtract, but which maintained their authority independent of the will of the sovereign. (This would explain, for instance, how the laws might remain in force even with the death of the king.) As such, the idea was not terribly consequential, but it became much more important once the suggestion was made that there might be a division of labor within the state, with one "branch" of government responsible solely for administering and applying existing laws and another branch responsible for making changes. In England, of course, this was not so much a suggestion as an acknowledgement of how things were, since "the common law"—which was, in effect, a body of law assembled by judges over the course of centuries—was the older and dominant tradition, with the phenomenon of "statutory law" being a more recent innovation. When combined with the idea of natural rights, however, the arrangement became extremely powerful, because it led to the suggestion that if the legislature takes some action that impinges upon an individual's rights, the individual might appeal to the judiciary to defend those rights, and to declare the legislative decision void. This makes individual rights justiciable, in the sense that individuals can go to the courts seeking defense of them.

As a result, with the introduction of the division of powers, and the idea of an independent judiciary, the concept of inalienable natural rights, which is something of a residual category in Hobbes's framework, suddenly becomes extremely consequential. One can see this clearly in Locke, who posits a "right of resistance" against a legislature that oversteps its authority and violates the natural rights of individuals. This, in turn, makes the idea of limited government much more important. Hobbes created the blueprint for a system of limited government, but in his framework, the limits are purely conceptual, there is nothing that can limit the power of the sovereign *in practice* (other than individual resistance). The introduction of a division of powers creates the possibility of institutionalizing these conceptual limitations, creating a state that is limited not just conceptually, but is also self-limiting in practice. This finds expression in the idea, given its canonical formulation by Montesquieu, that the different branches of government might serve to check one another, to prevent abuses of political authority (or that "power must check power by the arrangement of things"[31]). In other words, we might divide up state powers, not for convenience, or to get the benefits of a division of labor, but to preserve individual freedom.

The modern liberal schema, in which the state is thought of as divided into three branches—the legislative, the executive, and the judicial—is a descendant of Montesquieu's framework. The objective is to separate out the power to make laws (legislature), to interpret and apply those laws (judiciary), and to implement or enforce these decisions (executive):

> When legislative power is united with executive power in a single person or in a single body of the magistracy, there is no liberty, because one can fear that the same monarch or senate that makes tyrannical laws will execute them tyrannically. Nor is there liberty if the power of judging is not separate from legislative power and from executive power. If it were joined to legislative power, the power over the life and liberty of citizens would be arbitrary, for the judge would be the legislator. If it were joined to the executive power, the judge could have the force of an oppressor.[32]

What is important is not just the separation of legislative from judicial functions. It is that the power to use actual force is sequestered in the executive— thus the police, the military, and the penal system are all part of the executive branch. This means that for the state to coerce someone, all three branches must be aligned: the legislature must pass a law, the judiciary must accept it, and the executive must enforce it.

One can see here the defining ideas of modern constitutionalism, where the purpose of the constitution is to provide an authoritative statement of the *limits* of state power, both in terms of its scope and the way in which it is to be exercised—the former in terms of an enumerated list of individual rights, the latter in terms of a statement of the division of powers. The tradition of modern constitutionalism is one that has become so familiar, and so influential, that we struggle sometimes to see how historically anomalous and, in some ways, peculiar it is. Perhaps its most important feature is that it introduces a distinction between morality and law. In a liberal political order, the mere fact that something is immoral, or even harmful to others, does not mean that it should be illegal—or even that it can be made illegal. Whether it is subject to legal regulation depends on whether the power to suppress that particular form of conduct falls within the scope of legitimate state power. Similarly, the fact that an action is morally obligatory does not mean that the *state* has an obligation to do it, or to make people do it.

Edmund Burke articulated this distinction quite clearly, in his insistence that the government not provide "relief" or food aid to the poor in times of famine. In his "Thoughts and Details on Scarcity," presented to William Pitt in 1785, he argued that even though "charity to the poor is a direct and obligatory duty upon all Christians," this does not mean that it falls within the "province" of the magistrate.[33] On the contrary, provision of poor relief by the magistrate would be "a violation of the property which it is his office to protect." Thus he encouraged Pitt "manfully to resist" the idea "that it is within the competence of Government, taken as Government" to supply the poor with "those necessities which it has pleased the Divine Providence for a while to with-hold from them."[34]

One can see quite clearly here the feature of liberalism that many people find profoundly counterintuitive. We are inclined to think that if provision of food aid is "the right thing to do," or if it is morally obligatory, then "society" ought to do it. If we imagine the state as simply the organized representative of "society," then it would seem to follow that that state should do it. Liberalism, however, makes the rather surprising suggestion that the state not only may have no obligation to do it, but may be positively prohibited from doing so. Whether or not one agrees with Burke's specific application of this principle should not be allowed to distract from its novelty and significance. Although our political culture has become more sympathetic to the provision of food aid over the years, there are many cases in which liberal societies have been highly resistant to the legal enforcement of obligations arising from "private morality."

This feature of liberalism, however, has tended to become obscured by the modern discourse of "human rights," which typically blurs the distinction between "rights" and "goods." The liberal conception of rights, the distinction between morality and law, and the concept of limited government are all rather counterintuitive political arrangements. The idea that political leaders who possess enormous power might voluntarily refrain from using it, even when there is nothing obviously stopping them, seems unlikely to many people. Limited government involves a form of self-restraint on the part of the powerful that is, in the broad sweep of human history, a rather improbable accomplishment. Similarly, the idea of rights as protections against state interference is neither anodyne nor self-evident. Rights protect individuals who want to say and do despicable things, and that may foreseeably result in harm to others. They offer legal protection for certain forms of immoral behavior, on the grounds that the behavior falls outside the scope of legitimate state action.

This is why liberalism is an unintuitive political arrangement, and why it has always been necessary to make the case for it. Perfectionism and perfectionist ideas are in many ways much more natural. In fact, around the world, in every major civilization, some form of perfectionism represents the older, indigenous strain of political thinking.[35] This may be because perfectionism takes the resources that we use to organize small-scale communities and attempts to scale them up, to apply them at the level of the nation-state. Liberalism, by contrast, has no correlates at the small-scale or community level, and so it is extremely non-obvious, as a template for the organization of human society.

3.3. The triumph of classical liberalism

Given the evident peculiarity of certain liberal ideas, as well as the fanciful character of the "state of nature"—which was the standard way of motivating both modern constitutionalism and individual rights doctrines during the Age of Enlightenment—one might wonder how this way of thinking came to exercise such enormous influence in the world. The short answer is that it produced societies that were extremely successful, in several different dimensions. In other words, it was not so much the intellectual appeal of liberalism, or the supposed "self-evidence" of its fundamental postulates, that led to its emulation. It was the fact that liberal societies became both wealthy and powerful, in large part *because* they were liberal. Most obviously, liberalism provided something very close to a definitive resolution to the problem of religious warfare. But it also laid the foundations for the development of what we would call the "modern" state, able to exercise genuine control over its entire territory. This included, for instance, the power to impose universal conscription, and the power to directly tax all real property—both of which dramatically increased the organizational capacity of the state. And finally, liberalism somewhat inadvertently gave rise to capitalism—or the coordination of economic activity through a relatively autonomous market—which dramatically increased the wealth of liberal societies.

The formula that proved so successful was that of the "minimal" state, in which the government was only involved in a very narrow range of activities—areas in which one could imagine the grant of power from citizens being unanimous. David Hume provided the canonical articulation of this conception of the state with a list of three "goods" that the liberal state may legitimately provide: security, property, and contract:[36]

1. *Security.* This is perhaps the most obvious good. While there are benefits to be had from being able to commit acts of aggression against others, the disadvantages associated with everyone else doing the same are enormous. It seems unproblematic to assume that a renunciation of the *private use of force* would be in everyone's interest, leaving it the responsibility of the state to provide security for all. Thus what would later become the Weberian definition of the state—the institution "that (successfully) claims the *monopoly*

of the legitimate use of physical force within a given territory"[37]—was established as an important *normative* idea in the early liberal tradition.

2. *Property.* This is less obvious, particularly property in land, since partitioning up the entire territory and allocating it once and for all to individuals, under a system of inheritable property rights, foreseeably results in some individuals getting shut out of the allocation. This gives rise to a serious question about how such a system could ever attract universal consent. The central response to this was the *labor theory of value*, defended most influentially by Locke, who argued that since all property gets its value from the labor invested in it, no one is ever entirely shut out of the system, because each is born possessing his own labor power. The case for property in land then involved a rather subtle argument, based on the claim that private ownership of land produces superior incentives for improvement, which, in turn, raises the productivity of labor, so that even those born without land were nevertheless better off than under a system of common ownership.[38]

3. *Contract.* Finally, there is the enforcement of contracts. We have already seen in the discussion of Hobbes how it can be mutually advantageous for individuals to be able to enter into enforceable agreements. What is original to liberalism is the insistence that the state's role in this should be limited to enforcing the will of the parties, whatever that will happens to be. A contract should be enforced, according to this view, merely because it was entered into in the correct way, without coercion, etc.[39] The state has no role in assessing the merits of what was agreed to, or determining whether the terms of the contract are "fair" to all parties. Thus, the liberal doctrine of contract involved a commitment to what Weber would later call "legal formalism."[40]

To refer to property, security, and contract as "goods" provided by the state is, of course, to risk blurring the distinction between a liberal state and a perfectionist order. This, at one level, is merely a reflection of the fact that evaluative vocabulary is expressively quite robust, and so almost any norm can be described as involving a commitment to some "good" or "value." Yet there appears to be an important difference between a state that is committed to promoting a list of virtues, of the sort that Aristotle provided, and a state that is committed to providing physical security, defending property rights, and enforcing contracts. It is not just that the latter type of state is doing *less*, it is that the "goods" it is promoting are far less *specific* than the ones promoted by a perfectionist state. They are, one is tempted to say, goods that individuals can be expected to value regardless of their more specific conceptions of the good.

Consider, for instance, the question at the heart of the fundamental disagreement that divided Protestants and Catholics: Is the good life one that involves quiet contemplation and prayer, in an environment isolated from the concerns of everyday life, or does the good life require engagement with the world, and success in practical affairs? It would seem that, whatever one's ultimate view on this question, there are still significant benefits to be had from living in a society in which the state guarantees one's personal security, one's property, and the integrity of one's contracts. The current way of framing this contrast is to suggest that the liberal state strives to pursue objectives that are *neutral* with respect to the particular conceptions of the good adhered to by its citizens. At the risk of some confusion, the list of state activities enumerated by Hume can be described as the pursuit of "neutral goods." (As we shall see, many modern liberals drop this formulation, choosing instead a more deontological mode of expression, according to which the state is governed by normative *principles* that are, in some sense, neutral with respect to the various conflicting conceptions of the good at play in the society.)

It is important to be clear about what this concept of neutrality entails, since it has attracted a measure of criticism.[41] A commitment to state neutrality does not require some sort of "view from nowhere," or a basis for determining state objectives that is independent of what individuals happen to value. Liberal neutrality is not equivalent to normative neutrality. What it means for a particular state objective to be neutral is that one can justify it without having to affirm the correctness of any particular controversial conception of the good.[42] This does not prevent one, however, from making certain presuppositions about human value. To claim that security is a neutral good, for instance, is still to make certain presuppositions about what individuals want. This much is clear from the social contract thought experiment, because the motivation that people have for entering the civil condition is that it allows them to better promote their own good. The commitment to neutrality, in this case, falls out of the unanimity criterion, whereby *everyone* must agree to surrender a power for it to be transferred to the state. Locke, for instance, argues for religious toleration on the grounds that imposition of a single religious view could never attract universal agreement, given the disagreements that exist over religious questions. On the contrary, he claims, it is protection from such imposition that would be agreed upon: "For force from a stronger hand to bring a man to a religion, which another thinks to be true, being an injury which in the state of nature everyone would avoid, protection from such injury is one of the ends of commonwealth, and so every man has a right to toleration."[43] The key inference is from the claim that a particular injury is one that "everyone would avoid" to the conclusion that limiting it becomes one of the "ends" that government may legitimately promote.

One can imagine that, in different cultural contexts, in which circumstances are different, the list of powers that might attract unanimity could differ. It follows that what is considered "neutral" in one society might not be considered neutral in another. For instance, other social contract theorists, including both Hobbes and Rousseau, thought that the state could enforce a "civic religion," because they considered it essential to public order that there be *some* shared religion. Thus, they wanted the state to distill out an extremely abstract essence of Christianity, or a very basic set of rites, to be publicly promoted, but then leave all further details as matters of individual conscience. Given the need for a shared religion, they claimed, a proposal to establish a set of public religious institutions could attract unanimous approval. Since that time, however, estimates of the indispensability of a shared religion have changed, leading most liberals to want to further constrain the role of the state in religious matters, and in many cases, to endorse either a strict separation of church and state or else a commitment to public secularism. The idea that there must be a civic religion, which is in some way neutral toward the specific sects, has largely passed away.

In this respect, the minimal state sets out to do *less* than its feudal or ancien regime forebearers had. It is important to recognize, however, that a state that sets out to do less is not necessarily weaker than a state that sets out to do more—it very much depends on how well it accomplishes its aim. And it is also worth noting that during the high-water mark of Enlightenment liberalism, there was a significant withdrawal of the state from many domains in which it had traditionally been involved. This was particularly noticeable in Great Britain, where "as late as 1880, the British state was chiefly notable for its virtual absence from broad areas of social and economic life."[44] At the same time, by eliminating some of the major sources of internal discord, and providing a governing ideology more broadly acceptable to the population, liberal states became capable of organizing more concerted collective action. So even though *intellectually* the liberal state seemed to lack a powerful source of unity (viz., a shared conception of the good), in practice it wound up creating much greater unity. More importantly, liberal thinking served as a powerful source of disintermediation in the relationship between individuals and the state, which wound up—somewhat counterintuitively—dramatically increasing the power of central governments.

It is important, when looking back on hierarchically organized societies, feudal ones in particular, not to imagine that they were like modern bureaucracies, in which there is a clear chain of command and any superior has authority over any subordinate. Medieval hierarchies are better understood on the model of a recursive application of a basic relationship of personal loyalty and subordination between two individuals. Thus, if one were a peasant, it was entirely clear what was owed to one's local (or "liege") lord, but beyond that, things became much less clear, and there were at various times active debates about what was owed to those with authority over one's lord, such as the king. At many points in time, the answer was "nothing." This meant that to make something happen at the lower levels of the hierarchy, the king was usually not in a position to issue direct commands to the occupants of those levels. He was obliged to pass the command down to his immediate subordinate (or "vassal"), who would then decide whether to pass it down to his own subordinate, and so on. Obviously, there were many ways that this arrangement could break down, and the king had very limited powers of enforcement when it did. Thus "the king of France in the tenth and eleventh centuries was indeed the nominal lord over the great feudal princes, but he had no real power over the dukes and counts who were his vassals because he was not the liege lord over their subvassals . . . The duke of Normandy had a much better army than the king had, and the Norman knights did not recognize the king as their overlord in any way."[45]

Under the ancien regime, this showed up most clearly in two areas: the conscription of soldiers and the collection of taxes.[46] Generally speaking, the king had no power to raise an army, he instead had to rely on the local nobility, who could conscript peasants from their land. Since there was no census, or even inspectors to send around, only the local lord was in a position even to know how many men were available for recruitment. Taxation similarly relied upon a great deal of local knowledge, which the central state did not possess.[47] This is one reason for the heavy reliance on customs and excise taxes—trade was one of the few areas in which the center had adequate information, because it could control key ports and waterways. It is also why kings often relied on borrowed money and mercenaries to fight their wars—these were the only funds and manpower that they could access directly, without having to go through the (often uncooperative) nobility.

Social contract theory reconceptualizes public authority, positing a direct relationship between the individual and the state, not mediated by any of the traditional institutions of feudal society. As a result, the center acquired much greater direct control over individuals. By abolishing all the intermediate institutions and traditional power structures of feudal society, liberal egalitarianism wound up, perhaps paradoxically, increasing the power of the state. The clearest example of this is seen in the development of universal conscription, one of the great legacies of the French Revolution (beginning with the *levée générale* of 1793). Napoleon was able to conquer most of Europe, not because of any technological or tactical superiority, but rather because of the superior organizational capacity of the French state, not least its power to impose universal male conscription upon the population, which made it possible for Napoleon to field massive armies. Napoleon's success in turn pushed neighboring states to adopt a more liberal model, either directly, by having it imposed upon them by Napoleon, or indirectly, under the pressure to achieve similar organizational outcomes to defend themselves militarily.[48]

The second important consequence of liberalism is that it gave rise, almost accidentally, to capitalism. This is largely a consequence of the separation of law and morality that liberalism introduced, along with the development of legal formalism, particularly in the area of contracts. Economic transactions, in particular, the prices at which goods were exchanged, had always been subject to moral evaluation. The doctrine of the "just price," from Aristotle through Aquinas, had developed largely in response to the intuition that it is immoral to charge too much or offer too little for goods (including labor). In a perfectionist political order, in which the law is nothing other than the enforcement of morality, this led naturally to the extensive legal regulation of the prices at which goods could be exchanged (regulations that were imposed either by the state, or by agencies with the delegated power to do so, such as guilds). As a result, it was impossible for competitive markets to emerge, or for the price system to be used as a way to improve the allocation of goods and labor. So there was trade, but it was nothing resembling what we would now call a market economy.

All this changes when the state adopts a more formal approach to contract enforcement. If two people agree to the exchange of certain goods at a certain price, and enter into a contract, then a liberal political order is committed to enforcing that contract, regardless of the specific terms that the parties agreed to. So when adjudicating a commercial dispute, judges in a liberal society are no longer encouraged to ask, "Is this a just price?"; instead, they are urged to focus strictly on the voluntariness of the contract. In perfectionist societies, by contrast, the legal system tends to be either too much involved, or too little involved, in commercial affairs. Abstractly, the idea that the state should enforce private contracts is not entirely obvious. If one person cheats another person, why does this concern the state? What does it have to do with the good? If one person blasphemes, then the public interest is obvious. But if one person cheats another? The *public* interest there is not so obvious. Yet to the extent that it is possible to make the case for state involvement, there will be a tendency to want to evaluate the transaction in substantive terms. Were the terms of the contract just? If not, was the person right to violate it? The idea that the state should *merely* enforce the contract, whatever its terms, is highly unintuitive.

In other words, within a perfectionist political order, making the case for state involvement in private contracting involves showing that there is a good at stake in the transaction. But if there is some good involved in the transaction, then it stands to reason that adjudication should involve direct enforcement of that good. What liberalism introduces is the rather novel idea that what the state should be enforcing is merely the *ex ante* will of the parties—regardless of whether the outcome conforms to any substantive conception of the good.

Similarly, liberalism is what permitted the emergence of so-called free labor. Technically, labor is "free" when the absence of the worker from his or her place of employment is not regarded as a criminal matter (and so employers could not compel workers to perform, or imprison them for abandoning their employment).[49] Much of this was due to the way that liberal thinking disaggregated the feudal concept of "dominion" into two distinct ideas: that of private property and of political sovereignty.[50] Locke was an important influence in this transition, which led to the suggestion that a ruler might exercise legal and political jurisdiction over members of the working class, without at the same time having the right to dispose over their labor power. Thinking of labor in terms of property rights controlled by the individual, and thus as freely contracted, is an important precondition for the emergence of a labor market, since it is only once workers are free to quit their jobs that differences in the wage rate being offered can begin to direct labor to its best employment.

The market economy is sometimes described, by its more enthusiastic advocates, as a "moral-free zone," where not only does the invisible hand relieve people of the obligation to exhibit moral constraint in their actions, but where the smooth operation of the price mechanism actually precludes a lot of everyday cooperative behavior.[51] This is an exaggeration. It is, however, true that to get a competitive market up and running, people must be willing to set aside some of the concern for others that tends to be encouraged by everyday morality. And so, to the extent that the legal order is saturated with moral constraints, there will be formidable legal obstacles to the emergence of a market economy. It was by evacuating the law of a great deal of its moral content, and by focusing on formal statuses, such as property deeds and signed contracts, that liberalism created the space within which internal markets could develop. This in turn led to dramatic improvements in economic efficiency.

I am emphasizing these points because I think it is important not to be overly intellectualistic about the successes of liberalism. Just because the American Declaration of Independence starts out by proclaiming certain truths to be self-evident, it does not mean that people who gravitate toward the American model of governance also find those propositions to be self-evident, or even terribly persuasive. In many cases, they accept them merely because doing so seems to be a necessary precondition for duplicating certain attractive features of the American polity, such as the standard of living of its people. Indeed, there have been many attempts to duplicate the successes of capitalism without reproducing the liberal political order—many of them failures, although the jury is still out on several others.

There is, however, a great deal of confusion on this score, often exacerbated by theorists who try to identify one or more "values" as serving as the foundation for liberal societies. This tends to suggest that the spread of liberal ideas was a consequence of the attractiveness of these values—as opposed to the attractiveness of the "outputs" of liberal political institutions and the social orders that they created. It tends also to obscure or diminish the major accomplishment of liberal societies, which is that they have been able to produce a stable political order under conditions of value pluralism. Too often, the "values" that are posited as the foundation of liberalism are actually just thinly veiled redescriptions of liberal principles, and so are not really values in the strict sense of being "conceptions of the good." The commitment to "free speech," for instance, or the "free exchange of ideas," is best described not as a value, but rather as a prohibition on the imposition of value-based restrictions on speech.

In other cases, the values that are posited as essential commitments of liberalism are actually epiphenomenal, or merely by-products, of liberal institutions. For instance, some form of commitment to "individualism" or "autonomy" is often posited as a fundamental liberal value.[52] And certainly, there can be no question that liberal societies are, in some sense of the term, individualistic, and that they promote individual autonomy. The question is whether or not these "values" drive the adoption of liberal political institutions, or whether they are a consequence of those institutions.[53] The analysis that I have been presenting here suggests that they are by-products. What the classical liberal theorists were primarily concerned about was imposing limits on the scope of state power, not so that individuals could be given free rein to develop their faculties, but in order to pacify armed conflict and prevent civil war. The social contract thought experiment was a way of motivating this arrangement, with the suggestion that there were certain powers that individuals would have no interest in surrendering to the state. Thus, a line gets drawn between the "public" and the "private" in liberal thinking. But this has nothing to do with a sudden valuation of the private sphere; it is driven by a desire to impose limits on public authority. The fact that this creates a sphere of individual freedom is merely a downstream consequence.

Thus, the focus on individualism as the foundation of liberalism is highly misleading, for two reasons. First, there is the fact that the background culture in European societies was already highly individualistic. In the broad scope of human affairs, the primary alternative to individualism is not communalism, but rather familialism, and it was Christianity that broke the back of familialism in Europe, not liberalism. Christianity destroyed the ancestor cult of Roman families, undermined the authority of the *paterfamilias*, eliminated the tribalism of Judaism, promoted celibacy among the priesthood, and made salvation a one-on-one relationship between the sinner and God.[54] Christianity assigns no moral status to the family at all—indeed, Jesus encouraged his disciples to abandon their families, and gave them new "apostolic" names in part to symbolize the break. And yet all of this individualism—much of it quite revolutionary—had no tendency to produce liberal political orders. Indeed, historians of ideas have had an easy time showing that the "individualistic" values supposedly associated with liberal societies long predate the rise of liberalism in the West.[55]

Second, there is the fact that early liberal and Enlightenment thinkers had little to say about the individual, and seldom appealed to the importance of individual freedom or personal autonomy when making the case for their preferred political arrangements. Hobbes's introduction of the social contract thought experiment—by far the most important framework for liberal political thinking—was motivated by his desire to develop a normative theory of the state that would minimize armed conflict and civil war, not by a desire to valorize the individual. Even Locke, whose "rights" framework is in many ways quite individualistic, has nothing laudatory to say about the individual. The exception that proves the rule is perhaps Wilhelm von Humboldt, who in 1792 wrote *The Limits of State Action*, which does explicitly appeal to the value of the individual as an argument for limits on state power.[56] The fact that Humboldt's argument was regarded as something of a novelty reveals the extent to which earlier liberal writers were not relying upon a direct appeal to individualism to make the case for their views. Indeed, Humboldt's argument received little uptake until seventy years later, when John Stuart Mill drew upon it in *On Liberty* to argue against state paternalism. All of this lends support to the suggestion that a commitment to individualism was never really *driving* the liberal project; that the valorization of "private life," which became more pronounced in Europe beginning in the late 18th century, was rather a *consequence* of political liberalism.

Much the same could be said for the liberal commitment to equality. There is a highly simplistic view of political history, which says that people used to think everyone was unequal, but one day they opened their eyes and realized that, as a matter of fact, "all men are created equal" (and that, a century or so later, they began to realize that women might be equal as well). Although the language of equality figures much more prominently in liberal political writing—unlike individualism, of which there is practically no explicit articulation—serious doubts can be raised about how much work it actually did in driving the liberal project. The appeal to equality obviously figured prominently in the French Revolution, both in the revolutionary slogan *liberté, égalité, fraternité,* and in the Declaration of the Rights of Man and Citizen. Yet even then, the Declaration put much greater emphasis on the idea of imposing limits on state power. Furthermore, the excesses of the French Revolution tended to diminish the prestige of the ideal of equality. Thus, for instance, the gradual dismantling of class privileges that occurred in Britain during the first half of the 19th century occurred under the banner of "disinterestedness"—the idea that the state should not take sides in favor of some people's interests against others—rather than equality.[57] And, of course, the persistence of slavery in the United States until 1865 made something of a mockery of the commitment to equality in that nation.

Finally, and perhaps most importantly, it is essential to recognize that there is no sense in which liberal ideas are derived from Christianity or depend upon any aspect of the Christian religion for their justification. Liberalism arose against a background culture that was Christian, but as we have seen, it was motivated primarily by the inability of Christians to resolve their doctrinal disputes, and the enormous hardship wrought by the tendency to enlist the state on one side or another of the resultant conflicts. In this respect, liberalism arose as a remedy for Christian intolerance. Similarly, the doctrine of individual rights is sometimes portrayed as an outgrowth of Christian thinking. Yet it is difficult to see how this could be. In over a thousand years of reflection on political topics, from Augustine's *City of God* through the works of the Renaissance, Christian thinkers never once suggested that individuals might have "rights" in anything like the sense in which Hobbes, Locke, and Rousseau would use that term. Indeed, the suggestion that certain forms of immoral behavior should enjoy legal protection is extremely foreign to the Christian sensibility. And again, it is worth recalling that toleration of religious difference was itself condemned as a heresy by Christian thinkers, and thus, declared to be intolerable.

It is, therefore, very misleading to think that the triumph of liberal ideas was due to a shift in European *values*. This way of framing the development tends to portray it as a cultural phenomenon. The important innovation in the classical liberal political project was not cultural, it was a structural idea about constraining the use of state power, limiting its employment to areas in which everyone could agree to surrender his or her natural rights. This is best articulated using the language of *neutrality,* which is perhaps the closest one can find to a single, guiding normative idea in liberal thought.[58]

3.4. The decline of classical liberalism

Given the evident success of liberal societies, not to mention the "long peace" that prevailed in Europe from the end of the Napoleonic Wars in 1815 until the outbreak of the First World War in 1914, one of the most puzzling features of 19th- and early 20th-century European history is the decline of liberalism as a political philosophy and the growing appeal of totalitarianism, a tendency that culminated in the Second World War, which despite some involvement of the democratic states, was primarily a conflict fought between rival totalitarian states: fascist Germany and the communist Soviet Union. Indeed, it was this vivid illustration of the dangers of totalitarianism that led to the great resurgence of liberal thinking in the postwar era—it is certainly not an accident that two of the greatest 20th-century liberal theorists had been soldiers in that war (John Rawls served in the US military in the Pacific, and witnessed firsthand the consequences of the atomic blast at Hiroshima; Jürgen Habermas was indoctrinated into the Hitler Youth, and sent to the front at age fifteen, just a few months before the war ended.) As a result, there is a sense in which contemporary political philosophy is much closer in spirit to the thinking of the 18th century than it is to that of the 19th. Indeed, much of what happened in the late 19th century and early 20th century, with the rise of fascism and revolutionary communism, not to mention the vituperative denunciations of liberalism that become surprisingly common on both right and left, has become quite opaque, even mysterious, to the modern observer.

For example, to read Nietzsche's enthusiastic defense of the "spirit of war," and his critique of liberalism *on the grounds that it dampens that spirit*, is to be transported to an intellectual milieu that is both deeply foreign and shockingly irresponsible:

> Sometimes the value of a thing is not what you get with it but what you pay for it,—what it *costs*. Here is an example. Liberal institutions stop being liberal as soon as they have been attained: after that, nothing damages freedom more terribly or more thoroughly than liberal institutions. Of course people know *what* these institutions do: they undermine the will to power, they set to work levelling mountains and valleys and call this morality, they make things small, cowardly, and enjoyable,—they represent the continual triumph of herd animals. Liberalism: *herd animalization*, in other words . . . As long as they are still being fought for, these same institutions have entirely different effects and are actually powerful promoters of freedom. On closer inspection it is the war that produces these effects, the war *for* liberal institutions . . . war is what teaches people to be free . . . Freedom means that the manly instincts which take pleasure in war and victory have gained control over the other instincts, over the instinct of 'happiness,' for instance. People who have *become free* . . . wipe their shoes on the miserable type of well-being that grocers, Christians, cows, females, Englishmen, and other democrats dream about.[59]

Modern readers sometimes dismiss a passage of this sort as a rhetorical flourish, or a consequence of Nietzsche's declining mental state. Yet sentiments like these were not at all unusual in the late 19th century. Nietzsche's work received an enthusiastic reception at its time of publication, and his keenness for war was by no means exceptional. Support for the First World War was nearly unanimous among the intellectual classes in Germany at the onset, as it was in France and throughout the British Empire. Furthermore, one can find Nietzsche's ideas about the importance of war being picked up and crafted into a more detailed political philosophy by Carl Schmitt, who became one of the major intellectual defenders of the Third Reich.

Anti-liberalism was prevalent not just on the right wing of the political spectrum. As Stephen Holmes has observed, "In Europe during the 1920s and 1930s implacable hostility to liberalism was the one attitude on which extreme rightists and extreme leftists could agree."[60] Karl Marx, in particular, had been an uncompromising critic. Most of his attacks were focused on the idea of individual rights (or, as he put it, "the so-called rights of man"), which he took to be nothing more than an ideology, a sort of collective fantasy, created to mask the relations of exploitation that existed in the exchange of labor power for wages. Liberalism, in his view, served exactly the same function under capitalism that Christianity had under feudalism—it provided a set of rationalizations needed to maintain the structures of exploitation in the society. The concept of agreement in a "state of nature" through a "social contract" was, in his view, a construct that played the same role for the industrial proletariat that the promise of "eternal life" and admission to "heaven" did for medieval peasants. The way to deal with it, he thought, was not to engage with it intellectually, but rather to overthrow the material conditions that made it necessary to entertain such fantasies. And since the latter would invariably require the use of force, there is a very clear sense in which Marx encouraged his followers to take up violence as an alternative to argumentation as a way of resolving political disputes. The justice of their actions would become apparent only retrospectively, within the intellectual framework that would emerge *after* the revolution.

Thus, it is not entirely surprising that the 20th century saw the emergence of both right-wing and left-wing totalitarian states. After all, what made these states "totalitarian" is precisely the fact that they rejected the liberal principle of limited government, and thus rescinded the distinction between "public" and "private." This went hand-in-hand with a rejection of the idea of individual rights, and an undoing of the numerous procedural safeguards of these rights that liberal societies had developed over the years (including, in many cases, the right to a trial as a prelude to punishment). Indeed, the distinction between totalitarian societies and ones that are merely authoritarian, or dictatorial, is that totalitarianism seeks to abolish entirely the distinction between public and private life. "Every aspect of a person's life is politicized under totalitarian rule, whether this be in the areas of science, economic activity, or family relationships. Nothing is left outside the scope of politics."[61] Thus there is a close connection between the decline of liberalism in the 19th century and the rise of totalitarian states, which dominated the first half of the 20th century—and led European civilization to the moral catastrophe of the Second World War.

There is a temptation, when confronting this troubled period in European history, to treat it as an anomaly, as though Europeans just "went crazy" for a few decades, before settling back into their old routines. This is particularly tempting when one is seeking to explain Nazi Germany and the Holocaust. This tendency, however—to treat totalitarianism as a period of "exception"—is worth resisting, since there were clear intellectual currents that led to its triumph, many of which focused on the weakness of liberalism in its classical form. Most of the European countries that became totalitarian states underwent a period of "weak" liberal government—the Weimar Republic in Germany (1915–1933), the Duma in Russia (1905–1917), and "Liberal Italy" (1861–1922). It was the inability of these governments to manage, in a satisfactory manner, the most pressing issues of the day that sealed their fate. Thus understanding the currents of anti-liberalism that developed in the 19th century is important, not just out of historical interest, but also to understand the rise of the distinctively modern form liberalism has taken in the present day. That is because *modern* liberal thinkers—Rawls in particular—have sought to reform the doctrine in a way that allows them to address the vulnerabilities that led to its decline in the 19th century, and that made totalitarianism seem an attractive alternative to so many people. Modern liberalism must be understood in part as a response to the extremely powerful socialist critique of liberalism that arose in the 19th century.

Here, I would like to pick out two threads of the story—although admittedly a great deal more could be said on the subject. Two developments, however, had the effect of greatly eroding the status of liberalism and, in particular, led many people to regard the liberal fixation on the public/private distinction, and on the limited state, as a weakness rather than a strength of the theory. The first involves the rise of what might be referred to as "liberal morality"—or, at least, secular morality—which began to erode the important distinction early liberal theorists had drawn between morality and politics. By reforming morality, to bring it closer to liberal political principles, Immanuel Kant, Jeremy Bentham and others ended up making the strict separation of the two, which had been the hallmark of liberal thinking, seem much less important. This, in turn, tended to obscure or undermine the force of liberal neutrality. Thus, the idea that the state might take on, as a project, the comprehensive moral reform of society, began to seem much less undesirable.

The second major trend was, ironically, a consequence of liberalism itself. By permitting the development of a capitalist economy, and with it the growing process of industrialization, liberalism wound up creating a vast new range of social problems that it was, in turn, ill-equipped to deal with. This is because the theory of classical liberalism was quite narrowly focused on the state and the uses of state power, and it licensed only a very narrow range of "neutral goods" that the state could provide. As a result, classical liberalism did not have a great deal to say about the economy, other than that people should be free to do whatever they liked, and that government should not intervene. Yet as the economy became a more important feature of public life, many more situations arose that appeared to require some form of organized social response. Classical liberalism not only had nothing to say about this, in many cases, it actively impeded efforts to address the problems. Thus the weaknesses of the theory became increasingly obvious. In the end, liberalism wound up creating a conceptual vacuum, which various forms of socialism then rushed to fill.

The tendency of both these trends was to create a return to "comprehensive" political doctrines, or normative approaches that held out the idea of ordering all of society in accordance with a set of shared moral principles. What Marx derided as "utopian socialism"—which primarily consisted of schemes to re-order political and economic life following the dictates of some form of comprehensive utilitarianism—was the highest expression of this tendency. Indeed, the 19th century was the high-water mark of utopian social planning, which Marx, despite his rhetoric, did a great deal to encourage. Unfortunately, the way that this tendency manifested itself politically was in the form of totalitarianism. The idea that law was nothing but the enforcement of morality created a great deal of mischief during the period in which this was interpreted as an injunction to create a Christian commonwealth. Yet the extent of the damage was limited by the fact that feudal states had very limited organizational capacity—they were simply not able to bring that much force to bear upon the population. The *modern* state, by contrast, was vastly more powerful (several possessed military or police forces that were prepared to murder literally millions of people, for no other reason than that they had been given the order to do so). Thus the removal of all the safeguards that had constrained the use of state power in the modern period resulted in the creation of institutions that were astonishingly dangerous, not just to neighboring states, but to their own citizens.

3.4.1. Liberal morality

To begin with, consider the phenomenon of liberal morality. One of the major differences between the early social contract theorists and their later followers is that the early theorists all subscribed to private moral views that were essentially Christian, and that retained a strong teleological, if not positively Aristotelian, flavor. Certain theorists were clearly unconventional Christians, not to mention deists, and there remains the special case of Baruch Spinoza.[62] The important point, however, is that although early liberals were proposing a radically different way of thinking about the state, one that was purged of traditional perfectionist modes of thought, they were by no means proposing a change in moral thinking. Indeed, many were quite content to endorse the traditional, perfectionist way of thinking about moral questions. One can see the tension quite clearly in Locke's *Second Treatise of Government*, in the section dealing with paternal power. When addressing the question of how the family should be organized (i.e., in the private sphere), Locke does not hesitate to posit a set of "ends" or "intentions" established by "the great Creator," appealing to these teleologically ordered natural relations as the basis of a hierarchy within the family.[63] This casual justification of patriarchal authority is possible only because the "natural order" that Locke posits is doing most of the work. But when it comes to political relations, this Aristotelian mode of thinking is dropped entirely—there is no longer a natural order, or pre-established "ends"; everything is strictly contractual. Indeed, Locke's central criticism of Robert Filmer's *Patriarcha* (in his *First Treatise of Government*) is that Filmer attempts to extend principles from the private realm to the public realm. Locke's acceptance of these principles in the private realm shows why he was so eager to distinguish it from the public realm, and why he had, therefore, no tendency to collapse the moral and the political. The reason is that his moral views, as well as his ideas about how private life should be ordered, were *thoroughly illiberal*. He was what we would now call a strictly *political* liberal, in that his liberal principles applied only to the state.

One of the most striking developments in the late 18th century, however, is the revolution in moral thinking that began with the emergence of both utilitarianism and Kantianism as new ways of thinking about the structure of our moral obligations. Both are secular theories in that they explicitly seek to establish a foundation for morality that is independent of any theistic belief. They are also, in their own ways, liberal moralities. This is most obvious in the case of Kant's "categorical imperative," which is basically an interiorized version of the social contract (most obviously, in the injunction to act as though one were a "legislator in the kingdom of ends").[64] There is a straight line to be drawn between Rousseau's social contract theory, his principle of universalization, and the various formulations of Kant's categorical imperative. Utilitarianism, by contrast, remains somewhat more traditional, in the sense that it maintains an essentially teleological way of thinking about ethics—as action oriented toward the attainment of a good. Where it differs is in how it interprets the good. The crucial innovation in utilitarian thinking lies in its insistence that the common good is nothing but the sum, or the aggregate, of individual goods. This is, again, an attempt to define a common good that will be *neutral* among the various competing conceptions. By giving everyone's "happiness" equal weight in the calculation, the utilitarian cannot be accused of privileging any one view. Bentham's famous claim, that when it comes to happiness, "pushpin is as good as poetry," reflects this underlying commitment to neutrality (one, I should note, that many people found a little bit *too* neutral). The adoption of preference-based conceptions of utility, already apparent in Mill ("the sole evidence it is possible to produce that anything is desirable is that people do actually desire it"[65]) solidified this movement toward neutrality.

It is important to recognize that these developments did not just result in a change in how philosophers thought about our moral commitments; they also generated, over time, a change in what was popularly regarded as right and wrong. Consider, for example, an area like sexual morality, which in its traditional form was a very direct consequence of Aristotelian teleological reasoning. Christians began by asking what the "end" or "purpose" of sexual relations was, or what God had in mind when he created creatures with male and female sex organs. The obvious answer is reproduction. From this, it is not difficult to derive a list of virtues and vices. Virtuous or "natural" forms of sexuality will be all those that are conducive to childbearing and child-rearing, which is to say, sex within heterosexual relationships structured by long-term commitment. Sexual vices, or "unnatural" forms of sexuality, will be all those that are non-procreative. From this we get the traditional catalogue of sexual vice associated with Christian morality: sodomy, fellatio, masturbation, homosexuality, pedophilia, bestiality, contraception, and fornication.

A liberal approach to sexuality, by contrast, instead of taking a conception of the good as its point of departure, assumes that people will disagree about the ultimate purpose, and so focuses on the consensuality of sexual relations. Liberal morality thus takes issue with coercive sexual relations, such as rape and sexual harassment. For example, marital rape, which had never been considered problematic from a perfectionist perspective (on the contrary, it was generally considered the wife's obligation to have sex with her husband, precisely to serve the ends of procreation), begins to show up as an offense, from a liberal perspective. Sexual assault also begins to seem to be more than just an offense against a woman's male relatives. Pedophilia remains prohibited, but for a different reason now, based on the inability of children to consent to sexual relations (rather than their lack of fecundity).

One can see here how consent starts out as a political idea, about what could make an exercise of state power legitimate, but then migrates into the moral realm, to become a more general way of thinking about how relations between individuals should be ordered. Rousseau, in *La Nouvelle Heloise*, articulated the *political* principle that "man is too noble a creature to be used as a mere tool by others. He must not be used for their purposes, without concern also for his own wishes"[66]—an idea that goes on to become *moral* in Kant's second formulation of the categorical imperative, with its injunction to treat humanity as an end, and never as a means only. Yet it is important to recognize that as the conception of morality shifts, in accordance with these ideas about consent, the difference between the political principles governing a liberal state and the private moral convictions of its citizens begins to narrow.

A similar dynamic can be observed among the early utilitarians, who were in many respects the most radical reformers of the 19th century.[67] William Godwin, for instance, was quick to draw the conclusion that the older Christian sexual morality was indefensible, and launched a spirited attack on the idea that sexual relations should be confined to marriage.[68] (Another early utilitarian, Soame

Jenyns noted, somewhat less enthusiastically, that adultery "may bring heirs, and good humour too, into many families, where they would otherwise have been wanting."[69]) Godwin's larger ambition, however, in his *Enquiry Concerning Political Justice*, was to challenge the separation of the political from the moral. In his view, earlier writers had made a great mistake by focusing strictly on the constitution of the government, as opposed to the more general question of the organization of society. In his view, it was the latter that had to be addressed, and with the same set of principles being deployed across all domains. So, while Godwin was clearly a "progressive" writer—as one would expect from the husband of Mary Wollstonecraft—there is also a clear sense in which he rejected the major tenet of political liberalism. Subscribing, as he did, to a thoroughly liberalized morality, he saw no reason the law could not simply be the enforcement of morality. Godwin was, in this respect, representative of a broader trend. As the structure of moral thinking became closer to that of liberal political thinking, people began to lose sight of the motivation for the strict distinction between the moral and the political (see Figure 3.1).[70]

It may be, in hindsight, difficult to see in what way utilitarianism could have posed a deep threat to liberalism. Contemporary utilitarians are almost invariably political liberals as well (e.g., they find some way of incorporating a system of individual rights into their framework), using some form of rule-utilitarian or indirect-strategy consequentialism.[71] But this is in large part a *response* to the experience of totalitarianism in the 20th century, which drove home the importance of those constraints. Early utilitarians, by contrast, were far more radical in their instrumentalism, and their willingness to apply the act-utilitarian calculus. Bentham, after all, had declared the idea of "natural rights" to be "nonsense." Thus, the fact that utilitarianism collapses the distinction between the moral and the political was, in the 19th century, much more apparent. One can see this in the number of strikingly illiberal projects, such as eugenics, that enjoyed widespread support among the more "enlightened" classes during that period. This doctrine acquired a bad name after the Second World War, when the extent of the atrocities perpetrated by the Nazis under the guidance of this ideal became clear—in particular, the fact that they had gone beyond forcible sterilization, and had undertaken mass executions of individuals deemed "defective" or "degenerate." Yet before the war, support for eugenics had been widespread in Europe, receiving the enthusiastic endorsement of Winston Churchill, George Bernard Shaw, John Maynard Keynes, and Sidney Webb, among others. The international eugenics movements began in England and the United States, grounded in a combination of social Darwinism and utilitarianism. Criminality, for instance, was at the time generally thought to be an inherited form of degeneracy, and could therefore be eliminated through selective breeding and sterilization of convicted criminals. Yet eugenics is quite obviously illiberal, contemplating as it

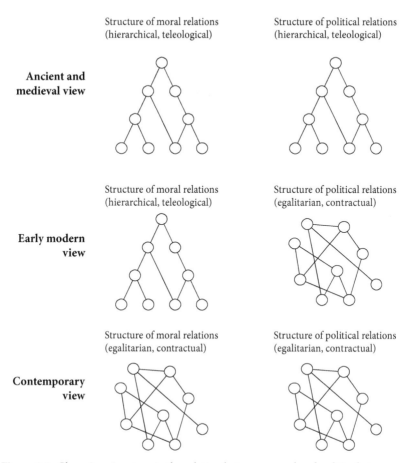

Figure 3.1 Changing structure in the relation between moral and political views.

does state interference in the most private of personal affairs, and abrogation of the individual's right to bodily integrity.

3.4.2. Capitalism

Early social contract theory developed in the context of societies in which almost all wealth was agricultural in origin. This is why Locke, writing in the 17th century, had a great deal to say about the ownership of land (as well as labor), but very little to say about any other form of wealth. Furthermore, because control of land was the basis of the political power of the feudal aristocracy, there was no clear separation between "the state" and "the economy," and so a political theory was also, necessarily, an economic theory. After the separation between political sovereignty and private property became more pronounced, owing in no small measure to Locke's influence, the economy became increasingly detached from the political realm. This tendency was amplified by the industrial revolution and the growth of factory labor, which resulted in large concentrations of wealth developing outside the control of the traditional aristocracy. It also resulted in a new set of social relations developing—most importantly, between workers and employers—outside the confines of the traditional political system.

Along with these new economic arrangements came a new set of social problems. For example, while there had always been some unemployment in the British economy, feudal institutions were such that it tended to manifest itself in the form of generalized underemployment spread across the countryside. As such, unemployment was both invisible and, for the most part, nondisruptive. Circumstances changed, however, with the growth of factory labor, particularly after the development of the steam engine, which encouraged large-scale installations at a single location, organized around the power source. This was accompanied by the development of large tracts of worker housing—the infamous "factory slums"—which sprang up in a completely unplanned and haphazard fashion across England. Along with this came a transformation in the nature of unemployment. Instead of being dispersed, it became highly localized, as the closure of a factory would throw hundreds of workers into the street. And rather than spread the shortfall in demand for labor across all workers, it would drop it entirely on some, who would find themselves completely out of work. Needless to say, a situation in which hundreds of poor, able-bodied men find themselves in a single neighborhood, with nothing to do, and no way to earn money for their next meal, much less support their families, can be a *highly* disruptive force in society. Even in the absence of any eleemosynary concern for the welfare of the working classes, the presence of a mob of angry, desperate, unemployed workers in the streets can be considered a social problem from a variety of perspectives.

Yet in response to this emerging set of problems, classical liberalism had practically nothing to say, and certainly no solutions to offer. Because the conception of state neutrality tended to focus on a narrow list of goods, in particular, the three that Hume had enumerated (security, property, and contract), it had very few resources for dealing with problems that arose from the free operations of the market economy. Furthermore, the only normative standard that it could deploy, in assessing these problems, was the entirely formal commitment to freedom of contract, which tended to suggest that nothing should be done to interfere with market outcomes. Thus, liberalism became practically synonymous with the doctrine of laissez faire. Whether it was workplace safety and accidents, wages, work hours and conditions, or unemployment, the liberal presumption was that any arrangement agreed to by the parties was just *eo ipso*. If employers wanted to hire workers one day and fire them the next, it was a matter that concerned the employers and the workers, in which the state had no business interfering. The liberal position at the time was well summed up in the 1905 *Lochner v. New York* decision, in which the United States Supreme Court struck down a New York statute that would have limited the number of hours that bakery employees could work to sixty per week. The court deemed the limitation on work hours an "unreasonable, unnecessary and arbitrary interference with the right and liberty of the individual to contract."[72] Beyond this, the commitment to the integrity of private property and security of the person meant that the primary liberal impulse, in response to worker unrest or demands for improved conditions was to send in armed men to defend the rights of property owners.

Furthermore, if in certain cases liberalism was merely unhelpful—in the sense that it had nothing to offer those who were concerned about what Frederick Engels memorably described as "the condition of the working classes"—in other cases it was positively obstructionist. Increased urbanization, for instance, brought with it many challenges that seemed to call for some kind of a collective response. Until the mid-19th century, there had been practically no urban planning in Europe. Cities just sprang up spontaneously; land was used in whatever way people chose; street design was erratic. As urban areas became larger, this made transportation more difficult, exacerbated pollution problems and fire risks, created conflict between neighbors, and generated a host of other difficulties. Yet the demand for planning, regulation, building codes, and even sewage systems was strongly resisted by those who adhered to a classical liberal framework, on the grounds that these things constituted unjust interference in the rights of property.[73]

Similar issues arose concerning public health and the growing awareness of the importance of clean water in preventing outbreaks of diseases such as cholera and typhus. Throughout the 19th century, the city of London was served by eight different water companies, each of which strongly resisted any attempt to regulate their affairs. The Metropolis Water Act of 1852 was considered especially bold, because it prohibited these companies from drawing water from the filthy Thames River, and required filtration.[74] Again, the companies appealed to freedom of contract to resist government intervention. A series of additional acts followed, each one strongly opposed by the water companies and their supporters. A Royal Commission recommended public ownership of the companies in 1869, but this was not implemented until 1903, with the creation of the Metropolitan Water Board, which brought all the companies under a single public authority. Similarly, the Public Health Act of 1875 represented a major victory of reformers and trade union groups over a liberal opposition.

By steadfastly opposing these developments, liberal thinkers went from being a revolutionary vanguard in the fight against the ancien regime to reactionary defenders of the status quo, steadfast opponents of all "schemes of improvement."[75] Yet, as David Keir put it, "the growth of industry, of banking, of joint-stock enterprise, of maritime transport, of inland communications, especially railways, of town-life and the consequent need for police, sanitation, water-supply, education, and poor-relief created problems which, whatever the theoretical merits of laissez-faire, could not be disregarded."[76] As a result, people hoping to address the major social problems of their age no longer turned to liberalism as a source of guidance or inspiration. Increasingly, they turned to some form of socialism, because whatever their other deficiencies, socialists at least had something to say, or some plan, to address the social consequences of capitalism and industrialization. Liberalism, particularly the version derived from social contract theory, became increasingly marginal to the conversation, because of its insistence that nothing should be done about these problems. As a result, it was not difficult to dismiss the doctrine, as Marx did, as nothing more than an ideology concocted to advance the class interests of the bourgeoisie.

3.5. The rise of modern liberalism

As I suggested earlier, the success of liberalism is not entirely based on intellectual factors, or on the power of its central ideas. Liberalism represents, in many ways, a second-best solution to the problem of political order. By and large, people would prefer to live in close-knit communities, with neighbors who share their values, and a set of laws that both articulate and reproduce those values. The problem with this first-best arrangement is that it is, in practice, unobtainable on a large scale, and the attempt to achieve it—particularly in a modern nation-state, which possesses an unprecedented capacity for organized coercion—is positively dangerous. The willingness to settle for a second-best arrangement, however, appears to be highly dependent upon peoples' estimation of the obtainability of a first-best arrangement. Over the course of the 19th century, and into the beginning of the 20th, many Europeans convinced themselves that the rules had changed, that "this time is different," and thus that a first-best arrangement was once again within their grasp. Much of this thinking owed to industrialization, and the widespread perception that the "curse of Adam" was about to be lifted by broad-based economic growth. This is what gave rise to the massive experiments in social reorganization that dominated 20th-century history, and generated such enormous bloodshed and disillusionment.

Indeed, if the emergence of liberalism in the 17th century is best understood as a response to the "wars of religion" that had plagued European societies in the wake of the Reformation, the remarkable resurgence of liberalism in the late 20th century can be understood in similar terms, as a reaction to the "wars of totalitarianism" that dominated the first half of that century, and were not definitively resolved until 1989. These served, if nothing else, as a reminder of how dangerous the state can be when it is stripped of all the constraints that social contract theory and "modern constitutionalism" had fought so assiduously to impose upon it. With the benefit of hindsight, and considering the total collapse of the rule of law experienced in both the Soviet Union and Communist China, it is difficult to read Marx's breezy dismissal of "bourgeois right" as anything other than a staggering miscalculation. More generally, these episodes served as an important reminder of the enduring value of liberal "virtues" such as tolerance and compromise.

There is a particular way of recounting history, according to which both social contract theory and liberalism all but died out in the 19th century, until they were suddenly and miraculously revived in 1971 with the publication of John Rawls's *A Theory of Justice*. Like most popular accounts, it contains an element of truth. Certainly, it would be difficult to overstate the impact of Rawls's book. Furthermore, the fact that such a seemingly unassuming piece of work could achieve such complete dominance over the philosophical imagination is something that cries out for explanation. While it is not true that all of Western philosophy is a footnote to Plato, there is a clear sense in which almost all contemporary political philosophy is structured by, and represents an elaboration of, arguments developed by Rawls (with the sole exception of democratic theory, where Habermas is the important figure). At the same time, Rawls did not invent his views from whole cloth. Liberalism may have gone out of fashion among political theorists and philosophers, but in one corner of the academy it was never abandoned, and that is in economics. Indeed, the economics profession clearly constituted the major carrier stratum for liberalism in the early 20th century. In part, this is because economists felt the socialist challenge most acutely, and struggled to formulate an effective response to it. This is what drove the development of "welfare economics," which culminated in the proof of the so-called invisible hand theorem, a vindication of Adam Smith's claim that a competitive market would not just maximize aggregate welfare, but would in fact maximize the welfare of *each individual*.[77] Welfare economics also gave rise to the theory of "public goods," which represented for the first time a rigorous development of the case for state involvement in the economy, in the provision of goods such as clean water, sewers, vaccinations—precisely the issues that had animated 19th-century reformers.[78] The result was a framework that was still recognizably liberal, and yet offered a remedy for many of the social problems that classical liberalism had insisted the state must ignore. This made it possible to adopt a progressive position with respect to issues like urban planning, or public health, without necessarily committing oneself to socialism.

Among economists, the commitment to liberal neutrality was expressed, somewhat crudely, in the doctrine of "consumer sovereignty," or the idea that society should be concerned with maximizing the satisfaction of preferences, whatever those preferences happen to be. Central to this was the principle of Pareto efficiency, which almost completely displaced utilitarianism as the normative framework used by 20th-century welfare economists. The crucial feature of the Pareto principle is that it does not require interpersonal comparisons of utility, it simply states that a social state is to be preferred if it makes at least one person better off, by his or her own lights, and no one worse off. Thus, there is a close conceptual connection between Paretianism and liberal neutrality, as the central attraction of the former is the desire to make normative judgments without taking sides on controversial conceptions of the good.

Rawls's great achievement is to have grasped the normative principles being used by welfare economists (such as Kenneth Arrow and Paul Samuelson), as well as nascent developments in game theory, and to have generalized them, to show how they could be used as the basis for a complete political philosophy, or for a theory of justice that could be applied to all major social institutions, both economic and political. Whereas early liberals used the social contract thought experiment as a way of deriving principles to govern the state, and economists focused almost entirely on the market, Rawls developed a normative framework at a level of abstraction that allowed him to make claims about both. The issue for him is how individuals come together to establish *systems of cooperation*. The state is one such system, but crucially, so is the set of property relations underlying the market economy. Thus Rawls attempts to address the basic questions of normative political philosophy at a much higher level of generality than that undertaken by first-generation social contract theorists. In doing so, he inaugurated the modern resurgence of liberalism, which is founded on an abstract reconceptualizing of the ideas that animated classical liberalism.

Rawls makes the foundation of his approach clear in the opening pages of *A Theory of Justice*, where he explains what a "theory of justice" is, and what problem it attempts to solve:

> Let us assume, to fix ideas, that a society is a more or less self-sufficient association of persons who in their relations to one another recognize certain rules of conduct as binding and who for the most part act in accordance with them. Suppose further that these rules specify a system of cooperation designed to advance the good of those taking part in it. Then, although a society is a cooperative venture for mutual advantage, it is typically marked by a conflict as well as by an identity of interests. There is an identity of interests since social cooperation makes possible a better life for all than any would have if each were to live solely by his own efforts. There is a conflict of interests since persons are

not indifferent as to how the greater benefits produced by their collaboration are distributed, for in order to pursue their ends they each prefer a larger to a lesser share. A set of principles is required for choosing among the various social arrangements which determine this division of advantages and for underwriting an agreement on the proper distributive shares. These principles are the principles of social justice: they provide a way of assigning rights and duties in the basic institutions of society and they define the appropriate distribution of the benefits and burdens of social cooperation.[79]

This paragraph requires a great deal of unpacking, although it is worth the effort, because almost all the major ideas that separate modern from classical liberalism can be found therein. First, it should be noted that Rawls is using the term "cooperation" in the game-theoretic sense, usually illustrated using the interaction known as a "prisoner's dilemma." The goal is to focus on a set of situations in which individuals are in a position to achieve mutual benefit, but where no one has an individual incentive to act in a way that will produce that benefit. Thus, individuals are called upon to exercise restraint in their pursuit of self-interest, narrowly conceived. When they do so, they are said to be acting "cooperatively." Social institutions, in Rawls's view, are essentially sets of rules that codify these constraints, and thus establish systems of cooperation. (Rules are required because of the free-rider incentive that individuals possess. They do well by cooperating, but they stand to do even better by persuading others to cooperate, but then defecting themselves.)

Cooperation, however, creates its own unique set of problems. While self-interest, broadly construed, may encourage individuals to enter into cooperative relations with one another, it fails to determine the specific modalities of cooperation. There are, in other words, many different ways in which individuals could cooperate with one another. (To take an example from Rousseau, individuals hunting alone may be able to catch rabbits, but in order to catch a deer, they will need to work together. Agreeing to hunt together, however, raises a whole set of new questions—questions that never came up when each individual was hunting alone. Should there be a division of labor, and if so, who should do which job? How should the rewards be divided up if the hunt is successful? Or to use Rawls's language, what is the appropriate "distribution of the benefits and burdens of social cooperation"?) Principles of justice, in Rawls's view, are designed to answer precisely this question—to determine the specific modalities of cooperation.

The basic idea can be illustrated quite clearly using a conventional two-person prisoner's dilemma (or a "collective action problem"). Consider the interaction shown in Figure 3.2. The range of possible outcomes can be represented as in Figure 3.3, with Player 1's payoffs on the horizontal axis and Player 2's on the vertical. Each point in the space represents a possible outcome—a certain quantity

Player 2

		C	D
	C	(2,2)	(0,3)
Player 1			
	D	(3,0)	(1,1)

Figure 3.2 Collective action problem.

of benefits, as well as a distribution of those benefits between the two individuals. (The standard one-shot prisoner's dilemma is in this respect overly simplified, since it has only one cooperative outcome. If, however, the interaction is repeated over time and the numbers represent average payoffs, or if the individuals used randomized strategies, then the entire set of outcomes in the diamond shown in Figure 3.3, with vertices at the "pure strategy" outcomes, is a possible expected outcome of the interaction between the two players.) This representation allows one to see the problem faced by the two players quite clearly—they both have an interest in cooperating, but there are a very large number of different cooperative arrangements available to them, and so they require some basis for choosing one.

Rawls's suggestion is that the principles of justice can be formulated as a way of solving the problem of cooperation posed at this level of abstraction. One can think of the objective as simply narrowing down the set of outcomes, from the very large set shown in Figure 3.3 to a single point. There are an infinite number of ways to do this, but one way to think about the problem is to consider what it would take to get the parties to *agree* upon an outcome. This is where the social contract comes in. The parties may, of course, have certain "thick" cultural

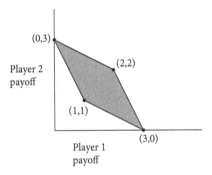

Figure 3.3 Possible payoffs in collective action problem.

resources—such as a shared system of values—that will allow them to agree on a specific outcome. Failing that, there are certain principles that are suggested simply by the structure of the decision problem. Rawls presents his thought experiment of the "original position" as a way of selecting such principles. His central suggestion is that the participants be thought of as choosing principles of justice from behind a "veil of ignorance," which denies them any knowledge of which position they will wind up occupying in the eventual institutional arrangement. This is intended to prevent them from choosing arrangements that favor their own specific values or interests. Rawls's thought is that if everyone makes a choice under conditions that preclude any partiality, then everyone should be expected to make the same choice, and so agreement can be achieved.

Critics were not slow to point out problems with Rawls's specific proposals.[80] In part as an acknowledgment of this criticism, Rawls put less and less emphasis on the original position in his later work. My own preference is to maintain the focus on cooperation, but to adopt a more minimal approach to the selection of principles, so that instead of trying to construct an idealized decision procedure, one approaches the problem using a general heuristic of conflict avoidance. For instance, if one were to heed the injunction to avoid outcomes that generate obvious *complaints* from one or both players, then a number of basic principles of justice suggest themselves. Three in particular have significant pragmatic and intuitive appeal.

The first involves reducing the set of options to those that are superior to the non-cooperative outcome of (1,1)—what John Nash referred to as the "feasible set," shown in Figure 3.4.[81] The thought is that if each player can guarantee himself an outcome of 1 by "going it alone" and acting non-cooperatively, then the social interaction should guarantee an outcome that is at least as good. (The non-cooperative outcome, in this respect, provides a way of conceptualizing what early social contract theorists had in mind with the "state of nature," and it serves

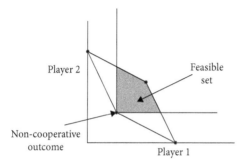

Figure 3.4 The feasible set.

a similar role in providing a baseline for the benefits provided by any scheme of cooperation.)

Once the problem is pared down in this way, one can see the force of Rawls's observation that there is both a "conflict" and an "identity" of interests in every cooperative interaction. On the one hand, both players are interested in maximizing the available benefits—here, there is a common interest—but on the other hand, they would like to direct as much of that benefit to themselves as they can—here, there is a conflict of interest. One can imagine the choice of outcome moving along two axes within the space of cooperative outcomes (illustrated in Figure 3.5). The first, the "common-interest" axis, moves from the southwest to northeast, while the second, the "conflict-of-interest" axis moves from northwest to southeast. The problem of choosing a set of principles to determine the modalities of cooperation then involves answering two questions, namely, where should the parties be on each axis? The natural suggestion, with respect to the common-interest axis, is that the parties should want to *maximize* along this dimension. The conflict-of-interest axis is more controversial, precisely because it involves a conflict of interest, but one attractive suggestion is that the parties should seek to *equalize* in this dimension. The reason is that doing so neutralizes an obvious source of objection. If one player receives more than the other, it gives the second an incentive to "switch places" with the first. The only way to eliminate this source of dissension is to give each player the exact same amount.

A compelling "theory of justice" can be constructed out of three principles. The first is a principle of liberty, which states that interactions should be ones to which individuals could, in principle, consent, by virtue of the benefits that they receive. This reduces the set of options to those in the feasible set. The second is a principle of efficiency, which prescribes maximization along the common-interest axis. The most persuasive interpretation of this is the principle of Pareto efficiency. (Again, it is easy to see how any violations of Pareto efficiency would

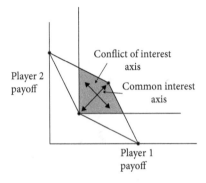

Figure 3.5 Common and conflict of interest axes.

generate an objection, from either or both players.) Graphically, this means that any point to the northeast of the status quo is preferred. Pareto optimality can then be defined as the limit of such Pareto improvements. It represents an outcome in which it is not possible to improve the outcome for anyone without worsening it for someone else. Thus the efficiency principle reduces the problem to a choice of points along what is known as the Pareto frontier, or the set of Pareto optima. Finally, we can draw a ray out from the origin, identifying the set of outcomes that are symmetric, or where the outcome received by one player is the same as the outcome received by the other (and so the two have no incentive to switch places). This is the set of *equal* outcomes. We can define the third general principle, that of equality, as specifying that outcomes closer to the equal outcome are to be preferred to ones that are more remote. (See Figure 3.6.)

Thus, instead of the rather concrete set of "neutral goods" endorsed by classical liberalism: property, security, and contract, modern liberalism endorses three very abstract principles of justice: liberty, equality, and efficiency. The framework remains recognizably liberal, however, in that these principles can reasonably claim to be neutral among competing conceptions of the good. This is, of course, one of the things that Rawls hoped to achieve by insisting that the "veil of ignorance" denied individuals any knowledge of their own conception of the good, which in turn prevented them from selecting principles that favored any particular conception. A similar commitment to neutrality is implicit in Figure 3.6, in that the principles are specified in a way that is independent of what the x and y axes represent. Thus, the x axis can be taken to represent "what player 1 cares about most," and the y can represent "what player 2 cares about most." If we think of an agent's *first-order conception of the good* as a system of values that determine that agent's ranking of outcomes, then it follows that principles of efficiency, equality, and liberty can be formulated in a way that is neutral with respect to such conceptions. The principles are, of course, not normatively

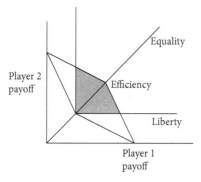

Figure 3.6 Three liberal principles of justice.

neutral—in that they clearly rank some states of affairs as *better than* others—but they can be expected to be dramatically less controversial than the first-order conceptions of the good that inform the more specific preferences of agents.

There is, I should note, still some resistance to this sort of analysis and the central role it assigns to neutrality in the formulation of the liberal ideal. Yet most forms of perfectionist liberalism, which insist on embracing the language of the good, wind up positing "goods" that are nothing but the translation into evaluative language of these basic liberal principles. Henry Richardson, for instance, rejects the idea of liberal neutrality, claiming that "it is always a mistake to think of liberalism in this way." Yet, when it comes time to articulate the good that he intends to "take a stand on," it winds up being "the good of fair cooperation among free and equal citizens."[82] This seems like a distinction without a difference, and indeed, it is very difficult to see what conceptual gain Richardson sees in calling this a "good." It is, in any case, not a first-order conception of the good, since "cooperation" can only be conceived of as a good insofar as it allows individuals to better advance their own, more-specific conceptions of the good. Furthermore, the central virtue of cooperation is that, unlike other forms of joint action, it has a "you help me, I help you" structure, which allows individuals to advance their interests despite whatever disagreements they may have about ultimate ends. Privileging cooperation already entails a commitment to neutrality, the question is only whether it should remain implicit or be made explicit.

It is the neutrality of the efficiency principle that persuaded many economists that it could be introduced as merely a technical postulate, or a non-normative proposition. Underlying this is often a confusion between neutrality and objectivity, resulting in the view that efficiency is somehow "scientific," whereas all other normative judgments are merely "subjective." (As my undergraduate economics textbook stated approvingly, back in 1988: "Because it is possible to talk about efficient and inefficient allocations, but not about better or worse distributions of income without introducing normative considerations, much of economics concerns efficiency and neglects effects on the distribution of income."[83]) Part of Rawls's achievement is to have clarified this issue, making it obvious that both efficiency and equality are normative principles—in fact, ones that have very similar standing. The difference is merely that efficiency is less controversial, because it mediates win-win transformations, whereas equality will always be more controversial, because of the win-lose structure of distributive questions. Nevertheless, there is a clear sense in which, despite first-order disagreement about the good, individuals can still be treated equally with respect to their capacity to pursue their own conception. Thus, a commitment to equality, like the commitment to efficiency, can be made while still abjuring controversial *value* judgments about what goals individuals should be pursuing.

Setting aside these confusions about its status, one can see how the articulation of the Pareto principle produced significant changes in the way that economists thought about the normative foundations of the market economy. Instead of seeing it through the lens of individual rights, as a domain of private contracting, modern liberalism encouraged them to see the economy as a system of cooperation like any other. The central weakness of classical liberalism was either that it had nothing to say about the problems that arose within the economic sphere, or else what it did say was unhelpful. From a classical liberal perspective, the most basic argument for laissez faire policies was that they followed from the combination of property rights and freedom of contract. While there was widespread awareness of "invisible hand" arguments, to the effect that all this trading would promote general happiness, this was often seen as something of a bonus, not a foundational consideration. This is why, as instances of market failure accumulated, and it began to look as though promoting general happiness might require some interference with the rights of property, utilitarianism became a major force driving people to embrace socialism.

Modern liberalism reframes this debate, by offering an argument for the market that assigns an important role to both property and contract but does not treat either as inviolable. Once the Pareto principle is articulated, it becomes clear that the classical liberal arguments for property and contract appeal to the fact that both institutions are Pareto improving. This is most obvious in the case of Locke's argument for property, which focuses on showing that the individual appropriation and exchange of goods generates benefits for some, while producing no harm to anyone else.[84] This argument can be seen to produce a general presumption in favor of property rights, but these rights are also defeasible (unlike the strict property rights of classical liberalism, which can never be overturned by the state), most obviously in cases where there is good reason to think that interference with specific property rights would be Pareto improving (e.g., expropriating land for an infrastructure project or introducing municipal zoning regulations or imposing taxes to finance the provision of public goods). It also starts to make the list of classical liberal goods seem rather partial, perhaps even arbitrary. If the state is to be in the business of solving collective action problems, then it should do more than just provide personal security, defend property rights, and enforce contracts. It should also provide education, infrastructure, environmental goods, and so on.

Focusing on the Pareto principle also transforms the classical understanding of the market. Rather than being based on individual rights, the presumption in favor of market outcomes comes to be seen as a consequence of the fact that each individual trade is Pareto improving. The important modern argument for laissez faire, developed by Friedrich Hayek, is that only individuals have the information required to determine which exchanges will be advantageous, and so only private exchange will be able to maximize efficiency.[85] This implies, however, that in circumstances in which there is good reason to think that market contracting will *not* maximize welfare, the case can be made for other institutional arrangements. One can see the consequences of this type of thinking in a variety of areas, but one of the earliest issues to come up was that of natural monopoly. A major scourge of 19th-century capitalism was that many markets were dominated by either cartels or monopolistic firms. Again, states were loath to interfere, because both property and contract were regarded as sacrosanct, and monopolies often developed without any interference with either. The problem is that monopolies generate price distortions, which in turn generate Pareto inefficiencies (or, in the economist's term, "deadweight losses"). Thus one of the earliest reforms in the transition to what we might think of as "modern capitalism" was the development of active competition policy, which involved overseeing markets (and interfering with private contracting) to ensure that they remained reasonably competitive, or, in cases where a competition could not be organized, moving management and ownership of the industry into the public sector.

3.6. Conclusion

This discussion has taken us a long way from the everyday world of public administration, and so it may be helpful to connect it back to the central theme of the book. My goal has been to show that when civil servants act on the basis of an independently developed conception of the public interest that is based on liberal principles of justice, they are not behaving like philosopher kings, privileging one conception of the good among many. Standard textbooks on normative political theory, which typically feature a chapter on liberalism, alongside chapters on communitarianism, Marxism, libertarianism, and other philosophical theories, can unfortunately produce this impression.[86] The difference between liberalism and these other doctrines is that liberalism has played a constitutive role in the emergence of the particular constellation of institutional arrangements that make up the modern state. Liberalism is, as it were, part of the DNA of the societies that we refer to (for that reason) as "liberal-democratic." As a result, liberalism is not just one political philosophy among others. And because liberal principles are already embedded in our state institutions, asking state employees to be guided by liberal principles in their discretionary judgments is not likely to sow chaos, in the way that asking them to follow some other set of principles would.

The history that I have been recounting focuses on what I take to be the central current of liberal theory and liberal institutions. It is aimed at showing that there is much greater continuity between 18th-, 19th-, and 20th-century liberalism than has often been maintained. In particular, it is important to see that the classical liberal framework, which informs a great deal of contemporary libertarianism, is just a more concrete way of expressing the logic of the liberal position. This early formulation may have been suitable for addressing the circumstances and challenges of the societies in which it was developed, but it is manifestly inadequate for dealing with the social changes that arose as a result, in no small measure, of its own application. A more reflexively stable version of the doctrine could only be achieved through the type of radical abstraction that gave us modern liberal principles. The result is a set of doctrinal commitments that may strike some as platitudinous—efficiency, equality, and liberty, all conceived of at a high level of generality—but that is precisely the point. They are, as I have attempted to show, not intrinsically platitudinous, much less self-evident, since they have been rejected in most human societies throughout most of human history. They are platitudinous only in our society, because they cohere with the deep normative structure of the institutional arrangements that we by and large approve of, and usually take for granted. And it is precisely because they are platitudinous in this way that they can serve as the normative basis for a conception of the public interest that the executive can advance without interfering with the prerogatives of the legislature.

Of course, there is an important distinction to be drawn between liberalism construed institutionally, as the general set of ideas that inform the organization of liberal societies, and the specific conceptions of liberal justice that have been articulated by political philosophers. The latter tend to be far more controversial, in part because they move beyond just the abstract articulation of liberal principles, to propose specific principles or procedures for ordering or weighting them (such as Rawls's "difference principle"). As a result, they invariably move into the realm of political ideology (which is to say, they make claims that belong in the domain of legitimate democratic contestation). While it is important to note that, under perfectly idealized conditions, there is no conflict between these principles, under real-world conditions, there will often be tensions, and so trade-offs will be required. Under these circumstances, the way that the principles are ordered, or the weight that they are given in deciding on acceptable trade-offs, is subject to intense disagreement. The politically "centrist" position assigns paramount importance to welfare maximization, or to resolving collective action problems. The left assigns much greater weight to equality, to the point of being willing, under appropriate circumstances, to "level down" (i.e., to prefer Pareto-inferior arrangements that are more egalitarian).[87] The righ attaches much greater significance to liberty, to the point of defending the right of individuals to free ride, thus creating the potential for states of "dysphoric freedom." There are also, of course, many who reject the fundamental premises of liberalism (e.g., Christian social conservatives), or else its modern formulation (e.g., libertarians who adopt some form of classical liberalism). Nevertheless, the very broad center of contemporary politics, and the major axis of disagreement in political ideology, concerns the appropriate weighting of the three major principles that characterize modern liberalism.

Because of this, there are good reasons for civil servants, while being committed to these principles, to remain agnostic on the question of how they should be ordered. Again, it is worth noting that the conflicts between them are not conceptual but rather pragmatic—it is the imperfections of the world that force us to make trade-offs between them. Thus, there are also circumstances in which we are able to produce gains on all fronts simultaneously, and these obviously should be sought out and valued. Nevertheless, it is important to recognize that despite sometimes sharp disagreements over political ideology, liberal societies have tended to drift toward a particular ordering over time. As I will attempt to show in the next chapter, the development of the welfare state is largely a consequence of governments choosing to assign greater weight to efficiency than to other concerns.

4

Efficiency and the Rise of the Welfare State

In the same way that classical liberalism, with its triumvirate of property, security, and contract, provided the reigning ideology of laissez faire capitalism, modern liberalism, with its commitment to abstract principles of equality, efficiency, and liberty, provides the central rationale for the modern welfare state. One of the central features of this new framework is that, unlike classical social contract theory, which is specifically a theory of the state, modern liberalism articulates a set of principles that are intended to govern all major systems of cooperation in society, and thus not just the state. (John Rawls articulated this point, somewhat cryptically, as the claim that the "basic structure" of society forms the "subject" of justice.[1]) An immediate consequence of this is a measure of institutional pragmatism with respect to the role of the state in society. Whereas liberal courts used to police the boundary between the private and public sectors quite zealously, rejecting any state "intrusions" into the realm of private property and contract, the shift to modern liberal principles in the 20th century left it very much an open question whether any particular economic activity should be undertaken in the private or the public sector, or whether the state should get involved in regulating the conditions under which private contracting could occur.[2]

The development of this institutional pragmatism led to a dramatic expansion of the size of the state and the scope of its activities. State spending in Canada, as a fraction of GDP, rose from less than 2 percent in 1900 to a peak of 45 percent in 1998. Concretely, this increased spending, over the course of the 20th century, manifested itself in the Canadian state (including the provinces), besides owning and controlling all major utilities, telecommunications, roads, air- and seaports, schools and universities, and most of the healthcare system, also at various times owning and operating an airline, an oil company, both freight and passenger rail companies, passenger ferries, nuclear reactors, several mining companies, a bank, a hotel chain, a steamship and telegraph company, and intercity bus companies, as well as radio and television broadcast firms in both official languages. Of course, there have been significant changes in the pattern of ownership, the state having withdrawn from many of these sectors beginning in the 1980s. The history of how this came to pass, and of the ideological struggles that were involved, is well-known: the challenge posed to Western states by the Great Depression; the ascension to power of social-democratic parties in the postwar era and the expansion of the welfare state; the

The Machinery of Government. Joseph Heath, Oxford University Press (2020). © Oxford University Press.
DOI: 10.1093/oso/9780197509616.001.0001

right-wing backlash of the Reagan-Thatcher era resulting in widespread privatization of public services, etc. What is less well understood is the ideological convergence that occurred during this same period of time, not just on broadly liberal norms, but also on a particular "flavor" of liberalism, one that assigns significant weight, if not priority, to the principle of efficiency.

From the standpoint of this welfarist liberalism, market arrangements are generally favored because the price system allows for an extremely efficient allocation of productive assets and labor inputs, as well as of final goods and services. This is, however, subject to some well-known qualifications—the market must be reasonably competitive; there must not be significant externalities; certain sorts of information asymmetries must be absent, etc. When these conditions are not satisfied, markets may fail to produce efficient outcomes. That alone is insufficient to make the case for state involvement, because bureaucratic coordination of economic activity is also subject to notorious inefficiencies. The question of how a particular economic activity should be organized is therefore determined by the relative merits of different institutional arrangements. Typically, state involvement becomes desirable only when markets fail *egregiously*, which is to say, when they are so inefficient that the state becomes the more efficient provider.

This is a thumbnail sketch of a very standard story about the welfare state, which can be found in any public economics textbook, and it is widely subscribed to in the public sector. When one turns to the *normative* literature on the welfare state, however, the focus on efficiency disappears almost entirely from view.[3] There is broad, though not universal, agreement among political philosophers that the welfare state makes society more just than it otherwise would be. However, when it comes to saying in what *way* it makes society more just, any semblance of agreement disappears. Even among the most enthusiastic supporters of the welfare state there are several different accounts of what it is thought to achieve, or in what way it increases the achieved level of social justice.

Perhaps the most discordant note is struck by those who think that the welfare state represents a rejection of liberalism. Liberalism, from this perspective, is associated with a certain atomistic individualism, which when acted upon generates the competitive relations of the market. Thus liberalism (or "neoliberalism") comes to be seen as giving rise to the market, which then begins to crowd out more traditional forms of community. The state provides a haven from the atomistic norms of the marketplace, allowing individuals to cultivate relationships and pursue shared goods that would be impossible to achieve under market norms. We can refer to this as the "communitarian" model of the welfare state.[4] According to this view, the welfare state is not a product of liberalism at all, but is rather an institutional arrangement that offers individuals protection from some of the consequences of liberalism.

The more commonly held view is that the welfare state is an essentially liberal institution, but that it is committed to promoting equality rather than efficiency. The market economy, according to this view, is extremely successful at producing wealth, but the wealth winds up being very unequally distributed—or winds up being distributed in a way that violates widely shared intuitions about justice. Thus the state intervenes, redistributing a certain amount of the wealth, in order to make the overall results of the economy more just or, at least, palatable to a sufficiently large number of people that the arrangement remains stable. We can think of this as the "egalitarian" model of the welfare state.

Each of these two views has something to be said for it, insofar as each provides an intuitively natural account of certain specific features of the welfare state. Yet when it comes to the broader picture, they suffer from the same deficiency, which is that both fail to make any sense of a great deal of what the welfare state actually does, or why its programs are organized and operated in the way that they are. By contrast, the standard "public-economic" view, which sees the welfare state as committed, first and foremost, to resolving market failures (i.e., promoting Pareto efficiency), is able to provide a unified account of all the major features of the welfare state, ranging from the big spending programs (health, pensions, education) to the regulatory interventions to the social safety net. Furthermore, it provides an intuitively natural account of one feature of the welfare state that neither model is able to explain, which is its spectacular growth over the course of the 20th century. Both the communitarian and egalitarian models are quite static in their orientation, and as a result have no explanation for why the state might come to take on new roles and responsibilities. Thus they have difficulty explaining the seeming inexorability of welfare-state growth, and in particular, why the political ideology of governing parties had relatively little impact on this growth trend during the major period of welfare-state expansion.[5]

My central objective in this chapter is to rescue the public-economic model of the welfare state, in order to show that it should be, not just the economist's preferred understanding of why the welfare state does what it does, but also the political philosopher's preferred normative standard for assessing the contribution made by the welfare state to the realization of social justice. In the long run, this will help us to better understand the normative ideas that have come to inform the practice of public administration, and in particular, the central role that considerations of efficiency have come to play.

I should note that the bulk of the discussion in this chapter is focused on views that are taken to provide sound justification for the scope and nature of welfare-state activity, held by people who might loosely be described as "friends" of the welfare state. There are, however, theories in circulation that provide a largely negative assessment of the welfare state. The most theoretically well-articulated of these is the "public-choice" model, which bears a certain resemblance to the egalitarian model, insofar as it regards the welfare state as being primarily in the business of effecting unproductive transfers between individuals. The difference is that, rather than regarding these transfers as motivated by a laudable commitment to equality, it regards them instead as a consequence of unprincipled rent-seeking by interest groups. The other negative assessment of the welfare state, less well articulated but still widely held, is that it is a "nanny state," whose growth over time represents little more than the accretion of a set of essentially paternalistic policies. There is no doubt a grain of truth in both of these negative assessments, and there are some specific cases and policies that fit these models. Nevertheless, I will try to show that they fail to account for the core features of the welfare state, not to mention its growth over time. In both cases, I will argue, the negative perception arises primarily through confusion about the insurance functions of the welfare state. Once the latter are correctly understood, it is much easier to see the efficiency rationale underlying these programs.

4.1. The egalitarian model

The egalitarian model is probably closest to what might be considered the received view of the welfare state among political philosophers. The central claim is that *redistribution* is the most important activity of the state, and that the major objective of the welfare state is to promote greater equality. There are more or less moralized versions of this view. The Marxian tradition, for instance, has encouraged the suggestion that capitalist societies are riven by class conflict, which generates a fundamental antagonism between the interests of the bourgeoisie and the proletariat. The true interest of the proletariat lies in the creation of a classless society, and thus the working class is constantly threatening to dispossess the bourgeoisie. The bourgeoisie, knowing this, have an incentive to "buy off" or "co-opt" segments of the working class, by providing them with enough of a payoff to motivate them to defend the existing order. (People who take this view often talk about "the welfare-state compromise"—the idea being that the bourgeoisie agrees to tolerate some seizure and redistribution of its wealth, in order to stave off the threat of revolution, while the working class agrees to tolerate ongoing exploitation and alienation, in return for the satisfactions of the consumer lifestyle.) This commits the state to a range of economic—in the broadest sense of the term—activities:

1. *Co-optation of the proletariat.* The working class must be given enough of a stake in the existing order that its members come to regard any radical economic reform or seizure of property as an undesirable risk. This is achieved

mainly through transfer payments (with perhaps state pension benefits being the best example), funded by a progressive income tax.

2. *Deradicalization of the lumpenproletariat.* The state transfers just enough resources to those *outside* the labor market (through welfare, workers' compensation, healthcare, subsidized tuition, etc.) to forestall any radical political action on the part of those actors. As a result, the centrality of the market in determining the fate and fortune of individuals becomes more tolerable, and forestalls the radicalization of women, students, the disabled and the unemployed.

3. *Control of exploitation.* The state limits the rate of exploitation in order not to motivate radical resistance to the corporate system on the part of the population. It engages in regulation, and sometimes ownership, of natural monopolies. The state also imposes consumer protection, environmental and workplace safety rules, and similar forms of legislation, in order to protect the public from some of the sharper edges of marketplace competition.

4. *Wasteful spending.* Finally, there is the post-Keynesian idea that the state must engage in various forms of demand management to maintain the stability of the system in the face of endogenous crisis tendencies. Without constant growth, the (moderately) positive-sum character of the economy becomes zero-sum, which then exacerbates all forms of latent distributive conflict. (For example, during the Cold War, it was often claimed that the state engaged in wasteful military expenditure to keep the economic pump primed, and that this was ultimately motivated by a need to pacify class conflict.[6])

The Marxian version of the model focuses very much on the interests of the parties involved, and tends to assume therefore that the bourgeoisie, through the medium of the welfare state, accepts the minimum level of redistribution needed to stabilize the capitalist system. The model is, of course, still organized around a conception of social justice—namely, the ideal of a classless society—it simply does not regard the welfare state as the *embodiment* of that ideal, but treats it rather as a *concession* in the direction of that ideal, adopted by the ruling class for largely prudential reasons.[7]

There are a variety of more moralized versions of this model as well, which share the focus on redistribution as the central activity of the welfare state, but claim that the objective of this redistribution is not merely to modify individual incentives in such a way as to preserve the stability of the system, but rather to satisfy a moral criterion required for political legitimacy. "Liberal egalitarian" views in particular consider the welfare state to be the institutional embodiment of a conception of justice along these lines.[8]

The most persuasive foundation for this view can be found in Rawls's work, with its emphasis on the principles of efficiency and equality (and the difference principle, which represents his formula for trading off one against the other). The follow-up suggestion, which many people find irresistible, is that the market and the state are the institutional embodiment of these two different principles: that the market promotes Pareto efficiency, while the state renders the entire arrangement more equal, by reallocating initial endowments and adjusting final outcomes (in order to maintain what Rawls called "background justice," which in turn confers a presumption of legitimacy upon all private contractual arrangements entered into by individuals). On this view, the normative "logic" of the state is completely different from the "logic" of the market.

The most obvious evidence that supporters of this view can point to is the progressivity of the income tax system, combined with the fact that this progressivity is typically justified through appeal to some notion of "fairness." The benefits that are then provided using this tax revenue are either available to all citizens equally (roads, postal service, national broadcasting, policing and fire services, public education, national defense, etc.) or in a way that is progressive with respect to income (welfare, unemployment benefits, workers' compensation, etc.), or else targeted at those who are subject to some disadvantage (healthcare, pensions, etc.). Ability to pay is almost never a criterion for the receipt of government services. The net result is a dramatic enhancement in the achieved level of distributive justice. The central objective of the welfare state, on this view, is to help those who are, in one way or another, left behind by the market.

An important variant of this view claims that the distributive pattern being sought by the state is not so much about achieving equality as it is about ensuring that a basic minimum is maintained. According to this "sufficientarian" view, there is a certain threshold level of resources, opportunity or welfare that must be provided, in order to ensure that everyone is able to participate effectively in society.[9] Thus the role of the state is to ensure that everyone has this, by providing public education and healthcare, and by guaranteeing that basic living conditions (e.g., food and shelter) are met. Because each individual has an entitlement to satisfaction of these "basic needs," the goods must be provided by the state. Once these needs have been met, then it is acceptable for all other discretionary advantages to be allocated through the free play of the market.

4.2. The communitarian model

According to the egalitarian model, the economic role of the welfare state is organized around a set of core tasks that are fundamentally *different* from those that are carried out by the market. While the private sector produces, and is therefore concerned with efficiency, government redistributes, and is therefore concerned with equality. The most obvious difficulty with this view is that the state does many things that do not appear to be redistributive, and which seem in fact to be quite productive. States in various parts of the world own and operate hundreds of departments, bureaus, enterprises, and agencies, all of which have employees doing work that is productive and, in many cases, not all that different from what similarly situated employees in the private sector are doing. (Compare the case of a police officer patrolling the streets to a private security guard sitting at the front desk of a condominium or office tower, or a bodyguard protecting a celebrity.[10] All are doing essentially the same job.) Thus, many theorists feel the need to provide some explanation for why the state is engaged in the provision of so many goods and services. If the goal were merely redistributive, this could usually be achieved more efficiently through the economist's preferred method of taxation and cash redistribution; it is not necessary to have state employees actually deliver the goods. Furthermore, state provision often takes the form of "universal" rather than targeted programs, which can have regressive consequences. The benefits of subsidized higher education, for instance, flow disproportionately to those in the upper-middle and upper classes, and so cannot be motivated entirely by distributive concerns.

One particularly prominent response to this line of criticism has been to suggest that the state is engaged in producing these goods and services out of a desire to impose limits on the scope of the market. Michael Walzer has provided what is perhaps the most rigorous defense of this view, arguing that basic human needs should not just be guaranteed by the state, but should be satisfied through communal provision. The moral imperative to ensure the satisfaction of needs has the effect of blocking the "free exchange" of the goods that satisfy them.[11] Thus "needed goods are not commodities"—or more precisely, they ought not be treated as such.[12] The reason for communal provision, in Walzer's view, is not that it achieves greater equality. He is quite emphatic that, although communal provision is likely to have distributive consequences, it is not *justified* through appeal to any particular conception of distributive justice.[13] What determines the question of whether a particular economic activity should be discharged by the private or the public sector, according to this perspective, is whether commodification of the good or service is morally permissible.

I refer to this as the "communitarian" model of the welfare state. (There is some risk of confusion here, since Robert Goodin uses the term in a different way.[14] I might have referred to it as the "anti-commodification" model instead, although that makes it sound less attractive.) According to this view, the most important feature of the welfare state is that is constitutes a *nonmarket* institution capable of producing and delivering goods and services. Its function, as Goodin describes it, is "to supplant ordinary market mechanisms for certain limited purposes."[15] Consider the following particularly concise articulation of the view, presented by Joel Bakan in his book *The Corporation*:

> The twentieth century was unique in modern history for the widely held belief that democracy required governments to protect citizens' social rights and meet their fundamental needs. Essential public interests, and social domains believed to be too precious, vulnerable, or morally sacred to subject to corporate exploitation, were inscribed by law and public policy within protective boundaries. Human beings could not be owned and children could not be exploited, either as workers or as consumers. Institutions essential to human health and survival (such as water utilities and health and welfare services), human progress and development (such as schools, universities, and cultural institutions), and public safety (such as police, courts, prisons, and firefighters), were deliberately placed beyond the corporation's exploitative grasp, as were precious natural domains, which were turned into parks and nature reserves.[16]

As the analogy to slavery contracts and child labor suggests, the issue is not one of distributive justice, or of welfare per se. The standard view of slavery contracts is that they are prohibited—regardless of how much benefit both parties might derive from them—on the grounds that they are incompatible with human dignity. Or consider the case of organs for transplant. There is widespread agreement that the sale and purchase of human organs should be prohibited, not just because of the problematic incentive effects of such a market, but because treating parts of the living human body as commodities constitutes an affront to the dignity of the person.[17] The moral stigma associated with buying and selling has very deep roots. Recall Immanuel Kant's contrast between things that have a *price* and those that have *dignity*:

> Whatever has a price can be replaced by something else as its equivalent; on the other hand, whatever is above all price, and therefore admits of no equivalent, has a dignity. That which is related to general human inclinations and needs has a *market price* . . . But that which constitutes the condition under which alone something can be an end in itself does not have mere relative worth (*price*), but an intrinsic worth (*dignity*).[18]

The communitarian understanding of the welfare state is, essentially, an application of this moral intuition to the distinction between the public and private sectors. One can see it quite clearly in the extension of rights discourse to include "social rights."[19] The most prominent line of defense of traditional negative liberties is that they are central to the dignity of the individual—that freedom of conscience, freedom of association, and freedom of speech are preconditions for the exercise of our rational faculties. Many theorists have been inclined to extend this list to include the material conditions necessary for the exercise of these same faculties: food, shelter, clothing, and medical care, and to argue that the core set of entitlement programs run by the welfare state should be understood as the articulation of a set of social rights possessed by the individual, the denial of which constitutes an affront to the dignity or autonomy of the person.[20] The state, on this view, does not just redistribute wealth; it also provides goods and services, in circumstances in which it would violate human dignity to have them delivered through the market.

As with the social justice model, there are some paradigm cases in which this intuition is quite plausible. With basic police services, for instance, there is a widely held conviction that provision should occur outside "the cash nexus." Not only is there an egalitarian intuition, which says that all citizens should be afforded equal protection, there is also what one might call the "anti-commodification intuition," which says that the relevant service should not be charged for. Even if everyone had the ability to pay, it seems preposterous to suggest that people should be billed for calling the police when they are violently assaulted or their property is stolen. Indeed, the ubiquitous police slogan, "to serve and to protect," is intended to suggest that officers are motivated by a sense of duty, rather than some lowly pecuniary interest.

Yet despite clear cases like the police, the extension of the same intuition to other domains of state activity quickly becomes problematic. Consider the case of healthcare. The last major federal review of the socialized medicine system in Canada defended public delivery of healthcare on the communitarian grounds that it was the only modality consistent with Canadian values, because "Canadians view medicare as a moral enterprise, not a business venture."[21] This is very far from obvious, in part because most healthcare in Canada is delivered by the private sector, and doctors are overwhelmingly paid on a fee-for-service basis (unlike, say, police officers). Strictly speaking, the Canadian state only provides health *insurance*, and it is not clear that many people experience moral revulsion at the thought of insurance products being bought and sold as though they were mere commodities.

Insofar as there is a cogent defense of the communitarian view, the strongest argument no doubt hinges on the observation that welfare-state benefits are typically provided in kind, and citizens are not entitled to "cash them in" for something else. This feature of the system appears to be the most incompatible with the liberal egalitarian distributive justice view.[22] For example, a person cannot renounce her right to government health insurance in return for a one-time cash payment (even though in many jurisdictions with socialized medicine, this policy would not be difficult to administer). In the United States, the Supplemental Nutrition Assistance Program (SNAP), which provides food stamps, takes this even further—beneficiaries of the program are typically cut off if they are caught trying to exchange their benefits for cash or other non-food items. One way of interpreting this is simply as paternalism (in the case of food stamps, for instance, a central objective is to stop people using them to purchase alcohol or other drugs). Another interpretation, central to the communitarian view, is that non-fungibility is central to the logic of state provision, and that this sort of "cashing in" is morally odious, comparable to a transaction on the black market for transplant organs.

It should be noted that, in the realm of political debate, the communitarian model of the welfare state is usually based on fairly brute moral intuitions about which things should and should not be bought and sold. The report on health-care in Canada, for instance, did not attempt to explain why the provision of certain goods being a "moral enterprise" precluded the possibility of it being also a "business venture." (After all, as Debra Satz observes, few if any Christians object to the buying and selling of Bibles, proving that mere sacredness is no impediment to commodification.[23]) When the issue is pressed, the specter of people being denied access to the service because of an inability to pay is usually invoked. Yet this confuses the issue of commodification with that of distributive justice. The communitarian is committed to the view that certain things should not be provided on a commercial basis *even if* everyone could afford them.

Thus, the burden of proof on the communitarian is to answer the question, "What's so bad about commodification?" (or, perhaps, "What's so abhorrent that the state must control entire sectors of the economy?").[24] Although several political philosophers have offered sophisticated responses to this question, the standard argument in the public political sphere simply taps into a general unease with the role pecuniary motives play in the private sector (either with respect to the profit orientation of corporations or the role of self-interest in motivating individual economic actors). The thought is that the public sector is able to neutralize these incentives: first, because the state as a whole is nonprofit, and is explicitly committed to promoting the public interest, and second, because of an organizational culture that encourages dedication to the public interest on the part of public-sector employees. Here is Walzer again:

> Needed goods cannot be left to the whim, or distributed in the interest, of some powerful group of owners or practitioners. Most often, ownership is abolished, and practitioners are effectively conscripted or, at least, "signed up" in the public service. They serve for the sake of the social need and not, or not simply, for their own sake: thus, priests for the sake of eternal life, soldiers for the sake of national defense, public school teachers for the sake of their pupils' education. Priests act wrongly if they sell salvation; soldiers, if they set up as mercenaries; teachers, if they cater to the children of the wealthy.[25]

The issue, for communitarians, often comes down to one of motive. Expressed in its crudest form, this means that individuals in the private sector are thought of as acting egoistically, while those in the public sector are thought of as acting altruistically. The scope of the welfare state is determined by moral abhorrence at the suggestion that the provision of essential needs should be instrumentalized and subjected to the corrupting influence of ultimately self-interested actors.

4.3. The public-economic model

This brings us finally to what is often called the "economic" view of the welfare state, according to which its basic role is to resolve collective action problems.[26] The classical liberal state institutionalizes the market economy through the enforcement of property rights and civil contract. The welfare state then emerges in those areas where conventional markets fail to produce reasonably efficient outcomes. State involvement can take the form of regulatory agencies (in cases where the rules of marketplace competition need to be adjusted), state-owned enterprises (SOEs; typically in sectors where efficient competition cannot be organized, because of economies of scale or network externalities), and public goods and services (in cases where a system of effective property rights cannot be instituted, or where the transaction costs associated with a system of voluntary exchange would be prohibitive). According to this analysis, the welfare state essentially does the same thing as the market—both are in the business of enabling mutually beneficial forms of cooperation to emerge—it merely organizes the transactions under somewhat different terms, using administrative authority rather than market exchange in order to realize gains from trade and a division of labor.[27]

Despite the popularity of this view among economists, political philosophers have not been particularly enthusiastic about it for two reasons (above and beyond a general unease with forms of thought that are regarded as "economistic"). First of all, the general objective of resolving collective action problems is often articulated in terms of a commitment to promoting Pareto efficiency. As noted in chapter 3, the economics profession for a long time touted efficiency as a purely technical, value-free standard for measuring the performance of economic systems, not as a principle of justice. Despite the efforts of Rawls and others to show that this is not so, there is still a residual sense that Pareto efficiency is simply not "moral enough" to count as the core of an acceptable normative model of the welfare state.[28] Goodin, for instance, adopts a very common way of speaking when he presents an invidious contrast between "*unfairness*" and "mere inefficiency."[29] He makes it clear that he considers the former a much more serious matter, from the moral point of view, than the latter. This is unfortunate, since there is a clear sense in which inefficiency is much worse than unfairness.

The Pareto principle states that the transition from one social state to another constitutes an improvement if it does not make anyone worse off and makes at least one person better off. There are a variety of more "moralizing" ways of redescribing this. For example, violations of the Pareto principle create outcomes in which at least one person is made worse off, without anyone else receiving any benefit. We might refer to this as "gratuitous suffering." One way of formulating the Pareto principle would therefore be to say that it recommends the elimination of gratuitous suffering. From this perspective, inefficiency seems much worse than mere inequality. With redistributive transfers, even regressive ones, the loss to one individual is at least offset by the gain to some other. It is a win-lose transformation. Inefficient outcomes, on the other hand, are lose-lose. Thus, inequality has a silver lining; inefficiency has none.[30]

The second barrier to the more widespread endorsement of the economic model of the welfare state is that it is often identified with the view that the state should provide "public goods" in the very narrow sense that Paul Samuelson used that term (viz., goods that are "nonrival" and "nonexcludable").[31] Samuelson's adoption of this restrictive definition was driven by his desire to provide what he called a "pure theory"; it was not intended to be a realistic description of what states actually do—rightly so, because there are almost no public goods in the sense in which Samuelson used the term, and providing such goods constitutes an almost imperceptibly slight component of the actual activities of the welfare state. Most of what it does provide are better thought of as "club goods."[32] Samuelson's influential formulation, however, has made it difficult to appreciate the generality of the "market failures" perspective, and the way that it provides a unifying explanation for a superficially heterogeneous set of state activities.

A better framework for understanding the economic theory of the welfare state is the transaction-cost perspective, developed by Ronald Coase and further refined by Oliver Williamson.[33] It was introduced as a way of understanding the existence of corporations, but it applies equally to the state. The analysis begins by positing two elementary institutional forms that can be used to organize "transactions," understood here as cooperative interactions between two or more individuals. There are markets, or, more generally, private contracts, and there are hierarchies, or interactions governed by an authority. The benefits of these transactions take the form of collective action problems that are resolved. For example, two parties may be able to achieve the advantages that stem from a division of labor if they are able to institute an orderly system of property rights and contract, which will permit them to exchange the fruits of their labor. They can achieve the same advantages in a "command and control" system if a superior authority assigns them each a specialized task, then allocates the goods that are produced.

Coase drew this distinction in order to explain the success of corporations within the market economy. "Outside the firm," he observed, "price movements direct production, which is co-ordinated through a series of exchange transactions on the market. Within a firm, these market transactions are eliminated and in place of the complicated market structure is substituted the entrepreneur-coordinator, who directs production."[34] The reason this arrangement makes sense is that, although each different mode of organization generates transaction costs, these costs differ depending on the nature of the transaction. Sometimes, markets have the advantage; other times, hierarchies do. When firms are able to purchase generic inputs from suppliers, for instance, it is fairly easy to organize a competitive market, and so the transaction costs associated with the market form of organization will be relatively low. When firms try to purchase highly specialized inputs, production of which would require suppliers to make asset-specific investments (e.g., purchasing specialized equipment), they set themselves up as potential monopsonists.[35] This raises the cost of market transactions (a cost that includes the potential deadweight losses associated with suppliers being unwilling to make such investments). Under these circumstances, it may make sense for the firm to produce these inputs "in-house," or to take over the supplier and then simply direct its managers to make the needed investments.

One way of describing this theory would be to call it a "market failures" theory of the firm.[36] It is often the case that hierarchies are not a particularly efficient way to organize production when compared to markets. However, sometimes markets fail, in the sense that they do not correct a particular set of collective action problems. Of course, if the benchmark is Pareto optimality, then markets almost always fail. What matters for practical purposes is that this failure is sometimes so egregious that it is possible to achieve a better outcome using a hierarchy to organize the transaction. Thus hierarchical organizations, such as the corporation, succeed in precisely the areas where markets fail (and conversely, markets succeed in precisely the areas where hierarchies fail, because it is all about the *relative* effectiveness of different organizational forms). Market failure can have a variety of causes, but the four most important are incompleteness in the system of property rights (hence the presence of externalities, both positive and negative); information asymmetries (and hence principal-agent, moral hazard, and adverse selection problems); economies of scale (hence varying degrees of imperfect competition); and, finally, difficulties in drawing up and enforcing contracts.

Corporations are able to resolve some but not all of these problems. Their central limitation is that, while they can exercise great power over their members, they are ultimately voluntary organizations. This means that there are certain free-rider problems that they are unable to control. What distinguishes the state, in this context, is that it is the only organization in society that can impose its authority on anyone found within the scope of its territory. (Joseph Stiglitz articulates this idea by saying that membership in the state is "universal" and "compulsory," which captures the spirit of Weber's definition, but obviously requires some qualification in order to be literally correct.[37]) This characteristic—and this characteristic alone—gives the state a unique role to play in the economy, because it gives it the capacity to organize certain transactions in a way that will be much less costly than voluntary contracting, whether on the market or within a firm. Of course, in the case of voluntary transactions, there is a strong presumption that the transaction will be efficiency promoting for the parties involved (otherwise why would they agree to it?). In the case of state-imposed transactions, however, there is no such presumption. And indeed, state power can be used to effect redistributions, as proponents of the egalitarian model of the welfare state correctly observe. But none of this changes the fact that the state can also use its authority to control free riders, and thereby to eliminate some of the more recalcitrant collective action problems, in a way that has significantly lower transaction costs than would any private remedy.

The public-economic model of the welfare state should be interpreted as the view that the state should strive to resolve collective action problems whenever it can do so more efficiently than other institutional forms. This analysis has considerable explanatory power, providing an intuitively natural account of the following set of state activities, at least:

1. *Control of natural monopolies.* In cases where it is inefficient to have more than one supplier of a service (typically because of economies of scale or network externalities), then private markets will not be competitive. Examples include roads, sewers, ports, and electricity-distribution grids. The state can avoid the social costs associated with monopoly pricing, either by assuming ownership of the supplier or by regulating it (in particular, controlling the prices it can charge). Either way, it can impose marginal cost pricing, and therefore achieve both the efficiency gains associated with a single supplier and the level of supply that would be produced in a competitive market.

2. *Control of imperfections in existing markets.* The state very actively discourages the production of negative externalities and encourages the production of positive ones. This involves the regulation of existing markets (e.g., banning harmful environmental contaminants, establishing food safety standards, regulating pharmaceutical products, etc.), imposing Pigovian taxes (e.g., carbon taxes), and subsidizing activities that produce useful spillover effects (e.g., public transit, scientific research, primary education, vaccination, weather forecasting, etc.). The state also tries to limit information asymmetries, particularly between producers and consumers (through truth-in-advertising laws, mandatory warranties, etc.).

3. *Public provision.* When the private sector is left to its own devices, many markets will simply be "missing," in the sense that particular goods or services will not be provided at all (or not in particular areas, or not to particular consumers, etc.) In this case, the state can achieve efficiency gains by imposing taxes or fees, then using the revenue to provide these missing goods. Examples include pest control, national defense, and certain types of police services, along with many forms of insurance. Also, although public provision is the norm, there are cases in which a private firm does the providing (e.g., prisons, military aircraft, mercenaries), in which case the state acts like a "market maker" in the private sector—raising revenue on one side, then making the (collective) purchase on the other. Finally, it should be noted that the state sometimes opts for public ownership with the goal of limiting the production of negative externalities—nuclear power plants and liquor stores are good examples.

4. *Social safety net.* A set of welfare-state programs, including healthcare, old-age pensions, unemployment insurance, and welfare, are often grouped together and referred to as "the social safety net." These are often described as "transfer programs," which is potentially misleading, since they are more accurately described as universal state-run insurance programs.[38] This is particularly obvious in the case of "single-payer" healthcare systems, where healthcare *provision* remains primarily private, but the state exercises a monopoly in the market for health *insurance*. It is also sometimes forgotten that both life annuities and defined benefit pension schemes are fundamentally insurance products, and that most state-run pension schemes amount to the provision of this type of insurance on a national scale. The social safety net, from this perspective, is just a special instance of state provision in the face of missing or inefficient private markets. It merits its own heading, however, because these forms of social insurance are often misclassified as redistributive transfer schemes rather than as risk-pooling arrangements.

These four points are what might be thought of as "bread and butter" public-economics claims.[39] There are several other ways, however, in which the state can use its organizational resources to resolve collective action problems, which have received considerably less discussion:

5. *Minority public goods.* The most important "public goods"—in the non-Samuelson sense of the term—that the welfare state delivers are ones that benefit almost everyone in the society. There are, however, certain goods that stand to benefit only a relatively small number of people, where the group is difficult to identify and for various reasons is unlikely

to self-identify.[40] Examples would include hosting the Olympic games and sponsoring athletes, having national parks, constructing monuments or monumental architecture, and promoting cultural heritage events. Partisans of state involvement often try to posit subtle positive externality effects that enhance the welfare of everyone, in order to defend against the charge that these goods involve interest group rent-seeking. A more forthright defense would simply be to admit that the state is catering to a minority taste in these cases—a taste that would otherwise not be satisfied, because of contracting problems among private parties—but that if the state caters to a very wide range of such minority tastes over time, everyone is likely to benefit from some such activity at some point. Thus, the overall activity of "providing a wide variety of minority public goods" can be seen as a general public good.

6. *Governance failures.* In private-sector discussions of "markets and hierarchies," there is a strong tendency to equate "hierarchies" with "corporations." Private hierarchies are, however, organized under a surprisingly large number of governance structures. There are, of course, different types of corporations (most importantly, partnerships and limited liability corporations). There are also different types of cooperatives, along with "special purpose" corporate forms, such as condominiums, which are essentially consumer cooperatives. And finally, there are nonprofits. Part of the reason for this proliferation of governance structures is that the standard business corporation is sometimes not the most efficient *ownership structure* for a particular economic activity.[41] This is why certain types of economic activity are often undertaken by cooperatives (e.g., insurance) and nonprofits (e.g., universities, daycares). In many cases, however, state intervention is required to guarantee adequate levels of supply. This is particularly so in the case of nonprofits, where private individuals typically lack any economic incentive to create them, but where, once created, they are able to resolve collective action problems caused by the governance structure of investor-owned firms.

7. *Human capital formation.* There is a somewhat exotic class of market failures caused by what are referred to, following John Stuart Mill, as the prohibition of "slavery contracts." The law imposes rather severe restrictions on the ability of individuals to transfer rights over their own future labor to other persons. This means that investments in human capital will be suboptimal because workers, being unable to pledge their future labor as collateral, will find it difficult to obtain loans to finance training and education. More generally, firms will be unwilling to invest in training, because they cannot stop their workers from leaving (and taking their human capital with them). The more general the skills, the more serious the commitment problem,

and so the state must play an active role to provide education and training (and to offer guarantees or financing for student loans). The same problem impedes the formation of worker cooperatives, and so the state may take on a role to promote or subsidize that sector.[42]

These examples show that the characterization of the public-economic model usually found in the literature is often too narrow, especially when it takes the Samuelson definition of public goods as the point of departure. When presented in its full generality, using a transaction-cost analysis, it is an exceedingly robust theory, in that it provides a unified account of regulation, state ownership, and the social safety net. In particular, what might be thought of as the "big-ticket items" of the welfare state—health, education, and pensions (which usually add up to about a quarter of the economy)—can all be understood as a response to different sorts of market failure. Furthermore, the model is able to explain why the state is actually involved in the production and delivery of these goods and services, as opposed to just the financing.

4.4. Assessing the models

All three of these normative models—egalitarian, communitarian, and public-economic—are intended to be "reconstructive," in Jürgen Habermas's sense of the term; that is, they are not merely prescriptive, but instead try to articulate the norms and ideals that are implicit and play a structuring role in our practices.[43] It is always possible that the state should confine itself to providing redistributive transfers, or to protecting communal goods from the incursions of the market; the question is whether the pursuit of these objectives provides a plausible characterization of how existing welfare states are organized. As I have already suggested, the communitarian model is the weakest from this perspective, since it is not able to describe or capture the fine grain of how the welfare state works. For example, from the mere fact that a particular good is, as Bakan puts it, "too precious, vulnerable, or morally sacred"[44] to be subject to commercial exchange, not much seems to follow about the way that good should be provided or consumed. One can see the problem quite clearly in the quotation from Walzer (see section 4.2), in which he lists a set of professionals who, in his view, are prohibited from engaging in market contracting for their services. Priests are supposed to work "for the sake of eternal life," which prohibits them from "selling salvation."[45] Yet this does not require that they be employed in the public sector. Indeed, the only consequence of the focus on salvation seems to be that priests must be paid flat salaries, rather than work on a fee-for-service basis (although this is unsurprising, given how difficult it would be to determine their success rate). Soldiers, however, are obliged to work in the public sector. If they work in the private sector, even on flat salaries, they become "mercenaries" and are subject to opprobrium. With teachers, there is no prohibition on working in the private sector, or even on a fee-for-service basis (presumably, tutoring is permitted). Walzer's only constraint is that public school teachers must not confine their attention to "the children of the wealthy."[46]

One can see from the capriciousness of these strictures that Walzer is not really working out the consequences of his model in a principled fashion, but simply taking existing arrangements and working backward to provide a rationale. The problem is that the moral considerations he adduces are too vague to justify the specific arrangements that prevail, and which he appears to endorse. This is a common feature of communitarian thinking about the welfare state. For example, Maude Barlow and Tony Clarke have written and campaigned extensively against the commodification of water resources. Their central argument for keeping water in "the commons" is that it is "essential to life" and therefore is not just a "need" but a fundamental human "right."[47] This requires that water be publicly owned and provided to all, without charge, by the public sector. Barlow and Clarke vigorously oppose privatizing water services, and where they have been privatized, they call for nationalization. Yet this opposition extends only to water delivered to the home through pipes. When it comes to the bottled water industry, they express concern about environmental impact but do not call for nationalization. Why not? If water is sacred, then it should be sacred whether it is delivered through a pipe or in a bottle. A market failures theory explains the difference quite easily—it's not about the water, it's about the *distribution system*. Water pipes are a natural monopoly, which is why they should be owned by the state. Bottled water is not, and so, despite the various other public policy issues that bottled water raises, there is no case to be made for public ownership of those companies.[48] (One can see the same dynamic in telephone service. There is nothing intrinsic to the nature of telephony that requires state provision, it's just that land lines are a natural monopoly. When mobile phones came along, with a technology that made it possible to organize a competitive market, it was natural that these services would be provided by the private sector.)

Another "fine grain" aspect that the communitarian model has difficulty accommodating is the prevalence of purchaser-provider splits in the delivery of public goods and services. Indeed, communitarians routinely conflate two quite distinct claims: first, that the provision of a particular good should be publicly *funded* (guaranteeing, inter alia, that access will not be limited to those with the ability to pay), and second, that a particular good should be publicly *provided* (which is to say, produced and delivered by employees of the state). When Walzer talks about a moral imperative to "abolish the market" for a particular good, he simply assumes that the two must go together. In his discussion of healthcare, for example, he claims that the requirement to allocate healthcare according to need "can be fulfilled only by turning physicians, or some substantial number of them, into public physicians . . . and by abolishing or constraining the market in medical care."[49] Yet outside the National Health Service (NHS) in the United Kingdom, this is not the typical welfare-state arrangement. Most public healthcare systems guarantee universal access by ensuring that care is publicly *funded* (through state-owned or subsidized insurance schemes and grants to hospitals), but they rely on the private sector (both for-profit and nonprofit), in varying degrees, to provide the healthcare. Similarly, roads, government buildings, military hardware, and, increasingly, services such as garbage collection, are paid for by the government, but supplied by private contractors. Even more common are arrangements in which goods are provided by public-sector employees but paid for privately by consumers. Prominent examples include (in many jurisdictions) postal service, electricity, natural gas, and automobile insurance. Even household water is usually metered, which means that consumers pay for it by volume, as they do with many other commodities.

Again, this is a detail that can be explained quite easily from a market failures perspective. In many cases, the conditions that create the market failure occur on only one *side* of the market: either the supply side or the demand side. Public provision with private purchase is an attractive arrangement when the failure is primarily on the supply side (e.g., natural monopoly); private provision and public purchase is attractive when the failure is on the demand side (e.g., nonexcludability); and, of course, public purchase combined with public provision is best when the market is compromised on both sides. In principle, the communitarian model could provide an account that mirrored this one, focusing on which side of a transaction was morally odious. For example, Walzer's central preoccupation is typically on the demand side; his usual objection to the market is that it is wrong for certain goods to be distributed based on "ability to pay." This could generate an argument for public purchase combined with private provision. Bakan, on the other hand, is more concerned with supply-side considerations, believing that it is immoral for certain goods to be "subject to corporate exploitation."[50] Here, one might imagine a circumstance in which it is wrong to make money from selling something, but there is nothing particularly wrong with buying it, which might, in turn, justify an arrangement involving public provision combined with private purchase. A communitarian theory that developed a more nuanced account of why certain exchanges are prohibited—one that distinguished between supply-side and demand-side issues—might then be able to supply a more robust account of existing welfare-state arrangements.

This, however, raises an interesting question, which is why—factoring out egalitarian concerns about distribution and ability to pay—communitarians consider state provision less odious than private provision. Part of the answer lies in the fact that the communitarian model, unlike either the egalitarian or the market failures perspectives, places great stock in the "public sector ethos."[51] What makes the state distinctive, according to this view, is not just that it has superior powers of coercion (to redistribute or to resolve collective action problems), but that its agents act on the basis of a different sort of *motivation*. Private corporations are motivated by profits, which means that they can be expected to take advantage of consumers whenever they can. The state, on the other hand, is motivated by the public interest, and so is thought to be more trustworthy in dealing with morally sensitive transactions (e.g., when one party is particularly vulnerable, or where the production of externalities is a concern)

This argument must be handled carefully, to avoid the temptation to assume that, because corporations try to maximize profits, the individuals they employ must be motivated by self-interest, whereas in the public sector, where the primary concern is the public interest, civil servants are more likely to act morally. Both private corporations and the state are large bureaucratic organizations, whose employees are motivated by a similar mixture of self-interest and moral constraint. Furthermore, no bureaucratic organization could function at all if its members acted in a purely self-interested fashion; it would fall victim to insuperable agency problems.[52] Thus every organization, private or public, must be able to elicit a degree of cooperative behavior from its employees. To do so, it will typically use a combination of incentives and moral suasion. Thus it is problematic to assume that the public-sector ethos gives the state distinctive organizational capabilities that allow it to achieve objectives that the private sector is unable to achieve, entirely because of its ability to elicit a greater degree of intrinsic, prosocial motivation from its employees. Well-managed corporations also spend a great deal of time and energy inculcating a set of "corporate values," in recognition of the fact that the willingness of employees to set organizational objectives above their narrow self-interest is necessary to the operations of any complex bureaucracy.

There are, no doubt, specific instances in which public-sector work requires selfless commitment—the administration of criminal justice is probably the best example. Here, it is essential to the proper functioning of the system that officers of the court be motivated by non-pecuniary concerns. Privatizing the system simply wouldn't work, not because competitive markets could not be developed, but because the buying and selling of judicial services would erode the deontic structure of legal adjudication. There is, however, a tendency to generalize from examples such as this, and so to imagine that a doctor who works in the public sector will be less likely to perform unnecessary surgery than one who works in the private sector, or that a teacher who works in the public sector will be more concerned about the integrity of the curriculum than a private-sector counterpart, or that a railway ticket agent will be less likely to take advantage of a tourist by selling him a more expensive ticket than he needs, if he works for an SOE.[53] This assumption, that working in an organization dedicated to serving the public interest makes an employee less likely to act in a self-interested fashion, and more likely to act in the public interest, is a straightforward logical fallacy, which can easily translate into a dangerous political illusion. Whether the state is, as a matter of fact, able to motivate its employees to better serve the public is mainly a question of organizational psychology.

Much of the motivation for the widespread expansion of SOEs after the Second World War was the belief that public ownership would result in better service to the public. Thus, Western governments became involved in a variety of enterprises for which there was no obvious efficiency or equality reason for intervention, such as airlines, railroads, mining, and heavy manufacturing. The result of this experiment was the discovery that public ownership did not, in general, translate into better service to the public. In many cases, it did not even translate into effective public control.[54] State-owned enterprises in competitive sectors of the economy often performed worse than private enterprises on every measure—not only did they lose money, but they failed to live up to their public-interest mandate as well. (To take just one example, state-owned nuclear reactors in the United States have a worse record of safety violations than those that are privately owned.[55]) Furthermore, SOEs often formed powerful special interest groups within the state, and pursued their own advantage in a way that was highly detrimental to the public interest.[56] This was one of the major motivations for the widespread movement toward the "commercialization" or "corporatization" of these enterprises.[57] It is noteworthy that this occurred under predominantly left-wing governments (Francois Mitterrand in France, Pierre Trudeau in Canada), prior to the wave of privatization occurring in the 1980s. The objective of commercialization was to reorganize these enterprises in such a way as to make profitability (i.e., revenue to the state) the central criterion for the evaluation of their performance. This grew out of the realization that the earlier public interest mandate was generating what we now refer to as "multitask" agency problems. By specifying too many objectives, many of which were in tension with one another, the state had made it almost impossible to assess the performance of these organizations, which effectively made them unmanageable.[58] It was not just that managers could not be held accountable for failing to advance the public interest; it was that managers often had no way of even *knowing* whether they were effectively advancing the public interest.

As a result, the late 20th century was characterized by greater humility about the state's organizational abilities and, in particular, its ability to motivate its employees to act in a public-spirited way. To the extent that the public-sector ethos has been studied, empirical work has suggested that it plays a fairly small role in the motivation of low-level government employees. It is only at higher levels of the organization that it becomes detectable, and can reasonably be thought to play a significant role in the way that public organizations function.[59] This is pretty much what one would expect from looking at the wage structure in the public service, which is quite flat compared with the private sector (with a higher floor and a much lower ceiling). Thus, low-level state employees typically enjoy a wage premium over their counterparts in the private sector, whereas high-level civil servants suffer a rather significant wage penalty. This means that not only must the state rely more heavily on moral suasion to motivate its high-level employees, but there is also a significant selection effect, whereby employees with stronger pecuniary concerns are more likely to leave the public service once they reach a level at which their outside options become more attractive. Thus at the senior management level, the state is able to expect a fairly distinctive motivational structure among its employees, but at the lower level—the level at which most services get delivered to the public—the state functions in very much the same way as any other large bureaucratic organization. This corresponds, I am sure, to the experience of anyone who has interacted with a front-line state employee and found that the exchange did not involve being transported into a realm of intimate, trusting, communal relations.

To the extent that the communitarian model does provide a coherent conception of what the welfare state should look like, it recommends a strategy for demarcating the public from the private that was essentially abandoned more than three decades ago. Contemporary welfare states are largely structured by the idea that, insofar as the state has a distinctive role to play in the economy, it is not because of the peculiar moral character of its employees, but because of its distinctive institutional powers, in particular, the power of compulsion. This power, however, can be (and is) used in two ways: the first is to redistribute wealth and thereby promote greater equality, and the second is to resolve free-rider problems and thereby promote greater efficiency. The first use, of course, is emphasized by proponents of the egalitarian model, and the second is emphasized by proponents of the public-economic model.

There is no doubt that the state does engage in some economic interventions that are primarily aimed at promoting equality, and some that are primarily aimed at promoting efficiency. There is, furthermore, no contradiction in principle between pursuing these two objectives simultaneously.[60] Thus there is nothing incoherent about a hybrid "egalitarian economic" view of the welfare state. However, the amount of actual egalitarian redistribution that goes on in a typical welfare state is often dramatically overstated. This is because many theorists treat the social safety net, which is essentially a set of government-run insurance programs, as a system of redistribution, and hence governed by an egalitarian logic. This is quite misleading.[61] There is, of course, a sense in which any system of insurance is redistributive, in that its net effect will be to transfer money from the lucky to the unlucky. But this is true whether it is public or private, and whether the unlucky are, in the grand scheme of things, rich or poor. Car insurance transfers money from those who do not have accidents to those who do, just as health insurance transfers money from those who do not get sick to those who do. In both cases, the logic of the redistribution is not egalitarian.[62] This is suggested by the fact that, first, people buy insurance voluntarily, because the transaction is Pareto improving *ex ante,* and second, there is nothing to stop the transfers from being regressive with respect to income.[63] If everyone buys health insurance, but only the rich get sick, then the poor will wind up paying for the healthcare of the rich.

Thus, the reason for the state to be involved in sectors such as health insurance cannot be the redistribution that occurs at the "front end," in the way that medical services are delivered to the public. Making payments to the sick is something that all health insurance does, whether private or public. If there is an egalitarian reason for public involvement, it must be at the "back end," in the redistribution that is achieved by funding the system out of general tax revenues or payroll deductions, rather than charging individuals an actuarially fair premium.[64] But if this sort of redistribution were the only objective, there would be no reason for massive state involvement in the sector. This follows rather closely from the suggestion, made by egalitarians, that markets are best at delivering efficiency, and the state is best at promoting equality. If this were true, then the best policy for the state to pursue, when confronted with any particular inequality, would be to not interfere with the way goods are being traded, but rather, just to redistribute income so that the pattern that emerges out of the set of market transactions is less offensive to the egalitarian sensibility.[65] As Abba Lerner put it, "If a redistribution of income is desired it is best brought about by a direct transfer of money income. The sacrifice of the optimum allocation of goods is not economically necessary."[66] The only reason for state involvement in the provision of goods, on the egalitarian view, would be a paternalistic concern that individuals would not spend cash transfers wisely. The easiest way to handle this, however, is not through state provision or purchase, but simply through the introduction of constraints on the fungibility of transfers to individuals. Egalitarianism, in other words, even when leavened with a generous dose of paternalism, tends to militate in favor of what Ronald Daniels and Michael Trebilcock have called "government by voucher"—where most government-provided services, including health and education, would be privatized, and individuals would be given vouchers that they could use to purchase services—not a conventional welfare state.[67]

Indeed, conservative critics of the welfare state often recommend dismantling state healthcare systems and replacing them with a set of individual health savings accounts.[68] If the objective of the system is simply to ensure that poor people can afford care, they argue, this can be achieved by having the state make a minimum deposit into each individual's account, enough to cover a standard package of healthcare services. If the objective of the system is paternalistic (to force people to purchase healthcare that they need rather than something else), this can be accomplished by making the balances in these savings accounts subject to various restrictions on use, and perhaps even replacing them with vouchers. Either way, there is no reason for the state to get involved in providing or paying for healthcare directly. Healthcare could be delivered by the market, in much the same way that education is provided in charter schools, or food is provided to SNAP recipients.

What the argument for health savings accounts misses is the very powerful efficiency arguments in favor of state-run health insurance systems. The problem with healthcare spending—what makes it quite different from spending on things like food and shelter—is that at the individual level it is extremely unpredictable. It typically follows what is known at the 80/20 rule, namely, that 20 percent of the population accounts for 80 percent of the spending.[69] Thus the average person has very little idea how much to save for his or her future healthcare needs. Saving the average amount required is almost guaranteed to result in under- or oversaving. For example, one large study in the Netherlands showed a huge difference in the average cost of healthcare for individuals in the last year of life (€14,908) compared to other years (€1,102).[70] Even more striking, however, was the standard deviation in final-year expenditure, which was €18,751. This means that even if (*per impossible*) every member of the population set aside a generous €34,000 to cover the cost of end-of-life care, more than 15 percent of the population will still not have saved enough. This makes the case for pooling healthcare savings overwhelming.

The problem is that health insurance is subject to rather severe adverse selection and moral hazard problems (and, therefore, huge administrative costs associated with attempts to *control* adverse selection and moral hazard). State health insurance schemes are able to achieve better results on both fronts, by eliminating adverse selection entirely (in the case of single-payer systems) and eliminating several of the collective action problems that private insurers face when it comes to controlling moral hazard.[71] Indeed, if one looks at any serious proposal for a system of health savings accounts, there is usually a *public* insurance system underlying it, to cover "catastrophic care," or the like. This is in recognition of the fact that forcing individuals to self-insure against extremely costly, unpredictable events is inefficient (i.e., it lowers everyone's welfare). Yet when one examines the numbers carefully, it soon becomes apparent that the insurance mechanism proposed will likely cover the bulk of expenditures in the system.[72] Because of this, the "savings account" winds up being just a complex way of imposing a deductible on an insurance plan.

One can see that the real driving force behind state involvement in the health-care sector is not a general concern about equality, but rather a response to market failure in the health insurance sector.[73] The normative logic of these systems is one of efficiency. The way that public healthcare systems are *financed* is implicitly redistributive, being progressive with respect to income, but this is a property of the tax system, not the healthcare system. Health insurance is provided on terms that are more advantageous to the poor than the wealthy, in the same way that primary education, weather forecasting, national defense, and myriad other public goods are provided on terms that are more advantageous to the poor than the wealthy. This does not make the *rationale* for these programs egalitarian. Of course, socialized medicine systems are often defended through appeal to egalitarian principles in public political discourse.[74] Furthermore, a lot of state intervention in this sector was initiated to achieve egalitarian objectives. Yet what keeps these systems in the public sector, and what creates the political constituencies prepared to defend them against cuts, is the set of efficiency gains they create.

The tendency to misclassify social insurance programs as redistributive, and thus to assume an egalitarian rationale, is quite firmly entrenched in the literature. This is even more common when it comes to pension systems, which actually do take money from one person and give it to another, and so seem like paradigm instances of the state redistributing wealth. For example, in *The Myth of Ownership*, Liam Murphy and Thomas Nagel discuss the US Social Security plan as though its central function was to achieve an egalitarian redistribution of income. The reason it mainly benefits seniors, they claim, is that redistribution toward those who have left the workforce has fewer perverse incentives than redistribution that favors the working-age population. This redistributive intent is "somewhat disguised," they claim, by the fact that "benefits are a function of contribution." Nevertheless, "the program is clearly redistributive: low earners get back more than they put in, and high earners less."[75]

As a matter of fact, the extent to which the retirement-benefit component of Social Security is progressive with respect to lifetime income within cohorts is subject to dispute.[76] Much of the talk about Social Security as a whole fails to factor out the disability insurance program—which will obviously be progressive with respect to *lifetime* income, since it is intended to cover those who are forced to drop out of the labor market prematurely—and the auxiliary benefit. The retirement benefit taken alone, which makes up the bulk of spending, is significantly less progressive than the other components of the system.[77] There is, though, one respect in which the retirement benefit is obviously redistributive—namely, it transfers money away from those who die young and gives it to those who live a very long time. Indeed, one of the factors that diminishes the level of progressivity of the system as a whole is that the rich tend to outlive the poor, and the core function of the system is to redistribute from those who die young to those who live for a long time. This is because the retirement system in the Social Security program is essentially a defined benefit pension scheme, which is to say, a collectively purchased life annuity. And a life annuity is an *insurance product*, designed to protect individuals from the risk of outliving their savings.[78] Just as people do not know how much they should save to meet their healthcare needs, they also do not know how much they should save to meet their need for retirement income. The risk is that one will live too long and thus fall into penury. Average life expectancy at age ten in high-income countries is to age 80 or so, but the standard deviation is very high—close to fifteen years.[79] Assuming retirement at age 65, this means that while the average person will have to save for around fifteen years of retirement, more than 15 percent of the population will, in fact, be retired for more than thirty years. So again, there is a strong case to be made for pooling retirement savings, which is precisely what a life annuity does. The market for private life annuities, however, is subject to adverse selection problems, which means that there are efficiency gains to be achieved through the public administration of such a program.

The US Social Security system is admittedly confusing in this regard, since it bundles together a rather disparate group of programs. The normative logic of government pension schemes is easier to discern in more-developed welfare states, such as Canada's, where there are three distinct programs, each serving a distinct objective. First, there is the Canada Pension Plan (CPP), which is a pay-as-you-go defined benefit pension scheme, governed entirely by social insurance principles (and as such, aimed exclusively at promoting efficiency).[80] Then there is the Old Age Security (OAS) program, which is a universal social program that provides payments to all elderly citizens regardless of their past history of labor-force participation. Finally, there is the Guaranteed Income Supplement (GIS), which is a means-tested transfer scheme designed to supplement the OAS for those without private pensions or savings. The latter two programs have an obvious egalitarian logic. What is important to recognize, however, is that the two egalitarian programs are significantly smaller than the CPP, in terms of total expenditure. (Furthermore, because almost all CPP recipients receive OAS benefits, the CPP benefits are lower than they otherwise would be.) The program that accounts for the majority of spending is the one that is organized around the objective of increasing efficiency.

If one looks at the three major categories of welfare-state expenditure: health, pensions, and education, there is a powerful efficiency-based rationale for each program. This is not to deny that the programs have been implemented in a way that was intended to achieve a measure of implicit redistribution as well. The point is that the redistribution does not explain why these activities are being undertaken in the public sector, whereas the efficiency arguments do explain this. This is why the principle of equality should be seen as subordinate to the principle of efficiency when it comes to understanding these programs. The reasoning underlying the redistributive dimension is something like this: "these services must be provided by the public sector, because the private sector is unable to do so efficiently. However, as long as they are being done in the public sector, we may as well finance them in a way that is progressive with respect to income. This will allow us to carry about a measure of redistribution without suffering too much from the efficiency-equality tradeoff."[81]

Figure 4.1 shows a status quo point *s*, which involves an unequal distribution between two individuals ("rich" and "poor"), which we can take to be the result of a market allocation of income. Points *a* through *e* represent a set of program options. Point *a* represents a Pareto improvement over the status quo, but one that leaves the market pattern of inequality unchanged. Point *b*, by contrast, is also a Pareto improvement, but one that shifts the distribution in a more egalitarian direction, because it benefits poor more than rich, relatively speaking. By contrast, points *c* and *d* are more "purely" redistributive, in that they create a gain for poor and a loss for rich. The chief difference is that the redistribution *c* is welfare-maximizing, because the gain to poor is larger than the loss to rich. Redistribution to *d* is non-welfare-maximizing, in that rich loses more than poor gains. Finally, there is point *e*, which is a "leveling-down" redistribution—it brings the social state closer to equality, but in a way that leaves both individuals worse off (i.e., it is Pareto inferior).

The egalitarian model suggests that the welfare state is primarily in the business of moving the market outcome *s* in the direction of outcomes like *c*, *d*, and possibly *e*. The public-economics view, by contrast, says that the welfare state actually moves society to outcomes like *a* and *b* (and that, to the extent it is egalitarian, this manifests itself primarily as a preference for outcomes like *b*). There is a sense in which *b* is redistributive, because it involves provision of goods to the poor on better terms than they would get on the market, which results in

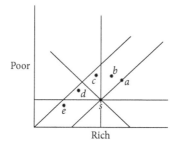

Figure 4.1 Forms of "redistributive" policy.

an overall reduction in inequality. So, for example, when health insurance is financed primarily through general tax revenue, much of which comes from a progressive income tax, then the poor receive this insurance on much better terms than they would get from private insurers. But this desire to provide the good to the poor on better terms is not what justifies the public provision of the good; it is the Pareto improvement that motivates state involvement. If the state were actually a less-efficient health provider, yet exercised a monopoly in the sector to prevent the emergence of undesirable inequalities—as the egalitarian model suggests—then intervention would actually be leveling down (i.e., equivalent to moving to point *e*). Thus, both communitarianism and egalitarianism fail to offer a plausible reconstruction of the dominant logic of the welfare state. Indeed, these accounts typically harbor significant misunderstandings about how welfare-state programs operate (such as Walzer's failure to see the role of purchaser-provider splits in socialized medicine, or Murphy and Nagel's failure to see that US Social Security is essentially an insurance system).

4.5. Wagner's law

One of the most striking features of the welfare state is its extraordinary growth over the course of the 20th century. This growth pattern largely confirmed what is known as "Wagner's law of expanding state activity," which claims that public-sector expenditure can be expected to increase as a percentage of GDP as a society becomes more affluent. This is why richer countries tend to have bigger states.[82] Indeed, welfare-state spending in the 20th century did not just grow along with everything else, but steadily increased its relative share of GDP. This tends to be taken for granted, but it is actually difficult to explain on either the communitarian or the egalitarian model.

One of the most striking features of this growth pattern, in particular, is that it was largely unaffected by the ideological complexion of the political party in power. With very few exceptions, the welfare state continued to expand—in some cases, quite dramatically—under the custodianship of right-wing political parties that explicitly rejected both egalitarian and communitarian ideals.[83] Conservative governments have often introduced changes in the *tax system*, to make income taxes less progressive, or else shifted the burden of revenue-collection to more regressive taxes (such as consumption taxes). But at the same time that the tax system was being made significantly less egalitarian (under, say, Ronald Reagan or Margaret Thatcher), state spending as a whole was still increasing, almost always at a pace that exceeded the rate of economic growth. If the core normative logic of the welfare state involved a commitment to promoting equality, or protecting certain spheres of interaction from commodification, one would naturally expect to see a certain ebb and flow in the activities of the state, expanding after the election of political parties that endorsed this moral vision, and contracting during periods after the election of parties that explicitly rejected it. And yet the actual pattern is not like this. If, however, one regards the major set of welfare-state programs as public goods, in the broad sense of the term, then it is easier to see why they are so notoriously difficult to cut. When a redistributive program is eliminated, those who had been winners in the transfer can be expected to resist, while those who were losers will tend to support the initiative. With a Pareto improvement, on the other hand, the outcome is win-win, and so there is no "natural" constituency to press for its elimination. Thus, the only groups who support cuts tend to be ones motivated by either anti-welfarist political ideologies (such as libertarians) or free-rider incentives. Neither of these are particularly strong or disciplined political constituencies (the former have ideas but no aligned interests: the latter have interests but no plausible ideas).

If indeed the function of the welfare state were to take certain domains of social interaction and have them "inscribed by law and public policy within protective boundaries," as the communitarian view has it, then it is difficult to see why state spending should not remain constant over time, or even constitute a diminishing share of the per capita national product. This is particularly so in cases where the protected domains are interpreted in "basic needs" terms. Once basic needs—say, food, water, shelter, and security—are satisfied, one would expect economic growth to constitute primarily expansion of the sphere of discretionary needs. Thus, one would expect the state sector to *shrink* as a fraction of GDP over time. Even if one interprets "basic needs" in relative terms, so that the list of needs, or the quantity of goods required to satisfy them, expands as overall wealth increases, this still would lead us to expect the state share of spending to remain, at best, constant.[84]

One can see the same problem with egalitarian theories. If the major goal of the welfare state were to redistribute wealth to redress the inequalities produced by the operations of the market economy, why should the *fraction* of wealth that it seeks to redistribute increase steadily over time? The answer cannot be that the state starts out modestly, then works its way closer to the egalitarian ideal. If this were so, then one would expect to see more ebb and flow in spending, corresponding to the level of commitment to egalitarian ideals in the governing party. So why the seemingly inexorable growth in spending?

There have been attempts by egalitarians to explain this phenomenon, none of which have been particularly persuasive. For instance, some have suggested that increased pre-tax income inequality is an endogenous effect of the welfare state, so that the government must increase the amount that it redistributes every year merely to maintain a constant inequality level.[85] The argument is that income-support programs, by cushioning individuals from the ill effects of labor-market failure, encourage riskier career strategies, along with more specialized human-capital investments. This may be efficient overall, but it increases the variability of returns—some people make a lot of money; more people wind up unemployed (or unemployable). The state must redistribute more aggressively to counteract these effects. This becomes an autocatalytic process, the net effect of which is a steady (and, possibly, unsustainable) expansion of state spending as a fraction of GDP over time.

What is noteworthy about this view is that it is the right *kind* of theory. It is, in other words, the sort of theory that proponents of the egalitarian model need in order to explain the expansion of welfare-state spending but have generally failed to provide. As for its merit, much of it rests on empirical claims that are controversial. The general tendency toward increased inequality in Western nations—which is particularly pronounced in the United States—is a puzzling and empirically complex phenomenon. But among the leading contenders for an explanation, the moral hazard effects of social insurance programs do not rank very high, especially because the United States provides so little in the way of social insurance.

The public goods perspective, on the other hand, offers a simple explanation for the expansion of the welfare state. Indeed, Wagner's law is sometimes formulated as the claim that "the income elasticity of demand for public goods is greater than unity."[86] This is actually not a formulation of the law, but rather a proposed explanation for it—one that presupposes the correctness of the public goods framework. Unpacking things a bit, the view is as follows: The state taxes people in order to provide public goods. As people become wealthier, they want to spend an increasing fraction of their income gains on public goods, and so, to the extent that the state is responsive to public preferences, growth in per capita GDP will lead to an increase in state spending as a fraction of GDP.

One feature of this view that is worth drawing attention to is the fact that it actually asserts the opposite of the "basic needs" or "sufficientarian" claim, which says that the job of the state is to ensure that everyone has the basic goods required for a decent life. If anything, these sorts of basic goods (food, clothing, shelter) are the ones that the *market* does a good job of providing. What the state provides, by contrast, are discretionary goods (in the sense that they are goods for which there is low demand at low income levels), which is precisely why the demand for state services increases disproportionately with gains in income. One can see this trajectory very clearly in developing nations, where at early stages of growth the population puts enormous emphasis on consumer durables (refrigerators, bicycles, televisions, mobile phones, etc.), as well as food (particularly meat) and housing, all of which the market delivers quite efficiently. Only once these "basic needs" are satisfied do people begin to worry about various "quality of life" issues, such as sanitation, water and air quality, healthcare, and insurance of various types—all of which are best delivered by the state.

Of course, many welfare-state programs are engaged in what Gøsta Esping-Andersen and John Myles refer to "horizontal redistribution"—namely, reallocation of income over the individual's own life cycle. This characterizes not only social insurance programs, such as healthcare and pensions, but a lot of education spending as well (insofar as education generates higher employment earnings later in life). As income (and life expectancy) increases, it is natural that individuals would want to engage in more horizontal redistribution, and because many of these transfers are mediated by the state, it will show up as increased state spending. Thus, it is not always increased demand for public goods, as such, that generates the increase in state spending. An increased taste for leisure—understood broadly to include time spent in school and in retirement—will generate increased demand for horizontal transfers of income, making it unsurprising to see that these transfers increase as a fraction of GDP over time.

Other cases seem to fit the "increased demand for public goods" pattern more clearly. There is a sense in which private goods are the "low hanging fruit," when it comes to organizing production, simply because markets have such low transaction costs. Even if the public sector has lower transaction costs than the private sector when it comes to delivering a specific service such as mass transportation, there may be close substitutes, such as private transportation, that have lower costs still. Thus production and consumption will initially be focused on these private goods, and it is only with increased satiation (or crowding) in these areas that the transaction costs associated with the public good will begin to seem like a price worth paying. The importance of negative externalities (such as congestion and pollution) will also tend to grow over time, not always because the absolute magnitude of their welfare effects increases, but also because their relative significance increases, simply because they remain unchecked, while the marginal value of increased consumption of private goods declines.

Finally, it should be noted that with increased wealth comes a relative decline in the consumption of material goods and increased consumption of what Fred Hirsch referred to as "positional goods."[87] This is codified in the form of what I call Hirsch's Law, which states that "as the level of average consumption rises . . . the satisfaction that individuals derive from goods and services depends in increasing measure not only on their own consumption but on consumption by others as well."[88] Thus wealthy individuals spend an increasing portion of their income on goods that are valued for the positional advantage that they confer: status, exclusivity, style, design, beauty, trendiness, hipness, or location (in real estate). The satisfaction generated by consumption of these goods is zero-sum in the aggregate. This decreases the relative value of these goods, as a class, compared to public goods, which tend to be non-positional (in particular, when they are supplied universally).[89] The overall effect, again, will be a shift toward increased state spending as the society becomes wealthier.

4.6. The rent-seeking view

Before we leave the topic, it is important to acknowledge an important alternative to all the positions canvassed here, which differs primarily in that it regards the growth of the welfare state over time as primarily a negative development. It takes as its point of departure the acknowledged fact that the state is distinguished from all other social institutions by its ability to coercively impose transfers between individuals.[90] From a certain perspective, this makes all its activities somewhat suspicious. After all, if a transaction is mutually beneficial, then there is no need to get the state involved; individuals can be expected to undertake it voluntarily. The state's getting involved then naturally arouses the suspicion that one party is trying to force the other to do something that it does not want to do. So unlike the egalitarian model, which views the market as the domain of efficiency and the state as the domain of equality, this view regards the market as the domain of the voluntary (and efficient) and the state the domain of the involuntary (and non-efficient or, perhaps, inefficient). The two positions agree, however, in seeing the state as primarily the locus of "unproductive transfers" between individuals.

If all individuals were similarly positioned, able to wield equal influence over state policy, then redistributive transfers would be difficult to achieve. The interests of the potential winners would be checked by those of the potential losers. Because of collective action problems, however, some individuals who share a particular interest are easier to organize than others (because there are fewer of them or they are geographically concentrated, or they are in regular communication with one another, etc.). If the potential winners are better organized than the potential losers, they may be able to secure such a transfer. For example, farmers may be able to successfully lobby for protective tariffs, because the higher food prices this generates for consumers are practically imperceptible, and consumers typically lack sufficient incentive to create the organizations needed to resist such policies. Because this type of limitation on competition generates an economic "rent," which is, in turn, appropriated by the farmers, this model of the welfare state can be referred to as the "rent-seeking" model.

Of course, this is not a positive normative account of the welfare state. On the contrary, it encourages the view that the welfare state is a parasitic accretion on the otherwise healthy market economy. I mention it because it shares with the egalitarian perspective an understanding of the welfare state as primarily redistributive in function, and has therefore tended to enhance the plausibility of the idea that the fundamental logic of the state is different from that of the market. Both views share an understanding that the primary institutional characteristic of the state is its capacity to impose transfers; the disagreement arises only at the normative level: is the redistribution that goes on mainly good or mainly bad? The rent-seeking model also constitutes an important challenge to the egalitarian view, insofar as it puts pressure on the liberal egalitarian to explain what sort of decision mechanisms or institutional constraints prevent the egalitarian state from becoming simply a rent-seeking free-for-all.

The challenge is made somewhat more pressing by the fact that it is not difficult to find state policies that are a consequence of precisely the logic that the rent-seeking model criticizes, and where the dynamic that sustains these policies also quite clearly fits the model. The most commonly cited example, in the Canadian context, is the dairy supply management system, which imposes domestic quotas on the production of milk and eggs for commercial sale (combined with significant tariffs on imports from the United States). By limiting entry to the market, the system has the effect of driving up the price of dairy products quite significantly. Consumers, however, are a diffuse and poorly organized group, while dairy farmers are highly organized and extremely vocal. (Ownership of quotas has also become more concentrated over time, reducing the number of farmers in the system from more than 145,000 when it was instituted to slightly more than 9,000 in 2017.[91]) Whatever the rationale for the system may have been at the time it was adopted, it persists only because politicians are not interested in invoking the wrath of farmers, especially given that they are not subject to any countervailing pressure from consumers. Indeed, food manufacturers have been the most vocal opponents of the system, especially those in the pizza industry, who are the major bulk purchasers of cheese. Their interest in the matter, of course, is less than that of consumers, the difference is merely that they are *organized* in a way that consumers are not. All this serves to illustrate the basic point, central to the rent-seeking analysis, that these asymmetries in organizational capacity set the stage for the state to impose unproductive transfers (and for various organizations to waste resources campaigning for such transfers).

There are many other domains in which an institutional arrangement that could plausibly be construed as promoting efficiency in some instances has been extended in dubious ways that seem to be a consequence of rent-seeking. One example is professional licensing, through which the state prohibits individuals from offering certain services unless they possess appropriate certification. This can in some cases be a legitimate way of resolving a market failure caused by information asymmetries.[92] The canonical example involves providers who are able to make a costly investment that allows them to provide a genuinely high-value service (in, say, education). However, if consumers are unable to distinguish this genuinely high-value service from a low-value one provided by those who have not made the relevant investment, then the market price will be bid down to the point where it is no longer economical for anyone to make the investment. Typically, the way this market failure gets resolved is that the high-value service providers form a professional association and limit entry to those who have demonstrated the capacity to provide the service. In some cases, the professional association is able to establish a strong enough "brand" that consumers will naturally gravitate to it, but in other cases, the association turns to the state for enforcement, to limit market entry to those who possess the appropriate certification. With groups such as doctors and lawyers there is reason to think that this arrangement is efficiency promoting on the whole. Nevertheless, since the basic mechanism involves limiting entry to the market in order to allow incumbents to charge higher prices, it is inevitable that other occupational groups will want to copy the arrangement, even in cases where it takes little effort for consumers to distinguish low-value providers from high-value providers. When this is combined with the credulity or venality of politicians, the result has been a wild proliferation of occupational licensing regimes, for example, restricting the market for haircuts to licensed beauty parlors, for decorating advice to licensed interior decorators, and so on.

There are many subtler ways in which economic actors can use the state apparatus to limit competition, and thereby to secure economic rents. Many American manufacturers with a history of opposing regulation reversed course when they began to experience serious competition from China. Several, in fact, began to lobby the US government for stricter, more detailed product-safety regulations.[93] The goal was to prevent the entry of foreign goods into US markets. In general, the more detailed and complex a set of regulations, the more difficult it will be for new firms, smaller firms, and foreign firms to comply. This produces economic rents for incumbents. The patent regime also produces formidable barriers to entry. Technology corporations accumulate an arsenal of extremely vague and general patents, then enter into exclusive cross-licensing arrangements with one another.[94] No money changes hands, but the arrangement generates a legally enforceable barrier to entry for all new firms, which are denied access to the patents.

Finally, it is important to recognize that state employees are also an interest group, quite capable of engaging in rent-seeking behavior. William Niskanen made the influential suggestion that it is in the nature of bureaucratic organization for managers to want to maximize their budgets.[95] (This tendency must surely be familiar to all university professors, who consider it an essential function of the department chair to constantly press for an increase in the department's budget and faculty complement.) With private-sector bureaucracies, this growth tendency is constrained by the fact that budgets must ultimately be financed by voluntary transactions. Considering the state's powers of compulsion, however, there is no reason that state bureaucracies cannot expand continuously, until they choke off all other economic activity. Even setting aside these managerial imperatives, wage pressure from state employees also tends to increase spending over time. Whereas private-sector wage demands are moderated by the desire to keep the firm solvent, no such constraint prevails in the public sector, and the state can, in principle, simply raise taxes to finance ever-higher wages (and pensions).

Again, it would be foolish to deny that these pathologies exist or to say that one cannot find such *tendencies* in the modern welfare state. It is also important to recognize that some countries are worse than others, based on innumerable features of the state system that make rent-seeking more or less likely to be successful. The question is whether what we can observe are just that—tendencies, hazardous dynamics that must be resisted—or whether they actually constitute the core logic of the welfare state. In other words, is rent-seeking the engine that has been driving welfare-state growth, or is it an unfortunate by-product? This question cannot be answered at the level of theory. It is, however, important to notice a significant difficulty with the rent-seeking model, at least in its cruder forms. In my original statement of the view, I began by claiming that "if a transaction is mutually beneficial, then there is no need to get the state involved, individuals can be expected to undertake it voluntarily." This is a fallacy, since individuals often fail to contract to mutually beneficial outcomes. So to the extent that the rent-seeking view is founded on claims of this sort, the suspicion will be that it simply fails to take the possibility of collective action problems and market failure seriously enough.[96] Recognizing that coercion is often necessary to bring about efficient outcomes disrupts the equivalency that is drawn in the rent-seeking model between the voluntary and the efficient, on the one hand, and the involuntary and the inefficient, on the other.

The major problem with the rent-seeking model, however, is empirical. If the welfare state is nothing but a parasitic accretion on the market economy, it follows that there should be a negative correlation between economic growth and the expansion of the state sector. Looking back over the 20th century, however, high levels of social transfers are positively correlated with wealth—the most affluent societies are also the ones with the most developed welfare states. As Peter Lindert has observed, "Nine decades of historical experience fail to show that transferring a larger share of GDP from taxpayers to transfer recipients has a negative correlation with either the level or rate of growth of GDP per person. The average correlation is essentially zero."[97] Nations with large welfare states tend to be rich, and to enjoy both high levels of labor productivity and leisure. This suggests, in turn, that the more pessimistic diagnoses of the welfare state may have misunderstood many of the transfers that are occurring. In particular, the rent-seeking model shares with the social justice model a tendency to misclassify social insurance arrangements as redistributive, and therefore to ignore the efficiency rationale for much of the social safety net.[98]

4.7. Conclusion

Many people would count themselves supporters of the welfare state, on the grounds that its activities make society a great deal more just than it otherwise would be. If pressed for further details, however, what tends to emerge is a hazy amalgam of communitarian, egalitarian, and public-economic ideas. In some cases, this is not a problem, since these normative accounts are not strictly incompatible with one another, and it is possible to find some programs that fit each different model. Nevertheless, for policy purposes it is important to be clear about the dominant logic of the welfare state, and about the normative basis of particular state programs.

Consider, for example, debates that have arisen in the domain of healthcare. Commitment to a communitarian model of the welfare state has tended to favor what Evan Davis calls the "traditional public sector model," where goods are both paid for and provided by the state. This suggests that the health system should function as a single, vertically integrated service provider, in which physicians work as salaried state employees, on the model of the NHS. The contracting out of even minor services will seem problematic from this perspective. This is a highly inflexible arrangement, one that imposes significant efficiency losses. The temptation then is to retreat to an egalitarian position and argue that some contracting out is permissible as long as the principle of equal access to timely, quality care is guaranteed. The problem is to explain why *all* services should not be contracted out or why socialized medicine systems should not be abolished entirely, in favor of a system in which individuals are given an income supplement or voucher that they can use to purchase care (as recommended, for instance, by the "Ryan plan" passed by the US Congress in 2011, which would have abolished the federal program that currently provides health insurance for all Americans over the age of 65). It is simply impossible to explain what is wrong with such proposals without pointing to the problem of market failure in the health insurance sector. And once this has been pointed out, nothing more needs to be said to make the case for a socialized medicine system (along "single payer" lines). One can appeal to egalitarian principles in deciding how this system should be *financed*. But the boundary between public and private with respect to service delivery can be drawn entirely through appeal to efficiency considerations.

Thus the public-economic model of the welfare state provides both the best theoretical reconstruction of the existing configuration of welfare-state services, and the most useful set of principles to guide any proposed expansion or modification of these services. Indeed, the usual complaint against the model is not that it lacks explanatory adequacy, but that it is not "moral enough" to count as a guide to policy. This is, as I have attempted to show, largely a consequence of a misunderstanding of the Pareto principle. (In the domain of healthcare, for instance, the term "inefficient" is simply another way of referring to arrangements that generate unnecessary suffering and death. Eliminating "inefficiency" in this sense—by resolving the collective action problems that produce it—is clearly a morally significant enterprise.)

It should be acknowledged that many of the historical processes that gave rise to these programs did not come about through an explicit commitment to efficiency. There are some exceptions, such as the 1942 Beveridge Report in the United Kingdom, which laid out the efficiency rationale for the social insurance system quite clearly. In many other cases, however, the state's involvement in particular sectors was motivated by nation-building considerations, or by more ambitious socialist projects that had an explicitly egalitarian rationale. Public health insurance in Canada, for instance, was introduced primarily as a way of ensuring the provision of services in rural and geographically remote regions. The reason that these programs survived, however, through subsequent rounds of cutbacks and privatization, is that they wound up being efficiency-promoting, which meant that there was no natural constituency pressing for their abolition. Thus, the win-win structure of these arrangements winds up explaining their persistence, even in cases where it does not explain their origins.

The important point is that, through a combination of direct and indirect mechanisms, liberal principles of justice, and in particular, the principle of Pareto efficiency, have become institutionalized in the welfare state. The overarching commitment to neutrality has meant that liberal principles are conflict-minimizing, which has not only served to recommend them as guiding principles for the design of welfare-state institutions; it has also given programs organized along these lines greater survivability over time. While the liberal conception of neutrality is highly contentious in the academic literature, it does not take much to grasp the thought that citizens have a number of fundamental disagreements with one another, yet despite this, still have opportunities to create systems of cooperation that will produce win-win outcomes. As a result, the principle that recommends setting aside the disagreements to focus on the potential gains, is the one that becomes effective, not because academics have succeeded in articulating an uncontroversial conception of efficiency, but because the principle succeeds in minimizing actual social conflict and thus in promoting cooperation under conditions of value pluralism.

This commitment to liberal principles, it should be noted, extends through all three branches of the state. This is why the portrait I sketched in chapter 2 of members of the executive branch developing an independent conception of the public interest, based upon a commitment to liberal principles, is not one that we should find alarming. If the morality in question were a purely theoretical construct, or an abstract doctrine like Rawls's difference principle, then this sort of autonomy would seem to be a recipe for chaos or insubordination (e.g., one can imagine liberal civil servants facing off against communitarian civil servants, each group coming to an entirely different conclusion about what political morality requires in a particular circumstance). The way to dissolve the anxiety is to observe that liberalism is not just one theory among many; it represents the set of principles that are institutionalized in the welfare state. As a result, when civil servants who are developing policy proposals or exercising discretionary power are guided by principles such as Pareto efficiency, they are actually just acting in ways that are consistent with, and perhaps extending slightly, the core logic of the welfare state. Furthermore, because liberal principles have been guiding the development of Western states for over two centuries, they are also institutionalized in the professional culture of the civil service. The public-sector ethos entrenches a set of fundamentally liberal norms. So again, we need not worry about the disorder that might result from state employees following their own private moral convictions. Acting ethically, in most cases, simply involves following the norms, or the best practices, of the civil service.

One can see the influence of liberal principles quite clearly in the way that the civil service conceives of the public interest. Nowhere is this more evident than in the growing influence of cost-benefit analysis over the course of the 20th century and into the 21st. Indeed, cost-benefit analysis is regarded by many as the biggest hammer in the toolbox of "technocratic" decision-making. In the next chapter, I will argue that it represents an extension of the efficiency logic that has guided the development of the welfare state. Subsequent chapters will then examine the role of equality (which is expressed primarily in terms of a commitment to the rule of law), and liberty (which takes the form of an anti-paternalism constraint).

In recent years, the civil service has become insistent that public policy be evidence-based. Evidence of what? would be the natural follow-up question. The answer cannot be just evidence of effectiveness, because there are always more or less costly ways of achieving the same effects. What the demand for evidence amounts to, increasingly, is a demand for evidence that the benefits of a policy are greater than the costs. This is offered not merely as "advice" to elected officials; it is a demand being made by the executive, reflecting an independently formulated conception of good policy. At the same time, it is extremely unpopular in some quarters, and is often perceived as involving a commitment to controversial philosophical or political doctrines. Thus my central objective in chapter 5 is to show that cost-benefit analysis *as institutionalized and employed in contemporary welfare states* is a straightforward extension of modern liberal principles.

5

Cost-Benefit Analysis as an Expression
of Liberal Neutrality

The past few decades have seen a steady expansion in the use of cost-benefit analysis (CBA) as a tool for policy evaluation in the public sector. In 2003, the *Green Book* was introduced in the United Kingdom, with its requirement that "all new policies, programmes and projects, whether revenue, capital or regulatory, should be subject to comprehensive but proportionate assessment, wherever it is practicable, so as best to promote the public interest . . . This is achieved through identifying other possible approaches which may achieve similar results; wherever feasible, attributing monetary values to all impacts of any proposed policy, project and programme; and performing an assessment of the costs and benefits for relevant options."[1] The book as a whole is described as providing "binding guidance for departments and executive agencies."[2] And in the United States, where CBA has been mandatory for all major regulatory initiatives since 1981, many progressive groups that had historically refused to participate in such exercises (based on the perception that CBA was part of a broader antiregulatory agenda), have slowly come around to the view that they need to learn to accept the approach, and work toward using it to their advantage.[3]

One of the most striking features of the slow, steady advance of CBA across a range of jurisdictions is that it typically arises through the initiative of the executive branch of government (e.g., via an executive order in the United States, or as Treasury guidance in the United Kingdom). Part of this stems from a simple desire on the part of the civil service to impose greater consistency on the hodgepodge of evaluative standards that legislatures write into statutes in different domains, at different points in time.[4] For example, environmental hazards and health hazards in the United States are governed by different statutes, which impose inconsistent standards. Thus, there is an understandable desire to develop a common basis of evaluation to curtail the obvious irrationalities that would arise from a mechanical application of legislatively imposed standards. In other respects, the pressure to adopt CBA stems from a set of more substantive commitments that arise endogenously from the executive branch.[5] As noted, the push for evidence-based policy generates significant pressure in the direction of CBA, since in addition to purely scientific and technical analysis, the type of

The Machinery of Government. Joseph Heath, Oxford University Press (2020). © Oxford University Press.
DOI: 10.1093/oso/9780197509616.001.0001

"evidence" sought generally includes some indication that the benefits of a policy are likely to exceed its costs.

Yet despite its practical merits, the growing popularity of CBA has been a source of consternation to many philosophers and political theorists, who are inclined to view it as simply a variant of utilitarianism, and consider utilitarianism to be completely unacceptable as a public philosophy.[6] This interpretation of CBA—as a type of applied utilitarianism—is rendered more plausible by the fact that many of its most prominent academic defenders are in fact utilitarians (or moral consequentialists), and defend it on the grounds that it approximates what they take to be the correct comprehensive moral view.[7] Furthermore, there is the obvious fact that CBA has at its core a calculation that is consequentialist, aggregative, and appears to presuppose a welfarist theory of value—all positions that are associated with utilitarianism. Finally, and perhaps most problematically, CBA seems to exhibit what many people take to be the central flaw of utilitarianism, namely, that it does not respect the distinctness of persons. This is reflected in a variety of ways, including an apparent commitment to distributive neutrality (the view that, as long as the total quantity of welfare is constant, it is a matter of indifference from the standpoint of society how that welfare is distributed) as well as its willingness to place a valuation on human life (suggesting that, if one person's death would produce a sufficient compensating benefit to others, then society should be willing to let that person die).

These observations do conspire to present what is, admittedly, a rather damning circumstantial case. The situation, however, is more complex than it may at first appear. The first and most important thing to appreciate is that CBA is not literally a decision procedure, which is to say, it is never applied "baldly" to any particular policy question. It is always embedded in a set of more complex institutional decision procedures, which impose a set of constraints that reflect essentially non-utilitarian concerns.[8] My central objective in this chapter is to show that, because of this, CBA *as institutionalized* in representative modern welfare states is better understood as reflecting a commitment to a set of concerns that are widely shared by political liberals. First and foremost, it is used to determine what outcome private individuals would have contracted to—which is to say, agreed upon—absent some market failure. The underlying normative principle is therefore Pareto efficiency, not full-blown utilitarianism. The basic commitment is to resolving collective action problems, not promoting social welfare in the aggregate.

Because the introduction of CBA has been so controversial, its use has generated a bewildering array of objections, along with replies to the objections, replies to the replies, and so on, creating a body of literature that is very difficult to survey and assess. As my point of entry, therefore, instead of trying to present a synoptic overview, I will instead present what I think of as a "primrose path," which starts with a fairly uncontroversial form of liberalism, but ends with a full-fledged commitment to comprehensive CBA of the sort mandated by the *Green Book*. I invite the reader to imagine a junior analyst, who shows up for work on the first day of her new job in the civil service, having not one speck of sympathy for utilitarianism, but affirming rather the basic principles of modern liberalism. As she confronts a series of public policy questions, she finds herself accepting the reasonableness of CBA as a way of picking out the best policy. The process is not entirely one-sided—certain constraints get added to the CBA procedure along the way, in order to make it acceptable. What emerges in the end is a more complicated, but normatively more sophisticated, decision procedure, whose basic framework I will try to articulate.[9]

5.1. Embedded CBA

It is important to recognize from the very beginning that CBA *as institutionalized* is very different from the abstract decision procedure described in introductory public finance textbooks.[10] (I will use the terms "bald" CBA to refer to the textbook version, and "embedded" CBA to refer to the procedure within its broader institutional context.[11]) The overall impact of CBA, for instance, is strongly affected by the choice of problems to which it is applied. Most importantly, governments do not apply CBA to programs that are purely, or even primarily, redistributive. It is not difficult to see why. Suppose one were to propose a new program called "taking money away from the rich and giving it to the poor." Using a standard willingness-to-pay (WTP) willingness-to-accept (WTA) framework for measuring the benefits and costs (respectively), this program would be guaranteed to be at least CBA-neutral. (The amount that a person should be willing to pay, to receive a transfer of $1,000, should be exactly the same as the amount that a person would need to be paid, in order to accept a loss of $1,000, viz., $1,000.) Also, because money is subject to diminishing utility, the UK *Green Book* recommends imposing a set of distributional weights on the WTP/WTA amounts, stipulating that benefits to the lowest-income quintile ("the poor") be subject to a multiplier in the range of 1.9 to 2.0, while benefits to the upper quintile ("the rich") be discounted, with a multiplier in the range of 0.4 to 0.5. Using the high end of these values suggests that taking $1,000 away from a rich person and giving it to a poor person produces a net benefit to society of $1,500 (i.e., above and beyond the $1,000 itself, which nets out).

Of course, the fact that bald CBA has this consequence should come as no surprise to anyone, since this sort of derived egalitarianism is a well-known implication of utilitarianism (when applied to a world in which money, or consumption generally, is subject to diminishing returns). So the fact that CBA is not applied to this sort of problem (e.g., "How high should GIS payments be?"), should serve as the first hint that, underlying CBA, there is not actually a commitment to utilitarianism.

When one looks at the problems that CBA is applied to, what one finds is that they are almost exclusively instances of market failure (or, more generally, collective action problems). In the United States, Executive Order 12866, issued by President Clinton, makes this reasonably explicit with respect to regulations: "Federal agencies should promulgate only such regulations as are required by law, are necessary to interpret the law, or are made necessary by compelling public need, such as material failures of private markets to protect or improve the health and safety of the public, the environment, or the well-being of the American people. In deciding whether and how to regulate, agencies should assess all costs and benefits of available regulatory alternatives, including the alternative of not regulating."[12] Despite a somewhat complex history of subsequent amendment, the impact of this order has been to put the burden squarely upon agencies proposing new regulations to specify the market failure they are responding to.[13] Thus the goal of a regulation cannot simply be to increase social welfare, it must be to solve a collective action problem that private parties are unable to resolve through voluntary contracting. This suggests that the underlying rationale for CBA is actually Paretian (i.e., aimed at producing Pareto improvements), rather than utilitarian.

Given the importance of this distinction, it is worth dwelling on it for a moment, to ensure that it is not subject to any misunderstanding. An intuitive way of representing the difference between Paretianism and utilitarianism is to show how they resolve a two-person distribution problem. Figure 5.1 shows a set of possible social states, with the status quo corresponding to an allocation of utility between two individuals. The line U shows the set of other social states with the same aggregate utility level as the status quo.[14] Utilitarianism therefore ranks any point to the northeast of this *line* as superior to the status quo. The Pareto principle, by contrast, ranks every social state to the northeast of the *point* that represents the status quo—including those strictly north and strictly east—as superior. Informally, this is the set of win-win (or at least no-lose) outcomes. Changes that make one person better off but leave the other worse off are Pareto-noncomparable and are not ranked by the Pareto principle. Thus, it has nothing to say about the more controversial set of proposals, to the northwest and the southeast of the status quo. Utilitarianism, by contrast, makes the controversial claim that it is acceptable to harm one person, to the benefit of another, as long as the magnitude of the benefit is greater than or equal to that of the harm. Thus, the Pareto principle is about as attractive and uncontroversial as a normative principle can get (although it achieves this through the somewhat dubious means of simply saying nothing about the set of cases most likely to arouse controversy).

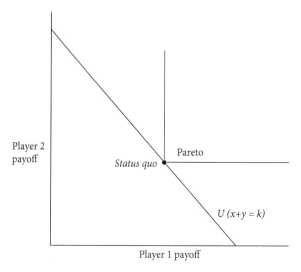

Figure 5.1 Utilitarianism versus Paretianism.

In textbook treatments, the way that CBA is usually presented to students is not by starting with the moral case for utilitarianism. Typically, the argument starts with the Pareto principle, which is often treated as either self-evident or self-recommending. The argument then moves along quickly to the observation that, under real-world conditions, we are unlikely to find many pure Pareto improvements. Making an omelet always seems to require breaking at least one egg. (For example, no matter how magnificent and useful a certain infrastructure project will be, there always seems to be one landowner who refuses to sell at any price.) We do not want it to be the case that a harm to a single person is able to hold up a vast project that could benefit many others. So, we need a way to articulate the idea that the benefits to the many should, on occasions such as this, outweigh the harm to the few. The Kaldor-Hicks principle is then proposed as an alternative criterion—that if the gains to the winner are great enough that they *could* be used to compensate the loser, then the proposal is ranked better than the status quo. This is sometimes known at the "potential Pareto" principle, because whenever it is satisfied, it means that one could, in principle, carry out the compensation, which would then make the outcome an actual Pareto improvement.[15]

Mild sleight of hand is often involved in presenting this argument. The Kaldor-Hicks principle is usually made to sound like only a slight modification of the Pareto principle. Once it is clear, however, that compensation need not actually be paid, it is obvious that the principle is practically equivalent to full-blown utilitarianism (they diverge only in cases where, even though a particular change would increase aggregate utility, compensation is not possible because of differing attitudes toward the medium in which compensation would be paid). This observation has led some critics, such as Amartya Sen, to argue that the Kaldor-Hicks principle is either redundant or unacceptable.[16] If the intention is actually to pay the compensation, then there is no need for a "potential" Pareto principle; one only needs the Pareto principle, because after the compensation has been paid, an actual Pareto improvement will have been achieved. So for the principle to have any purpose, there must not be any intention to pay compensation. But if that is the case, then the principle is subject to all the traditional objections to utilitarianism. In particular, it seems difficult to justify imposing a loss on someone just by saying, "Well someone else is gaining more than you are losing."

The major claim I make in the discussion that follows is that, even though bald CBA uses the Kaldor-Hicks criterion, embedded CBA does not (in practice) but is instead used in the pursuit of actual Pareto improvements. It primarily achieves this through the choice of problems to which it is applied. Formally, this can be represented by subjecting the basic calculus to two "screening" procedures, one on the input side and the other on the output side.[17] On the input side, policy proposals that are not essentially a response to collective action problems (e.g., questions about the progressivity of the tax code, changes to the criminal law) are set aside as being unsuitable for CBA. Once the CBA is conducted (and, as we shall see, an enormous number of further normative judgments go into determining how it should be conducted), the results are weighed against other considerations. Most obviously, in cases where significant costs would be imposed upon some people, the question of whether they will *actually* be compensated becomes important. If it is impossible to compensate them (e.g., because they cannot be identified or one cannot exclude impostors), then one might decide not to pursue the policy, and so the potential welfare gain would be screened out on the output side.

The major commitment at the heart of CBA can be expressed in the form of a principle of efficiency:

1. *Pareto improvement.* The state should seek to resolve collective action problems that private actors are either unable to resolve, or unable to resolve at reasonable cost through voluntary contracting.

This is combined with a second set of commitments, which are central to liberalism, and closely connected to the privileging of the Pareto standard. The first is a commitment to liberal neutrality, broadly construed:

2. *Liberal neutrality.* The state should avoid adopting policies that can only be justified through appeal to particular controversial values.

There is obviously a close connection between this commitment to neutrality and the Pareto principle, since the central attraction of a Pareto improvement is that it allows the state to bring about an outcome that is deemed better for all, each from his or her own perspective—which is to say, according to each individual's own conception of the good, or system of values. Pareto efficiency is therefore the paradigm instance of a normative principle that the state can act on without presupposing the correctness of any first-order conception of the good.

As we shall see, a great deal of the resistance to CBA is a consequence of the difficulty many people have accepting the constraints imposed by the principle of liberal neutrality when it comes to their own most deeply-held values. It is, after all, much easier to say that the state should not take a particular set of values as a basis for policy when one considers those values to be woefully mistaken than it is when they are values that one considers correct. For example, in the area of environmental policymaking, many of the objections to CBA are, at bottom, objections to the fact that the procedure treats a very broad range of values— including those that in various ways instrumentalize nature—on par. More pro- saically, CBA treats the interests of loggers and conservationists as having equal standing, not trying to evaluate their substantive correctness. This makes it diffi- cult to accept for those who regard the values of conservationists as substantively correct.[18]

Yet if the state "does not have a view" on the correctness of certain questions, and still it needs to regulate in that area, what is it supposed to do? The answer is that, as much as possible, it should defer to citizens' judgments about these questions, and to the extent that it does so, it should assign their views and interests *equal* weight. This is very closely connected to the idea of neutrality as well. In the same way that the state should not just pick a winner among a contested set of values (or pursue what Michael Oakeshott described as "favorite projects"[19]) neither should it privilege any particular subset of these values by assigning them greater weight in its deliberations. Thus, the third principle, which also expresses a very standard liberal commitment, is to a certain form of equality:

3. *Citizen equality.* In areas of reasonable disagreement, the state should as- sign equal weight to the values and interests of each citizen in deciding which policies to pursue.

It is this commitment to equality that explains one of the most controversial features of CBA, which is that it uses money as a "metric" to compare the magni- tude of the gains and losses that a given policy would produce. It is a well-known feature of utilitarian moral systems that to aggregate happiness, they require some basis for making interpersonal comparisons of utility. That finding such a basis can be difficult is often thought to be a powerful argument against such systems. Seldom noted, however, is the fact that egalitarianism also requires some way of making interpersonal comparisons, since in order to say that two people are unequal with respect to some endowment, one must be able to say how much each one of them possesses. If the endowment in question consists of utility, or welfare, then the egalitarian confronts the exact same problem as the utilitarian. If the endowment involves a complex bundle of goods (such as with Rawls or Ronald Dworkin), then the problem is only slightly different, because a person may have more of one good and less of some other good, so to compare this to the endowment of another person, one must be able to come up with a "score" that reflects how much the entire bundle is worth. This is not a metaphysical exercise, but a pragmatic one—the purpose is not to say anything deep about the true value of each person's endowment, it is simply a matter of finding some way to compare these endowments against one another, in order to say whether, or when, equality has been satisfied.[20]

One of the most important claims I will make in this chapter is that the use of money as a "metric of value" in CBA—in particular, through the use of WTP/ WTA values—is not a consequence of any underlying commitment to utilitarianism, or "economism"; it is a consequence of an underlying commitment to equality. The need for CBA typically arises when the state must choose between employing some bundle of resources to achieve one outcome rather than some other (say, x or y), in which many people want x, while many others want y. This may reflect just a difference in interests, but it may also reflect a deeper disagreement about questions of value. Neutrality prevents the state from simply declaring one set of values to be correct, while equality commits the state to assigning equal respect to both concerns. But how is this done? Treating citizens equally does not mean assigning the same weight to their interests, because citizens themselves regard some interests as more important than others. Indeed, one of the problems with voting as a decision procedure is that it gives equal weight to everyone's preferences, even though some may have a great deal at stake in a particular question, whereas others have only a trivial interest. A better procedure would be one that recognizes that interests have a certain weight, within each individual's system of values, and so respects individual equality by assigning interests that have comparable weight the *same* weight in the decision procedure regardless of who holds them.

To do this, it will be necessary first to figure out how strong people's feelings are about a particular question, or how much they care about the values that are generating the conflict. One strategy for getting this information is to ask them what they would be willing to sacrifice to get their way—or more specifically, how much of something else they would be willing to give up to get their favored outcome. If one can find a "something else" that one has good reason to think will be valued roughly the same by all parties, then it can be used as a metric of value, to ascertain the relative intensity of the value commitments in conflict. There are various candidates for such a metric, but one that has many attractive qualities is *money*. This is the primary reason that the "costs" and "benefits" in a CBA are expressed in monetary terms.

So despite the fact that the Kaldor-Hicks criterion at the heart of bald CBA is notorious for assigning no weight to distributive considerations, I will try to show that a commitment to citizen equality is an important feature of the way that CBA is practiced. Although textbooks often describe a perfectly general decision procedure, CBA as institutionalized is done quite differently in different areas. If one looks at the way it treats life, for instance, one sees that sometimes CBA assigns a value to "lives saved," but in other cases it assigns a value to "life years saved." The difference between the two is quite significant, in that the latter may privilege the interests of the young over the old in a way that the former does not. The fact that the calculations are done differently in different domains is not just eclecticism; it constitutes a principled difference. It reflects the fact that, underlying the application of CBA is a commitment to a particular conception of equality among citizens, but that the way equality gets interpreted differs in different policy domains (e.g., in workplace safety compared to healthcare resource allocation).

Each of the foregoing three principles has been formulated in an intentionally loose way (for example, through inclusion of a "reasonability" constraint). That is because my goal is not to show that CBA can be formally derived from the central tenets of modern liberalism. My goal is merely to show that the commitment to a vague form of liberalism, of the sort represented by these three principles, is sufficient to motivate the use of cost-benefit analysis in most if not all of the policy domains in which it is currently being applied. This, I will argue, is what explains its appeal—departures from CBA seem to violate one of these three principles, and are, to that extent, widely perceived to be unacceptable (or else motivated by political ideologies that are, at some level, illiberal). There are some circumstances in which CBA considerations should be overridden in favor of certain other liberal constraints—cases in which the rights of individuals or minorities would be violated are the most obvious example. But the more common circumstance is that opposition to CBA involves an interest group wanting to put a "thumb on the scales" in favor of a set of perfectionist values.

It is worth noting, perhaps just in passing, that none of the three principles seem to involve any commitment to moral consequentialism. While most consequentialists—particularly utilitarians of one stripe or another—would be inclined to endorse them, all three principles could just as easily be justified in a non-consequentialist fashion. For example, they all follow from the minimally controversial contractualism sketched out in chapter 3 (section 3.5). The principles obviously create a normative structure within which consequences will be *relevant* to the evaluation of a policy. After all, a collective action problem is defined in terms of the consequences of individuals' maximizing choices. This does not mean, however, that the Pareto principle must be justified through appeal to these consequences (and nothing *but* these consequences, as the consequentialist would have it). For example, it might be justified by its capacity to bring about agreement, or to minimize complaints.[21] Thus the framework that has been presented here is perfectly compatible with all but the most implausibly strict deontological moral views. This is just to accentuate my basic point, which is that there is a lot more daylight between CBA and utilitarianism than is commonly realized.[22] Indeed, to use the Rawlsian term, one might say that CBA is a good candidate for being a "freestanding" component of a more general conception of justice for a liberal state. (There is some irony in this, since one of Rawls's stated objective, in the early passages of *A Theory of Justice*, was to displace utilitarianism from its dominant position in public decision-making. This was normally taken to imply an opposition to CBA. My claim here is that the basic conceptual framework of Rawls's work, far from displacing CBA, provides support for it.)

My goal in the next five sections is to describe the primrose path that might lead a person committed to these three principles to accept CBA, including some of its most controversial aspects, such as the practice of assigning a monetary value to lives lost. I do so by way of a series of examples of policy scenarios in which state officials are inclined to use CBA. Some of these are rather stylized for purposes of exposition—in real life, they would not, for a variety of reasons, be subject to CBA, including the fact that they fall below the "threshold of significance" (e.g., because a CBA is very expensive to carry out properly, in the United States only regulations with an impact over $100 million require a full-blown CBA). In the discussion that follows I ignore these complications, choosing instead examples that bring out in the most transparent way possible the normative issues at stake in the decision to use CBA.

5.2. Provision of a public good

Suppose that a municipality comes into possession of some land (perhaps it has seized a derelict property for nonpayment of taxes) and must decide what to do with it. There are two proposals for its use: first, the land could be cleared and converted to a neighborhood park, or second, it could be sold to a developer. It is the responsibility of the planner to decide which constitutes the best use. How should this decision be made?

If the choice were between selling it to a developer who wanted to build a shopping mall and selling it to a developer who wanted to build a condominium complex, then there would be no real difficulty. One could simply sell it to the highest bidder, with reasonable confidence that in so doing, one would be ensuring that the land was being put to its best use. The underlying question is what "people" want most. The market is the mechanism through which their desires are transmitted and aggregated. If there are a lot of people who really want to live in that neighborhood, and there is not enough housing, relatively speaking, then they will be willing to pay a lot for the condominiums, making that venture the more profitable one. If there is instead a shortage of stores in the area, then the shopping mall will be the more profitable venture, and so the commercial real-estate developer will be willing to bid more for the land.

It is noticeable, however, that there are never any developers lined up to buy land and convert it to public parks. The reasons for this are obvious—they could never get their money back because they couldn't charge admission, or if they did, very few people would come. Thus, much of the benefit associated with the construction of a public park takes the form of positive externalities (and thus, the "value stream" created by the park is difficult to monetize). Markets will therefore systematically underproduce these goods (this is the "market failure"). We refer to them as public goods in the informal sense of being *relatively* non-rival and non-excludable.

It is worth dwelling for a moment on the nature of the market failure in this case, because it is not actually all that difficult to exclude people from a park; one need only build a fence around it and charge admission. Many people have backyards, which are essentially private parks (open green space in the city for recreational use), condominiums have grounds, which often function as parks for building residents, and some neighborhoods even have gated parks, where only residents in adjoining houses have the key. So it is perfectly possible to provide parks and park-like amenities as a private or as a club good.[23]

What is important to observe is that in all these cases, a different *type* of good is being provided. This is a key point made by Fred Hirsch, who observed that having to pay for certain goods may change their character, in a way that amounts to quality degradation.[24] The most compelling example he gives of this is sexual intercourse, which most people are inclined to regard as a *different good* when paid for with cash than when supplied through systems of informal reciprocity. Similarly, the changes that must often be made to a good to make it excludable, such as building a wall or a fence around a piece of land, change the character of the good. Thus a public park, like a public beach or a public festival, is a distinct type of good, where part of the enjoyment that people get from its consumption arises precisely from the fact that entry is free and open to all. Because of this, provision of such a good will often generate a collective action problem. Voluntary contribution will not generate the optimal level of provision, because of free-rider problems (and the fact that it is impossible to identify some potential users—such as tourists, or people who live far away but occasionally pass through the neighborhood). Thus people's desire for a park will not be transmitted faithfully into market demand for a park. Even *actual* willingness to pay for a park through a contributory arrangement may fail to generate market demand.

The fact that the good generates this problem is in one sense quite accidental. The good itself has no special moral property, such that it must be provided by the government; it's just an ordinary good that people like to consume, the provision of which happens to be very difficult to organize through any institution other than government. There is no reason to think that there is a morally correct level of provision, other than what people themselves want to consume. After all, there is no point providing parks if people are not going to use them (just as there is no point in lowering peoples' taxes, if what they would really like to buy is more parks). And if some strange technological intervention were to make the underlying market failure go away (or if some burst of public spiritedness made voluntary financing by "passing the hat" feasible), there would be no special objection to allowing market forces (i.e., supply and demand) to determine the level of provision.

Thus, what the state needs to engage in, when deciding whether to build the park, is a market-simulating exercise. It needs to produce the outcome that the market would have produced, had the market failure not occurred. (Again, this is not because the market is special, but because the market is a general mechanism for channeling resources to their best employment, and in this case, the state shares the same objective.) We know how much people want the condominium project, because this takes the form of actual market demand, which is what generates the price that the developer is willing to pay. What we do not know is how much people want a park, because that does not show up as market demand. The only way to get at it is to try to ascertain a hypothetical WTP. This can be done using a variety of methods, the main ones being the stated preference method (e.g., do a telephone survey of the neighborhood and ask people what they would be willing to pay to have a new public park) and the indirect valuation (or "revealed preference") method (e.g., do a comparative study to look at what impact public parks have on property values in the surrounding neighborhood—this allows one to estimate how much people are *actually* willing to pay for access to parks).

Once we've done this, we need to compare one value to the other, to see which project is more desirable. This is, of course, just what it means to do a cost-benefit analysis, since the "cost" of any one project is just its opportunity cost, which is to say, the benefit that is foregone when a decision is made *not* to do any of the alternative projects. Thus the cost of building a park is that the land is then not used for private development; this is reflected in the price of the land, which constitutes the revenue that the state will *not* be receiving if it decides to build the park. Thus, the focus on "cost" in CBA is potentially misleading. When performing a CBA, what one is really doing is comparing the benefits of a particular project to the benefits of the presumptively second-best use of the resources to see which is greater. It could be called "benefit-benefit comparison" or "relative benefit assessment," which would in some ways be more confusing, but would have the advantage of emphasizing the fact that the comparison of costs and benefits in a CBA is not the same thing as the balancing of "gains to the winners" and "losses to the losers" that one would see in a utilitarian calculus.

I think it can be shown that making any decision in this case other than the CBA-justified one would violate one of the three principles. First, the basic rationale for state action is to resolve a collective action problem among potential users of the park. The case is somewhat complicated by the fact that the park is a "minority public good," namely, it will not be used by everyone.[25] This appears to give the project a Kaldor-Hicks quality, where some people are asked to forgo a benefit that they want (e.g., whatever they would buy with their tax savings if the land were sold to a developer), so that others may enjoy having a park. This is why, as we have seen, it is important that the state provide a balanced mix of such goods, in the hopes that in general and over the long term everyone will benefit to a reasonable degree. (Not everyone benefits equally from snow removal and pothole repairs, since some people do not drive; not everyone benefits equally from mosquito control, since some people do not enjoy sitting outdoors; and so on.) This, combined with Tiebout sorting in the municipal context (people can move to neighborhoods that provide the balance of amenities most closely matched to their tastes), creates a general presumption that these government activities are Pareto-improving.

The next question then concerns the *level* of provision of these public goods. Here what is important to the justification of CBA is the idea that there is no correct level of provision independent of what people happen to want. This follows from neutrality and equality, because any deviation from it would seem to require taking sides on the question of whose proposed use is better and assigning greater weight to the interests of that party. This sort of partiality is not unheard of. In the early 20th century, many urban planners were persuaded that parks would produce "moral improvement" in the working classes—a judgment that was particularly influential in the decision to raze working-class slums and replace them with residential towers surrounded by green space. This backfired spectacularly, as the green space remained largely unused, making it a magnet for crime.[26] As a result, the "parks are good for you" judgment that prevailed in the first half of the 20th century is now regarded as involving an impermissible partiality toward a particular set of values. Some people like trees and green spaces, some people do not. Planners tend to share the values of those who do, but it is a clear violation of liberal neutrality to use that as a basis for decision. No matter how much planners may like parks, they must ultimately defer to patterns of use.

5.2.1. The commodification objection

Perhaps the most global and all-encompassing critique of CBA is the argument that it "commodifies" public goods, and therefore represents a fundamentally wrong-headed way of thinking about goods that are, as Elizabeth Anderson puts it, "not properly regarded as mere commodities."[27] There is no doubt an element of truth to this, since when calculating a WTP value, then using it as the basis for a decision, we are in effect asking "what would the market do?" where "the market" in question is a hypothetical market in which all goods are available, and all costs and benefits are fully reflected in their prices. Yet if all that it meant to "commodify" something was to subject it to such acts of the imagination, then it is not clear where the harm would lie in "commodification." After all, no one is planning to turn public parks into actual commodities. Indeed, it is precisely because the municipality is considering building a public park, free and open to all, that there is a need to do a CBA. Asking people "how much would you pay for a new park?" as a way of deciding whether to build it or how large it should be does not really change anything about the eventual status of the park as a public good. In fact, a casual visitor to the park, sitting on a bench enjoying the afternoon sun, might be surprised to discover that the surrounding environment had been turned into a "mere commodity" by the fact that a CBA was performed prior to the decision to turn the land into a public park.

This suggests that the commodification charge needs to be made a bit more carefully. When it comes to debates over, say, the buying and selling of transplant organs, the question is whether a certain good should become an *actual commodity*, which can be bought and sold on private markets. But when the government performs a CBA to determine how large a park should be (or, for example, to decide whether the public health service should provide free vaccinations to the public, or whether a new road to a remote community should be built, etc.), there is no question of actually commodifying the good in question.[28] Just thinking about the good as if it were a commodity is not itself a harm, and does not violate any taboo against the buying and selling of it. To show that there is a harm, those who make the criticism must show that this way of thinking will distort decision-making, leading to incorrect levels of provision of the good (including perhaps, in some instances, failure to provide it at all).

Anderson does make an effort to show this, although there are significant problems with the exposition. She starts by providing a definition of what she means by commodification: "A good is treated as a commodity if it is valued as an exclusively appropriated object of use and if market norms and relations govern its production, exchange and distribution."[29] From this definition, it seems perfectly clear that using CBA to determine the provision of public goods does not commodify anything. But she goes on to claim that CBA "measures people's valuations of these goods in market transactions and hence, only as they are valued as privately appropriated, exclusively enjoyed goods. This assumes that the public nature of some instances of these goods is merely a technical fact about them and not itself a valued quality. The possibility that national parks . . . might be valued as shared goods does not enter into its evaluations."[30]

It is difficult to know what to say here, other than to observe that all the substantive allegations made are false. It is simply not true that calling someone up on the phone and asking, "How much would you pay to have a public park in your neighborhood?" is the same as asking, "How much would you pay to have a private park in your neighborhood that only you can use?" (this would be equivalent to asking, "How much would you pay for a larger backyard?") Apart from the fact that one would not need to ask this (one could just look at how much people actually pay for larger backyards), what one is asking about specifically is the private value (i.e., the value to the individual) of a *public* amenity. It is false to claim that CBA tries to estimate the value of public goods as if they were "privately appropriated" or "exclusively enjoyed."

The same is true of revealed preference methods, such as looking at property values in surrounding neighborhoods. Even though one is looking at the value of private commodities, one is doing so as a way of estimating the value of nearby *public* amenities. It is a well-known feature of the real estate market that houses in "nice" neighborhoods sell for a lot more money than houses in "not-so-nice" neighborhoods. Many cities have a housing stock that is architecturally fairly homogeneous, so it is possible to find what amounts to the same house in a number of different neighborhoods. Because the private good (i.e., the actual house and lot) in each case is the same, the differences in price must be due to externalities, both positive and negative. With a good data set and sufficiently refined statistical techniques, this allows one to determine how much people value these externalities (which will include public goods, such as proximity to good schools and clean parks, the availability of transit, etc., as well as public "bads," such as crime, freeway noise, traffic congestion, etc.) This, in turn, permits one to calculate how much people really care about these various things (so that if it turns out that schools make a huge difference, but parks only modestly so, it might make sense to invest more money in schools instead of parks). There is simply nothing commodifying about this. More generally, there is nothing paradoxical about the idea of eliciting people's private valuation of a public amenity, or in thinking that the *public* valuation of public amenities should be a function of these private valuations.

It should be mentioned that, when the numbers come back, the results can sometimes put pressure on one's commitment to liberal neutrality. That is because the planners who do these studies all tend to belong to roughly the same social class and to have similar educational backgrounds, and therefore their views on these questions tend to be both similar and strongly held. For example, there is a marked tendency to think that people ought to value neighborhood green space over proximity to a freeway. So if it turns out that people in certain neighborhoods have the "wrong" preferences, according to one's perfectionist values, there is a temptation to want to impugn the methodology of the study, or the validity of a decision procedure that assigns those "incorrect" preferences the same weight as one's own. It is important to observe, however, that the problem lies not in the details of how CBA aggregates preferences; the source of the tension is actually the more fundamental liberal commitments that are embodied in CBA. When a critic like Anderson suggests that a process of "deliberation" should be used instead of CBA, one suspects that this is motivated, at least in part, by the thought that such a process would result in everyone having preferences much closer to her own. (In other words, it is unlikely that she is promoting deliberation as a way of giving herself the opportunity to discover the error of her own ways. It is more likely motivated by a desire to give greater weight to her own values in the eventual outcome, in a way that CBA does not permit.)

5.2.2. The inequality objection

There is a second objection that can be made, which is far more serious than the "commodification" claim. The example that I chose of a neighborhood park was intended to neutralize it to some degree, but still it will have occurred to many people. The point of a CBA is basically to determine how much people, in the aggregate, want something, and whether they want it enough to justify foregoing what they would have to forego should the state choose to provide it. This sort of aggregative exercise requires interpersonal comparisons, and so any CBA must select some metric to serve as a basis for these interpersonal comparisons. Standard CBA uses money. Given the rhetorical appeal of the commodification objection, it is important to emphasize that the reason for assigning a dollar value to costs and benefits has nothing to do with imposing "market norms," and it certainly does not reflect any underlying commitment to actually selling the good in question. Money is used simply as a basis for comparing the benefits going to one person to the benefits going to some other person. But of course, money is an

imperfect metric, because it is not valued equally by all persons. It is instead subject to diminishing utility, which means that it is more highly valued the less of it
one has. As a result, a poor person will be willing to give up less of it, in order to
achieve some benefit, than a rich person (which is to say, the WTP of the wealthy
will be greater than the WTP of the poor for benefits that are of the same magnitude, in terms of utility.)

As a result, it has seemed obvious to many that WTP numbers are going to
be skewed, to the benefit of the wealthy.[31] This is an analytic consequence of the
idea that money has diminishing marginal utility, as can be seen in Figure 5.2.
A person with b amount of money (and thus at utility level 2) would be willing to
pay c-b for a single-point gain in utility, while a person with d amount of money
(and thus at utility level 4) would be willing to pay e-d for a single-point gain.
Thus, if one were to auction off a good that promised a single-point gain in utility,
the wealthier person would be willing to pay much more for it.

This means that if one does a CBA, eliciting WTP figures from people in different social classes, one will get numbers that are distorted by the value that
individuals place on money. Whether or not this is a problem, however, depends
very much on the project being contemplated, as well as the class profile of those
affected. It may not be a problem if one is contemplating a project that will affect
the entire population, and what one is looking for is an average WTP. In this case,
the high WTP values one gets by asking the rich will counterbalance the low
WTP values that one gets from asking the poor, producing the average value. The
difference becomes problematic only when one is considering projects that will

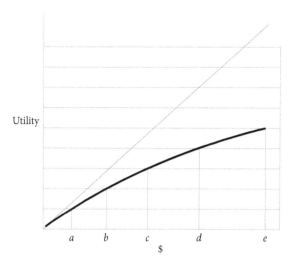

Figure 5.2 Diminishing marginal utility of money increases willingness to pay.

have a differential impact on the rich and the poor. In such cases, it is true that using an unadjusted WTP value will systematically privilege the interests of the wealthy.

To see this, one need only consider a case in which a large municipality found itself with the funds to purchase land for a new park, and had to decide which neighborhood to build it in. If it decided to find out where a park was most needed by surveying residents from one end of town to the other, asking people how much they would be willing to pay for it, the consequence of this would almost certainly be a recommendation that the park be built in a wealthy neighborhood, simply because the residents there would have the greatest willingness to pay for a park. But this is not because they value the park *more*, it is because they value money (i.e., the marginal dollar) *less*. Thus, if one were to sketch out the social welfare function reflected in bald CBA, it is easy to see that it is anti-egalitarian.

Figure 5.3 represents these social welfare functions (SWF) as indifference curves (where every point along the curve is considered just as good as any other, from the standpoint of social welfare). The utilitarian indifference curve U, just as in Figure 5.1, is a straight line, indicating that as long as the sum of individual satisfaction is the same, the utilitarian is indifferent with respect to distribution. CBA with a monetary metric, by contrast, generates the convex curve A, where the more unequal the two parties are, the more the richer one is willing to pay, relative to the poorer one, and so the greater the weight assigned to her interests. By contrast, as Sen has observed, it is generally thought that a plausible SWF should

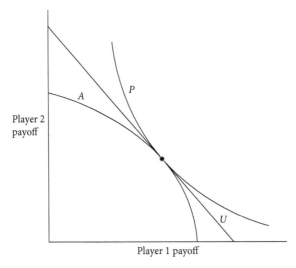

Player 2 payoff

Player 1 payoff

Figure 5.3 Prioritarian and anti-prioritarian social indifference curves.

be concave, as in the prioritarian indifference curve P.[32] Such a SWF tolerates deviations from equality, but as the level of inequality increases, the greater the benefits to the better-off must be to justify any further deviation.

Now some people have argued that the A curve is just fine, since this is how the market distributes most other goods.[33] Cass Sunstein, for instance, has observed that if the city were to build the park in a poor neighborhood, even though the WTP there was quite low, it would essentially be forcing the residents to accept a good that they themselves would willingly give up in exchange for money (if, for example, a developer were to come along and offer to buy the land). This starts to look a bit like forcing people to consume a good that they do not want. Nevertheless, there are many theorists who feel that, given the range of unde-served inequalities in the distribution of wealth, the state is under an obligation to do more in the way of promoting equality than merely mimicking the pattern of distribution favored by private markets. This is reflected in the fact that, at the "back end," goods are typically paid for by a tax system that incorporates a measure of progressivity. And at the "front end," goods are often—although not always—distributed in ways that are intended to be independent of either ability or willingness to pay. Ideally, it might be the case that all transactions should be organized in this way, but practical difficulties in implementing such a scheme leave us no choice but to defer to the market pattern of allocation in most cases. But this represents nothing more than a concession to practicality. In cases where the state is providing a good directly, there is no reason to privilege the market pattern.[34]

As a result, planners will in some cases adjust the WTP values in a CBA, in order to reflect the income level of respondents. If there is reason to think that one proposal is likely to benefit the poor disproportionately, while another is more likely to benefit the rich, then one can simply impose a multiplier on the reported WTP values, reflecting one's best estimate of the diminishing marginal utility of money. This has the effect of "unbending" the A curve, so that it more closely approximates the utilitarian curve U. One can even give the CBA an egal-itarian bias, by increasing the weights until the curve more closely resembles P. (For instance, one could look at the progressivity of the income tax system, infer from it the shape of the implicit SWF, then derive from it a set of multipliers that will give the CBA the same shape.) None of this is technically difficult, and as mentioned earlier, the UK government *Green Book* recommends that it be done whenever it is appropriate and feasible, using multipliers in the ranges set out in Table 5.1.

Now the use of such multipliers does raise a number of delicate issues. My point is merely to show that CBA is a very flexible tool, which can be made more or less egalitarian. Furthermore, it is worth observing that it is very difficult to find anyone willing to endorse bald CBA, with its convex

Table 5.1 Distributive weights suggested by UK *Green Book*

Quintile	Weight
bottom	1.9–2.0
2nd	1.3–1.4
3rd	0.9–1.0
4th	0.7–0.8
top	0.4–0.5

SWF, across the board. Even Sunstein, who endorses strict market simulation in the standard run of cases, draws the line when it comes to the VSL (or "value of a statistical life") measure. This will be dealt with more thoroughly in section 5.4, but for now suffice it to observe that if one uses WTA to price the risk of death associated with various activities, then one will find that the poor are willing to pay less than the rich are for a reduction of risk of given magnitude. This implies that the VSL for a poor person should accordingly be lower than for a rich person. If taken seriously, this would mean that employers need not spend as much on workplace safety if their workers are poor, that the state need not spend as much money on road safety in poor neighborhoods, and so on. To avoid this outcome, a standard VSL, the same for every person, is used.

One way of thinking about these adjustments in the way that the CBA is performed is to imagine that another value, such as equality, is trumping the concern for aggregate social welfare that is articulated by the CBA. This is, I believe, not the best way of framing the issue. On the contrary, the concern for equality is not trumping the concern for welfare; the concern for equality is already built into the CBA. A better way of thinking about it is to see that every CBA presupposes a particular conception of equality—some more persuasive than others—and that respecting this may require some reweighing of the WTP/WTA values.

That having been said, there is no question that a concern for equality can raise some difficult informational challenges. For example, it is important that if one is using distributive weights on one side of a calculation, one must use them on the other as well. This can be difficult if, as is often the case, one has a market valuation of the costs but not the benefits. It becomes particularly important if there is an asymmetry between the two, e.g., if the poor would be the major users of the park, but the rich would benefit most from a condominium development. In this case, it is not enough to merely ask about income when surveying for

WTP values, and then adjust the valuations of the benefits up if the respondents are low income. One must also adjust the market valuation of the costs down, if one has reason to believe that the primary beneficiaries of the alternative use would be high income. The latter is, needless to say, very difficult to do.

If the problems raised by the use of a monetary WTP measure are significant enough, there may be the option of abandoning it in favor of some other metric. In this regard, it is important to keep in mind that there is nothing intrinsically significant about money in CBA (pace proponents of the "commodification" critique), it is merely being used as a basis for interpersonal comparisons. If one can find some other metric of value, which is not subject to the same distortions, then one may well be better off using that.[35] In healthcare resource allocation, for example, life expectancy is used as the basic metric, rather than WTP. Similarly, municipal planners may choose to use "commute time" as a metric of comparison for transit planning. There may be an element of stipulation in this—for example, even if an extra year of life expectancy may not be of equal value to all persons, the state may nevertheless be justified in treating it as though it were. These metrics all have their flaws and limitations, the point is simply that if they are able to provide the basis for a more compelling assessment of the relative benefits of a set of policy options, then there is no barrier either in principle or in practice to using them.

Finally, it is important when considering the possibly inegalitarian features of CBA not to commit the "nirvana fallacy," of comparing it against some entirely idealized decision procedure, particularly not one that makes use of impossible-to-obtain information. There are many examples in the United States of statutes that specifically prohibit the use of cost-benefit information in determining the way that they will be administered. There is no evidence that these operate to the benefit of the poor. On the contrary, the political system, the judicial system, as well as the informal will-formation mechanisms of civil society, are all substantially biased against the poor. As a result, it is not clear that the poor will fare any better under a "democratic" decision-making process (such as the professorial favorite, "deliberation," which transparently favors the well educated) than under a technocratic CBA. Kip Viscusi, to take just one example, has observed that the distribution of "superfund" environmental cleanup resources in the United States—a well-known example of non-CBA-justified spending—basically mirrors the distribution of "pork barrel" spending. By contrast, there can be little doubt that the imposition of CBA with a standard valuation of life has had equalizing consequences. So while I am not aware of any systematic investigation of the distributive consequences of CBA versus other decision procedures, it is important to remain realistic about the challenges involved in designing an alternative to CBA that will not exhibit many of the same defects that critics have been hoping to correct.

5.3. Imposing a regulation

Suppose that our municipality has recently made a number of zoning changes, to allow mixed-use development in the downtown core. Slowly, people are beginning to migrate back to the city from the suburbs. Several warehouse conversion projects are underway, being turned into condominiums, but also mixed-use commercial-industrial-residential complexes. This is successful in attracting not just new residents but also new businesses—bars and restaurants, small-scale manufacturing, and the like. Unfortunately, with success comes conflict. The residents are beginning to complain about a number of things, including noise levels. They want new regulations, constraining the amount of noise that businesses can produce (and at what hours). In particular, they want manufacturers to install noise-abatement technology (such as sound-proof insulation).

Unlike the case of a public park, which is not so difficult to imagine being a Pareto improvement, regulation seems to have a more win-lose structure. Any noise regulation that is introduced (assuming that there is currently none) is clearly going to impose a cost on business, while generating a benefit for residents. The question that CBA can be used to answer is whether the benefit to residents is large enough to justify the cost imposed on business. This seems very much like a utilitarian calculation—and indeed, it is often described that way (e.g., "regulations seek to counteract externalities by restricting behavior in a way that imposes harm on an individual basis but yields net societal benefits"[36]). These appearances, however, are misleading. The purpose of CBA, when examining a regulation, is to determine where the Pareto-efficient outcome lies (and thus, whether the status quo could have arisen through contracting, or is due only to market failure).

This is one of the important points Ronald Coase made in his foundational paper, "The Problem of Social Cost." His argument, however, is quite subtle on several points and so merits exposition. One of Coase's ambitions was to criticize the assumption, made by Alfred Pigou, that *merely* because there was an externality being produced in a particular market, the resulting outcome would be inefficient.[37] Coase showed that market outcomes may still be efficient, even in the presence of externalities, depending on how important those externalities are. He illustrated this with a classic example of a railroad track that passes through several farmers' fields. The faster the trains travel, the more sparks they throw off, and the more likely they are to set the fields ablaze. Under the status quo, the sparks are a negative externality, the cost of which is manifest in the form of crops lost to fire. There are two solutions to the problem: either the railroad could run the trains at slower speeds, or the farmers could increase the setback between the railbed and the land on which they grow their crops. Naturally, the farmers prefer that the trains run slower, while the railroad prefers that the set-back be increased.

Coase used this example to make one obvious point, which no reader has failed to grasp, and two less obvious ones, which are sometimes overlooked. The obvious point is that one need not necessarily impose a *regulation* to resolve this problem; all it would take is a clear assignment of rights. Furthermore, there is one sense in which it doesn't really matter which party is given the rights, be-cause the two sides can be expected to negotiate to the efficient outcome regard-less of their starting positions.[38] Suppose, for example, that the farmers would suffer a loss of $80 from increasing the setback, while the railroad would suffer a loss of $100 by slowing down the trains. If one gives the railroad the right to run its trains as fast as it likes, then it will continue to do so, and farmers will have to absorb the $80 loss. But if instead one gives farmers the right to have their fields protected from sparks, it will not actually change the outcome—the railroad will still run the trains fast, it is just that the railroad will be forced to negotiate with the farmers and pay them $80 to increase the setback. Either way, the parties will negotiate to the efficient outcome. The difference between the two outcomes is purely one of *distribution*—which party must bear the $80 loss. If the right is given to the railroad, the farmers bear the loss; if the right is given to the farmers, then the railroad has to bear it (by paying the farmers).

This separation of the distribution issue from the efficiency issue is the first rather counterintuitive point that Coase makes.[39] The second is that the mere presence of a negative externality (in this case) is not necessarily inefficient; it all depends on how much the externality costs the person who suffers it, and how much it benefits the person producing it. In the case of the railroad and the farmers, the status quo ante, with the production of the sparks, is the efficient outcome—as witnessed by the fact that, even if the farmers are given the right to block production of the externality, they would choose not to do so, by selling the right to the railroad. So while the presence of the unregulated externality creates what many people are inclined to regard as a *distributive* injustice (i.e., the farmers receive no compensation for their lost farmland or ruined crops), it was not actually producing an inefficiency.

Now there are many circumstances in which externalities are being produced, but the parties are not able to negotiate a solution (typically because of transac-tion costs, understood broadly). The state cannot just assign rights and let the parties decide; it must actually impose an outcome. To do so, it should be guided by some conception of what the parties *would* have decided, had they been able to negotiate freely. First and foremost, it must decide whether the parties would actually have negotiated a limit on the externality (and thus, whether the state should even regulate at all) and then, if it determines that they would have agreed to reduce it, what level of output they would have settled on. This is precisely what a CBA does. The important point is that this calculation is independent of the distributive justice decision. For instance, if the state decided to look at the situation between the farmers and the railroad, with an eye to regulating the externality, a CBA would recommend against it, on the grounds that the cost of slowing down the trains ($100) exceeded the benefit ($80). It might, however, also decide that the farmers were owed some compensation by the railroad, but this would be based on separate, distributive justice considerations, not the CBA.

In the case of the condominium residents and their noisy neighbors, the logic is much the same. Suppose that in this case, the residents would be willing to pay $100 for a quieter environment, while it would only cost the manufacturers $80 to reduce the noise level of their operations. What this means is that the current state of affairs is inefficient—there is a mutually beneficial (i.e., Pareto improving) transaction between the residents and the manufacturers that could be taking place (i.e., the residents could pay the manufacturers $80 to reduce the noise level, leaving them with a welfare gain worth $20). The only reason it is not occurring is incompleteness in the system of property rights, as well as transaction costs that prevent bargaining. The current inefficient state of affairs, in which the manufacturers make too much noise, persists only because of a market failure. This is precisely what the CBA shows when it comes back positive. So when the state imposes through regulation the outcome that the parties would have contracted to, it is realizing a Pareto improvement over the status quo ante, in which it is not yet determined whether there should be noise or silence.

The regulation, of course, creates only a *potential* Pareto improvement over the existing state of affairs because it imposes the cost of noise abatement on the manufacturers without requiring any transfer from the residents. The question of whether or not to turn it into an *actual* Pareto improvement is a separate issue, which must be decided by considerations of distributive justice, such as whether the manufacturers were "entitled" to make the noise they were making in the first place. In general, whenever the state regulates, it has the option of compensating parties based on who "should" have had the rights in question. In the case of these classic pollution externalities, it usually does not compensate, on the grounds that the rights would typically not have gone to the emitter, but rather to those affected. So the cost impact of the regulation is more like a seizure of ill-gotten gains. It is important to be clear, however, that the regulation is motivated by (Pareto) efficiency concerns, and efficiency concerns alone. The subsequent decision, whether to compensate those who are adversely affected by it, is a separate, distributive justice decision. Put the two together, and it looks like a utilitarian decision, but it is actually two separate decisions, one about efficiency, the other about distribution. If there is a loss imposed on one party, this is due to the distributive justice decision—in which the CBA plays no role.

Figure 5.4 sketches out the situation. The two diagonal lines show the benefits that are obtainable under the two scenarios (regulation or no-regulation), and the possible distributions of those benefits between the manufacturers and the residents. One can easily see that any arrangement that features an absence of regulation is Pareto inferior to a set of arrangements in which there is a noise regulation, and thus the parties, had they been in a position to negotiate an arrangement, would never have settled on one in which the noise is produced. Nevertheless, if one takes the "no regulation" outcome as the point of departure, then the move to regulation without compensation is clearly not a Pareto improvement; it is only Kaldor-Hicks. Starting with this outcome, however, begs the question, because the manufacturers should never have been entitled to produce the noise—and absent the market failure that prevents negotiations with the residents, they might never have done so. Thus the status quo point from which all regulatory decisions should be assessed is the outcome in which neither party is exercising any of the rights that are in question (or the "status quo prior to interaction"). From that point of departure, one can see that if one is motivated by the Pareto principle, one would not choose an outcome in which the manufacturers were allowed to make noise. Even if the state decides to impose the noise regulation without requiring compensation, it can do so without making any essential appeal to the Kaldor-Hicks principle. Instead, there are two

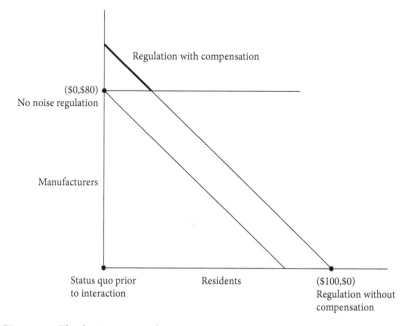

Figure 5.4 The decision to regulate.

decisions going on. The first decision, to impose the regulation, is justified by the Pareto principle. Here, the state is imposing the outcome that the parties would have contracted to, had empirical circumstances (i.e., high transactions costs) not intervened. The second decision, not to compensate, is made on the basis of a distributive justice consideration. This is based on the fact that one party was able to free ride, in the absence of a negotiated agreement.

So, despite appearances, the state is not doing anything very different when it imposes a regulation from what it does when it decides to build a park. In both cases, it is trying to bring about an outcome that would have been brought about had there not been transaction costs and incompleteness in the system of property rights. Provision of public goods is a response to the market's underproduction of positive externalities; regulation is typically a response to the market's overproduction of negative externalities.

5.3.1. The rights objection

One of the complaints often made against CBA is that it does not recognize, or assign any status to, the "rights" of individuals affected by a decision. Thus one might object to the very idea that residents should have to negotiate with manufacturers regarding noise levels, on the grounds that they have a "right" to a good night's sleep (or, more plausibly, that farmers should not have to negotiate with the railroad, on the ground that they have a "right" not to have their crops set on fire). The issue becomes even more significant when the externality in question poses a danger to people's health, or even their lives. For example, many people who object to the use of CBA in deciding on carbon abatement policies to address global climate change insist that the issue must instead be addressed within a "rights" framework.[40]

There are two responses to this. Implicit in the objection is the idea that rights function as "trumps," in the way that Ronald Dworkin defined them, as strict deontic constraints ("rights are best understood as trumps over some background justification for political decisions that states a goal for the community as a whole"[41]). In some circumstances, rights do function this way, so that no matter how much welfare is at stake, the state cannot take action aimed at realizing it if doing so violates an individual's rights. For example, prior to the *Kelo v. City of New London* decision in the United States, it was understood that the "power of eminent domain" could only be used to seize private property, or forcibly transfer title, if the property was to be put to a "public use"—such as for the construction of a road or a park.[42] So while the state might contemplate all sorts of development projects, it is only worth doing a CBA on ones that involve permissible forms of land appropriation; the rest are simply "trumped" by the property rights of individual landholders. This can be handled on the "input filter" side of the embedded CBA procedure, when it comes to selection of problems.

The fact that CBA is done so broadly, however, is a reflection of the reality that very few rights actually function as trumps in this way, despite the assertions of some philosophers.[43] For example, Simon Caney argues that CBA is inappropriate as a framework for thinking about climate change, and urges that we instead think about the problem within a rights framework. He then posits a set of very broad rights, which he goes on to claim that climate change violates, such as: "HR2, the human right to health: All persons have a human right that other people do not act so as to create serious threats to their health."[44] One need only reflect upon this to see that such a right could only trump other concerns if one construes both "serious" and "health" in an extremely narrow way. For example, we are hesitant to enforce quarantines on people with contagious diseases, even though they may pose serious health threats to others. This suggests that HR2 is not a strict constraint, but is routinely traded off against other interests, such as the liberty interests of those who are sick. But even more prosaically, every time I get into my car, I impose any number of "health" risks upon other people. I impose a risk of death and injury upon pedestrians, cyclists, and, to a lesser extent, other drivers. My car produces tailpipe emissions that, in urban areas, contribute to a large number of health problems (such as asthma and bronchitis), including thousands of preventable deaths—a far more serious impact on human health than those associated with the carbon emissions.

Thus whatever right people may have to health clearly does not often play the role of a trump card, but is rather a right of the sort that Joseph Raz had in mind when he described an individual as having a right "if an interest of his is sufficient to hold another to be subject to a duty."[45] On this Razian view, "rights" are basically a subset of the person's more general interests, distinguished only by the fact that we consider them unusually important. Thus the "right to health" does not mean that no one can do anything that risks impairing my health, even in the slightest way. It simply means that my health is important enough an interest that my desire to protect it may generate *pro tanto* duties for others, for example, not to recklessly or unreasonably endanger it. But what counts as "reasonable" in this context?

It is here that the rights framework requires some supplementation, since as soon as two rights are in tension with one another, and some "balancing" is required, a normative criterion must be introduced in order to determine how a balance should be struck. The alternative is simply "moral gridlock," where no one can do anything because every course of action violates someone's rights.[46] So, for example, people have a right to a reasonably quiet environment, particularly at night, but at the same time, people also have a right to make a certain amount of noise, particularly when it is a by-product of a productive activity aimed at satisfying other essential needs. So how do we decide which "right" should prevail in cases of conflict? When one construes the issue as fundamentally a matter of conflicting *interests*, then it becomes clear that liberal neutrality prevents the state from merely siding with one group. The natural procedure is therefore to try to determine how *important* the various interests at stake are to the individuals involved, in the particular circumstances that are generating the conflict, and to weigh these interests against one another, subject to the overarching constraint that the interests of each individual be given equal weight. One way of doing this—not the only way, but a plausible way—is to figure out how much people are willing to give up to protect those interests. This is essentially what the WTP/WTA measure in CBA tries to get at.

The example I have chosen may be trivial, but it is important to recognize that most of the difficult and controversial choices confronting the state have this structure. Both the railroad and the noisy-neighbors cases are simplified in several dimensions, the most important being that costs and benefits in the real world are generally not lump sum, but rather continuous. Typically, the situation will be one in which reducing production of the externality is associated with increasing marginal cost, along with decreasing marginal benefit. (For example, cutting the noise level in half may be relatively inexpensive to do, and will significantly improve the lives of residents. Cutting it in half again will be a lot more expensive and will generate a lot less benefit.) Figure 5.5 illustrates the usual structure of such an interaction, with marginal cost increasing with abatement level, while marginal benefit decreases. The point *r* indicates the outcome that an optimal regulation would achieve (i.e., that the parties would have contracted to).

Many different normative frameworks can generate the conclusion *that one should regulate*. The difficult question is *how much* one should regulate. For

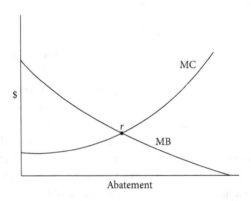

Figure 5.5 Increasing marginal cost, declining marginal benefit.

example, the days when particular environmental pollutants could be banned outright are for the most part long gone (primarily because all the low-hanging fruit, from a regulatory perspective, has been picked). The question now is almost always how much of the pollutant should be allowed. Unless cost-benefit considerations are introduced, agencies can easily fall victim to what Stephen Breyer calls the "last 10%" problem.[47] By ignoring the dramatic increase in marginal cost, they expend vast resources trying to solve a problem completely. For example, with respect to environmental cleanup, instead of removing 90 percent of contaminants from 100 percent of sites, an agency may insist that 100 percent of contaminants be removed, but in so doing, restrict itself to cleaning up only a small percentage of sites. There are many examples to suggest that this was a real problem in American regulatory law prior to the widespread adoption of CBA.

To take a specific example, it is not difficult to arrive at the conclusion that the problem of global warming requires us to price carbon. The question is how high the price should be. It makes no sense to do nothing, but it also does not make sense to do too much. So we need to be able to say how much we should be doing. Should carbon taxes be set at $30 per tonne of CO_2, or $300? Here the other normative frameworks tend to fall silent, leaving CBA as the "only game in town." While point r may be difficult to find empirically, at least it offers a clear and coherent conception of what we are looking for. If we want to solve a collective action problem, and we cannot rely upon the parties to negotiate their way to a solution, then we have to estimate where that solution would be. CBA is the only known methodology for doing so. The rights framework has nothing to say on this question. CBA not only has something to say, but what it says can plausibly be construed as reflecting our commitment to equality and neutrality.

5.3.2. The "garbage in garbage out" objection

Proponents of CBA sometimes defend the procedure on the grounds that it is more "rational" than the alternatives or, at least, less likely to be subject to cognitive bias.[48] Yet these arguments tend to cut both ways. The value of CBA as a procedure depends entirely on the quality of the valuations it uses as inputs, which it must take as given. It is therefore susceptible to a version of the "garbage in garbage out" principle, which states that no matter how good a procedure may be, if the input is worthless, then the output will also be worthless. And if cognitive bias is such a serious difficulty that it impairs ordinary deliberative decision-making, as many proponents of CBA claim, then what reason is there to hope that the WTP values that are taken as "input" will not also be hopelessly compromised by many of the same cognitive biases?

This is the central contention made by Peter Diamond and Jerry Hausman in an influential article entitled "Contingent Valuation: Is Some Number Better Than No Number?"[49] They make several extremely important observations. The first is that calling people up on the phone and asking, "How much would you pay for x?" is practically worthless as a way of ascertaining the value of an outcome. In particular, it is subject to all the familiar biases, such as framing effects and anchoring effects.[50] Perhaps the most damning example of this comes from a well-known study that showed that the WTP values for rescuing birds was roughly the same, regardless of whether the number of birds to be saved was 2,000, 20,000, or 200,000.[51] Similar problems afflict certain "revealed preference" methods. For example, the idea that workers' valuations of life and injury will be revealed through the wage premium associated with dangerous employments is solidly contradicted by empirical studies that fail to find any such premium.[52] There are no doubt many factors that contribute to this, but the most important seems to be that workers suffer from optimism bias and control illusions, which cause them to underestimate the chances that they will be victims of a workplace accident.

It is disingenuous for proponents of CBA to respond to this, as they sometimes do, by pleading modesty, and suggesting that their analysis is only one consideration in a complex decision-making process, which no one should assign greater weight to than is warranted by the quality of the underlying data. There are two things wrong with this response. The first lies in a failure to acknowledge that numbers themselves can have a biasing impact (as studies on the anchoring effect have shown), leading to quantitative measures having an outsized role in deliberations, even when this is unwarranted by the reliability of the underlying data. (For example, there is widespread awareness of the limitations of GDP, and by extension, GDP growth, as a measure of economic progress or well-being. And yet growth still exercises something like a magnetic attraction in debates over development, government economic management, etc. Indeed, the effort to develop alternative measures of progress, such as the Human Development Index, was in part a reaction to the fact that just attaching caveats and qualifications to GDP data has not been sufficient to eliminate the biasing effect it can have upon deliberations.) The second important consideration is that in certain jurisdictions and policy areas, all major regulations will be litigated, and so must be defensible in court. In an adversarial context such as this, quantitative measures are much more defensible than qualitative ones, and so if both are available, courts will gravitate toward assigning the most authority to a CBA, even if the numbers it is based on represent little more than a guess.

Thus the "number" provided by CBA is not just one data point among many. What Diamond and Hausman refer to as the "some number is better than no number" fallacy arises from the fact that information of equal quality will often be given greater credence, or deliberative weight, when presented in a quantitative form rather than a qualitative one.[53] Thus if a particular decision requires weighing two considerations, people are more likely to achieve an appropriate balancing if both considerations are expressed quantitatively or both are expressed qualitatively. But if one is presented quantitatively, and the other qualitatively, the former is likely to be overweighted. In this case, it is better to have no number than to have some number.

Thus, the mere insistence on methodological transparency is not an adequate response to the "garbage in garbage out" objection. A better response lies in the observation that in almost every case in which CBA is used, there is already at least one number available—namely, the number that reflects the *cost*. This will be true, for example, whenever a regulation is imposed on economic activity, or whenever resources are directed to the provision of a public good. It is usually the *benefit* that is intangible, because it lacks a market valuation (which is why the state must provide the good). Thus the question is not whether we want to have one number or no number, but whether we want one number—reflecting only the cost—or two numbers—reflecting both the cost and the benefit. The logic of Diamond and Hausman's position suggests that, if there is always going to be one number available and, furthermore, if this number is always going to be on the same side of the scale, then deliberation will be enhanced by generating a second number to balance out the effects of the first.

From this perspective, the one thing that can be said for the WTP value is that, whatever its shortcomings—and I certainly have no desire to understate these— it represents at least an *attempt* to measure the right thing. When market prices are used to calculate the cost of a policy, what is essentially being measured is the aggregate WTP for the associated resources in some other employment (keeping in mind that the cost of a particular policy is its opportunity cost, which is simply the foregone benefit of *not* implementing some other policy). The danger is that, if one does not construct a similar measure of WTP for the resources needed to enact that policy (i.e., the "benefits"), then one will not be comparing like with like. Furthermore, misstatement of the benefits will typically err in the direction of underestimation.

This is, in fact, precisely what happens. Consider an environmental regulation that we now regard as uncontroversial, such as the ban on leaded gasoline. At the time it was implemented, the ban was quite controversial, largely because it was not subjected to proper CBA, which, in turn, made it difficult to make the case for it. The problem was that the cost of the regulation was easily calculable because it primarily took the form of impacts that had market prices. Thus petroleum companies were able to calculate how much their refining costs would go up to achieve the same octane level in their fuels without the lead additives (thus, how much the price of gasoline would go up). By contrast, the benefits of the regulation—primarily health benefits associated with the reduction of airborne lead—had no market value. What CBA recommends in such cases is to take the primary welfare gains and estimate their value, by asking people "How much would you pay to avoid exposure to an atmospheric contaminant that gives you a chance of brain damage and/or kidney failure, according to the following risk/exposure schedule?" But instead of doing this—trying, however, imperfectly, to measure the direct welfare gain—analysts at the time chose downstream beneficial consequences that *did* have a market value, such as a savings to the healthcare system from not having to treat those conditions, or increased worker productivity.[54] This is completely arbitrary, because the question of which benefits happen to have a market value is determined by contingent features of the world, such as where the cost of implementing a system of property rights is high and where it is low. Furthermore, the effect of doing this sort of ad hoc CBA is that it consistently overstates the relative cost of regulation.

Thus in the real world of regulation, the choice is not really between doing a CBA and not doing a CBA, but rather between doing a proper, complete CBA and doing an improper, incomplete CBA.[55] In the usual case of regulation, industry lobby groups can be counted on to do their half of the CBA—the one that adds up the total costs. The question is whether the state will do the other half of the CBA—the one that adds up the diffuse, difficult-to-quantify benefits that flow to the population generally (the population whose interests elected officials are responsible for protecting). When it comes to articulating the latter, some number really is better than no number, and a good estimate is better than a bad one.

Finally, it should be observed that most critics of CBA do not reject it categorically, but instead believe there is some *other* decision procedure that is in some way superior. The most commonly cited candidate procedure is some form of participatory democratic deliberation.[56] It is worth observing, however, that such a procedure could *also* be used to increase the quality of the inputs to CBA. There have been small-scale experiments that involve using community deliberation as a way to improve WTP values, and there is some measure of enthusiasm for the technique among proponents of CBA.[57] There is also increased interest in the development and use of standard valuations, constructed by comparing and cleaning up the data sets from many different studies to develop a model of the impact on the quality of life of the average person from various interventions.[58] Thus there are a variety of ways of improving the inputs to the CBA procedure, which can help to minimize the concern that the numbers are garbage.

5.4. Assessing safety

Let us suppose now that our municipality receives a large provincial grant for road improvement. There is immediate consensus that the highest-priority spending area is road safety since the rate of motor-vehicle-accident fatalities in the municipality is above the national average. This category, however, includes not just the safety of drivers, but also pedestrians, cyclists, and users of public transit. A number of improvements could be made to make travel in the city safer: one could spend the money on new crosswalks, left-turn lanes at intersections, bicycle lanes, improving highway embankments, arborism to improve sight lines, barriers on level rail crossings—the list goes on and on. The question then is how the money should be spent. What are the high-priority areas? And so, the municipality commissions a study.

Two overarching principles govern this exercise. The first follows immediately from the Pareto principle, and it is a commitment to maximization. The available funds should be spent in such a way as to produce the greatest attainable reduction of mortality. (If this is not done, then a reallocation could improve the condition of at least one person without worsening that of anyone else.) The second is an application of the principle of citizen equality, which suggests that the interests of all users of the road should be assigned equal weight, there should be no privileging of any one category, such as drivers, pedestrians, or cyclists. The first requires evaluating each potential improvement to see how effective it would be at reducing mortality, and at what cost. To compare and rank projects of different scale, one must then calculate the cost of each project *per life saved*. The second requires that one do so comprehensively, examining projects that affect all users, and that one should choose projects with the lowest cost per life saved. (If, for example, one were to recommend a project that reduced driver fatalities at a cost of $7 million per life over one that reduced pedestrian fatalities at a cost of $5 million per life, then pedestrians could reasonably complain that their interests were not being assigned equal weight to the interests of drivers.) This is implicit in the commitment to maximization, but it is nevertheless worth observing that the cost-per-life calculation is necessary to ensure that the egalitarian principle is being satisfied.[59]

One can see here that we are moving into the neighborhood of one of the most controversial features of cost-benefit analysis, which is the valuation of life. At this point we are technically not yet valuing life, because what is being proposed is a cost-effectiveness analysis (CEA), rather than a full-blown cost-benefit analysis. What makes it a CEA is that monetary valuation is only being used on the "cost" side of the ledger; some other metric is being used on the "benefit" side. (The fact that one can do this illustrates the point, made earlier, that monetary valuation in CBA is simply used as a metric for comparison across individuals. There is nothing essential or important about money. Thus if one can use some other metric to compare different projects, such as "lives saved," where one can safely assume or stipulate that a life saved is of equal value regardless of whose life it is, then this can also be used as a metric.) Since saving lives is the benefit of the policy, while the cost is the actual financial cost, then one is not really assigning a monetary value to life within this framework, because lives only show up on the benefit side; money stays on the cost side.

CEA is useful if one has a budget that is exogenously determined and a single policy objective (such as "improving road safety"). One can then just look at alternative employments of the fixed budget and pick the most effective projects. So one calculates the cost in monetary terms, but on the benefit side, one uses a certain quantity of "whatever it is that we are trying to accomplish" as the unit (in this case, it would be reduction in road fatalities). This eliminates the need to monetize the value on the benefit side of the ledger. There is, it should be noted, an implicit valuation of life here—determined at the point at which the money runs out. So if the least cost-effective project to be funded has a cost-per-life-saved of $5,347,000, then this means that anything beyond this threshold is deemed "too expensive," and thus life is being implicitly valued at that sum. This decision, however, is not being made in the CEA, it is an implicit consequence of the budget decision that was made when a certain amount of money was allocated to road safety. In this case the CEA just makes explicit what was implicit in the earlier decision.

Where the CEA approach does not work so well is when the budget is endogenous to the policy choice (e.g., when the question of how much money should be spent on road safety depends, at least in part, on how expensive it is to improve road safety[60]), or when the budget is designated for multiple objectives that are rather different in character from one another. Suppose, for instance, that the money given to the municipality is for "road improvement" in general, a category that includes not just safety improvements, but also maintenance, construction, and various other forms of improvement. One of the questions that must be answered is therefore *how much* to spend in each area, and as is typical with these things, spending in each domain is subject to diminishing returns. (The first million dollars spent on pothole repair will produce much more benefit than the second million spent on it, just as the first million dollars spent on safety improvements will save more lives than the second million dollars will.) Furthermore, in the case of safety, it will likely be the case that marginal cost tends toward infinity as the level of fatalities approaches zero, which is to say that, absent a stopping rule, one could easily spend the entire budget on safety and still not get the level of traffic fatalities down to zero.

There is good reason to think, however, that users of the road are interested in more than just safety. For example, people also want to get to their destinations quickly, even when it involves putting themselves at risk: drivers exceed the speed limit, pedestrians jaywalk, cyclists ride the wrong way on one-way streets. The list could be extended considerably. In each case, the person is trading off the need for safety against the desire for expeditious passage. Their personal preferences are going to be reflected in their collective preferences as well—people are not going to want the government to spend its entire budget on safety if the result is a significant increase in travel times. Thus one must compare the benefits that would come from increased safety with the benefits that would come from reduced travel times, and decide how to balance the two spending priorities. A CEA will not be adequate to do this, because it requires a metric that will enable comparisons of "lives saved" against travel-time improvements. This leaves little choice in practice but to convert to a CBA, by assigning a monetary value to each life saved, as well as a monetary value to a given reduction in average travel time. The state must then determine at what point individuals themselves would want to stop spending on increased safety and start spending on other priorities. The point at which they do will imply a monetary valuation of life.

Two points should be noted here. First, whenever spending decisions are made that affect, in any way, human mortality, or even just longevity, subject to a budget constraint, there is always an implicit valuation of life. States that do not perform CBA still have budgets, which they use to improve road safety, as well as to accomplish myriad other objectives, many of which involve merely enhancing quality of life (such as park maintenance). To the extent that they do so, they are clearly letting some people die so that others can enjoy what may be, taken singly, minor benefits. Cost-benefit analysis merely articulates, or makes explicit, what is implicit in these decisions; it does not provide any independent justification for them. Second, the only way to tell whether citizens are being treated equally is to compare the valuation of life across policy domains. Where CBA calculations are not performed, the valuation of life is likely to be quite arbitrary. Thus it would not be surprising to find workplace safety rules that impose over $3 million in costs to save a single life, even as the Ministry of Transportation balks at making infrastructure improvements that would cost only $1 million per life saved. To the extent that citizens are equally exposed to all these risks, the arbitrariness of the valuations does not translate into any significant inequality between citizens. But if exposure to certain risks is correlated with other forms of disadvantage, then the arbitrariness does have the capacity to exacerbate inequality.[61] In particular, if budgets are determined through the political process, then "sympathetic victims" are more likely to attract funding for the issues that affect them. To the extent that individuals with low socioeconomic status are less sympathetic, they are more likely to receive equal concern and respect from the state if all agencies are forced to use a standard life valuation that is equal across all projects and policy domains.

5.4.1. The aggregation objection

In his influential critique of utilitarianism, Bernard Williams presents a scenario in which an individual (Jim), wanders into a small South American town, where the military is about to execute twenty randomly chosen civilians (the "Indians"), as an act of collective punishment against their village for supporting anti-government rebels.[62] The commander makes Jim an offer: if he (Jim) is willing to choose one of the villagers at random and personally execute him then the other nineteen will be spared. Williams's intuition (not universally shared) is that it would be permissible, perhaps even obligatory, for Jim to refuse. This appears to suggest that there is a deontic prohibition on killing the innocent, even when a foreseeable consequence of not violating the prohibition is that others will. Thus *aggregationism* (e.g., adding up the number of lives saved or lost under different conditions, or the number of rights violations that occur) ignores morally signif-icant features of the choices that we face. To the extent that CBA is committed to aggregationism, especially regarding human life, it runs afoul of these intuitions.

The standard response to this argument on the part of moral consequentialists is to say, "Surely there must be *some* point at which you would be willing to vi-olate the constraint. What if the commander is threatening to kill 100 Indians, or 1,000?" and then to chip away at the position from that end, with the goal of showing that there is something irrational or indefensible about any strict deontic prohibition. There is no reason, however, for proponents of CBA to be drawn into philosophical controversies of this nature. After all, in claiming that it is permissible for Jim to refuse to execute the innocent, Williams is granting that it is permissible for Jim to take actions that will foreseeably result in the death of twenty innocents, including the one that Jim was unwilling to kill. So, what is the difference between these two ways of bringing about someone's death? Typically, the way that deontologists have tried to articulate the difference is by distin-guishing *intended* outcomes from merely *foreseen* consequences. If Jim were to shoot one innocent, that individual's death would be the intended outcome of an action chosen by Jim. If Jim refuses, the same individual will die, but merely as a by-product of Jim's action—a foreseen consequence, but not an intended outcome.

As the subsequent literature on trolley problems has illustrated, everyday mo-rality imposes deontic constraints in the realm of intended outcomes and actions but is much less restrictive of aggregative calculation in the realm of the foreseen. (This is taken to explain the judgment that it is permissible to divert a runaway trolley onto a side-track where it will kill an innocent maintenance worker, if doing so will save a larger number of innocent passengers waiting on a platform.[63]) Thus the standard defense of CBA lies in the observation that, because of the policy areas in which embedded CBA is applied, the deaths that it deals with are entirely in the realm of the foreseen, not the intended. Furthermore, to the extent that these deaths do occur, it is typically the result of an omission on the part of the state (i.e., a failure to spend the extra money through which that death could have been averted). Satisfaction of either of these conditions may be sufficient to establish a context in which strict deontic constraints do not apply.

For example, when the state limits the amount that it spends on shelters for the homeless, it has the foreseeable result that some people will freeze to death on the street; when it limits the amount that it spends on chemotherapy drugs, it has the foreseeable result that some people will be denied access to life-extending treatment; when it limits the amount that it spends on road safety, it has the foreseeable result that more motorists will die in accidents. But this is not the same thing as killing the homeless, cancer patients, or drivers to achieve some other policy objective. Thus, the actions simply do not fall under the scope of any deontic prohibition. It is therefore perfectly permissible to ask whether one is really maximizing the number of lives saved by upgrading a highway to provide an additional passing lane, instead of providing expanded outreach services to the homeless. If one discovers that the lives of motorists are being implicitly valued much more highly than those of the homeless, and so one decides to reduce spending on road safety while putting new funds into "in from the cold" programs, then one is not killing motorists to save homeless people. One is, however, letting motorists die who otherwise might be saved, so that one can save a larger number of homeless people.

Thus there need not be any conflict between CBA and the deontic constraints that we feel should govern decision-making in certain policy areas (and there is no need for proponents of CBA to commit themselves to the sort of controversial modifications of everyday morality implied by moral consequentialism). Deontic constraints can be accommodated through a set of "input filters" in embedded CBA, which determine the set of problems to which it will be applied. For example, the mining industry is subject to a variety of workplace safety regulations, all of which are eligible for CBA. There are no doubt certain safety procedures, or equipment, or mining techniques that are not mandated, simply because they would be too expensive, relative to the number of lives that would be saved. As a result, some mining accidents will occur that could have been prevented, had "we" been willing to spend more money to prevent them. At the same time, once an accident has occurred and a group of miners is trapped underground, it is not permissible to apply a CBA to the rescue attempt. On the contrary, states are usually willing to spend what seems like arbitrarily large amounts of money rescuing trapped miners (even though the same money, if saved and spent later on preventative safety measures, might actually save the lives of many more miners). Nevertheless, it is impermissible to abandon specific people to their deaths merely to save money. That is because the accident triggers a "duty of rescue" that overrides the more general consequential calculus governing budgeting.

Of course, reasonable people may differ on whether a certain problem should trigger a deontic context that prohibits CBA. For example, after the terrorist attack on the World Trade Center in 2001, the US government declared something like a "state of exception" with respect to airline safety and other aspects of antiterrorism policy. Thus the large number of the changes to airport security were exempted from ordinary CBA. This eventually became controversial, simply because the costs imposed by these changes (mainly in the form of lost time for travelers) were gigantic, while the number of lives saved seemed to be quite low. This led to widespread speculation that none of the enhanced security measures (except for the hardened cockpit doors) could pass a CBA test. (It led as well to questions about why lawmakers, who in many cases were eager to assign standard valuations to the victims of workplace accidents, should suddenly lose their resolve when it came to valuing the lives of victims of terrorist attacks). The important point, however, is that the state will typically pick and choose which problems to evaluate using CBA, and this gets decided by the political process, an area in which the various deontic constraints governing the treatment of life carry full sway. Thus, the commitment to CBA involves much less than a commitment to moral consequentialism, which in turn makes the type of aggregationism it employs less problematic.

5.4.2. The dignity objection

The second major objection to the valuation of life in CBA appeals to the suggestion that human life has an inherent "dignity," which is incompatible with the assignment of a price. Critics often quote the passage from Immanuel Kant cited in chapter 4.[64] Setting aside concerns about aggregationism (trading off lives for lives), there is a separate concern that arises when one contemplates trading off a human life against something of lesser value, such as a basket of ordinary economic goods. This is thought to diminish the inherent dignity and value of life, and it should be strictly prohibited for that reason.[65]

The preceding discussion has shown that CBA does not justify anything that the state is not already doing whenever it makes decisions affecting human life subject to a budget constraint. There are, however, two further points that are worth making in response to the dignity objection. First, proponents of CBA have tried to explain that when they talk about the value of "life" it is, in most cases, a shorthand way of talking about something quite different, namely, the disvalue that people assign to very small risks of death. So when one says that the valuation of a "life" is $5 million, it is not actually any known individual's life that is being valued; rather, it is the aggregate disvalue of very small risks of death distributed over a very large number of persons. This is flagged by the insistence that the dollar figures in question represent the "value of a statistical life" (VSL), not the value of an *actual* life (VAL). The thought is that if 100,000 people are each willing to pay $100 to eliminate exposure to a pollutant that generates a 1/50,000 risk of death, then the total "budget" of $10 million represents a WTP of $5 million *per life saved* (since the pollutant can be expected to kill two people out of the 100,000 people affected). In deliberations about whether to ban the pollutant, the question that is asked is not whether it is worth spending the money to save these two people's lives; the question is whether it is worth spending the money to deliver the benefit of a small *ex ante* reduction in risk to the entire group.

One way of responding to the "dignity" objection is simply to state that, although human life may be priceless, *risks* to human life are not. Even if one could never be justified in killing a person to achieve some good consequence, it is not so obvious that one could not be justified in imposing a risk of death on a person to achieve some such consequence, as long as the risk is not excessive.[66] After all, every time we get behind the wheel of a car, we are imposing some risk of death on other users of the road. Thus embedded CBA can avoid the general concern about human dignity simply by avoiding any application in areas that would require the use of a VAL rather than a VSL.

A second line of argument that defenders of CBA appeal to is that individuals themselves make choices, quite often, in which they trade off risks of their own deaths against other goods. Nobody wants to spend infinite amounts of money on safety, and very few people take living as long as is humanly possible to be central to their vision of the good life. On the contrary, safety is just one good among many that make up a balanced and healthy life. (As Jonathan Wolff puts it, "It is clear that purchasing—or declining to purchase—devices or services that make small differences to one's safety, or that of one's family, is an ordinary part of life, taking its place alongside other consumer decisions."[67]) Deciding on an appropriate balance to strike among these various goods is an expression of individual autonomy. Yet if individuals, taken singly, have the right to decide what risks they are willing to accept, then there seems to be no reason that individuals, acting collectively, should not have the right to make that same decision. And since the state, in its "public economic" functions (which are the focus of CBA), is just acting as the agent of individuals, it seems that it should be able to make choices that reflect these individual preferences.

There are, of course, problems that arise in the transition from individual to collective autonomy, particularly given that the state is often obliged to make "one size fits all" decisions about the levels of risk that individuals will be exposed to. Setting aside these issues, however, it is worth pausing to consider how dramatically handicapped the public sector would be if it were somehow prevented from performing the ordinary cost-benefit calculations that inform individuals' private choices about safety and, in particular, their market behavior. It would mean that a very large number of collective action problems simply could not be resolved, because private individuals are unable to contract their way to a solution (i.e., there is a market failure), yet the public sector is unable to step in and resolve the issue, because doing so would implicitly treat human life as less than infinitely precious. To take just one example, if human life really does have an "inherent dignity" that prevents the state from trading off risks to individuals against other goods, then the state would be unable to operate public transit systems. Transportation is inherently risky, and so one can spend arbitrarily large sums of money on improving safety.[68] When choosing private transportation options (e.g., buying a car), individuals necessarily trade off the benefits of safety against other considerations. But if the state is unable to make the same calculations, then the cost of state administration of transit would skyrocket. As a result, collective forms of transit like subways or buses would fall through the cracks—too costly to be provided privately, but too unsafe to be provided publicly.

This is, of course, not what proponents of the dignity argument have in mind. In fact, much of the concern over valuation of life seems not to be a concern over valuation per se, but rather a concern that using standard methods will result in a VSL that is simply too *low* (and that the benefits of certain kinds of regulations will therefore be understated). Critics focus a great deal on the use of wage premiums in risky occupations as a revealed preference mechanism for inferring the valuation that workers put on their own lives. These are perfectly legitimate concerns, since we know that cognitive bias results in these premiums being far too low. The appropriate response, however, is simply to increase the assigned VSL to a more acceptable level, not to treat it as infinitely large. And in fact, if one looks at the practice of most states that make extensive use of CBA, one can see that the VSL figure is set through what amounts to an exercise in reflective equilibrium. Most importantly, a standard valuation is selected that is applied in *all* policy domains.[69] This value is typically the result of lengthy reflection and negotiation. In Canada, for instance, Environment Canada and Health Canada jointly sponsored an internal review of CBAs to determine the range of VSL values. They found a "mean VSL of $5.2 million with a range from a low of $3.1 million to a high of $10.4 million in 1996 dollars."[70] This mean value ($5.2 million in 1996 dollars), adjusted for inflation, was picked up by the central agencies and became the standard valuation used in all departments of the federal government.

5.5. Rationing healthcare

In 1992, the pharmaceutical company Bristol-Myers Squibb raised eyebrows when it began charging $4,000 a year for Taxol, a new drug for patients with breast cancer that avoided many of the side effects of traditional chemotherapy. Although there were some complaints, insurers had little choice but to pay that price. This had the unfortunate consequence, however, of setting a precedent. In 1998, Genentech introduced another breast cancer drug, Herceptin, at a price of $20,000 a year. In 2002, Bristol and ImClone Systems began charging as much as $100,000 for Erbitux, a drug for patients with advanced colon cancer.[71] In 2011, the company Alexion set a new record with the drug Soliris, for which they charged more than $500,000 a year.

What is striking about these drugs is not just the extraordinary price tag, but how little benefit they offer to patients. A study of Erbitux (Cetuximab) conducted by the National Cancer Institute of Canada Clinical Trials Group found that treatment with the drug led to an average gain of only 0.12 life years, which is to say, 43 days. When quality of life was factored in, the gain was only 0.08 quality-adjusted life years (QALYs). At the worldwide average price—which was at the time approximately half that charged in the United States—this amounted to $199,742 per life year, or $299,613 per QALY gained.[72] By way of comparison, colorectal cancer screening programs cost between $10,000 and $25,000 per life year saved.[73] Thus the drug treatment was literally an order of magnitude more expensive than other options for combating the same condition (from a population perspective).

The introduction of these ultra-expensive drugs has led to a "day of reckoning" for health insurers, particularly those in the public sector, where budget constraints are more sharply felt. There was a time when insurers could promise to pay for the "best available" care for their policyholders in the event of illness. Now it is no longer feasible to pay for all the therapies that patients might be inclined to consume (or doctors to prescribe). Furthermore, very few people would be willing to pay the premiums on a health-insurance policy that paid for *every* life-extending therapy (and few citizens are interested in paying the taxes that would be required for public health-insurance systems to provide such coverage). The result is that patients in public healthcare systems are sometimes denied therapy, particularly with respect to pharmaceuticals. There may be a drug available, which the patient could be taking and which would increase that patient's life expectancy, but which the state simply refuses to pay for on the grounds that it is too expensive—and that the money would be better spent elsewhere, providing other, more cost-effective therapies for other patients.

One does not need to be a moral philosopher to see that this sort of healthcare rationing *looks* as though it rests on a utilitarian calculation. The patient who is being denied treatment is harmed, and the resources that could have been used to help him are being given to some other patient, where they can be expected to do more good. And yet, as Ronald Dworkin observed, appearances in this case can be misleading.[74] This is because of the role that health insurance plays in mediating the transaction, and the way it obscures the relationship between the patient's own prior choices and the subsequent rejection of the claim. That relationship would be easier to discern if the market for health insurance were less subject to market failure.

Consider, for the moment, what an ideal market for health insurance would look like. It would feature close to an infinite number of different insurance policies for sale, each providing a specific level of indemnity against a specific range of conditions, and each charging an actuarially fair premium, reflecting the precise expected loss that each individual brought to the insurance pool. Thus anyone who wanted to have the option of receiving Erbitux in the event of developing colon cancer could buy a policy that offered to pay for that specific treatment. The premium associated with such a policy would, of course, be higher than the premium for a policy that was identical save for an exclusion of Erbitux. In a perfect market, both policies would be available, so it would be possible for a person to see exactly how much difference coverage of that specific drug made to the monthly payments. The person could then decide, based on this price information, whether he thought it was worth it to pay extra for the policy that covered Erbitux.

Now imagine that this person opts for the policy that does not cover Erbitux, but ten years later develops colon cancer and finds that he could benefit from a course of it. He requests the drug, but his insurer refuses. He might be tempted to challenge the decision, but in this case it is almost pointless to do so, because the justification for the refusal is too obvious: "You cannot have Erbitux because you chose the policy that doesn't cover Erbitux. Furthermore, you benefited from paying lower health-insurance premiums for ten years, precisely because you chose the policy that excluded Erbitux. So you cannot turn around now and demand it."

Under these circumstances, it will still be a fact about the insurance scheme that the money that could have been used to pay for the person's Erbitux will be used to pay for other treatments, for other patients, that are presumably more cost-effective. It will look as though one person is being denied a life-extending therapy in order to provide a greater benefit to someone else. But this is misleading. The greater benefit to someone else does no work in justifying the denial of Erbitux to the individual in question, it is just a by-product of the way insurance systems are organized, along with the fact that the policyholders in these schemes seek maximum value *ex ante*.

The same structure is preserved when the example is changed from an ideal market to the real world. Private insurers, of course, are not able to offer a continuum of policies, and they do not have the information required to charge an actuarially fair premium to each potential policyholder. Thus they aggregate and average across groups, then offer a limited selection of add-ons and exclusions (and deductibles). Health insurers may offer a choice between "basic," "comprehensive," and "deluxe" policies. Individuals will then sort themselves into groups, depending on their willingness to pay for various levels of coverage. In this case, a person may be denied Erbitux on the grounds that she bought the "basic" package instead of the "deluxe" one, but the principle is the same.

Nothing changes fundamentally when the state takes over provision of health insurance, except that now the aggregation and calculation of WTP has to be done over the entire population. Because private health-insurance markets are so inefficient, the state is in a position to offer a comparable product at far lower cost (and with less distortion of the healthcare market, because of its superior ability to control moral hazard and, thus, to limit cost inflation). To do so, the state must calculate approximately what individuals themselves would be willing to pay for health insurance (i.e., what fraction of lifetime income the average person would want to spend).

The situation with single-payer healthcare systems is really no different from when the state gets involved in providing public goods like parks. When it comes to choosing the size of their backyards, individuals can find private markets that offer an enormous range of options, and so everyone is likely to find something that is a close match to her particular tastes. Individuals can then further customize, by spending as they like on landscaping, playground equipment, a swimming pool, and so on. However, if some individuals want to trade backyard space for access to a communal park, to be provided for the neighborhood as a whole, the government is forced to make a number of extremely rough-and-ready calculations to determine how to satisfy something like the average preference in the neighborhood. Thus a variety of decisions get made about public park size, landscaping, playground equipment, dog runs, and wading pools, which are not likely to satisfy any one individual perfectly, but provide rough satisfaction to a very large number of people. Public health-insurance schemes are the same. They provide one-size-fits-all coverage, rather than the continuum of individually tailored policies that an ideal market would provide. This will be based on average healthcare needs and average WTP. Because we cannot create a market in which individuals are free to choose the exact policy they want, the state has to choose a level of provision on their behalf that comes as close as possible to satisfying as many people as possible. Such a policy will necessarily include spending limits, simply because people's willingness to pay for health insurance is not unlimited. And when those spending limits are reached, it will look as though the state is engaging in utilitarian redistribution of resources, but in fact, it is not doing so. The justification for the denial will simply be that the individual's insurance policy does not cover it.

The need to make calculations about relative value of therapies has led to the emergence of decision-making bodies such as the National Institute for Health and Care Excellence (NICE) in the United Kingdom, which uses an "embedded" QALY framework to decide, inter alia, when the National Health Service (NHS) should pay for pharmaceuticals. This eliminates the problem associated with drugs like Erbitux, since NICE has established a WTP threshold in the range of £20,000 to £30,000 per QALY. Patients are, of course, free to buy such drugs privately should they so desire.[75]

5.5.1. The death panels objection

During the debates that preceded the adoption of the Patient Protection and Affordable Care Act (PPACA, also known as "Obamacare") in the United States, which sought to extend health insurance to a broader segment of the American population, much of the discussion was sidetracked by the allegation that the proposed legislation sought to implement "death panels," or committees that would withdraw care from the elderly or disabled. This had been set in motion by an online post by former governor of Alaska Sarah Palin, who wrote: "The America I know and love is not one in which my parents or my baby with Down Syndrome will have to stand in front of Obama's 'death panel' so his bureaucrats can decide, based on a subjective judgment of their 'level of productivity in society,' whether they are worthy of healthcare. Such a system is downright evil."

In part to avoid this accusation, and in part in response to lobbying by physicians and the pharmaceutical industry, the Patient-Centered Outcomes Research Institute (PCORI) that was created as part of the PPACA was expressly prohibited from engaging in cost-effectiveness analysis of the sort that is performed by NICE in the United Kingdom. It could only engage in "comparative effectiveness analysis," which can look at how different therapies compare to one another but does not take cost into consideration. The legislation specifies that the PCORI "shall not develop or employ a dollars-per-quality adjusted life year (or similar measure that discounts the value of a life because of an individual's disability) as a threshold to establish what type of healthcare is cost effective or recommended. The Secretary shall not utilize such an adjusted life year (or such a similar measure) as a threshold to determine coverage, reimbursement, or incentive programs."[76]

As we have seen, the mere fact that cost-effectiveness may result in the refusal to fund overly expensive care is not "evil"; it is a legitimate feature of all insurance schemes, whether they are run in the private sector or public sector. Thus, the restrictions built into the mandate of the PCORI are probably best understood as a consequence of rent-seeking by the pharmaceutical industry. There are, however, other issues raised in the famous "death panels" post. One of these is the concern that the cost-benefit calculations underlying the availability of medical care will consider, not just the health benefits to the individual patient, but also the contribution that the patient makes to society more generally. In the background, of course, is the specter of eugenics movements, including that of the Nazis in Germany, who executed large numbers of disabled people on the grounds that they were a burden on society.

This issue is closely related to a view, widely debated among philosophers, about whether healthcare is "special," such that its distribution should be largely independent of the distribution of other goods in society.[77] Some of this debate is based on a confusion that is caused by the fact that healthcare is paid for through insurance schemes, and as a result is distributed in accordance with "need" rather than "ability to pay." This is not a consequence of any egalitarian commitment arising in the domain of health, it is just how insurance systems work.[78] People whose houses burn down have "need" of a new house, and their home insurance provides them with one (whether they are rich or poor, deserving or undeserving, etc.). This is not because houses are special, it is because the insurance they bought indemnified them against the specific eventuality of losing their home. Similarly, health insurance indemnifies individuals against the specific eventuality of needing healthcare, and so that is precisely what it provides.

Thus much of the way that healthcare provision is "insulated" from the patterns of distribution of goods in other domains is a consequence of the way that our purchase of it is mediated through health insurance systems (or quasi-insurance systems, such as one finds in an HMO or a large provider like the NHS in the United Kingdom). This in turn explains why the allocation of healthcare resources is almost entirely an exercise in "local justice,"[79] where there is no compensation across allocative spheres. The rich get the same as the poor, the talented get the same as the untalented, the prudent get the same as the irresponsible, and the disabled get the same as the able-bodied (above and beyond, of course, what they get for their disability). The question is whether CBA threatens this, as Palin suggested, or whether it is possible to preserve healthcare as a domain of local justice. More narrowly, the question is whether one can preserve health as a domain of CEA, with a health-specific value, such as a QALY, as the metric of comparison, or whether the framework creates an irresistible dynamic toward monetization in order to facilitate comparisons *across* policy domains.

It seems to me that there is nothing inevitable about the use of full-blown CBA, and therefore no reason that healthcare resource allocation decisions cannot continue to be made within a CEA framework. Because healthcare funding is mediated through what amounts to an enormous insurance scheme, and because it is possible to ascertain individual willingness to pay for health insurance at a very general level, the healthcare budget tends to be relatively self-standing. This means that there is no particular need to do CBA in the area of healthcare; one can instead ask people questions along the lines of "how much of your income do you want to spend on protection from disease and injury?" and then do a CEA with the budget that results.

Cost-effectiveness analysis is attractive in this domain as well, because there is good reason to think that the health outcomes that are sought provide a plausible basis for interpersonal comparisons. As has been mentioned, there are solid normative grounds for assigning a gain in life expectancy the same value, regardless of who experiences it (and regardless of what they are willing to pay for it), based simply on the obligation the state has to treat all citizens as equals. Thus, a gain in life expectancy can provide the benchmark against which various states of morbidity can be assessed, generating the well-known QALY framework for assessing gains in health outcome. Using a QALY framework, in turn, allows proponents of CEA to avoid all the problems that stem from using money as the metric of comparison between individuals.

Overall, then, there is no reason to think that the creation of an institute like NICE is the first step on a slippery slope that ends with eugenics. As long as individuals are unwilling to spend their entire income on healthcare, and they are pooling together their healthcare spending in response to the uncertainty of their future needs, whoever manages that pool is going to have to make decisions about what expenses will and will not be paid by the group. When the state manages the pool, then it has no choice but to make those decisions. As is typically the case, the only real question is whether those decisions will be made in accordance with explicit, fully articulated criteria, as in a CEA, or implicit, poorly articulated criteria.

5.5.2. The discrimination objection

One of the striking features of the decision to bar PCORI from assessing the cost-effectiveness of medical spending is that the two major interested parties, namely, the pharmaceutical industry and physicians, were able to persuade disability rights groups to support their position, by arguing that the CEA framework discriminates against the disabled.[80] This turns up in the language of the statute, where the QALY framework is described as a system that "discounts the value of a life because of an individual's disability." Thus, another objection to the use of cost-benefit considerations in the allocation of healthcare resources is that it is discriminatory.

This is a spurious charge. As long as individuals are concerned not just with avoiding death, but also with avoiding pain, suffering, and indignity, then they are going to want to allocate resources in a way that reflects not just mortality risk, but also the disvalue of different states of morbidity. Hip-replacement surgery, for instance, does not extend anyone's life, yet it vastly improves a patient's quality of life. Chemotherapy, by contrast, extends life, but often at great cost, and with significantly reduced quality of life. So how much should be spent on hip-replacement surgery versus chemotherapy drugs? To make this decision, there must be some basis of comparison between the two, so that changes in the quality of life can be weighed against changes in quantity (i.e., expectancy).

The core idea of the QALY framework, again, is to defer to patients' own autonomous choice in this domain. Individuals living in various states of morbidity (or disability) typically would prefer to be restored to full health (or normal ability). In the standard run of cases, this preference is strong enough that they would be willing to accept a reduction in life expectancy if it meant being able to live out their remaining years without the condition. (Or conversely, and more commonly, people would like to live longer and are willing to accept a reduction in quality of life in order to extend their lives.) Through a standard titration procedure, it is possible to determine how much life expectancy people would be willing to trade off against various states of morbidity. So if a person is willing to accept a reduction in life expectancy from ten years to nine years, to alleviate a particular condition, it suggests that she values a year spent living with that condition as worth one-tenth less than a year spent living without it. Thus, if we assign a year lived in perfect health a value of 1, then a year spent living with the condition would be worth 0.9. By finding the precise point at which that person becomes indifferent between a reduction in life expectancy and an improvement in quality of life, it is possible to assign a QALY value for life with the condition. This can then serve as a metric for comparing gains or losses in quality of life with gains or losses in life expectancy.

So, for example, the "badness" of confinement to a wheelchair might be reflected in a year living in that condition being assigned a QALY value of 0.8. As a result, offering hip-replacement surgery to a population with an average life expectancy of ten years, although it would not increase anyone's actual life expectancy, would be *equivalent*—for resource-allocation purposes—to increasing each person's life expectancy by two years (because the QALY value of living with the condition makes the ten years confined to a wheelchair equivalent to only eight years with full mobility). Now this all *sounds* a bit like saying that the lives of people who are confined to wheelchairs are somehow worth less than the lives of those who aren't, but this is not in fact what is being said. "Life" is being used as a metric of comparison, not as a unit of evaluation. The simple fact is that people care about more than just survival; they care about their quality of life.

234 THE MACHINERY OF GOVERNMENT

This is why they are willing to pay a great deal of money to relieve chronic pain, for instance. Thus, every healthcare system is going to make trade-offs between investing in interventions that extend life and those that improve quality of life. The QALY framework is an attempt to make explicit, and hence to systematize, the criteria for doing so.

Far from being discriminatory, the use of QALY measures in healthcare resource allocation reflects a commitment to a particular form of egalitarianism. It is based on the view that the opportunity to live life for a given duration, in a particular state of health, is of equal value regardless of whose life it happens to be (or, conversely, that death and disease are of equal disvalue, regardless of whom they may strike). But that having been said, it should be acknowledged that there are a number of other egalitarian intuitions at play in the healthcare sector, which are clearly in tension with the egalitarian intuition that is at the heart of the QALY framework. For example, the American Association of Retired Persons has at various times mobilized in opposition to CEA, on the grounds that the use of QALYs discriminates against the elderly—as does any framework that assesses benefit by considering the *duration* of gains. This is because young people have greater life expectancy, and so an appendectomy performed on a 30-year old will produce much more "benefit" than an appendectomy performed on a 90-year old, even if it has the immediate effect of restoring each to perfect health.

Now it is important to issue a small cautionary note to make it clear that CEA is not used to make individual patient-care decisions. It is used instead to determine what therapies will be made globally available through the insurance system. It would not be the case that if two patients were lying in hospital beds side by side, one of them younger, the other one older, a particular therapy would be offered only to the younger one, but not the older one (on the grounds that offering it to the older one did not produce enough benefit to justify the cost). Similarly, a disabled person would never be denied a therapy on the grounds that the extra years added to that person's life counted for less because of the pre-existing disability. On the contrary, the value of a therapy is calculated using the average life-expectancy gain of the average patient receiving it, and it is then made available to everyone or to no one, on the basis of that assessment. Thus, there is no danger of differential clinical treatment based on age or disability.[81]

What is true, however, is that the use of a QALY framework at the global level will tend to favor funding for therapies that disproportionately benefit the young. On a per patient basis, for example, the treatment of childhood leukemia is going to be assigned higher priority than the treatment of Alzheimer's disease, because "saving the life" of a child winds up saving more life than "saving the life" of an elderly person. In this sense, CEA does discriminate against the elderly, because it does not treat all persons as having equal claim on a given quantum of resources. This gets confusing, however, because many people find such "discrimination" to be both intuitively correct and fully justified. Many people's thinking about these questions is informed by what is called the "fair innings" intuition[82]—that everyone is entitled to a certain amount of life, and that there is something more unfair (or at least tragic) about a child contracting a deadly disease than an older person contracting it, since the child hasn't had her fair share of life yet. From this perspective, there is something untoward about the elderly "hogging" vast quantities of healthcare resources, despite having already led full lives.

Complicating matters is the fact that some people also have a luck-egalitarian intuition, which says that in cases where people are not responsible for suffering from various conditions, the fact that these conditions are more or less expensive to treat should not be allowed to determine their prospects. From this perspective, one person should not be entitled to less healthcare than someone else just because the disease he happens to have caught is more expensive to treat than the other person's.

People also have a strong tendency to direct resources to the person who is in the worst condition, not necessarily to the place where they will do the most good.[83] At the limit, this takes the form of the duty of rescue, which involves a strict deontic prohibition on "letting people die," and therefore entails a willingness to spend arbitrarily large quantities of resources to keep someone alive. Both allocation formulas are, of course, in tension with the practice of triage, which requires pretty much the opposite—that "lost causes" be identified and denied resources altogether, so that attention can be focused on cases where there is greater opportunity for improvement.

The point of these examples is to show that people have a number of very strong deontic intuitions in the domain of healthcare resource allocation, and that although many of these intuitions are in tension with the basic principles that inform QALY-based CEA, they are also in tension with one another. As Larry Temkin and others have shown, it is extremely difficult to get *any* consistent set of principles for the distribution of resources in the healthcare domain.[84] Thus it is typically not the case that the aggregative framework recommended by CEA runs headlong into a single unified egalitarian or deontic principle. It tends instead to run into a morass of confused and contradictory principles. That tension is diffused through institutional arrangements. The QALY framework is only used as a basis for healthcare resource allocation decisions made by the state. Medical decisions on the ward, by contrast, are made on a more deontological basis, based on a set of principles that constitute the traditional professional ethic of doctors and nurses. This can generate a variety of tensions, but not ones that undermine the validity or usefulness of CEA as the basis of high-level budget decision-making.

5.6. Environmental goods

With the safety upgrades complete, the municipality is now considering expanding its highway network, by building a new expressway in a ravine that cuts through the city. Doing so, however, will disrupt the natural ecosystem in and around the river that formed the ravine, producing significant habitat destruction for local wildlife. The municipality decides to do a CBA to determine whether the expressway project is worth undertaking. The advantages and disadvantages of the roadway—including pollution, noise, and impact on downtown congestion—are considered. Questions arise, however, over how to handle the environmental impacts of the project. Recreational use of the ravine is minimal. It is too inaccessible to be used as a park; hunting is not permitted in it; and no one fishes in the river. Thus, the impact of the wildlife habitat and ecosystem destruction on human welfare is quite small.

Nonetheless, many citizens are profoundly concerned about the environmental consequences of the project. So the planners decide to incorporate an "existence value" into the CBA.[85] Residents of the municipality are asked how much they would be willing to pay to preserve the ravine ecosystem, regardless of whether they make any direct use of it (e.g., such as through recreational use). This provides an estimate of an additional cost associated with construction of the roadway. When this cost is taken into consideration, it turns out that construction of the expressway fails the CBA test.

This result is, of course, controversial, and soon a group of citizens who had supported the expressway project step forward to challenge it. They argue that the use of "existence values" in the CBA was illegitimate and unfairly tipped the scales against the project. Such values are, according to their brief, a type of "intrusive preference," which should not be counted when it comes to determining the level of social welfare a particular project produces. The inclusion of existence values, they argue, is a form of gerrymandering of the CBA by environmentalists, based on the introduction of a preference that no one would be willing to accept in other areas of decision-making. For example, a person might have very strong views about what color his neighbor's house should be painted and might become quite distraught when the neighbor decides to change it. Or a person might have strong views about what books other people should read, or what sort of food they should eat. But unless it is possible to show a tangible "harm"—as John Stuart Mill argued long ago—then whatever loss of welfare this person suffers should not count as an argument in favor of social regulation.

In other words, for people to claim that the destruction of a natural ecosystem lowers their welfare, even though they have never interacted with that ecosystem or have any concrete intention of doing so, is an abusive concept of welfare. Allowing it to count as a consideration that speaks against the proposal, on par with the concerns of drivers who want to reduce their morning commute time, opens up a Pandora's box, making the entire CBA framework unworkable. For example, when people eat pork, even in the privacy of their own homes, should the disgust this evokes among observant Jews and Muslims, at the very thought that someone is eating pork, count as an "externality," whose cost must be taken into consideration by the state (justifying, perhaps, a special tax on pork)? Presumably, the answer is no. However, trying to specify why this disgust reaction, and the attendant loss of welfare, should *not* count is surprisingly difficult.[86] There are several candidate theories, and what they all have in common is some reference to the lack of close connection or involvement between the event that occurs (the consumption of pork) and the loss of welfare the individual who is upset by it suffers. Yet this would seem to apply to the environmental case as well. The mere fact that some people do not want a piece of land to be developed, and will get upset if it is developed, does not appear to be the right sort of preference to count as an argument against development. In fact, it seems more like a moral judgment, to the effect that the piece of land *ought not* to be developed. But this is what the CBA is supposed to determine. To do so, the CBA needs to start with a characterization of the *interests* that are at stake in the decision. To allow people's moral attitudes toward those interests to count as interests creates a variety of problems, including opening the door to an objectionable form of double counting.

Supporters of the "existence value" practice, however, respond by emphasizing that the desire to set aside land for conservation is an extremely common preference, which markets already cater to quite extensively at both an individual and a club level. Wealthy individuals buy ecologically sensitive land to protect it from destruction. Conservationist Douglas Tompkins owns more than two million acres in Chile and Argentina, purchased with the goal of protecting biodiversity, and CNN founder Ted Turner purchased 128,000 acres of Patagonian wilderness with the same end in mind.[87] Celebrities and wealthy environmentalists have been buying large tracts of Amazonian rainforest. There are also a number of popular nonprofit organizations, such as the World Land Trust, the Nature Conservancy, the Rainforest Conservation Fund, and Nature Trust in Canada, which allow less-wealthy individuals to pool their funds to purchase land, which is, in turn, set aside in perpetuity as a private conservation trust. Most of these people, it should be noted, will never have occasion to visit these properties, or to interact with them in any significant way.

Thus, unlike the case of the books other people read, the food they eat, or the color they paint their houses, the interest that people have in preserving land for conservation is one that private markets already cater to. This suggests that it cannot be overly intrusive. Of course, some of the conservationist impulse seems directed toward "existence value," but at the same time, a certain element of it can also be construed as the preservation of an "option value," particularly when it comes to protection of biodiversity. Ecosystems tend to be easy to destroy, but extremely expensive, difficult, and time-consuming to rebuild. Thus, even a very small possibility that one might want to make use of an ecosystem in the future can make it straightforwardly rational to preserve it. (This issue arises quite often with the biodiversity of the rainforest, where many plant species have not even been cataloged, and there is a suspicion that some may have useful medicinal properties.) Furthermore, in the same way that having a hospital, or a fire station, in the neighborhood can be of value to residents, even if they never make direct use of it, the presence of a nature preserve can also generate value for those who never directly enjoy its charms or benefits. The knowledge that it is there, and that they can make use of it if they wish, can have positive value.

Thus the burden of proof, in the case of ecosystem preservation, is not to show that the relevant existence values are legitimate, it is merely to show that there is some sort of a market failure, which explains why the *state* should be undertaking the conservation effort, rather than a nonprofit organization or an individual conservationist.

5.6.1. The intrinsic value objection

For theorists who approach these issues from a background in environmental ethics, the cost-benefit approach to environmental valuation is a non-starter. In many ways, the cornerstone of modern environmental ethics is the critique of "anthropocentric theories of value," of which all major schools of thinking in normative ethics are taken to be variants. As J. Baird Caldicott described it, "An anthropocentric value theory (or axiology), by common consensus, confers intrinsic value on human beings and regards all other things, including all other forms of life, as being only instrumentally valuable, that is, valuable only to the extent that they are means or instruments which may serve human beings."[88] He claims that it represents an arbitrary limitation on the scope of moral concern.

It seems obvious that standard CBA embodies this kind of anthropocentric approach, because for any consideration to *count*, in the analysis, it must first be translated into an object of human concern. When a CBA considers the "cost" involved in the destruction of a natural ecosystem, it does not consider the cost to the ecosystem, but the cost to humans of the destruction of that ecosystem. The problem with this is often expressed, as Caldicott does, by saying that the CBA treats the ecosystem as having only *instrumental* value and fails to recognize that it has *intrinsic* value. As a result, though CBA may be an appropriate guide to decision-making when the primary impacts of a policy involve human welfare, it is inappropriate for thinking about environmental questions, where the primary impacts of a policy involve the natural world.

This argument may appear straightforward; however, it does involve a few complications that are worth flagging. First is the assumption, often made, that the categories of "intrinsic value" and "instrumental value" map onto the "natural" and the "artificial," so that anything humans have made by will have been built for some purpose, and so will have instrumental value. This is not correct, however, since under any reasonable definition of intrinsic value, human artifacts also have intrinsic value. Great works of art are the example most often given.[89] Consider, for instance, the way that Richard Routley illustrated the concept of intrinsic value, using a "last man" scenario: if you were the last person alive on earth, about to die, would it be permissible for you to kill and destroy as much of the natural world as you could, before the lights go out?[90] He considers the fact that many would regard this as impermissible as a sign that the natural world has intrinsic value, which, in turn, calls for a new environmental ethic that transcends our species chauvinism. Yet many people would be equally alarmed at the thought of the "last man" going through art galleries and libraries, slashing paintings and burning books. It is doubtful, however, that these artifacts of human creation could have a value that is independent of human valuation.

These reflections suggest that intrinsic and instrumental values do not correspond to "natural" and "human" values, they represent merely two different modes of *human* valuation. Further argument would have to be given to show that it is possible for values to be ontologically independent of human valuers— merely pointing to the existence of things with intrinsic value is not enough. Now it may be possible to make such an argument, but the ultimate outcome would have little impact on the basic case for CBA. Even if it were possible to show that some values are "out there," completely independent of human valuation, it is not clear what role these would play in human deliberation over questions of environmental policy. For these values to play any effective role, people would have to know what they are, and somehow advocate for or represent them. And whatever was ultimately put forth would undoubtedly be controversial. For example, even among environmental ethicists there is deep disagreement over whether individual animals have intrinsic value, or whether value lies in animal populations, or species, or, rather, entire ecosystems. The difference becomes important when one is deciding, for example, whether there is a moral obligation to intervene to prevent predators from killing other animals.[91] Thus what Rawls described as the "fact of pluralism" obtains just as much in this domain of value as in any other (and perhaps even more so, since the emphasis on the objective independence of these values makes it much more difficult to know what they are, and practically impossible to agree on any procedure for determining their significance).

As a result, what is typically taken to be a commitment to an anthropocentric theory of value in CBA is better understood as just a consequence of liberal neutrality. When it comes to ecosystems, for instance, there is disagreement about what sort of value they possess—some people value them instrumentally; others value them intrinsically; still others value them quite highly, while others assign them only negligible value, and so on. The liberal state is committed to remaining neutral on these questions, and so is not willing simply to take sides on the basic question of how to value natural ecosystems. Instead, it looks to how individuals in society estimate their value, to gauge the intensity of their commitments. It does so by trying to determine how much the individual would be willing to give up for the sake of those values (which is to say, what the individual's WTP is). However, in recognition of the fact that certain environmental goods are valued both instrumentally and intrinsically, the CBA takes into consideration not just the use value of the land to drivers, but also the existence value of the ecosystem to conservationists.

Thus, the inclusion of "existence value" in a CBA is essentially a response to the criticism that CBA focuses only on instrumental value to the neglect of intrinsic value. Since money has only instrumental value, the use of money as the metric of comparison is misleading, because it suggests that everything is "reduced" to instrumental value. In fact, monetary valuation is only used to make instrumental values commensurable with intrinsic values—something that must necessarily be done, no matter what the decision procedure, since no one thinks that intrinsic value categorically trumps instrumental value. This has, of course, been the subject of considerable misunderstanding, and it is entirely possible that the optics of using money and WTP values in environmental CBA are so irremediably bad that a different metric should be chosen. When one scratches the surface, however, it becomes apparent that much of the opposition among environmentalists to the use of CBA as a guide to decision-making is not based on anything specific to CBA; it is opposition to liberal neutrality as such. In other words, it is really a demand that certain first-order environmental values be used as a direct basis for legislation. Formulated as such, the demand obviously has troubling implications—which take us, however, beyond the scope of these reflections on CBA, and relate back to the more fundamental arguments that have been developed, over the years, for the wisdom of liberal political arrangements.

5.6.2. The precautionary principle objection

A second objection that is often made to the use of CBA in environmental decision-making, particularly with respect to ecosystem protection, is based on an appeal to the "precautionary principle," and the suggestion that this principle is more appropriate than the standard decision-theoretic approach to risk employed by CBA. Unfortunately, this criticism is difficult to assess, because there is no single, widely accepted formulation of the precautionary principle.[92] The general idea, stated at a high level of abstraction, is that if there is some possibility of harm from an action and yet some uncertainty as to whether this harm will materialize, the burden of proof should fall upon the proponents of the action to show that the harm will *not* materialize, and until this burden has been discharged the action may not proceed. This is an all-purpose principle for dealing with situations of epistemic uncertainty, but it is often thought to be particularly relevant to actions that involve making changes in complex ecosystems, because it is so difficult to anticipate what the effects of an intervention will be, and to undo damages after they occur.

The precautionary principle is also often appealed to as an objection to the introduction of new synthetic chemicals to the environment, or genetically modified organisms. Opponents insist that scientists should be obliged to "prove that it is safe," before they are allowed to act. Not knowing what the exact consequences of, say, a new pesticide will be should count as an argument *against* introducing it, not as an argument in favor of its use. When formulated in this way, however, the principle is far too restrictive—since it is seldom possible to entirely rule out the possibility of an "unknown unknown." Furthermore, if formulated as a response to Knightian uncertainty, the principle does not offer much guidance for dealing with the *known* probability of harm. Most importantly, it does not permit the balancing of possible harms with expected benefits. Depending upon the exact formulation, it might wind up blocking an action with enormous known benefits, because of a tiny probability of an insignificant harm. Finally, there is the fact that, in many cases, both action and inaction may have unknown effects, and so precaution winds up either gridlocking decision-making, or else arbitrarily privileging the status quo.[93]

To avoid these untoward consequences, several theorists have attempted to formulate more moderate versions of the principle. Stephen Gardiner, for instance, has argued that the precautionary principle can be understood as the application of maximin reasoning to particular cases.[94] The idea is that, when making a decision, one must focus on the "worst-case scenario," and select the action that is best in that case. (A similar idea informs the Final Declaration of the First European "Seas at Risk" Conference: "If the 'worst case scenario' for a certain activity is serious enough then even a small amount of doubt as to the safety of that activity is sufficient to stop it taking place."[95]) And yet the idea that one should assign lexical priority to the worst-case scenario seems far too extreme. It is one thing to be risk-averse in one's decision-making—this can easily be incorporated into standard CBA—but to assign *lexical* priority to one's concern over a potential loss requires ignoring all other scenarios and, thus, ignoring foregone gains of arbitrarily large magnitude. It is difficult to avoid the suspicion that, in the standard sort of environmental case, where a small risk of great harm to the environment is being weighed against a reasonable certainty of a moderate economic benefit, the reason for assigning an outsized importance to the small risk is not that anyone considers this an appropriate way of managing small risks, but merely that proponents of precaution assign much greater *value* to the environment than they do to the economic benefits. The decision principle is essentially being gerrymandered to ensure that the "right" set of values wins—while nevertheless maintaining the appearance of neutrality among the competing values.

The easiest way to determine whether this is the actual motive underlying one's own endorsement of the precautionary principle is to take the proposed decision rule and apply it in a policy domain in which one is not sympathetic to the values that win out when an outsized importance is given to small risks. For instance, environmentalists might hesitate to endorse the use of the precautionary principle for the management of national security risks. Under the George W. Bush administration, vice president Dick Cheney articulated a version of the precautionary principle for dealing with terrorism: "If there was even a 1% chance of terrorists getting a weapon of mass destruction—and there has been a small probability of such an occurrence for some time—the United States must now act as if it were a certainty."[96] The invasion of Iraq (along with its $1.1 trillion price tag) could thus be justified as a "precautionary" measure, given that no one was able to *completely* rule out the possibility that Saddam Hussein had weapons of mass destruction and was willing to give them to terrorists.

Many people would not hesitate to describe Cheney's principle, not as prudent, but rather as paranoid. The real problem, however, is that it does not allow any balancing, in this case between the probability of terrorists acquiring weapons of mass destruction, on the one hand, and the enormous cost that Americans (and Iraqis) were asked to shoulder to rule out that possibility. So, while this version of the precautionary principle is clearly an alternative to CBA, it is not clear that many people would consider it very compelling as a general principle of decision-making under uncertainty. People likely find it compelling in the environmental case only because, as a matter of private comprehensive doctrine, they assign very high value to environmental preservation. Thus, the real question is whether there is anything specific to the environment that would justify precaution in this area, but not others. If the answer is no, then there will be a strong suspicion that the common appeal to it in this area is really an attempt to put a thumb on the scale in favor of environmental values.

Objections like these have generated an impetus to further weaken the precautionary principle. Many of these modifications, however, have the effect of dissolving the tension between the precautionary principle and CBA. For example, some theorists focus on the *epistemic* issues that arise, emphasizing the way the precautionary principle assigns the burden of proof when it comes to determining the impacts of a policy. Most obviously, the precautionary principle rules out using Laplace's principle of insufficient reason to assign probabilities to outcomes. It imposes an obligation to *figure out* a reasonable basis for assignment of probabilities. When someone challenges a particular action by asking "how do you know it's safe?" one cannot just reply "how do you know it's not safe?" CBA, however, only addresses the question of which policy should be adopted, *given the information that we have*. The question of how much information we should collect before making a decision is, as Adrian Vermeule puts it, "a distinct and logically prior question."[97] To the extent that the precautionary principle addresses this prior question, it is not really in tension with CBA.

It is worth noting that the epistemic values at work in scientific inquiry may lead scientists to adopt an attitude toward potential risks that is overly casual from the standpoint of practical decision-making. This is because, as Sven Ove Hansson has observed, scientists put much greater emphasis on avoiding type I errors (false positives) than type II errors (false negatives).[98] (In other words, within scientific circles, thinking that something is there when in fact it isn't is considered a much more serious error than failing to detect something that is there.) Yet when it comes to making decisions under conditions of risk, policymakers must be *equally* concerned with both false positives and false negatives. Thus, it is important to recognize that the intuitions that scientists have about how we should deal with "unknowns" will often be biased, in a way that can easily lead to excessive risk-taking. In comparison, the policymaker will appear to be more cautious. Yet imposing an appropriate degree of caution does not require the introduction of any special principle, CBA alone incorporates the appropriate core attitude toward risk. But again, this may lead to policymakers having to force scientists to go out and collect information that they might otherwise have neglected.

5.7. The three-step procedure

I suspect that no one who has followed the argument so far will fail to be struck by the amount of flexibility and variation there is in the way that CBA is applied to real-world decision-making. Many of the objections that have been presented are legitimate with respect to the use of bald CBA as a decision procedure, or to the use of a plain-vanilla WTP/WTA calculus. What has happened in practice is that the basic calculus and procedure have been adapted to the specific needs of different policy domains. One can see the divergence of methods this creates most clearly in the growing use of QALY-based CEA in the area of healthcare resource allocation, compared to the use of VSL-based CBA, with standardized valuations of life, in the area of safety regulation. The decision to focus on life years saved as the central outcome, as opposed to lives saved, has significant implications (not to mention the fact that in neither of these two domains is there any use of expressed WTP values). From a utilitarian perspective, this might seem unacceptably ad hoc. I would like to suggest that these variations are not the results of path-dependency, gerrymandering, or any other sort of arbitrariness; rather, they flow from the interpretation and application of the liberal principles articulated at the beginning of the chapter: (1) Pareto improvement, (2) liberal neutrality, and (3) citizen equality. Governments want to put their resources to the best use (1), yet in many different policy areas, citizens disagree in their evaluations of the outcomes that might be achieved. Instead of just picking a winner based on first-order values (2), governments strive instead to show equal concern and respect for the values of all citizens, by giving their evaluations equal weight (3) in determining the overall ranking of outcomes.

The variation in the way that embedded CBA is carried out is largely a consequence of differences in the interpretation and application of the principle of citizen equality in different domains. For instance, the fact that we use a VSL calculus in certain areas reflects the fact that we tend to think of accidents in terms of unnecessary injury and death. So we articulate our policy objectives in this area by saying things like "we want to reduce the number of deaths that occur." But of course, no one can prevent death, the most that we can do is delay it. When we say that we are "saving lives," technically all we are doing is extending them. In the case of workplace safety, however, it doesn't seem relevant to ask by how much we are extending a particular life. If we did, then we would tend to favor initiatives that reduced the accident rate among employees who are younger, or female, on the grounds that doing so resulted in greater benefit.

Of course, the thought that we might take into consideration such factors as "how much longer a person expects to live" when it comes to workplace safety is not entirely beyond the pale. In the wake of the Fukushima Daiichi nuclear disaster in 2011, a 72-year old engineer assembled a volunteer corps of over 160 retired civil and nuclear engineers to work in dangerous radiation zones. The rationale was that, being already quite old, most of them would not live long enough to develop the various forms of cancer the radiation exposure would likely cause. Of course, it was crucial to the public acceptance of this arrangement that the work group consisted entirely of volunteers. What the example shows, however, is that considerations about life expectancy are not *irrelevant* to the question of who can be exposed to which workplace hazards. And if one were a utilitarian, it would be difficult to explain why it would ever be permissible to *avoid* taking them into consideration. In a standard safety CBA, however, we choose not to take them into consideration, in a way that reflects a relatively formal conception of equality. We are, in most of these areas, talking about the risk of a highly unexpected, extremely negative event, which no one has done anything to deserve. The template that such a problem evokes is something like the "choosing straws" procedure, where everyone gets an equal chance to choose the short straw, regardless of any differences there may be among individuals. It is therefore this conception of equality that is reflected in the way CBA is carried out, with the use of a standard VSL.

The situation with healthcare is quite different. Here we are dealing with situations in which everyone affected has already suffered from bad luck, creating a need for medical intervention, but where there are not enough resources to fully satisfy everyone. There is, however, significant gradation in the extent to which needs can be met. For example, patients who are denied very expensive chemotherapy drugs will still receive "standard of care" cancer treatment. Since there is largely a fixed envelope of healthcare spending, sliding one patient up on the scale of treatment will almost necessarily involve sliding some other patient, or patients, down on the scale of treatment. Thus there is reason to think that the relevant conception of equality will focus much more on ensuring that the system is impartial with respect to individuals, when determining what claim each one can make on the pool of resources that are being set aside to meet healthcare needs.

Both of these cases are quite different from ones in which resources are being claimed by individuals who disagree more profoundly about what uses these resources should be put to. In the case of regulatory intervention, for instance, or environmental preservation, deep disagreement often underlies the conflict. Unlike healthcare, where people seek roughly the same outcome, in these cases there is no shared outcome to serve as a metric for interpersonal comparison. One could just hold a vote, of course, and count heads to see who should win in the contest over resources. The problem with that procedure is that it fails to take into consideration how *strongly* people feel about the issue. Thus, a large group having little at stake in an issue might easily outvote a small group with much at stake. A CBA tries to ascertain how much people care, or how much benefit they would derive from a particular use of resources, by asking them how much they would be willing to give up in the way of *other* resources to secure it (which is to say, what their WTP/WTA value is). The concern for efficiency is obviously in the foreground here, but one can see also a concern for equality in the insistence that no one group's interests should be privileged.

This shows that CBA should not be thought of as a generic procedure that ideally would be applied in the same way in all domains. My suggestion is that it reflects a combined commitment to three distinct principles, each of which admits of different interpretations, depending upon the situation to which they are being applied. The application of the approach involves, either implicitly or explicitly, answering a fairly lengthy series of questions. This is why I think it is useful to treat the core procedure as being framed by two "filters," one on the input side and another on the output side.[99]

5.7.1. Input filters

The following is not an exhaustive list, but it represents a series of questions that are useful (and in some cases essential) to pose *before* embarking upon a CBA. And, of course, a set of completely pragmatic questions must be asked as well, involving, for instance, the threshold of significance (a proper CBA is costly to carry out, and so may not be worth doing, simply because the cost involved in identifying the best policy exceeds the largest possible benefit of adopting that policy). What I present, by contrast, are principled considerations, dealing with the question of whether a CBA represents the right set of normative principles to be applied to a particular problem, and if it does, precisely how they should be applied:

1. *Is this an appropriate problem for CBA?* The most valuable heuristic for determining the appropriateness of CBA is to ask, "Where's the market failure?" As we have seen, policies that primarily involve considerations of distributive justice, rather than correcting a market failure, are not candidates for CBA. Consider the structure of social transfers to the elderly in Canada, as described in chapter 4. The Canada Pension Plan is based on lifetime contributions through workforce participation, and it exists primarily because of inefficiency in the market for private life annuities. It is therefore quite reasonable to look to cost-benefit considerations in determining a benefit level. The Guaranteed Income Supplement, by contrast, is a means-tested transfer program designed to alleviate the problem of poverty among the elderly. It clearly is *not* motivated by a market failure but is intended merely to improve the distribution of income from the standpoint of equality (or sufficiency). It would be inappropriate to determine the benefit level of a program such as this through appeal to cost-benefit considerations.

2. *Are there individual rights that trump the policy?* During the highwater mark of the "law and economics" movement, certain legal theorists were fond of claiming that the criminal law could be justified through reference to cost-benefit considerations. Richard Posner made the unfortunate suggestion that rape was illegal because it was inefficient.[100] If men and women were to negotiate, in the Coasian style, women would be willing to pay more for the right not to be raped than men would be willing to pay for the right to

rape them, and so the efficient outcome requires the assignment of the right to control their own bodies to women. Many people found this line of reasoning outrageous, for a variety of reasons, perhaps the most obvious being that control over one's own body is not usually regarded as something that is "up for grabs"—so that if someone else is able to make better use of your body than you are, he might be granted control over it. On the contrary, the rights that we exercise over our own bodies are normally considered "trumps" with respect to projects that others might have. There is no point in doing a CBA on a policy that involves violation of such rights; it is ruled out *ab initio*. It is worth noting as well that even when rights do not render a CBA entirely otiose, they may significantly constrain the policy space within which the CBA is conducted, by ruling out certain options.

3. *Are there other deontic constraints that preclude the policy?* Even if a policy is not ruled out by individual rights, there may be other deontic constraints that preclude the sort of balancing, or consideration of consequences, that is involved in CBA. For example, when it comes to dealing with the loss of life, it is important that CBA involves statistical lives, not known individuals, and that the deaths are not the intended outcome of the policy. When these conditions do not obtain, policy may be dictated by the set of rules or deontic constraints. Alpine search and rescue, for instance, is probably not cost-benefit justified, but it continues to be carried out because the situation triggers a deontic constraint—namely, the duty of rescue. (The case, however, is not reducible to one involving individual rights, because individuals are not normally taken to have a "right" to expensive rescue operations.) Some argue that the CBA should be done anyway, so that everyone knows how much the commitment to that particular deontic constraint costs us, as a society. The perception, however, is often that such an exercise is a thinly veiled attempt to erode public commitment to the constraint.

4. *Is there a compelling metric for establishing interpersonal comparability?* As we have seen, since a CBA typically involves comparing the proposed use of resources by one set of actors against the proposed use by some other(s), the value of the analysis depends heavily on the quality and fidelity of the metric used as a basis for interpersonal comparison. Every measure has serious deficiencies, but the seriousness of those deficiencies depends in part on the domain in which they are used. For example, a money metric (hence WTP/WTA) has major defects, but these are far more severe in the area of medical decision-making than they are in the area of consumer goods. For example, in one study, participants were asked to rank different medical interventions based on their perceptions of the benefits, and then were asked how much they would be willing to pay for each one. For a significant fraction of respondents, the WTP values failed to respect

the earlier ranking; that is, subjects in some cases were willing to pay *more* for interventions that they considered *less* beneficial.[101] Thus if there is not something like the QALY measure available, and one is forced to use WTP/ WTA values, one might easily conclude that it is not worth doing a CBA for medical resource allocation, simply because the decisions are so far removed from the everyday context of consumer choice, and there are so many other complicating factors, that money simply does not serve as a plausible basis of interpersonal comparison.

5. *What is the scope of the analysis?* Finally, there is a preliminary question that must be asked about what the scope of the CBA will be, and thus, what factors are to be taken into consideration. Unlike moral consequentialism, which essentially offers a "global" standard of justice—used to evaluate the total benefit that individuals receive over their lifetimes—the way that we apply norms of equality is for the most part responsive only to local justice considerations. This in turn affects what counts as a cost or a benefit. Preventing the death of a worker with a family to support may produce more benefit than preventing the death of a worker who is single, but the benefits to the family do not count in a typical CBA. It is therefore important, before initiating a CBA, to clearly identify the range of effects that one is planning to take into consideration.[102]

5.7.2. Performing the analysis

Once the policy area has been defined, and a CBA has been selected as both appropriate and feasible for that domain, a series of further questions arise that are, as it were, "internal" to how the CBA is to be conducted:

1. *Which costs and benefits should count?* Selecting the policy domain already involves excluding certain costs and benefits from consideration, particularly if the CBA is being undertaken as an exercise in local justice. Yet even once that is complete, serious questions may arise about which costs and benefits should be taken into consideration within that domain. One of the most significant dangers—commonly warned against in all textbook treatments—is that of double counting either costs or benefits (e.g., counting the increase in property values due to construction of a new school as a benefit), or simple confusion about what counts as a benefit (e.g., counting the creation of jobs as a benefit). In other cases, certain preferences may be excluded on the grounds that they are either antisocial or inauthentic. For example, many CBAs on cigarette smoking do not count

the enjoyment smokers get from smoking as a benefit (presumably on the grounds that they are addicted). Also, as Wolff has observed, people who are exposed to certain hazards because they have broken the law (e.g., by trespassing), might have their interests assigned less significance than those who have respected the law.[103]

2. *What metric to use?* It may only be possible to make a final decisions about which metric to use after the CBA has been initiated and some data collected. For example, if there is significant tension between expressed and revealed WTP (e.g., residents claim that a transit project would confer an enormous benefit, yet there is no reflection of this elsewhere in property values), then one might want to look for some other metric.

3. *Should the quality of preferences be enhanced?* One of the reasons that expressed preference methods with a monetary metric are weak in certain areas, such as healthcare resource allocation, is that the choice problem is one that is unfamiliar to most individuals. In general, monetary valuations are likely to be more coherent and plausible when the problem resembles or parallels consumer choices that individuals make on a routine basis. Thus, one might decide to take measures to enhance the quality of preferences—ranging from the provision of supplementary information to the organization of a full-scale deliberative exercise.

4. *How to measure preferences, given the metric?* No matter which metric is chosen, there are different ways of getting at the information one is looking for. Furthermore, the different methods for getting at it can yield dramatically different results. With WTP/WTA, for instance, one can choose between stated, revealed, standardized, or negotiated values. Similar indeterminacy affects QALY measures, where one can get dramatically different results on the quality-of-life scale depending on whether one asks patients before they have the condition or after. Indeed, both before and after valuations are so compromised by cognitive bias that some QALY scales seek input from *caregivers* in doing the quality evaluation.[104]

5. *What corrections should be made to establish comparability?* As we have seen, some metrics must be adjusted to establish a normatively compelling basis for interpersonal comparison—most obviously, any metric that is itself subject to diminishing returns. This is a major issue with using money as a basis for comparison, and it generates a set of problems that, in my view, most proponents of CBA do not taken seriously enough. At the same time, simply attaching distributional weights, as the UK *Green Book* recommends, is not an adequate response in all cases—especially if one adjusts only stated WTP values but not market prices.

6. *What social discount rate should be applied?* In some cases, the question of whether to apply a social discount rate, and if so, what the rate should be, is

one of the most difficult to arise "internal" to the CBA procedure. In medical decision-making, it is common to apply *no* discount rate (which is, to say, a discount rate of zero). In other cases, such as infrastructure investment, a simple "opportunity cost" framework seems unproblematic. Then there are a variety of mixed cases, including most environmental ones, where neither approach seems appropriate (zero is too low, but the rate of return on capital is too high). The literature on this is too vast to be usefully summarized here, but it is important to flag the question as one that must be answered, to determine how the CBA should be carried out.[105]

5.7.3. Output filters

After the CBA has been performed and the best option identified, a number of questions must still be asked before that option can be recommended.

1. *If potential Pareto is satisfied, is it possible to achieve actual Pareto?* As we have seen, notwithstanding the use of the Kaldor-Hicks criterion, the underlying commitment in CBA is to resolving collective action problems, which is to say, promoting Pareto efficiency. Satisfying Kaldor-Hicks shows that it is possible for the winners under the policy to compensate the losers. In many cases, a policy can only go forward if it is possible to *actually* compensate them as well. For example, landowners who suffer expropriation so that a public infrastructure project can go through receive *actual* compensation. If for some reason it is not possible to compensate the losers, then that might count as an argument against pursuing the project. Or, where the losers are not to be compensated (as is the case with many regulations), some distributive justice argument would have to be adduced to show why there is no obligation to do so.[106]

2. *Would implementation conflict with rights or other deontic constraints?* Even if individual rights or other deontic constraints do not preclude the policy *ab initio*, there may be conflict once the CBA is conducted. With rights that do not function as "trumps" but rather have a threshold of application, for example, it may not be possible to know if a threshold would be surpassed without conducting a CBA. A policy might also have a negative effect on gender, racial, linguistic, or religious equality or raise issues pertaining to indigenous treaty rights.

3. *Would the policy have adverse distributive impacts?* A CBA may find a policy to be worth implementing based on people's expressed WTP, but the question of how it *actually* will be paid for is a quite different one. Whether it

is financed through income taxes, consumption taxes, payroll taxes, or user fees will have important implications for the distributive effects of the policy. If the impacts under any feasible modality are considered unacceptable, then that would provide a reason not to proceed with the policy.

4. *Is it in tension with other qualitatively expressed considerations?* There are a variety of other, purely qualitative considerations, which might speak in favor of or against a policy. For example, it is entirely possible that the state's subsidization of amateur athletics is not cost-benefit justified, but that it plays an important role in promoting national unity. Instead of trying to quantify these benefits and insert them into the calculus, it might make sense just to introduce them as qualitative considerations on the "output" side. Sunstein suggests, along these lines, that certain risks have qualitative features, such as "the voluntariness of the risk, its potentially catastrophic character, whether it is especially dreaded,"[107] which one might want to take into consideration after the CBA is complete. That having been said, it is important not to engage in double counting. For example, it is sometimes suggested that CBA articulates our commitment to just one value—namely, efficiency—and that once the results are known this must be balanced against all other values. This is incorrect. CBA already takes into consideration the value commitments of all citizens (to the extent that these inform their WTP). The efficiency and equality principles at the heart of CBA are not just "values" like the others; they are principles that we employ to provide a basis for public decision-making in the context of first-order value pluralism. Thus, whenever one applies "qualitative considerations" as an output filter on a CBA, it is important to be able to specify quite clearly why those considerations could not have been represented *within* the CBA.

5.8. Conclusion

As I noted at the outset of the discussion, the growth of CBA over the years has largely been a consequence of pressure from the executive branch. Legislatures seldom require it, and if they mention it at all in a statute, it is often with the goal of prohibiting it. Similarly, while courts in the United States have increasingly come to regard CBA as the "gold standard," when it comes to evaluating agency regulations, they also stop well short of imposing it—and are often quite aware of the limitations of their own abilities, when it comes to conducting such analyses. Furthermore, their decisions in other areas, particularly those touching on individual rights, are often made with flamboyant disregard for the balance of costs and benefits. (The series of US superior court decisions involving school busing, aimed at achieving racial integration, are an often-cited example.) Even in tort law, where Coase's reasoning has had considerable influence, there is seldom any effort made to determine whether the punitive damage awards imposed in civil suits achieve an optimal level of deterrence.

I do not think it is unreasonable to suggest that CBA arises out a set of normative ideals that have developed endogenously within the civil service. This would be troubling, if it were the case the CBA reflected a commitment to full-blown utilitarianism, simply because utilitarianism is a controversial doctrine, elements of which more properly belong in the domain of political ideology and, hence, of democratic contestation. This would make it a violation of civil service neutrality for the executive branch to push for the use of CBA. What I have tried to show instead is that the commitment to CBA stems from a set of far more minimal principles, all of which can plausibly be construed as structural features of a *liberal* political order. So, while the use of CBA has obvious normative implications, these norms are ones that transcend, or stand outside, democratic contestation, precisely because they provide the structure within which democratic contestation can occur. When the state undertakes a CBA, it is asking the fundamental question, "What would the parties themselves have contracted to, absent the market failure that renders state involvement necessary?" Yet CBA is obviously controversial, which would seem to be in tension with this claim. My objective in this chapter has been to show that these controversies arise mainly from the "optics" of the procedure, and that most objections are based on rather diffuse intuitions that are difficult to sustain under analysis, or that apply with equal force to any other feasible decision procedure. This goes a long way toward explaining why, despite the generally critical tone of both the public and the academic discussions, CBA continues its long march through the institutions.

As we have seen, the growth of the welfare state over the course of the 20th century was largely the consequence of a relentless application of the logic of Pareto efficiency in the context of a market economy. Deference was shown to the market, and to private contracting, as a general strategy for resolving collective action problems (and promoting the division of labor). Yet in cases where private contracting proved insufficient—in domains suffering from what I have been referring to as egregious market failure—efforts were made to substitute state institutions for private contracting. This proved most successful in areas where an appropriately competitive market could not be maintained (e.g., infrastructure); where the preponderance of value took the form of positive externalities (e.g., education, defense, public health); and in insurance markets, where adverse selection made it exceedingly costly to exclude free riders (e.g., health, pensions). Of course, the way these programs are usually financed has made them implicitly redistributive, which led many political philosophers to conclude, erroneously, that the fundamental rationale for state involvement in these sectors was to effect a redistribution, or to distribute these goods in accordance with nonmarket principles. This analysis, though superficially plausible, collapses under more careful scrutiny. Liberal equality represents an important *constraint* on the way that these programs are designed and administered, but the basic objective is to achieve Pareto-efficiency gains. The fact that the Pareto principle attracts such a wide and overlapping consensus explains the steady expansion in the use of CBA in the assessment of state activities. Furthermore, the reason that a market-simulating procedure like CBA is an appropriate basis for decision-making, in domains ranging from environmental regulation to health-care provision, is precisely that the welfare state has been trying to achieve the outcome that markets would have achieved, had private contracting not been limited by various contingencies of the world.

6

Administrative Discretion and
the Rule of Law

One of the most prominent features of the *Value and Ethics Code for the Public Sector* in Canada is a commitment on the part of civil servants to respect the "rule of law."[1] This could easily be passed over as self-evident. Understood as an injunction to obey the law, it amounts to little more than a prohibition on official corruption. Within the civil service, however, the "rule of law" is understood to enjoin much more than mere obedience to law. It refers instead to a set of general constraints on the exercise of state power. Following John Adams's dictum that governments should be "of laws, and not of men," the rule of law is normally taken to prohibit various forms of arbitrariness in the use of state power. The thought is that, even when the exercise of state power does not involve the direct application of a statute, it should still exhibit an essentially law-like quality. This means, at the very least, that the rules must apply equally to everyone (including public officials), that like cases should be treated alike, that decisions should be consistent over time and between officials, and that some structure of accountability should be in place to ensure that actions can be reviewed for conformity to these principles.

In the international context, the United Nations has defined the rule of law even more broadly:

> For the United Nations, the rule of law refers to a principle of governance in which all persons, institutions and entities, public and private, including the State itself, are accountable to laws that are publicly promulgated, equally enforced and independently adjudicated, and which are consistent with international human rights norms and standards. It requires, as well, measures to ensure adherence to the principles of supremacy of law, equality before the law, accountability to the law, fairness in the application of the law, separation of powers, participation in decision-making, legal certainty, avoidance of arbitrariness and procedural and legal transparency.[2]

Although this might reasonably be classified as an "expansive" conception of the rule of law, it is important to note that it stops short of requiring that the law be fully just. If one were to imagine a continuum, with mere conformity to

The Machinery of Government. Joseph Heath, Oxford University Press (2020). © Oxford University Press. DOI: 10.1093/oso/9780197509616.001.0001

written rules on the one end and perfect justice on the other, the "rule of law" ideal is intended to fall somewhere in the middle (and is a necessary but not sufficient condition for justice[3]). Thus one can imagine a tax code that falls short of achieving the distribution of burdens that an ideal conception of justice would recommend, yet is nevertheless applied in a way that satisfies the rule of law. Similarly, one can imagine various ways of applying a tax code that would satisfy the literal terms of the relevant statutes, yet would fail to respect the rule of law, on the grounds that decisions were being made that were arbitrary, capricious, discriminatory, unaccountable, or secretive.

The discussion of the rule of law, it should be noted, for the most part deals with constraints that the *legal* structure of the society should respect. But it is important to recognize that extensive domains of what we refer to as the "public sector" are not subject to detailed legal regulation. For instance, despite the enormous reach of the criminal law, and its specificity with respect to punishment, in most countries criminal law is virtually silent on the question of how prisons should be organized and run. The division of correctional institutions into low-, medium-, and high-security facilities, for instance, along with the assignment of prisoners to these institutions, is entirely an administrative matter, despite the fact that it has enormous repercussions for the punitiveness of any jail term imposed. The same can be said for the organization and administration of public-housing projects, primary schools, military bases, hospitals, drug rehabilitation centers, planning departments, grant agencies, schools, daycare centers, and hundreds of other organizations in which state officials make decisions that have a direct impact on the public. In all of these institutional settings, decisions made by officials are only loosely constrained by acts of legislation, yet they can have a dramatic impact on the life chances of individuals, by granting or denying them access to important goods.

The existence of these extensive administrative bureaucracies poses an obvious challenge to the rule of law. This is often expressed as a concern over the *discretion* state officials in these domains enjoy. Public servants are empowered to make certain decisions, but are often given little guidance on what standards or principles they should use to make those decisions.[4] For instance, should they take their past decisions as precedents, which, in turn, constrain future decisions, or should officials remain free to decide each case on its own merits? What if two officials are interpreting the rules differently, generating inconsistencies in their decisions? If a citizen objects to a decision that has been made, what recourse does he or she have? Do members of the executive branch even have an obligation to explain their decisions? We know what constraints the *courts* are subject to in these cases, but what about prison wardens, or welfare caseworkers, or workplace safety inspectors, or municipal bylaw officers?

It is not difficult to see why the growth of the administrative state over the course of the 20th century, which dramatically expanded the realm of official discretion, was widely seen as posing a challenge to the rule of law.[5] Consider a regulatory agency that is charged with ensuring that all "feasible" efforts are made to ensure the "health and safety" of workers. This arrangement seems to be one that necessarily generates a reversion from the rule of "law" to one of "men." For instance, the separation of powers—between those who decide on the rules, those who apply them in real-life circumstances, and those who punish transgressions—has essentially been abolished. Agency officials are now in a position to promulgate rules (e.g., specifying acceptable levels of exposure to various environmental hazards in the workplace), to apply those rules in specific circumstances (e.g., deciding whether an investment in a particular abatement technology is feasible for an employer), and to determine punishments (e.g., imposing a citation or fine for violation).[6] What is to stop agency inspectors from abusing their power, using it to harass or intimidate those who question their authority?

In his influential 1885 text, *An Introduction to the Study of the Law of the Constitution*, A. V. Dicey declared that the rule of law was "opposed to the influence of arbitrary power, and excludes the existence of arbitrariness, or prerogative, or even of wide discretionary authority on the part of the government."[7] Both Friedrich Hayek and Michael Oakeshott thought this problem was so significant that it provided grounds for viewing the welfare state as an essentially illiberal institution.[8] It is worth noting, of course, that the basic problem was identified quite early on, and mitigated to some degree by the introduction of various measures aimed at limiting official discretion, by both the legislature and judiciary.[9] The centerpiece of this response has been the self-regulation of state operations through the development of administrative law. The United States stands out as having taken a particularly legalistic approach, developing a set of "rules for the creation of rules." The Administrative Procedures Act (APA) of 1946 requires that all administrative agencies of the US government develop an explicit set of rules, specifying and constraining the exercise of their own discretion. It also imposes extensive procedural obligations on any executive rule-making exercise, including a requirement to give advance notice of the intention to regulate, consultation with all affected parties, publicization of the corpus of rules, and justification of all decisions. There was also a widespread movement to create administrative tribunals, staffed by "administrative law judges," which would give individuals an opportunity to contest bureaucratic decisions. The net effect was to reproduce, within the executive branch, many of the functions that had previously been carried out by the legislature and the judiciary.

This approach reflects a deep distrust of administrative discretion, amplified by the rather extreme formal division of powers in the US system, which gives

Congress little ability to control the executive except through legislation. The result has been the development of an extremely frustrating system, characterized by enormous bureaucratic rigidity, and judicial review of almost every important exercise of administrative power. The US legislature has, on occasion, attempted to resolve these problems with *more* legislation, aimed at limiting the impact of its prior requirements (from the Paperwork Reduction Act of 1980 to the Plain Writing Act of 2010). In other jurisdictions, the approach has been to let discretion stand, but to focus more on the cultivation of a "rule of law culture" within the executive branch, along with more informal mechanisms of oversight.[10] There has, of course, been a steady growth of administrative law over time in all jurisdictions, as well as court and tribunal decisions that have set important precedents. Nevertheless, the primary mechanism through which discretion has been managed, particularly in parliamentary systems, has been through the internalization, by the civil service, of the norms associated with the rule of law. This is what accounts for its prominent position in the Canadian public-sector ethics code. Ideally, this arrangement preserves the benefits of discretion, while still limiting arbitrary or capricious decision-making.

One can see how this "rule of law culture" fits well with the tradition of civil service neutrality. As mentioned earlier, a commitment to the rule of law stops well short of a commitment to any complete conception of justice. While the latter falls naturally within the domain of democratic contestation, the basic principles of the rule of law can legitimately be placed outside the partisan fray. The conception of equal citizenship, for instance, which is implicit in the concern over arbitrariness in the use of state power, is quite minimal compared to the more robust conceptions of equality debated in partisan politics. And in cases where rule-of-law norms do become politically controversial, there is good reason to think that the executive should continue to adhere to them.

Although a great deal has been written about the role of the judiciary in maintaining adherence to the rule of law, it is important to recognize that the behavior of the executive branch is far more consequential than the judicial branch in terms of the overall quality of governance. Courts offer redress only in cases of the most egregious violations, and then only after the fact. It is the members of the executive branch—particularly those Michael Lipsky refers to as "street-level bureaucrats"—who have the most immediate and wide-ranging impact on people's lives, and who determine whether the power of the state is experienced as despotic or liberal. In this chapter, I examine how the "rule of law" ideal has been interpreted and institutionalized in the civil service. The most important feature of the rule of law, I will argue, is that it gives direct expression to the liberal principle of equality, since the constraint on arbitrariness corresponds to a requirement of equal citizenship.

6.1. Discretion

Anyone who has had more than a passing encounter with public-sector bureaucracy will understand, implicitly if not explicitly, why administrative discretion is both important and desirable. I was reminded of it quite forcefully a few years ago, when I received a phone call from a public health official in the province of Ontario, informing me that my daughter's vaccinations were not up to date, and that unless the problem was corrected she would not be allowed to return to school. The official drew my attention to a vaccination, which my daughter was supposed to have received at age one, but which was missing. Looking over my own copy of her medical records, I saw that the vaccination had in fact been administered but that our appointment with the doctor had been three days before her birthday, so that the vaccination record showed her as having received it at the age of 11 months instead of at age one. Nevertheless, the form showed quite clearly the date on which the vaccination had been administered. I presented it to the public health official, assuming it would resolve the issue. Unfortunately, she replied, the Ontario Immunization Schedule specifies that the vaccination must be received at an age "greater than or equal to one," and the Immunization of School Pupils Act is quite explicit that the child's vaccinations much be in compliance in the immunization schedule. Surely, I said, it must be possible to make an exception. No exceptions, she replied. But what if the doctor refuses to re-administer the vaccine, I asked, given that my daughter has already received it? In that event, she replied, I would have to obtain a letter from the physician stating the medical reason for the child's non-compliance with the immunization schedule, which would then be reviewed by the ministry. The only alternative, she said, would be to file Form 014-4897-64E, Statement of Conscience or Religious Belief, which permits exemptions for non-medical reasons.

Since the latter was clearly the least onerous course of action, I filled out the form and joined the ranks of conscientious objectors to childhood vaccination. This is a typical example of what happens when public officials refuse or are unable to exercise discretion. The story illustrates several problems that can arise. The first, and most obvious, is that administrative rules seldom have independent deontic significance; they are instead aimed at achieving some objective. This is usually articulated in terms of the rules having a "point." Yet there will often be ways of applying the rules that defeats their point (e.g., by being overly literal, or insensitive to circumstances, or by ignoring the interaction with other rules). Sometimes, applying the rules too mechanically can actually defeat the point. This sort of formalism—an insistence on following the rules even when doing so does not serve their objective[11]—is the quality of bureaucracy most often described as "Kafkaesque." In this case, the public health official was applying the rules in a way that was oblivious to their point, which was to ensure that preventable contagious diseases would not be spread through the public school system. Substantively, my daughter was in compliance with the regulation, even though formally she was not.

The second feature of the interaction worth noting is the fact that it occurred in a dealing with a state official, whose decisions were backed by the force of law. I do not believe it maligns civil servants unfairly to observe that frustrating encounters with bureaucracy occur more often in the public sector than in the private (in the private sector they occur more often in uncompetitive markets). An important feature of the public sector is that, in most instances, officials have no intrinsic reason to be concerned about how much inconvenience is being caused by their decisions (as a result of which, clients may experience remarkable difficulty finding a sympathetic ear). The problem is that the costs of administrative decisions are completely externalized. (In this case, the public health official was asking me to make an appointment with my doctor, take time off work and take my daughter out of school for several hours, and then either redo a vaccination or secure a letter granting a medical exemption, which typically would involve paying a fee.) In the private sector, organizations must worry, at least a little bit and perhaps a lot, about how much inconvenience they are imposing on clients or customers, simply because the latter have exit options. Because there typically is no exit option when one is dealing with public authorities, the social cost of bureaucratic formalism can be quite high.[12]

Finally, it is no accident that the public official, after being pressed for a while, offered me a "work-around" to the self-evidently absurd outcome that would result from an inflexible application of the primary rule. This illustrates a general tendency, often observed, that the attempt to eliminate discretion in a particular domain can wind up merely displacing it into another. The official I dealt with knew perfectly well that I was not a conscientious objector to vaccination. When I examined Form 014-4897-64E, however, I found that it did not actually require any statement of the nature of my objection. As a result, there was nothing to stop either her or me from using the submission of the form as a way of circumventing the primary rule, which required strict adherence to the immunization schedule. And so I wound up being formally in compliance with the secondary rule, despite substantively violating it (i.e., using the form in a way that was not intended), and that was contrary to its point (which was to accommodate religious believers). From an administrative perspective, the entire arrangement was perverse. The refusal to allow a minor variance, with respect to the primary rule, resulted in more serious deviance, as officials substantively misused a secondary rule to achieve an outcome that was substantively correct with respect to the primary rule. (Indeed, I felt a slight pang of guilt a few months later, when I read several newspaper reports expressing concern over the growing number of "conscientious objectors" to vaccination in Ontario.[13])

From the standpoint of both personal experience and common sense, most people will agree that bureaucratic discretion is something that should be valued. Who does not want public officials able to apply rules in a flexible, intelligent, and when circumstances warrant, compassionate manner? Particularly for those who believe that there is an important role for the state in promoting social welfare, there should be a reluctance to tie the hands of officials with rigid rules that will reduce the comparative advantage of the state with respect to other organizational forms. Yet if one turns to the literature in political philosophy, two things immediately stand out. The first is how seldom it mentions or discusses administrative discretion. Although discretion is an important topic in both law and social science, it has largely been ignored by political philosophers. Second, the literature that does exist is almost uniformly hostile to discretion. Here, the "liberal" objection, that discretion undermines the rule of law, is less important than what might be called the "democratic" objection, that discretion involves an exercise of state power that cannot be traced back to any democratic source of legitimacy (paradigmatically, the decision of an elected official). Philip Pettit, for instance, though he discusses the issue only in passing, is predictably suspicious of discretion.[14] Given that he assigns a central role to the ideal of non-domination in his "republican" political philosophy, understood as freedom from *arbitrary* interference with one's goals, it is unsurprising that he is inclined to think that there is an inherent tension between discretion and justice, because the only thing that can defeat arbitrariness, in his view, is some kind of democratic procedure.

The most sustained philosophical discussion of discretion to date has been by Robert Goodin, who also views it as deeply problematic, and calls for curtailing it whenever possible. He outlines four specific objections:

1. *Illicit power.* Goodin's first concern is that discretion serves as a source of illicit power for administrative officials, which may be used to manipulate or exploit citizens.[15] Goodin also takes issue with the way that discretion may permit public officials to pursue objectives that are unrelated to the purpose of the program or regulation.[16] He mentions, for instance, the way that discretion exercised by the police gives them the ability to pursue the independent objective of maintaining social order.

2. *Arbitrariness.* Goodin's second major objection is that administrative officials are not obliged to give reasons for their decisions, which makes it impossible to ensure that the decisions are justifiable, or even rational.[17] Specific examples he gives are the denial of welfare benefits and the decisions of parole boards. Of particular concern is the possibility that decisions will be based upon illicit prejudice.

3. *Undermines legal certainty.* Discretion also has the potential to make administrative decisions unpredictable, which undermines legal certainty.[18] For instance, when a regulation is written in precise language, businesses know exactly what they must do to comply. If the language is vague and subject to interpretation, then businesses do not know if their compliance efforts are sufficient until they actually receive a ruling. Furthermore, if the regulator does not consider past practices to be binding, then even the history of past rulings may not be predictive of future ones.

4. *Intrusiveness.* Finally, Goodin expresses the concern that discretion frees public officials from having to respect individual privacy, which is an important feature of liberal government. Certain means-tested social programs are infamous in this regard. For instance, welfare services that offer single parents more generous benefits than those who are married or cohabiting often conduct intrusive searches, to ensure that the parent is, in fact, single. (Unlike the police, who must have a warrant to search one's home, welfare recipients are not in a position to deny entry to inspectors, since the penalty for refusal will often be termination of benefits. Thus, the burden of proof is effectively reversed—the only way the welfare recipient can avoid punishment is to prove the absence of cohabitation.)

It should also be mentioned that, while this concern does not always show up explicitly, another reason for the deep suspicion of discretion among Americans is a concern about racial prejudice. This often combines with the view that, among whites, racism is strongly related to social class, so that as one descends the organizational hierarchy, more state employees are likely to be racist. (One can see this most clearly in the visceral horror most liberal Americans experience at the thought of police discretion.) Mary Baumgartner articulates a commonly held view when she says that "left to their own devices, agents of the law routinely favor some sorts of people over others." As a result, "discretion, in practice, amounts to what is commonly known as discrimination."[19] This perception generates a very strong desire to always push decision-making up to the highest level possible, and to do whatever can be done to limit discretion, based on the suspicion that if low-level employees are given any freedom they will immediately use it to indulge their taste for racial prejudice. As a result, administrative legalism enjoys broad-spectrum political support in the United States, which is perhaps why state power in that country is so often exercised in a way that is peculiarly inflexible, adversarial, and coercive.[20]

The problems Goodin enumerates are all possible, and perhaps even likely outcomes of arrangements that involve what he refers to as "complete" discretion, where there is an explicit grant of authority, subject to little or no constraint, and where the decision is not subject to review.[21] But for reasons that are not entirely clear, Goodin is quite pessimistic about the possibility that self-regulatory measures might limit the potential for such abuses and still preserve discretion. The only solution, he claims, is to abolish discretion entirely. ("These problems are inherent in the practice of discretion and can be overcome (if at all) only by removing discretion from officials."[22]) While recognizing that a certain amount of administrative discretion is inevitable, he makes it clear that, from his perspective, the ideal arrangement would be one in which discretion is was eliminated entirely. (He endorses what Mirjan Damaska describes as the hierarchical ideal of legislation: "Essentially, the exercise of discretion represents a necessary evil in the hierarchical model, an evil to be tolerated so long as more precise guidelines for official action cannot be formulated."[23])

One recent exception to this otherwise negative assessment of discretion is Bernardo Zacka's *When the State Meets the Street*, which develops a much more nuanced position (strongly influenced by Lipsky's *Street-Level Bureaucracy*).[24] Partly this is due to the fact that Zacka did fieldwork for eight months as a volunteer at a social services center in the United States. So while he also has concerns about discretion (he identifies partiality, unpredictability, lack of accountability, and absence of democratic legitimacy as the major problems), he also has a clear understanding of how ubiquitous it is, and the extent to which the organizational culture of the workplace constrains the way that state employees respond to it. Furthermore, he has seen how the exercise of discretion makes possible greater responsiveness, which is required to deal with the unique circumstances and needs of the agency's clients. He is therefore inclined to regard discretion, not just as an inevitability, but also as a desirable feature of street-level bureaucracy.

Zacka's defense of discretion involves showing the useful role that it plays in the work environment of public officials who exercise a great deal of it. Another approach to the normative evaluation of discretion would be to look at situations in which it is *not* being exercised, or where it has been legislatively precluded. For example, "fear of discretion" has been one of the major factors driving the regulation of government procurement practices.[25] This is an area that is notorious for the amount of "red tape" that must be worked through. As Herbert Kaufman famously observed, one person's "red tape" is usually someone else's "due process."[26] In other words, the rules and regulations have their origin in the desire to limit discretion, as a way of achieving greater accountability. In the case of procurement, this has resulted in an extremely rigid set of rules, designed to limit the accusations of corruption or favoritism that seem to accompany the granting of public contracts. Because of this, however, procurement is regarded in many countries as one of the *least* satisfactory domains of government operations.

The perversities of government procurement systems are so extensive that they are impossible to survey in an economical way. The most well-known problem is that public agencies are almost always required by law to take the lowest bid. This is contrary to common sense, since the outlying bids (both high and low) come from the firms most likely to have misestimated the cost of the job, or who plan to cut the most corners. (Thus, the successful firm suffers from the "winner's curse."[27]) Homeowners who solicit multiple estimates for a renovation are routinely advised never to take the lowest bid. Government officials, however, often find themselves locked into doing business with suppliers or contractors whom they know have submitted unrealistic or non-credible bids, and so will be unable to deliver on time, or at all, or will be able to deliver only by cutting corners or cheating. To avoid this problem, many states have layered on an additional batch of rules, creating a pre-approval process aimed at limiting the firms that can bid to those that are reliable. This then undermines the competitiveness of the bidding process, as only the most sophisticated firms have the resources and experience to qualify, while new entrants face enormous upfront costs and very uncertain rewards.

More generally, the procurement system prevents the purchaser and provider from engaging in the sort of "conditional cooperation" that underlies most productive supply relationships in the private sector. As Steven Kelman observes:

> The fear of discretion makes it more difficult to select the right vendor because public officials cannot use important information that could help predict vendor performance if that use requires judgment that the system forbids officials to exercise. The most dramatic example of the information that may not be used is information regarding the past performance of vendors on earlier contracts with the organization . . . Moreover, unwillingness to allow officials the discretion to depart from "free and open competition" can prevent the government from obtaining more value from vendors. Officials cannot offer as an incentive for good performance a promise to award future contracts.[28]

Because vendors' performance cannot help them obtain future contracts, they also have no incentive to cultivate any good will with the state (e.g., by overperforming with respect to the terms of the contract, or volunteering innovative solutions, etc.) There is an extraordinary amount of gamesmanship in government contracting, involving compliance with the strict terms of the contract while failing to offer good value. (To take just one petty, but ultimately consequential example, some firms will systematically assign new and inexperienced employees to work on government contracts, and once they become experienced, transfer them to private-sector contracts.[29]) This is what produces the workplace culture reflected in the folk saying, used to excuse shoddy results, that "it's close enough for government work."

The pathologies of procurement systems are just one example of how attempts to limit administrative discretion can easily result in a cure that is worse than the disease. Furthermore, while many of these attempts succeed in imposing additional rules and procedures, they do not actually succeed in limiting official discretion. Readers of Ludwig Wittgenstein will be familiar with the paradox that can arise, in the application of rules, when one tries to limit indeterminacy in one set of rules by introducing a new set of rules aimed at specifying how the first set of rules are to be applied. Since the same indeterminacy will infect the second set of rules, there may be a temptation to introduce a third set of rules, to control the application of the second. An obvious regress arises.[30] Yet while Wittgenstein considered this primarily a conceptual problem, the US government has turned it into a real-world one. Apart from the inefficiencies it produces, there is a point at which the sheer volume and complexity of the rule set itself can become a source of discretion. For instance, if application procedures for a benefit become so complex that individuals are unable to complete the necessary paperwork without assistance, then officials acquire enormous discretionary power, by virtue of their ability to decide which applicants to help. Or if the requirements become so onerous that it is practically impossible for anyone to have their paperwork completely in order, then officials acquire the power to pick and choose which applications to accept and which to disqualify.

6.2. Varieties of discretion

When it comes to analyzing administrative discretion, it is conventional to distinguish two types. The first involves cases in which the law, or a derived set of regulations, rules, or procedures, is reasonably specific, and discretion arises primarily in the application of these rules. This is the form of discretion usually exercised at the street or "site" level. Social workers, for instance, may have a set of "eligibility criteria" that they use to determine whether elderly members of the community can access in-home support services. In principle, the goal is merely to ascertain whether certain factual circumstances obtain. Yet determining these facts involves a great deal of judgment. To take just one, entirely typical example, the questionnaire may ask whether or not the person is "at risk of being socially isolated."[31] Not only is the meaning of "social isolation" intrinsically vague, but the criterion calls for evaluating, not the individual's actual level of isolation, but merely the risk that such isolation will develop. This is determined through an at-home visit, combined with discussions with family or caregivers. So, in deter-mining whether this criterion has been met, the organization is entirely reliant upon the individual case worker's say-so.

The second form of discretion involves cases in which the civil service is charged with providing a specification or interpretation of the law, or with developing rules to achieve objectives set out in the law.[32] Binding rules may take the form of "regulations," "bylaws," or "orders"; less binding ones may be known as "directives," "guidelines," "manuals," "rulebooks," and, internally, as "standard operating procedures" (SOPs).[33] For instance, OSHA's mandate "to assure so far as possible every working man and woman in the Nation safe and healthful working conditions" requires significant elaboration, not to mention compromise, to be of any use at all.[34] OSHA has, since its inception, undertaken a series of rule-making exercises in which it proposes regulations governing specific workplace hazards, and then goes through the onerous APA process of consulting the parties, holding hearings, responding to objections, revising its proposals, and eventually adopting a set of rules. For instance, one of OSHA's major initiatives during the 1970s was to regulate exposure to cotton dust in garment factories. To do so, it had to determine acceptable levels of exposure, and then decide whether these should be achieved through worker safety equip-ment (e.g., masks or respirators), environmental changes (e.g., improved ven-tilation), technological changes to the production process (e.g., new filters on equipment), or some combination of two or more, at different stages of the pro-duction process. Only after working through all these issues could the agency say that it had a standard, which could, in turn, be enforced in the workplace.

Obviously, the distinction between discretion in rule-making and discretion in rule application is not hard and fast. One might claim that all this is just rule interpretation. Nevertheless, it can be useful to distinguish the situation that arises when OSHA is asked to develop a workplace standard for cotton dust ex-posure from the situation that an OSHA inspector is in when asked to determine whether a particular factory is in compliance with that standard.[35] In both cases, there is significant discretion, but in the former case the executive branch is en-gaged in something that more closely resembles law-making.

Beyond this, there is another important distinction to be made, between *de jure* and *de facto* grants of discretionary power.[36] In the former case, the delega-tion of powers is intentional, and often explicit in the statute. In the latter case, the discretion that arises is not official, and is often unwanted (although not al-ways unforeseen). Considering the full range of circumstances in which discre-tion arises is helpful in coming to see why discretion is not just unavoidable, but in many cases also desirable.

6.2.1. De jure delegation

It is worth noting that in the United States there is generally thought to be a constitutional constraint on the delegation of law-making powers to the executive (known as the "nondelegation doctrine"). This is based on an interpretation of article 1, section 1 of the US Constitution, which states that all legislative power is vested in Congress. There was a period in which the US Supreme Court struck down legislation that it took to be granting too much discretion to administrative officials. The court used this to overrule several pieces of New Deal legislation. After 1935, however, it essentially stopped applying the doctrine.[37] At the same time, the court never repudiated it, and as a result the US Congress remains somewhat circumspect when crafting legislation that delegates rule-making powers, compared to many other jurisdictions. As a result, de jure delegation of powers in the United States is often not fully explicit but is achieved instead through the use of vague terms and objectives. In other countries, the grant of discretion will usually be more explicit. For instance, the Quebec *Act Respecting Alcoholic Liquor*, made famous by the *Roncarelli v. Duplessis* decision (see section 6.5), stated that "the Commission may cancel any permit at its discretion."[38]

The following are some of the reasons that legislatures engage in explicit grants of discretion:

1. *Inherent in the task.* In many cases, the nature of the task is such that the legislature is simply not capable of producing laws at a sufficient level of specificity. There can be a number of reasons for this, the most obvious being that the crafting of rules requires a great deal of technical information or expertise. OSHA's cotton dust regulations are an example of this. There is simply no scenario in which legislators have the time, the attention, or the staff to consider the question of whether the acceptable level of cotton dust exposure should be 200 $\mu g/m^3$ or 100 $\mu g/m^3$.[39] Furthermore, in areas of rapid change, rules and regulations must be constantly updated (particularly when they mandate specific technologies). Whether it be financial products, pharmaceuticals, food additives, or industrial chemicals, it is difficult to imagine an arrangement other than one in which the legislature appoints a decision-making body, giving it the power to examine each case and decide what should be permitted and what should not.

2. *Incompleteness of rules.* H. L. A. Hart argued that judicial discretion was inevitable, because of the "open texture" of language.[40] While terms have a core meaning, even the most straightforward ones are surrounded by a penumbral region of vagueness. Thus rules are not self-applying; they always

involve an exercise of judgment, but with this judgment comes discretion. This has been a major topic in the discussion of legal discretion, but the observation applies with equal force to the actions of the executive. As has already been mentioned, legislatures often write bills in very abstract language, precisely because they want the executive to work out the details.[41] Even when laws use very specific language, it is inevitable that cases will arise that push the boundaries of the terms used. For instance, should an SUV be considered a "passenger vehicle" or a truck for purposes of emissions regulation?[42] The answer to this question wound up restructuring the entire US automotive industry, and had a determinative impact on global climate change policy. Crucially, however, it came from the US Department of Transportation, not Congress.

3. *Incompatibility, or the weighing of goals.* Legislation often specifies more than one objective. These are usually not fully complementary, and so trade-offs must be considered, which, in turn, requires a weighing of those goals. In some cases, such goal conflict will be an inadvertent feature of legislation, but in other cases, the legislature both wants and intends the conflict to be resolved at the administrative level.[43] In particular, since different political constituencies often favor different outcomes, politicians are tempted to offer comfort to them all by passing legislation that commits the state to the advancement of everyone's goals. Disappointment arises only later, at the "implementation" stage, when (inevitably) these goals are traded off against one another. For example, the US Toxic Substances Control Act of 1976 has the primary purpose of protecting Americans from "unreasonable risk of injury to health or the environment" from chemicals, but then also instructs the regulator not to "impede unduly or create unnecessary economic barriers to technological innovation."[44] As noted, the terms "unreasonable," "unduly," and "unnecessary" allow an enormous amount of room for interpretation. But beyond this, discretion is created because the two goals are often in tension. The agency cannot be overly risk-averse, when it comes to considering the introduction of new chemicals, because it has been instructed to avoid creating barriers to technological innovation. As a result, almost any decision can be justified through appeal to one or the other objective.

4. *To discourage gaming.* Private actors often stand in an adversarial, rather than a cooperative, relation with the state. As a result, they have an incentive to interpret the rules in a way that favors their own interests. When the ways that public officials can apply these rules are narrowly constrained, it can encourage gaming of the rules (or "gamesmanship"). This involves acting in ways that conform to the literal text of the statute but are contrary

to its purpose or point. This often generates cycles of "tit-for-tat" escalation, where public officials act "legalistically" in their interpretation of the rules, in ways that private actors consider unreasonable, which leads them to retaliate by being more "aggressive" in their use of gaming strategies.[45] In some cases, the state responds by adjusting the rules, but this is a slow and cumbersome process. The more effective response is to grant officials greater discretion.[46] A particularly clear-cut example of this is the introduction of General Anti-Avoidance Rules (GAARs) into tax codes.[47] The version introduced in the United Kingdom in 2013, for instance, gives revenue authorities the power to invalidate any "tax arrangement" that is deemed "abusive."[48] This essentially gives authorities the discretion to tax corporations on what they regard as the economic *substance* of a transaction or entity, rather than its legal form. The motivation for the introduction of this rule was the desire to reduce the amount of revenue lost to gaming (or in the vernacular, to "loopholes"). GAARs are particularly interesting because of the way they retroactively change rules-based tax systems into principles-based ones. A great deal of ordinary legislation, however, builds in discretion from the start, to discourage a culture of gaming from arising in the first place.

5. *To avoid bureaucratic rigidity.* There are often circumstances in which legislatures may believe that granting discretion, or "flexibility," to the executive will result in better outcomes. For example, with regulations that mandate specific technologies (such as safety features to be installed on consumer products), any particular standard is likely to become obsolete, often quite quickly, depending on the rate of technological change. The legislature often lacks the "bandwidth" to deal with an issue domain more than once per generation, and so instead of writing specific rules, it will adopt general goals that will not require much updating. Legislators might also want to allow room for learning processes, which can lead to revisions once the real-world effects of rules are understood. In such cases, it makes sense to delegate rule-making or decision-making authority to the executive, which is in a position to adjust practices as the need arises. Another important class of cases are ones in which there is a desire to violate formal equality, for instance, by treating different regulated firms differently. This aim may not be avowable in legislation, but it can often be achieved through granting discretion. Finally, it is important to recognize that discretion is often sought for enforcement purposes. An inspector who enjoys a degree of flexibility in the application of the law will be able to bargain to secure compliance, and therefore develop a more cooperative relationship with regulated firms.[49]

6.2.2. De facto delegation

While legislatures often create statutory discretion with complete foresight, discretion may also be an inadvertent or unwanted feature of legislation. We can refer to this as *de facto* discretion. De facto discretion often arises as a perverse consequence of attempts made to limit it. Discretion is sometimes like the proverbial bump under the carpet—it can be moved around but not eliminated. In other cases, the attempt to limit discretion winds up increasing it. (The same dynamic is reproduced within the executive, since official rule-making exercises at the higher levels may wind up increasing discretion at the "street" level.) Again, many of the best-known examples of this are American, because the United States has arguably gone further than any other country in its efforts to limit or eliminate discretion. The US approach to regulation is notoriously formal, or legalistic—it sticks close to the literal text of the rules. The society is also highly litigious, and so both the rules and the specific rulings must be made in a way that will be "court proof." There is a heavy emphasis on documentation, as well as a preference for very specific rules, whose application is easier to defend in court. Yet despite all of this, it is widely acknowledged that the US regulatory system is rife with discretion. This shows how, even when the intention is to eliminate it, discretion often winds up re-entering through the backdoor. It also shows that de facto discretion is as important, if not more important, than de jure discretion.

1. *Too many rules.* It should hardly come as a surprise to learn that, as the number of rules increases, the amount of discretion that can be exercised in the administration of these rules almost always increases as well.[50] In part, this is because the world is complex, and so the rules will interact with one another in unpredictable ways, leading to novel situations that call for the exercise of judgment. In other cases, the rules will conflict with one another, forcing the official to prioritize them, or to pick and choose which ones to apply. As Damaksa has observed, "[T]here is a point beyond which increased complexity of law, especially in loosely ordered normative systems, objectively increases rather than decreases the decisionmaker's freedom. Contradictory views can plausibly be held, and support found for almost any position."[51] Ironically, many of these extra rules may have been added to try to limit administrative discretion. In doing so, however, legislatures often create situations in which the volume of rules has become so great that it becomes unreasonable to expect full compliance, and so administrators gain the freedom to pick and choose which ones to enforce. It may also create a situation in which *all* actions are prohibited. If, however, a decision still must be taken, then discretion has been expanded, because it

has become necessary to break a rule. It will, of course, be up to officials to decide which rule to break.

There are many regulatory domains in the United States in which this situation obtains. The overcriminalization of behavior, for instance, is thought to be an important source of both police and prosecutorial discretion. Business sectors, as well, are often subject to so much regulation that enforcement becomes highly discretionary. Consider the meat-packing industry:

> It is a commonplace in the industry, denied only by official USDA spokesmen, that if all meat-inspection regulations were enforced to the letter, no meat processor in America would be open for business... The inspector is not expected to enforce strictly every rule, *but rather to decide which rules are worth enforcing at all.* In this process, USDA offers no official guidance, for it feels obliged, like all public agencies, to maintain the myth that all rules are rigidly enforced. Unofficially, the inspector is admonished by his USDA superiors to "use common sense," to do his job in a "reasonable way."[52]

In some cases, US agencies have decided to drop the pretense that they are enforcing all rules. The FDA, for instance, has so many rules governing food production that enforcing them all is basically impossible. Thus the agency itself at one point initiated a program aimed to instruct inspectors on which rules should be enforced.[53] The public disclosure of such practices, however, is typically embarrassing to a government agency, producing a perverse state of affairs in which the *actual* enforcement practices of the agency can only be reproduced through the informal culture of the civil service, they cannot actually be written down or publicly acknowledged.

2. *Inadequate resources.* Inadequacy of program resources is a major source of administrative discretion. Resource insufficiency, however, is a structural feature of many government programs, most obviously when goods or benefits are being provided at below-market rates (in which case, "it has often been observed that utilization increases when public services are expanded").[54] The standard strategy for the management of scarcity is means-testing, or the imposition of eligibility criteria. This alone introduces substantial discretion because determining eligibility usually involves a great deal of judgment. On top of this, divergence may arise between "official" and "unofficial" eligibility criteria. For instance, an agency may respond to fluctuations in its budget by tightening or loosening its application of the eligibility criteria, creating in effect a set of "unofficial" criteria.[55]

In addition to eligibility criteria, scarcity—including time scarcity—is often managed through queuing. Wherever there is a queue, there must be someone who manages the queue. In some cases, such as access to public housing, the potential for abuse that control over the queue generate is so extreme that specific rules are put in place to govern it. But in many other cases, public officials are free to manage their own queues. (For example, in Canada queues for access to healthcare, public school programs, and daycares are not subject to any formal oversight, and so are managed by individual doctors, principals, and managers respectively.) This obviously gives street-level bureaucrats control over access to the resource, but beyond that, control over the queue can often be leveraged into the power to pursue other, non-official ends. Zacka gives the example of a social service agency whose wait time to see a case manager is more than a week. Clients often do not have all their documents in order when they arrive at these meetings, and so must return on a subsequent occasion. At this point, the case manager must decide whether to send the person to the back of the line or "squeeze in" a follow-up appointment sometime in the interim. As Zacka observes, the option of sending the person to the back is often used as a way of punishing clients who are regarded as having inappropriate "attitude," or who are thought to be abusing the program.

3. *Inadequate enforcement.* One form of resource scarcity that deserves its own heading is scarcity that results in limited enforcement of the law. Generally speaking, the police do not have enough resources to investigate more than a fraction of the crimes that are reported (and beyond this, have very limited capacity to engage in any preemptive actions aimed at encouraging compliance). This is partially due to resource constraints, along with limited tolerance on the part of the populace for the level of intrusiveness and surveillance that would be needed to impose full compliance. As a result, the police have considerable discretion to pick and choose the crimes they wish to pursue. The situation is even more extreme in other domains. In the United States, the IRS (Internal Revenue Service) has the capacity to audit only a miniscule fraction of the tax returns that are filed in any given year. As a result, there is significant room for what amounts to policy discretion in making decisions about where, when, and with respect to whom the rules should be enforced. Immigration officials often find themselves in the same position of not having anything close to the resources that would be required to deport everyone who is in the country illegally. As a result, agencies and officials will develop and act upon their own priorities.

4. *Compliance is impossible or undesirable.* As we have seen, sets of laws will often interact in such a way as to make compliance impossible. In other cases, the laws will be written in a way that is essentially aspirational, as

a result of which they cannot literally be obeyed.[56] For instance, the US Congress has passed statutes requiring that worker health "not be impaired," or that "no cancer risks will be permitted."[57] As Gary Bryner has observed, "statutes include such unrealistic promises for understandable political reasons."[58] In other cases, however, there is no explicit political calculation, legislators simply may not realize that they are asking for something impossible. They may not be aware that certain trade-offs will be required, and so will use absolute language that, when translated into policy, cannot be complied with. In such cases, compromises will have to be worked out on the executive side.

In other cases, the rules that are formulated make sense in some contexts but cannot be applied in others. For instance, food safety regulations governing one US apple orchard required personnel "to check the orchard each morning for mouse and deer droppings and address the problem before picking begins."[59] Although it is an unreasonably onerous task, it is at least possible to check a 300-acre orchard each morning for deer droppings. Eliminating mouse droppings, on the other hand, is simply not possible. Thus, a work-around was developed, in collaboration with regulatory authorities.

5. *Work is unsupervised, or unsupervisable.* As Baumgartner observes, "[A]ll law is to some extent decentralized in actual practice, requiring scattered officials to respond to incidents on their own and without supervision. This necessarily creates opportunities for the use of discretion, authorized or otherwise."[60] Because there is no way of supervising the employee's activities, a great deal of work in the public sector is done on what amounts to an honor system (often with a thin overlay of accountability). Despite a great deal of talk about "results-based management," it is often impossible to determine, in any precise way, the results of any particular action. Inputs of time and energy can be equally difficult to ascertain. Even when the work is done in plain sight, information asymmetries can make it impossible for anyone other than the employee to know what is really being done. In other cases, the work itself is unobservable, because it happens "in the field," away from the prying eyes of a supervisor.[61] A great deal of regulation, for instance, is enforced by inspectors who work entirely alone, outside direct observation. Efforts to improve observability are usually difficult to implement. For instance, there is a strong temptation to impose reporting and documentation requirements on unsupervised workers. This is, however, usually ineffective, because there is no independent way to check the accuracy of those reports—so all that is really being checked is the ability of employees to maintain a *consistent* official record of their

activities and decisions. In addition to this, oversight is often severely restricted by union rules. Motivational crowding out also means that efforts to introduce oversight may produce worse results than simply allowing an honor system to prevail. As a result, attempts to impose additional rules, aimed at constraining the discretion of unsupervised agents, will often result in nothing more than the development of unofficial "work-arounds," so that traditional practices can continue.[62]

Perhaps the most widely discussed example of a class of public officials who enjoy substantial de facto discretion are the police. What is particularly striking about the police is that they are granted practically no de jure discretion, and yet in practice have considerable autonomy.[63] The latter arises through a confluence of at least four of the five factors just listed. Prior to the advent of patrol and body cameras, their interactions with the public were almost entirely unsupervised (and in the case of disputed accounts, enormous deference was shown to the police version). Because of overcriminalization, the police have the power to interfere with, and often arrest, citizens in almost any circumstance. Yet because of resource constraints, most law breaking goes unpunished. With only a few exceptions, police have the power to pick and choose which laws they want to enforce, under which circumstances. A surprising amount of police work involves talking, negotiating, and giving warnings. Because of this, the overwhelming majority of arrests are discretionary.[64] It is generally agreed, in the sociological literature, that the police then use this discretionary power to advance an independent (non-statutory) interest in preserving social order. Some people find this scandalous, although that judgment does seem a bit precipitous. Experiments that involve removing all discretion from police decision-making have been done, and the results have been decidedly mixed. For instance, people often call the police to defuse what they consider to be a dangerous situation, but not necessarily to make an arrest. If the police are compelled by policy to make an arrest—as they were under several US statutes aimed at removing discretion in cases of domestic violence—then potential victims may delay, or even avoid, calling the police.

Overall, these examples show how otherworldly it is to imagine a public service that is free from discretion. Not only is discretion inevitable but attempts to reduce it often make things worse. At a minimum, they make government inefficient. The formalism that is imposed sometimes succeeds in limiting discretion, but at the cost of undermining the legislation. Compliance with the rules increases, but advancement of the major objective of the legislation is thwarted. And finally, efforts to limit discretion are often perversely self-undermining, in that they wind up increasing it. Attempts to eliminate de jure discretion often just turn it into de facto discretion.

These observations, however, should not be allowed to overshadow the positive case that can be made for discretion. Discretion is not just inevitable; it is also desirable. Support for this claim has been implicit in the preceding discussion, but it is worth restating the points in a more organized form. Major advantages of discretion in public administration include:

1. *Greater flexibility.* Consider a relatively simple problem, such as devising an abatement plan to reduce the production of arsenic and sulfur dioxide in copper smelters. According to one occupational health study, conducted at a time when there were only sixteen copper smelters operating in the United States, it was practically impossible to articulate a general rule:

    Some smelters use old reverberatory furnaces, some use electric models, some modern flash ovens; some use "Pierce-Smith converters," some use very different "Hoboken converters," and some use both; some plants use anode furnaces for further purification, while others do not. Each of these different variations yields different concentrations of emissions and engineering problems in collecting and "cleaning" gases and fumes, and presents widely divergent costs of control. A single government-prescribed control technology, such as acid plants or sulfur dioxide liquefiers—machinery that can cost millions of dollars—has worked well in some plants but has proved utterly ineffective in others. Variations in raw materials complicate the picture further.[65]

    Under such circumstances, the most reasonable way to proceed is to set general goals, then allow inspectors to respond flexibly to the circumstances in each plant, negotiating with individual firms to develop an abatement plan that is tailored to their specific situation. If this is true with respect to copper smelters, which pose a set of essentially technological problems, consider how much more so it will be in the social realm, when attempting to devise a home-care plan for an elderly person, or a job-training program for unemployed miners.

    Regulation is often also a discovery process. The legislative process is governed entirely by *estimates* of the likely effects of intervention. It is quite common to discover only after the regulation is in place that the real compliance costs are quite different, or that benefits are greater or less than expected. In the case of environmental regulation, for instance, a number of regulated substances have proven to be significantly less hazardous than had initially been feared.[66] This has prompted calls for a more "dynamic" approach to regulation, so that learning processes can be incorporated into the regulatory system. In practice, however, this can only be implemented through administrative discretion, because the legislature is seldom capable of revising these statutes once they have been enacted.[67]

2. *Use of local knowledge.* The knowledge that public officials need to achieve certain policy goals will often be impacted, and not amenable to direct observation. Thus, the only way to elicit this information is to establish cooperative relations with private actors. These contacts are unlikely to occur higher up in the organization, at the level at which rules and regulations are formulated. Granting discretion to street-level officials greatly heightens the ability to tap into these local knowledge sources, and informal social networks.

3. *Better substantive outcomes (less gaming).* The problem with formalism is that it can sometimes impede the attainment of the very objectives that are sought under the legislation. For instance, in 2005 the US government, in an effort to promote the use of environmentally friendly fuel sources, created a 50-cent subsidy per gallon for using "hybrid" fuels—those that blended old-fashioned fossil fuel with a biofuel, such as ethanol. Normally, this subsidy would have been of no interest to the pulp and paper industry, because the paper-making process, which involves stewing the wood until cellulose fibers can be removed, leaves behind a sludge, called black liquor, that serves as a perfect fuel source to power the process. As a pure biofuel, the black liquor was not eligible for the government subsidy. In 2008, however, someone had the perverse idea of adding diesel fuel to the black liquor, then declaring it to be a hybrid fuel and applying for the subsidy. This was, of course, exactly the opposite of what the legislation expected to achieve, which was a *reduction* in fossil fuel consumption. Nevertheless, the "blended" black liquor satisfied the letter of the law, and so the application was approved and the subsidy was granted. As a result, the pulp and paper industry was able to extract a rather astonishing amount of money from the US government.[68]

   Denying the payment would, of course, have been an exercise of discretion—in this case, involving a ruling that was contrary to the letter of the statute. This is just one example of the way that a tension can develop between the obligation to follow the rules and the desire to advance the objectives the rules are intended to promote. So, while discretion has the worrying consequence of opening the door to unprincipled decision-making, in some cases the only way to promote instrumental efficacy is by allowing officials to act in an unprincipled fashion.

4. *Improved compliance.* Perhaps the most pernicious misconception about the law is the assumption that compliance is motivated by fear of punishment. As criminologists have been at pains to emphasize, the overwhelming preponderance of compliance with laws is voluntary, based on an essentially cooperative disposition. Punishment is important, but it is reserved for the minority of cases in which voluntary compliance cannot be secured. As a result, it is important that those whom the law addresses perceive it to be legitimate, or in some sense

reasonable, so that they can in turn see themselves as having an internal reason to comply, and not just an external incentive. Legal and bureaucratic formalism has an unfortunate tendency to undermine this, by decoupling the application of rules from the objectives that they are intended to achieve. Making compliance "pointless" in this way deprives those whose actions the law constrains of any internal reason for obedience. As a result, formalism is often coupled with a deterrence-oriented approach to enforcement, generating the syndrome known as legalism, in which both rules and penalties are applied in a highly nondiscretionary way. In certain, very specific circumstances legalism can be appropriate, but as a general approach to enforcement it is widely regarded as a costly and ineffective way of securing compliance.

For example, in many countries, firms that discover inadvertent environmental violations, develop a compliance plan, then self-report the infraction, can expect leniency from regulators—and, in many cases, exemption from penalties. The legalistic culture of US regulation, by contrast, does not permit the EPA such discretion.[69] Firms have no incentive to self-report infractions, and because there are no benefits to be had from self-reporting, there is also nothing to be gained from remediating the problem before detection. Failure to remediate, of course, turns the infraction from an unintentional to an intentional one, but again, the penalties for the two are the same, and so there is no incentive to fix the problem. Thus, the lack of discretion in the system—based on the perception that leniency is equivalent to "going easy" on corporate criminals—generates perverse incentives that undermine voluntary compliance.

These are the most important benefits that flow from administrative discretion. When assessing the issue, it is important to keep in mind the transaction-cost analysis of the welfare state (see chapter 4). The development of the welfare state depends crucially upon its comparative advantage as an organizational form when it comes to meliorating collective action problems that remain unresolved, or inefficiently resolved, through private contracting. As a result, anything that impairs the efficiency of the state as an organization puts pressure on the public-private boundary and tends to call for a reduced role for the state in the economy. To the extent that the state is engaged in implicit redistribution, in the way that it finances the services it delivers, this retrenchment, in turn, has the potential to exacerbate social inequality. Thus, the question of how efficient the state is, in its administrative or regulatory interventions, is not one to be taken lightly, but rather one that has serious implications for social justice.

At the same time, it is important to acknowledge that the four advantages of discretion I have listed do not in any way nullify the four problems identified by

Goodin. Those are still serious concerns. My suggestion is that contemplating the advantages should immunize us against the temptation, which Goodin succumbs to, of wanting to eliminate discretion as much as possible. It should instead lead us to consider more carefully whether there is not a way to address the dangers without losing the advantages. In this respect, Goodin's pessimism seems to be based on a rather striking oversight. He considers three ways to curtail discretion, short of legal constraint. The first is by empowering citizens to promote a more vigorous assertion of their rights. He dismisses this on the grounds that it would require an implausible level of mobilization and collective action.[70] His other two options involve external supervision, the first through administrative rules, and the second through control of outcomes. He dismisses both for reasons that are familiar from principal-agent theory. What he does not consider is the possibility of internalized systems of control, such as professional self-regulation, organizational values, or even just workplace culture. Although he considers systems of "control from below" and "control from above," he ignores the possibility of peer-level regulation of decisions.

Zacka, by contrast, argues that peer-level regulation, though easily underestimated by outsiders, is a powerful force constraining the exercise of administrative discretion:

> In the course of everyday work, peers relentlessly observe and probe each other's working styles. They intervene directly to praise, criticize, mock, or confront one another. They raise questions, give advice, demand explanations, and pass judgment. Peers serve as a constant, panoptic presence. Their influence is both disciplining and formative, and it makes itself felt at each step of the process of casuistic reasoning: in determining what is morally salient about a situation, in deciding what label is most appropriate, and in assessing what to do once a label has been assigned.[71]

Zacka does not hesitate to describe the workplace culture, and the system of informal peer assessment that sustains it, as a "regime of accountability." As several commentators have pointed out, the power of this informal system of constraint is what accounts for the fact that, in most domains where officials enjoy substantial discretion, decision-making is very far from being arbitrary, capricious, or unpredictable. On the contrary, it is eminently predictable, and often quite regimented. Police discretion, for example, does not confer upon individual officers the freedom to pursue their own, idiosyncratic conceptions of justice. What discretion does is create the space for the reproduction of an independent set of norms, a "police culture," that is in its own way highly constraining. Those who are familiar with this code understand that police behavior is highly predictable, and that much of the concern about discretion undermining "legal certainty" is overblown.[72]

There is no need to stand idly about, hoping that such a workplace culture will develop. Positive steps can be taken to inculcate it, through training, mentorship programs, and active management initiatives. Most new employees find it anxiety provoking to be asked to exercise judgment. They quite naturally look to older, more experienced coworkers as role models to guide them. Because of this, the capacity of organizations to create and sustain a workplace culture is not insignificant—simple initiatives like mentorship programs for new employees can have a powerful effect. This workplace culture can significantly reduce the tension between discretion and the rule of law. It is, of course, natural to assume that the rule of law must be achieved through the actual adoption and implementation of *laws*. Another possibility, however, is that it can be promoted through a moral commitment, on the part of public officials, to "rule of law values," a commitment that can, in turn, be institutionalized through a system of peer evaluation and enforcement. In other words, even when officials are exercising discretionary power, there can still be a commitment to exercising that power in a way that is lawlike, or that respects the basic principles governing legitimate law. This is what, at its best, the existing public-sector ethos accomplishes.

6.3. Discretionary enforcement

One of the greatest points of divergence between expert and lay opinion concerning the power of the state is that the public at large tends to dramatically overestimate the effectiveness of coercion. Coercion can be extremely powerful *when perceived as legitimate*, but it cannot create its own conditions of legitimacy. As a result, when applied within a legal order that is generally perceived to be legitimate, it may be quite effective. But this is to some extent an illusion, since the perception of legitimacy is doing a great deal of the work. Coercion on its own, when seen as *illegitimate*, can just as easily generate resistance, general disorder, escalating cycles of violence or unrestrained repression.

As a result, enforcement of the law is a far more complex matter than it is often taken to be, because it is as much about the cultivation and preservation of public authority as it is about the application of sanctions. There is, however, a tendency, when thinking about the division of powers in the state, to assume that the executive has the most straightforward and theoretically uninteresting task, that of merely providing individuals with incentives to elicit compliance. Yet if one looks at even the most instrumental of executive functions, which is the police power, one can see that this is a dramatically oversimplified view. What one finds instead is that not only is a great deal of judgment involved, but in many cases the creation of an effective enforcement regime necessarily involves the discretionary use of power.

One can see this illustrated quite vividly in the debate that has been underway, for the past half-century, about the most effective approach to securing regulatory compliance. Corporations are, in general, much more difficult to deter than individual citizens.[73] This generates a series of dilemmas when it comes to determining an effective enforcement strategy. The most basic involves the question of how best to threaten them. Perhaps the most obvious approach is to threaten them with financial penalties for non-compliance. In the economist's ideal world, the state simply associates higher costs with socially dispreferred courses of action, causing profit-oriented firms to recalculate their best strategy and choose a socially optimal level of pollution, product safety, information disclosure, etc.[74] The major problem with this ideal is that firms that do engage in law breaking can be extremely adept at avoiding detection, and so to compensate for the relatively low probability of apprehension, the penalties for non-compliance must often be implausibly large. Since limited liability protects investors in most firms from seizure of their personal assets, any fine larger than the amount that would drive a firm into bankruptcy has no additional deterrent value. Furthermore, since states have an interest in protecting the viability of domestic firms, excessively large fines are often not credible when threatened against them (and often cannot be collected when imposed on foreign firms). Finally, there is the problem of determining the *incidence* of these fines. Ideally, if the firm has broken the law and been caught, one would like the consequent penalty to be imposed on all those within the organization who did the law breaking, as well as those who benefited from the law breaking. Yet the firm has the capability to displace costs internally, which it may use to protect favored constituencies. Banks, for instance, usually do not have mechanisms in place to claw back the bonuses paid to employees who have concluded fraudulent transactions. Furthermore, although it is usually shareholders who have benefited the most from corporate crime, the imposition of significant fines will often result in greater hardship for workers or consumers. As a result, while the penalty may seem to deter the "firm" in the abstract, it may not deter the individuals in the firm who are responsible for the law breaking, because they have ways to insulate themselves from the negative consequences.

These difficulties have led many people to the conclusion that it is better to set economic incentives aside and to pursue criminal sanctions against firms that break the law. The criminal law has the advantage of allowing officials to pick out the specific individuals in the firm that they want to punish. It also has the advantage of emphasizing the deontic force of the law, to make it clear that the penalties associated with law breaking cannot merely be treated as another cost of doing business. However, these advantages are offset by some important disadvantages.

First, criminal prosecution is almost always directed against employees, managers, or directors, and therefore lets shareholders off the hook. Second, picking out particular individuals within the employee class to prosecute may involve some arbitrariness, since corporate crime often involves the participation, in some capacity, of many individuals. Therefore the tendency is to focus on senior management, on the grounds that they were directing the actions of the others. Senior managers, however, know this, and so often set up structures that give them plausible deniability of law breaking.

The more fundamental problem, however, is simply that it is very difficult to conduct a successful prosecution against business managers. The criminal law, along with the prosecutorial apparatus that enforces it, is basically organized to handle street crime.[75] The overwhelming majority of street crime is perpetrated by relatively isolated individuals acting in an impulsive manner (i.e., without much planning). As a result, a major concern of the judiciary over the years has been the enormous asymmetry between the individual who stands accused of a crime and the highly organized, overwhelmingly powerful state bureaucracy that seeks his conviction. This has resulted in the introduction of a series of important "due process" rights for the individual defendant, aimed at redressing, at least in part, this asymmetry. Nevertheless, a significant fraction of the convictions the state obtains are a result of the remaining power asymmetry. For example, the police still rely heavily on their ability to extract confessions from suspects, a practice that depends almost entirely upon those individuals not having adequate legal representation.

When it comes to prosecution of corporate offenders, however, the asymmetry of power often runs in exactly the opposite direction. The corporation is highly organized, which enhances its ability both to commit crime and to conceal evidence after the fact. Perhaps more importantly, the corporation is often able to mobilize greater legal resources in service of the defense than the state is able to marshal for the prosecution. Corporate offenders can pay for high-quality legal representation, while public prosecutors are notoriously underpaid and underresourced. Nevertheless, corporate defendants still enjoy all the due-process protections that were designed to protect street criminals from police and prosecutors. As a result, in many jurisdictions, it is almost impossible to secure convictions in white-collar cases involving organizationally competent corporations.

Thus there is a general dilemma, when it comes to deterring corporate crime, between adopting an "economic" or a "criminal" approach, or some mixture of the two. Beyond this, the fact that corporations are complex organizations adds an additional layer of complexity. There may be different reasons they break the law, which may, in turn, favor one enforcement strategy over another. Robert Kagan and John Scholz, in an influential contribution, argued that there are three primary types of corporate offenders.[76] The first is the stereotypical one, familiar from economic theory, of the corporation as an amoral calculator that simply pursues the profit-maximizing course of action, drawing no distinction between a fine, a tax, and a business expense. Some firms no doubt fit this characterization, but many others act in ways that are completely inconsistent with it. For instance, as Kagan and Stolz observe, some firms will balk at making minor investments in safety equipment that they consider ineffective, but willingly comply with other regulations that impose much greater costs.[77] Corporations will also sometimes spend more money to challenge regulations in court than they would have had to spend simply to comply with them. Furthermore, they often adopt different stances toward different regulatory agencies, pushing back against some and complying with others, in ways that bear no systematic relation to cost and benefit. This second type of corporate offender is concerned with the *reasonableness* of regulation, and adopts something like a "citizenship" orientation toward compliance. And finally, there the third class of offender, which is firms that break the law through simple organizational incompetence.[78] The most common scenario is one in which senior management is committed to compliance, but does not have adequate control over lower-level employees, who then break the law in self-serving ways. Criminality, in this case, is a symptom of internal agency problems in the firm.

The differences between these three types of corporate offender are important because they determine the appropriateness of different enforcement strategies. In the case of the amoral calculator, the most effective enforcement strategy will be one that focuses on deterrence—compliance can be improved by increasing the probability of apprehension and the certainty or severity of punishment. In the other two cases, however, classic deterrence is often ineffective. In the case of organizational incompetence, the problem is that penalties imposed on the firm are not communicated down to those who are breaking the law, and so do not actually deter anyone. In this case, an effective enforcement strategy involves the regulator acting like a consultant, suggesting to management various best practices, such as ways to improve internal control and monitoring systems. And in the case of corporations that are acting as disputatious citizens, the most effective enforcement strategy involves adopting an essentially "political" approach—entering into dialogue with the firm, seeking to persuade it that there are good reasons for the relevant regulations, and negotiating an arrangement that will bring it into compliance.

Unfortunately, regulators sometimes struggle to determine the sort of firm they are dealing with. This can make it difficult to develop an appropriate enforcement approach, because the wrong strategy may be ineffective, or worse, may generate a backlash that further reduces compliance. In particular, adopting a deterrence approach with firms that have an essentially political orientation may be counterproductive, as it may evoke an adversarial response that transforms the firm into more of an amoral calculator. To take just one example, Kagan and Scholz describe an American steel firm that initially appointed a safety engineer to act as the go-between with OSHA, but finding the agency too inflexible, it dismissed the engineer and replaced him with a lawyer, who proceeded to stonewall all requests.[79]

These difficulties account for the popularity of the so-called *responsive regulation* approach, which involves giving firms the benefit of the doubt initially, engaging with them constructively on the assumption that they want to be in compliance, but then escalating the severity of enforcement action when they fail to respond to these overtures.[80] The steps involved in escalation are illustrated in the "enforcement pyramid" introduced by John Braithwaite and Ian Ayres.[81] It begins with education, persuasion, and other forms of informal engagement at the bottom, then ascends through warning letters, or statements of non-compliance, the issuing of commands, and, finally, extrinsic punishments. The pyramid shape reflects the fact that the interventions at the bottom are the ones most often used, because they are all that is needed, while the more forceful interventions are uncommon, and are used only in cases of recalcitrance. For instance, in a study of the regulation of the nursing-home industry, Braithwaite and his collaborators found that the most common intervention involved education and the provision of management advice (i.e., dealing with the firm as organizationally incompetent); after that came persuasion (i.e., dealing with the firm as citizen); the "get tough" approach (i.e., dealing with the firm as amoral calculator) was reserved for a small number of cases.[82]

The important point, for our purposes, is that responsive regulation is *inherently discretionary*, in at least two ways. First, constructive engagement is possible only if enforcement agents have some measure of discretion. Strict adherence to the letter of the law is the primary source of "regulatory unreasonableness," which is the most common objection that firms have to compliance. Inspectors who listen to objections, and have the discretion to waive particular rules (or to ignore certain technical infractions), are then able to bargain for other objectives (e.g., "I will agree to overlook the following, as long as you focus on remedying this issue."). Discretion is what makes it possible for them to offer something to the firm, which, in turn, permits reciprocity, and through that, cooperation. Second, and most importantly, the decision to escalate sanctions, moving from constructive engagement to a deterrence orientation, is inherently discretionary. As Kagan and Scholz put it, because there are different types of firms, "inspectors should be prepared to shift from strict policemen, to politician, to consultant and back again according to their analysis of the particular case."[83] This is why it is called "responsive" regulation. There are some firms that go through the motions with regulators, pretending to be making a sincere effort to come into compliance, but in fact just stalling for time in order to maximize the advantages stemming from their non-compliance.[84] The regulator must be aware of this possibility, and in such cases, must decide at what point to abandon the constructive approach and adopt a more instrumental stance, and, ultimately, when to become overtly punitive. None of this can be decided a priori, or second-guessed by observers, it will be based on judgments that are made based on the interactions that have occurred between the regulator and the firm, as each side responds to the actions and reactions of the other.

The primary challenge that proponents of responsive regulation face is that outsiders look at it and see a "cozy" relationship between government agencies and firms, which seems to them indicative of capture. As a result, as Scholz has observed, it is often those who are politically most inclined to support regulation who wind up making demands that undermine regulatory effectiveness.[85] Indeed, much of the desire to limit discretion in regulatory agencies is motivated by a concern over capture. For example, the impulse to compel inspectors to issue fines every time they observe a violation, regardless of how minor or technical it is, is driven by the suspicion that if one allows any discretion, it will give rise to collusion between government officials and industry. The willingness to allow a responsive enforcement style to develop requires a relatively high degree of public trust in public officials, the central question being how susceptible to corruption the officials are. There is a close connection therefore between the existence of a robust sense of professional ethics in the public sector and the availability of discretionary enforcement approaches. While external sanctions no doubt play a role, the most powerful defense against regulatory capture is the existence of a strong commitment to the public interest on the part of public officials, along with a professional culture that offers a clear sense of how that interest is to be served.

In circumstances in which trust in public officials is impaired or absent, the tendency will be to limit official discretion. This, in turn, makes constructive engagement more difficult, which pushes enforcement in the direction of a more punitive deterrence-oriented model. This gives rise to the problem of unreasonableness in site-level enforcement, which, in turn, generates adversarial rather than cooperative relations between industry and government officials. Lack of discretion means that rules will often be enforced in ways that "make no sense," relative to the purpose of the regulation. This leads to a decline in the moral authority of the law, encouraging corporate actors to think of themselves as complying only to avoid sanctions. This naturally leads to a more instrumental orientation toward the rules on the part of the firm. If public officials retaliate, it can generate a highly undesirable spiral, as the relationship becomes increasingly adversarial, punitive, and costly for both sides.[86]

Thus when we look at the enforcement activities of the state, it is not just that some measure of discretion is inevitable, it is that discretion—and the willingness of politicians and the public more generally to tolerate official discretion—is actually the cornerstone of an effective enforcement system, and thus of the bindingness of law. The development and reproduction of a workplace culture that limits the abuse of discretion, and guides its appropriate exercise, is therefore one of the most important factors determining the quality of governance in a liberal state. Furthermore, the executive branch makes its own contribution to the legitimacy of the state, to the extent that it develops an enforcement style that permits citizens to believe that they are not just being controlled by the law, but also addressed by it as rational individuals.[87] No matter how impeccable the democratic pedigree of a statute may be, its legitimacy can still be undermined by an enforcement regime that relies too heavily on coercion, while failing to bring the force of rational argument to bear upon legal subjects.

6.4. The morality of law

It is important to remember that the coercive power of society over the individual does not begin with the state. Small-scale societies without a formal hierarchy are governed by a set of social norms, which are common knowledge among members and enforced in a decentralized manner, through a general propensity to impose punitive sanctions on those who violate them. Although such a system has the ability to generate a very stable social order, it is also associated with certain inconveniences. Disagreement about the content or application of norms has the potential to generate intractable conflict, and the reliance on a purely informal enforcement system can give rise to collective action problems. Thus political power has, historically, tended to crystallize around the judicial function of adjudicating conflicts, as well as the development of specialized enforcement roles.[88] Political authority, in other words, begins as the power to interpret and enforce a pre-existing normative order.

Yet the power to interpret the rules can easily develop into the power to change them, and lead to the emergence of the "steering" or leadership functions of political authority. This has certain obvious advantages, as it allows the development of much greater flexibility in response to changed circumstances, as well as the capacity to adapt more quickly to new environments. On this model, the political leadership has the power to make changes in the norms (typically following certain procedures), norms that will, in turn, be imposed by specialized enforcement agents. The arrangement, however, gives rise to an unfortunate temptation for those who occupy positions of political authority to short-circuit the relationship between political leadership, the normative order and the system of enforcement, so that instead of the norms being enforced, and the leadership exercising its influence though its capacity to change these norms, enforcement becomes directly associated with the will of the leadership. This is what marks the transition that Adams described, away from the rule of "laws" towards that of "men." Less diplomatically put, it represents the emergence of what is traditionally referred to as "tyranny"—the ability of the powerful to coercively impose their will upon others using the apparatus of the state. Such an arrangement violates the central legitimacy condition of the state, which is that its use of coercive power is justified by the claim that it is enforcing the normative order, not merely imposing the arbitrary will of the leader or leadership class.

Thus a commitment to the "rule of law" represents much more than a commitment to "mere legality," or to the requirement that state officials be able to justify acts of coercion by pointing to some form of legislative authorization. As Hayek and many others have pointed out, elected officials could easily pass a law conferring upon themselves, or some designated person, arbitrary and unlimited power.[89] Instead, the rule of law represents a broader vision of how the political order should be structured, in particular, how the use of coercion should be regulated. It is a vision of society as *governed by a set of general rules*, with the legitimate use of force restricted to the enforcement of these rules. This, among other things, is why the legislative branch only has the power to make laws, not to issue orders, and why it does not have the power to enforce its decisions.

On Hayek's view of things, there is a very close conceptual connection between the rule of law and the standard liberal division of powers. Each branch of the state serves a specific function regarding the law, which stands above them all. Because the law cannot be fixed forever, the legislature has the power to amend it, and to create new law as circumstances warrant. In doing so, however, it must restrict itself to formulating perfectly general rules, which stop short of singling out certain individuals or circumstances. The role of the judiciary, then, is to serve as an intermediary between the law and social reality, providing definitive interpretations of how the law is to be applied to particular individuals and specific circumstances. And finally, because not everyone is motivated to respect the rules, the executive ensures that legally mandated actions are actually carried out, and it punishes those who fail to comply.

Beyond this, Hayek adds three specific constraints, which he sees as necessary corollaries of the notion of a society ordered by a set of laws:

1. *Known and general rules.* To say that the society is genuinely governed by rules, it must be the case that the rules are known to everyone *prior* to any decision to act. This constraint must be satisfied for there to be a reasonable expectation that individuals will actually comply with the rules. Furthermore, the rules must be "general," which means that they must

provide a fairly abstract specification of which actions are allowed and disallowed, under fairly generic descriptions (i.e., "containing no references to specific persons, places or objects"[90]). This is intended to capture our sense of what it means that something is a rule, as opposed to a command.

2. *Legal certainty.* It must be possible to predict, with relative confidence, how the rules will be interpreted when it comes to assessing an individual's conformity to them. Ideally, this will be achieved by having statutes that are unambiguous and clear, and legal procedures that are predictable in their application. When this is not the case, however, it means that the way state officials interpret the law must be at least consistent across individuals and over time, as well as publicly known. Read more strictly, it implies the judicial doctrine of *stare decisis*, or the idea that legal decisions generate precedents, which in turn constrain future decisions.

3. *Citizen equality.* Finally, Hayek maintains that the rule of law commits the state to recognizing a certain form of "equality before the law" of citizens. In a minimal sense, equality follows from the principle that the law must treat like cases alike, such that people cannot be treated differently unless there is some relevant difference between them. In other words, for the law to have different implications, it cannot be just that the people to whom it is being applied are different; the situation must also be somehow different. Hayek goes somewhat further than this, claiming that when the law does draw distinctions between classes of people relevant to the application of the law, these distinctions must be recognized as legitimate by people on both sides of the divide (i.e., they cannot just be imposed by one group on the other).

These three constraints, it should be noted, do not rule out the administrative state. Hayek's hostility to the latter was grounded more in a mental image he had of liberal society (which Oakeshott shared [91]), according to which the administrative state is structurally incapable of respecting the rule of law. On this view, private individuals have various goals and purposes. They accept the constraint of rules because, on the whole, doing so allows them to better achieve their goals. The role of the state is to be an impartial arbiter of the rules To do so, however, it cannot have any purposes of its own. One can see in the background of this conception a commitment to liberal neutrality, along with the idea that the state should not favor the goals of one class of individuals over another. This is, however, bolstered by an hypertrophied distinction between deontological and teleological modes of reasoning, with the guarantee of neutrality being that the state will only engage in the deontological task of enforcing rules, while the prerogative of reasoning teleologically is reserved for private individuals.

One can see how this conception of the rule of law is compatible with the state's commitment to modern liberal principles of liberty and equality, both of which Hayek endorsed in some form. Where it runs into difficulty is in dealing with the principle of efficiency. Hayek at various points made use of the Pareto principle to justify a variety of coercive institutional arrangements, including, most obviously, the market.[92] Yet, as we have seen, the rise of the administrative state can largely be seen as an attempt to achieve greater efficiency. An objective like "solving market failure," however, tends to slip through the cracks of Hayek's analysis. When the state adopts a policy on such grounds, it is not violating neutrality (at least, no more so than when it adheres to principles of liberty or equality). Nor is it imposing a purpose, since by and large it is merely helping individuals to achieve their own purposes. For example, when it makes investments in mass transportation systems, it is not telling people where to go, it is merely helping them to get where they want. At the same time, the pursuit of efficiency in this sense imposes a certain direction or purpose on state activity and has given rise to some of the largest and most powerful state bureaucracies. This, in turn, has put pressure on the separation of powers, and shown that there is no necessary connection between that separation and state neutrality.

Thus the growth of the welfare state has had the effect of forcing a choice between the efficiency gains that can be achieved through regulation, social insurance, and public provision of goods, on the one hand, and the safeguard against violation of individual freedom that is provided by a strict separation of powers, on the other. Western states have answered this question overwhelmingly in favor of the former. This is not so surprising, since the standard Montesquieuian justification for the separation of powers is essentially pragmatic, even instrumental. The institutional arrangement is presented as the one best suited to protecting the individual from the arbitrary or tyrannical use of state power. There is no doubt a great deal to be said for preserving it at the highest levels of political authority, but it does not follow from this that it should be preserved all the way down the organizational hierarchy, such that each branch must make its own distinct contribution each and every time a state official interacts with a citizen. Furthermore, if some *other mechanism* is put in place to protect individuals from the abuse of state power, then the underlying normative conditions—the ones that tolerate no abridgment—may be just as well satisfied. Thus, in some administrative domains, the separation of powers seems like a *desideratum* that could be traded off against other valued objectives or properties, including the desire to increase social welfare by resolving various forms of market failure.[93]

As a result, modern conceptions of the rule of law tend to focus much less on the separation of powers and more on the qualities that exercises of power must possess to be considered applications of a *rule*. For instance, Lon Fuller's influential conception of the rule of law can be seen as an attempt to render more specific Hayek's first two constraints, while setting aside the broader picture that required a strict separation of powers. Fuller argues that *failures* of the rule of law can take the following forms: (1) a lack of explicit law, leading to ad hoc adjudication; (2) failure to publicize or make the rules known; (3) retroactive legislation; (4) unclear or obscure legislation that is impossible to understand; (5) contradictions in the law; (6) demands that are beyond the power of citizens to obey; (7) unstable legislation (e.g., daily revision of laws) and (8) lack of consistency between the rules as announced and the rules as administered.[94] The focus is very much on the insistence that individuals only be punished if they have been given fair warning of the rules and reasonable opportunity to conform to them, and yet have failed to do so. For this to be the case, agents of the state must conduct themselves in a highly disciplined and transparent fashion.

Legal theorists sometimes deride Fuller's constraints as platitudinous. Yet if one considers them as a set of constraints on, not just judges, but also the practice of public administration—and in particular, on the behavior of street-level bureaucrats—then one can see that they are very far from being platitudinous. If one were to examine the ways that teachers organize their classrooms, or prison guards work the floor, or welfare caseworkers conduct investigations, violations of these principles would not be difficult to find. Indeed, one would have to count any bureaucratic organization that succeeded in satisfying most of these constraints, most of the time, as exceptionally well managed.

The other major feature of Fuller's conception of the rule of law is that it focuses quite specifically on the idea of rule-following, and on what conditions must be satisfied for conduct to be governed by rules. It does so at a sufficiently high level of generality that one can imagine the ideal as one that governs action within any branch of the state. Hayek and Oakeshott, by contrast, present conceptions that are so closely wedded to the traditional understanding of the division of powers that they provide little guidance about the conduct of individuals working within any particular branch. Other theorists, such as Joseph Raz or Jeremy Waldron, have offered conceptions that are tailored quite specifically to the judiciary.[95] Fuller's doctrine, by contrast, has the advantage of leaving it open as to whom it is addressed, and thus it can serve more easily as a specification of the rule of law that can inform the practice of public administration.

Furthermore, it is not difficult to see that Fuller's conception has *some* normative content (which is what leads him to claim that he is articulating the inner "morality" of law). The rule of law, one may recall, is a normative ideal intended to fall somewhere between mere legality and perfect justice. Where Fuller falls short of Hayek's conception, in this regard, is in failing to articulate any conception of equal citizenship. The latter is often closely associated with the prohibition on arbitrariness in the treatment of individuals, something that Fuller's principles do not explicitly exclude. One can see as well in "expansive" conceptions of the rule of law, such as the United Nations proposal quoted at the beginning of the chapter, an attempt to extend the equality provisions even further, by requiring not only that laws be compatible with human rights norms, but also explicitly acknowledge "equal standing" and "fairness" in the application of law.

As far as the practice of public administration is concerned, there may be no theoretically correct answer to the question of how far these equality commitments should go, other than the pragmatic one, of how assertive the civil service can be on this question without violating political neutrality.[96] This will be determined largely by the political culture of the nation. The principle of equality is, by its very nature, more controversial than Pareto efficiency, precisely because it is used to mediate conflicts of interest, instead of just expressing the common interest that all individuals share in maximizing the benefits of cooperation. Thus, despite its neutrality (in the liberal sense), it is nevertheless more likely to be contested politically, simply because whatever particular conception becomes institutionalized will always generate a constituency with an interest in promoting some *other* conception. As a result, it is possible for the civil service to be relatively assertive in its pursuit of efficiency (first and foremost, through its promotion of cost-benefit analysis), whereas the commitment to equality will require far more deference to elected officials. Thus, what the civil service needs to concern itself with primarily is the minimal conception of equality, implicit in the rule of law, that serves as a constraint on popular sovereignty. In this respect, the courts have played the most important role in drawing the appropriate boundaries, and the executive largely takes direction from these judicial decisions. In most liberal-democratic jurisdictions, there are key rulings in which courts have overturned particular acts of legislation or administrative decisions, on rule of law grounds. These have often provided important guidance for the civil service (which is why otherwise obscure cases, such as *Roncarelli v. Duplessis* in Canada, are so well-known in the higher civil service).[97] This is the best place to look for a baseline conception of equality that the executive can rightfully consider nonnegotiable in its dealing with elected officials.

6.5. Administrative law

Although some degree of administrative discretion is inevitable, a great deal of the autonomy of the executive branch that arose during the 20th century occurred with the foresight of the legislature, and in many cases through the explicit delegation of legislative power. This is what created the state of affairs that, I have claimed, requires the cultivation of a "rule of law culture" within the executive. Some will disagree with this. As we have seen, the rise of the administrative state coincides with the development of administrative law, some of which is statutory (particularly in the United States), but much of which stems from the application of common law principles of justice and constitutional norms, by the courts, to the actions of administrative officials (or in civil law countries such as France, the application of the case law developed in administrative law tribunals). This suggests that, if the legislature is failing to write laws at a level of granularity sufficient to curtail executive discretion, the courts might step in to perform that function. On this view, the rule of law would remain the preserve of the judiciary, and the executive could be assigned a more instrumental role.

Judges, of course, will always be tempted by this suggestion. Although doctrines such as the supremacy of Parliament may make them loathe to interfere in legislative decision-making, there is no such reticence when it comes to asserting authority over the executive. Save for the areas in which "royal prerogative" insulates executive action from judicial oversight, there are few constitutional obstacles to prevent judges from issuing orders to administrative officials. At the same time, the complex bureaucratic apparatus of the administrative state exists for a reason. If one considers the sometimes awe-inspiring difficulty of the rule-making exercises undertaken by agencies involved in regulating health and safety, for instance, along with the formidable range of specialized scientific and technical data that must be taken into consideration in developing such rules, one can see why the courts might hesitate to second-guess the outcomes of these procedures.[98] Many of the epistemic difficulties that prevent the legislature from writing detailed statutes occur with even greater force in a judicial review undertaken by non-specialized courts. These problems are particularly acute in jurisdictions where judges have limited ability to appoint their own experts, and so must rely on litigants to put forward expert testimony (which is typically contested by the other side).[99] So while judges may be temperamentally inclined to assert their authority over the executive, in practice, they have exhibited a certain degree of restraint. Determining the correct degree of restraint has been at the heart of the question, which features centrally in the development of administrative law, over the appropriate "standard of review" when executive decisions are challenged and wind up before the court.

Overall, the treatment of this question has been somewhat disorderly, characterized by the emergence of significant differences in different jurisdictions, a fair amount of instability, and sometimes outright incoherence over time. If one can discern an overall trajectory of development, however, it is in the direction of judicial deference to the *content* of particular administrative decisions, combined with a willingness to impose a set of procedural constraints that amount to what I have been calling a "rule of law culture." In other words, the idea that judicial review might serve as an alternate route to the control, or abolition, of executive discretion, has not been realized. What courts have done, instead, is insist that when the executive exercises the discretion it has, that it respect the rule of law, understood in terms of a set of constraints more-or-less along the lines articulated by Fuller. Rather than regard themselves as the custodians of the rule of law, courts have instead insisted that the executive develop its own commitment to those principles.

To see the dilemma that the rise of the administrative state posed for the judiciary, consider the classic formulation of the common law right to due process. Dicey took it to be an essential feature of the rule of law that no one "can be lawfully made to suffer in body or goods except for a distinct breach of law established in the ordinary legal manner before the ordinary courts of the land."[100] Historically, of course, this meant that before a person could be punished, some sort of judicial proceeding had to occur, up to and including a full trial. This is the familiar structure of the criminal law. Yet it is clear that a wide variety of administrative decisions may also cause individuals to "suffer in body or goods." For example, many economic activities can only be undertaken after a license or permit has been issued. Someone whose license to practice a certain occupation is revoked is clearly being punished. Similarly, denying someone a permit to engage in some trade may be equivalent to destroying his business. Yet these decisions are not made by courts; in almost all cases, they are made by administrators who have been appointed to regulate these professions or trades. Thus Dicey's claim about due process, even at the time it was written, was more normative than descriptive.[101] Since then, the scope of administrative power over the "body and goods" of the individual has expanded dramatically.

The welfare state provides individuals with a wide range of different benefits, very few of which involve unconditional entitlements. Administrative officials charged with determining eligibility wind up having the power to deny or revoke benefits. In the United States, for instance, individuals who are caught or suspected of abusing the SNAP can be subjected to a lifetime ban from the receipt of any further food stamps. Technically, this is not a punishment; it is the denial of a discretionary benefit, but in practice, it is difficult to see any substance to the distinction. (Further confusing the issue is the fact that individuals may be banned from receiving food stamps for having certain felony convictions, even though the denial of access to the program is not part of their judicially imposed sentence.) Similarly, it has been observed that the small army of government "inspectors," charged with enforcing all sorts of regulations, are police officers in everything but title.[102] Furthermore, they often have the power to write citations and impose fines "on the spot," in response to any perceived infraction of the rules.

If one were to take Dicey's view seriously, then every one of these decisions should be, if not the outcome of a judicial proceeding, then at least subject to appeal and review by the courts. Furthermore, it means that if and when the courts do review the decisions made, they should use the lowest standard of deference, what is commonly known as the "correctness" standard. In other words, the court, when reviewing an administrative decision, should be committed to determining whether the administrative body made the right decision, given all of the considerations and circumstances at play. This, of course, commits the court to recapitulating the entire process of reasoning that led the administrative body to its decision, a task that is obviously quite onerous—and in some cases, one is tempted to say, impossible. Perhaps more importantly, it imposes obligations on public servants that would undermine the efficacy of the executive branch. For instance, for a court to be able to determine whether the correct decision was made, it must have a complete record of how the administrative body went about making its decision, and the information it took into account. This, in turn, requires that the administrative body carefully document the entire process that led to the decision (and that it do so as a matter of course, in every case, to ensure that its decisions can withstand judicial scrutiny). Such an obligation would be onerous in the extreme, and would make certain administrative activities, for all practical purposes, impossible to perform. Thus, as one commentator has observed, Dicey's view "amounts to a prohibition against reconciling law with the imperatives of administration."[103]

One strategy for heading off this difficulty is for the administrative agency itself to create a quasi-judicial "tribunal" to make certain decisions, or to hear appeals from those who want to contest decisions. Most developed welfare states have hundreds, if not thousands of these administrative tribunals (in keeping with the principle that if one cannot respect the separation of powers, one can at least reproduce the other two functions *within* the executive branch). Prominent instances include tribunals that hear immigration and refugee cases, settle residential rental disputes, apply human rights or civil rights law, provide labor arbitration, and deal with planning and bylaw disputes. In most cases, the tribunals offer "expedited" claims settlements, often in a non-adversarial context, with minimal documentation, and few of the "due process" constraints that one associates with the courts. Individuals are often encouraged to represent themselves rather than retain counsel. The overriding imperative is usually one of efficiency, providing individuals with a relatively accessible forum that gives them a fair chance to express their point of view, but that at the same time imposes a relatively rapid resolution of claims. In some cases, these tribunals are created through legislation, sometimes at arms-length from the administrative agency (e.g., the legislation that created OSHA in the United States also created the Occupational Safety and Health Review Commission, an independent federal agency whose task is to review OSHA's decisions). In other cases, however, the tribunal is created by, and staffed by members of, the agency that is involved in the exercise of administrative power. The creation of tribunals therefore does not really solve the problem of due process or accountability, if anything it just pushes it up one level, because a certain fraction of individuals whose claims are denied by tribunals will be unsatisfied by the outcome, and so will demand judicial review of the decision, on the grounds that their right to due process was not respected by the tribunal procedure.

The French solution to this problem was to add additional administrative tribunals to hear appeals concerning the decisions of lower administrative tribunals (the Conseil d'Etat being the highest). In one sense, this approach reproduces the entire structure of the judicial system, with its escalating hierarchy of appeals courts, within the executive branch. In another sense, it blurs the distinction between the executive and the judiciary, so that it becomes difficult to say what the difference is, at a certain level, between a tribunal and a court. In common law jurisdictions, however, this approach has not been favored, in part because of the unwillingness of the judiciary to accept the necessary limitations on its power to overturn administrative decisions based on such factors as conformity to principles of "natural justice." Yet, if one develops this idea along the lines that Dicey suggested, it implies the implausible view that the courts have, not just the jurisdiction, but also the obligation, to review any and all tribunal decisions, to ensure that the correct decision was made.

The obvious solution for the courts was to insist on their authority, but to reconcile it with the imperatives of administration by adopting a more deferential standard of review (e.g., by refraining from overturning administrative decisions in all but cases of "patent unreasonableness"). This accommodation was in most cases further encouraged by the legislature. Keeping in mind that most administrative agencies were created by legislatures that intended to grant them fairly broad discretionary powers, it was not difficult to see that their operations would be frustrated if the courts insisted on inserting themselves into every decision-making process. And so, to restrict broad assertions of judicial authority, it became common in the early 20th century for legislatures to insert "privative" clauses into legislation, which explicitly exempted certain administrative decisions from judicial review. To take just one, entirely typical example, the New Zealand Industrial Arbitration and Conciliation Act of 1900 created a Court of Arbitration—in effect, an administrative tribunal—intended to provide expedited resolution of labor disputes. At the same time, the act protected the decision of this "court" from judicial review with the following privative clause: "Proceedings in the Court shall not be impeached or held bad for want of form, nor shall the same be removable to any Court by *certiorari* or otherwise; and no award, order or proceeding of the Court shall be liable to be challenged, appealed against, reviewed, quashed, or called in question by any Court of judicature on any account whatsoever."[104] It is not difficult to detect in this a rather forceful message to the judiciary.

It should also be mentioned that the total wars of the early 20th century had a substantial impact on the legal culture, the overall tendency being to encourage much greater deference to executive power. Even in countries that remained liberal and democratic throughout, military operations were obviously conducted without any judicial oversight. More importantly, however, central governments commandeered large segments of the economy, including, essentially, all industrial facilities (particularly during the Second World War). Even in the United States, which for the most part fought the war only at a distance, the federal government created a series of "mobilization" agencies, which engaged in the large-scale planning of production across the economy as a whole. The work of each high-level agency was supplemented by more specific agencies, such as the War Manpower Commission, for the administration of labor; the Maritime Commission, to direct civilian shipbuilding; the Office of Price Administration, to set prices; the War Food Administration, to ensure that civilian needs were met, and so on. This period is sometimes described as one in which the "state" assumed control of the economy, which is true, although it would be more precise to say that it was not the state as a whole, but rather the executive that took over the economy. And while some effort was made to include business and labor groups in the decision-making processes of these agencies, the fact remained that they ruled with essentially dictatorial power, and their decisions were obviously not subject to meaningful oversight or review by either the legislature or judiciary.

Most of this, of course, occurred in a "state of exception," and things reverted to normal when the war ended. (Modern "emergency power" laws and declarations have a similar effect, giving the executive extraordinarily far-reaching powers, all exempt from judicial scrutiny, but for a limited period of time.) The widespread insertion of privative clauses into legislation, by contrast, posed a standing difficulty, which courts had little choice but to address. Taken at face value, a privative clause looks like an attempt by the legislature to challenge the rule of law or, at least, the traditional separation of powers, by giving the executive the power to enforce laws without the intervening judgment of the courts. How is this any different from giving the police the power to throw people in jail without trial? It is certainly not difficult to imagine reasons for considering such legislation unconstitutional. Yet, in part because of the changing legal climate, the courts by and large shrank from direct confrontation with the legislature on this point. Instead, as David Dyzenhaus has argued, they decided to treat the privative clause as presenting them with a "puzzle" that they were entitled to solve.[105]

It is impossible to tell a unified story of the development of administrative law from this point forward, since courts have adopted different strategies in different jurisdictions. However, one point of general agreement has emerged, which is that privative clauses could not protect administrative decision-making entirely from the jurisdiction of the courts, for the obvious reason that a particular administrative action might be ultra vires—which is to say, it might exceed the boundaries of the power the enabling statute confers upon the administrative agency. For instance, an official might try to assert authority outside his territorial jurisdiction, or in domains that are not part of his mandate. And tribunals could not be allowed to decide their own jurisdiction. Thus, ultra vires challenges to executive power must always remain possible, even in the presence of privative clauses.[106]

It is not difficult, however, to expand this ultra vires rationale for review into a more general evaluation of "reasonableness." In particular, when the enabling legislation specifies some kind of overarching goal, it is natural to think of the administrative agency's proper jurisdiction as the set of actions that are instrumental to the attainment of that goal. Yet one cannot simply defer to the agency's judgment in this matter; otherwise, the agency could make any exercise of administrative power intra vires just by deeming it necessary to that goal, as it conceives it. As a result, it remains up to the courts to decide if a particular decision can *reasonably* be construed as advancing that goal, to decide whether it is ultra vires or not.

Courts have used similar reasoning to constrain the exercise of administrative discretion, in cases where statutes directly confer what would appear to be unlimited discretion. In the United Kingdom, for instance, statutes are littered with the "fitness" formulation, wherein officials are granted the authority to create such rules as they "think fit," impose such fares or taxes as they "think fit," grant or revoke licences as they "see fit," and so on. Yet the concept of "fitness" can be read normatively—there must be some plausible connection between the administration action contemplated and the goal sought, to think that the former is "fit" to produce the latter—which gave an opening to the courts to introduce a reasonability constraint on the exercise of what would appear, at first glance, to be a grant of unlimited discretion.[107] For instance, the "think fit" constraint is often taken to prohibit officials from giving weight to considerations or objectives that are irrelevant to the purpose of the statute. Thus, "the discretion of a statutory body is never unfettered. It is a discretion which is to be exercised according to law. That means at least this: the statutory body must be guided by relevant considerations and not by irrelevant. If its decision is influenced by extraneous considerations which it ought not to have taken into account, then the decision cannot stand."[108]

In Canada, it was the *Roncarelli v. Duplessis* judgment in 1959 that established the definitive constraint on administrative discretion. Superficially, the case involved the revocation of a restaurant's liquor license, but underlying it was an issue of freedom of religion. The premier of Quebec at the time of the incident, Maurice Duplessis, was trying to prevent Jehovah's Witnesses from proselytizing in the province. The legislature passed a law preventing the distribution of free newspapers in the streets, which led to widespread civil disobedience by Jehovah's Witnesses, who were promptly arrested for violating the law. Roncarelli was a restaurant owner sympathetic to their cause, who began to bail Jehovah's Witnesses out of jail so that they could return to distributing papers in the streets. In retaliation, Duplessis ordered the liquor commissioner to revoke Roncarelli's license to serve alcohol in his restaurant. The commissioner complied, which soon led to the failure of Roncarelli's business. Roncarelli tried several avenues of redress, all of which were denied by the provincial courts, until finally, when Duplessis left office, Roncarelli started a civil suit against him (which he eventually won). The ruling, however, was more noteworthy for the way that it defined the obligations of the liquor commissioner, not the premier.

The central challenge in the case involved the fact that, although the liquor commissioner's decision seemed intuitively improper, the statute that granted him his authority contained what appeared to be a grant of arbitrary power. Specifically, it stated that "the Commission may cancel any permit at its discretion." In the most famous line from the Supreme Court judgment, however, Ivan Rand declared that:

> In public regulation of this sort there is no such thing as absolute and untrammelled "discretion," that is that action can be taken on any ground or for any reason that can be suggested to the mind of the administrator; no legislative Act can, without express language, be taken to contemplate an unlimited arbitrary power exercisable for any purpose, however capricious or irrelevant, regardless of the nature or purpose of the statute. Fraud and corruption in the Commission may not be mentioned in such statutes but they are always implied as exceptions. "Discretion" necessarily implies good faith in discharging public duty; there is always a perspective within which a statute is intended to operate; and any clear departure from its lines or objects is just as objectionable as fraud or corruption. Could an applicant be refused a permit because he had been born in another province, or because of the colour of his hair? the legislature cannot be so distorted.[109]

As with judicial interpretation of the "think fit" formulation, the idea is that the legislature grants discretion for a particular purpose, specific to the act in question. Thus discretion is always implicitly bounded by the purpose it serves, and any particular exercise can be assessed based on whether there are reasonable grounds for thinking that the action serves the purpose. This opens up the exercise of this discretion to judicial review, as the English case *Padfield v. Minister of Agriculture, Fisheries and Food* affirmed: "Parliament must have conferred the discretion with the intention that it should be used to promote the policy and objects of the Act; the policy and objects of the Act must be determined by construing the Act as a whole and construction is always a matter of law for the court."[110]

Thus, courts have had no difficulty reasserting their right to intervene in cases where administrative decisions are irrational, abusive, or arbitrary. At the same time, they have not found any formula to resolve the fundamental dilemma underlying the "standard of review" problem, which stems from the fact that, even though courts have always found clever ways of asserting their authority, they do not have the "institutional competence, capacity, or legitimacy to intervene in any administrative setting as they wish."[111] Where there has been greater convergence is in the insistence that, in cases where the court cannot directly guarantee the rule of law, it can insist that executive decision-making satisfy rule of law constraints, in something like the sense Fuller described.[112] Courts, in other words, instead of acting as guarantors of the rule of law, have taken to outsourcing this obligation to the executive branch.

As Cass Sunstein and Adrian Vermeule have argued, despite the legalistic tradition in the United States, American courts have nevertheless imposed a series of highly Fullerian constraints on executive agencies. For example, while the APA explicitly grants agencies the option of proceeding through rule-making or through case-by-case adjudication, the onerous procedural requirements that govern rule-making exercises generate a perverse incentive for agencies to rely entirely on adjudication.[113] Perhaps the most high-profile example of an agency that rules by adjudication is the Securities and Exchange Commission. The problem with case-by-case adjudication, of course, is that it need not be consistent over time, and so it violates Fuller's most basic constraint, concerning the need for settled rules. Courts, however, have put significant pressure on agencies to make rules. In *Hornsby v. Allen*, for instance, another case involving liquor licenses, an applicant who had been refused a license in Atlanta complained that there was no ascertainable basis on which decisions were being made. The court held that the system of discretionary licensing violated the due-process clause of the US Constitution.[114] In other cases, agencies have been chastised for applying rules retroactively, for failing to follow their own rules, or for acting in ways that made it difficult to anticipate the decisions they would make. What is significant is that, in each case, the courts did not set *themselves* up as the guarantor of the rule of law, but rather insisted that the executive branch develop the competence to conduct itself in a way that embodies respect for those principles.

One can see in these developments increasing acknowledgment that the judiciary cannot serve as a custodian of the rule of law, any more than the legislature can. No one doubts that the extraordinary expansion of administrative power over the past century creates the potential for serious abuse, while simultaneously removing many of the checks that had been put in place under the classical liberal arrangement. Legislatures have tried to control this growth in administrative discretion by writing more detailed laws, or by writing laws intended to control the way that discretion is exercised. Courts have at various times tried to control it by imposing limits on discretion or by insisting that the exercise of discretionary power be subject to judicial review. Both strategies have encountered very significant constraints. Generally, the legislature is not in a position to write laws at a level of granularity that would constrain executive discretion in any meaningful way, hence the growth of delegated and secondary legislation. The judiciary lacks the competence and the resources required to exercise effective oversight, hence the abandonment of the "correctness" standard of review. As a result, it has become a significant responsibility of the executive to restrain itself in the way that it exercises power. Since the executive cannot be effectively controlled from the outside, it becomes all the more important to ensure that it control itself from the inside.

6.6. Conclusion

The easiest mistake to make, when thinking about administrative discretion, is to imagine that the alternative to regulation through formal rules is a regime of capricious individual choice. In fact, the alternative to regulation by formal rules is typically regulation by informal rules. In other words, it will not be individual preference but, rather, the workplace *culture* that determines how discretion is exercised. As Zacka has emphasized, the typologies and cognitive schemata used to classify clients, and to determine their subsequent treatment, are not something workers bring with them to the job; rather, they are a product of the workplace.

If there is a problem with that workplace culture, the temptation will often be to address it by squeezing out the culture, imposing more formal rules and regulations. Yet discretion has a way of creeping back in. A better solution in many instances would be to recognize the inevitability of statutory discretion, and to seek instead to reform the informal norms that govern the workplace. This can be extremely difficult to do, but it is often the only effective solution. Part of the difficulty stems from the fact that it can be hard to change informal institutions through formal rules, since people are quite adept at developing work-arounds to any formal system.[115] In many ways the informal culture can only be changed through informal mechanisms.

All of this is important when it comes to thinking about the rule of law. As I have tried to show, the most important institutional "backstop" for the rule of law is the workplace culture of state officials. Admitting this allows us to think more seriously about the use of informal means to promote a rule of law culture, as opposed to trying to squeeze it out through formal rules. For instance, instead of attempting to codify decision procedures and expand the rule book, it is possible instead to create less formal arrangements, through which officials are encouraged to present cases and discuss the basis for decisions made. Similarly, inspectors who might normally work alone can be assigned to teams and given group projects.[116] This encourages not just information sharing, but can also be expected to produce greater consistency in decision-making.

None of these informal measures will be particularly reassuring for those who like to see explicit "checks and balances" in state decision-making. But given that the existing system of checks and balances—those provided by the legislature and the judiciary—are almost completely ineffective, and yet the specter of bureaucratic tyranny has been kept largely at bay, it is important to recognize that self-restraint on the part of the executive is currently the most important guarantor of the rule of law, and there is nothing naive or implausible about the suggestion that explicit initiatives be undertaken to strengthen it.

7

Paternalism and Individual Freedom

The growth of the welfare state has not been greeted by everyone as an unmixed blessing; on the contrary, its expansion has been accompanied at every stage by an ongoing chorus of resistance and anxiety. There are numerous grounds for this, but one constant refrain has been the concern that the state is directly curtailing, or else just crowding out, human freedom and individual rights. Ludwig von Mises's *Man and State* and Friedrich Hayek's *The Road to Serfdom* forcefully articulated this critique, and, of course, a great deal of conservative politics has been animated by opposition to "big government" and the "nanny state." In certain respects, the encroachments that served as the focal point of anxiety were a natural consequence of the ways that a normative commitment to welfarism interacted with the broader trajectory of economic development. In the early stages of economic liberalization, there were enormous welfare gains to be had from instituting just the three neutral goods of classical liberalism (security, property, and contract), since these provided the foundation for the development of a market economy, which, in turn, became a remarkably effective mechanism for satisfying the basic material needs of the population (for food, clothing, shelter, transportation, etc.) At this stage, there was little obvious tension between the commitment to Pareto efficiency and respect for individual rights and freedoms—on the contrary, many people saw them as necessarily aligned.[1] Only much later, when the consumption of material goods became subject to more sharply diminishing returns, did other collective action problems begin to loom large, and the appetite for state curtailment of individual freedoms (or at least the freedom to free ride) begin to grow. Negative externalities that had once been ignored, such as various forms of pollution, began to register as serious impairments to quality of life. Risks that had been accepted with resignation became a source of increased anxiety and unhappiness. And, of course, life expectancy increased dramatically, giving rise to significant changes in the organization of consumption over time. The demand for state action—for regulation, for public goods, for social insurance, and for "horizontal" redistribution—began to grow.

This process is one that, as we have seen, disrupts the sharp distinction, drawn by classical liberalism, between the public and the private spheres. The commitment to limited government begins to change in its formulation, away from a concern over prohibited *domains* of interaction and toward an emphasis on the

The Machinery of Government. Joseph Heath, Oxford University Press (2020). © Oxford University Press.
DOI: 10.1093/oso/9780197509616.001.0001

types of interventions the state can legitimately undertake, or on what the permissible grounds for coercion are. Most conspicuously, the domain of private economic contracting loses its immunity from legislative intervention, leading the state to impose the restrictions on contracting that have become a central feature of modern labor law and workplace and consumer safety regulation, as well as civil rights and anti-discrimination law. The need to implement this legislation contributed, in turn, to the growth of the administrative state, along with its tendency to violate the traditional separation of powers. Accompanying all this has been the development of modern liberal theory, which makes the distinction between public and private, as well as the status of the constitution, much more ambiguous. Individual rights, for instance, which had once been conceived of as circumscribing an inviolable domain, became increasingly reinterpreted as a way of articulating the state's more general commitment to respecting the equality of citizens.[2] This has produced an understandable anxiety about the growth of state power, as many of the bulwarks established in the 18th and 19th centuries, intended to protect the individual from the abuse of public authority, were circumvented or broken down. The entire set of institutional and intellectual developments has been perceived by many as a turn *away* from liberalism.

Yet there is something paradoxical about the narrative of decline that informs this concern over individual freedom. For if state power expanded dramatically over the course of the 20th century, so, too, did private autonomy. Indeed, the 20th century saw landmark victories that expanded individual freedom, particularly in the domains of speech and publication, sexuality, religious freedom, and cultural expression. Women, as well as racial, ethnic, religious, and sexual minorities, experienced unprecedented gains in the range of options available to them, as well as significantly expanded protections against discrimination, harassment, and abuse. Moreover, an increased social tolerance for difference vastly expanded the scope of what is referred to, somewhat euphemistically, as "lifestyle experimentation." Indeed, acts that were once prohibited as libertinage are now regarded as ordinary exercises of individual liberty. It is not difficult to work out how this happened, since it all occurred in plain view. The most powerful force driving the shift was a reinterpretation, primarily by the courts, of fundamental liberal principles. This change in the way state power is exercised, I have argued, is best understood as involving an evolution of liberal doctrine, rather than as an abandonment of it.

The person whose work most clearly influenced this shift was John Stuart Mill, particularly through his short book *On Liberty*, which can reasonably be credited with having done more to expand the sphere of personal freedom than any other work of liberal philosophy.[3] What is striking about Mill's arguments, however, is that he does not formulate them in terms of social contract theory, constitutional protections, an inviolable system of individual rights, or any of the other tenets of classical liberalism.[4] On the contrary, his argument is reso-lutely welfarist. Although he advocates a defense of individual autonomy against state power, he employs a *normative framework* that recognizes no principled distinction between the private and public domains. His most lasting contri-bution is to have reformulated the liberal conception of individual freedom as an anti-paternalism constraint. Instead of thinking about liberty in terms of a protected personal sphere, on the model of property, he thinks of it in terms of the *justifications* that are available to the state for intervening in a particular domain of interaction, or in terms of individual choice. He argues that such interventions are justifiable when they aim to prevent some harm that one indi-vidual may inflict on another individual; but that they are not justifiable when the aim is merely to prevent the individual from self-inflicted harm or, following the *volenti non fit injuria* principle, when the harm is to another, but consensual. This represents a significant departure from the classical liberal way of thinking about the issue, yet it has in many ways been more effective in expanding the sphere of individual liberty.

There is, however, a growing tension surrounding the constraint on paternal-istic legislation that emerged so forcefully from Mill's work. Part of this is due to the very success of the welfare state at resolving collective action problems. Mill's framework invites us to imagine the sum total of human misery as di-vided into two types: that which individuals inflict upon one another, and that which they inflict upon themselves. Throughout most of human history, the former has loomed larger. Given the way that people can get trapped in collec-tive action problems, there has seldom been any shortage of misery caused by individuals acting in a way that impose costs on their neighbors. By contrast, the various perversities of human nature that lead people to destroy their own happiness have been of relatively scant importance. Yet over time, the modern state's relentless focus on efficiency, along with more effective enforcement of the solutions developed, has led to a significant decline in the amount of misery that can plausibly be blamed on the actions of others. As a result, a great deal of the misery that one sees outstanding is of the self-inflicted variety. Furthermore, the social environment has changed in ways that have exacerbated many of these problems, by providing individuals with a greater range of opportuni-ties for self-destructive behavior—the proliferation and widespread availability of highly addictive drugs is the most obvious example. Thus many states find themselves "spending" millions of dollars in the area of health and safety or en-vironmental regulation to eliminate almost infinitesimally small cancer risks, but stand idly by as individuals smoke tobacco, barbecue their food, and eat cured meats, all of which are associated with cancer risks that are, by compar-ison, quite enormous.

This has generated an understandable pressure to revisit the question of paternalism and perhaps to chip away at some of the restrictions that had traditionally restrained the state from interfering in the realm of individual choice. Nowhere has this been more evident than in the enormous impact that Richard Thaler and Cass Sunstein's book *Nudge* has had in public policy circles.[5] With their concept of "libertarian paternalism," Thaler and Sunstein claimed to be offering a way to correct many of the poor choices that people make in such areas as health, safety, diet, and personal finance without violating the traditional Millian prohibition on state paternalism. At the same time, the reception of their work has revealed troubling weaknesses in the general level of understanding of the issue of paternalism in policy circles. Many readers of *Nudge* seemed not to realize that there is even a prima facie problem with state paternalism, and therefore missed the significance of Thaler and Sunstein's contribution. This is worrisome. Just as with the rule of law, the most important safeguard of individual liberty in a modern welfare state is the commitment, on the part of public servants, to respect the autonomy of citizens. And yet there is considerable unevenness, across the executive branch, in the depth and sophistication of the appreciation of these issues. Areas that touch upon criminal justice have perhaps the highest sensitivity to the issue. At the other extreme is the field of public health, where policy advocates often appear entirely oblivious to the idea that there are any problems with the paternalistic use of state power.

My goal, in the discussion that follows, is partially reconstructive but much more normative than in previous chapters. As the conceptual muddle that developed in the wake of *Nudge* showed, there is a great deal of confusion in the public service on the subject of paternalism. Thus I begin by reviewing Mill's influential case against paternalism, putting special emphasis on its reliance on the normative framework of modern liberalism—the commitment to state neutrality in particular—to justify his major claims. Of course, though Mill's argument may be quite modern, the strict prohibition that he imposes on state paternalism has a very 19th-century quality, particularly in the hardness of heart he exhibits in the face of certain forms of human suffering. With respect to alcohol consumption, for instance, Mill took the strict line that it was simply none of the state's business if individuals chose to destroy their lives, and abandon their dependents, through alcoholism. Even though Mill's basic arguments remain quite compelling, there is much less tolerance in the modern era for the policy lessons that he drew. I will therefore examine the various attempts to chip away at Mill's strict prohibition. Unlike the *Nudge* literature, which tends to group them all together in an unhelpful way, I will attempt to provide a more systematic catalog of different strategies that have been proposed.

7.1. Mill's argument

In 1968 the Government of Canada initiated a series of "liberalizing" reforms of the criminal code, which included decriminalizing both homosexuality and the use of contraceptives. The minister of justice at the time, Pierre Trudeau, justified the changes with the memorable assertion that "the state has no business in the bedrooms of the nation." This may have been a masterful piece of political rhetoric, but it is not a satisfactory statement of the normative principles that motivated the reforms. The 1965 *Griswold v. Connecticut* decision, which initiated the legalization of contraceptives in the United States, on the grounds that there is a right to privacy implicit in the Constitution, is misleading in a similar way. Both suggested that there is some spatial or territorial domain in which the individual reigns supreme and is, therefore, to be protected from state interference. Yet states that adopted a more permissive attitude toward consensual sexual relations also began to take a less permissive attitude toward non-consensual relations. The criminalization of marital rape, as well as heightened concern over the sexual abuse of children, obviously involved the state taking an interest in what happens "in the bedrooms of the nation," and it would be futile to appeal to one's right to privacy as a defense against prosecution for one of these offenses. So, what is the difference?

The most obvious way to draw the distinction, one might think, would be to say that the latter crimes involve a *harm* to some other person, while the former do not. This was not, however, the prevailing opinion at the time that liberalization began.[6] Most people believed that homosexual relations, as a matter of fact, involved a harm, both to the self and to one's partner. This was implicit in the widespread belief that homosexuality was sinful. Yet people also entered into homosexual relations voluntarily, which suggested that the parties involved did not regard the harm as a genuine one, or else thought that it was outweighed by some other good. What changed, over the course of the initial liberalizing process, was not the public assessment of the actions, but rather the willingness, on the part of the majority, to assert the superiority of its own assessment in such cases of disagreement. As Mill observed, the fact that a person chooses something provides strong pro tanto grounds for believing that the thing is good for that person.[7] This creates a difficulty for anyone who wants to claim that someone else is engaged in an act of self-harm. On the one hand, it is possible that this other person is making a mistake, and that the act really is not good for her. On the other hand, it is possible that she knows exactly what she is doing, and that she merely *disagrees* with the observer about where her own good lies, and thus about what constitutes a "harm." To want to interfere with the action, much less coercively impose an alternative, one must have reason to think that the first case is, at very least, more likely than the second.

This analysis is at the heart of Mill's argument against what has come to be known as paternalistic legislation. Roughly speaking, a law is paternalistic if the justification for it, when addressed to those who are constrained by it, contains some variant of the claim "it's for your own good."[8] More specifically, since law is a coercively imposed rule, a paternalistic law is one that coerces or punishes an individual to stop that person from harming himself, or from acting in a way that is somehow contrary to his own interests. Mill claims that this legislative objective is illegitimate: "[T]he only purpose for which power can be rightfully exercised over any member of a civilized community, against his will, is to prevent harm to others. His own good, either physical or moral, is not a sufficient warrant."[9] Note that *parents* often impose rules on their children "for their own good." The question is whether the *state* could be justified in imposing these rules on adult members of the community. There are, of course, many cases in which the state does impose paternalistic rules, such as the law that compels individuals to wear seatbelts when traveling in an automobile. But it is not difficult to see that there is something at least peculiar about these laws. If the prohibited action is contrary to the individual's own interests, then it would not appear necessary to threaten or punish that person to get him to stop. Because it is, by hypothesis, in his self-interest to act in the appropriate way, the law appears to be superfluous (and the coercion gratuitous). Legal regulation would only make sense if the individual is for some reason unable to recognize where his own interests lie, or is unable to act on them. Although this is not a common state of affairs, there are no doubt circumstances in which it does arise, and so one can imagine conditions under which a paternalistic law would be justified. Mill's argument shows only that there is something peculiar about these laws, such that a more complex set of conditions must be satisfied for them to be justified.

Another way of thinking about the issue is to note that in cases of putative harm, we normally leave it up to the person who is being harmed to determine what counts as a harm. For instance, if my music is too loud and my neighbor makes a noise complaint to the police, I cannot defend my actions by insisting that it is "great music" and that I am helping my neighbor to cultivate a higher aesthetic sensibility. The fact that my neighbor finds it unpleasant is sufficient to settle the question of whether it counts as a harm. Yet in the case of a paternalistic law, in which the purpose is to stop me from harming myself, it would seem that the presumption should lie with me, as the person suffering the putative harm, to determine what counts as a harm. Yet in this case, the fact that I am doing it provides strong grounds for thinking that I do *not* regard it as a harm— otherwise I would not be doing it. Thus the justification for a paternalistic law must necessarily meet a higher threshold, because of the need to show that those governed by it are making a mistake about their own interests, as opposed to just disagreeing with those who have crafted the law. Mill claimed that this higher threshold of justification will seldom be met—sufficiently so that, for all practical purposes, it can be ignored and a general prohibition on paternalistic state intervention enacted. He offered three arguments to support this conclusion: the epistemic, the agency, and the autonomy arguments.

7.1.1. The epistemic argument

The most obvious problem with the justification for a paternalistic regulation is that for the state to have a better sense than the individual does, of where that person's best interests lie, state officials would have to be in some sort of an epistemically privileged position.[10] Yet far from this being the case, it would seem to be the individual who is best positioned to know where his own good lies. Most people spend a great deal of time, in one way or another, trying to make themselves happy, and as a result they have considerable experience in the task. How likely is it that a state official can come along and make a superior judgment? Obviously, people make mistakes when it comes to advancing their own interests. But the suggestion that this could be improved by substituting someone else's judgment seems highly improbable, since other people are at least as likely to be mistaken, and probably more so. For example, everyone has no doubt had the experience of buying something, only to decide later that the purchase was a mistake. Compare this to the number of times one has received a gift that is tasteless, inappropriate, useless, or positively insulting. Considering how much family and friends may have struggled to find a gift that caters to one's taste or needs should provide a good sense of how little capacity state officials have to make the same determination.

Furthermore, in cases in which outside observers do disagree with individuals about where their best interests lie, though it is always possible that the observers have uncovered an error, there is another quite plausible explanation, which is that the disagreement is merely a symptom of an underlying value pluralism.[11] In other words, when the observer says something like "you should do x, because it is good for you," the claim that "x is good for you" may actually reflect an evaluative judgment being made by the observer, which the person addressed does not share, and possibly even rejects. For example, with respect to sexual desire, the traditional Christian view was that one ought to experience and act only on desires that are conducive to the satisfaction of the divine purpose, which is procreation. Using one's body in a manner contrary to God's intention, according to this view, is degrading and abusive (indeed, one traditional term for masturbation is "self-abuse"). This judgment underlies the impulse to prohibit non-procreative forms of sexuality.[12] Other people reject this judgment. Those who take the initial evaluative judgment seriously will always be inclined to say that those who reject it are mistaken; however, it is difficult to say how this mistake might have arisen, much less to imagine circumstances under which those making it might come to adopt a more 'enlightened' stance. Furthermore, the force of the evaluative judgment is likely to bias cognition quite significantly, leading the observer to overlook the possibility of reasonable disagreement.

Mill's view is that basic questions about the nature of the good life, and therefore about what we should desire, are very difficult to decide, and that what is right for one person is not necessarily right for another. Thus he calls for "experiments in living," and social tolerance of such experiments, to improve the chances of finding the right answer (or answers).[13] A great deal of paternalistic legislation, he suggests, is based on a failure to adopt the appropriate level of humility when approaching these questions. As a result, when an observer wants to prevent another person from engaging in a putatively self-destructive action, it is more likely that the observer is making the mistake—by failing to recognize the circumstances of reasonable disagreement—than that the other person is failing to recognize where his own best interests lie.[14]

7.1.2. The agency argument

One of the reasons that individuals are usually better at figuring out where their own interests lie, compared to strangers, is that they have a great deal more at stake in the question. After all, they are the ones who bear the cost of a failure to answer the question correctly. It is important not to assume that the state is a benevolent guardian that can be counted on to act either dispassionately or altruistically. The state is made up of people, just like any other large organization. For a third party to make a better judgment than the individual agent, not only must she be in an epistemically privileged position, but she must also be motivated to *care* about that individual's interests. Yet it is difficult to find any circumstances under which anyone cares about anyone else's interests as much as people care about their *own* interests.[15] This is important for not only the formulation, but also the execution of policy. Because individuals are the ones principally affected by the outcomes of their actions, they are likely to take much greater care in executing plans to bring about those outcomes.

With a paternalistic intervention, not only is the state substituting its own judgment for that of the individual when it comes to determining the appropriateness of some outcome, but because the individual rejects that outcome, the state will often have to employ its own agents to bring it about. The attractive thing about letting individuals pursue their own conception of the good is that they can be relied on to exercise a reasonable degree of diligence, not just in formulating their ends, but also in bringing them about. If one seeks to impose some other conception of the good, then the individual can no longer be relied upon to seek it, and so the state's agent will have to pursue that conception *for* the individual. This sort of agency relation, as we have seen, is fraught with moral hazard. Even if the state is right about where the individual's best interests lie, if agents of the state fail to act diligently to advance that interest, the costs are borne primarily by the individual, not the agent. It may therefore be better on the whole to let an individual engage in the diligent pursuit of an imperfect conception of the good than to try to impose on her a better conception of the good, carried out by a sloppy and uninterested state official (or one who occasionally goes on strike).

This is an extremely important point, one that again encourages a certain modesty about the ability of the state to improve people's lives. It is not difficult to find people who are doing a poor job at caring for themselves. Yet caring for *others* is not something that state officials are particularly good at doing either. One of the reasons, for instance, the child welfare services routinely leave children in conditions of severe deprivation is that for it to be in the "best interests of the child" to be removed from the home, the state must be able to provide an environment that is better. State institutions, however, such as orphanages, are generally terrible for children, in part because salaried employees working on shifts make very poor substitutes for parents. As a result, when children are removed from an abusive home, considerable effort is usually made to place them in a foster home rather than a state institution. The point is that, as child welfare services generally recognize, objectively bad parenting often produces better outcomes than more enlightened child-rearing practices executed by bureaucratic organizations. This is an *agency problem*—the state is simply not able to carry through on its good intentions, because it has to rely on employees who will never care as much about outcomes as do the actual individuals whose happiness is at stake.

7.1.3. The autonomy argument

Finally, Mill observes that, for most people, the power to formulate and pursue one's own conception of the good life is part and parcel of that very conception. Substituting someone else's conception will typically produce less value for the person on whom it is imposed, precisely because it is the conception of *someone else*. As Mill puts it (perhaps hyperbolically), for the individual agent, "all errors which he is likely to commit against advice and warning are far outweighed by the evil of allowing others to constrain him to what they deem his good."[16] In some cases, this "outweighing" involves a measure of petulance or grumpiness, which can be expected to fade away in time; but in other cases, there is something almost completely self-defeating in the attempt to impose a putatively correct conception of the good upon others. This is a particularly important observation in the case of religious observance, since most religions provide a great deal of guidance about the correct way to live, along with various encouragements to "enlighten" others about where their true interests lie. Yet forcible religious conversion has proven almost completely ineffective at reorienting individuals toward these higher goods. Coercively imposed atheism has also proven surprisingly ineffective at extinguishing the religious sensibility. As a result, a good case can be made for non-interference by the state in matters of conscience simply because of the way that commitments in this domain are valued for being self-chosen.

7.1.4. Additional observations

It is important to note that all three of these arguments rely on empirical generalizations. Thus, they do not rule out paternalistic legislation in principle, they merely claim that the conditions under which state paternalism will be able to improve people's lives will almost never be met. Since Mill's time, some philosophers have made the more radical claim that paternalism is wrong in principle, such that even *successful* paternalistic interventions are prohibited. This has generated a significant body of literature, most of it of limited relevance to policy, because it is tied to controversial comprehensive moral views.[17] Mill's argument, by contrast, focuses specifically on the political question of whether state officials should have the power to coerce citizens on the grounds that it is "for their own good." Of course, certain aspects of Mill's argument rely on his own comprehensive moral view (i.e., preference-based utilitarianism). However, his argument can easily be transposed onto the framework of modern liberalism.

From a policy perspective, the central problem with paternalistic state intervention is that it is a prima facie violation of liberal neutrality. Paternalism, by its very nature, seems to involve the state "taking sides" in a conflict over different conceptions of the good. If one person is doing x, we can safely presume that she thinks x is good.[18] If someone else comes along and wants to stop her, on the grounds that x is not really in her "best interests," but says that some other action y, would be better for her, then we are facing a situation of disagreement. There is nothing wrong with the second person making the *moral* judgment that "you ought to do y." (Although some philosophers do object to moral paternalism, this seems like an obvious instance of the migration of ideas from the political to the moral sphere, described in chapter 3.[19]) Problems arise only when the second person tries to use state power to force the first to do y. Here the state, faced with two different opinions about where the good lies—in x or y—is clearly "taking sides" by choosing to impose y. Thus, the law cannot be justified without reference to the correctness of the view that y constitutes the good. By contrast, refraining from intervention requires no such judgment. While such restraint results in the person doing x, rather than y, the justification for the state's position is simply that individuals should be left free to make these decisions by themselves. Thus, deferring to the individual's judgment does not involve any commitment with respect to the substantive merits of the goods under dispute, in the way that overriding the individual's judgment does.

Another way of thinking about the violation of neutrality involved in paternalistic legislation is to observe that it takes the individual being targeted outside the "feasible set." In other words, if one thinks that state institutions are fundamentally concerned with promoting cooperation, one must recognize that paternalistic interventions as such are not aimed at producing mutual benefit. Cooperation makes each individual better off from his or her own perspective. While paternalistic intervention may make one person better off from someone else's perspective, it does not make her better off from her *own* perspective. Thus it can be seen as violating the abstract "liberty" constraint that is one of the basic principles of modern liberalism.

Finally, it is worth emphasizing that the problem with paternalism is fundamentally about the proper use of state power, or the justification for coercive intervention. This, however, is not always how Mill expresses the point in *On Liberty*, where he is concerned not only about state coercion, but also the social regulation of behavior. He was, in other words, concerned as well about the tyranny of public opinion and the uses of informal social censure. Yet while most commentators note this aspect of his argument, it is seldom taken very seriously. After all, people are free to subscribe to perfectionist values in their private lives, and to express those values in various ways, including denouncing those who do not share them. This may be a problem, in some sense of the term, but it is not as serious a problem as when the state begins to draw invidious distinctions between citizens, and to sanction them for the values to which they subscribe.

The point about coercion is important, because it reveals a final weakness in the argument for paternalistic intervention. To make the case for interference, the observer must show that the individual targeted is making some sort of mistake. If this were genuinely the situation, it is difficult to see why one must jump so quickly to the use of coercion as a way to remedy the problem.[20] If the underlying problem involved a conflict of values, then it would not be surprising to find that coercion was required to change that person's behavior. But if the problem is simply that the person is making a mistake, then there would appear to be less drastic remedies available. One could, for example, provide the person with more information, to help him recognize where his best interests lie. Or, if the problem is that the person is not thinking clearly, then one could give him a "cooling off" period, so that he can gather his thoughts. This may involve some coercion—one might be obliged to forcibly restrain the person to provide the needed information or delay—but one would still leave the final decision up to that person.

Based on this line of thinking, Joel Feinberg drew the influential distinction between "soft" and "hard" paternalism.[21] Both involve interfering with the individual's choice, but the former is aimed only at ensuring that the conditions of informed, rational agency are fulfilled. The latter, by contrast, involves changing the incentives that lead to the ultimate choice. The classic example of "soft" paternalism, given by Mill, is that of waylaying a person who is trying to cross a damaged bridge. This is justifiable, he argues, if the intention is merely to warn him of the danger. But if the person, having been adequately warned, decides to press on, then one should not interfere, since "no one but the person himself can judge the sufficiency of the motive which may prompt him to incur the risk."[22] Thus Mill is willing to entertain the possibility of beneficial "soft" paternalism but not "hard" paternalism. This distinction has subsequently become the object of considerable controversy, in part because many contemporary philosophers have sought to expand the class of "soft" interventions, as a way of avoiding some of the harsher judgments that Mill's Victorian morality led him to make.[23] I mention it here only to note that proponents of "hard" paternalist interventions (e.g., fines) have an additional, sometimes overlooked burden, of explaining why a "soft" intervention (e.g., education) is insufficient.

7.2. Bureaucratic paternalism

Mill's primary goal was to persuade elected officials to refrain from enacting paternalistic legislation. In this respect, his arguments achieved only moderate success. Where they found a more receptive audience was with the judiciary. American courts were quite aggressive throughout the 20th century in striking down legislation that interfered unduly with the "liberty" of subjects. They initially did this through appeal to freedom of contract (such as the 1905 *Lochner v. New York* decision that declared a law limiting the work hours of bakery workers unconstitutional, on the grounds that they were not "wards of the state"). After *Griswold v. Connecticut*, the constitutional arguments relied more heavily on the newly discovered right to privacy, and the cases were focused on the decriminalization of consensual sexual behavior (and, more controversially, abortion). This history of judicial activism has led many people to assume that the courts are the most important bulwark against overly intrusive regulation of private affairs. Yet, just as in the case of the rule of law, the role the executive plays, and the level of restraint it exhibits, when it comes to interferences in the private lives and decisions of individuals, is far more consequential for the average citizen. Increasingly, the problem of paternalism is less concerned with the content of the laws than with the ways they are enforced.

First, and most obviously, paternalistic laws are of little concern if the executive chooses not to enforce them. This is, in fact, a surprisingly common arrangement, especially when there are paternalistic laws on the books that are widely considered problematic, but legislators do not want to go on record as favoring repeal because of the risk that this will be portrayed as endorsement of the behavior in question. More generally, the police are always and everywhere subject to resource constraints that make it difficult to engage in much proactive law enforcement. As a result, they tend to be highly reactive—their interventions are almost always responses to citizen complaints. In the case of genuinely paternalistic legislation, there are seldom any complaints to respond to, because the people "harmed" by the actions have either consented or else are the same as those who are perpetrating them. Thus, it is quite easy for the police to ignore violations of these laws, so long as the perpetrators are "not bothering anyone." In the United States, this is the status quo in states in which various forms of consensual sexual activity—including adultery—are still criminalized but the laws are not enforced. Similarly, laws prohibiting possession of "soft" drugs in small quantities are not enforced in many European states—the police may seize the drugs but will often not press charges. Laws against polygamy are also seldom enforced unless there are minors involved.

On the other hand, the police enjoy substantial discretion, which they often use, to enforce conceptions of the good that are in no way embodied in any statute or rule. As Mary Baumgartner and others have observed, the police tend to be far more concerned about crimes committed against "respectable" or "upstanding" members of the community.[24] In general, individuals who are engaged in a form of social deviance are at risk of being held responsible for their own victimization, and therefore benefit less from police protection. Through this mechanism, the police are essentially enforcing a set of social norms that have no statutory authority, and that may be highly intrusive with respect to individual conceptions of the good. Thus, the police preoccupation with maintaining social order can easily translate into a coercive imposition of paternalistic rules.

The police are not alone in this; other segments of the welfare and regulatory bureaucracy can be far more intrusive, because of the proactive character of their enforcement regimes. Promoting "health" or "safety" is not intrinsically paternalistic, but unless executive agencies exercise substantial self-restraint, these goals can easily be used to justify paternalistic measures. Legitimate food safety regulation, for instance, can shade over into illegitimate dietary interference. Given the amount of power and discretion of food safety inspectors (both at the production and retail levels), it is important that they maintain an institutional culture that is appropriately deferential to the choices made by consumers. There are, for instance, important cultural differences in the way that food is handled and prepared (including which foods are eaten raw and which are cooked; which animals, or parts of them, are eaten; where the line is drawn between "fermented" and "rotten," and so forth). Traditional Western practices tolerate certain trade-offs between safety and flavor (such as the use of unpasteurized milk in various cheeses, or raw egg yolk in salad dressing). Thus, one cannot treat food safety as an overriding priority, and so it is important that officials be open to the possibility that different people will evaluate these trade-offs in different ways.

There are, unfortunately, many examples of food safety regulation run amok. To take one small-scale example, consider the case of the City of Toronto's unfortunate A La Cart street-food program.[25] As in many first-world countries, the quality of urban life in Canada is significantly impaired by the unavailability of street vendors and "food carts." This is not due to the climate but to food safety regulations, which prohibit the sale of food prepared outside of licensed restaurants (with regularly inspected kitchens). Several decades ago, a group of East European immigrants achieved a partial reprieve from these regulations, obtaining permission to sell hot dogs from food carts, on the grounds that because the sausages were pre-cooked, they carried very little risk of food-borne illness. As a result, a strange arrangement prevailed in which only one food item could be purchased from street vendors—namely, hot dogs. As the years passed, other immigrants, particularly ones from countries with strong street-food cultures, protested this arrangement, until the municipal government finally relented, and agreed to license a small number of food carts as a pilot project. Unfortunately, elected officials passed control of the project to Toronto Public Health, which proceeded to bury it under a mass of bureaucratic regulations so absurd that it would have been comedic, had they not also appropriated the savings and destroyed the livelihood of all the unfortunate immigrants who chose to participate in the program.

It took public health officials very little time to decide that vendors could not be allowed to use their own carts to sell the food because without standardization, it would be impossible to have a uniform safety code. They struck a committee to come up with a design for the carts, which would then be custom manufactured and leased to the vendors. The committee, which included representatives of the departments of health, fire prevention, licensing and economic development (but none of the vendors) wound up producing a seventy-five-page list of specifications.[26] The carts, when manufactured, weighed 360 kilograms, cost over $30,000, and more importantly, were too large to be towed (a spokesperson for the department specified that these rules were developed "to minimize the public risk of foodborne illness and maximize fire safety, while also ensuring a durable, high-quality, easy-to-clean cart"[27]). Not finished yet, public health officials became concerned that the food being sold would be insufficiently healthy, and so, beyond requiring that all ingredients be locally sourced and sustainably produced, it also decreed that all menu items, and all subsequent changes in menus or ingredients, had to be approved by a new committee. Vendors were required to demonstrate the preparation of all proposed foods before the committee, which then imposed changes in the ingredients and cooking methods. Predictably, the committee chose to reduce the fat and salt content of most of the menu items. And in a final, entirely gratuitous flourish, the department decided to prohibit vendors from posting any pictures of the menu items, for the aesthetic reason that they did not want the uniform "look" of the carts disrupted. Predictably, all the vendors either abandoned the program or went bankrupt within a few years.

What is striking about this episode is that almost all of these regulatory encumbrances were paternalistic. City officials could have done what practically every other country in the world does, which is to let customers decide for themselves whether or not a food cart looks clean enough to order from. Unlike in a kitchen restaurant, which is typically out of sight, a street vendor's food is both stored and prepared in front of the customer. Similarly, in terms of whether the ingredients are "locally sourced" or sustainably produced, this is a decision normally left up to the vendor. The idea that administrative officials should be able to veto any menu item or ingredient is highly intrusive, to put it mildly. It is a clear symptom of an organizational culture that does not respect individual autonomy. (It is worth emphasizing, again, that this was done at the administrative level, not by elected officials.) More generally, it shows that, regardless of more abstract questions of political ideology, it is important not to be naive about the danger posed to personal freedom by well-meaning bureaucrats. People of good will are perfectly capable of destroying other people's happiness out of a misguided concern for their welfare (e.g., by treating "safety" or "health" as overriding values).

It is important also to be alert to the subtle forms that paternalism can take. State coercion is often described in terms of hard limitations imposed on individual freedom—as though individuals are literally being denied options that would otherwise have been available to them. In practice, however, what state coercion usually amounts to is merely a change in the incentives that the agent is facing. We may describe a "no parking" sign as prohibiting the individual from parking at a particular location, but the prohibition does not literally prevent anyone from parking there, it just imposes certain consequences, such as a fine, on those who defy the instruction. Naturally, a fine is not the same thing as a price, in that it has a certain deontic significance, such that one is not supposed to treat it as merely the cost of engaging in a particular behavior. It remains the case, however, that what the state is ultimately doing, when it prohibits parking at a certain location, is changing the incentives in such a way as to discourage people from parking there. This is nevertheless an exercise in coercion, since the only reason the state can change the incentives in this way is because of its powers of compulsion.

It follows from this that when the state changes the conditions of individual choice in a way that involves the manipulation of incentives, but has no deontic significance, it remains just as coercive, and therefore carries the same justificatory burden as when the state "prohibits" something. Thus, for example, the various "sin taxes" that are imposed on tobacco products and alcohol must also be classified as coercive, even though they only raise the price of these items, rather than prohibiting their sale.[28] The same goes for cases in which the state chooses to subsidize certain goods, such as symphony orchestras, to encourage individuals to choose them. While this generates less resistance from consumers, the subsidy is paid from tax revenue, which is coercively obtained. Thus, the subsidy represents a forced transfer from one individual to another—and must therefore be justified as an exercise of state power.

Mill's argument is therefore best understood as imposing a prohibition on state *interference* in a certain class of choices. A policy need not deprive people of their liberty entirely to count as paternalistic. Any change in the incentives that they face—most obviously, the economic incentives—generates the justificatory burden that paternalistic policies then struggle to discharge. Seen from this broader perspective, it is easy to understand how the administrative state poses a serious threat to individual liberty. Because of its outsized economic role, the state winds up intruding in almost every aspect of everyday life. Simply by imposing conditions on access to its services—especially its insurance products—the state can exercise enormous power over the lives of its citizens. The temptation to use this economic power, and the leverage it provides, to advance the "real" interests of citizens, as opposed to merely deferring to their "expressed" interests, can become overwhelming for public officials committed to promoting the general good.

The example of the food carts in Toronto is a relatively minor one, but it is not difficult to find more consequential examples. One issue that has become politically controversial in recent years involves the implicitly paternalistic structure of pharmaceutical regulation. Most states exercise "gatekeeping" authority over new pharmaceuticals, which means that drugs cannot be sold until they have received regulatory approval. The structure of this regulatory regime is precautionary, in that it puts the burden of proof on pharmaceutical companies to prove that their compounds are safe before going to market. Many other regulatory regimes operate in the reverse manner, in that they allow anything to be sold, requiring only that products be withdrawn from the market if they turn out to be unsafe. As Daniel Carpenter has shown, in the case of the FDA in the United States, this gatekeeping authority was not created by statute, but developed administratively.[29] As he puts it, "The bureaucratic regulation of pharmaceuticals arrived not starkly in the form of new laws, nor in scientific and medical upheavals, but continuously, haltingly, and ambiguously in regulatory practice."[30] The set of procedures that must be followed is not set out in law, but rather by the New Drug Application (NDA) form, which is by far the most important regulatory instrument in this domain. This form has the force of law, without actually being a law.

There is no doubt a great deal that can be said in favor of this arrangement, given the susceptibility of the public to chicanery in this domain. (As we will see, there are cases in which the burden of proof imposed by Mill's epistemic argument can easily be discharged. Situations in which ordinary citizens must assess complex scientific evidence, under the pressure of both confirmation and optimism bias, are obviously not ideal for the exercise of individual autonomy.) At the same time, there are situations in which individuals might rationally choose to ignore concerns over safety and efficacy. The case of individuals suffering from terminal diseases who have exhausted all other treatment options, and so would like access to unproven therapies, is a particularly compelling one. Thus the FDA has historically allowed exceptions to its gatekeeping principles, under an "expanded use" (or "compassionate use") program, which gave terminally ill patients access to drugs that were undergoing clinical trial, but not yet approved for general use. Several libertarian organizations, however, were unsatisfied with this arrangement, and they succeeded in passing the Right to Try Act in 2017, which attempted to cut the FDA out of the process, by allowing terminally ill patients to purchase drugs that had passed Phase I trial directly from pharmaceutical companies. Despite the intention of the statute, however, the FDA remained deeply involved in the process, because pharmaceutical companies have very little incentive to deal directly with these individuals, especially if doing so would jeopardize their ongoing clinical trials. In practice, "right to try" wound up differing very little from the preexisting "expanded use" program.

More generally, the episode shows that if the administrative agencies of the state are committed to paternalism—as the FDA no doubt is—it can be very difficult for the legislature to do anything about it, because politicians are not the ones actually interacting with the public, or overseeing the corporations involved. The reverse is true as well. If state officials are happy providing citizens with all the rope they need to hang themselves, then it can be extremely difficult to persuade them to feel any concern about the outcome of their actions. Thus the issue of paternalism, or of distinguishing admissible from inadmissible forms of paternalism, is, first and foremost, a challenge for the state bureaucracy. This is why the primary audience for Thaler and Sunstein's *Nudge* book was neither legislators nor judges, but mid-level bureaucrats—those charged with implementing state policies. Thaler and Sunstein's key examples of their nudge policies at work—involving the design of the energy-efficiency stickers used on appliances, the default options on a website for applicants to a drug benefit program, the arrangement of items in a cafeteria—are at much too fine a level of granularity to be decided by either legislatures or courts. One can see woven through these examples the myriad ways in which bureaucratic paternalism has become a far more pressing issue than legislative paternalism.

7.3. The Harm Principle

It will often be the case that the justification for a state action is overdetermined, in the sense that there is more than one argument that can be given for it. For example, social insurance schemes typically resolve a market failure, and therefore promote efficiency, but they also have the agreeable side effect of reducing economic inequality. One could provide an egalitarian rationale for them, although such an argument would typically be more controversial than the efficiency argument, not to mention that it would fail to provide an adequate normative model of such programs. Similarly, mandatory public pension schemes have the desirable effect of rescuing many individuals from self-harm, or from their own improvidence, since a substantial fraction of the population, left to its own devices, would fail to set aside any retirement savings. Because state pension systems force all workers to contribute, they have the effect of also ensuring that everyone has at least some retirement savings, thereby eliminating a great deal of misery. Nevertheless, the arrangement can be justified purely on efficiency grounds. Because the inefficiency in the market for life annuities is caused by adverse selection, state pensions achieve significant efficiency gains by forcing everyone to participate. Thus there is no need to rely upon a paternalistic argument to justify the mandatory savings arrangement—and indeed, the system would be organized quite differently if the primary objective had been the paternalistic one of imposing savings on the improvident. The same can be said for health insurance.

It is, of course, possible to abuse this argumentation strategy. For instance, Sunstein once argued that mandatory seat-belt laws are not really paternalistic, but can instead be seen as resolving a collective action problem. When a group of people get into a car, he suggested, they might all want to put on their seat belts, and yet also not want to appear overly nervous or cowardly in front of the others (much less critical of the driver's competence). Thus a situation might arise in which everyone would prefer to wear a seat belt, and yet no one wants to be the only one, or the first one, to strap in, and so everyone settles for the "non-cooperative" outcome of being unbelted. A mandatory seat-belt law, in this case, just forces them all to do what they would rather be doing anyway.[31] It is difficult to know how seriously one is supposed to take this argument, given the obvious problems with it (e.g., most drivers on the road are alone in their cars, and yet are equally subject to the seat-belt regulation). One is inclined to suspect that the collective action problem being posited is just a "fig leaf," being used to rationalize what is an essentially paternalistic policy.

Sunstein's seat-belt argument at least has the merit of being creative. The more common approach to rationalizing paternalistic policies has been to make up some harm to a third party, and then argue that the action is being prohibited, not because of the harm it causes to the person doing it, but as a way to protect others from the harm that it causes. (The claim, in other words, is that the action generates a negative externality. The only difference between this and the collective action argument is that, for an externality to generate inefficiency, it must be reciprocated. A "harm," by contrast, can be unilateral, and yet still provide grounds for prohibition.) For instance, during the intense debates that occurred over the decriminalization of homosexuality in the 20th century, defenders of the status quo often suggested that homosexual conduct produced a number of diffuse harms, such as "eroding the moral fabric of society" or "scandalizing the public conscience."[32] Given how easy it is to imagine harms of this sort as a consequence of any action that one disapproves of, many have concluded that Mill's harm principle is useless. Since almost every action undertaken has *some* effect on other people, Mill's attempt to protect "self-regarding" actions from state interference can easily be defeated, it would appear, simply by denying that there is any such thing.[33]

In particular, because of the way that people react to actions that are immoral, or that violate social norms, Mill's argument runs the risk of collapsing the distinction between the moral and the political. The central principle of limited government is that an action's being considered immoral does not mean that the state can legitimately prohibit it. Yet violations of a social norm typically generate anger and outrage among those who witness the transgression. If the mere fact that observers get upset when they witness the violation of a social norm is allowed to count as a harm against them, then it follows that every norm is, in principle, enforceable by the state.[34] For instance, when young men first began to wear beards in the 1960s, it was considered scandalous by many, and generated paroxysms of outrage. Yet one is inclined to regard questions of personal grooming as essentially self-regarding. It seems problematic to say that a young man growing a beard *harms* his neighbors, merely because the latter disapprove of it to the point of becoming upset.

Mill suggested several different responses to this difficulty, none of them satisfactory, and not all of them compatible with one another. At one point, he claimed that individuals have a core set of protected interests, and that an action counts as harmful only if it impinges on these interests. Elsewhere in the text, he argued that actions only count as harmful if they violate a "distinct and assignable obligation" toward some other person.[35] In other places, he appealed to a more general criterion of utility maximization to assess the overall effects of an interference.[36] The variety of his responses in many ways just reflects the difficulty of the problem. Obviously, we have intuitive criteria for determining what counts as a "harm" to others and what does not, but it turns out to be extremely difficult to provide any precise and defensible specification of these criteria.[37]

There is, however, one important and useful argument that Mill develops, which allows us to flush out certain "fig leaf" definitions of harm. The argument is essentially a reductio, used against those who accept the general prohibition on paternalistic intervention, but want to defend a particular interference using an expansive or overly generous definition of harm. The argument consists in showing that, if a particular effect counted as a legitimate harm, then there would no longer be any actions protected from state interference, and thus the effect of that definition of harm would be to eradicate the sphere of personal liberty completely. Mill used this argument to argue against temperance activists, who wanted to ban all consumption of "strong spirits" on the grounds that drinking violates the "social rights" of others. Alcohol consumption "destroys my primary right of security," the activists claimed, "by constantly creating and stimulating social disorder. It invades my right of equality, by deriving a profit from the creation of a misery, I am taxed to support. It impedes my right to free moral and intellectual development, by surrounding my path with dangers, and by weakening and demoralising society, from which I have a right to claim mutual aid and intercourse."[38] Mill's response to this argument was to observe that this definition of "social right" amounts to "nothing short of this—that it is the absolute social right of every individual that every other individual shall act in every respect exactly as he ought."[39] As a result, "there is no violation of liberty which it would not justify; it acknowledges no right to any freedom whatever."[40]

I refer to this argument as Mill's "death of liberty reductio." It consists in showing that the justification being offered for a particular policy could be used to justify any interference in any area of life. Assuming that one's interlocutor does not reject the principle of limited government, this then provides grounds for thinking that the definition of harm being adopted is too expansive. A more limited version of the argument, equally effective in certain contexts, would consist in showing that, to justify an interference that the advocate happens to support, she is adopting a definition of harm that would also license numerous interferences that she does not support. This again shows that the definition of harm is too expansive.

One can see that "eroding the moral fabric of society" arguments (or "setting a bad example for others") are vulnerable to this reductio. It may well be the case that violating one norm makes it more likely that other people will violate other norms. Some people are therefore tempted to claim that a particular normative violation may count as harmful, even if the action as such harms no one, because the action makes other people more likely to violate other norms, and some of *those* actions may be harmful. It is not difficult to see, however, that this mechanism is so indirect that, if this chain of effects is to count as a harm to others, then there is no contra-normative action that cannot be classified as harmful, and so the argument permits the unlimited laundering of actions from "socially disapproved" to "illegal." For instance, the claim that homosexuality "weakens the family," and therefore should be prohibited, could be used as an argument to support the prohibition of adultery, "swinging," divorce, and so on. Naturally, the argument has no force against someone who does in fact want to prohibit all these things, or who is not troubled to see the sphere of individual liberty eliminated. It is aimed only at those who accept a broadly liberal conception of limited government, and yet want to recommend paternalistic policies in very particular domains.

In contemporary policy debates, the most common form these expansive notions of harm take is in terms of "costs to the healthcare system." Almost any form of foolish or self-destructive behavior will, at some point, generate some demand for healthcare services that otherwise would not have occurred. In states with publicly funded healthcare systems, these costs are eventually borne by the taxpayer, and so it can be claimed that other people are harmed by the individual's actions. Thus it is common to defend particular instances of paternalistic legislation—such as mandatory seat-belt or motorcycle helmet laws, or else prohibitions on smoking—on the grounds that the prohibited behavior produces increased "costs to the healthcare system."

Before even getting to the Millian response to these arguments, it is worth noting that these abstract appeals to cost are usually not serious, because advocates of prohibition seldom look at the *net* costs to society, or even to the healthcare system. Smoking, for instance, is generally thought to produce net benefits to the healthcare system, because it increases the chances of early death from essentially untreatable conditions—that is, heart failure and lung cancer.[41] People who do not die of lung cancer inevitably die of something else, and so for treatment of lung cancer to count as a "cost" to the healthcare system, it would have to cost more than the sum total of healthcare expenditures that would otherwise have been incurred by the individual. The fact that the calculation of costs is so transparently fallacious should raise the suspicion that the argument is merely a fig leaf. The reason no one bothers to point out the inadequacy of the CBA is the tacit understanding that these calculations are not doing much of the work in supporting the policy, since the actual, unstated rationale is the paternalistic concern for the smoker's health.

The Millian objection to the "costs to the healthcare system" argument would be that it opens the door to unlimited state interference in the private lives of individuals. Consider the precedent that would be set, if the state could assert the power to compel motorcycle riders to wear helmets, because of the "cost" to society of the elevated risk of cranial injury among those who do not wear helmets. What other sorts of behavior would the state then have the power to compel? Certain sex acts produce much higher risk of HIV transmission, which in turn generates real costs for the healthcare system—because treatment options are expensive, and people live for a long time in various states of morbidity. Yet most people would hesitate to have the state legally require the use of condoms, or impose a ban on "high risk" sex acts, much less the lifestyles that are highly correlated with repeat performance of such acts. Similarly, we know that diet has a huge impact on future healthcare needs, and yet most people would be loathe to grant the state coercive power to impose healthy eating habits on the population. As a result, most "costs to the healthcare system" arguments in support of paternalistic policies involve cherry-picking of harms, since their proponents would not be willing to accept, as a matter of general principle, the definition of harm that they are implicitly adopting.

More generally, because the welfare state is involved in so many different areas of life, much of which is financed out of general taxation, a great deal of improvident behavior, such as dropping out of school, or having a child without the means to support it, generate "costs to the taxpayer," which in turn risks giving every citizen a claim to have been harmed by it. Treating these harms as a legitimate basis for state coercion would go a long way toward transforming the welfare state into the dystopian nightmare that many conservatives claim it is already. So despite the fact that the definition of harm remains a subject of ongoing controversy, not to mention negotiation, Mill's "death of liberty reductio" does provide a useful way of picking out illegitimate harms, and thus of identifying fig-leaf arguments. It is also of particular importance in an administrative context. Since legislatures and courts have already provided considerable guidance on the question of which harms can license interference (e.g., the definition of "nuisance" in tort law), the primary task within the executive can be understood as one of achieving consistency across policy domains, so that respect for individual autonomy is protected to roughly the same degree in all areas of life, and for all citizens equally.

There is one other fig leaf that should be mentioned, which involves the tendency that can be observed in modern societies to "medicalize" a range of social issues, to bring them under the jurisdiction of public officials. In many cases this is used to rationalize paternalistic policies, not by inventing dubious harms, but by attempting to shift the underlying disagreement about the nature of harm outside the space of reasonable disagreement. The suggestion made is that, whatever other disagreements people may have about the nature of the good life, the importance of health is one thing that everyone can agree upon.[42] Positing this as a consensus value allows one then to treat every issue that may arise in the field of health policy as merely a technical question, and therefore not one in which the state must defer to anyone's private judgment. One can see this most clearly in discussions of addiction, where the "disease model" remains the primary way of framing the issue in policy circles, even though it is a highly contested scientific theory.[43] The advantage to treating substance abuse as a disease, or as a condition that is completely outside the individual's control, lies in the implicit denial that it is a consciously chosen pattern of behavior. This makes it possible to deny that state policy in this area—which in almost all cases involves coercive discouragement of the addictive behavior—is genuinely paternalistic.

This argumentation strategy is no doubt one of the reasons that the field of public health has been a major source of paternalistic policy ideas in recent years. One of the most important advances in the field has involved the discovery and investigation of the various "social determinants of health." Poor health outcomes, it turns out, are associated not only with a lack of timely and effective healthcare, but also with a range of other social ills, such as poverty, low social status, stress, and unemployment. As a result, practitioners in the field have taken their mandate to improve general population health and sought to leverage it, to provide them with the authority to address a wide range of other problems, such as economic inequality, that lie far outside of what has traditionally been considered the field of "health." In many cases this is harmless. For example, if public officials want to treat school bullying as a health problem, on the grounds that it has adverse health impacts, they might stand accused of "expertise imperialism," but other than that there should be no particular objection.[44] After all, bullying is a type of harmful behavior with clearly identifiable victims, the seriousness of which has perhaps been underestimated. Where the medical model becomes more objectionable is when it is expanded into domains that lie beyond the traditional jurisdiction of the liberal state. For example, despite incessant repetition of the phrase, it is important to keep in mind that the "epidemic of obesity" is not actually an epidemic; it is rather the product of the choices made by autonomous adults. No matter how defective these choices may be, they remain choices, and so the state cannot deal with issues involving diet and exercise in the same way that it deals with vaccination or contagious disease. Medicalization, therefore, often serves as a fig leaf, used to conceal the paternalistic rationale for policies. By obscuring the fact that individuals are making choices, it seeks to avoid the justificatory burden that the state takes on when it coercively interferes with these choices.

In fairness, it should be noted that these fig-leaf arguments, although they contain an element of bad faith, are for the most part adopted by people who have the best of intentions. Their goal is the laudable one of helping other people lead happy and productive lives. Problems arise only when they try to use the *coercive power of the state* to achieve those ends. Unfortunately, the temptation to do so has grown over time, in part because the number of opportunities that individuals have to engage in self-destructive behavior has grown significantly since the time that Mill was writing. For example, inadequate planning for the future has always been a major source of self-inflicted misery. However, life expectancy in the United Kingdom in 1859, when Mill published *On Liberty*, was just forty-one years. Since then it has increased to over eighty years. Because of this, "saving for one's retirement" was not something that the average person had to worry about in Mill's time. Yet now, the need to set aside enough to live for fifteen years on average creates an enormous self-control problem for many people. Mill's suggestion that the greatest happiness will be served by leaving individuals alone to make their own decisions in these areas—and then to bear the consequences—seems deeply implausible.

It is helpful to picture the welfare gains that can be produced through public policy as a verdant pasture, ready to be grazed. Mill's harm principle is like a fence that runs through the pasture, dividing it into two halves. On the one side is the realm of "harm to others," which forms the legitimate domain of state intervention. On the other side is "harm to self," which is out of bounds. Initially, it is easy to produce welfare gains on either side of the fence. Yet over time, the "harm to others" side becomes more thoroughly grazed, so that the grass must be nibbled closer to the ground, and large green patches can be found only by carefully hunting for them. Meanwhile, the "harm to self" side has become lush and overgrown. Inevitably, policy entrepreneurs will find themselves gazing longingly over the fence, wishing that they could achieve even a fraction of the welfare gains that are so easily realizable on that side. In some cases, they lose their inhibitions, and try to demolish the fence entirely. (Many do so in brazen disregard of the time-honored principle that one should never tear down a fence without understanding why it was built in the first place.[45]) The more measured response involves, not tearing up Mill's fence but, rather, analyzing its construction, and perhaps seeking to rebuild it slightly, or just to move it over a bit.

This is, I will suggest, the appropriate metaphor for understanding the "nudge" movement in public policy—at least among those who take its "libertarian paternalism" claims seriously. The traditional approach to justifying paternalistic policy has been to invent non-paternalistic rationales for them.[46] For example, since the discovery of the link between cigarette smoking and cancer, most developed countries have enacted fairly successful tobacco control policies. These are self-evidently paternalistic, and yet many of them were defended publicly through appeal to the harmful effects of second-hand tobacco smoke. For the most part these were fig-leaf arguments, not just because the scientific evidence underlying the claims was thin, but because the scope of the damage was never great enough to justify the severity of the imposed restrictions. For example, the prohibition of smoking in bars and restaurants was often justified through reference to the health consequences for employees of exposure to second-hand smoke. Yet if that were the only concern, the issue could have been addressed at much lower cost, and with much less inconvenience to smokers, simply by mandating protective respiratory equipment for wait staff. The fact that this option was never even considered shows that the health benefits to smokers were being included as one of the "benefits" of the policy, even though, strictly speaking, they should not have been.[47]

The new way of thinking, illustrated by the nudge approach, has the advantage of being more forthright—it attempts to provide a direct justification for such policies, without denying their paternalistic character. In its strongest variants, it does so by accepting, and then seeking to discharge, the burden of proof that Mill imposed on the justification of paternalistic interventions. (This is why I was at pains to emphasize, in section 7.1, that Mill's argument does not rule out paternalistic policies in principle, it merely shows how difficult they are to justify.) Many of these new justificatory strategies rely on findings in the emerging discipline of "behavioral economics," which is organized around the identification and investigation of *systematic deviations from rationality* in human decision-making. Sunstein and Thaler, for instance, seize the bull by the horns in declaring that the traditional argument against paternalism, exemplified by Mill, is based on a false assumption: "The false assumption is that almost all people, almost all of the time, make choices that are in their best interest or at the very least are better, by their own lights, than the choices that would be made by third parties. This claim is either tautological, and therefore uninteresting, or testable. We claim that it is testable and false, indeed obviously false."[48] Of course, Mill's argument would still have considerable force if the mistakes that individuals made were unpredictable or random, because then there would still be no grounds for thinking that third parties could do better. Psychological research has revealed, however, a number of extremely systematic, and thus highly predictable, deviations from rationality in individual decision. This suggests that an observer, equipped with the relevant psychological research, might in some circumstances be able to do better than the individual at promoting the latter's own goals.

Behavioral economics, unfortunately, is a highly unsystematic body of research. Thaler, for instance, for a long time wrote a column for the *Journal of Economic Perspectives* called "Anomalies."[49] It has often been observed that behavioral economics has not progressed much beyond this point. It does not have a unified model of human action or psychology; it is basically just a long list of anomalies to the rational actor model. Each of these anomalies could, in turn, be appealed to in defense of a particular class of paternalistic policies. Several of the anomalies, however, are structurally quite different from one another, and so the "behavioral" approach to policy—again exemplified by the discussion in *Nudge*—winds up being something of grab bag of different ideas. To impose some order on this, I will break the proposals down into three broad categories. The first involves arguments that specifically have to do with attitudes toward time, and the difficulty many people have achieving intertemporal consistency in choice (section 7.4). After that, I will examine "hard nudge" arguments, which use attributions of cognitive bias as grounds for overruling individual choices (section 7.5). Having set aside these two mechanisms, I will then consider many of the "soft nudges" that Thaler and Sunstein focus on, such as the setting of default options or the reframing of decisions (section 7.6).

7.4. Hyperbolic discounting

Before we get into the details of this discussion, it is important to clarify a few points about the traditional economic model of rational action. One of the big changes that occurred, at the end of the 19th century, was a transition away from a hedonistic to a preference-based conception of utility. According to these later formulations, utility is not a representation of a psychological state, it is simply a measure of "whatever it is that individuals happen to want." The adoption of this preference-based conception of utility was in part motivated by the commitment to liberal neutrality, or the view that economists had no business worrying about which specific outcomes gave individuals satisfaction, but only with maximizing the amount of satisfaction that could be obtained, given a certain (limited) quantity of resources. This is why normative principles, such as Pareto efficiency, or conceptions of equality that can be formulated entirely in terms of utility, are thought to satisfy the liberal neutrality constraint—because any set of goals can be "plugged in" as a specification of the concrete outcomes that give individuals satisfaction.

Because of this open-ended conception of preference, the resulting theory of rational action is quite "thin," in the sense that pretty much any action can be rational, if the agent happens to have a strong enough preference for its consequence.[50] This is why Thaler and Sunstein say that, under one interpretation, the idea that people always act in their "best interest" is tautological. Where the theory of action becomes more interesting is when one takes a particular set of preferences over outcomes as fixed, then assumes that the individual wants to select the action that maximizes satisfaction of those preferences. This does generate significant constraints on individual action because it is possible to act in ways that are inconsistent with those goals, or that are otherwise non-maximizing. For example, people are entitled to have whatever attitude toward risk they like, but rationality requires that the attitude be *consistent* across options. Unfortunately, most people have a greater aversion to risk when considering potential gains than they do when contemplating losses. As a result, it is not difficult to construct scenarios in which their choices will be inconsistent. Furthermore, it is possible to take one and the same choice and elicit different decisions from the individual by manipulating the "frame"—presenting it as either a potential gain or a foregone loss. This is irrational, even according to the very thin theory of rationality that economists have traditionally employed.

There has never been any shortage of psychologists who are able to come up with objections to the economic conception of rational action. Most of these objections have been easily dismissed by economists, however, because the critics did not appreciate how thin the conception was, and thus how much behavior could be explained away just by positing unusual or idiosyncratic preferences. The importance of Daniel Kahneman and Amos Tversky's work is that they focused narrowly on structural features of the model, then produced a set of experimental results that could not be explained away using any of the conventional strategies. Thus, they were able to show that human decision-making exhibits persistent deviations from rationality, even when rationality is conceived of in minimal terms, as nothing more than a commitment to expected utility maximization. This is what gave rise to the field of behavioral economics, which consists in a style of analysis that takes seriously the points on which actual human behavior deviates from the standard economic model of rational action. (It is not a fully behaviorist theory, because it retains this model of rational action as a point of reference, and as the basis for default assumptions about behavior.)

All of this is of considerable relevance to government decision-making because a great deal of policy development and implementation is based on assumptions about how people will modify their behavior in response to changes in the incentives they face. The standard assumption is that people will respond rationally to these incentives—minimally, that negative sanctions will discourage behavior, while positive sanctions will encourage or reinforce it. This is, of course, valid as a general assumption, and behavioral economics has done nothing to dethrone it. If, however, there are specific instances in which it is not true, and especially if those instances are predictable, then there is a great deal to be gained, from a policy perspective, in knowing how people are likely to react in those cases. From this perspective, the central gain that has come from the rise of behavioral economics is the increased precision that it affords us. Instead of merely saying "people are often irrational"—something that everyone has always known—it provides a set of tools that allows us to identify the *specific* deviations from rationality that one can expect to find in different circumstances.

For example, one area of decision-making in which people have often been suspected of widespread irrationality involves our capacity to plan for the future. A number of quite distinct flaws show up in this domain, but perhaps the most basic is the trait that I have been referring to as improvidence, which is simply the tendency to ignore the future, or more specifically, to neglect the interests of one's future self. Although there is a colloquial sense in which we say that it is "irrational" to be overly short-sighted, any attempt to specify the irrationality involved quickly turns up a number of difficulties. While it is probably a bad idea to assign too little weight to one's future interests, it is an equally bad idea to assign too much weight to one's future interests. Caring for the future can easily crowd out the enjoyment of life in the present, and a person who assigns too much weight to the future can fall victim to the "paradox of the indefinitely postponed splurge"—constantly putting off some satisfaction, to achieve greater satisfaction in the future, but then never getting around to achieving any actual satisfaction. Thus, the appropriate attitude is probably one of moderation, giving considerable weight, but not too much weight, to one's future interests.

Whenever one calls for "moderation" in a particular domain, however, this is tantamount to recognizing the possibility of reasonable disagreement. It is not clear that rationality requires us to have any *particular* attitude toward our future satisfaction. Thus, economists have been inclined to treat the individual's attitude toward the future as just another preference. The traditional strategy for representing it involves the introduction of a "discount rate" into the agent's utility function, which specifies the rate at which the present value of future welfare declines, the further removed it is from the present temporally. This discount rate is modeled on, and essentially the opposite of, the interest rate. The standard (annualized) interest rate states how much *more* a person must be given, by way of compensation, to be willing to defer consumption by a year. The (annualized) discount rate, by contrast, states how much *less* some act of consumption is worth, in the present, when it is delayed by one year. The fact that people discount future satisfaction is thought to explain why interest must be paid on loans (i.e., because future consumption is worth less than present consumption, people must be compensated, to make them willing to defer consumption). On this basis, economists have often posited an "off the shelf" discount rate of 5%, based on a typical value of the rate of interest. What is noteworthy, however, is that they have never claimed that any particular value is the *right* value. While discount rates of 0% or 100% would be problematic, the standard assumption has been that any intermediate value is permissible under the doctrine of "consumer sovereignty." In other words, if people want to privilege their short-term over their long-term satisfaction, then that is their affair.

One might be tempted to conclude, on this basis, that an accusation of "improvidence" is essentially a perfectionist critique, not an accusation of irrationality. There is, however, more to the story than this. One of the features of the economist's way of modeling attitudes toward the future, using a standard discount rate, is that it imposes *consistency* on the agent's temporally modulated attitudes. The technical property is known as *stationarity*, and what it means, in this context, is that if *a* is preferred to *b* at some time *t*, then it will also be preferred at any other time.[51] As a result, the *mere* passage of time cannot change the individual's preference ordering. Modeling discount rates on interest rates has the effect of ensuring that the individual's utility function exhibits stationarity. In real life, however, individuals' choices appear to violate this principle. This is, in fact, an extremely familiar feature of human psychology, which is central to the phenomena of both temptation and regret. When a decision is at some remove from us, temporally, we often resolve to choose the greater over the lesser good. When the time comes to act, however, we succumb to temptation and choose the lesser good, only to regret the decision at some later time. What makes these episodes of temptation distinctive, and what distinguishes them from a mere change of view, is that they involve a *temporary preference reversal*. We prefer *a* to *b* both before and after, it is only during the critical period in which we must actually make the choice that we prefer *b* to *a*. What is striking is that, in many of these cases, nothing seems to have changed other than the passage of time, which would not appear to warrant a change in preference. This suggests that irrationality may be involved.[52]

Thanks to the work of psychologist George Ainslie, we have available an extremely powerful representation of the basic phenomenon.[53] One of the features of temptation is that it involves choosing a smaller but more immediate reward over a larger but temporally deferred one. This is the case whenever we choose fatty foods over our weight-loss goals, staying up late over being well-rested the next day, smoking a cigarette over avoiding cancer, and so on. A helpful mnemonic is to think of temptation as choosing the "smaller sooner good" (SS+) over the "larger later" one (LL+). When stated in this way, it is easy to see that procrastination—when we make things worse by putting them off—is the same phenomenon with the signs reversed.[54] It involves choosing the "larger later bad" (LL−) over the "smaller sooner" one (SS−). What Ainslie observed is that all animals, up to and including humans, seem to have a "warp" in the way we evaluate future benefits. Expressed in terms of a discount rate, we discount the future quite sharply in the near term, with a rate that subsequently declines, and approaches temporal neutrality in the longer term. Ainslie refers to this discount function as "hyperbolic" on the grounds that it is highly exaggerated in and around the present. So while the standard economic model would see $100 worth of consumption as losing 5% of its value like clockwork, for each year that it must be deferred, a more psychologically realistic model would see it losing half of its present value, for the first year that it must be delayed, perhaps only a sixth of its value in the second, and so on. As a first approximation, Ainslie suggests that one can calculate the present psychological value of some delayed satisfaction by *dividing it* by the number of years of delay plus one. (Thus, the present value of $100 in a year is $50, in two years $33, in three years $25, etc.)

If one were looking for a model that "fits the data" on human choice, some kind of hyperbolic discount rate along the lines suggested by Ainslie is a strong candidate.[55] The model, however, has an unexpected explanatory benefit, which is that it also predicts precisely the sort of temporary preference reversals that characterize the phenomena of temptation and procrastination. With a hyperbolic discount rate, future outcomes are subject to a large initial penalty, by virtue of being delayed. When all options are subject to this penalty, we have something like an impartial or dispassionate perspective, and so resolve to choose the greater good. Unfortunately, when the decision has an SS+/LL+ structure, the delay penalty on the smaller good "comes off" before the penalty on the larger one, which causes its present value to dramatically increase. This in turn leads us to choose it. Later, when the delay penalty on the LL good also comes off, we regret the decision, wishing that we had stuck with the initial resolution.

There is still some debate to be had over whether these temporary preference reversals are irrational or not, or more generally, whether it is irrational to discount the future hyperbolically.[56] Generally speaking, we lack a persuasive dynamic model of rational choice. The standard economic model takes preferences as given, and so imposes no requirement of preference stability—a rational person could want something one day, go out and buy it, hate it the next day, sell it at a penalty, then want it again the next day, repurchase it at a premium, and so on. There are, however, obvious prudential reasons for wanting to avoid having preferences that are unstable in this way (these are at the core of traditional "money-pump" arguments against intransitive preferences as well).[57] Similarly, individuals are all intimately familiar with their own tendency to succumb to temporary preference reversals, and so engage in a variety of self-management practices (or as economists say, "pre-commitment strategies"), aimed at preventing their own future selves from acting in these moments of weakness. As a result, it is not necessary to resolve the deeper question of whether the preference reversals are irrational to see the implications of these observations for the debate over state paternalism.

One of the assumptions of Mill's argument is that individuals have interests that are relatively stable, and that individuals pursue these in a relatively steadfast manner.[58] Once it is recognized, however, that peoples' interests may be unstable over time, it makes the question of where their "best interests" lie more complicated. If a person expresses a preference for a over b, but then later tries to choose b, only to discover that the option has been denied her in favor of a, should this denial count as paternalism? There are, of course, circumstances in which we would want to consider the later preference to be more authoritative than the earlier one. An important element of personal freedom is the freedom to change one's mind. Yet there are some circumstances in which one would want to consider the earlier preference more authoritative, especially if the later one is only temporary, and the individual will foreseeably revert to the earlier one after the point of decision has passed. In these cases, the paternalist's claim that "you'll thank me later" is much more than just a hollow assurance.

Another way of putting the point is to note that when we speak of the individual's "interests," we are speaking of them at a particular point in time. In cases where these interests change, from one point in time to another, then one must decide which set of interests should be considered authoritative. The default, of course, is that the individual's *present* conception of his interests is the authoritative one. But for certain policy purposes, especially when decisions are being made that will affect individuals over an extended period of time, it may not be so obvious that this is the correct frame. For instance, suppose one has an intervention that an individual will disapprove of at the beginning but approve of at the end, versus one that the individual will approve of at the beginning but disapprove of at the end. Which should one prefer? Free choice by the individual will favor the second, but it is not entirely obvious that policy always should. Of course, the mere fact that the individual will subsequently ratify the decision is not enough to justify imposing the first option. The formal criterion does not allow one to distinguish "experience goods," such as education, from cult membership. Thus, the question has to be answered by examining the merits of each case.[59] The point, however, is that it is difficult to justify a general presumption in favor of one option or the other.

This observation—that if you ask a person a question at different points in time, you may get different answers—creates opportunities for the type of light touch paternalism that Sunstein and Thaler recommend. Consider Thaler's "Save More Tomorrow" program, developed in collaboration with Shlomo Benartzi.[60] Most workers with elective-contribution retirement schemes save less than they themselves would like, given their own professed postretirement standard-of-living goals. Yet if one asks them to increase their retirement savings contribution rate, most will refuse. Thaler and Benartzi found, however, that if one asks workers *now* to commit some of their *future* pay increases toward increased retirement savings, a large majority of those who had previously refused to increase their current contributions will agree to the future increase. Since there is no a priori correct temporal perspective from which to choose one's retirement savings level (e.g., why should contributions rates be chosen once a year, instead of once every five years, or every ten?), then there is a lot to be said for selecting a temporal frame that promotes greater alignment between the individual's implementation choices and her long-term goals. It is not clear that this is even paternalistic; it is merely arranging the "choice architecture" in a way that enables individuals to most effectively pursue their own expressed interests.

There are, however, some more obviously paternalistic policies that could be justified through reference to hyperbolic discounting. The phenomenon of temporary preference reversal poses a challenge to Mill's agency argument against paternalism. Mill assumes that individuals will always be the most faithful and diligent when it comes to carrying out their own plans, and somewhat less diligent when it comes to advancing the interests of others. As a result, even if the state does have better knowledge of where the interests of the individual lie, it will have difficulty finding an agent able to carry out those plans as faithfully, and so the net effect of paternalistic intervention on the individual's welfare will usually be negative. These claims, however, are gainsaid by the fact that individuals often regard themselves as unreliable agents, when it comes to execution of their own plans, and so enlist the help of others. This is particularly common when they expect to undergo temporary preference reversals. Under such circumstances, they may engage others in what are known as "Ulysses contracts"—named after the episode in which Ulysses had himself bound to the mast of his ship, then instructed his crew to ignore his subsequent orders to release him, so that he could hear the song of the sirens without succumbing to the temptation to leap into the water and pursue them.[61]

This individual "scaffolding" of choice is ubiquitous in everyday life.[62] Given that individuals often solicit help from others, to help themselves to overcome these foreseeable failures of agency, the question is whether there is any reason why they should not be able to use the state in the same way—or why the people, collectively, could not choose to employ state power to implement a type of Ulysses contract. In the case of temporary preference reversals, the agent is unanimous at almost all times that a is to be preferred to b. There is only one small time-slice of the agent that happens to prefer b to a. Unfortunately, that one time-slice is the agent's present self, at the time the option to choose b becomes available. As a result, despite being "outvoted" by every other time-slice, the agent can see that she is going to wind up with b. From the perspective of the agent's earlier selves, this looks like a failure of agency.[63] But because of this, those earlier selves have an interest in changing the decision context, so that the option of choosing a is made available to them, or the option of choosing b is removed at the time that the later self gets to choose.

To pick an everyday example of this, most people who exercise effective control over their own eating habits do so by making choices earlier, in the grocery store, about what food to stock their pantry with. By refraining from buying unhealthy snack foods, they deprive their future (hungrier) self of the option of opening a bag of chips at midnight. People do a great deal of this on their own initiative and using their own resources, organizing their environment and interpersonal relations in such a way as to minimize the most obvious and pernicious temptations. The question is whether we should be obliged to rely exclusively on these individualized strategies, when social institutions can also be organized in ways that advance the same interests.

This issue has enormous contemporary relevance, primarily due to the problem of addiction. Mill essentially had nothing to say on this topic, not just because the concept was not available to him, but also because there were so few opportunities in 19th-century England to develop a dangerous addiction. Beer and wine are simply not strong enough to result in a lot of cases of serious alcoholism. Thus, it was only the consumption of "strong drink"—by which was meant distilled spirits, such as gin—that posed any serious threat of alcoholism. At the time, however, the most prominent issue was not the self-destructive consequences of excessive drinking, but rather the violence and public disorder that it caused. The British, of course, traded in opium in large volumes abroad, and were aware of its effects, but very little opium was sold domestically. Coca leaf was traded, but seldom consumed for anything other than its "medicinal" effects. Since this time, however, the widespread availability of these substances, the use of refinement techniques that have increased both their potency and addictive qualities, as well as the development of synthetic opioids (fentanyl, methadone, oxycodone, hydrocodone, hydromorphone, etc.), have made it impossible to ignore the enormous potential for self-destructive behavior that modern societies afford.

The central feature of addiction (and what distinguishes it from merely liking something a great deal) is not the fact of dependence on some stimulus, but rather the fact that so many people try to rid themselves of the dependence and fail. Thus, we describe smoking tobacco as addictive, not because it is bad for one's health and yet terribly enjoyable, but because so many people find it difficult or impossible to quit. Addiction, in other words, is associated with the familiar cycle of resolution, temptation, weakness of will, and regret. What motivates state interference with individual choice, in the case of tobacco use, is not that "it's bad for you," but rather the fact that so many people are unable to carry through on their professed intention to quit. Or at least, this is how the case for interference should be framed. Unfortunately, discussion of tobacco policy has been dominated to date by fig-leaf strategies—either the medicalization of the addiction, or else an appeal to the effects of second-hand smoke. A more honest approach would be to acknowledge that the primary rationale for the policy is paternalistic, but to argue that those affected are not univocal or consistent in their preferences, and that the state is interfering on the side of what it judges to be their more legitimate preference—which is to say, *not* the one that they express when experiencing the compulsive effects of a nicotine craving.

One attractive feature of this argumentation strategy is that understanding addiction as essentially a psychological phenomenon, involving temporary preference reversal, allows one to extend the framework of policy analysis beyond the traditional catalog of psychoactive addictive substances. There is a large body of evidence, for instance, suggesting that gambling, for certain people, can be just as addictive as smoking. The medical model, with its focus on the effects of chemicals, such as alcohol or opioids, that cross the blood-brain barrier, becomes quite implausible when extended to activities that provide stimulus through ordinary channels, as is the case with gambling or overeating. The hyperbolic discounting model provides a much better way to characterize these problems. Furthermore, because it accounts for procrastination as well, emerging problems such as the rather sharp decline in the average number of hours slept (which has surprisingly large negative health effects), can be thematized as a legitimate domain for policy intervention.[64] Thus it is possible to respect Mill's general restriction on paternalistic state policies, and yet recognize an important class of exceptions to the rule in cases involving addiction, improvidence, and procrastination.

7.5. Cognitive bias

The arguments for paternalistic intervention canvassed above involve challenges to Mill's agency argument for individual liberty. The more obvious target, however, is Mill's epistemic argument. The central finding of behavioral-economic research has been that human decision-making is subject to a large number of *cognitive biases*, which generate deviations from rationality. The term "bias" is used, not to indicate that individuals are somehow prejudiced in favor of certain decisions, but in the statistical sense, to indicate a *non-random* pattern of deviation from some norm. It is because failures of rationality are non-random that they are predictable (and also why they do not cancel one another out when multiple judgments, or the judgments of many people, are aggregated). Mill's epistemic argument, however, seems to presuppose that errors will be random, or unpredictable, which is why third parties will struggle to do better than the individual concerned, in trying to determine where the latter's interests lie. Psychological research has shown, however, that certain errors are highly predictable. Furthermore, the operations of a cognitive bias are not introspectively discernible by the affected person, which is one of the reasons that just teaching people about cognitive biases does not make them less likely to exhibit them. As a result, certain errors of judgment are not only predictable, but also highly persistent in the population, because people cannot tell when they are making them. This means that it is possible for experts (or other uninvolved third parties) to develop an epistemic advantage over the individuals who are making particular choices.

Sunstein and Thaler make note of this, but refrain from following the line of reasoning to its more daunting conclusion, which is that the state could in some instances simply substitute its judgment for that of individuals, on the grounds that "they don't know what's best for themselves." As Americans, both Sunstein and Thaler are writing in a cultural context that is extremely averse to government interference with individual freedom.[65] As a result, they blunt the force of their own position by insisting that paternalistic policy be limited to "light touch" interventions—even though their arguments seem to license much more. In Europe, by contrast, there are fewer inhibitions about state interference. Thus to appreciate the full force of the behavioral-economic critique of Mill's epistemic argument, and at the risk of reinforcing national stereotypes, we can turn to the work of two Swiss economists, Bruno Frey and Alois Stutzer, to see a defense of a far more heavy-handed form of paternalism.[66] In this section, I will focus on this more extreme position, which I refer to as "justified hard paternalism,"[67] before going on in the final section to examine the literature on nudges.

Psychological research has identified dozens of different biases, all of which could in principle serve as justifications for paternalistic policies. Frey and Stutzer focus on the phenomenon of *mispredicted utility*.[68] Many of the most important decisions that we make involve an attempt to satisfy, not our occurrent desires but, rather, our anticipated future desires. Our desires, however, change over time. The most commonly noted phenomenon is that of adaptation, whereby we "get used to" certain experiences, which causes their impact on us to be blunted. Through the process of psychological adaptation, things that are initially a source of distress to us become less distressing over time, just as things that are initially a source of pleasure become less pleasurable over time.

Unfortunately, individuals are not particularly good at predicting how the process of adaptation will affect their future satisfaction levels. For example, people often mispredict the satisfaction they will get from a larger living space. Those who feel cramped and confined in their current dwelling do get an increase in subjective satisfaction when they move to a larger space. Yet they very quickly adapt to the larger space (and fill it with new possessions), so that it no longer serves as a source of any ongoing satisfaction. This is not so much a problem, except when individuals have made significant sacrifices in other areas, less susceptible to adaptation, to be able to afford a larger living space. The most common trade-off is when people accept a longer commute to work to be able to buy a larger house. This is, unfortunately, a trade-off that usually works out rather poorly over time, because studies have shown that individuals tend not to adapt very well to the unpleasantness of commuting—particularly driving on congested roads.[69] As a result, a trade-off that seems advantageous at the point of decision becomes less advantageous over time, as people cease to derive any ongoing satisfaction from their larger home, and yet continue to experience dissatisfaction from fighting traffic every day on the way to and from work.

The underlying psychological mechanism is relatively well-understood.[70] People adapt very quickly and completely to environmental stimuli that are unchanging. If, however, the stimuli change over time, even very slightly, this serves to delay or even prevent adaptation. Thus, for example, people in general de-rive much greater ongoing satisfaction from a window with a pleasant view than from a painting hung on the wall. The painting quickly goes unnoticed, whereas the changes in the seasons make it so that the view out the window constantly undergoes slight modification, which ensures that its aesthetic qualities will never recede entirely into the background. A room with a view may therefore be a better investment than a painting, from a hedonic perspective. The size of a house, however, is an invariant feature, whereas traffic changes slightly every day, which means that people adapt much more quickly to the former than to the latter. Based on this observation, one might argue, as Robert Frank has, that public policy should discourage urban sprawl, based on the paternalistic grounds that individuals who choose to live in far-flung suburban developments are making a mistake in "affective forecasting."[71] Of course, one would still want to leave room for reasonable pluralism in this area, and so one would not want to impose an entirely uniform model of residential development. One could, how-ever, impose higher development charges on low-density or exurban develop-ment to raise the relative prices of houses in these areas, and thus correct the bias that people exhibit when calculating the expected benefits of living in such areas.

Frey and Stutzer go further, arguing that people exhibit a systematic bias in their utility predictions that leads them to overestimate the value of extrinsic satisfactions (such as money and consumer goods) over intrinsic ones (such as socializing with family and friends). There are a number of psychological reasons for this (including the aforementioned one, about the impact of small changes on rates of adaptation), but there is also an obvious environmental one, which is that we are bombarded with advertisements that accentuate the benefits of ex-trinsic attributes of goods, but seldom mention the merits of intrinsic ones.[72] Thus Frey and Stutzer call for policies that will encourage individuals to pursue intrinsic rather than extrinsic satisfactions. Examples include limitations on the number of allowable work hours, restrictions on opening hours for commercial enterprises, as well as generous parental leave policies.

It is worth noting that, unlike the hyperbolic discounting case, in which one can expect individuals to at some point endorse the policy, with cognitive bias one cannot be confident that they will ever come around to seeing things the right way. To see why, recall that the discovery of cognitive biases does not defeat Mill's epistemic argument *merely* by showing that certain errors are predictable. It must also be the case that the individuals afflicted are somehow impaired in their ability to overcome the error in a way that third parties are not (e.g., because it is not introspectable, or because they suffer from limited attention, etc.). Yet it follows from this that even when a policy is helping people to achieve their own ends, they may remain implacably opposed to it, precisely because the cognitive bias is so persistent. For example, they may want to work longer hours, or have more convenient access to the shops, and simply not see the connection between the quality of life that they enjoy and the restrictive policies that they dislike.

Because of this, one can expect paternalistic policies that seek to correct the results of cognitive bias to be a source of ongoing tension. At very least then, a government that wants to maintain such policies, on the grounds that public officials "know better" than individuals, must have very solid evidential foundations for this claim. For instance, the cognitive biases being ascribed should not be identified impressionistically, but rather should be empirically demonstrable both in a laboratory setting and in everyday environments. They should also have robust cross-situational predictive validity (so that, from the fact that people exhibit the bias in one decision, one can predict that they will exhibit it on other, structurally similar, decisions). Given the ongoing "replication crisis" in experimental psychology—in which a large number of highly publicized results turned out to be irreproducible—it is important to avoid excessive credulity when relying upon the results of psychological science. (In this context, it is worth noting that one study by Brian Wansink, which Thaler and Sunstein refer to in *Nudge* as a "masterpiece," has since been retracted.[73]) Again, because paternalistic policies are coercively imposed, it is important that the evidence on which they are based be of the highest caliber.

7.6. The nudge framework

Some commentators have complained that Sunstein and Thaler's discussion of "nudges" is not so much a coherent theory as it is a series of provocative examples.[74] The amount of clarification that has been required here, as a prelude to the discussion of their work, tends to support this contention. Yet even with cases of hyperbolic discounting and cognitive bias set aside, further qualifications are needed. Most importantly, it is essential to distinguish two quite distinct ideas that Sunstein and Thaler present, which they tend to run together: the idea of a "nudge" and that of "libertarian paternalism." A "nudge" is the more general concept, which they define as "any aspect of the choice architecture that alters people's behavior in a predictable way without forbidding any options or significantly changing their economic incentives."[75] Stated this way, a nudge has nothing to do with paternalism; it could be introduced as a way of advancing any public policy goal. For instance, the Behavioral Insights Team in the United Kingdom experimented with using nudges as a way of improving tax compliance. There should be nothing particularly controversial about this, in part because the UK government also coerces people who do not pay their taxes. If the state can throw people in prison for nonpayment of taxes, what objection could there be to the introduction of public service billboards that use the "watching eyes effect" to encourage payment? These nudges are theoretically un-interesting (though perhaps useful in practice). Their central attraction is merely that they may turn out to be a less costly way of securing compliance.

Similarly, Sunstein and Thaler give the example of an organ-donation program switching the default rule, so that people would have to opt out if they do not want to donate, as opposed to opting in if they do. They consider this a nudge, be-cause the cost of doing the paperwork is relatively low, and the change can have a significant impact on participation rates. This policy is also relatively uncon-troversial, because all it does by imposing the paperwork requirement on those who want to opt out is to penalize a certain sort of free-riding. After all, most people who opt out still expect to be eligible to receive an organ donation, if they happen to need one; they just do not want to contribute their own organs. The government could justifiably impose a system of strict reciprocity, as the govern-ment of Singapore does, where those who opt out of the organ-donation system are assigned lowest priority on the wait lists for receipt of organs. This seems a bit heavy-handed to many Western governments, who prefer the "light touch" intervention of adopting just an opt-out scheme. There should be nothing espe-cially controversial about this, however, because a far more coercive scheme such as Singapore's (which effectively denies transplant organs to non-contributors) could also be justified. The use of a nudge therefore does nothing to expand the frontiers of public policy.

What makes nudge theory controversial is Thaler and Sunstein's further claim that because nudges are non-coercive, the state can use them to advance policy objectives that it could not pursue through ordinary legal means. Specifically, while they endorse the traditional prohibition on the coercive imposition of hard paternalistic policies, they argue that there is no objection to the use of nudges to advance these same policies.[76] They take themselves to have found a third way of circumventing Mill's argument, by identifying a set of strategies that can have powerful effects on behavior, yet do not count as coercive. On this view, the use of force against citizens, or the coercive restriction of their freedom, has a high threshold of justification, which hard paternalistic policies generally cannot sur-mount. Various forms of psychological manipulation, by contrast, have a lower justificatory threshold, which paternalistic policies that rely on nudges may be able to clear. (Sunstein and Thaler claim that, with nudges, "since no coercion is involved, we think that some types of paternalism should be acceptable."[77]) This is the idea at the heart of "libertarian paternalism," which they claim is "a relatively weak, soft, and nonintrusive type of paternalism because choices are not blocked, fenced off, or significantly burdened."[78] This is the provocative and potentially transformative claim that is at the heart of their analysis.

One way of thinking about their position is to note that there has seldom been much concern over the use of *persuasion* by government officials to promote outcomes that, were they to be legally imposed, would clearly run afoul of the prohibition on paternalism. It was at one time common to describe the US president as having access to a "bully pulpit," which could be used to press Americans to reform themselves in various ways—whether it be through improved parenting, greater commitment to national service, or better diet and exercise. The Surgeon General (or chief health official) often plays a similar role. In a sense, all that Sunstein and Thaler are claiming is that various forms of psychological manipulation—of the sort that are routinely employed in the private sector, most obviously in advertising—should be counted as persuasion, not as coercion. The essence of their proposal is simply that the state should become less ad hoc, and more systematic, in the way that it frames and communicates the choices that it presents to citizens.

There are, it should be noted (and many commentators have), several unhelpfully vague terms used in the definitions of both "nudge" and of "libertarian paternalism."[79] Neither in fact can stand up to critical scrutiny as initially presented. As far as libertarian paternalism is concerned, the traditional Millian constraint is not that the state should refrain from actions that "significantly burden" particular choices, in the domain of self-regarding action, it is that the state should not be permitted to burden them *at all*. (For comparison, consider a freedom of religion policy that allowed the state to discourage certain faiths, the only restriction being that it refrain from making it "unreasonably difficult" to practice a particular religion. The fact that no religion is banned outright does not make this an acceptable conception of religious freedom, much less a "libertarian" one. Similarly, a law that banned abortion in one state, but left women free to travel to a neighboring state to obtain one, would not generally be regarded as consistent with libertarianism. Having to walk through a gauntlet of protestors on the way to an abortion clinic might also be construed as a nudge.[80]) A similar problem occurs in the definition of nudges, where it is specified that an intervention is just a nudge so long as it does not forbid any option, or significantly change the "economic incentives" that an agent faces. This is unreasonably narrow, since a policy that threatens individuals with an electric shock if they choose a certain option could be said to leave their "economic incentives" untouched. An incentive is an incentive, regardless of whether it is psychological or economic, and the traditional restriction on paternalistic intervention is that the state not be allowed to intervene in cases of primarily self-regarding action in such a way as to restructure *any* incentives.[81]

Suppose that an employer, to promote better fitness among its employees, introduces a benefit plan that consists of a gym membership, paid for by a new automatic payroll deduction. In recognition of the fact that some employees would rather not exercise, they offer a provision under allowing those who want to decline the benefit (and avoid the payroll deduction) to file some paperwork and opt out. Studies suggest that enrollment in such a plan will be higher under this opt-out arrangement than it would be under an opt-in arrangement, because some employees who would rather not participate will simply never get around to filing the necessary paperwork. Critics of the opt-out benefit plan might argue that it is objectionably paternalistic, on the grounds that it makes the choice of withdrawing from the plan more costly than the choice of joining by imposing the paperwork requirement on those who withdraw. Therefore, they claim, it fails to respect neutrality. Those who want to opt out are being penalized, in effect, because the employer deems them to be making the wrong choice about their own exercise and activity level.

How could one defend such a plan? The wrong strategy, it seems to me, would be to argue that the opt-out arrangement is not genuinely paternalistic, because the cost involved in filling out some forms is relatively small. The economic cost is obviously trivial, what deters people from completing the paperwork is the psychological aversiveness of the task. How aversive is it? The claim that it is just a "nudge" is reminiscent of the Monty Python sketch in which the waiter offers a restaurant patron a "wafer-thin mint." The mere fact that some individuals will continue to pay for a gym membership that they do not use rather than fill out the form suggests that it is a very large psychological cost. Thus it seems question-begging to justify displacing it onto some option, on the grounds that it is a "weak" or "soft" constraint—the fact that it deters a substantial number of people from making that choice would appear to belie the description.

A bit later in the text, however, Sunstein and Thaler offer a much more promising characterization of a nudge. They begin by distinguishing between what they call "Econs," or individuals who act in accordance with the economic conception of rationality, and "Humans," who are subject to the usual cognitive biases that compromise ordinary human decision making. A nudge, they say, is "any factor that significantly alters the behavior of Humans, even though it would be ignored by Econs."[82] According to one plausible definition, an incentive is anything that changes the *rational* structure of a decision problem. The threat of punishment, the anticipated loss of money, the expectation of an unpleasant psychological state—these all provide us with reasons to avoid performing some action. Yet because we are not perfectly rational, there are other features of the choice situation that may influence our decision, but not by giving us reasons. For example, while the content of a message may give us a reason to perform some action, the color of the font in which it is communicated may also influence our decision, yet it does not give us a reason one way or the other. (Typically, even if font color were shown to have such an effect, individuals would deny that the color had influenced their decision.) According to the definition of an incentive given earlier, these sources of influence do not constitute incentives. It follows that manipulation of these non-rational features of the choice problem does not count as changing incentives, and as a result, does not violate the traditional pro-hibition on paternalistic intervention. A nudge can therefore be more produc-tively defined as a modification of the choice architecture that does not change the rational structure of the decision.

To take the simplest, least controversial example of this, consider the framing effect in the presentation of risks. It is well-established that people are risk-averse with respect to potential gains, yet often risk-seeking when it comes to avoiding losses. As a result, the way that a particular gamble is presented can af-fect whether or not the individual accepts it. If a doctor presents a surgical option as having a 90 percent survival rate, it is more likely to be accepted than if it is presented as having a 10 percent mortality rate. Rationally speaking, the way the choice is presented should have no effect on the patient's preference, yet it does. According to Sunstein and Thaler, the "choice architect" should therefore think carefully about how the options are presented to the patient, and then frame the choice in a way that is most likely to elicit the answer that is in the patient's best interest. The state should act in the same way, across a wide range of choices that it offers to citizens.

Market actors are generally aware of the impact that framing can have. The most celebrated example are the various lawsuits by credit card companies aimed at preventing merchants from imposing a surcharge on customers for credit card use, but instead limiting them to offering a discount for cash payments. The ec-onomic effect is exactly the same, but the number of consumers who pay cash is dramatically lower with this framing, because a foregone gain is treated as less consequential than a loss. States confront a similar issue with the payment of taxes, where tax payments are resented much more than taxes that are withheld at source—as a result of which most taxpayers treat their annual tax refund as a windfall gain rather than as the reduction of a loss. Thus it is possible for the state to increase tax compliance by adopting more behaviorally sophisticated framing strategies.[83] It is also possible to pursue various paternalistic strategies using the same approach (e.g., the imposition of monthly wage withholdings could be justified as a way of ensuring that individuals save enough to cover their tax liabilities.)

To the extent that nudges like this work, in the sense that they actually change the decision that a subject makes, it is only because the person so influenced is acting, or would otherwise have acted, irrationally. As a result, it is always pos-sible to avoid the nudge *just by choosing rationally*. This does not necessarily mean that the nudge can be easily avoided—it may in fact be quite hard to act rationally. The point is that, if one succumbs to the influence of the nudge, one cannot criticize the state for failing to respect one's rational autonomy, since one has already admitted to a failure to act rationally in acknowledging the influence of the nudge.

With respect to opt-in/opt-out schemes, for instance, one of the reasons the small cost of having to fill out some paperwork can nevertheless have a large effect on behavior no doubt owes to the effects of hyperbolic discounting. It is not just the psychological aversiveness of the task that discourages people from opting out. When we consider the choice at some remove, the idea of filling out a few forms may seem trivial, and we are willing to grant that it is a very small cost. Yet when it comes time to do it, the aversiveness of the task looms large, while the benefits of avoiding the payroll deduction are more distant. Thus, we procrastinate, and fail to pursue our own best interest, which is to opt out. In this case, the choice architect is basically taking advantage of our weakness of will. If the net effect is that we become more likely to exercise (e.g., having paid for the gym membership, we decide to use it), then one type of weakness of will has been used to combat some other. And thus, as David Hume suggested long ago, one can arrange things so that this "infirmity of human nature becomes a remedy to itself."[84]

In other cases, the "irrationality" that people exhibit is somewhat more difficult to classify, as it involves a lack of clear preferences, and thus a susceptibility to suggestion. ("In many domains, people lack clear, stable, or well-ordered preferences. What they choose is strongly influenced by details of the context in which they make their choice, for example default rules, framing effects (that is, the wording of possible options), and starting points. These contextual influences render the very meaning of the term "preferences" unclear."[85]) People are often happy to have what everyone else is having, or to do what everyone else is doing. This may be perfectly rational, like "following the smart money." By copying the choices of informed consumers, an ignorant consumer can often make better choices. Yet in other cases, it winds up becoming a self-fulfilling prophecy, as everyone simply copies what they think others are doing, and no one actually has superior knowledge. In this case, the choice architect can have a significant impact on outcomes by making one particular outcome more focal than the others. The power of a default, for instance, is that many people interpret it as an indication of what most people choose, or what most people find satisfactory. The nudge can be avoided by anyone who comes to the decision with determinate preferences and ignores the "social" aspect of the choice.

Finally, there is a minor category of interventions, in which the presentation of the options will inevitably result in some choices being more costly than others as a consequence of the choice architecture. The example that Sunstein and Thaler repeatedly reference, that of the organization of food choices in a cafeteria, fits this description. It is inevitable that some items will be presented before others, and some will be given placements that are more prominent. This generates a psychological cost for those who want to make the relatively disfavored choices— they are obliged to pay more attention, and perhaps be more patient as they move through the cafeteria. Under these circumstances, Sunstein and Thaler argue, it would make sense to organize the food items in a way that favors the healthier choices over the unhealthy ones. This is perfectly reasonable, but if the rationale is that "some choice must be favored, and so it ought to be the one that's best for you," this is not an example of libertarian paternalism, it is actually just hard paternalism, justified through reference to its inevitability.

The cafeteria examples serves one useful purpose, however, which is to remind us that we are surrounded, in everyday life, by a built environment that is almost entirely structured in ways that are largely inimical to the pursuit of our interests.[86] Commercial environments, in particular, are designed to exploit every conceivable bias and error to increase revenue for the retailer. In a grocery store, for instance, each shopper must slowly pass through a gauntlet of unhealthy snack foods and other "impulse buys" while waiting in line for a cashier. The packaging of food, the layout of the store, the positioning of the fresh foods, the remoteness of the dairy section, the lighting level, the music being played—all are designed to advance goals that are, if not positively contrary, than at least orthogonal to the goals of the average shopper. A great deal of the outrage expressed over Sunstein and Thaler's proposals involves something of a double standard, given the level of "nudging" that we have reconciled ourselves to in the private sector, where as long as the manipulation falls somewhere short of outright fraud, we shrug our shoulders and say "buyer beware."[87] In this context, it does not seem so unreasonable to expect that, in dealing with the public sector, citizens be offered at least a hiatus from the nonstop sales job that they endure elsewhere, so that they can relax their vigilance, with the confidence that their interests will be the ones guiding the way that choices are structured.

7.7. Conclusion

The image of a fence running through a pasture remains an apt metaphor for thinking about the impact of Mill's critique of state paternalism. There are pressures on it coming from both directions. Some people would like to dismantle the fence entirely, others would like to strengthen it, or move it over. On the one hand, the modern environment is one in which the individual faces increased jeopardy, which makes it much harder to avoid self-destructive behavior using only the power of one's own reasoning and will. As Keith Stanovich has observed, the development of more complex societies and advanced technologies has resulted in a growing "mismatch" between the set of innate problem-solving heuristics that evolution has provided us with and the cognitive demands that are put on us by our environment. Evolution has endowed us with a visual system that adapts to changes in natural light, in order to preserve the illusion of color constancy throughout the day, yet some forms of artificial lighting, such as a sodium vapor lamp, cause this system to misfire, leaving us unable to distinguish certain colors. Modern society, Stanovich argues, is like a sodium vapor lamp, which increasingly causes our innate heuristics to misfire:

> The cognitive equivalent of the sodium vapor lamps are: the probabilities we must deal with; the causation we must infer from knowledge of what *might* have happened; the vivid advertising examples we must ignore; the unrepresentative sample we must disregard; the favored hypothesis we must not privilege; the rule we must follow that dictates we ignore a personal relationship; the narrative we must set aside because it does not square with the facts; the pattern that we must infer is not there because we know a randomizing device is involved; the sunk cost that must not affect our judgment; the judge's instructions we must follow despite their conflict with common sense; the contract we must honor despite its negative effects on a relative; the professional decision we must make because we know it is beneficial in the aggregate even if unclear in this case.[88]

As the challenges thrown up by the world become more complex, and the cognitive burden more demanding, it is not surprising that more and more people are failing to keep up. Thus an increased fraction of human misery winds up being self-inflicted, not just because we have become much better at resolving collective action problems, but also because the tasks involved in caring for the self have become that much more difficult. As Stanovich observes, we live in a world in which it is easy, through mere inadvertence, to eat in a single snack more grams of fat than should be eaten in an entire day.[89] The suggestion that "society" should take no responsibility for the consequences that this environment has for the individual seems untenable (just as the 19th-century conviction that the state should have no involvement in the economy became untenable).

At the same time, there are other pressures that push in the direction of increased deference to individual choice. As Rawls once suggested, the exercise of practical reason, under conditions of freedom and equality, tends to produce more, not less, disagreement about the good life.[90] Experience largely supports this assessment, that there is an endogenous tendency toward increased pluralism within liberal societies. All of this is dramatically amplified by the increased mobility associated with globalization. Immigration, in particular, is increasing the level of ethnic and religious pluralism within every Western society. As a result, it is more important than ever that the state—along with its officials—show considerable deference to the choices made by individuals. The line between paternalism and intolerance is easy to cross. Perhaps the most obvious cases involve an unwillingness to recognize the consent given by members of minority cultural or religious groups to practices that seem distasteful or oppressive in the eyes of the majority.

The tension produced by these two movements, I would suggest, is what accounts for the dramatic impact that Sunstein and Thaler's book had on thinking about public policy (both in government and in the academy). Unfortunately, the level of clarity in their presentation of the view left something to be desired. My primary objective in this chapter has been to remedy that deficit. This involved first clarifying the background presumption against paternalism, against which their argument was presented. There are good reasons for us to be suspicious of paternalistic policies—they represent a use of state power that is strongly in tension with both the commitment to state neutrality and the traditional liberal conception of limited government. Mill's arguments, apart from being highly influential, provide a useful framework for separating the different strands of thinking that one can find emerging from a "behavioral-economic" perspective. This analysis allows one to see how recent advances in psychological research about human decision-making have made it easier to meet the special burden of justification that paternalistic policies are subject to.

8

Conclusion

The central challenge around which the discussion in this book has been structured involves reconciling the tension between the traditional commitment to *political neutrality* on the part of the public service with the fact that administrative discretion inevitably involves making normative judgments. State employees, from the mandarin class down to the street-level bureaucrat, are in many cases unable to do their job effectively without developing some conception of where the public interest lies. Yet defining the public interest has traditionally been seen as the prerogative of the legislature, or of elected officials more generally. The civil service therefore seems to be caught in something of a bind. On the one hand, it is compelled to develop its own conception of the public interest—indeed, it is sometimes instructed to do so by legislation. On the other hand, it appears to be prohibited from doing so, both by democratic theory and constitutional convention.

The discussion began by considering two mechanisms through which democratic institutions could provide some specification of the public interest— the first through the traditional institutions of electoral democracy, the second through various forms of direct public engagement or participatory democracy. I spent some time showing the weakness of these two mechanisms in order to cast doubt on the suggestion that they might bear the burden of defining the public interest. The limitations of these two mechanisms are what leave the public service with no alternative but to develop its own, independent conception of where the public interest lies. Yet it seems inevitable that this will conflict with the commitment to political neutrality, since this conception of the public interest might well be tension with that of elected officials.

The solution to the dilemma, I argued, lies in careful development of the "liberal" portion of the "liberal democratic" equation that governs our polity. It is well and widely understood that we do not live in a regime of unrestricted popular sovereignty. Most obviously, the courts play an important role in checking the power of democratic publics, as well as of elected officials, when their impulses conflict with basic principles of liberalism. I argued that the executive branch—and more specifically, the class of permanent officials—is also the custodian of these basic liberal principles. In the extreme, this means that the executive may be called upon to serve as a countermajoritarian check on the legislature. In the more common run of cases, it means that the public service

The Machinery of Government. Joseph Heath, Oxford University Press (2020). © Oxford University Press.
DOI: 10.1093/oso/9780197509616.001.0001

works as a moderating influence, lending greater stability and rationality to state decision-making. In all circumstances, what guides the decision-making of the executive is a commitment to a "minimal" liberal theory of justice. Thus, the discussion in the book advanced reconstructively, starting with an articulation of the theory of liberal justice in terms of three basic principles: efficiency, equality, and liberty. It went on to show how each principle underlies a particular set of "public service values" and decision-making practices.

Among these principles, efficiency is without doubt the most important, yet it is also the most neglected in the philosophical literature on the welfare state. Partly, this is due to confusion between efficiency in the Pareto sense, which is basically an injunction to maximize the benefits of cooperation, with efficiency in the technical sense, which is merely an instrumental principle. The confusion is exacerbated by a widespread tendency to overestimate how much redistribution is undertaken by the welfare state, and thus to imagine that institutional arrangements such as state pensions or health services must have an egalitarian rationale. This is caused, I argue, by a tendency to misclassify insurance arrangements, which are undertaken in the public sector largely for reasons of efficiency (i.e., to correct a market failure), as egalitarian redistributions. Careful attention to the structure of these programs shows that they are almost all undertaken in the public sector for reasons of efficiency, not equality.

The final reason for the relative neglect of efficiency is that it is the least controversial of the core principles of modern liberalism. Indeed, it is so uncontroversial that many theorists—economists in particular—have been misled into thinking that efficiency can be treated as merely a technical principle, and therefore outside the scope of normative contestation. This is clearly mistaken. And yet it is true that the efficiency principle, being *relatively* uncontroversial, is the normative commitment that the civil service can most assertively promote without violating political neutrality. One can find this commitment expressed in various ways, but the most important has been through the growing importance, over the past few decades, of cost-benefit analysis in government decision-making. Although it is sometimes mistaken for a species of applied utilitarianism, cost-benefit analysis—I argue—is best understood as a consequence of the state's commitment to resolve various forms of market failure, which implies a Pareto rationale, not a utilitarian one.

Somewhat more controversial is the liberal principle of equality, which has been the subject of vigorous philosophical contestation in recent decades. Controversy is, in a sense, a built-in feature of the principle of equality, because its central role is to mediate distributive conflict, which necessarily has a win-lose structure. This produces the commonly noted tendency of egalitarian arrangements to be more popular among the winners than among the losers. The latter, in many cases, form a mobilized political constituency. As a result, the requirement of non-partisanship, or political neutrality, imposes much more significant constraints on the public service when it comes to promoting any specific conception of equality, or policies that have a purely egalitarian rationale. Nevertheless, the dramatic expansion of administrative discretion that accompanied the development of the welfare state has left the public service no choice but to develop its own conception of equality, especially to govern its "street-level" relations with citizens. This is typically articulated within the civil service (somewhat misleadingly) in terms of a commitment to the rule of law. Thus the second major component of my discussion of public service values focused on the evolution of a "rule of law culture" in the executive (a process that has involved not only a broadening of our understanding of the rule of law, but also a move away from the classical liberal conception, which placed too much emphasis on the separation of powers).

The final element of my discussion focused on the changing understanding of individual liberty, away from classical rights doctrines (which tended to conceive of liberty as a protected sphere) toward a general anti-paternalism constraint (which focuses instead on the type of *justification* that can be offered for coercive measures). Again, while the judiciary has, in numerous jurisdictions, played an important role in promoting this principle (by ruling certain forms of paternalistic legislation unconstitutional), the extent to which state power is experienced as intrusive depends quite heavily on the actions of the executive. Thus, it is important that a general culture of deference to individual autonomy be promoted within the public service—most obviously, in the police forces. At the same time, there is a broader dynamic within liberal societies that tends to increase the opportunities for self-destructive behavior among individuals (of which the current opioid crisis is but one manifestation). This has put increased pressure on the traditional prohibition on paternalistic state policies. The resulting tension, I argue, is what accounts for the most important recent trend in public policy, which is the use of "behavioral-economic" analysis as an approach to justifying state paternalism. By situating these proposals in the broader history of reflection on this topic within the liberal tradition, it is possible to articulate criteria that will allow us to sort the good from the bad in these discussions.

The overall ambition of this discussion has been to take the central concepts of a liberal theory of justice, understood in terms of an abstract commitment to efficiency, equality, and liberty, and to show how these principles can be used to illuminate some of the most important practices and norms of the public service. The development of the welfare state has resulted in important changes in the nature of government. Most obviously, it has resulted in a vast expansion of both administrative power and bureaucratic autonomy. At no point has anyone ever failed to notice the extraordinary challenge this poses to the traditional liberal commitment to limited government and the rule of law. The growth of the state has thus been accompanied by a wide range of responses aimed at mitigating these negative effects. Most of these have been of the "muddling through" variety. The medium of reform has in some cases been legal—through the widespread development of administrative law—but a great deal has also occurred through the informal workplace culture of the civil service.

It is the latter that state officials try to articulate when formulating a "code of ethics" or "statement of values" for the public service. These efforts, however, have traditionally produced only a laundry list of values, with little in the way of guidance on how they are to be applied. By rearticulating these values in terms of the fundamental principles of modern liberalism, and connecting them up to a broader story about the development of the welfare state, I hope to have developed an intellectual framework that will provide better guidance for those thinking about specific questions and dilemmas that may arise. Along the way, I hope to have provided the resources to question, to criticize, and sometimes to defend the arrangements and accommodations that currently prevail. In particular, I hope to have provided an alternative to the old civil service statement of duty, "fearless advice, loyal implementation." It will no doubt remain useful to say this when politicians are in the room, but the phrase dramatically understates the amount of raw power that is directly exercised by the civil service. Unfortunately, between civil servants not wanting to be impolitic and academics being enamored of highly idealized conceptions of democracy, there has been something of a conspiracy of silence around this reality. This unwillingness to acknowledge or admit the degree to which state power is wielded by permanent officials has, in turn, posed a significant barrier to any discussion of the normative principles that should guide its exercise. At very least, I hope to have initiated a more serious philosophical discussion of these issues.

Notes

Preface

1. Will Kymlicka, *Multicultural Citizenship* (Oxford: Oxford University Press, 1996).
2. Joseph Heath, *Morality, Competition, and the Firm* (New York: Oxford University Press, 2014).
3. John Stuart Mill, *Considerations on Responsible Government* (New York: Harper & Brothers, 1862), pp. 98, 100.

Chapter 1

1. Thomas Hobbes, *Leviathan*, edited by Richard Tuck (Cambridge: Cambridge University Press, 1991), p. 9.
2. For an overview, see Kenneth J. Meier and Laurence J. O'Toole Jr., "Political Control versus Bureaucratic Values: Reframing the Debate," *Public Administration Review* 66 (2006): 177–192.
3. James Kitfield, *Prodigal Soldiers* (New York: Simon & Shuster, 1995), p. 144.
4. Lewis Sorley, *Thunderbolt* (New York: Simon & Schuster, 1992), p. 363.
5. Ibid., p. 150.
6. Ibid.
7. Andrew J. Bacevich, *The New American Militarism* (Oxford: Oxford University Press, 2005), p. 39.
8. Kitfield, *Prodigal Soldiers*, p. 150.
9. Sorley, *Thunderbolt*, p. 364.
10. James Jay Carafano, "The Army Reserves and the Abrams Doctrine: Unfulfilled Promise, Uncertain Future," *Heritage Lectures* 869 (2005): 1–12 at 3.
11. Arthur Kroeger, *Retiring the Crow Rate* (Edmonton: University of Alberta Press, 2009), p. 14.
12. Ibid., p. 15.
13. Ibid., p. 44.
14. Ibid., pp. 51–52.
15. Ibid., p. 148.
16. "Canadian Soybean Production (Metric Tonnes)," Production Statistics, SoyCanada, http://soycanada.ca/statistics/production/, accessed Jan. 9, 2019.
17. Brandon Harder, "For the First Time, Canada Seeds More Canola Than Wheat," CBC News, June 30, 2017, accessed Jan. 9, 2019, http://www.cbc.ca/news/canada/saskatchewan/canola-takes-national-lead-from-wheat-1.4186606.

18. Daniel Carpenter, *Reputation and Power* (Princeton, NJ: Princeton University Press, 2010), p. 21.
19. Ibid.
20. Ibid., p. 78.
21. Cited in Carpenter, *Reputation and Power*, p. 151.
22. Ibid., p. 153.
23. Ibid., p. 255.
24. Ibid., p. 269.
25. Ibid., p. 228.
26. Ibid., p. 192.
27. The distinction between policy and administration is normally attributed to Woodrow Wilson, "The Study of Administration," *Political Science Quarterly* 2 (1887): 197–222, although of course it is implicit in much earlier work.
28. Tony Evans, *Professional Discretion in Welfare Services* (Farnham, UK: Ashgate, 2010).
29. Daniel Carpenter, *The Forging of Bureaucratic Autonomy* (Princeton, NJ: Princeton University Press, 2001).
30. Michael Lipsky, *Street-Level Bureaucracy* (New York: Russell Sage, 1980); Richard B. Stewart, "The Reformation of American Administrative Law," *Harvard Law Review* 88 (1975): 1669–1813; Keith Hawkins, ed., *The Uses of Discretion* (Oxford: Oxford University Press, 1995). There is also, it should be noted, an extensive literature on judicial discretion, which despite sharing certain themes, is largely distinct.
31. Henry Parris, *Constitutional Bureaucracy* (London: Allen and Unwin, 1969), p. 201.
32. Ibid., p. 191.
33. Ibid.
34. It has been suggested that one of the structural weaknesses of "illiberal democracies" is that they tend to destroy the value of their own currency, precisely because they undermine the independence of both the judiciary and the executive (and thus the central bank). "How Turkey Fell from Investment Darling to Junk-Rated Emerging Market," *The Economist*, May 19, 2018. It is also worth observing that US President Donald Trump's attempt to politicize the Federal Reserve Board through appointment of partisans is one of the very few points on which he was rebuffed by the (Republican-controlled) Senate.
35. See Pierre Rosanvallon, *Democratic Legitimacy*, trans. Arthur Goldhammer (Princeton, NJ: Princeton University Press, 2011), p. 37.
36. Cited in Gary C. Bryner, *Bureaucratic Discretion* (New York: Pergamon Press, 1987), pp. 150–151.
37. Sean Gailmard, "Accountability and Principal-Agent Theory," in Mark Bovens, Robert E. Goodin, and Thomas Shillemans, eds., *Oxford Handbook of Public Accountability* (Oxford: Oxford University Press, 2014), pp. 90–105 at 95. The literature discussed is Theodore Lowi, *The End of Liberalism*, 2nd ed. (New York: Norton, 1979), pp. ; Hugh Heclo, *A Government of Strangers* (Washington, DC: Brookings, 1977); and William Niskanen, *Bureaucracy and Representative Government* (Chicago: Aldine, 1971).

38. Joseph Heath, "Public-Sector Management Is Complicated: Comment on Farrell," in Jack Knight and Melissa Schwartzberg, eds., *NOMOS LX: Privatization* (New York: New York University Press, 2019), pp. 200–222.

39. Robert Millward, *Private and Public Enterprise in Europe* (Cambridge: Cambridge University Press, 2005), p. 261.

40. Keith Dowding, *The Civil Service* (London: Routledge, 1995), pp. 96–98.

41. Michel Foucault, *History of Sexuality*, vol. 1, trans. Robert Hurley (London: Penguin, 1979), pp. 88–89.

42. One of the few exceptions to this is Jürgen Habermas, *Between Facts and Norms*, trans. William Rehg (Cambridge, MA: MIT Press, 1992).

43. Peter K. Manning and John van Maanen, eds., *Policing: A View From the Street* (Santa Monica, CA: Goodyear, 1978).

44. John R. Huber and Charles R. Shipan, *Deliberate Discretion?* (Cambridge: Cambridge University Press, 2002), pp. 68–69.

45. Pollution Prevention Act of 1990, 42 USCA §13101-13109, https://www.epa.gov/p2/pollution-prevention-act-1990, accessed Mar. 30, 2020. Similarly, the Consumer Product Safety Commission is charged with developing product safety rules whenever a rule is "reasonably necessary to eliminate or reduce an unreasonable risk of injury," and the creation of such a rule is in "the public interest." Bryner, *Bureaucratic Discretion*, p. 149.

46. John Rohr, *Ethics for Bureaucrats*, 2nd ed. (New York: Marcel Dekker, 1989), p. 41. This list is cited from Philip J. Cooper, *Public Law and Public Administration* (Palo Alto, CA: Mayfield, 1983), p. 221, where it is credited to Ernest Freund.

47. Terry L. Cooper, *The Responsible Adminstrator*, 5th ed. (San Francisco: Jossey-Bass, 2006), p. 78.

48. Habermas, *Between Facts and Norms*, pp. 39–40. The term is of course more widely used, see Rosanvallon, *Democratic Legitimacy*, p. 48.

49. G. W. F. Hegel, *Philosophy of Right*, trans. Alan White (Indianapolis, IN: Hackett, 2002). Rosanvallon, *Democratic Legitimacy*. Some would argue that Carl Schmitt, *Constitutional Theory*, trans. Jeffrey Seitzer (Durham, NC: Duke University Press, 2008) should be inserted between these two.

50. Irvin Studin, *The Strategic Constitution* (Vancouver: UBC Press, 2014), pp. 17–19.

51. Graham Wallas, *Human Nature in Politics*, 2nd ed. (London: Constable, 1919), p. 262.

52. The term "civil service" is used throughout most of the commonwealth. "Public service" is preferred in Canada, presumably because it translates better into French. I use the two terms interchangeably.

53. See Leonard D. White, *The Jacksonians: A Study in Administrative History* (New York: Macmillan, 1954).

54. William G. Resh, *Rethinking the Administrative Presidency* (Baltimore: Johns Hopkins University Press, 2015).

55. Steven M. Teles, "Kludgeocracy in America," *National Affairs* 17 (Fall 2013): 97–114.

56. Adrian Ellis, "Neutrality and the Civil Service," in Robert E. Goodin and Andrew Reeve, eds., *Liberal Neutrality* (London: Routledge, 1989), pp. 84–105.

57. William J. Stuntz, *The Collapse of American Criminal Justice* (Cambridge, MA: Harvard University Press, 2011). See also John Pfaff, *Locked In* (New York: Basic Books, 2017).

58. Alan Jacobs, *Governing for the Long-Term* (Cambridge: Cambridge University Press, 2011).

59. Gordon Tullock, *Rent-Seeking* (Brookfield, VT: Edward Elgar, 1993).

60. Alan S. Blinder, "Is Government Too Political?," *Foreign Affairs* 76 (1997): 115–126 at 123–124.

61. The constitutional bill of rights in Canada is known as the Canadian Charter of Rights and Freedoms. Thus a "Charter-proof" piece of legislation is one that is able to (or expected to be able to) survive a "Charter challenge" in the courts.

62. Gary Lawson, "The Rise and Rise of the Administrative State," *Harvard Law Review* 107 (1994): 1231–1254.

63. Friedrich Hayek, *The Road to Serfdom* (London: Routledge, 2001).

64. Miriam Golden and Ray Fisman, *Corruption: What Everyone Needs to Know* (Oxford: Oxford University Press, 2017).

65. This admirable summary is from Ian Brodie, "In Defense of Political Staff," *Canadian Parliamentary Review* 35 (2012): 33–39. On the fourth point, recall Arthur Kroeger's account, in *Retiring the Crow*, p. 51, of how he was able to use his contacts in the Privy Council Office to insert material into the prime minister's briefing notes.

66. Specifically, John Snobelen and Al Palladini, both Cabinet ministers in the government of Premier Mike Harris.

67. Kelly Grant, "Former Surgeon to Shake Up Ontario's Health Ministry," *Globe and Mail*, March 27, 2014.

68. Key informant interview, Ministry of Health and Long-Term Care, Province of Ontario, April 2016 (anonymized).

69. E.g., Henry S. Richardson, *Democratic Autonomy* (Oxford: Oxford University Press, 2002).

70. Kroeger, *Retiring the Crow*, p. 225.

71. Quoted in Parris, *Constitutional Bureaucracy*, p. 106.

72. Graham Steele, *What I Learned about Politics* (Halifax, CAN: Nimbus, 2014), pp. 36–44. Constituency work is also, I should note, undertheorized, given the amount of time it occupies in the life of the average parliamentarian.

73. Jürgen Habermas, "Popular Sovereignty as Procedure," in Habermas, *Between Facts and Norms*, pp. 463–490.

74. It is sometimes thought that this principle prevails only in parliamentary systems. In fact, it is more general. The alternative candidate most often posited is a principle of "judicial supremacy," where the country's higher court is given the "last word" over the legislature. Yet this is largely an illusion, in part because there are always provisions for democratic amendment of the constitution, and so any court ruling can be overturned if a sufficiently concerted effort is made. In the United States, however, where the Supreme Court is quite active at striking down legislation on constitutional grounds, there is in fact no constitutional basis for this authority, it is merely a practice that evolved during the 19th century. In other words, constitutional review of legislation is part of the unwritten constitution of the United States.

75. Similarly, as Paul du Gay notes, ministerial accountability "never required that ministers should be policy-makers and officials merely the administrators, but only that the minister should have the final word and be publicly accountable." Paul du Gay, *In Praise of Bureaucracy* (London: Sage, 2000), p. 116.

76. John Stuart Mill, *Considerations on Responsible Government* (New York: Harper & Brothers, 1862), p. 100.

77. Lorne Sossin, "Defining Boundaries: The Constitutional Argument for Bureaucratic Independence and Its Implication for the Accountability of the Public Service," *Research Studies* 2 (2006): 25–72.

78. This issue came to the forefront in Canada during the "sponsorship scandal," the Gomery Commission, and the subsequent Accountability Act passed in 2006. The general verdict was that the civil service had crossed the line, engaging in activities that served to support the Liberal Party rather than the Government of Canada (Sossin, "Defining Boundaries," pp. 40–42). A less consequential, but more illustrative, example occurred in 2015, when a federal minister used departmental resources and staff to shoot a "campaign-style" video, promoting a policy that had not yet been enacted. Jordan Press, "Opposition Demands Explanation for Pierre Poilievre's 'Vanity' Video," *Ottawa Citizen*, May 15, 2015.

79. Du Gay, *In Praise of Bureaucracy*, p. 141.

80. Adrian Ellis, "Neutrality and the Civil Service," in Robert E. Goodin and Andrew Reeve, eds., *Liberal Neutrality* (London: Routledge, 1989), pp. 84–105 at 87.

81. Max Weber, "Politics as a Vocation," in H. H. Gerth and C. Wright Mills, eds., *From Max Weber: Essays in Sociology* (London: Routledge, 1948), pp. 77–128 at 95.

82. Ellis, "Neutrality and the Civil Service," p. 87.

83. Donald Savoie, *Breaking the Bargain* (Toronto: University of Toronto Press, 2003). See also Kenneth Kernaghan, "Political Rights and Political Neutrality: Finding the Balance Point," *Canadian Public Administration* 29 (1986): 639–652.

84. Anecdotally, I should mention that this feature of the arrangement is the one that has been met with the greatest incredulity by the Chinese state officials I have taught.

85. This generates what is sometimes described as the "iron triangle" of political neutrality, ministerial responsibility, and civil service anonymity. See Geoffrey Marshall, *Constitutional Conventions* (Oxford: Oxford University Press, 1984), p. 210.

86. Ken Rasmussen, "Saskatchewan's Deputy Ministers: Political Executives or Public Servants?," in Jacques Bourgault and Christopher Dunn, eds., *Deputy Ministers in Canada* (Toronto: University of Toronto Press, 2014), pp. 239–261 at 257–258.

87. For example, see John C. Tait, *A Strong Foundation: Report of the Task Force on Values and Ethics in the Public Service* (Ottawa: Canadian Centre for Management Development, 2000). See also the 1985 UK "Armstrong Memorandum," accessed Sept. 1, 2018, https://www.civilservant.org.uk/library/1996_Armstrong_Memorandum.pdf.

88. Canadian Environmental Law Association, "Radon in Indoor Air: A Review of Law and Policy in Canada," accessed Mar. 30, 2020, https://carst.ca/resources/Documents/Radon-Report-with-Appendices.pdf.

89. Brian Cubbon, "The Duty of the Professional," in Richard A. Chapman, ed., *Ethics in Public Service* (Ottawa: Carlton University Press, 1993), pp 7–14 at 9.

90. Cubbon, "Duty of the Professional," p. 8.

91. Rohr, *Ethics for Bureaucrats.*

92. In this I am following Jürgen Habermas, *Moral Consciousness and Communicative Action*, trans. Christian Lenhardt and Shierry Weber Nicholson (Cambridge, MA: MIT Press, 1999), p. 97.

93. Pierre Rosanvallon, *Counter-Democracy*, trans. Arthur Goldhammer (New York: Cambridge University Press, 2008); Rosanvallon, *Democratic Legitimacy*, trans. Arthur Goldhammer (Princeton, NJ: Princeton University Press, 2011); Rosanvallon, *The Society of Equals*, trans. Arthur Goldhammer (Cambridge, MA: Harvard University Press, 2013); Rosanvallon, *Good Government*, trans Arthur Goldhammer (Cambridge, MA: Harvard University Press, 2018). It should be noted that Habermas also takes administrative power quite seriously, given that he describes the state as an autonomously steered subsystem. And yet he treats it mainly as a problem that needs to be controlled. See Habermas, "Popular Sovereignty as Procedure," in Habermas, *Between Facts and Norms.*

94. Rosanvallon, *Good Government*, p. 106.

95. Rosanvallon, *Democratic Legitimacy*, p. 17.

96. Ibid., p. 29.

97. Rosanvallon, *Good Government*, p. 96.

98. Ibid.

99. Rosanvallon, *Democratic Legitimacy*, pp. 88–94.

100. Ibid., p. 87.

101. Rosanvallon, *Good Government*, pp. 106–110.

102. Ibid., pp. 107–108.

103. Juan J. Linz, "The Perils of Presidentialism," *Journal of Democracy* 1 (1990): 51–69.

104. Arthur M. Schlesinger Jr., *The Imperial Presidency* (Boston: Houghton Mifflin, 1973).

105. For a vigorous critique of this tendency, see Vincent Ostrom, *The Intellectual Crisis in American Public Administration*, 3rd ed. (Tuscaloosa: University of Alabama Press, 2008).

106. Ian Brodie, *At the Centre of Government* (Montreal: McGill-Queen's University Press, 2018), pp. 160–166.

Chapter 2

1. Noteworthy contributions include John Rohr, *Ethics for Bureaucrats*, 2nd ed. (New York: Marcel Dekker, 1989); Terry Cooper, *The Responsible Administrator*, 5th ed. (San Francisco: Jossey-Bass, 2006); Carol W. Lewis, *The Ethics Challenge in Public Service* (San Francisco: Jossey-Bass, 1991); Dennis Thompson, "The Possibility of Administrative Ethics," *Public Administration Review* 45 (1985): 555–561; Thompson, *Restoring Responsibility* (Cambridge: Cambridge University Press, 2005); and Arthur Applbaum, "The Remains of the Role," *Governance* 6 (1993): 545–557.

2. The only journals with a sustained focus on ethics are *Public Integrity* and the more general *Governance.*

3. E.g., Allan Buchanan, "Toward a Theory of the Ethics of Bureaucratic Organizations," *Business Ethics Quarterly* 6 (1996): 419–440; David Luban, Alan Strudler, and David Wasserman, "Moral Responsibility in the Age of Bureaucracy," *Michigan Law Review* 90 (1992): 2348–2392.

4. Douglass C. North, John Joseph Wallis, and Barry R. Weingast, *Violence and Social Orders* (Cambridge: Cambridge University Press, 2009), p. 159.

5. Patrick Dunleavy provides a useful categorization of different agency types belonging to the state: delivery, regulatory, transfer, contract, control, taxing, trading and servicing. "The Architecture of the British Central State, Part II: Empirical Findings," *Public Administration*, 67 (1989): 391–417. For précis see Keith Dowding, *The Civil Service* (London: Routledge, 1995), pp. 88–89.

6. For the Canadian federal government code, see *Value and Ethics Code for the Public Sector* (Ottawa: Treasury Board, 2011). The UK Civil Service Code can be found at https://www.gov.uk/government/publications/civil-service-code (accessed Sept. 25, 2017). The United States is more complicated. A useful compendium of codes can be found at the Illinois Institute of Technology's *Ethics Codes Collection,* http://ethics.iit.edu/ecodes/ (accessed Sept. 25, 2017), which provides links to all important federal government executive orders, supplementary agency codes, as well as state codes.

7. The American literature represents a partial exception to this generalization, because of the enormous attention lavished on the President.

8. Daniel Carpenter, *Reputation and Power* (Princeton, NJ: Princeton University Press, 2010), p. 192; Carpenter, *The Forging of Bureaucratic Autonomy* (Princeton, NJ: Princeton University Press, 2001).

9. John Kingdon, *Agendas, Alternatives, and Public Policies*, 2nd ed. (New York: Pearson, 2003).

10. Rohr, *Ethics for Bureaucats*, p. 3.

11. For discussion, see Joseph Raz, *The Authority of Law* (Oxford: Clarendon Press, 1979), p. 27. Raz discusses the work of Robert Paul Wolff.

12. One can find a similar argument in Carol W. Lewis, *The Ethics Challenge in Public Service* (San Francisco: Jossey-Bass, 1991), criticizing what she calls the "integrity" approach: "When reduced to simplistic do-good exhortation, it overlooks the competing claims that perplex an ethical manager. By neglecting the decision-making environment and focusing exclusively on autonomous moral individuals, the integrity approach sweeps aside organizational and other influences that affect behavior" (p. 11). What she proposes, however, is a "fusion" between a "compliance" framework and the "integrity" framework. Fusion is an unfortunate term, because it suggests that moral conduct involves meeting institutional demands halfway. This obscures the fact that the institutions themselves may be the source of the moral demands.

13. Cooper, *Responsible Administrator*, pp. 100–105.

14. As Paul du Gay puts it, "The ethical attributes of the 'good' bureaucrat—adherence to procedure, acceptance of sub- and superordination, commitment to the purposes of the office and so forth—. . . should be regarded as a positive moral and ethical achievement in their own right. They represent the product of particular ethical techniques and practices through which individuals develop the disposition and

capacity to conduct themselves according to the ethos of bureaucratic office." *In Praise of Bureaucracy* (London: Sage, 2000), p. 4.

15. As a point of entry, see David Luban, *Lawyers and Justice* (Princeton, NJ: Princeton University Press, 1988).

16. Arthur Applbaum, *Ethics for Adversaries* (Princeton, NJ: Princeton University Press, 2000).

17. For some further examples of the sort of dilemmas public servants may face, see Lewis, *Ethics Challenge in Public Service*, p. 1.

18. David H. Rosenbloom, "Public Administration Theory and the Separation of Powers," *Public Administration Review* 43 (1983): 219–227.

19. Robert K. Christensen, Holly T. Goerdel, Sean Nicholson-Crotty, "Management, Law, and the Pursuit of the Public Good in Public Administration," *Journal of Public Administration Research and Theory*, suppl. 1 (2011): i125–i140 at i130. David H. Rosenbloom and Katherine Naff, *Public Administration and Law*, 2nd ed. (New York: Marcel Dekker, 1997).

20. Kathryn G. Denhardt and Bayard L. Catron, "The Management of Ideals: A Political Perspective on Ethics," *Public Administration Review* 49 (1989): 187–193 at 188–189.

21. I use the term "discretion" in Robert Goodin's sense, to describe "an area of conduct which is generally governed by rules but where the dictates of the rules are indeterminate." Robert Goodin, *Reasons for Welfare* (Princeton, NJ: Princeton University Press, 1988), p. 186.

22. John D. Huber and Charles R. Shipan, *Deliberate Discretion?* (Cambridge: Cambridge University Press, 2002), pp. 44–77.

23. Michael Lipsky, *Street-Level Bureaucracy* (New York: Russell Sage, 1980), p. 3.

24. Dennis Thompson, "Bureaucracy and Democracy," in *Restoring Responsibility: Ethics in Business, Government and Healthcare* (Cambridge: Cambridge University Press, 2005), pp. 50–70.

25. Thompson, "Bureaucracy and Democracy," p. 57.

26. The term "accountability" refers to the explicit institutional obligation, where accountability relations determine who has to provide an account to whom; whereas "responsibility" deals with moral relations of obligation, such as who owes loyalty to whom. The difference is most clear-cut when the person who is responsible for a particular mistake differs from the person who is held accountable.

27. The classic work in this tradition in the United States is Paul H. Appleby, *Morality and Administration in Democratic Government* (Baton Rouge: Louisiana State University Press, 1952).

28. In the United States, it should be noted, the question of which elected official an administrator owes allegiance to does not admit of any simple answer. There are, on the one hand, the president and his or her appointed agency head or cabinet official and, on the other hand, the congressional committee that exercises oversight of the agency. There is also the statute, or collection of statutes, from which the agency derives its authority. In part because of legislative gridlock, there is room for significant divergence between the latter two (i.e., the current congressional majority may be entirely unsympathetic to the statute that granted authority to the agency, but is

unable to change it). One gets the sense that most US career officials feel primary allegiance to the enabling statutes, which define the "mission" of the agency.

29. Woodrow Wilson, "The Study of Administration," *Political Science Quarterly* 2 (1887): 197–222. See also Paul H. Appleby, "Toward Better Public Administration," *Public Administration Review* 7 (1947): 93–99.

30. Carl J. Friedrich, "Public Policy and the Nature of Administrative Responsibility," in Carl J. Friedrich and Edward S. Mason, eds., *Public Policy* (Cambridge, MA: Harvard University Press, 1940), pp. 5–7; Paul H. Appleby, *Policy and Administration* (University: University of Alabama Press, 1949).

31. Lorne Sossin writes, with respect to the constitutional status of the civil service:

> It is true that no express provisions in any of Canada's constitutional texts accord the public service constitutional status (as they do, for example, the judiciary), but it is equally true that a range of unwritten constitutional conventions and principles clearly give rise to obligations, responsibilities and constraints on decision-making by members of the public service which arguably together confer constitutional status on the public service as an organ of government. Thus, in my view, it is misleading to suggest that public servants have no constitutional identity independent of their Minister, or to suggest that public servants are subject to no constitutional or legal accountability beyond loyalty to their Minister.

See Lorne Sossin, *Defining Boundaries: The Constitutional Argument for Bureaucratic Independence and Its Implication for the Accountability of the Public Service* (Ottawa: Gomery Inquiry, 2006), p. 27.

32. Arthur Applbaum's paper, "Professional Detachment: The Executioner of Paris," *Harvard Law Review* 109 (1995): 458–486, moves from a discussion of Sanson, the executioner of Paris, to a fairly lengthy discussion of Adolph Eichmann and Nazi war crimes. Interestingly, the revised version of the paper that appeared as a chapter of Applbaum's book *Ethics for Adversaries* (Princeton, NJ: Princeton University Press, 1999), contains no reference to the Nazis. This is, I would hope, in recognition of the fact that the "Nazi card" has been played one too many times in moral philosophy, and seldom helps to advance any discussion.

33. William H. Whyte, *The Organization Man* (New York: Simon & Schuster, 1956). See also William G. Scott and David K. Hart, *Organizational America* (Boston: Houghton Mifflin, 1979).

34. Donald J. Savoie, *Breaking the Bargain: Public Servants, Ministers and Parliament* (Toronto: University of Toronto Press, 2003), pp. 50–51.

35. Allan Buchanan, "Toward a Theory of the Ethics of Bureaucratic Organizations," *Business Ethics Quarterly* 6 (1996): 419–440.

36. Paul Milgrom and John Roberts, *Economics, Organization and Management* (Englewood Cliffs, NJ: Prentice Hall, 1992), p. 170.

37. For more extensive discussion, see Joseph Heath, "The Uses and Abuses of Agency Theory," in *Morality, Competition and the Firm* (New York: Oxford University Press, 2014), pp. 263–293.

38. Buchanan, "Toward a Theory of the Ethics of Bureaucratic Organizations," p. 422.

39. I say "functionalist-sounding" because there are a variety of ways of explaining how these norms could arise that need not appeal to any "function."

40. Buchanan, "Toward a Theory of the Ethics of Bureaucratic Organizations," p. 427.

41. It is worth noting that the Nolan principles were formulated primarily to apply to politicians, but they have ramified throughout the civil service, so that "in the public sector a rather catch-all Nolan code is supported by a mountain of guidance and regulatory best practice." William L. Hutton and Andrew Massey, "Professional Ethics and Public Service: Can Professionals Serve Two Masters?," *Public Money and Management* 26 (2006): 23–30 at 25.

42. On the latter, see Dennis F. Thompson, "Moral Responsibility of Public Officials: The Problem of Many Hands," *American Political Science Review* 74 (1980): 905–916.

43. Halsey Rogers and Margaret Koziol, *Provider Absence Surveys in Education and Health* (Washington, DC: World Bank, 2011); also Nazmul Chaudhury, Jeffrey Hammer, Michael Kremer, Karthik Muralidharana, and F. Halsey Rogers, "Missing in Action: Teacher and Health Worker Absence in Developing Countries," *Journal of Economic Perspectives* 20 (2006): 91–116.

44. An early, influential formulation of this criticism can be found in Friedrich, "Public Policy and the Nature of Administrative Responsibility," pp. 5–7.

45. Carol W. Lewis, *The Ethics Challenge in Public Service* (San Francisco: Jossey-Bass, 1991), p. 8.

46. Herman Finer, *The British Civil Service* (London: Allen and Unwin, 1937), p. 196.

47. Brian Cubbon, "The Duty of the Professional," in Richard A. Chapman, ed., *Ethics in Public Service* (Edinburgh: Edinburgh University Press, 1993), p. 10.

48. Henry Parris, *Constitutional Bureaucracy* (London: Allen and Unwin, 1969), p. 299.

49. Oliver Williamson, *Markets and Hierarchies* (New York: Free Press, 1983), p. 31.

50. Kenneth J. Meier and Laurence J. O'Toole Jr. "Political Control versus Bureaucratic Values: Reframing the Debate," *Public Administration Review* 66 (2006): 177–192.

51. Tony Evans, *Professional Discretion in Welfare Services* (Farnham, UK: Ashgate, 2010), p. 37.

52. Statistics Canada, *Table 10-10-0025-01 Public Sector Employment, Wages and Salaries, Seasonally Unadjusted and Adjusted*, http://www.statcan.gc.ca/tables-tableaux/sum-som/l01/cst01/govt62d-eng.htm, accessed July 7, 2018.

53. János Kornai, Eric Maskin, and Gérard Roland, "Understanding the Soft Budget Constraint," *Journal of Economic Literature* 41 (2003): 1095–1136.

54. Graham Steele, *What I Learned About Politics* (Halifax: Nimbus, 2014), pp. 120–121.

55. See Joseph Heath and Wayne Norman, "Stakeholder Theory, Corporate Governance and Public Management," *Journal of Business Ethics* 53 (2004): 247–265.

56. Huber and Shipan, *Deliberate Discretion?*

57. Gary C. Bryner, *Bureaucratic Discretion* (New York: Pergamon Press, 1987), p. 141.

58. As Richard B. Stewart notes, "Individual politicians often find far more to be lost than gained in taking a readily identifiable stand on a controversial issue of social or economic policy." Richard B. Stewart, "The Reformation of American Administrative Law," *Harvard Law Review* 88 (1975): 1669–1813 at 1695.

59. Government Legal Department, *The Judge over Your Shoulder: A Guide to Good Decision-Making*, Gov.uk, https://www.gov.uk/government/publications/judge-over-your-shoulder, accessed May 16, 2019.

60. Dowding, *Civil Service*, p. 178.

61. Savoie, *Breaking the Bargain*, pp. 9–11.

62. In the United States, a somewhat delayed version was initiated under the banner of "reinventing government," usually associated with the early years of the Clinton administration. See David Osborne and Ted Gaebler, *Reinventing Government* (New York: Penguin, 1993).

63. Philip H. Jos and Mark E. Tompkins, "Keeping It Public: Defending Public Service Values in a Customer Service Age," *Public Administration Review* 69 (2009):1077–1086.

64. Per Lægreid writes, "NPM tends to supplement the vertical mandatory accountability relationship with more voluntary horizontal accountability arrangements such as social accountability to customers and users of public services as well as market-based forms of accountability. Instead of being integrated elements of responsible, collective public bodies, public administrators are supposed to be autonomous and entrepreneurial and pay attention to signals they receive from their clients or customers." Per Lægreid, "Accountability and New Public Management," in Mark Bovens, Robert E. Goodin, and Thomas Schillemans, eds., *The Oxford Handbook of Public Accountability* (Oxford: Oxford University Press, 2014), pp. 324–338 at 326. See also du Gay, *In Praise of Bureaucracy*, p. 108.

65. For an overview of the limited impact this model had in North America, see Andrew Graham and Alisdair Roberts, "The Agency Concept in North America," in Christopher Pollitt and Colin Talbot, eds., *Unbundled Government* (New York: Routledge, 2004): 157–163; Donald J. Savoie, "What Is Wrong with the New Public Management?," *Canadian Public Administration* 38 (1995): 112–121. For general discussion of the difficulties, see H. George Frederickson, "Ethics and the New Managerialism," *Public Administration and Management* 4 (1999): 299–324.

66. Roberto R. C. Pires, "Beyond the Fear of Discretion: Flexibility, Performance, and Accountability in the Management of Regulatory Bureaucracies," *Regulation and Governance* 5 (2010): 43–69.

67. Avinash Dixit, "The Power of Incentives in Private versus Public Organizations," *American Economic Review* 87 (1997): 378–382; George Baker, "Incentive Contracts and Performance Measurements," *Journal of Political Economy* 100 (1992): 598–614; Robert Gibbons, "Incentives in Organizations," *Journal of Economic Perspectives* 12 (1998): 115–132.

68. Friedrich, "Public Policy and the Nature of Administrative Responsibility," p. 19.

69. Donald Savoie, *What Ever Happened to the Music Teacher?* (Montreal: McGill-Queen's University Press, 2013).

70. Francis Fukuyama, *Political Order and Political Decay* (New York: Farrar, Straus and Giroux, 2014), pp. 377–380.

71. Emily Harris-McLeod, "Incentives for Public Service Workers and the Implications of Crowding Out Theory," *Public Policy and Governance Review* 4. no. 2 (2013): 5–21.

72. Dan Ariely, *Predictably Irrational* (New York: HarperCollins, 2008).

73. Ariely, *Predictably Irrational*, p. 86.

74. This phrase is from the implementation guidelines, adopted in 1985, for the 1984 Code of Ethics of the American Society for Public Administration, https://www.aspanet.org/ASPADocs/1984-Guidelines.pdf, accessed July 22, 2019.

75. Donald Savoie writes, "Imagine, if you will, an opposition member saying that the opposition accepts that the local manager made two—or even just one—high-profile mistakes because that is the price to pay for empowerment." "What Is Wrong with the New Public Management," p. 115.

76. Paul G. Thomas, "The Changing Nature of Accountability," in Guy Peter and Donald J. Savoie, eds., *Taking Stock: Assessing Public Sector Reforms* (Ottawa: Canadian Centre for Management Development, 1998), pp. 375–378; Henry Mintzberg, "Managing Government, Governing Management," *Harvard Business Review* (May-June 1996): 75–83 at 79; Lægreid, "Accountability and New Public Management," p. 327.

77. Savoie, *What Ever Happened to the Music Teacher?* p. 127.

78. Bourgault, "Federal Deputy Ministers," p. 396.

79. An example of partisan criticism: "In the real world, people show up for work and they get a salary. They don't get extra 'performance pay' for doing what they're supposed to do. Not so with Ontario's Liberal government." "Wynne Must Scrap Performance Pay," *Toronto Sun*, Oct. 15, 2013.

80. Daniel J. Fiorino, "Citizen Participation and Environmental Risk: A Survey of Institutional Mechanisms," *Science, Technology, and Human Values* 15 (1990): 226–243. For an overview of relative merits of different instruments, see Gene Rowe and Lynn J. Frewer, "Public Participation Methods: A Framework for Evaluation," *Science, Technology, and Human Values* 25 (2000): 3–29.

81. Vivien Lowndes, Lawrence Pratchett, and Gerry Stoker, "Trends in Public Participation: Part 1—Local Government Perspective," *Public Administration* 79 (2001): 205–222 at 210.

82. Thompson, "Bureaucracy and Democracy," p. 66.

83. Jack Knight and James Johnson, "Aggregation and Deliberation: On the Possibility of Democratic Legitimacy," *Political Theory* 22 (1994): 277–296 at 283.

84. Barry Checkoway, "The Politics of Public Hearings," *Journal of Applied Behavioral Science* 17 (1981): 566–582 at 568–569; Fiorino, "Citizen Participation and Environmental Risk," p. 231.

85. For discussion, see Christian Hunold, "Corporatism, Pluralism, and Democracy: Toward a Deliberative Theory of Bureaucratic Accountability," *Governance* 14 (2001): 151–167.

86. Genevieve Fuji Johnson, *Democratic Illusion* (Toronto: University of Toronto Press, 2015), p. 121.

87. Lowndes, Pratchett, and Stoker, "Trends in Public Participation," p. 212.

88. As Pierre Rosanvallon notes, this means that in France the number of engaged members of the public is only slightly larger than the number of people who hold elected office of one sort or another. *Democratic Legitimacy*, p. 207.

89. Julie Dolan and David H. Rosenbloom, *Representative Bureaucracy: Classic Readings and Continuing Controversies* (Armonk, NY: M. E. Sharpe, 2003).
90. Terry L. Cooper, "Citizenship and Professionalism in Public Administration," *Public Administration Review* 44 (1984): 143–151.
91. *The 2009 Citizen Panel's Recommendations to Edmonton City Council* (Edmonton: City of Edmonton, 2009).
92. For discussion of these issues, see Ian Brodie, *At the Centre of Government* (Montreal: McGill-Queen's University Press, 2018), pp. 160–166.
93. Friedrich's "Public Policy and the Nature of Administrative Responsibility," is probably the first attempt to articulate such a model. It differs from my own in that it does not attempt to articulate a professional ethic specific to the public service; instead, in keeping with the "scientific management" fashion of the day, it tries to assimilate public-sector professionalism to that of science. See also Rosanvallon, *Democratic Legitimacy*, p. 41.
94. For more detailed discussion, see Sareh Pouryousefi, "A Normative Model of Professionalization" (unpublished PhD diss., University of Toronto, 2013).
95. Arthur Applbaum, "The Remains of the Role," *Governance* 6 (1993): 545–557 at 550.
96. Applbaum, "Remains of the Role," p. 550. See also Jørgen Grønnegård Christensen and Niels Opstrup, "Bureaucratic Dilemmas: Civil Servants between Political Responsiveness and Normative Constraints," *Governance* 31 (2018): 481–498.
97. Patrick Overeem and Jelle Verhoef, "Moral Dilemmas, Theoretical Confusion: Value Pluralism and Its Supposed Implications for Public Administration," *Administration and Society* 46 (2014): 986–1009. Also Michael W. Spicer, *In Defense of Politics in Public Administration* (Tuscaloosa: University of Alabama Press, 2010); Hendrik Wagenaar, "Value Pluralism in Public Administration," *Administrative Theory and Praxis* 21 (1999): 441–449.
98. Denhardt and Catron, "Management of Ideals."
99. Ideally, it should also be neutral with respect to the partisan ideological positions taken by various political parties, although Rawls's specific conception of justice obviously fails this test (the difference principle articulates a very controversial egalitarian commitment). The principles of modern liberalism that I articulate in chapter 3 are intended to be "more neutral" in this regard, primarily because they are unranked vis-à-vis one another.
100. Or, of course, in the United States, France, and many other countries, the direct election of individuals to positions within the executive.
101. Bo Rothstein, *The Quality of Government* (Chicago: University of Chicago Press, 2011), pp. 77–82. In the Canadian context, see Campbell Sharman, "Political Legitimacy for an Appointed Senate," *IRPP Choices* 14 (2008): 1–26.
102. See Kevin Olson, *Reflexive Democracy* (Cambridge, MA: MIT Press, 2006), pp. 94–99.
103. The passage continues "far more than on when, how and by whom it was created." Ian Shapiro, *Politics against Domination* (Cambridge, MA: Harvard University Press, 2016), p. 47.
104. Rosanvallon, *Democratic Legitimacy*, p. 87.

105. Glen Rangwala, "The Democratic Transition in Iraq and the Discovery of Its Limitations," in Alex Danchev and John MacMillan, eds., *The Iraq War and Democratic Politics* (London: Routledge, 2005), pp. 157–176 at 161.

106. There has also been some discussion of the issue with respect to transnational institutions, e.g., Ruth W. Grant and Robert O. Keohane, "Accountability and Abuses of Power in World Politics," *American Political Science Review* 99 (2005): 29–43, articulate seven different ways that organizations can be accountable *other* than classic democratic accountability.

107. Fritz W. Scharpf, "Interdependence and Democratic Legitimation," in Susan J. Pharr and Robert D. Putnam, eds., *Disaffected Democracies* (Princeton, NJ: Princeton University Press, 2000).

108. Francis Fukuyama, *Political Order and Political Decay* (New York: Farrar, Straus and Giroux, 2014), p. 499.

109. Fukuyama, *Political Order and Political Decay*, p. 498.

110. Rothstein, *Quality of Government*, p. 80.

111. Of course, the public is free to elect politicians who are committed to dismantling any or all of these sectors of the welfare state (although it is worth noting that many such politicians actually change their minds about the desirability of doing so once they are in office). Yet even if this were to occur, there would still be a commitment to dismantling (or, typically, privatizing) the relevant apparatus in an orderly fashion to ensure continuity of service to the public. For example, it would be a deep betrayal of the public trust for the state to simply close down an urban transportation system, on the grounds that it no longer has any desire to be in the business of providing transportation services, without putting into place some plan for a transition to private transportation.

112. For more extensive discussion, see Joseph Heath, *The Efficient Society* (Toronto: Penguin, 2001).

113. Rothstein, *Quality of Government*, p. 95.

114. Ibid.

115. Ibid.

116. Rothstein distinguishes his notion of impartiality from the rule of law on the grounds that the former is broader, applicable in areas of public administration that are not directly governed by law (e.g., education, healthcare, etc.). Rothstein, *Quality of Government*, p. 29. My own notion of "rule of law values," elaborated in chapter 6, is intended to have the same generality.

117. Rothstein, *Quality of Government*, p. 12.

118. John C. Tait, *A Strong Foundation: Report of the Task Force on Public Sector Values and Ethics* (Ottawa: Canadian Centre for Management Development, 1996), p. 18.

119. Cubbon, "Duty of the Professional," p. 9.

120. For theoretical defense of this model, see Hugh Heclo, "OMB and the Presidency: The Problem of Neutral Competence," *Public Interest* 38 (1975): 80–98.

121. Michael Quinlan, "Ethics in the Public Service," *Governance* 6 (1993): 538–544 at 542. The Tait Report points to the enthusiasm with which the Canadian public service set about constructing, and then dismantling, the National Energy Program as a sign of its capacity for loyal implementation.

122. Jacques Bourgault, "Federal Deputy Ministers: Serial Servers Looking for Influence," in Jacques Bourgault and Christopher Dunn, eds., *Deputy Ministers in Canada* (Toronto: University of Toronto Press, 2014), pp. 3654–400 at 378.

123. The Tait Report, for instance, argues that "faithful execution of democratic decisions is what a public service is for, not to substitute for them some other definitions of the public good" (*Strong Foundation*, p. 16), and claims that in a democratic system of government, it is the prerogative of elected officials "to define the public interest" (p. 17).

124. Sossin, *Defining Boundaries*, p. 50.

125. James C. Scott, *Seeing like a State* (New Haven, CT: Yale University Press, 1998).

126. Cooper, *Responsible Administrator*, p. 75.

127. Jane Jacobs, *The Death and Life of Great American Cities* (New York: Random House, 1961).

128. J. M. Granatstein, *The Ottawa Men: The Civil Service Mandarins, 1935–1957* (Toronto: Oxford University Press, 1982).

129. Bourgault, "Federal Deputy Ministers," p. 379.

130. For classic statement, see Luther Gulick, "Notes on the Theory of Organization," in Luther Gulick and Lyndall Urwick, eds., *Papers on the Science of Administration* (New York: Columbia University Press, 1937), pp. 1–49 at 9.

Chapter 3

1. See M. Rainer Lepsius, *Max Weber and Institutional Theory* (Geneva: Springer, 2017), pp. 23–34.

2. Rainer Forst, *Toleration in Conflict*, trans. Ciaran Cronin (Cambridge: Cambridge University Press, 2003).

3. For discussion, see Benjamin J. Kaplan, *Divided by Faith* (Cambridge, MA: Harvard University Press, 2007), pp. 15–22.

4. For discussion, see Larry Seidentop, *Inventing the Individual* (Cambridge, MA: Harvard University Press, 2014), p. 308.

5. On the relation between vice and sin, see Jean Delumeau, *Sin and Fear*, trans. Eric Nicholson (New York: St. Martin's, 1990), pp. 189–195.

6. Delumeau, *Sin and Fear*, p. 192.

7. See David Wootton, ed., *Divine Right and Democracy* (London: Penguin, 1987). Also Jacques-Benigne Bossuet, *Politics Drawn from the Very Words of Holy Scripture*, trans. Patrick Riley (Cambridge: Cambridge University Press, 1990).

8. Max Weber, *The Sociology of Religion*, trans. Ephraim Fischoff (Boston: Beacon Press, 1993).

9. E.g., see Jonathan Robinson, *William of Ockham's Early Theory of Property Rights in Context* (Leiden: Brill, 2013).

10. A good example of this tendency can be found in Alan Ryan, *On Politics* (London: Allen Lane, 2012).

11. Abu Nasr al-Farabi, *On the Perfect State*, trans. Richard Walzer (Oxford: Oxford University Press, 1985).

12. In *On Monastic Vows* he declared monasticism to be "contrary to both common sense and reason," Helmut Lehmann, ed., *Luther's Works*, vol. 44 (Philadelphia: Fortress Press, 1965), p. 251.

13. Charles Taylor, *Sources of the Self* (Cambridge: Cambridge University Press, 1989), p. 211.

14. "Of Geneva, and of Calvin," in T. Francklin, ed., *The Works of M. de Voltaire*, vol. 4 (London: S. Crowder et al., 1779), pp. 77–81 at 79.

15. For the first definition, see Aristotle, *Nicomachean Ethics*, trans. Martin Ostwald (New York: Macmillan, 1962), pp. 14–19 (1097a–1098b), for the second, see p. 292 (1178a–b).

16. For discussion, see John Marshall, *John Locke, Toleration and Early Enlightenment Culture* (Cambridge: Cambridge University Press, 2006), p. 215.

17. For discussion, see J. S. McClelland, *A History of Western Political Thought* (London: Routledge, 1996), p. 120.

18. St. Thomas Aquinas, *Summa Theologica*, trans. Fathers of the English Benedictine Province (New York: Benzinger, 1947), Pt. II-II q. 11 art. 3.

19. On England, see G.W. Bernard, "The Dissolution of the Monasteries," *History* 96 (2011): 390–409.

20. John Stuart Mill, *On Liberty*, ed. Elizabeth Rapaport (Indianapolis: Hackett, 1978), p. 84.

21. Kaplan, *Divided by Faith*, p. 21.

22. "For even when highly educated, well-intentioned Christians interpreted the Bible, beginning in the early 1520s, they did not and manifestly could not agree about its meaning or implications." Brad S. Gregory, *The Unintended Reformation* (Cambridge, MA: Harvard University Press, 2012), p. 368. The difficulty was compounded by widespread commitment to the Protestant doctrine of *sola scriptura*, which held that only biblical texts were authoritative.

23. Plato, *The Republic*, trans. Francis Cornford (Oxford: Oxford University Press, 1941), p. 44.

24. A good example of this can be found in Jean Bodin, *The Six Books of the Commonwealth*. He starts from the premise that religion underlies the authority of the state and the law, as a result of which the state must actively suppress all forms of doubt and dissent. If, however, the state finds itself in a situation where a substantial portion of the population consists of religious dissidents, and forcible conversion is not an option, then pragmatic considerations speak in favor of showing "indulgence" toward them. See Jean Bodin, *On Sovereignty*, trans. Julian H. Franklin (Cambridge: Cambridge University Press, 1992).

25. See Reinhart Koselleck, *Critique and Crisis* (Cambridge, MA: MIT Press, 1988), pp. 23–25.

26. Thomas Hobbes, *Leviathan*, ed. Richard Tuck (Cambridge: Cambridge University Press, 1991), p. 39.

27. Koselleck, *Critique and Crisis*.

28. John Locke, *Second Treatise of Government*, ed. C. B. Macpherson (Indianapolis: Hackett, 1980), p. 29 (§49).

29. Hobbes, *Leviathan*, p. 87.

30. Hobbes, *Leviathan*, p. 98. For survey of Hobbes's statements on this issue, see Susanne Sreedhar, *Hobbes on Resistance* (Cambridge: Cambridge University Press, 2010).

31. Montesquieu, *The Spirit of the Laws*, trans. Anne M. Cohler, Basia Carolyn Miller, and Harold Samuel Stone (Cambridge: Cambridge University Press, 1989), p. 155 (pt. 2, bk. 11, chap. 4).

32. Montesquieu, *Spirit of the Laws*, p. 157 (pt. 2, bk. 11, chap. 6).

33. Edmund Burke, *Thoughts and Details on Scarcity* (London: F. and C. Rivington, 1800), p. 18.

34. Burke, *Thoughts and Details on Scarcity*, p. 32.

35. For instance, the Confucian tradition in China is thoroughly perfectionist. As Joseph Chan describes it, "The Confucian ethical ideal is to be achieved through transformation of individual moral life and through implementing the basic social relationships in society and politics. The emperor and ministers are expected to behave according to the ethical requirements and to act benevolently and righteously so as to promote the material and ethical well-being of the common people. There is no fundamental separation between the familial, the social, and the political spheres. All parts should be ordered in mutually supportive ways to achieve the ethical ideal. This ideal, if achieved, can at once solve problems of individual morality, social harmony, and political stability." Joseph Chan, "Confucian Attitudes toward Ethical Pluralism," in Daniel A. Bell, ed., *Confucian Political Ethics* (Princeton, NJ: Princeton University Press, 2008), pp. 113–138 at 123.

36. David Hume, *A Treatise of Human Nature*, ed., P. H. Nidditch, 2nd ed. (Oxford: Oxford University Press, 1978), pp. 484–501.

37. Max Weber, "Politics as a Vocation," in H. H. Gerth and C. Wright Mills, eds., *From Max Weber: Essays in Sociology* (London: Routledge, 1948), pp. 77–128 at 78.

38. Locke, *Second Treatise of Government*, pp. 25–26 (§41).

39. For a modern formulation, see Michael J. Trebilcock, *The Limits of Freedom of Contract* (Cambridge, MA: Harvard University Press, 1993).

40. Max Weber, *Economy and Society*, vol. 2, Guenther Roth and Claus Wittich, eds. (Berkeley: University of California Press, 1978), p. 809.

41. Classic statements of the commitment to neutrality include Ronald Dworkin, "Liberalism," in Stuart Hampshire, ed., *Public and Private Morality* (Cambridge: Cambridge University Press, 1978); Charles Larmore, *Patterns of Moral Complexity* (Cambridge: Cambridge University Press, 1987). For debates, see Alexa Zelletin, *Liberal Neutrality* (Berlin: De Gruyter, 2012); Robert Goodin and Andrew Reeve, eds., *Liberal Neutrality* (London: Taylor and Francis, 1989); Steven Wall and George Klosko, *Perfectionism and Neutrality* (Lanham, MD: Rowman and Littlefield, 2003).

42. This is "justificatory neutrality." See typology in Peter Jones, "The Ideal of the Neutral State," in Robert Goodin and Andrew Reeve, eds., *Liberal Neutrality* (London: Routledge, 1989).

43. John Locke, "Third Letter for Toleration," in Richard Vernon, ed., *Locke on Toleration* (Cambridge: Cambridge University Press, 2010), p. 141.

44. Philip Harling, *The Modern British State* (Cambridge: Polity, 2001), p. 112. See also discussion at pp. 78–88.

45. Norman F. Cantor, *The Civilization of the Middle Ages*, rev. ed. (New York: HarperPerennial, 1994), pp. 202–203.

46. Jürgen Osterhammel, *The Transformation of the World*, trans. Patrick Camiller (Princeton, NJ: Princeton University Press, 2014), p. 572.

47. James C. Scott, *Seeing like a State* (New Haven, CT: Yale University Press, 1998).

48. James Robinson and Daron Acemoglu, *Why Nations Fail* (New York: Crown, 2012), p. 294.

49. Robert J. Steinfeld, *The Invention of Free Labour* (Chapel Hill: University of North Carolina Press, 1991).

50. James Tully, *A Discourse on Property* (Cambridge: Cambridge University Press, 1982).

51. David Gauthier, *Morals by Agreement* (Oxford: Clarendon Press, 1986).

52. E.g., Catherine Audard, *Qu'est ce que le libéralisme?* (Paris: Gallimard, 2009), p. 29; Joseph Raz, *The Morality of Freedom* (Oxford: Clarendon Press, 1986), p. 394.

53. See Charles Larmore, "Political Liberalism: Its Motivation and Goals," in David Sobel, Peter Vallentyne, and Steven Wall, *Oxford Studies in Political Philosophy*, vol. 1 (Oxford: Oxford University Press, 2015): 63–88 at 67–68.

54. Francis Fukuyama, *The Origins of Political Order* (New York: Farrar, Straus and Giroux, 2011), pp. 229–239.

55. Seidentop, *Inventing the Individual*, pp. 352–360.

56. Wilhelm von Humboldt, *The Limits of State Action*, trans. J. W. Burrow (Cambridge: Cambridge University Press, 1969).

57. Harling, *Modern British State*, p. 78.

58. "The history of the emergence of the theory of the modern state is also the history of the state's emerging claim to neutrality." McClelland, *History of Western Political Thought*, p. 289.

59. Friedrich Nietzche, "Twilight of the Idols," in *The Anti-Christ, Ecce Homo, Twilight of the Idols and Other Writings*, ed. Aaron Ridley and Judith Norman (Cambridge: Cambridge University Press, 2005), p. 213.

60. Stephen Holmes, *The Anatomy of Antiliberalism* (Cambridge, MA: Harvard University Press, 1993), p. xi.

61. Michael Halberstam, *Totalitarianism and the Modern Conception of Politics* (New Haven, CT: Yale University Press, 1999), p. 40.

62. Jonathan Israel, *Radical Enlightenment* (Oxford: Oxford University Press, 2001).

63. Locke, *Second Treatise of Government*, p. 44 (§82).

64. Immanuel Kant, *Grounding for the Metaphysics of Morals*, trans. James W. Ellington (Indianapolis: Hackett, 1981), p. 40 (at 434).

65. John Stuart Mill, *Utilitarianism*, ed. George Sher (Indianapolis: Hackett, 1979), p. 34.

66. Jean-Jacques Rousseau, *La nouvelle Héloïse* (Paris: Firmin Didot Frères, 1843), p. 493; my translation.

67. See Elie Halévy, *The Growth of Philosophical Radicalism*, trans. Mary Morris (New York: Macmillan, 1928).

68. William Godwin, *Enquiry Concerning Political Justice*, vol. 2. (London: G. G. and J. Robinson, 1798), p. 507.

69. Soame Jenyns, *A Free Inquiry into the Nature and Origin of Evil*, 4th ed. (London: R & J Dodsley, 1761), pp. 114.

70. The triumph of liberal political ideas in the moral sphere is now so complete that many philosophers have difficulty even conceptualizing a framework under which an activity such as masturbation could be considered immoral. The philosopher Ruwen Ogien began a recent book by defending what he calls a "minimal morality" in the following terms: "Imagine a world in which one could be judged 'immoral,' not just for one's actions, but also for one's thoughts, one's desires, one fantasies or one's 'character' traits; not only for what one does to others, but also for what one does to oneself . . . Who would really want to *live* in such a world?"*L'éthique aujourd'hui* (Paris: Gallimard, 2007), p. 11. Indeed, modern liberals are often pressed to explain in what sense they are not simply imposing their particular moral views upon others.

71. See, e.g., L. W. Sumner, *The Moral Foundation of Rights* (Oxford: Clarendon Press, 1987).

72. *Lochner v. New York*, 198 U.S. 45, 62 (1905).

73. Parris, *Constitutional Bureaucracy*, pp. 268–271.

74. David Owen, *The Government of Victorian London* (Cambridge, MA: Belknap Press of Harvard University Press, 1982), pp. 134–136.

75. See, for example, Herbert Spencer, *Social Statics* (London: John Chapman, 1851). His "equal freedom" framework leads him to be extremely "progressive" with respect to the question of democracy and enfranchisement, yet at the same time, he denies that the state should have any role in education, health, poor relief, planning, infrastructure, or environment.

76. David Lindsay Keir, *The Constitutional History of Modern Britain* (New York: D. Van Nostrand, 1938), p. 419. Cited in Parris, *Constitutional Bureaucracy*, p. 16.

77. Mark Blaug, *Economic Theory in Retrospect*, 4th ed. (Cambridge: Cambridge University Press, 1985), pp. 592–596.

78. Paul Samuelson, "The Pure Theory of Public Expenditure," *Review of Economics and Statistics* 36 (1954): 387–389.

79. John Rawls, *A Theory of Justice* (Cambridge, MA: Harvard University Press, 1971), pp. 3–4.

80. Most importantly, John Harsanyi, "Can the Maximin Principle Serve as a Basis for Morality? A Critique of John Rawls's Theory," *American Political Science Review* 69 (1975): 594–606; Allan Gibbard, "Disparate Goods and Rawls' Difference Principle: A Social Choice Theoretic Treatment," *Theory and Decision* 11 (1979): 267–288.

81. John Nash, "The Bargaining Problem," *Econometrica* 18 (1950): 155–162.

82. Henry S. Richardson, *Democratic Autonomy* (Oxford: Oxford University Press, 2002), p. 39. See also Daniel M. Weinstock, "Neutralizing Perfection: Hurka on Liberal Neutrality," *Dialogue* 38 (1999): 45–62. Similarly, George Sher, after writing a book-length critique of liberal neutrality (*Beyond Neutrality*, Cambridge: Cambridge University Press, 1997), posits the following as a "good" for the polity: "the formation and execution of reason-based plans—what Parfit tersely designates 'rational

activity' and Brink more elaborately calls the 'reflective pursuit of agents' reasonable projects,'" p. 204. Alasdair Macintyre crowns his trenchant critique of liberal neutrality by asserting that "the good life for man is life spent in seeking the good life for man," *After Virtue*, 3rd ed. (London: Bloomsbury, 2007), p. 254.

83. Richard G. Lipsey, Douglas D. Purvis, and Peter O. Steiner. *Economics*, 6th ed. (New York: Harper and Row, 1988), p. 478.

84. Locke, *Second Treatise of Government*, pp. 18–24 (§§25–38).

85. Joseph Heath, "The History of the Invisible Hand," in *Morality, Competition, and the Firm* (New York: Oxford University Press, 2014), pp. 205–229.

86. E.g., Will Kymlicka, *Contemporary Political Philosophy*, 2nd ed. (Oxford: Oxford University Press, 2003).

87. Larry S. Temkin, *Inequality* (New York: Oxford University Press, 1993).

Chapter 4

1. John Rawls, "The Basic Structure as Subject," *American Philosophical Quarterly* 14 (1977): 159–165.

2. Indeed, Rawls even claimed that the organization of the economy along capitalist or socialist principles should be up for debate, to be resolved by determining which would best satisfy the terms of a liberal theory of justice. John Rawls, *A Theory of Justice*, 2nd ed. (Cambridge, MA: Belknap Press of Harvard University Press, 1999), pp. 234–242.

3. For instance, Stuart White, in his survey of the normative arguments for the welfare state, does not even mention efficiency. See his "Ethics" in Francis G. Castles, Stephan Leibfried, Jane Lewis, Herbert Obinger, and Christopher Pierson, eds., *The Oxford Handbook of the Welfare State* (Oxford: Oxford University Press, 2010), pp. 19–31.

4. Michael Walzer, *Spheres of Justice* (New York: Basic Books, 1983); Michael Sandel, *Liberalism and the Limits of Justice* (Cambridge: Cambridge University Press, 1982).

5. Peter Lindert, *Growing Public*, vol. 1 (Cambridge: Cambridge University Press 2004), pp. 11–15.

6. Jürgen Habermas, *Legitimation Crisis*, trans. Thomas McCarthy (Boston: Beacon Press, 1975), p. 35.

7. One can find a recent, particularly stark—though non-Marxian—formulation of this claim in Daron Acemoglu and James A. Robinson, *Economic Origins of Dictatorship and Democracy* (Cambridge: Cambridge University Press, 2006), pp. 23–31.

8. Ronald Dworkin, *Sovereign Virtue* (Cambridge, MA: Harvard University Press, 2000), pp. 102–104.

9. Influential proponents of this view are Elizabeth Anderson, "What Is the Point of Equality?," *Ethics* 109 (1999): 287–337; Nancy Fraser, *Justice Interruptus* (London: Routledge, 1997); Philip Van Parijs, *Real Freedom for All* (Oxford: Oxford University Press, 1995). The commitment to sufficiency is typically taken to be an interpretation of the principle of equality, which is why I am presenting this view as a subcategory of the "egalitarian" model. There are also versions of the "basic needs" model that are motivated by communitarian commitments.

10. Joseph Heath, *Filthy Lucre* (Toronto: HarperCollins, 2008), pp. 87–88.

11. Michael Walzer, *Spheres of Justice* (New York: Basic Books, 1983), p. 89.

12. Walzer, *Spheres of Justice*, p. 90.

13. Walzer, p. 85.

14. Goodin, *Reasons for Welfare*, p. 70.

15. Goodin, p. 27.

16. Joel Bakan, *The Corporation* (Toronto: Penguin, 2004), pp. 112–113.

17. For a popular exposition of this view, see Michael J. Sandel, *What Money Can't Buy: The Moral Limits of Markets* (New York: Farrar, Straus and Giroux, 2012). Note that Sandel does not make the older, more ambitious claim that welfare state provision of goods is explained by these "moral limits of markets."

18. Immanuel Kant, *Foundations of the Metaphysics of Morals*, trans. Lewis White Beck (New York: MacMillan, 1990), pp. 51–52.

19. Thomas H. Marshall, *Citizenship and Social Class and Other Essays* (Cambridge: Cambridge University Press, 1950).

20. David Braybrooke, *Meeting Needs* (Princeton, NJ: Princeton University Press, 1987); Elizabeth Anderson, *Value in Ethics and Economics* (Cambridge, MA: Harvard University Press, 1993), pp. 143–144; David Copp, "Equality, Justice and Basic Needs," in Gillian Brock, ed., *Necessary Goods* (Lanham, MD: Rowman and Littlefield, 1998), p. 126; Lawrence Hamilton, *The Political Philosophy of Needs* (Cambridge: Cambridge University Press, 2003).

21. Commission on the Future of Heath Care in Canada, *Building on Values: The Future of Health Care in Canada* (Final Report, no. CP32-85/2002E-IN; Ottawa: Government of Canada, Nov. 2002), p. xx. Commissioner Roy Romanow made the implications of this phrase clear in a speech at Yale University, just prior to the release of the report, when he claimed that healthcare was a moral venture, and "not a commodity." Dorie Baker, "In Canada, Publicly-Funded Health Care Is 'Moral Enterprise', says Official," *Yale Bulletin and Calendar* 31 (2002): 8.

22. Debra Satz, *Why Some Things Should Not Be for Sale* (Oxford: Oxford University Press, 2010), p. 76.

23. Satz, *Why Some Things Should Not Be for Sale*, p. 82.

24. For an example of such a challenge, see Jason Brennan and Peter Jaworski, *Markets without Limits* (London: Routledge, 2015).

25. Walzer, *Spheres of Justice*, pp. 89–90.

26. An "economic" model should not be confused with the "economic theory of democracy," which is closely associated with the public choice model of the welfare state.

27. Joseph Stiglitz, *The Economic Role of the State*, ed. Arnold Heertje (Oxford: Blackwell, 1989); Nicholas Barr, *The Economics of the Welfare State*, 3rd ed. (Stanford, CA: Stanford University Press, 1998), pp. 68–85.

28. Rawls, *Theory of Justice*, pp. 59–63.

29. Robert E. Goodin, "Vulnerabilities and Responsibilities: An Ethical Defense of the Welfare State," *American Political Science Review* 79, no. 3 (1985): 775–787 at 770.

30. Evan Davis, *Public Spending* (London: Penguin, 1998), p. 65.

31. Paul Samuelson, "The Pure Theory of Public Expenditure," *Review of Economics and Statistics* 36 (1954): 387–389.

32. See James M. Buchanan, "An Economic Theory of Clubs," *Economica* 32 (1965): 1–14; also Joseph Heath, *Filthy Lucre* (Toronto: HarperCollins, 2008), pp. 85–88.

33. Ronald Coase, "The Nature of the Firm," *Economica* 4 (1937): 386–405; Oliver E. Williamson, *The Economic Institutions of Capitalism* (New York: Free Press, 1985).

34. Coase, "Nature of the Firm," p. 388.

35. Williamson, *Economic Institutions of Capitalism*, pp. 32–35.

36. Alan Shipman, *The Market Revolution and Its Limits* (London: Routledge, 1999), p. 290; Abraham Singer, *The Form of the Firm* (Oxford: Oxford University Press, 2018).

37. Stiglitz, *Economic Role of the State*, p. 21.

38. David A. Moss, *When All Else Fails* (Cambridge, MA: Harvard University Press, 2004).

39. For textbook treatment, see Nicholas Barr, *The Economics of the Welfare State*, 3rd ed. (Stanford, CA: Stanford University Press, 1998).

40. Davis, *Public Spending*, pp. 83–84.

41. Henry Hansmann, *The Ownership of Enterprise* (Cambridge, MA: Harvard University Press, 1996).

42. Gregory K. Dow, *Governing the Firm* (Cambridge: Cambridge University Press, 2003).

43. Jürgen Habermas, *Between Facts and Norms*, trans. William Rehg (Cambridge, MA: MIT Press, 1996), p. 287.

44. Bakan, *The Corporation*, p. 112.

45. Walzer, *Spheres of Justice*, p. 90.

46. Walzer, *Spheres of Justice*, p. 90. There is actually some ambiguity in his phrasing, such that it is not clear whether he intends to prohibit all teachers from educating only the children of the wealthy, or just teachers who work in the public sector. The fact that Walzer spent his career teaching at Harvard and Princeton suggests that it cannot be the former. It is also possible that by "public school" he means grade school, and so excludes himself and other university professors from the constraint. It is not clear what sort of principled basis could be provided for such an exclusion.

47. Maude Barlow and Tony Clarke, *Blue Gold* (Toronto: Stoddart, 2002), pp. 79–81.

48. Similarly, Barlow and Clarke raise no objection to the installation of water meters in private homes, so that individuals can be charged for the amount of water they consume, rather than receive it as a public good (financed through taxation). Most people on the left support such measures for environmental reasons, despite it being an important step in the direction of the "commodification" of water. Again, it suggests that the concern is really about the distribution system, not some inherent quality of the good.

49. Walzer, *Spheres of Justice*, p. 88.

50. Bakan, *The Corporation*, p. 112.

51. Davis, *Public Spending*, pp. 36–41.

52. Allan Buchanan, "Toward a Theory of the Ethics of Bureaucratic Organizations," *Business Ethics Quarterly* 6 (1996): 419–440.

NOTES TO PAGES 169–172

53. The last example is from Evan Davis. "Did the Old British Rail ticket-seller lie about which ticket to buy? In fact, the old British Rail did go to some trouble to disguise from travellers the existence of cheap commuter services that were slower substitutes for the British Rail Gatwick Express. Indeed, the company used to go so far as lying about the destination of trains . . . in order to herd people on to the service the company desired. In as far as the ticket-seller offered best advice, it was normally in contravention of his employer's desire." See Davis, *Public Spending*, p. 56.

54. Charles E. Lindblom, *Politics and Markets* (New York: Basic Books, 1980), p. 113.

55. Joseph Stiglitz, *Whither Socialism?* (Cambridge, MA: MIT Press, 1996), p. 250.

56. Joseph Heath and Wayne Norman, "Stakeholder Theory, Corporate Governance and Public Management," *Journal of Business Ethics* 53 (2004): 247–265. Again, to pick just one example, resource ownership in Canada is provincial, whereas environmental regulation is under federal jurisdiction. As a result, provincial mining SOEs have often been more successful at lobbying against environmental regulation than privately owned firms are, because they always have an "inside track" when it comes to securing the support of regional politicians.

57. Anthony Ferner, *Governments, Managers and Industrial Relations* (Oxford: Basil Blackwell, 1988).

58. Heath and Norman, "Stakeholder Theory, Corporate Governance and Public Management," p. 259.

59. Lawrence Pratchett and Melvin Wingfield, "Petty Bureaucracy and Woolly-Minded Liberalism? The Changing Ethos of Local Government Officers," *Public Administration* 74 (1996): 639–656 at 645.

60. Stiglitz, *Whither Socialism?*; Heath, *Filthy Lucre*, pp. 279–281.

61. Davis, *Public Spending*, p. 86; Moss, *When All Else Fails*.

62. François Ewald, *L'État providence* (Paris: Grasset, 1986).

63. Gøsta Esping-Andersen and John Myles, "Economic Inequality and the Welfare State," in Wiemer Salverda, Brian Nolan, and Timothy M. Smeeding, eds., *Oxford Handbook of Economic Inequality* (Oxford: Oxford University Press, 2009), p. 640.

64. On actuarial fairness, see Xavier Landes, "How Fair Is Actuarial Fairness?," *Journal of Business Ethics* 128 (2014): 519–533.

65. Satz, *Why Some Things Should Not Be for Sale*, pp. 76–79; James Tobin, "On Limiting the Domain of Inequality," *Journal of Law and Economics* 13 (1970): 263–277.

66. Abba Lerner, *The Economics of Control* (New York: A. M. Kelley, 1970), p. 48.

67. Ronald J. Daniels and Michael J. Trebilcock, *Rethinking the Welfare State* (London: Routledge, 2005).

68. David Gratzer, *Code Blue* (Toronto: ECW Press, 1999). A proposal of this type also featured prominently in the US presidential campaign of John McCain in 2008.

69. Paul Krugman and Robin Wells, "The Health Care Crisis and What to Do about It," *New York Review of Books*, March 23, 2006.

70. Johan J. Polder, Jan J. Barendregt, and Hans van Oers, "Health Care Costs in the Last Year of Life—the Dutch Experience," *Social Science and Medicine* 63 (2006): 1720–1731.

71. Joseph Heath, *The Efficient Society* (Toronto: Penguin, 2001), p. 188.

72. E.g., David Gratzer, "The ABCs of MSAs," in David Gratzer, ed., *Better Medicine* (Toronto: ECW Press, 2002), pp. 296–297.

73. An integrated state health provider, such as the NHS, merely represents a different way of resolving the market failure in the insurance sector, in much the same way that a health maintenance organization (HMO) does in the United States.

74. Or quasi-egalitarian principles, such as solidarity. Indeed, one of the attractions of the "solidarity" language, as it is used in France, for example, is that it is systematically ambiguous between equality and efficiency concerns, particularly when applied to social insurance systems.

75. Liam Murphy and Thomas Nagel, *The Myth of Ownership* (Oxford: Oxford University Press, 2002), p. 183.

76. Don Fullerton and Brent D. Mast, *Income Redistribution from Social Security* (Washington, DC: American Enterprise Institute, 2005).

77. Congressional Budget Office, *Is Social Security Progressive?* (Report, CBO, Washington DC, December 2006), p. 4, https://www.cbo.gov/publication/18266, accessed Sept. 12, 2018.

78. Moss, *When All Else Fails*, pp. 205–206.

79. Ryan D. Edwards, "The Cost of Uncertain Life Span," *Journal of Population Economics* 26 (2013): 1485–1522.

80. Technically, there is also the Quebec Pension Plan, which has the same structure but is "devolved" to the provincial level.

81. I have referred to this position elsewhere as "opportunistic egalitarianism," and it very much characterizes the way that egalitarian objectives are integrated into public policy. See Heath, *Filthy Lucre*, p. 287.

82. Lindert, *Growing Public*, vol. 1.

83. Clem Brooks and Jeff Manza, *Why Welfare States Persist* (Chicago: University of Chicago Press, 2007), pp. 62–63.

84. Goodin, "Vulnerabilities and Responsibilities," p. 181.

85. Hans-Werner Sinn, "Social Insurance, Incentives and Risk Taking," *International Tax and Public Finance* 3 (1996): 259–280.

86. Mahmood Yousefii and Sohrab Abizadeh, "Wagner's Law: New Evidence," *Atlanta Economic Journal* 20 (1992): 100–110 at 100.

87. Fred Hirsch, *The Social Limits to Growth* (Cambridge, MA: Harvard University Press, 1978).

88. Hirsch, *Social Limits to Growth*, p. 2.

89. Robert H. Frank, *Luxury Fever* (New York: Free Press, 1999).

90. Gordon Tullock, "The Rhetoric and Reality of Redistribution," *Southern Economic Journal* 47 (1981): 895–907 at 904–906.

91. Martha Hall Findlay, "Canada's Supply Management System for Dairy Is No Longer Defensible," *Globe and Mail*, Aug. 18, 2017.

92. Kenneth Arrow, "Uncertainty and the Welfare Economics of Medical Care," *American Economic Review* 53 (1963): 941–973.

93. Eric Lipton and Gardiner Harris, "In Turnaround, Industries Seek U.S. Regulation," *New York Times*, Sept. 16, 2007.

94. Seth Shulman, *Owning the Future* (Boston: Houghton Mifflin, 1999), p. 173.

95. William A. Niskanen, *Bureaucracy and Representative Government* (Chicago: Aldine-Atherton, 1971); Niskanen, "The Peculiar Economics of Bureaucracy," *American Economic Review* 58 (1968): 293–305.

96. Michael J. Trebilcock, *The Limits of Freedom of Contract* (Cambridge, MA: Harvard University Press, 1993).

97. Lindert, *Growing Public*, vol. 1, pp. 17–18.

98. Consider the following typical conservative homily: "If you pay people not to work (through welfare payments or other income transfers) or put a hefty tax penalty on them if they do work, it's human nature that they won't work." Arthur B. Laffer, Stephen Moore, and Peter J. Tanous, *The End of Prosperity: How Higher Taxes Will Doom the Economy* (New York: Threshold, 2008). One could use this argument to condemn *any* insurance arrangement: "If you pay people to have car accidents, then it's human nature that they will have more car accidents." What is being described here is simply a moral hazard effect of the insurance arrangement. This is why it is important, in any insurance system, whether public or private, to have some controls that serve to limit moral hazard. One cannot conclude, however, that there should be no insurance arrangement. The question is whether the efficiency gains produced by the risk-pooling arrangement remain greater than the inefficiencies occasioned by the moral hazard.

Chapter 5

1. HM Treasury, *The Green Book*, Gov.uk, 2003, p. 1, https://www.gov.uk/government/publications/the-green-book-appraisal-and-evaluation-in-central-governent, accessed Sept. 22, 2014.

2. *Green Book*, p. v.

3. Richard L. Revesz and Michael A. Livermore, *Retaking Rationality* (Oxford: Oxford University Press, 2008).

4. Gary C. Bryner, *Bureaucratic Discretion* (New York: Pergamon Press, 1987), pp. 44–47.

5. Indeed, the Reagan-era executive order that imposed CBA on all agencies, via the Office of Management and Budget (OMB), was initially considered to be of dubious legality, because it overruled the decision rules articulated in the enabling statutes of various agencies, including the EPA and OSHA. Bryner, *Bureaucratic Discretion*, p. 44.

6. Donald C. Hubin, "The Moral Justification of Benefit/Cost Analysis," *Economics and Philosophy* 10 (1994): 169–194 at 170.

7. For example, see Matthew D. Adler and Eric A. Posner, *New Foundations of Cost-Benefit Analysis* (Cambridge, MA: Harvard University Press, 2006); or Eric Schokkaert, "Cost-Benefit Analysis of Difficult Decisions," *Ethical Perspectives* 2 (1995): 71–84; Cass Sunstein, *The Cost-Benefit Revolution* (Cambridge, MA: MIT Press, 2018).

8. A point emphasized by Lewis A. Kornhauser, "On Justifying Cost-Benefit Analysis," *Journal of Legal Studies* 29, no. S2 (2000): 1037–1057 at 1053.

9. It may interest or amuse some to know that this journey is semi-autobiographical, save for the part about being a junior analyst.

10. The textbook I happen to own provides a good example of the standard treatment. See Harvery Rosen, Beverly George Dahlby, Roger Smith, and Paul Boothe, *Public Finance in Canada*, 2nd ed. (Toronto: McGraw-Hill, 2002).

11. Cass Sunstein, having started as an academic advocate of CBA, then accepted an administrative position in the US government, where he was involved in assessing CBAs for a broad range of federal agencies, has written a number of interesting articles that attempt to describe the differences between textbook CBA and CBA as practiced. See, especially, Cass Sunstein, "The Real World of Cost-Benefit Analysis: Thirty-Six Questions (and Almost as Many Answers)," *Columbia Law Review* 114 (2014): 167–211.

12. This can be found in the US Federal Register of Oct. 4, 1993: https://www.govinfo.gov/app/collection/fr, accessed Sept. 17, 2018.

13. Sunstein, "Real World of Cost-Benefit Analysis," pp. 191–193.

14. For purposes of illustration, it is helpful to set aside the issue of interpersonal comparability in the utility scales. Disagreement about what one person's utility is "worth," in terms of the other's, concerns the *slope* of U, but not the basic form of the social welfare function.

15. For an example of this mode of presentation, see Daniel Farber, *Eco-Pragmatism* (Chicago: University of Chicago Press, 1999), pp. 44–45.

16. Amartya Sen, "The Discipline of Cost-Benefit Analysis," *Journal of Legal Studies* 29 (2000): 931–952 at 947.

17. See Rosemary Lowry and Martin Peterson, "Cost-Benefit Analysis and Non-utilitarian Ethics," *Politics, Philosophy and Economics* 11 (2011): 258–279.

18. Farber, *Eco-Pragmatism*, pp. 106–110.

19. Michael Oakeshott, "On Being Conservative," in *Rationalism in Politics, and Other Essays* (London: Methuen, 1962), pp. 191.

20. Joseph Heath, "Political Egalitarianism," *Social Theory and Practice* 34 (2008): 485–516.

21. Jules L. Coleman, "Efficiency, Utility, and Wealth Maximization," *Hofstra Law Review* 8 (1980): 509–551 at 516.

22. An observation that has been made by David Schmidtz, "A Place for Cost-Benefit Analysis," *Philosophical Issues* 11 (2001): 148–171, but not defended in detail.

23. On club goods, see James Buchanan, "An Economic Theory of Clubs," *Economica* 32 (1965): 1–14.

24. Fred Hirsch, *The Social Limits to Growth* (London: Routledge, 1977), p. 92.

25. Evan Davis, *Public Spending* (London: Penguin, 1998).

26. Jane Jacobs, *The Death and Life of Great American Cities* (New York: Vintage, 1961), p. 94. "In orthodox city planning, neighborhood open spaces are venerated in an amazingly uncritical fashion, much as savages venerated magical fetishes. Ask a houser how his planned neighborhood improves on the old city and he will cite, as a self-evident virtue, More Open Space. Ask a zoner about improvements in progressive codes and he will cite, again as a self-evident virtue, their incentives toward leaving More Open Space. . . More Open Space for what? For muggings? For bleak vacuums between buildings?" (p. 90).

NOTES TO PAGES 200–209

27. Elizabeth Anderson, *Value in Ethics and Economics* (Cambridge, MA: Harvard University Press, 1993), p. 190.

28. Many critics of CBA are either confused on this point, or write in a way that encourages significant confusion. Steven Kelman, for example, makes it sound as though CBA involves *actually* assigning prices to things, "Cost-Benefit Analysis: An Ethical Critique," *Regulation* 33 (1981): 33–40 at 39. See also Anderson, *Value in Ethics and Economics*, p. 193.

29. Anderson, *Value in Ethics and Economics*, p. 193.

30. Ibid., p. 193.

31. David Copp, "The Justice and Rationale of Cost-Benefit Analysis," *Theory and Decision* 23 (1987): 65–87.

32. Amartya Sen, "Discipline of Cost-Benefit Analysis," p. 938.

33. Cass Sunstein, "Cognition and Cost-Benefit Analysis," *Journal of Legal Studies* 29, no. 2 (2000): 1059–1103. See also Kip Viscusi, "Risk Equity," *Journal of Legal Studies* 29 (2000): 843–871 at 857–858.

34. For more extensive discussion, see Joseph Heath, "Efficiency as the Implicit Morality of the Market," in *Morality, Competition and the Firm* (New York: Oxford University Press, 2014), pp. 173–204.

35. It is worth noting that when some other metric is used on the benefit side, with cost being still expressed in monetary terms, the analysis is referred to as a "cost-effectiveness analysis." I am ignoring this distinction for now but will return to it in section 5.4.2.

36. Colin Camerer, Samuel Issacharoff, George Loewenstein, Ted O'Donoghue, and Matthew Rabin, "Regulation for Conservatives: Behavioral Economics and the Case for 'Asymmetric Paternalism,'" *University of Pennsylvania Law Review* 151 (2003): 1211–1254.

37. Pigou's view is quite intuitive, and still very widely held. Elizabeth Anderson, for example, assumes it when she says, "Markets do not produce efficient outcomes when market transactions impose welfare changes or 'externalities' on third parties." *Value in Ethics and Economics*, p. 192. What Coase showed was that markets *may* not produce efficient outcomes when there are externalities, not that they *do* not.

38. This is the claim that has come to be known as the "Coase theorem," although Coase does not present it as such.

39. This is one of the points that separates the way many economists think about social questions from more common-sense moral perspectives. According to this way of thinking, there is no reason to be overly concerned about theft, as such, because it is *merely* redistributive. If someone sneaks into your house and takes something, the total wealth of the nation is neither increased nor decreased; a portion of it simply passes out of your hands into someone else's. But if you go out and change your locks, or install a burglar alarm, in response to the theft, then that *is* a concern, because now real resources are being expended, not to increase to stock of wealth, but merely to ensure that a particular redistribution of that wealth does not occur. Thus the amount spent on theft deterrence is a loss, from the standpoint of efficiency.

40. Simon Caney, "Climate Change, Human Rights, and Moral Thresholds," in Stephen Humphreys, ed., *Climate Change and Human Rights* (Cambridge: Cambridge University Press, 2009). Henry Shue, "Bequeathing Hazards: Security Rights and Property Rights of Future Humans," in Mohammed Dore and Timothy Mount, eds., *Limits to Markets: Equity and the Global Environment* (Malden, MA: Blackwell, 1998), pp. 38–53.

41. See Ronald Dworkin, "Rights as Trumps," in Jeremy Waldron, ed., *Theories of Rights* (Oxford: Oxford University Press, 1984), pp. 153–167.

42. *Kelo v. City of New London*, 545 U.S. 469 (2005).

43. Steven Kelman writes, "The notion of human rights involves the idea that people may make certain claims to be allowed to act in certain ways or to be treated in certain ways, even if the sum of benefits achieved thereby does not outweigh the sum of costs. It is this view that underlies the statement that 'workers have a right to a safe and healthy work place' and the expectation that OSHA's decisions will reflect that judgment." Kelman, "Cost-Benefit Analysis: An Ethical Critique," p. 36. The first sentence constitutes a typical expression of the "rights as trumps" idea, but then the second sentence goes on to specify a right that could not possibly serve as a trump, simply because no workplace is ever perfectly safe or healthy. For example, anyone who has to drive a vehicle as part of his or her job is thereby exposed to a non-negligible mortality risk.

44. Caney, "Climate Change, Human Rights, and Moral Thresholds," p. 167.

45. Joseph Raz, "Legal Rights," *Oxford Journal of Legal Studies* 88 (1984): 1–21.

46. John Broome, "Trying to Value a Life," *Journal of Public Economics* 9 (1978): 91–100.

47. Stephen Breyer, *Breaking the Vicious Circle* (Cambridge, MA: Harvard University Press, 1994), p. 11.

48. Cass Sunstein, "Cognition and Cost-Benefit Analysis."

49. Peter A. Diamond and Jerry Hausman, "Contingent Valuation: Is Some Number Better Than No Number?," *Journal of Economic Perspectives* 8 (1994): 45–64.

50. Amartya Sen makes the narrower, but nevertheless very significant, point that with any sort of public good, the amount that any individual is willing to pay will be, in part, a function of his or her beliefs about what other people are going to pay. Thus the question is better suited to ascertaining the value of goods that are exclusive in consumption. Sen, "Discipline of Cost-Benefit Analysis," pp. 948–949.

51. William Desvousges, F. Reed Johnson, Richard W. Dunford, Sara P. Hudson, K. Nicole Wilson, and Kevin J. Boyle, "Measuring Natural Resource Damages with Contingent Valuation: Tests of Validity and Reliability," in Jerry Hausman, ed., *Contingent Valuation: A Critical Assessment* (Amsterdam: North Holland Press, 1993), pp. 91–164. For discussion, see Diamond and Hausmann, "Contingent Valuation," p. 51.

52. See Richard Dorman and Paul Hagstrom, "Wage Compensation for Dangerous Work Revisited," *Industrial and Labor Relations Review* 52 (1998): 116–135. For discussion, see David A. Moss, *When All Else Fails* (Cambridge, MA: Harvard University Press, 2002), pp. 162–169; Cass Sunstein provides a useful summary of studies in *Risk and Reason* (Cambridge: Cambridge University Press, 2002), p. 174.

53. Diamond and Hausmann, "Contingent Valuation," p. 58. There are important cases, of course, when the opposite is true. A telling anecdote, for instance, can often overwhelm any consideration of statistical data.

54. See Joel Schwarz, Jane Leggett, Bart Ostro, Hugh Pitcher, and Ronnie Levin, *Costs and Benefits of Reducing Lead in Gasoline* (Washington, DC: US Environmental Protection Agency, 1984).

55. Another example is that, prior to the introduction of the "valuation of life" measure based on willingness to pay, US Government agencies used a "cost of death" measure consisting of the discounted sum of lost earnings. See Viscusi, "Risk Equity," pp. 854–855. The latter sum is morally arbitrary. Future earnings are of no value to a dead person, and as far as society is concerned, the individual's death is a wash, since that individual's lost contribution to the social product is accompanied by a closely matched decline in consumption.

56. E.g., Anderson, *Value in Ethics and Economics*, pp. 210–216; or Mark Sagoff, "Aggregation and Deliberation in Valuing Environmental Public Goods: A Look beyond Contingent Valuation," *Ecological Economics* 24 (1998): 213–230.

57. See Douglas Craig Macmillan, Lorna Jennifer Philip, Nick Hanley, and Begoñia Alvarez-Farizo, "Valuing the Nonmarket Benefits of Wild Goose Conservation: A Comparison of Interview and Group-Based Approaches," *Ecological Economics* 43 (2002): 49–59; Begoñia Alvarez-Farizo, Nick Hanley, Ramón Barberan, and Angelina Lázaro, "Choice Modeling at the 'Market Stall': Individual versus Collective Interest in Environmental Valuation," *Ecological Economics* 60 (2007): 743–751. For discussion, see Giles Atkinson and Susana Mourato, "Environmental Cost-Benefit Analysis," *Annual Review of Environmental Resources* 33 (2008): 317–344 at 322.

58. Atkinson and Mourato, "Environmental Cost-Benefit Analysis."

59. Cass Sunstein suggested, in 1996, that the implicit cost per life year saved in transportation in the United States was $56,000; for occupational regulation, $346,000; and for environmental regulation, $4,207,000." Sunstein, "The Cost-Benefit State" (Coase-Sandor Institute for Law and Economics Working Paper No. 39), *Law and Economics Working Papers* 39 (1996): 1–43 at 10).

60. There is a somewhat esoteric, but philosophically significant point that arises when one considers comparison across policy areas. As long as the overall objective is the same, one could compare by taking the "benefit" side of a CEA and converting it to a monetary value, but one could also take the "cost" side and convert it to a "lives saved" value. How? By looking at how much it costs to save a life in other domains, such as healthcare. Every million dollars spent on road safety is a million dollars not spent in other areas. One can calculate how many lives will *not* be saved in those other areas—this is the "cost" of spending a million dollars on roads, expressed though in terms of lives saved. One can then convert the monetary cost of a policy into the "lives not saved" equivalent to determine which policy generates the highest net number of lives saved (as opposed to the highest net monetary benefit).

61. Viscusi, "Risk Equity."

62. Bernard Williams, "A Critique of Utilitarianism," in J. J. C. Smart and Bernard Williams, *Utilitarianism: For and Against* (Cambridge: Cambridge University Press, 1973).

63. See Judith Jarvis Thomson, "The Trolley Problem," *Yale Law Journal* 94 (1985): 1395–1415. See also John Mikhail's analysis in *Elements of Moral Cognition* (Cambridge: Cambridge University Press, 2011).

64. Immanuel Kant, *Foundations of the Metaphysics of Morals*, trans. Lewis White Beck (New York: MacMillan, 1990), pp. 51–52.

65. Kelman, "Cost-Benefit Analysis: An Ethical Critique."

66. This fact has generated problems for strict anti-aggregationist theories, because the most plausible way of handling risk seems to readmit aggregationism through the back door. See Rahul Kumar, "Risking and Wronging," *Philosophy and Public Affairs* 43 (2015): 27–49; Johann Frick, "Contractualism and Social Risk," *Philosophy and Public Affairs* 43 (2015): 176–223.

67. Jonathan Wolff, "What Is the Value of Preventing a Fatality?," in Tim Lewens, ed., *Risk: Philosophical Perspectives* (London: Routledge, 2007), pp. 54–67.

68. Wolff provides an excellent example of this involving British Rail, which was under pressure to install a computerized signaling system, at a cost of approximately £6 billion, that would have saved perhaps two lives per year. See Jonathan Wolff, *Ethics and Public Policy* (Oxford: Routledge, 2011), p. 89.

69. Viscusi, "Risk Equity," p. 855.

70. Treasury Board of Canada, *Canadian Cost-Benefit Analysis Guide: Regulatory Proposals* (Ottawa: Treasury Board, 2007), p. 20.

71. All the information on drug prices is from Alex Berenson, "Cancer Drugs Offer Hope, but at a Huge Expense," *New York Times*, July 12, 2005.

72. Nicole Mittmann, Heather-Jane Au, et. al. "Prospective Cost-Effectiveness Analysis of Cetuximab in Metastatic Colorectal Cancer: Economic Evaluation of National Cancer Institute of Canada Clinical Trials Group CO.17 Trial," *Journal of the National Cancer Institute* 101 (2009): 1182–1192 at 1190.

73. K. Robin Yabroff and Deborah Schrag, "Challenges and Opportunities for Use of Cost-Effectiveness Analysis," *JNCI: Journal of the National Cancer Institute* 101, no. 17 (Sept. 2009):1161–1163 at 1161.

74. Ronald Dworkin, *Sovereign Virtue* (Cambridge, MA: Harvard University Press, 2002).

75. The fact that this option is not available in Canada (under the commitment to "single-tier" medicine) is the source of ongoing controversy in that country. See Colleen M. Flood and Lorian Hardcastle, "The Private Sale of Cancer Drugs in Ontario's Public Hospitals: Tough Issues at the Public/Private Interface in Health Care," *McGill Health Law Publication* 1 (2007): 1–21. Such drugs are available de facto, because any Canadian who can afford a drug like Erbitux can also afford a trip to the United States to purchase it.

76. Cited in Alan M. Garber and Harold C. So, "The Role of Costs in Comparative Effectiveness Research," *Health Affairs* 29, no. 10 (2010): 1805–1811. See also Peter J. Neumann and Milton C. Weinstein, "Legislating against Use of Cost-Effectiveness Information," *New England Journal of Medicine* 363 (Oct. 14, 2010): 1495–1497.

77. Shlomi Segall, "Is Health Care (Still) Special?," *Journal of Political Philosophy* 15 (2007): 342–361 at 343; Norman Daniels, "Justice, Health and Healthcare," *American Journal of Bioethics* 1 (2001), 2–14 at 2.

78. See Lendell Chad Horne, *Health, Risk and Luck* (unpublished PhD diss., University of Toronto, 2014).

79. Jon Elster, *Local Justice in America* (New York: Sage, 1995), p. 133.

80. In the United States, it remains common practice for physicians to be paid a commission for prescribing drugs, often a percentage of the sale price. This is one of the reasons that drug prices are so high in the United States, and that physicians often prescribe brand-name pharmaceuticals instead of generics. Politically, it means that there is a strong alignment of interest between physicians and the pharmaceutical industry.

81. Again, this is why it is important to emphasize that CBA/CEA is a procedure used to guide correction of the large-scale market failure besetting the insurance system, and is thus unlike moral consequentialism, which is a theory that could be used to guide the treatment of individual patients.

82. Erik Nord, *Cost-Value Analysis in Health Care* (Cambridge: Cambridge University Press, 1999), p. 57.

83. Nord, *Cost-Value Analysis in Health Care*, pp. 64–69.

84. Larry Temkin, "Equality or Priority in Health Care Distribution" (unpublished manuscript).

85. Burton Weisbrod, "Collective Consumption Services of Individual-Consumption Goods," *Quarterly Journal of Economics* 78 (1964): 471–477. For critical discussion, see John Quiggin, "Existence Value and the Contingent Valuation Method," *Australian Economic Papers* 37 (1998): 312–329.

86. For my reflections on a similar set of issues, see Joseph Heath, "Envy and Efficiency," *Revue de philosophie economique* 13 (2006): 1–16. More generally, see Nils Holtung, "The Harm Principle," *Ethical Theory and Moral Practice* 5 (2002): 357–389.

87. John Vidal, "The Great Green Land Grab," *The Guardian*, Feb. 13, 2008, http://www.theguardian.com/environment/2008/feb/13/conservation, accessed Sept. 23, 2018.

88. J. Baird Callicott, "Non-anthropocentric Value Theory and Environmental Ethics," *American Philosophical Quarterly* 21 (1984): 299–309 at 299.

89. See Elizabeth Willott and David Schmidtz, introduction to Elizabeth Willott and David Schmidtz, eds., *Environmental Ethics* (New York: Oxford University Press), pp. xv–xxiii at xvii.

90. Richard Routley, "Is There a Need for a New, an Environmental, Ethic?," *Proceedings of the XVth World Congress of Philosophy* 1 (1973): 205–210.

91. Mark Sagoff, "Animal Liberation and Environmental Ethics: Bad Marriage, Quick Divorce," *Osgoode Hall Law Journal* 22 (1984): 297–307.

92. See discussion in Cass Sunstein, *Laws of Fear: Beyond the Precautionary Principle* (Cambridge: Cambridge University Press, 2005): 18–20.

93. This is Sunstein's central argument against the principle, in *Laws of Fear*, pp. 26–27. Proponents of the precautionary principle avoid gridlock by applying the principle only to action, which neglects the harms that might result from inaction. If one adopts a precautionary approach to the latter as well, then typically every option turns out to be impermissible.

94. Stephen M. Gardiner, "A Core Precautionary Principle," *The Journal of Political Philosophy* 14 (2006): 33–60 at 48.

95. Final Declaration of the First European "Seas at Risk" Conference, Annex 1, Copenhagen, 1994. Cited in Sunstein, *Laws of Fear*, p. 20.

96. Ron Suskind, *The One Percent Doctrine* (New York: Simon and Schuster, 2006), p. 62.

97. Adrian Vermeule, "Rationally Arbitrary Decisions in Administrative Law," *Journal of Legal Studies* 44 (2015): S475–S507 at S482.

98. Sven Ove Hansson, "Risk and Ethics," in Tim Lewens, ed., *Risk: Philosophical Perspectives* (London: Routledge, 2007), pp. 21–35 at 23.

99. There are several good discussions in the literature, providing lists of "questions" that should be asked when contemplating a particular CBA exercise. See, for instance, Michael F. Drummond, "Allocating Resources," *International Journal of Technology Assessment in Health Care* 6 (1990): 77–92 at 81; or Dan Brock, "Ethical Issues in the Use of Cost-Effectiveness Analysis for the Prioritization of Health Resources," in George Khushf, ed., *Handbook of Bioethics* (Dordrecht: Kluwer, 2004), pp. 352–380. My purpose here is to provide a bit more structure, by organizing the questions into a sequence.

100. Richard Posner, *Sex and Reason* (Cambridge, MA: Harvard University Press, 1992), pp. 357–358.

101. Jan Abel Olsen, "Aiding Priority Setting in Health Care: Is There a Role for the Contingent Valuation Method?," *Health Economics* 6 (1997): 603–612.

102. One of the places where this arises involves the treatment of citizens and non-citizens. Historically, there has been a tendency for national governments to take into consideration only the effects on their own citizens. This, however, generates obvious absurdities, and effectively renders certain cross-border collective action problems unsolvable. It is also a non-starter when it comes to dealing with issues like global climate change.

103. Wolff, "What Is the Value of Preventing a Fatality?," pp. 63–64.

104. Nord, *Cost-Value Analysis in Health Care*, p. 34.

105. For an overview, see David Pearce, Ben Groom, Cameron Hepburn, and Phoebe Koundouri, "Valuing the Future," *World Economics* 4 (2003): 121–141.

106. For discussion, see Michael Trebilcock, *Dealing with Losers* (Oxford: Oxford University Press, 2014).

107. Sunstein "Cost-Benefit State," p. 39.

Chapter 6

1. Government of Canada, *Value and Ethics in the Public Sector* (Ottawa: Treasury Board, 2011), p. 4.

2. Cited in Lorne Sossin and Vasuda Sinha, "International Civil Service Ethics, Professionalism and the Rule of Law," in Vesselin Popovski, ed., *International Rule of Law and Professional Ethics* (Oxford: Routledge, 2016), pp. 151–152.

3. T. R. S. Allan notes that "the more ambitious in scope one makes the 'rule of law', the less plausible one's claim to describe a necessary feature of any and every model of decent government, worthy of anyone's allegiance." *Liberal Constitutionalism* (Oxford: Oxford University Press, 2001), p. 5.

4. D. J. Galligan, *Discretionary Powers* (Oxford: Clarendon Press, 1986) defines discretion as "an express grant of power conferred on officials where determination of the standards according to which power is to be exercised is left largely to them" (p. 1).

5. Galligan, *Discretionary Powers*, p. 85.

6. Eugene Bardach and Robert A. Kagan, *Going by the Book* (Philadelphia: Temple University Press, 1982), p. 32.

7. A. V. Dicey, *An Introduction to the Study of the Law of the Constitution*, 10th ed., edited by E. C. S. Wade (London: Macmillan, 1959), p. 202.

8. Michael Oakeshott, "The Rule of Law," in Oakeshott, *On History and Other Essays* (Indianapolis, IN: Liberty Fund, 1999). See also Gary Lawson, "The Rise and Rise of the Administrative State," *Harvard Law Review* 107 (1994): 1231–1254.

9. For example, the publication in 1929 of Lord Hewart's *The New Despotism* (London: Ernest Benn, 1929) led to various reforms in the United Kingdom. See D. C. M. Yardley, *Principles of Administrative Law* (London: Butterworths, 1981), pp. 35–37.

10. The term "rule of law culture" is used by Sossin and Sinha, "International Civil Service Ethics," p. 150.

11. Speaking more precisely, David Dyzenhaus defines formalism (in a legal context) as follows: "Formalism is formal in that it requires judges to operate with categories and distinctions that determine results without the judges having to deploy the substantive arguments that underpin the categories and distinctions." Dyzenhaus, "Constituting the Rule of Law: Fundamental Values in Administrative Law," *Queen's Law Journal* 27 (2002): 445–509 at 450.

12. See Bardach and Kagan, *Going by the Book*.

13. Reports were prompted by the following study, from Public Health Ontario: Sarah E. Wilson, Chi Yon Seo, Gillian H. Lim, Jill Fediurek, Natasha S. Crowcroft, and Shelley L. Deeks, "Trends in Medical and Nonmedical Immunization Exemptions to Measles-Containing Vaccine in Ontario: An Annual Cross-Sectional Assessment of Students from School Years 2002/3 to 2012/13," *Canadian Medical Association Journal* 3 (2015): E317–E332.

14. Philip Pettit, *Republicanism* (Oxford: Oxford University Press, 1997), p. 65.

15. Robert Goodin, "Discretion," in *Reasons for Welfare* (Princeton, NJ: Princeton University Press, 1988), 184–223 at 194.

16. Goodin, "Discretion," p. 198.

17. Ibid.

18. Goodin, "Discretion," p. 201. Goodin's discussion here echoes a long-standing debate in accounting over the merits of rule-based versus principles-based systems. A rule-based approach, such as is employed in the United States, checks only for formal compliance with the rules as articulated, and does not look beyond that to consider the substance of a transaction. This creates an enormous number of "loopholes," but also offers greater certainty, in the sense that if the books are formally in compliance with legal requirements, there is very little chance that they will subsequently need to be revised.

19. M. P. Baumgartner, "The Myth of Discretion," in Keith Hawkins, ed., *The Uses of Discretion* (Oxford: Clarendon Press, 1992), pp. 129–162 at 157.

20. Bardach and Kagan, *Going by the Book.*
21. Goodin, "Discretion," pp. 188–190.
22. Goodin, p. 204.
23. Mirjan Damaska, "Structures of Authority and Comparative Criminal Procedure," *Yale Law Journal* 84 (1975) 480–544 at 485.
24. Bernardo Zacka, *When the State Meets the Street* (Cambridge, MA: Harvard University Press, 2017), pp. 171–182.
25. See Steven Kelman, *Procurement and Public Management: Fear of Discretion and the Quality of Government Performance* (Washington, DC: AEI Press, 1990).
26. Herbert Kaufman, *Red Tape* (Washington, DC: Brookings Institution Press, 1977), p. 35. See also James Q. Wilson, *Bureaucracy* (New York: Basic Books, 1989), p. 121.
27. Richard H. Thaler, *The Winner's Curse* (New York: Free Press, 1992).
28. Steven Kelman, *Procurement and Public Management* (Washington, DC: AEI Press, 1990), p. 10.
29. Kelman, *Procurement and Public Management*, p. 5.
30. Ludwig Wittgenstein, *Philosophical Investigations*, 4th ed., trans. G. E. M. Anscombe, P. M. S. Hacker, and Joachim Schulte (Oxford: Blackwell, 2009).
31. Tony Evans, *Professional Discretion in Welfare Services* (London: Routledge, 2010), p. 113.
32. Gary C. Bryner, *Bureaucratic Discretion* (New York: Pergamon Press, 1987), p. 6.
33. Geneviève Cartier, "Keeping a Check on Discretion," in Colleen Flood and Lorne Sossin, eds., *Administrative Law in Context* (Toronto: Emond Montgomery, 2008), pp. 269–288 at 272.
34. Pub. L. No. 91–596, § 2(b)(1954), 29 U.S.C. § 651, (b)(3)(1970).
35. Bardach and Kagan, *Going by the Book*, p. 7.
36. Tony Evans, *Professional Discretion in Welfare Services* (London: Routledge, 2010), p. 31.
37. Peter H. Aranson, Ernest Gelhorn, and Glen O. Robinson, "A Theory of Legislative Delegation," *Cornell Law Review* 68 (1982): 1–67 at 10.
38. *Roncarelli v. Duplessis*, Supreme Court of Canada (1959) S.C.R. 121. Some British examples include the Housing Act 1925, which specified that "the Order of the Minister when made shall have effect as if enacted in this Act," and the Finance (No 2) Act 1940, which conferred upon the Commissioners of Customs and Excise the power to make rules concerning "any matter for which provisions appear to them to be necessary." Yardley, *Principles of Administrative Law*, pp. 30–31.
39. This is a decision that was made, and periodically revised, by OSHA. See Bryner, *Bureaucratic Discretion*, pp. 136–137.
40. H. L. A. Hart, *The Concept of Law* (Oxford: Oxford University Press, 1961), pp. 124–125.
41. John Huber and Charles Shipan present an interesting comparison of an Irish employment equity statute, which spent 400 words developing a detailed definition of sexual harassment, to the German statute, adopted at around the same time, which dedicated less than one-third the number of words to the topic, and provided only a general definition. Huber and Shipan, *Deliberate Discretion?*, pp. 3–5.

42. Keith Bradsher, *High and Mighty* (New York: Public Affairs, 2002).

43. Zacka, *When the States Meets the Street*, p. 45.

44. Toxic Substances Control Act of 1977, 15 USCA, §2601(b), cited in Keith Hawkins and John M. Thomas, "The Enforcement Process in Regulatory Bureaucracies," in Keith Hawkins and John M. Thomas, eds., *Enforcing Regulation* (Boston: Kluwer-Nijhoff, 1984), pp. 3–22 at 6.

45. Bardach and Kagan, *Going by the Book*, pp. 105–116.

46. Lee Fritschler, *Smoking and Politics* (Englewood Cliffs, NJ: Prentice-Hall, 1984), describes the problem: "The [Federal Trade] commission was trying to regulate cigarette advertising on a case-by-case basis. Each time the commission ruled a particular advertisement deceptive, the industry came up with a variation that could squeak by under the rule of the previous case. This was proving to be an endless and fruitless process. The commission needed to write general regulations for the whole industry" (p. 69).

47. John Prebble QC, "Kelsen, the Principle of Exclusion of Contradictions, and General Anti-avoidance Rules in Tax Law," in Monica Bhandari, ed., *Philosophical Foundations of Tax Law* (Oxford: Oxford University Press, 2017). pp. 79–100.

48. "Arrangements are 'tax arrangements' if, having regard to all the circumstances, it would be reasonable to conclude that the obtaining of a tax advantage was the main purpose, or one of the main purposes, of the arrangements. Tax arrangements are 'abusive' if they are arrangements the entering into or carrying out of which cannot reasonably be regarded as a reasonable course of action in relation to the relevant tax provisions, having regard to all the circumstances." Finance Act 2013, c. 29. http://www.legislation.gov.uk/ukpga/2013/29/part/5/enacted, accessed Dec. 2, 2018.

49. Hawkins and Thomas, "Enforcement Process in Regulatory Bureaucracies," p. 16.

50. In some cases, there are so many rules that officials literally cannot remember them all. This alone can generate considerable selectivity in their application. See Evans, *Professional Discretion in Welfare Services*, p. 93. University professors should be familiar with this from their own work environment. Very few have actually read all of the rules that govern the administration of courses at their universities. They have instead learned how to structure a course as a *cultural practice*, by copying how their peers do it, subject only to occasional correction by administrative officials in cases of egregious error. It is important to recognize that universities are very typical bureaucracies in this regard, and that this is how large segments of the state function as well.

51. Mirjan Damaska, "Structures of Authority and Comparative Criminal Procedure," *Yale Law Journal* 84 (1975): 480–544 at 528.

52. Peter Schuck, "The Curious Case of the Indicted Meat Inspectors," *Harper's Magazine*, Sept. 1, 1972, pp. 81–88 at 82. Also cited in Bardach and Kagan, *Going by the Book*, p. 37.

53. Joseph Hile, "Food and Drug Administration Inspections—A New Approach," *Food, Drug and Cosmetic Law Journal* 2 (1972): 1010–1106.

54. Lipsky, *Street-Level Bureaucracy*, p. 33.

55. Evans, *Professional Discretion in Welfare Services*, p. 108.

56. Ibid., p. 94.

57. Bryner, *Bureaucratic Discretion*, p. 207.

58. Ibid.

59. Steve Eder, "When Picking Apples on a Farm with 5000 Rules, Watch Out for the Ladders," *New York Times*, Dec. 17, 2017. The concern was that workers would step in the droppings and contaminate the rungs of ladders, which would then transfer the fecal matter to their hands, and from there to the apples. The compromise involved training workers to grasp ladders only by the sides, not the rungs, to avoid potential transfer of fecal matter from shoes to hands.

60. Baumgartner, "Myth of Discretion," p. 161.

61. Robert A. Kagan, "Police and inspectors both work 'in the field', out of sight of their supervisors. They make decisions about the meaning of the law in face-to-face contact with complainants and suspects, directly exposed to offenders' expressions of outrage, pleas for mercy, and, on occasion, threats and offers of bribes." Robert A. Kagan, "On Regulatory Inspectorates and Police," in Hawkins and Thomas, *Enforcing Regulation*, pp. 37–64 at 39.

62. Lipsky offers an excellent example of such a work-around in US Veterans Administration hospitals, *Street-Level Bureaucracy*, pp. 20–21.

63. Albert Reiss, "Discretionary Justice in America," *International Journal of Criminology and Penology* 2 (1974): 181–205.

64. For the classic discussion, see John van Maanen, "The Asshole," in Peter K. Manning and John Van Maanen, eds., *Policing: A View from the Street* (Santa Monica, CA: Goodyear, 1978), pp. 221–238.

65. Bardach and Kagan, *Going by the Book*, p. 59.

66. Daniel A Farber, *Eco-Pragmatism* (Chicago: University of Chicago Press, 1999), pp. 183–192.

67. Farber, *Eco-Pragmatism*, pp. 191–192.

68. The industry as a whole is thought to have received approximately $8 billion by the time the subsidies expired on January 1, 2010. Greg Beato, "Black Liquor Binge," *Reason*, Dec. 29, 2009; also Christopher Hayes, "Pulp Nonfiction," *The Nation*, April 20, 2009.

69. Matthew Potoski and Aseem Prakash, "Voluntary Programs, Regulatory Compliance and the Regulation Dilemma," in Christine Parker and Vibeke Lehmann Nielsen, eds., *Explaining Compliance* (Cheltenham, UK: Edward Elgar, 2011), pp. 245–262 at 256.

70. Goodin, "Discretion," pp. 213–216.

71. Zacka, *When the State Meets the Street*, pp. 182–183.

72. James Q. Wilson, *Bureaucracy* (New York: Basic Books, 1989), pp. 37–38.

73. Sally S. Simpson, *Corporate Crime, Law, and Social Control* (Cambridge: Cambridge University Press, 2002).

74. Frank H. Easterbrook and Daniel R. Fischel, "Antitrust Suits by Targets of Tender Offers," *Michigan Law Review* 80 (1982): 1155–1178 at 1177. For a critique, see John Braithwaite, "The Limits of Economism in Controlling Harmful Corporate Conduct," *Law and Society Review* 16 (1981–1982): 481–504.

75. This discussion follows Simpson, *Corporate Crime, Law, and Social Control*, pp. 50–51.

76. Robert A. Kagan and John T. Scholz, "The 'Criminology of the Corporation' and Regulatory Enforcement Strategies," in Keith Hawkins and John M. Thomas, eds., *Enforcing Regulation* (Boston: Kluwer-Nijhoff, 1984), pp. 67–95.

77. Kagan and Scholz, " 'Criminology of the Corporation' and Regulatory Enforcement Strategies," p. 71.

78. Ibid, p. 80.

79. Ibid., p. 74.

80. John Braithwaite, "The Essence of Responsive Regulation," *UBC Law Review* 44 (2011): 475–520.

81. Ian Ayres and John Braithwaite, *Responsive Regulation* (New York: Oxford University Press, 1992); John Braithwaite, *Regulatory Capitalism* (London: Edward Elgar, 2008).

82. Valerie Braithwaite, John Braithwaite, Diane Gibson, and Toni Makkai, "Regulatory Styles, Motivational Postures, and Nursing Home Compliance," *Law and Policy* 16 (1984): 363–394.

83. Kagan and Scholz, " 'Criminology of the Corporation' and Regulatory Enforcement Strategies," p. 86.

84. E.g., Volkswagen stalled US regulators for over eighteen months, concealing the software "defeat device" installed in their diesel vehicles that allowed them to pass emissions tests. See Jack Ewing, *Faster, Higher, Farther* (New York: W. W. Norton, 2017).

85. John T. Scholz, "Cooperative Regulatory Enforcement and the Politics of Administrative Effectiveness," *American Political Science Review* 85 (1991): 115–135 at 115.

86. As Eugene Bardach and Robert Kagan observe, relations in the United States are so acrimonious that FDA inspectors were at one point given instructions not to provide regulated firms with any advice or information on how to comply with labeling regulations, on the grounds that anything said might later be used by the firm as a defense in subsequent legal disputes with the agency. Bardach and Kagan, *Going by the Book*, p. 118.

87. On the significance of this, see Jürgen Habermas, *Between Facts and Norms*, trans. William Rehg (Cambridge, MA: MIT Press, 1992). See also R. A. Duff, *Answering for Crime* (Oxford: Hart, 2007).

88. Jürgen Habermas, *The Theory of Communicative Action*, vol. 2, trans. Thomas McCarthy (Boston: Beacon Press, 1987), p 177.

89. Friedrich Hayek, *Constitution of Liberty: The Definitive Edition* (Chicago: University of Chicago Press, 2011), p. 205.

90. Hayek, *Constitution of Liberty*, p. 208.

91. Michael Oakeshott, *On History and Other Essays* (Oxford: Basil Blackwell, 1983), pp. 136–139 (e.g., "The expression 'rule of law', taken precisely, stands for a mode of moral association exclusively in terms of the recognition of the authority of known, non-instrumental rules (that is, laws) which impose obligations to subscribe to adverbial conditions in the performance of the self-chosen actions of all who fall within their jurisdiction" (p. 136).

92. F. A. Hayek, *Law, Legislation and Liberty*, vol. 2 (London: Routledge and Kegan Paul, 1976), p. 64.

93. Joseph Raz, *The Authority of Law* (Oxford: Clarendon Press, 1979), p. 229.

94. Lon Fuller, *The Morality of Law*, rev. ed. (New Haven, CT: Yale University Press, 1965), pp. 38-39.

95. Jeremy Waldron, "The Rule of Law and the Importance of Procedure," in James E. Fleming, ed., *Nomos 50: Getting to the Rule of Law* (New York: New York University Press, 2011), pp. 3-31; Raz, "Rule of Law and Its Virtue," in Raz, *Authority of Law*.

96. Although not directly concerned with this issue, T. R. S. Allen, *Liberal Constitutionalism*, has useful suggestions on how equality considerations should be taken into consideration when state power is exercised.

97. *Roncarelli v. Duplessis*, Supreme Court of Canada (1959) S.C.R. 121.

98. Bryner, *Deliberate Discretion*, chap. 3.

99. Robert A. Kagan, *Adversarial Legalism* (Cambridge, MA: Harvard University Press, 2003).

100. Dicey, *Law of the Constitution*, pp. 183-184.

101. Harry W. Arthurs, "Rethinking Administrative Law: A Slightly Dicey Business," *Osgoode Hall Law Journal* 17 (1979): 1-45 at 9.

102. Robert A. Kagan, "Regulatory Inspectors and the Police," in Keith Hawkins and John M. Thomas, eds., *Enforcing Regulation* (The Hague: Kluwer, 1984), pp. 37-64.

103. Arthurs, "Rethinking Administrative Law," p. 22.

104. New Zealand Industrial Conciliation and Arbitration Act (64 Vict. 1900, No 561), §90, p. 431.

105. David Dyzenhaus, *The Constitution of Law* (Cambridge: Cambridge University Press, 2006), pp. 103-106. The puzzle was something like this: "Since on a literal reading these clauses would be obviously unconstitutional, what could they mean, given that they cannot mean what they appear to mean?"

106. Yardley, *Principles of Administrative Law*, p. 29.

107. Ibid., pp. 49-51.

108. Ibid., p. 58.

109. J. E. Bickenbach, Keith C. Culver, and Michael Giudice, *Canadian Cases in the Philosophy of Law*, 5th ed. (Peterborough: Broadview Press, 2018), p. 209.

110. *Padfield v. Minister of Agriculture, Fisheries and Food* (1968) AC at 1030.

111. Sossin, *Administrative Law in Context*, p. 78.

112. Dyzenhaus, *Constitution of Law*, p. 136.

113. Cass R. Sunstein and Adrian Vermeule, "The Morality of Administrative Law," *Harvard Law Review* 131 (2018): 1931-1978 at 1934.

114. Sunstein and Vermeule, "Morality of Administrative Law," p. 1939.

115. Of interest in this context is Gerald Mars, *Cheats at Work* (London: Unwin, 1983).

116. Pires, "Beyond the Fear of Discretion: Flexibility," pp. 57-59.

Chapter 7

1. For a diagnosis of this tendency, see Michael Trebilcock, *The Limits of Freedom of Contract* (Cambridge, MA: Harvard University Press, 1997).

2. Sophia Moreau, "What Is Discrimination?," *Philosophy and Public Affairs* 38 (2010): 143–179; Sophia Moreau, "Discrimination and Negligence," *Canadian Journal of Philosophy* 40:sup1 (2010): 123–149.

3. John Stuart Mill, *On Liberty*, ed., Elizabeth Rapaport (Indianapolis: Hackett, 1978).

4. As Alan Ryan puts it, "It was, and is, a bold move to defend the right to liberty as something other than a *natural* right." "Mill in a Liberal Landscape," in Alan Ryan, *The Making of Modern Liberalism* (Princeton, NJ: Princeton University Press, 2012), pp. 292–325 at 296.

5. Richard Thaler and Cass Sunstein, *Nudge* (New Haven, CT: Yale University Press, 2008). For some of the discussion it has prompted, see Sherzod Abdukarirov, ed., *Nudge Theory in Action* (Switzerland: Palgrave Macmillan, 2016); Alberto Alemanno and Anne-Lise Sibony, *Nudge and the Law* (Portland, OR: Hart, 2015); David Halpern, *Inside the Nudge Unit* (London: W. H. Allen, 2016); Peter John, Sarah Cotterill, Alice Moseley et al., *Nudge, Nudge, Think, Think* (London: Bloomsbury, 2011); Peter John, *How Far to Nudge?* (Cheltenham, UK: Edward Elgar, 2018); Riccardo Rebonato, *Taking Liberties: A Critical Examination of Libertarian Paternalism* (New York: Palgrave Macmillan, 2012); Mark D. White, *The Manipulation of Choice: Ethics and the Libertarian Paternalism* (New York: Palgrave Macmillan, 2013); Jason Hanna, "Libertarian Paternalism, Manipulation, and the Shaping of Preferences," *Social Theory and Practice* 41 (2015): 618–643; Richard J. Arneson, "Nudge and Shove," *Social Theory and Practice* 41 (2015): 668–691; Julian Le Grand and Bill New, *Government Paternalism: Nanny State or Helpful Friend?* (Princeton, NJ: Princeton University Press, 2015).

6. E.g., see "Wolfenden Report" in the United Kingdom, *Report of the Committee on Homosexual Offences and Prostitution* (London: Home Office and Scottish Home Office, 1957), p. 22.

7. This is the upshot of Mill's much-derided line in *Utilitarianism*, cited earlier, that "the sole evidence it is possible to produce that anything is desirable is that people do actually desire it." John Stuart Mill, *Utilitarianism*, ed. George Sher (Indianapolis: Hackett, 1979), p. 34.

8. See Gerald Dworkin, "Paternalism," *The Monist* 56 (1972): 64–84. These definitions have become more complicated over time. See Gerald Dworkin, "Defining Paternalism," in Christian Coons and Michael Weber, eds., *Paternalism: Theory and Practice* (Cambridge: Cambridge University Press, 2013), pp. 25–38. The "for your own good" claim, however, forms the conceptual core of most definitions.

9. Mill, *On Liberty*, p. 9.

10. Mill, p. 74.

11. One can see this in gift giving as well. Many people are not good at choosing gifts for others because instead of giving them what they want, they give them what they think they *should* want.

12. See Alan Hunt, "The Great Masturbation Panic and the Discourses of Moral Regulation in Nineteenth- and Early Twentieth-Century Britain," *Journal of the History of Sexuality* 8 (1998): 575–615.

13. Mill, *On Liberty*, p. 54.

14. Strictly speaking, a utilitarian would want to intervene if the ex ante probability of being right, multiplied by the benefit of intervention, was greater than the probability of being wrong, multiplied by the cost imposed on the individual subject to the intervention. So-called asymmetric paternalism is considered justified by some in cases in which the cost of intervention is relatively low, while the benefits of intervention are significant, leading to greater tolerance for the possibility of error.

15. For discussion of this issue, see Jennifer Conly, *Against Autonomy* (Cambridge: Cambridge University Press, 2013), pp. 113–118. She acknowledges as a disadvantage of paternalistic legislation that for it to be beneficial, legislators must be "reasonably altruistic." She contrasts this with the advantage that, unlike individuals, legislators are not "tempted by imprudence" (p. 116). And yet she does not assess the relative likelihood of these two failures, and so ignores the obvious objection that failures of altruism are far more common than failures of individual prudence.

16. Mill, *On Liberty*, p. 75.

17. For discussion of these arguments, see Jason Hanna, *In Our Best Interest* (Oxford: Oxford University Press, 2018), p. 36. For survey of recent perspectives, see Kalle Grill and Jason Hanna, eds., *Routledge Handbook of the Philosophy of Paternalism* (Oxford: Routledge, 2018).

18. See Sergio Tenenbaum, *Appearances of the Good* (Cambridge: Cambridge University Press, 2007) for a defense of this claim.

19. For an example of opposition to moral paternalism, see Ruwen Ogien, *L'éthique aujourd'hui* (Paris: Gallimard, 2007). Admittedly, many recent authors have blurred the distinction between moral and legal paternalism, e.g., Seana Shiffrin, "Paternalism, Unconscionability Doctrine, and Accommodation," *Philosophy and Public Affairs* 29 (2000): 205–250; also Hanna, *In Our Best Interest*, pp. 24–25.

20. Ryan, "Mill in a Liberal Landscape," p. 303.

21. Joel Feinberg, *The Moral Limits of the Criminal Law*, vol. 1: *Harm to Others* (Oxford: Oxford University Press, 1984); Joel Feinberg, *The Moral Limits of the Criminal Law*, vol. 3: *Harm to Self* (Oxford: Oxford University Press, 1986). See also Michael N. Goldman and Alan H. Goldman, "Paternalistic Laws," *Philosophical Topics* 18 (1990): 65–78.

22. Mill, *On Liberty*, p. 95.

23. For discussion, see Hanna, *In Our Best Interest*, pp. 145–198.

24. M. P. Baumgartner, "The Myth of Discretion," in Keith Hawkins, ed., *The Uses of Discretion* (Oxford: Clarendon Press, 1992), p. 138, referring to Lynda Lytle Holmstrom and Ann Wolbert Burgess, *The Victim of Rape: Institutional Reactions* (New York: Wiley, 1983), pp. 42–43.

25. David Rider, "Why Toronto's Street Food Program Is in Shambles," *Toronto Star*, Sept. 17, 2010.

26. Robert Furtado, "Filion on the Toronto a la Cart Fiasco: 'The One Thing the City Messed Up on Was the Carts,'" *Toronto Life*, March 17, 2010.

27. Hall, "Why Toronto's Street Food Program Is in Shambles."

28. As Mill puts it, "To tax stimulants for the sole purpose of making them more difficult to be obtained is a measure differing only in degree from their entire prohibition, and

would be justifiable only if that were justifiable. Every increase in cost is a prohibition to those whose means do not come up to the augmented price; and to those who do, it is a penalty laid on them for gratifying a particular taste." *On Liberty*, p. 99.

29. Daniel Carpenter, *Reputation and Power* (Princeton, NJ: Princeton University Press, 2010), pp. 157–159.

30. Ibid., p. 118.

31. Cass Sunstein, *After the Rights Revolution* (Cambridge, MA: Harvard University Press, 1990), p. 51. The template for this argument is the mandatory helmet rule in the National Hockey League, which does appear to have resolved a collective action problem among players. The difference is that hockey is a competitive sport, and so those who put on helmets unilaterally put themselves at a competitive disadvantage relative to those who did not. Sitting in a car does not have the same structure. See Thomas Schelling, *Micromotives and Macrobehavior* (New York: W. W. Norton, 1978).

32. For a principled defense of such a view, see Patrick Devlin, *The Enforcement of Morals* (Oxford: Oxford University Press, 1970).

33. Mill, *On Liberty*, p. 78.

34. Mill, p. 82.

35. Mill, p. 79.

36. Mill, p. 94.

37. For a sample of these difficulties, see Nils Holtung, "The Harm Principle," *Ethical Theory and Moral Practice* 5 (2002): 357–389.

38. Mill, *On Liberty*, p. 87

39. Mill, p. 87.

40. Mill, p. 87.

41. W. Kip Viscusi, "Cigarette Taxation and the Social Consequences of Smoking," in James Poterba, ed., *Tax Policy and the Economy*, vol. 9 (Cambridge, MA: MIT Press, 1995), pp. 51–101.

42. E.g., Hanna, *In Our Best Interest*, p. 91.

43. Don Ross, Harold Kincaid, David Spurrett, and Peter Collins, *What Is Addiction?* (Cambridge, MA: MIT Press, 2010).

44. On "expertise imperialism," see Allan Buchanan, "Toward a Theory of the Ethics of Bureaucratic Organizations," *Business Ethics Quarterly* 6 (1996): 419–440.

45. Consider, for instance, Hanna (*In Our Best Interests*) and Conly (*Against Autonomy*). Both develop rhetorically powerful denunciations of traditional anti-paternalism. Yet their discussions contain practically no reference to the hard-won personal freedoms that were achieved through the elimination of paternalistic state powers, particularly in the domain of sexuality. Their enthusiasm for paternalism seems to be motivated primarily by a desire to defend tobacco-control policies, along with some minor dietary interferences, such as soda taxes. It is difficult not to see an alarming politically *naïveté* at work here. As I will attempt to show below, there are ways to defend these policies without tearing down the fence that Mill erected.

46. For a survey of such efforts, see Le Grand and New, *Government Paternalism*, pp. 64–72.

390 NOTES TO PAGES 324–329

47. Peter de Marneffe, "Self-sovereignty and Paternalism," in Christian Coons and Michael Weber, eds., *Paternalism: Theory and Practice* (Cambridge: Cambridge University Press, 2013), pp. 56–73 at 65.

48. Thaler and Sunstein, *Nudge*, p. 9. Note that Thaler and Sunstein are misstating the burden of proof here, in the same way that Hanna does in *In Our Best Interests*, pp 31–32. People do not need to be right about their own good "almost all of the time" to be better than third parties; they only need to be right more often than those third parties.

49. These are collected in Richard H. Thaler, *The Winner's Curse* (New York: Free Press, 1992).

50. The issue of preferences for actions is more complicated. See Joseph Heath, *Following the Rules* (New York: Oxford University Press, 2008), pp. 72–80.

51. Kris N. Kirby and R. J. Hernstein, "Preference Reversals Due to Myopic Discounting of Delayed Reward," *Psychological Science* 6 (1995): 83–89.

52. David Hume described the phenomenon with extraordinary lucidity:

> In reflecting on any action, which I am to perform a twelve-month hence, I always resolve to prefer the greater good, whether at that time it will be more contiguous or remote; nor does any difference in that particular make a difference in my present intentions and resolutions. My distance from the final determination makes all those minute differences vanish, nor am I affected by any thing, but the general and more discernible qualities of good and evil. But on my nearer approach, those circumstances, which I at first over-looked, begin to appear, and have an influence on my conduct and affections. A new inclination to the present good springs up, and makes it difficult for me to adhere inflexibly to my first purpose and resolution. This natural infirmity I may very much regret, and I may endeavour, by all possible means, to free my self from it. I may have recourse to study and reflection within myself; to the advice of friends; to frequent meditation, and repeated resolution: And having experienced how ineffectual all these are, I may embrace with pleasure any other expedient, by which I may impose a restraint upon myself, and guard against this weakness. (David Hume, *A Treatise of Human Nature*, ed. P. H. Nidditch, 2nd ed. [Oxford: Oxford University Press, 1978], p. 536)

53. George Ainslie, *Picoeconomics* (Cambridge: Cambridge University Press, 1992).

54. For a defense of this definition, see Joseph Heath and Joel Anderson, "Procrastination and the Extended Will," in Chrisoula Andreou and Mark D. White, eds., *The Thief of Time* (Oxford: Oxford University Press, 2010), pp. 233–252.

55. Note that it is not the only candidate. There is also something to be said for models that feature an exponential rate with a fixed penalty imposed on the first unit of delay. See Jess Benhabib, Alberto Bisin, and Andrew Schotter, "Present-Bias, Quasi-Hyperbolic Discounting, and Fixed Costs," *Games and Economic Behavior* 69 (2010): 205–223.

56. See Heath, *Following the Rules*, pp. 226–257.

57. Johanna Thoma, *Advice for the Steady* (unpublished PhD diss., University of Toronto, 2017).

58. The individual, Mill writes, must use "discrimination to decide, and when he has decided, firmness and self-control to hold to his deliberate decision," *On Liberty*, p. 56.

As for those who are unable to exercise this "firmness and self-control," Mills seems to think that any recognition of this would impugn their character so gravely that it would better to avoid any such suggestion.

59. See Andrew Franklin-Hall, "Binding the Self: The Ethics of Ulysses Contracts" (forthcoming).

60. Described in Thaler and Sunstein, *Nudge*, pp. 114–116.

61. Jon Elster, *Ulysses and the Sirens* (Cambridge: Cambridge University Press, 1979).

62. Heath and Anderson, "Procrastination and the Extended Will." See also Gharad Bryan, Dean Karlan, and Scott Nelson, "Commitment Devices," *Annual Review of Economics* 2 (2010): 671–98.

63. David Laibson, "Mental Accounts, Self-Control and an Intrapersonal Principal-Agent Problem," Working Paper (1994).

64. Sanne Nauts, Bart A. Kamphorst, Wim Stut, Denise T. D. De Rideer, and Joel H. Anderson, "The Explanations People Give for Going to Bed Late: A Qualitative Study of the Varieties of Bedtime Procrastination," *Behavioral Sleep Medicine* (2018): 1–10.

65. See Cass Sunstein, "Boundedly Rational Borrowing," *University of Chicago Law Review* 73 (2006): 248–270.Both Hanna (*In Our Best Interests*) and Conly (*Against Autonomy*) provide further examples of American authors developing rhetorically powerful condemnations of the classic anti-paternalist position, but then using the position only to defend extremely minimal state interferences.

66. Bruno Frey and Alois Stutzer, "Mispredicting Utility and the Political Process," in Edward J. McCafferey and Joel Slemrod, eds., *Behavioral Public Finance* (New York: Russell Sage, 2006), pp. 113–140.

67. My use of the term "justified" should not be taken to prejudge the question of whether it is actually justified. I use the phrase descriptively, to pick out the position Frey and Stutzer are defending. They are calling for hard paternalism in certain cases, and they argue that it is justified because the individuals involved are victims of cognitive biases that compromise their judgment.

68. Frey and Stutzer, "Mispredicting Utility and the Political Process," p. 114.

69. Robert H. Frank, *Luxury Fever* (New York: Free Press, 1999), pp. 80–83.

70. Shane Frederick and George Loewenstein, "Hedonic Adaptation," in Daniel Kahneman, Ed Diener, and Norbert Schwarz, eds., *Well-Being: The Foundations of Hedonic Psychology* (New York: Russell Sage, 1999).

71. Frank, *Luxury Fever*, pp. 80–83.

72. Frey and Stutzer, "Mispredicting Utility and the Political Process," p. 118.

73. Thaler and Sunstein, *Nudge*, p. 43. See James Hamblin, "A Credibility Crisis in Food Science," *The Atlantic*, Sept. 24, 2018.

74. Daniel Hausman and Brynn Welch, "Debate: To Nudge or Not to Nudge," *Journal of Political Philosophy* 18 (2010): 123–136.

75. Thaler and Sunstein, *Nudge*, p. 6.

76. This statement of the position is more clear in Cass Sunstein, *Why Nudge?* (New Haven, CT: Yale University Press, 2014), pp. 87–90.

77. Thaler and Sunstein, *Nudge*, p. 11.

78. Richard H. Thaler and Cass R. Sunstein, "Libertarian Paternalism," *American Economic Review* 93 (2003): 175–179 at 175.

79. See the overview in Pelle Guldborg Hansen, "The Definition of Nudge and Libertarian Paternalism: Does the Hand Fit the Glove?," *European Journal of Risk Regulation* 7 (2016): 155–174; Pelle Guldborg Hansen and Andreas Maaløe Jesperson, "Nudge and the Manipulation of Choice," *European Journal of Risk Regulation* 4 (2013): 3–28.

80. Tyler Cowen, "Why Conservatives Should Celebrate Thaler's Nobel," *Bloomberg Opinion*, Oct. 9, 2017.

81. Sunstein and Thaler acknowledge this in a footnote (*Nudge*, p. 8), but do not seem to regard it as a problem.

82. Thaler and Sunstein, *Nudge*, p. 8.

83. See collected papers in McCaffery and Slemrod, *Behavioral Public Finance*.

84. Hume, *Treatise of Human Nature*, p. 536.

85. Richard H. Thaler and Cass Sunstein, "Libertarian Paternalism Is Not an Oxymoron," *University of Chicago Law Review* 70 (2003): 1159–1202 at 1161.

86. For discussion, see Joseph Heath, *Enlightenment 2.0* (Toronto: HarperCollins, 2014), pp. 168–172.

87. See, e.g., White, *Manipulation of Choice*; Eric Cave, "What's Wrong with Motive Manipulation?," *Ethical Theory and Moral Practice* 10 (2007): 176–200.

88. Keith Stanovich, *The Robot's Rebellion* (Chicago: University of Chicago Press, 2004), pp. 136–137.

89. Stanovich, *Robot's Rebellion*, p. 138.

90. John Rawls, *Political Liberalism* (New York: Columbia University Press, 1993), p. xvi.

Bibliography

Abdukarirov, Sherzod, ed. *Nudge Theory in Action*. Switzerland: Palgrave Macmillan, 2016.

Ainslie, George. *Picoeconomics*. Cambridge: Cambridge University Press, 1992.

al-Farabi, Abu Nasr. *On the Perfect State*. Translated by Richard Walzer. Oxford: Oxford University Press, 1985.

Acemoglu, Daron, and James A. Robinson. *Economic Origins of Dictatorship and Democracy*. Cambridge: Cambridge University Press, 2006.

Adler, Matthew D., and Eric A. Posner. *New Foundations of Cost-Benefit Analysis*. Cambridge, MA: Harvard University Press, 2006.

Allan, T. R. S. *Liberal Constitutionalism*. Oxford: Oxford University Press, 2001.

Álvarez-Farizo, Begoña, Nick Hanley, Ramón Barberán, and Angelina Lázaro. "Choice Modeling at the 'Market Stall': Individual versus Collective Interest in Environmental Valuation." *Ecological Economics* 60, no. 4 (2007): 743–751.

Anderson, Elizabeth S. "What Is the Point of Equality?" *Ethics* 109, no. 2 (1999): 287–337.

Anderson, Elizabeth. *Value in Ethics and Economics*. Cambridge, MA: Harvard University Press, 1993.

Andreou, Chrisoula, and Mark D. White, eds. *The Thief of Time*. New York: Oxford University Press, 2010.

Applbaum, Arthur Isak. "The Remains of the Role." *Governance* 6, no. 4 (1993): 545–557.

Applbaum, Arthur Isak. "Professional Detachment: The Executioner of Paris." *Harvard Law Review* 109, no. 2 (1995): 458–486.

Applbaum, Arthur Isak. *Ethics for Adversaries*. Princeton, NJ: Princeton University Press, 2000.

Appleby, Paul H. *Morality and Administration in Democratic Government*. Baton Rouge: Louisiana State University Press, 1952.

Appleby, Paul H. *Policy and Administration*. University, AL: University of Alabama Press, 1949.

Appleby, Paul H. "Toward Better Public Administration." *Public Administration Review* 7, no. 2 (1947): 93–99.

Aquinas, St. Thomas. *Summa Theologica*. Translated by Fathers of the English Benedictine Province. New York: Benzinger, 1947.

Aranson, Peter H., Ernest Gelhorn, and Glen O. Robinson. "A Theory of Legislative Delegation." *Cornell Law Review* 68 (1982): 1–67.

Ariely, Dan. *Predictably Irrational*. New York: HarperCollins, 2008.

Aristotle. *Nicomachean Ethics*. Translated by Martin Ostwald. New York: Macmillan, 1962.

Arneson, Richard J. "Nudge and Shove." *Social Theory and Practice* 41 (2015): 668–691.

Arrow, Kenneth. "Uncertainty and the Welfare Economics of Medical Care." *American Economic Review* 53 (1963): 941–973.

Arthurs, Harry W. "Rethinking Administrative Law: A Slightly Dicey Business." *Osgoode Hall Law Journal* 17 (1979): 1–45.

Atkinson, Giles, and Susana Mourato. "Environmental Cost-Benefit Analysis." *Annual Review of Environmental Resources* 33 (2008): 317–344.

Audard, Catherine. *Qu'est ce que le libéralisme?* Paris: Gallimard, 2009.

Ayres, Ian, and John Braithwaite. *Responsive Regulation.* New York: Oxford University Press, 1992.

Bacevich, Andrew J. *The New American Militarism.* Oxford: Oxford University Press, 2005.

Bakan, Joel. *The Corporation.* Toronto: Penguin, 2004.

Baker, Dorie. "In Canada, Publicly-Funded Health Care Is 'Moral Enterprise', Says Official." *Yale Bulletin and Calendar* 31, no. 8 (2002).

Baker, George P. "Incentive Contracts and Performance Measurement." *Journal of Political Economy* 100, no. 3 (1992): 598–614.

Bardach, Eugene, and Robert A. Kagan. *Going by the Book.* Philadelphia: Temple University Press, 1982.

Barlow, Maude, and Tony Clarke. *Blue Gold.* Toronto: Stoddart, 2002.

Barr, Nicholas. *The Economics of the Welfare State.* 3rd ed. Stanford, CA: Stanford University Press, 1998.

Baumgartner, Mary P. "The Myth of Discretion." In Keith Hawkins, ed., *The Uses of Discretion,* pp. 129–162. Oxford: Clarendon Press, 1992.

Beato, Greg. "Black Liquor Binge." *Reason,* Dec. 29, 2009.

Benhabib, Jess, Alberto Bisin, and Andrew Schotter. "Present-Bias, Quasi-Hyperbolic Discounting, and Fixed Costs." *Games and Economic Behavior* 69, no. 2 (2010): 205–223.

Berenson, Alex. "Cancer Drugs Offer Hope, but at a Huge Expense." *New York Times,* July 12, 2005.

Bernard, G. W. "The Dissolution of the Monasteries." *History* 96, no. 324 (2011): 390–409.

Bickenbach, J. E., Keith C. Culver, and Michael Giudice. *Canadian Cases in the Philosophy of Law.* 5th ed. Peterborough: Broadview, 2018.

Blaug, Mark. *Economic Theory in Retrospect.* 4th ed. Cambridge: Cambridge University Press, 1985.

Blinder, Alan S. "Is Government Too Political?" *Foreign Affairs* 76, no. 6 (1997): 115–126.

Bodin, Jean. *On Sovereignty.* Translated by Julian H. Franklin. Cambridge: Cambridge University Press, 1992.

Bossuet, Jacques-Benigne. *Politics Drawn from the Very Words of Holy Scripture.* Translated by Patrick Riley. Cambridge: Cambridge University Press, 1990.

Bourgault, Jacques. "Federal Deputy Ministers: Serial Servers Looking for Influence." In *Deputy Ministers in Canada,* eds., Jacques Bourgault and Christopher Dunn, pp. 364–400. Toronto: University of Toronto Press, 2014.

Bradsher, Keith. *High and Mighty.* New York: Public Affairs, 2002.

Braithwaite, John. "The Essence of Responsive Regulation." *UBC Law Review* 44 (2011): 475–520.

Braithwaite, John. "The Limits of Economism in Controlling Harmful Corpo¬rate Conduct." *Law and Society Review* 16 (1981–82): 481–504.

Braithwaite, John. *Regulatory Capitalism.* London: Edward Elgar, 2008.

Braithwaite, Valerie, John Braithwaite, Diane Gibson, and Toni Makkai. "Regulatory Styles, Motivational Postures and Nursing Home Compliance." *Law & Policy* 16, no. 4 (1994): 363–394.

Braybrooke, David. *Meeting Needs.* Princeton, NJ: Princeton University Press, 1987.

Brennan, Jason, and Peter Jaworski. *Markets without Limits.* London: Routledge, 2015.

Breyer, Stephen. *Breaking the Vicious Circle.* Cambridge, MA: Harvard University Press, 1994.

Brock, Dan. "Ethical Issues in the Use of Cost-Effectiveness Analysis for the Prioritization of Health Resources." In George Khushf, ed., *Handbook of Bioethics*, pp. 352–380. Dordrecht: Kluwer, 2004.

Brodie, Ian. *At the Centre of Government*. Montreal: McGill-Queen's University Press, 2018.

Brodie, Ian. "In Defense of Political Staff." *Canadian Parliamentary Review* 35, no. 3 (2012): 33–39.

Brooks, Clem, and Jeff Manza. *Why Welfare States Persist: The Importance of Public Opinion in Democracies*. Chicago: University of Chicago Press, 2007.

Broome, John. "Trying to Value a Life." *Journal of Public Economics* 9, no. 1 (1978): 91–100.

Bryan, Gharad, Dean Karlan, and Scott Nelson. "Commitment Devices." *Annual Review of Economics* 2, no. 1 (2010): 671–698.

Bryner, Gary C. *Bureaucratic Discretion*. New York: Pergamon Press, 1987.

Buchanan, Allen. "Toward a Theory of the Ethics of Bureaucratic Organizations." *Business Ethics Quarterly* 6, no. 4 (1996): 419–440.

Buchanan, James M. "An Economic Theory of Clubs." *Economica* 32, no. 125 (1965): 1–14.

Burke, Edmund. *Thoughts and Details on Scarcity*. London: F. and C. Rivington, 1800.

Callicott, J. Baird. "Non-anthropocentric Value Theory and Environmental Ethics." *American Philosophical Quarterly* 21 (1984): 299–309.

Camerer, Colin, Samuel Issacharoff, George Loewenstein, Ted O'Donoghue, and Matthew Rabin. "Regulation for Conservatives: Behavioral Economics and the Case for 'Asymmetric Paternalism.'" *University of Pennsylvania Law Review* 151, no. 3 (2003): 1211–1254.

Canadian Environmental Law Association. "Radon in Indoor Air: A Review of Law and Policy in Canada." http://www.cela.ca/sites/cela.ca/files/Radon-Report-with-Appendices_0.pdf. Accessed Sept. 2, 2018.

Caney, Simon. "Climate Change, Human Rights, and Moral Thresholds." In Stephen Humphreys, ed., *Climate Change and Human Rights*, pp. 163–177. Cambridge: Cambridge University Press, 2009.

Cantor, Norman F. *The Civilization of the Middle Ages*. Rev. ed. New York: HarperPerennial, 1994.

Carafano, James Jay. "The Army Reserves and the Abrams Doctrine: Unfulfilled Promise, Uncertain Future." *Heritage Lecture*, No. 869. Washington, DC: Heritage Foundation, 2005.

Carpenter, Daniel. *The Forging of Bureaucratic Autonomy*. Princeton, NJ: Princeton University Press, 2001.

Carpenter, Daniel. *Reputation and Power*. Princeton, NJ: Princeton University Press, 2010.

Cartier, Geneviève. "Keeping a Check on Discretion." In Colleen Flood and Lorne Sossin, eds., *Administrative Law in Context*, pp. 269–288. Toronto: Emond Montgomery, 2008.

Cave, Eric. "What's Wrong with Motive Manipulation?" *Ethical Theory and Moral Practice* 10 (2007): 176–200.

Chan, Joseph. "Confucian Attitudes toward Ethical Pluralism." In Daniel A. Bell, ed., *Confucian Political Ethics*, pp. 113–138. Princeton, NJ: Princeton University Press, 2008.

Chaudhury, Nazmul, Jeffrey Hammer, Michael Kremer, Karthik Muralidharan, and F. Halsey Rogers. "Missing in Action: Teacher and Health Worker Absence in Developing Countries." *Journal of Economic Perspectives* 20, no. 1 (2006): 91–116.

Checkoway, Barry. "The Politics of Public Hearings." *Journal of Applied Behavioral Science* 17, no. 4 (1981): 566–582.

Christensen, Robert K., Holly T. Goerdel, and Sean Nicholson-Crotty. "Management, Law, and the Pursuit of the Public Good in Public Administration." *Journal of Public Administration Research and Theory*, suppl. 1 (2011): i125–i140.

Christensen, Jørgen Grønnegård, and Niels Opstrup. "Bureaucratic Dilemmas: Civil Servants between Political Responsiveness and Normative Constraints." *Governance* 31, no. 3 (2018): 481–498.

Coase, R. H. "The Nature of the Firm." *Economica* 4, no. 16 (1937): 386–405.

Coleman, Jules L. "Efficiency, Utility, and Wealth Maximization." *Hofstra Law Review* 8 (1980): 509–551.

Commission on the Future of Heath Care in Canada. *Building on Values: The Future of Health Care in Canada.* Ottawa: Government of Canada, 2002.

Committee on Homosexual Offences and Prostitution. *Report of the Committee on Homosexual Offences and Prostitution.* London: Home Office and Scottish Home Office, 1957.

Congressional Budget Office. *Is Social Security Progressive?* Congressional Budget Office Report. Washington, DC, Dec. 15, 2006. https://www.cbo.gov/publication/18266. Accessed Sept. 12, 2018.

Conly, Jennifer. *Against Autonomy.* Cambridge: Cambridge University Press, 2013.

Cooper, Philip J. *Public Law and Public Administration.* Palo Alto, CA: Mayfield, 1983.

Cooper, Terry L. *The Responsible Administrator*, 5th ed. San Francisco: Jossey-Bass, 2006.

Cooper, Terry L., and Luther Gulick. "Citizenship and Professionalism in Public Administration." *Public Administration Review* 44 (1984): 143–151.

Copp, David. "Equality, Justice and the Basic Needs." In Gillian Brock, ed., *Necessary Goods*, pp. 113–134. Lanham, MD: Rowman and Littlefield, 1998.

Copp, David. "The Justice and Rationale of Cost-Benefit Analysis." *Theory and Decision* 23, no. 1 (1987): 65–87.

Cowen, Tyler. "Why Conservatives Should Celebrate Thaler's Nobel." *Bloomberg Opinion*, Oct. 9, 2017.

Cubbon, Brian. "The Duty of the Professional." In Richard A. Chapman, ed., *Ethics in Public Service*, pp. 7–14. Ottawa: Carlton University Press, 1993.

Damaska, Mirjan. "Structures of Authority and Comparative Criminal Procedure." *Yale Law Journal* 84, no. 3 (1975): 480–544.

Daniels, Norman. "Justice, Health, and Healthcare." *American Journal of Bioethics* 1, no. 2 (2001): 2–16.

Daniels, Ronald J., and Michael J. Trebilcock. *Rethinking the Welfare State.* London: Routledge, 2005.

Davis, Evan. *Public Spending.* London: Penguin, 1998.

Delumeau, Jean. *Sin and Fear.* Translated by Eric Nicholson. New York: St. Martin's Press, 1990.

De Marneffe, Peter. "Self-Sovereignty and Paternalism." In Christian Coons and Michael Weber, eds., *Paternalism: Theory and Practice*, pp. 56–73. Cambridge: Cambridge University Press, 2013.

Denhardt, Kathryn G., and Bayard L. Catron. "The Management of Ideals: A Political Perspective on Ethics." *Public Administration Review* 49, no. 2 (1989): 187–193.

Desvousges, William, F. Reed Johnson, Richard W. Dunford, Sara P. Hudson, K. Nicole Wilson, and Kevin J. Boyle. "Measuring Natural Resource Damages with Contingent

Valuation: Tests of Validity and Reliability." In Jerry Hausman, ed., *Contingent Valuation: A Critical Assessment*, pp. 91–164. Amsterdam: North Holland Press, 1993.

Devlin, Patrick. *The Enforcement of Morals*. Oxford: Oxford University Press, 1970.

Diamond, Peter A., and Jerry A Hausman. "Contingent Valuation: Is Some Number Better Than No Number?" *Journal of Economic Perspectives* 8, no. 4 (1994): 45–64.

Dicey, A. V. *An Introduction to the Study of the Law of the Constitution*, 10th ed. London: Macmillan, 1959.

Dixit, Avinash. "The Power of Incentives in Private versus Public Organizations." *American Economic Review* 87 (1997): 378–382.

Dolan, Julie, and David H. Rosenbloom. *Representative Bureaucracy*. Armonk, NY: M. E. Sharpe, 2003.

Dorman, Peter, and Paul Hagstrom. "Wage Compensation for Dangerous Work Revisited." *Industrial and Labor Relations Review* 52, no. 1 (1998): 116–135.

Dow, Gregory K. *Governing the Firm*. Cambridge: Cambridge University Press, 2003.

Dowding, Keith. *The Civil Service*. London: Routledge, 1995.

Drummond, Michael F. "Allocating Resources." *International Journal of Technology Assessment in Health Care* 6 (1990): 77–92

Du Gay, Paul. *In Praise of Bureaucracy*. London: Sage, 2000.

Duff, R. A. *Answering for Crime*. Oxford: Hart, 2007.

Dunleavy, Patrick. "The Architecture of the British Central States. Part II: Empirical Findings." *Public Administration* 67, no. 4 (1989): 391–417.

Dworkin, Gerald. "Defining Paternalism." In Christian Coons and Michael Weber, eds., *Paternalism*, pp. 25–38. Cambridge: Cambridge University Press, 2013.

Dworkin, Gerald. "Paternalism." *The Monist* 56 (1972): 64–84.

Dworkin, Ronald. "Liberalism." In Stuart Hampshire, ed., *Public and Private Morality*, pp. 113–143. Cambridge: Cambridge University Press, 1978.

Dworkin, Ronald. "Rights as Trumps." In Jeremy Waldron, ed., *Theories of Rights*, pp. 153–167. Oxford: Oxford University Press, 1984.

Dworkin, Ronald. *Sovereign Virtue*. Cambridge, MA: Harvard University Press, 2002.

Dworkin, Ronald. "Sovereign Virtue Revisited." *Ethics* 113, no. 1 (2002): 106–143.

Dyzenhaus, David. "Constituting the Rule of Law: Fundamental Values in Administrative Law." *Queen's Law Journal* 27 (2002): 445–509.

Dyzenhaus, David. *The Constitution of Law*. Cambridge: Cambridge University Press, 2006.

Easterbrook, Frank H., and Daniel R. Fischel. "Antitrust Suits by Targets of Tender Offers." *Michigan Law Review* 80, no. 6 (1982): 1155–1178.

The Economist. "How Turkey Fell from Investment Darling to Junk-Rated Emerging Market." *The Economist*, May 19, 2018.

Eder, Steve. "When Picking Apples on a Farm with 5000 Rules, Watch Out for the Ladders." *New York Times*, Dec. 17, 2017.

Edwards, Ryan D. "The Cost of Uncertain Life Span." *Journal of Population Economics* 26, no. 4 (2013): 1485–1522.

Ellis, Adrian. "Neutrality and the Civil Service." In Robert E. Goodin and Andrew Reeve, eds., *Liberal Neutrality*, pp. 84–105. London: Routledge, 1989.

Elster, Jon. *Local Justice in America*. New York: Sage, 1995.

Elster, Jon. *Ulysses and the Sirens*. Cambridge: Cambridge University Press, 1979.

Esping-Andersen, Gøsta, and John Myles. "Economic Inequality and the Welfare State." In Wiemer Salverda, Brian Nolan, and Timothy M. Smeeding, eds., *Oxford Handbook of Economic Inequality*, pp. 639–664. Oxford: Oxford University Press, 2009.

Evans, Tony. *Professional Discretion in Welfare Services*. Farnham, UK: Ashgate, 2010.

Ewald, François. *L'État providence*. Paris: Grasset, 1986.

Ewing, Jack. *Faster, Higher, Farther*. New York: W. W. Norton, 2017.

Farber, Daniel. *Eco-Pragmatism*. Chicago: University of Chicago Press, 1999.

Feinberg, Joel. *The Moral Limits of the Criminal Law*. Vol. 1: *Harm to Others*. Oxford University Press, 1984.

Feinberg, Joel. *The Moral Limits of the Criminal Law*. Vol. 3: *Harm to Self*. Oxford: Oxford University Press, 1986.

Ferner, Anthony. *Governments, Managers and Industrial Relations*. Oxford: Basil Blackwell, 1988.

Finer, Herman. *The British Civil Service*. London: Allen and Unwin, 1937.

Fiorino, Daniel J. "Citizen Participation and Environmental Risk: A Survey of Institutional Mechanisms." *Science, Technology, and Human Values* 15, no. 2 (1990): 226–243.

Fleming, James E. *Getting to the Rule of Law: NOMOS L*. New York: New York University Press, 2011.

Flood, Colleen M., and Lorian Hardcastle. "The Private Sale of Cancer Drugs in Ontario's Public Hospitals: Tough Issues as the Public/Private Interface in Health Care." *McGill Health Law Publication* 1 (2007): 1–21.

Forst, Rainer. *Toleration in Conflict*. Translated by Ciaran Cronin. Cambridge: Cambridge University Press, 2003.

Foucault, Michel. *History of Sexuality*. Vol. 1. Translated by Robert Hurley. London: Penguin, 1979.

Frank, Robert H. *Luxury Fever*. New York: Free Press, 1999.

Franklin-Hall, Andrew. Forthcoming. "Binding the Self: The Ethics of Ulysses Contracts."

Fraser, Nancy. *Justice Interruptus*. London: Routledge, 1997.

Frederick, Shane, and George Loewenstein. "Hedonic Adaptation." In Daniel Kahneman, Ed Diener, and Norbert Schwarz, eds., *Well-Being: The Foundations of Hedonic Psychology*, pp. 302–311. New York: Russell Sage, 1999.

Frederickson, H. George. "Ethics and the New Managerialism." *Public Administration and Management* 4 (1999): 299–324.

Frey, Bruno, and Alois Stutzer. "Mispredicting Utility and the Political Process." In Edward J. McCafferey and Joel Slemrod, eds., *Behavioral Public Finance*, pp. 113–140. New York: Russell Sage, 2006.

Frick, Johann. "Contractualism and Social Risk." *Philosophy & Public Affairs* 43, no. 3 (2015): 175–223.

Friedrich, Carl J. "Public Policy and the Nature of Administrative Responsibility." In Carl J. Friedrich and Edward S. Mason, eds., *Public Policy*, pp. 165–175. Cambridge, MA: Harvard University Press, 1940.

Fritschler, Lee. *Smoking and Politics*. Englewood Cliffs, NJ: Prentice-Hall, 1984.

Fuji-Johnson, Genevieve. *Democratic Illusion: Deliberative Democracy in Canadian Public Policy*. Toronto: University of Toronto Press, 2015.

Fukuyama, Francis. *The Origins of Political Order*. New York: Farrar, Straus and Giroux, 2011.

Fukuyama, Francis. *Political Order and Political Decay*. New York: Farrar, Straus and Giroux, 2014.

Fuller, Lon. *The Morality of Law*. Rev. ed. New Haven, CT: Yale University Press, 1965.

Fullerton, Don, and Brent D. Mast. *Income Redistribution from Social Security*. Washington, DC: American Enterprise Institute, 2005.

Furtado, Robert. "Filion on the Toronto a la Cart Fiasco: 'The One Thing the City Messed Up on Was the Carts.'" *Toronto Life*, March 17, 2010.

Gailmard, Sean. "Accountability and Principal-Agent Theory." In Mark Bovens, Robert E. Goodin, and Thomas Shillemans, eds., *Oxford Handbook of Public Accountability*, pp. 90–105. Oxford: Oxford University Press, 2014.

Galligan, Denis James. *Discretionary Powers*. Oxford: Clarendon Press, 1986.

Garber, Alan M., and Harold C. So. "The Role of Costs in Comparative Effectiveness Research." *Health Affairs* 29, no. 10 (2010): 1805–1811.

Gardiner, Stephen M. "A Core Precautionary Principle." *Journal of Political Philosophy* 14, no. 1 (2006): 33–60.

Gauthier, David. *Morals by Agreement*. New York: Oxford University Press, 1987.

Gibbard, Allan. "Disparate Goods and Rawls' Difference Principle: A Social Choice Theoretic Treatment." *Theory and Decision* 11, no. 3 (1979): 267–288.

Gibbons, Robert. "Incentives in Organizations." *Journal of Economic Perspectives* 12, no. 4 (1998): 115–132.

Godwin, William. *Enquiry Concerning Political Justice*. Vol 2. London: G. G. and J. Robinson, 1798.

Golden, Miriam, and Ray Fisman. *Corruption: What Everyone Needs to Know*. Oxford: Oxford University Press, 2017.

Goldman, Michael N., and Alan H. Goldman. "Paternalistic Laws." *Philosophical Topics* 18 (1990): 65–78.

Goodin, Robert E. *Reasons for Welfare*. Princeton, NJ: Princeton University Press, 1988.

Goodin, Robert E. "Vulnerabilities and Responsibilities: An Ethical Defense of the Welfare State." *American Political Science Review* 79, no. 3 (1985): 775–787.

Goodin Robert R., and Andrew Reeve, eds. *Liberal Neutrality*. London: Taylor and Francis, 1989.

Government Legal Department (UK). *The Judge over Your Shoulder—a Guide to Good Decision-Making*. https://www.gov.uk/government/publications/judge-over-your-shoulder. Accessed May 16, 2019.

Government of Canada. *Value and Ethics in the Public Sector*. Ottawa: Treasury Board, 2011.

Granatstein, J. M. *The Ottawa Men: The Civil Service Mandarins, 1935–1957*. Toronto: Oxford University Press, 1982.

Grant, Kelly. "Former Surgeon to Shake Up Ontario's Health Ministry." *Globe and Mail*, March 27, 2010.

Grant Ruth W., and Robert O. Keohane. "Accountability and Abuses of Power in World Politics." *American Political Science Review* 99 (2005): 29–43.

Gratzer, David. "The ABCs of MSAs." In David Gratzer, ed., *Better Medicine*, pp. 296–297. Toronto: ECW Press, 2002.

Gratzer, David. *Code Blue*. Toronto: ECW Press, 1999.

Gregory, Brad S. *The Unintended Reformation*. Cambridge, MA: Harvard University Press, 2012.

Grill, Kalle, and Jason Hanna, eds. *Routledge Handbook of the Philosophy of Paternalism*. London: Routledge, 2018.

Gulick, Luther. "Notes on the Theory of Organization." In Luther Gulick and Lyndall Urwick, eds., *Papers on the Science of Administration*, pp. 1–49. New York: Columbia University Press, 1937.

Habermas, Jürgen. *Between Facts and Norms*. Translated by William Rehg. Cambridge, MA: MIT Press, 1996.

Habermas, Jürgen. *Legitimation Crisis*. Translated by Thomas McCarthy. Boston: Beacon Press, 1975.

Habermas, Jürgen. *Moral Consciousness and Communicative Action*. Translated by Christian Lenhardt and Shierry Weber Nicholson. Boston: MIT Press, 1999.

Habermas, Jürgen. "Popular Sovereignty as Procedure." In Jürgen Habermas, *Between Facts and Norms*, translated by William Rehg, pp. 463–490. Cambridge, MA: MIT Press, 1996.

Habermas, Jürgen. *The Theory of Communicative Action*. Vol. 2. Translated by Thomas McCarthy. Boston: Beacon Press, 1987.

Halberstam, Michael. *Totalitarianism and the Modern Conception of Politics*. New Haven, CT: Yale University Press, 1999.

Halévy, Elie. *The Growth of Philosophical Radicalism*. Translated by Mary Morris. New York: Macmillan, 1928.

Hall Findlay, Martha. "Canada's Supply Management System for Dairy Is No Longer Defensible." *Globe and Mail*, Aug 18, 2017.

Halpern, David. *Inside the Nudge Unit*. London: W. H. Allen, 2016.

Hamblin, James. "A Credibility Crisis in Food Science." *The Atlantic*, Sept. 24, 2018.

Hamilton, Lawrence. *The Political Philosophy of Needs*. Cambridge: Cambridge University Press, 2003.

Hanna, Jason. *In Our Best Interest*. Oxford: Oxford University Press, 2018.

Hanna, Jason. "Libertarian Paternalism, Manipulation, and the Shaping of Preferences." *Social Theory and Practice* 41 (2015): 618–643.

Hansen, Pelle Guldborg. "The Definition of Nudge and Libertarian Paternalism: Does the Hand Fit the Glove?" *European Journal of Risk Regulation* 7, no. 1 (2016): 155–174.

Hansen, Pelle Guldborg, and Andreas Maaløe Jesperson. "Nudge and the Manipulation of Choice." *European Journal of Risk Regulation* 4 (2013): 3–28.

Hansson, Sven Ove. "Risk and Ethics." In Tim Lewens, *Risk: Philosophical Perspectives*, pp. 21–35. London: Routledge, 2007.

Hansmann, Henry. *The Ownership of Enterprise*. Cambridge, MA: Harvard University Press, 1996.

Harder, Brandon. "For the First Time, Canada Seeds More Canola Than Wheat." *CBC News*, June 30, 2017.

Harling, Philip. *The Modern British State*. Cambridge: Polity, 2001.

Harris-McLeod, Emily. "Incentives for Public Service Workers and the Implications of Crowding Out Theory." *Public Policy and Governance Review* 4, no. 2 (2013): 5–21.

Harsanyi, John C. "Can the Maximin Principle Serve as a Basis for Morality? A Critique of John Rawls's Theory." *American Political Science Review* 69, no. 2 (1975): 594–606.

Hart, H. L. A. *The Concept of Law*. Oxford: Oxford University Press, 1961.

Hausman, Daniel, and Brynn Welch. "Debate: To Nudge or Not to Nudge." *Journal of Political Philosophy* 18 (2010): 123–136.

Hawkins, Keith, ed. *The Uses of Discretion*. Oxford: Oxford University Press, 1995.

Hawkins, Keith, and John M. Thomas. "The Enforcement Process in Regulatory Bureaucracies." In Keith Hawkins and John M. Thomas, eds., *Enforcing Regulation*, pp. 3–22. Dordrecht: Springer Netherlands, 1984.

Hayek, Friedrich. *Constitution of Liberty: The Definitive Edition*. Chicago: University of Chicago Press, 2011.

Hayek, Friedrich. *Law, Legislation and Liberty*. Vol. 2. London: Routledge & Kegan Paul, 1976.

Hayek, Friedrich. *The Road to Serfdom*. London: Routledge, 2001.

Hayes, Christopher. "Pulp Nonfiction." *The Nation*, April 20, 2009.

Heath, Joseph. *The Efficient Society*. Toronto: Penguin, 2001.

Heath, Joseph. *Enlightenment 2.0*. Toronto: HarperCollins, 2014.

Heath, Joseph. "Envy and Efficiency." *Revue de philosophie economique* 13 (2006): 1–16.

Heath, Joseph. *Filthy Lucre*. Toronto: HarperCollins, 2008.

Heath, Joseph. *Following the Rules*. New York: Oxford University Press, 2008.

Heath, Joseph. *Morality, Competition, and the Firm*. New York: Oxford University Press, 2014.

Heath, Joseph. "Political Egalitarianism." *Social Theory and Practice* 34, no. 4 (2008): 485–516.

Heath, Joseph. "Public-Sector Management Is Complicated: Comment on Farrell." In Jack Knight and Melissa Schwartzberg, eds., *NOMOS LX: Privatization*, pp. 200–222. New York: New York University Press, 2019.

Heath, Joseph, and Joel Anderson. "Procrastination and the Extended Will." "Procrastination and the Extended Will." In Chrisoula Andreou and Mark D. White, eds., *The Thief of Time*, pp. 233–252. Oxford: Oxford University Press, 2010.

Heath, Joseph, and Wayne Norman. "Stakeholder Theory, Corporate Governance and Public Management: What Can the History of State-Run Enterprises Teach Us in the Post-Enron Era?" *Journal of Business Ethics* 53, no. 3 (2004): 247–265.

Heclo, Hugh. *A Government of Strangers*. Washington, DC: Brookings Institution Press, 1977.

Heclo, Hugh. "OMB and the Presidency: The Problem of Neutral Competence." *Public Interest* 38 (1975): 80–98.

Hegel, G. W. F. *Philosophy of Right*. Translated by Alan White. Indianapolis: Hackett, 2002.

Hewart, Gordon. *The New Despotism*. London: Ernest Benn, 1929.

Hile, Joseph. "Food and Drug Administration Inspections—a New Approach." *Food, Drug and Cosmetic Law Journal* 2 (1972): 101–106.

Hirsch, Fred, 1976. *Social Limits to Growth*: Cambridge, MA: Harvard University Press.

HM Treasury. *The Green Book*, 2003. Gov. uk. https://www.gov.uk/government/publications/the-green-book-appraisal-and-evaluation-in-central-governent. Accessed Sept. 22, 2014.

Hobbes, Thomas. *Leviathan*. Edited by Richard Tuck. Cambridge: Cambridge University Press, 1991.

Holmes, Stephen. *The Anatomy of Antiliberalism*. Cambridge, MA: Harvard University Press, 1993.

Holmstrom, Lynda Lytle, and Ann Wolbert Burgess. *The Victim of Rape: Institutional Reactions*. New York: Wiley, 1983.

Holtug, Nils. "The Harm Principle." *Ethical Theory and Moral Practice* 5, no. 4 (2002): 357–389.

Horne, Lendell Chad. "Health, Risk and Luck." Unpublished diss. University of Toronto, 2014.

Huber, John D., and Charles R. Shipan. *Deliberate Discretion? The Institutional Foundations of Bureaucratic Autonomy*. Cambridge: Cambridge University Press, 2002.

Hubin, Donald C. "The Moral Justification of Benefit/Cost Analysis." *Economics and Philosophy* 10, no. 2 (1994): 169–194.

Hume, David. *A Treatise of Human Nature*. 2nd ed. Edited by L. A. Selby-Bigge and P. H. Nidditch. Oxford: Oxford University Press, 1978.

Hunold, Christian. "Corporatism, Pluralism, and Democracy: Toward a Deliberative Theory of Bureaucratic Accountability." *Governance* 14, no. 2 (2001): 151–167.

Hunt, Alan. "The Great Masturbation Panic and the Discourses of Moral Regulation in Nineteenth- and Early Twentieth-Century Britain." *Journal of the History of Sexuality* 8 (1998): 575–615.

Hutton, William L., and Andrew Massey. "Professional Ethics and Public Service: Can Professionals Serve Two Masters?" *Public Money and Management* 26, no. 1 (2006): 23–30.

Israel, Jonathan. *Radical Enlightenment*. Oxford: Oxford University Press, 2001.

Jacobs, Alan. *Governing for the Long-Term*. Cambridge: Cambridge University Press, 2011.

Jacobs, Jane. *The Death and Life of Great American Cities*. New York: Random House, 1961.

Jarvis Thomson, Judith. "The Trolley Problem." *Yale Law Journal* 94 (1985): 1395–1415.

Jenyns, Soame. *A Free Inquiry into the Nature and Origin of Evil*. 4th ed. London: R & J Dodsley, 1761.

John, Peter. *How Far to Nudge?* Cheltenham, UK: Edward Elgar, 2018.

John, Peter, Sarah Cotterill, Liz Richardson, Alice Moseley, Graham Smith, Gerry Stoker, and Corinne Wales. *Nudge, Nudge, Think, Think*. London: Bloomsbury, 2011.

Jones, Peter. "The Ideal of the Neutral State." In Robert Goodin and Andrew Reeve, eds., *Liberal Neutrality*, pp. 9–38. London: Routledge, 1989.

Jos, Philip H., and Mark E. Tompkins. "Keeping It Public: Defending Public Service Values in a Customer Service Age." *Public Administration Review* 69, no. 6 (2009): 1077–1086.

Kagan, Robert A. *Adversarial Legalism*. Cambridge, MA: Harvard University Press, 2003.

Kagan, Robert A. "On Regulatory Inspectorates and Police." In Keith Hawkins and John M. Thomas, eds., *Enforcing Regulation*, pp. 37–64. Dordrecht: Springer, 1984.

Kagan Robert A., and John T. Scholz. "The 'Criminology of the Corporation' and Regulatory Enforcement Strategies." In Keith Hawkins and John M. Thomas, eds., *Enforcing Regulation*, pp. 67–95. Dordrecht: Springer, 1984.

Kant, Immanuel. *Grounding for the Metaphysics of Morals*. Translated by James W. Ellington. Indianapolis: Hackett, 1981.

Kaplan, Benjamin J. *Divided by Faith*. Cambridge, MA: Harvard University Press, 2007.

Kaufman, Herbert, 1977. *Red Tape*. Washington, DC: Brookings Institution Press.

Keir, David Lindsay. *The Constitutional History of Modern Britain*. New York: D. Van Nostrand, 1938.

Kelman, Steven. "Cost-Benefit Analysis: An Ethical Critique." *Regulation* 33 (1981): 33–40.

Kelman, Steven. *Procurement and Public Management: Fear of Discretion and the Quality of Government Performance*. Washington, DC: AEI Press, 1990.

Kernaghan, Kenneth. "Political Rights and Political Neutrality: Finding the Balance Point." *Canadian Public Administration/Administration publique du Canada* 29, no. 4 (1986): 639–652.

Kingdon, John. *Agendas, Alternatives, and Public Policies*. 2nd ed. New York: Pearson, 2003.

Kirby, Kris N., and R. J. Herrnstein. "Preference Reversals Due to Myopic Discounting of Delayed Reward." *Psychological Science* 6, no. 2 (1995): 83–89.

Kitfield, James. *Prodigal Soldiers*. New York: Simon and Shuster, 1995.

Knight, Jack, and James Johnson. "Aggregation and Deliberation: On the Possibility of Democratic Legitimacy." *Political Theory* 22, no. 2 (1994): 277–296.

Kornai, János, Eric Maskin, and Gérald Roland. "Understanding the Soft Budget Constraint." *Journal of Economic Literature* 41, no. 4 (2003): 1095–1136.

Kornhauser, Lewis A. "On Justifying Cost-Benefit Analysis." *Journal of Legal Studies* 29, no. S2 (2000): 1037–1057.

Koselleck, Reinhart. *Critique and Crisis.* Cambridge, MA: MIT Press, 1988.

Kroeger, Arthur. *Retiring the Crow Rate.* Edmonton: University of Alberta Press, 2009.

Krugman, Paul, and Robin Wells. "The Health Care Crisis and What to Do about It." *New York Review of Books* 53, March 23, 2006.

Kumar, Rahul. "Risking and Wronging." *Philosophy and Public Affairs* 43 (2015): 27–49.

Kymlicka, Will. *Contemporary Political Philosophy.* 2nd ed. Oxford: Oxford University Press, 2003.

Kymlicka, Will. *Multicultural Citizenship.* Oxford: Oxford University Press, 1996.

Laibson, David. "Mental Accounts, Self-Control and an Intrapersonal Principal-Agent Problem." Mimeo, Harvard University, 1994.

Laffer, Arthur B., Stephen Moore, and Peter J. Tanous. *The End of Prosperity: How Higher Taxes Will Doom the Economy.* New York: Threshold, 2008.

Landes, Xavier. "How Fair Is Actuarial Fairness?" *Journal of Business Ethics* 128, no. 3 (2015): 519–533.

Larmore, Charles. *Patterns of Moral Complexity.* Cambridge: Cambridge University Press, 1987.

Larmore, Charles. "Political Liberalism: Its Motivation and Goals." In David Sobel, Peter Vallentyne, and Steven Wall, eds., *Oxford Studies in Political Philosophy*, vol. 1, pp. 63–88. Oxford: Oxford University Press, 2015.

Lawson, Gary. "The Rise and Rise of the Administrative State." *Harvard Law Review* 107, no. 6 (1994): 1231–1254.

Lægreid, Per. "Accountability and New Public Management." In Mark Bovens, Robert E. Goodin, and Thomas Shillemans, eds., *Oxford Handbook of Public Accountability*, pp. 324–338. Oxford: Oxford University Press, 2014.

Le Grand, Julian, and Bill New. *Government Paternalism: Nanny State or Helpful Friend?* Princeton, NJ: Princeton University Press, 2015.

Lehmann, Helmut, ed. *Luther's Works.* Vol. 44. Philadelphia: Fortress Press, 1965.

Lepsius, M. Rainer. "Interests and Ideas: Max Weber's Allocation Problem." In *Max Weber and Institutional Theory*, edited by Claus Wendt, pp. 23–34. Cham, Switzerland: Springer International, 2017.

Lerner, Abba. *The Economics of Control.* New York: A. M. Kelley, 1970.

Lewis, Carol W. *The Ethics Challenge in Public Service.* San Francisco: Jossey-Bass, 1991.

Lindblom, Charles E. *Politics and Markets.* New York: Basic Books, 1980.

Lindert, Peter. *Growing Public.* Vol. 1. Cambridge: Cambridge University Press, 2004.

Linz, Juan J. "The Perils of Presidentialism." *Journal of Democracy* 1 (1990): 51–69.

Lipsey, Richard G., Douglas D. Purvis, and Peter O. Steiner. *Economics.* 6th ed. New York: Harper & Row, 1988.

Lipsky, Michael. *Street-Level Bureaucracy.* New York: Russell Sage, 1980.

Lipton, Eric, and Gardiner Harris. "In Turnaround, Industries Seek U.S. Regulation." *New York Times*, Sept. 16, 2007.

Locke, John. *Second Treatise of Government.* Edited by C. B. Macpherson. Indianapolis: Hackett, 1980.

Locke, John. "Third Letter for Toleration." In Richard Vernon, ed., *Locke on Toleration*, pp. 123–163. Cambridge: Cambridge University Press, 2010.

Lowi, Theodore. *The End of Liberalism.* 2nd ed. New York: Norton, 1979.

Lowndes, Vivien, Lawrence Pratchett, and Gerry Stoker. "Trends In Public Participation. Part 1: Local Government Perspectives." *Public Administration* 79, no. 1 (2001): 205–222.

Lowry, Rosemary, and Martin Peterson. "Cost-Benefit Analysis and Non-utilitarian Ethics." *Politics, Philosophy & Economics* 11, no. 3 (2012): 258–279.

Luban, David. *Lawyers and Justice*. Princeton, NJ: Princeton University Press, 1988.

Luban, David, Alan Strudler, and David Wasserman. "Moral Responsibility in the Age of Bureaucracy." *Michigan Law Review* 90, no. 8 (1992): 2348–2392.

Macintyre, Alasdair. *After Virtue*. 3rd ed. London: Bloomsbury, 2007.

Macmillan, Douglas C., Lorna Philip, Nick Hanley, and Begona Alvarez-Farizo. "Valuing the Non-market Benefits of Wild Goose Conservation: A Comparison of Interview and Group-Based Approaches." *Ecological Economics* 43, no. 1 (2002): 49–59.

Manning, Peter K., and John Van Maanen, eds. *Policing: A View from the Street*. Santa Monica, CA: Goodyear, 1978.

Mars, Gerald. *Cheats at Work*. London: Unwin, 1983.

Marshall, Geoffrey. *Constitutional Conventions*. Oxford: Oxford University Press, 1984.

Marshall, John. *John Locke, Toleration and Early Enlightenment Culture*. Cambridge: Cambridge University Press, 2006.

Marshall, Thomas H. *Citizenship and Social Class and Other Essays*. Cambridge: Cambridge University Press, 1950.

McClelland, J. S. *A History of Western Political Thought*. London: Routledge, 1996.

Meier, Kenneth J., and Laurence J. O'Toole. "Political Control versus Bureaucratic Values: Reframing the Debate." *Public Administration Review* 66, no. 2 (2006): 177–192.

Mikhail, John. *Elements of Moral Cognition*. Cambridge: Cambridge University Press, 2011.

Milgrom, Paul, and John Roberts. *Economics, Organization and Management*. Englewood Cliffs, NJ: Prentice Hall, 1992.

Mill, John Stuart. *Considerations on Responsible Government*. New York: Harper & Brothers, 1862.

Mill, John Stuart. *On Liberty*. Edited by Elizabeth Rapaport. Indianapolis: Hackett, 1978.

Mill, John Stuart. *Utilitarianism*. Edited by George Sher. Indianapolis: Hackett, 1979.

Millward, Robert. *Private and Public Enterprise in Europe: Energy, Telecommunications and Transport, 1830–1990*. Cambridge: Cambridge University Press, 2005.

Mintzberg, Henry. "Managing Government, Governing Management." *Harvard Business Review*, May–June 1996, pp. 75–83.

Mittmann, N. et al. "Prospective Cost-Effectiveness Analysis of Cetuximab in Metastatic Colorectal Cancer: Evaluation of National Cancer Institute of Canada Clinical Trials Group CO.17 Trial." *JNCI: Journal of the National Cancer Institute* 101, no. 17 (2009): 1182–1192.

Montesquieu. *The Spirit of the Laws*. Translated by Anne M. Cohler, Basia Carolyn Miller, and Harold Samuel Stone. Cambridge: Cambridge University Press, 1989.

Moreau, Sophia. "Discrimination and Negligence." *Canadian Journal of Philosophy*. 40:sup1 (2010): 123–149.

Moreau, Sophia. "What Is Discrimination?" *Philosophy & Public Affairs* 38, no. 2 (2010): 143–179.

Moss, David A. *When All Else Fails*. Cambridge, MA: Harvard University Press, 2004.

Murphy, Liam, and Thomas Nagel. *The Myth of Ownership*. Oxford University Press, 2002.

Nash, John F. "The Bargaining Problem." *Econometrica* 18, no. 2 (1950): 155–162.

Nauts, Sanne, Bart A. Kamphorst, Wim Stut, Denise T. D. De Ridder, and Joel H. Anderson. "The Explanations People Give for Going to Bed Late: A Qualitative Study of the Varieties of Bedtime Procrastination." *Behavioral Sleep Medicine* (July 2018): 1–10.

Neumann, Peter J., and Milton C. Weinstein. "Legislating against Use of Cost-Effectiveness Information." *New England Journal of Medicine* 363, no. 16 (2010): 1495–1497.

Nietzsche, Friedrich. "Twilight of the Idols." In Friedrich Nietzsche, *The Anti-Christ, Ecce Homo, Twilight of the Idols and Other Writings*, edited by Aaron Ridley and Judith Norman, pp. 153–230. Cambridge: Cambridge University Press, 2005.

Niskanen, William A. *Bureaucracy and Representative Government*. Chicago: Aldine, 1971.

Niskanen, William A. "The Peculiar Economics of Bureaucracy." *American Economic Review* 58 (1968): 293–305.

Nord, Erik. *Cost-Value Analysis in Health Care: Making Sense Out of QALYs*. Cambridge: Cambridge University Press, 1999.

Douglass C. North, John Joseph Wallis, and Barry R. Weingast. *Violence and Social Orders*. Cambridge: Cambridge University Press, 2009.

Oakeshott, Michael. "On Being Conservative." In Michael Oakeshott, ed., *Rationalism in Politics, and Other Essays*, pp. 407–437. London: Methuen, 1962.

Oakeshott, Michael. "The Rule of Law." In Michael Oakeshott, ed., *On History and Other Essays*, pp. 119–164. Indianapolis: Liberty Fund, 1999.

Ogien, Ruwen. *L'éthique aujourd'hui*. Paris: Gallimard, 2007.

Olsen, Jan Abel. "Aiding Priority Setting in Health Care: Is There a Role for the Contingent Valuation Method?" *Health Economics* 6 (1997): 603–612.

Olson, Kevin. *Reflexive Democracy*. Cambridge, MA: MIT Press, 2006.

Osborne, David, and Ted Gaebler. *Reinventing Government*. New York: Penguin, 1993.

Osterhammel, Jürgen. *The Transformation of the World*. Translated by Patrick Camiller. Princeton, NJ: Princeton University Press, 2014.

Ostrom, Vincent. *The Intellectual Crisis in American Public Administration*. 3rd ed. Tuscaloosa: University of Alabama Press, 2008.

Overeem, Patrick, and Jelle Verhoef. "Moral Dilemmas, Theoretical Confusion: Value Pluralism and Its Supposed Implications for Public Administration." *Administration and Society* 46 (2014): 986–1009

Owen, David, 1982. *The Government of Victorian London*. Cambridge, MA: Belknap Press of Harvard University Press.

Parris, Henry. *Constitutional Bureaucracy*. London: Allen and Unwin, 1969.

Pearce, David, Ben Groom, Cameron Hepburn, and Phoebe Koundouri. "Valuing the Future." *World Economics* 4 (2003): 121–141.

Pettit, Philip. *Republicanism*. Oxford: Oxford University Press, 1997.

Pfaff, John. *Locked In*. New York: Basic Books, 2017.

Pires, Roberto R. C. "Beyond the Fear of Discretion: Flexibility, Performance, and Accountability in the Management of Regulatory Bureaucracies." *Regulation & Governance* 5, no. 1 (2011): 43–69.

Plato. *The Republic*. Translated by Francis Cornford. Oxford: Oxford University Press, 1941.

Polder, Johan J., Jan J. Barendregt, and Hans van Oers. "Health Care Costs in the Last Year of Life: The Dutch Experience." *Social Science & Medicine* 63, no. 7 (2006): 1720–1731.

Posner, Richard. *Sex and Reason*. Cambridge, MA: Harvard University Press, 1992.

Potoski, Matthew, and Aseem Prakash. "Voluntary Programs, Regulatory Compliance and the Regulation Dilemma." In Christine Parker and Vibeke Lehmann Nielsen, eds., *Explaining Compliance*, pp. 245–262. Cheltenham, UK: Edward Elgar, 2011.

Pouryousefi, Sareh, 2013. *A Normative Model of Professionalization*. Unpublished diss. University of Toronto.

Pratchett, Lawrence, and Melvin Wingfield. "Petty Bureaucracy and Woollyminded Liberalism? The Changing Ethos of Local Government Officers." *Public Administration* 74, no. 4 (1996): 639–656.

Prebble QC, John. "Kelsen, the Principle of Exclusion of Contradictions, and General Anti-avoidance Rules in Tax Law." In Monica Bhandari, ed., *Philosophical Foundations of Tax Law*, pp. 79–98. Oxford: Oxford University Press, 2017.

Press, Jordan. "Opposition Demands Explanation for Pierre Poilievre's 'Vanity' Video." *Ottawa Citizen*, May 15, 2015.

Quiggin, John. "Existence Value and the Contingent Valuation Method." *Australian Economic Papers* 37 (1998): 312–329.

Quinlan, Michael. "Ethics in the Public Service." *Governance* 6, no. 4 (1993): 538–544.

Rangwala, Glen. "The Democratic Transition in Iraq and the Discovery of Its Limitations." In Alex Danchev and John MacMillan, eds., *The Iraq War and Democratic Politics*, pp. 157–176. London: Routledge, 2005.

Rasmussen, Ken. "Saskatchewan's Deputy Ministers: Political Executives or Public Servants?" In Jacques Bourgault and Christopher Dunn, eds., *Deputy Ministers in Canada*, pp. 239–261. Toronto: University of Toronto Press, 2014.

Rawls, John. "The Basic Structure as Subject." *American Philosophical Quarterly* 14 (1977): 159–165.

Rawls, John. *Political Liberalism*. New York: Columbia University Press, 1993.

Rawls, John. *A Theory of Justice*. Cambridge, MA: Harvard University Press, 1971.

Rawls, John. *A Theory of Justice*. 2nd ed. Cambridge, MA: Harvard University Press, 1999.

Raz, Joseph. *The Authority of Law*. Oxford: Clarendon Press, 1979.

Raz, Joseph. "Legal Rights." *Oxford Journal of Legal Studies* 4, no. 1 (1984): 1–21.

Raz, Joseph. *The Morality of Freedom*. Oxford: Clarendon Press, 1986.

Rebonato, Riccardo. *Taking Liberties: A Critical Examination of Libertarian Paternalism*. New York: Palgrave Macmillan, 2012.

Reiss, Albert. "Discretionary Justice in America." *International Journal of Criminology and Penology* 2 (1974): 181–205.

Resh, William G. *Rethinking the Administrative Presidency*. Baltimore: Johns Hopkins University Press, 2015.

Revesz, Richard L., and Michael A. Livermore. *Retaking Rationality*. Oxford: Oxford University Press, 2008.

Richardson, Henry S. *Democratic Autonomy*. Oxford: Oxford University Press, 2002.

Rider, David. "Why Toronto's Street Food Program Is in Shambles." *Toronto Star*, Sept. 17, 2010.

Roberts, Alisdair. "The Agency Concept in North America." In Christopher Pollitt and Colin Talbot, eds., *Unbundled Government*, pp. 157–163. New York: Routledge, 2004.

Robinson, James, and Daron Acemoglu. *Why Nations Fail*. New York: Crown, 2012.

Robinson, Jonathan William. *William of Ockham's Early Theory of Property Rights in Context*. Leiden: Brill, 2013.

Rogers, Halsey, and Margaret Koziol. *Provider Absence Surveys in Education and Health*. Washington, DC: World Bank, 2011.

Rohr, John. *Ethics for Bureaucrats*. 2nd ed. New York: Marcel Dekker, 1989.

Rosanvallon, Pierre. *Counter-Democracy*. Translated by Arthur Goldhammer. New York: Cambridge University Press, 2008.

Rosanvallon, Pierre. *Democratic Legitimacy*. Translated by Arthur Goldhammer. Princeton, NJ: Princeton University Press, 2011.

Rosanvallon, Pierre. *Good Government*. Translated by Arthur Goldhammer. Cambridge, MA: Harvard University Press, 2018.

Rosanvallon, Pierre. *The Society of Equals*. Translated by Arthur Goldhammer. Cambridge, MA: Harvard University Press, 2013.

Rosen, Harvey, Beverly George Dahlby, Roger Smith, and Paul Boothe. *Public Finance in Canada*. 2nd ed. Toronto: McGraw-Hill, 2002.

Rosenbloom, David H. "Public Administration Theory and the Separation of Powers." *Public Administration Review* 43 (1983): 219–227.

Rosenbloom, David H., and Katherine Naff. *Public Administration and Law*. 2nd ed. New York: Marcel Dekker, 1997.

Ross, Don, Harold Kincaid, David Spurrett, and Peter Collins, eds. *What Is Addiction?* Cambridge, MA: MIT Press, 2010.

Rothstein, Bo. *The Quality of Government*. Chicago: University of Chicago Press, 2011.

Rousseau, Jean-Jacques. *La Nouvelle Heloise*. Paris: Firmin Didot Frères, 1843.

Routley, Richard. "Is There a Need for a New, an Environmental, Ethic?" *Proceedings of the XVth World Congress of Philosophy* 1 (1973): 205–210.

Rowe, Gene, and Lynn J. Frewer. "Public Participation Methods: A Framework for Evaluation." *Science, Technology, and Human Values* 25 (2000): 3–29.

Ryan, Alan. *On Politics*. London: Allen Lane, 2012.

Ryan, Alan. "Mill in a Liberal Landscape." In Alan Ryan, *The Making of Modern Liberalism*, pp. 292–325. Princeton, NJ: Princeton University Press, 2012.

Sagoff, Mark. "Aggregation and Deliberation in Valuing Environmental Public Goods." *Ecological Economics* 24, no. 2–3 (1998): 213–30.

Sagoff, Mark. "Animal Liberation and Environmental Ethics: Bad Marriage, Quick Divorce." *Osgoode Hall Law Journal* 22, no. 2 (1984): 297–307.

Samuelson, Paul A. "The Pure Theory of Public Expenditure." *Review of Economics and Statistics* 36, no. 4 (1954): 387–389.

Sandel, Michael J. *Liberalism and the Limits of Justice*. Cambridge: Cambridge University Press, 1982.

Sandel, Michael J. *What Money Can't Buy: The Moral Limits of Markets*. New York: Farrar, Straus and Giroux, 2012.

Satz, Debra. *Why Some Things Should Not Be for Sale*. Oxford University Press, 2010.

Savoie, Donald. *Breaking the Bargain: Public Servants, Ministers, and Parliament*. Toronto: University of Toronto Press, 2003.

Savoie, Donald. *What Ever Happened to the Music Teacher?* Montreal: McGill-Queen's University Press, 2013.

Savoie, Donald. "What Is Wrong with the New Public Management?" *Canadian Public Administration/Administration publique du Canada* 38, no. 1 (1995): 112–121.

Scharpf, Fritz W. "Interdependence and Democratic Legitimation." In Susan J. Pharr and Robert D. Putnam, eds., *Disaffected Democracies*, pp. 101–120. Princeton, NJ: Princeton University Press, 2000.

Schelling, Thomas. *Micromotives and Macrobehavior*. New York: W. W. Norton, 1978.

Schlesinger, Arthur M., Jr. *The Imperial Presidency*. Boston: Houghton Mifflin, 1973.

Schmidtz, David. "A Place for Cost-Benefit Analysis." *Philosophical Issues* 11, no. 1 (2001): 148–171.

Schmitt, Carl. *Constitutional Theory.* Translated by Jeffrey Seitzer. Durham, NC: Duke University Press, 2008.

Schokkaert, Eric. "Cost-Benefit Analysis of Difficult Decisions." *Ethical Perspectives* 2 (1995): 71–84.

Scholz, John T. "Cooperative Regulatory Enforcement and the Politics of Administrative Effectiveness." *American Political Science Review* 85 (1991): 115–135.

Schuck, Peter. "The Curious Case of the Indicted Meat Inspectors." *Harper's Magazine,* Sept. 1, 1972, pp. 81–88.

Schwarz, Joel, Jane Leggett, Bart Ostro, Hugh Pitcher, and Ronnie Levin. *Costs and Benefits of Reducing Lead in Gasoline.* Washington, DC: US Environmental Protection Agency, 1984.

Scott, James C. *Seeing like a State.* New Haven, CT: Yale University Press, 1998.

Scott, William G., and David K. Hart. *Organizational America.* Boston: Houghton Mifflin, 1979.

Segall, Shlomi. "Is Health Care (Still) Special?" *Journal of Political Philosophy* 15, no. 3 (2007): 342–361.

Seidentop, Larry. *Inventing the Individual.* Cambridge, MA: Harvard University Press, 2014.

Sen, Amartya. "The Discipline of Cost-Benefit Analysis." *Journal of Legal Studies* 29, no. S2 (2000): 931–952.

Shapiro, Ian. *Politics against Domination.* Cambridge, MA: Harvard University Press, 2016.

Sharman, Campbell. "Political Legitimacy for an Appointed Senate." *IRPP Choices* 14 (2008): 1–26.

Sher, George. *Beyond Neutrality.* Cambridge: Cambridge University Press, 1997.

Shiffrin, Seana Valentine. "Paternalism, Unconscionability Doctrine, and Accommodation." *Philosophy & Public Affairs* 29, no. 3 (2000): 205–250.

Shipman, Alan. *The Market Revolution and Its Limits.* London: Routledge, 1999.

Shue, Henry. "Bequeathing Hazards: Security Rights and Property Rights of Future Humans." In Mohammed Dore and Timothy Mount, eds., *Limits to Markets: Equity and the Global Environment,* pp. 38–53. Malden, MA: Blackwell, 1998.

Shulman, Seth. *Owning the Future.* Boston: Houghton Mifflin, 1999.

Simpson, Sally S. *Corporate Crime, Law, and Social Control.* Cambridge: Cambridge University Press, 2002.

Singer, Abraham. *The Form of the Firm.* Oxford: Oxford University Press, 2018.

Sinn, Hans-Werner. "Social Insurance, Incentives and Risk Taking." *International Tax and Public Finance* 3, no. 3 (1996): 259–280.

Sorley, Lewis. *Thunderbolt.* New York: Simon and Schuster, 1992.

Sossin, Lorne. "Defining Boundaries: The Constitutional Argument for Bureaucratic Independence and Its Implication for the Accountability of the Public Service." *Research Studies* 2 (2006): 25–72.

Spencer, Herbert. *Social Statics.* London: John Chapman, 1851.

Spicer, Michael W. *In Defense of Politics in Public Administration.* Tuscaloosa: University of Alabama Press, 2010.

Stanovich, Keith. *The Robot's Rebellion.* Chicago: University of Chicago Press, 2004.

Steele, Graham. *What I Learned about Politics.* Halifax: Nimbus, 2014.

Steinfeld, Robert J. *The Invention of Free Labor*. Chapel Hill: University of North Carolina Press, 1991.

Stewart, Richard B. "The Reformation of American Administrative Law." *Harvard Law Review* 88, no. 8 (1975): 1667–1813.

Stiglitz, Joseph. *The Economic Role of the State*. Edited by Arnold Heertje. Oxford: Blackwell, 1989.

Stiglitz, Joseph. *Whither Socialism?* Cambridge, MA: MIT Press, 1996.

Studin, Irvin. *The Strategic Constitution*. Vancouver: UBC Press, 2014.

Stuntz, William J. *The Collapse of American Criminal Justice*. Cambridge, MA: Harvard University Press, 2011.

Sumner, L. Wayne. *The Moral Foundation of Rights*. Oxford: Clarendon Press, 1987.

Sunstein, Cass. *After the Rights Revolution*. Cambridge, MA: Harvard University Press, 1990.

Sunstein, Cass. "Boundedly Rational Borrowing." *University of Chicago Law Review* 73 (2006): 248–270.

Sunstein, Cass. *The Cost-Benefit Revolution*. Cambridge, MA: MIT Press, 2018.

Sunstein, Cass. "The Cost-Benefit State." Coase-Sandor Institute for Law and Economics Working Paper No. 39. *Law and Economics Working Papers* 39 (1996): 1–43.

Sunstein, Cass. *Laws of Fear: Beyond the Precautionary Principle*. Cambridge: Cambridge University Press, 2005.

Sunstein, Cass. "The Real World of Cost-Benefit Analysis: Thirty-Six Questions (and Almost as Many Answers)." *Columbia Law Review* 114 (2014): 167–211.

Sunstein, Cass. *Risk and Reason*. Cambridge: Cambridge University Press, 2002.

Sunstein, Cass. *Why Nudge?* New Haven, CT: Yale University Press, 2014.

Sunstein, Cass, and Richard H. Thaler. "Libertarian Paternalism Is Not an Oxymoron." *University of Chicago Law Review* 70, no. 4 (2003): 1159–1202.

Sunstein, Cass, and Adrian Vermeule. "The Morality of Administrative Law." *Harvard Law Review* 131 (2018): 1931–1978.

Suskind, Ron. *The One Percent Doctrine*. New York: Simon and Schuster, 2006.

Tait, John C. *A Strong Foundation: Report of the Task Force on Values and Ethics in the Public Service*. Ottawa: Canadian Centre for Management Development, 2000.

Taylor, Charles. *Sources of the Self*. Cambridge: Cambridge University Press, 1989.

Teles, Steven M. "Kludgeocracy in America." *National Affairs* 17 (Fall 2013): 97–114.

Temkin, Larry S. "Equality or Priority in Health Care Distribution." Unpublished manuscript.

Temkin, Larry S. *Inequality*. New York: Oxford University Press, 1993.

Tenenbaum, Sergio. *Appearances of the Good*. Cambridge: Cambridge University Press, 2007.

Thaler, Richard H. *The Winner's Curse*. New York: Free Press, 1992.

Thaler, Richard H., and Cass R Sunstein. "Libertarian Paternalism." *American Economic Review* 93, no. 2 (2003): 175–179.

Thaler, Richard H., and Cass Sunstein. *Nudge*. New Haven, CT: Yale University Press, 2008.

Thoma, Johanna. *Advice for the Steady*. Unpublished diss. University of Toronto, 2017.

Thomas, Paul G. "The Changing Nature of Accountability." In Guy Peter and Donald J. Savoie, eds., *Taking Stock: Assessing Public Sector Reforms*, pp. 348–393. Ottawa: Canadian Centre for Management Development, 1998.

Thompson, Dennis F. "Moral Responsibility of Public Officials: The Problem of Many Hands." *American Political Science Review* 74, no. 4 (1980): 905–916.

Thompson, Dennis F. "The Possibility of Administrative Ethics." *Public Administration Review* 45 (1985): 555–561.

Thompson, Dennis F. *Restoring Responsibility: Ethics in Government, Business, and Healthcare*. Cambridge: Cambridge University Press, 2004.

Thomson, Judith Jarvis. "The Trolley Problem." *Yale Law Journal* 94, no. 6 (1985): 1395–1415.

Tobin, James. "On Limiting the Domain of Inequality." *Journal of Law and Economics* 13 (1970): 263–277.

Toronto Sun. "Wynne Must Scrap Performance Pay." Oct. 15, 2013.

Treasury Board of Canada. *Canadian Cost-Benefit Analysis Guide: Regulatory Proposals*. Ottawa: Treasury Board, 2007.

Trebilcock, Michael J. *Dealing with Losers*. Oxford: Oxford University Press, 2014.

Trebilcock, Michael J. *The Limits of Freedom of Contract*. Cambridge, MA: Harvard University Press, 1993.

Tullock, Gordon. *Rent-Seeking*. Brookfield, VT: Edward Elgar, 1993.

Tullock, Gordon. "The Rhetoric and Reality of Redistribution." *Southern Economic Journal* 47, no. 4 (1981): 895–907.

Tully, James. *A Discourse on Property*. Cambridge: Cambridge University Press, 1982.

Van Maanen, John. "The Asshole." In Peter K. Manning and John Van Maanen, eds., *Policing: A View from the Street*, pp. 221–238. Santa Monica, CA: Goodyear, 1978.

Van Parijs, Philip. *Real Freedom for All*. Oxford: Oxford University Press, 1995.

Vermeule, Adrian. "Rationally Arbitrary Decisions in Administrative Law." *Journal of Legal Studies* 44, no. S2 (2015): S475–S507.

Vidal, John. "The Great Green Land Grab." *The Guardian*, Feb. 13, 2008.

Viscusi, W. Kip. "Cigarette Taxation and the Social Consequences of Smoking." *Tax Policy and the Economy* 9 (1995): 51–101.

Viscusi, W. Kip. "Risk Equity." *Journal of Legal Studies* 29, no. S2 (2000): 843–871.

Voltaire. "Of Geneva, and of Calvin." In T. Francklin, ed., *The Works of M. de Voltaire*, vol. 4, pp. 77–81. London: S. Crowder et al., 1779.

von Humboldt, Wilhelm. *The Limits of State Action*. Translated by J. W. Burrow. Cambridge: Cambridge University Press, 1969.

Wagenaar, Hendrik. "Value Pluralism in Public Administration." *Administrative Theory & Praxis* 21, no. 4 (1999): 441–449.

Waldron, Jeremy. "The Rule of Law and the Importance of Procedure." In James E. Fleming, ed., *Nomos 50: Getting to the Rule of Law*, pp. 3–31. New York: New York University Press, 2011.

Wall, Steven, and George Klosko. *Perfectionism and Neutrality*. Lanham, MD: Rowman and Littlefield, 2003.

Wallas, Graham. *Human Nature in Politics*. 2nd ed. London: Constable, 1919.

Walzer, Michael. *Spheres of Justice*. New York: Basic Books, 1983.

Weber, Max. *Economy and Society*. Vol. 2. Edited by Guenther Roth and Claus Wittich. Berkeley: University of California Press, 1978.

Weber, Max. "Politics as a Vocation." In H. H. Gerth and C. Wright Mills, eds., *From Max Weber: Essays in Sociology*, pp. 77–128. London: Routledge, 1948.

Weber, Max. *The Sociology of Religion*. Translated by Ephraim Fischoff. Boston: Beacon Press, 1993.

Weinstock, Daniel M. "Neutralizing Perfection: Hurka on Liberal Neutrality." *Dialogue* 38, no. 1 (1999): 45–62.

Weisbrod, Burton A. "Collective-Consumption Services of Individual-Consumption Goods." *Quarterly Journal of Economics* 78, no. 3 (1964): 471–477.

White, Leonard D. *The Jacksonians: A Study in Administrative History*. New York: Macmillan, 1954.

White, Mark D. *The Manipulation of Choice: Ethics and the Libertarian Paternalism*. New York: Palgrave Macmillan, 2013.

White, Stuart. "Ethics." In Francis G. Castles, Stephan Leibfried, Jane Lewis, Herbert Obinger, and Christopher Pierson, eds., *The Oxford Handbook of the Welfare State*, pp. 19–31. Oxford: Oxford University Press, 2010.

Whyte, William H. *The Organization Man*. New York: Simon and Schuster, 1956.

Williams, Bernard. "A Critique of Utilitarianism." In J. J. C. Smart and Bernard Williams, *Utilitarianism: For and Against*. Cambridge: Cambridge University Press, 1973.

Williamson, Oliver E. *The Economic Institutions of Capitalism*. New York: Free Press, 1985.

Williamson, Oliver E. *Markets and Hierarchies*. New York: Free Press, 1983.

Willott, Elizabeth, and David Schmidtz. Introduction to Elizabeth Willott and David Schmidtz, eds., *Environmental Ethics*, 2nd ed, pp. xv–xxiii. New York: Oxford University Press, 2011.

Wilson, James Q. *Bureaucracy*. New York: Basic Books, 1989.

Wilson, Sarah E., Chi Yon Seo, Gillian H. Lim, Jill Fediurek, Natasha S. Crowcroft, and Shelley L. Deeks. "Trends in Medical and Nonmedical Immunization Exemptions to Measles-Containing Vaccine in Ontario: An Annual Cross-Sectional Assessment of Students from School Years 2002/03 to 2012/13." *Canadian Medical Association Journal* 3, no. 3 (2015): E317–E323.

Wilson, Woodrow. "The Study of Administration." *Political Science Quarterly* 2, no. 2 (1887): 197–222.

Wittgenstein, Ludwig. *Philosophical Investigations*. 4th ed. Translated by G. E. M. Anscombe, P. M. S. Hacker, and Joachim Schulte. Oxford: Blackwell, 2009.

Wolff, Jonathan. *Ethics and Public Policy*. London: Routledge, 2011.

Wolff, Jonathan. "What Is the Value of Preventing a Fatality?" In Tim Lewens, ed., *Risk: Philosophical Perspectives*, pp. 54–67. London: Routledge, 2007.

Wootton, David, ed. *Divine Right and Democracy*. London: Penguin, 1987.

Yabroff, K. Robin, and Deborah Schrag. "Challenges and Opportunities for Use of Cost-Effectiveness Analysis." *JNCI: Journal of the National Cancer Institute* 101, no. 17 (2009): 1161–1163.

Yardley, D. C. M. *Principles of Administrative Law*. London: Butterworths, 1981.

Yousefi, Mahmood, and Sohrab Abizadeh. "Wagner's Law: New Evidence." *Atlantic Economic Journal* 20, no. 2 (1992): 100

Zacka, Bernardo. *When the State Meets the Street: Public Service and Moral Agency*. Cambridge, MA: Harvard University Press, 2017.

Zelletin, Alexa. *Liberal Neutrality*. Berlin: De Gruyter, 2012.

Legal Cases Cited

Lochner v. New York, 198 U.S. 45, 62 (1905).

Kelo v. City of New London, 545 U.S. 469 (2005).

Roncarelli v. Duplessis, Supreme Court of Canada (1959) S.C.R. 121.

Padfield v. Minister of Agriculture, Fisheries and Food (1968) AC 997.

Index

National Aeronautic and Space Administration
(NASA), 83
National Cancer Institute of Canada, 227
National Health Service (NHS), 166–67, 184, 230
National Institute for Health and Care
Excellence (NICE), 230, 232
National Radon Program (Canada), 37
Nature Conservancy, 237
Nature Trust in Canada, 237
Nazi Germany, 125–26, 127–28, 230–31
negative externalities, 162, 163, 179, 208–9,
212, 300
Nelson (British Columbia), 4
Nelson, Erwin E., 9
neutral goods, 118, 128–29, 143–44
neutrality
civil service, 23–24, 33–34, 36–38, 39, 40–41,
46–47, 252, 257
liberal, 118, 128, 138, 144, 192–93, 202, 213–
14, 240, 286, 309–10, 325
political, 33–41, 92, 289, 345–47
the New Deal, 266
New Drug Application (NDA), 9, 315–16
New Public Management (NPM), 16–17, 66–
72, 75, 83–84
New Zealand, 293
Nicomachean Ethics (Aristotle), 97–98, 103–5
Nietzsche, 126
nirvana fallacy, 207
Niskanen, William, 182–83
Nixon, Richard, 2–3
Nolan principles, 57–58
nondelegation doctrine, 266
normative political theory, 17–18, 85, 146
not-in-my-backyard (NIMBY), 61–62
Nova Scotia, 61
nudge (concept), 323–25, 336–41
Nudge (Thaler and Sunstein), 303, 316–17,
324–25, 336

Oakeshott, Michael, 193, 256, 288
Obama, Barack, 18–19
Obamacare. *See* Patient Protection and
Affordable Care Act
Occupational Safety and Health Administration
(OSHA), 16, 265, 266, 281–82
Office of Price Administration (US), 293–94
Old Age Security (OAS), 174
Olympic games, 163–64
On Liberty (Mill), 124, 301–2, 310, 322–23
Ontario, 29–30, 60–62, 258
Ontario Immunization Schedule, 258
Ontario Municipal Board (OMB), 61–62

Opinions of the Inhabitants of the Virtuous City
(al-Farabi), 103–4
opportunity cost, 198–99, 249–50
option value (CBA), 237–38
Ottawa (Canada), 6
Oxford (university), 29

*Padfield v. Minister of Agriculture, Fisheries and
Food* (decision), 296–97
Palin, Sarah, 230, 231
Pareto
efficiency, 84, 138, 142–43, 154, 159, 184–86,
190–93, 208, 211–12, 250, 252–53, 300,
325, 346
frontier, 142–43
improvements, 142–43, 145–46, 170–71,
175–77, 191–93, 199, 208, 210
inefficiencies, 145–46
inferior, 175, 210
optima set, 142–43
optimality, 142–43, 161
principle, 88–89, 138, 145–46, 160, 184–85,
190–93, 195–96, 211–12, 219, 286–87
Parliament
accountabilty to, 34–35
acts of, 13
British, 20
description of, 42
dysfunctional, 82–83
members of, 20–21
supremacy of, 290
Parris, Henry, 59–60
participatory democracy, 72–78
patent medicine, 8
patents, 182
paternalistic legislation, 302, 305, 307, 309, 310,
311–12, 320
Patient Protection and Affordable Care Act
(US), 230
Patient-Centered Outcomes Research Institute
(PCORI), 230–31, 232
Patriarcha (Filmer), 129–30
peer assessment, 79, 277–78
pensions, 163, 173–74, 317
Pentagon, 2
Pépin, Jean- Luc, 5–7, 30
perfectionism, 100–1, 115–16
performance pay, 68, 69, 71–72
permanent officials, 24–27, 33–34, 44,
345–46, 348
Pettit, Philip, 260
pharmaceutical industry, 9–10, 230–31,
232, 315–16

Rawls's political philosophy, 81, 138
Raz, Joseph, 213, 288
Reagan, Ronald, 149–50
redistribution
   and the communitarian model, 154–55
   and the welfare state, 151–53, 174–75
   egalitarian, 170–71, 173, 177, 346
   horizontal, 179
   utilitarian, 229–30
Reformation, 102–3, 105
regulation of
   behavior, 310
   decisions, 276–77
   government procurement, 262
   interactions, 110
   markets, 162
   nursing homes, 282
   prices, 121
   private affairs, 311–12
   state operations, 256
regulation, 7–11
regulatory agencies, 7–8, 16, 159, 280–81, 283
regulatory capture, 70–71, 74, 283
regulatory compliance, 279
reinventing government. *See* new public
      management
religious
   authority, 102, 103–4
   consensus, 105–6
   conversion, 308–9
   disagreements, 106, 119
   dissidents, 97
   equality, 250
   freedom, 301, 338
   groups, 343–44
   institutions, 119
   intolerance, 96–97
   observance, 308–9
   pluralism, 107, 343–44
   questions, 105, 106, 118
   sensibility, 308–9
   specialists, 104
   terms, 104
   tolerance, 105–6, 118, 124–25
   uniformity, 105
   warfare, 96–97, 105–6, 116
Renaissance, 107, 124–25
rent-seeking, 26, 90, 151–52, 163–64,
      180–84, 230–31
Republic (Plato), 97–98, 106–7
Reserve Board Chair (central
      bank), 14–15
responsive regulation, 282–83
restaurants, 295–96, 313–14, 323–24

revealed preference method, 198, 201–2,
      216, 226
Richardson, Henry, 144
Right to Try Act (US), 316
rights
   as trumps, 212–13, 246–47, 250
   human, 115, 288–89
   inalienable, 112–13
   individual, 82, 94, 100, 114, 116, 124–25,
      145–46, 300–2
   justiciable, 113
   natural, 109–11, 112–14, 125, 132–33
   rejection of, 126–27
risk aversion, 241–42, 267, 325–26, 340
risk-pooling, 163
road safety, 219–22, 223
The Road to Serfdom (Hayek), 300
Rohr, John, 18–19, 39–40, 47–48, 52–53, 80–81
Roman
   empire, 97–98, 105
   institutions, 97–98
   views, 97–98, 101
Roncarelli v. Duplessis (decision), 266, 295–96
Rosanvallon, Pierre, 19–20, 41–44, 82
Rothstein, Bo, 83–85
Rousseau, Jean-Jacques, 41–42, 119, 124–25,
      130, 131
Routley, Richard, 239
Royal Mail. *See* British General Post Office
rule of law culture, 256–57, 289–91, 346–47

Samuelson, Paul, 160
SARS (first epidemic), 34–35
Saskatchewan, 5, 7
Save More Tomorrow (Thaler program), 330
Savoie, Donald, 34–35, 69, 71–72
Scharpf, Fritz, 82–83
Schlesinger, James, 3–4
Schmitt, Carl, 126
Scholz, John, 280–83
Second Treatise of Government (Locke), 129–30
Second World War, 125–26, 127, 132–33, 169
Securities and Exchange Commission
      (SEC), 297
self-destructive behavior, 307, 320, 322–23, 332,
      342–43, 347
self-interest, 84, 139, 158, 168–69, 305
Sen, Amartya, 191–92, 204–5
separation of church and state, 119
separation of powers, 23–24, 94–95,
      256, 286–88
sexual morality, 130–32
Shapiro, Ian, 82
Shaw, George Bernard, 132–33

Printed in the USA
CPSIA information can be obtained
at www.ICGtesting.com
CBHW061627290924
15102CB00018B/107